Lanier Travel Guides have set the standard for the industry . . .
Golf Resorts—The Complete Guide™   Golf Courses—The Complete Guide™
Golf Resorts International™

San Jose Mercury-News	"When traveling do you carry your clubs? You might pack *Golf Courses* by J.C. Wright . . . Each entry has information about fee structures, par, and reservation policies, each also has a description by a golf pro of the courses' characteristics and challenges."
Ft. Worth Morning Star-Telgram	"Golfers should have both these volumes . . . (*Golf Courses, Golf Resorts*) at hand along-side the clubs in the trunk."
Contra Costa Times	"Golfers plan their vacations around the game . . . a sampling of golf courses."
Houston Post	". . . descriptions and details on selected courses as well as a directory to 8,000 courses. . . ."
Fuzzy Zoeller	"I'm amazed at the number of golf resorts that have developed recently, and I'm delighted to see a reference guide of this scope and quality."
LPGA	"*The Complete Guide to Golf Resorts* is a wonderful golf destination guide. It points out the championship golf courses around the country and lists the various LPGA and PGA competitions held on them. But more than that, the Guide is a well-researched multi-purpose book with a special-interest index highlighting diversions such as shopping areas and suggestions for family entertainment near the resorts. This work is a comprehensive travel guide for anyone interested in planning a trip around the exhilarating sport of golf."
Washington Times	"If golf is your game, more to your liking will be *Golf Resorts*. Just reading the description of more than 400 golf resorts is likely to persuade duffer and expert alike to head for the fairway."

SO-CYE-351

Rees Jones	"This book is fantastic!"
Denver Post	"The first comprehensive guide to the more than 400 resorts nationwide. Rates, facilities and courses are described in detail."
Industry Week	"Executives who enjoy golf vacations may appreciate a new guidebook: *Golf Resorts*, by Pamela Lanier . . . details on 400 golf resorts, special facilities and the special challenge of each course."
Stephen F. Mona, Executive Director, Georgia State Golf Association	"The Guide is most impressive and well done. You should be congratulated on your fine effort in putting together this guide."
Franklin Mieuli, part-owner, San Francisco Forty-Niners	"There is much I don't know about golf, but there is nothing Pamela doesn't know about golf resorts."
Golf Lifestyle	"Golf Resorts includes everything you need to know about resort rates and special facilities . . . and the special challenges of each course."
Travel Age	"A guide to 400 golf resorts nationwide. Lists rates, special facilities, the course challenge. Available in bookstores."
Golden Years Magazine	"All the information you could want for the ideal golf vacation could be found in *Golf Resorts—The Complete Guide*."
John Stirling, Captain, British PGA	"I hope this comprehensive book inspires you to play the courses, and that you'll get as much fun out of the game as I have."
Barry McDermott, Golf Writer, Southern Links	"Don't leave home without it."
New York Times	". . . a useful guide."

Golf Courses

The Complete Guide™
to over 8,000 Courses Nationwide

J. C. Wright
Introduction by Arthur Jack Snyder

NATIONAL GOLF FOUNDATION

SPONSOR MEMBER

A *Lanier* Guide
▲

Acknowledgements: I wish to acknowledge and thank the following individuals for their help with this Guide: John Fite, Peter Morse, Del Goulet, Marianne Barth, Margaret Bolenbacher, Venetia Young, Seifu Haile, Hal Hershey, George Young, Phil Wood, JoAnn Deck, Brad Bunnin, Mariah Bear, Judy Berman, Sal Glynn, & Laura Heidt.

I especially want to thank Jack Elliot, President of the Northern California Golf Association for his assistance. The United States Golf Association, the National Golf Foundation, the Golf Course Architects Association, each of the states individual golf associations and Departments of Tourism.

Library of Congress Cataloging-in-Publication Data

Wright, J.C. (Julius C.)
    Golf Courses: the complete guide to over 8,000 courses nation-
wide / by J.C. Wright : introduction by Arthur Jack Snyder.
      p.   cm.
    ISBN No. 0-89815-514-2
    1. Golf courses–United States–Directories.   I. Title
GV981.W75 1993   92-19354
796.352'06'873–dc20   CIP

Published by Lanier Publishing International, Ltd.,

P.O. Box 20429, Oakland, CA 94620

Distributed by Ten Speed Press, P.O. Box 7123, Berkeley, CA 94707.

Printed in the United States of America

Dedication

This book is dedicated to the protection of our environment.

Greenspaces such as golf courses are important for the environment and enhance the quality of life.

No greenspace is as important to us all as the rain forest.

The rain forests are being destroyed at an alarming—no, terrifying—rate. We urge all of you who have learned to love nature to find out how you can help save the rain forests from destruction.

Rain Forest Action Network
301 Broadway, Suite A
San Francisco, CA 94133
415-398-4404

Other books from Lanier Guides:

Golf Resorts —
The Complete Guide™

Lanier Publishing
International, Ltd.

Golf Resorts International™

Condo Vacations—
The Complete Guide™

Elegant Small Hotels™

All Suite Hotel Guide™

The Complete Guide to Bed
& Breakfast Inns &
Guesthouses in the United
States and Canada™

22 Days In Alaska

John Muir Publications

Bed & Breakfast Cookbook

Running Press

To Contact the Guide, please write:

Golf Courses—The Complete Guide
P.O.Box 20429
Oakland, CA 94620

Table of Contents

A Good Golf Course (What Is It?)

How does one define what a "good" golf course really is? It means different things to different people. One definition might be that a "good", or successful, golf course is one that creates a desire in the golfer to return and play it again and again. He might not be able to explain why the attraction exists—it just feels good!

A good golf course is one that the real estate developer, municipality, daily fee operator, resort, or private club can afford to maintain. A golf course might be very dramatic, picturesque, and striking in its visual effect, but if it is too difficult to play, the average golfer, after playing it once or twice, will decide that he is not enjoying it and will never go back again. Income from green fees will diminish and the quality of maintenance will suffer. Poor maintenance will cause a further reduction in rounds of golf played. Also, because of excessively steep mounding and other design features, maintenance costs may be higher than usual. Can this be called a "good" golf course since it is not producing the results expected of it? Anticipated costs of maintenance *must* be considered during the design phase of the facility.

The design relationship between the parking area, the pro shop, the practice tee and green, the first and 10th tees, and the 9th and 18th greens is very important. This involves walking from the automobile to the pro shop, reaching the practice areas, starting and completing the 18 holes, and returning to the automobile. First and last impressions of the facility are developed during this process.

The design of a good 18-hole golf course first involves the development of a routing plan which takes advantage of existing topography. The goal is to have an interesting rotation of par for the course in which each hole would be followed by one of a different par, such as 4-5-4-3-4-5-4-3-4 for each nine holes. This example is not often possible because of topography and property boundary restrictions (I think it has happened to me twice in the last thirty years!), but an attempt must be made to achieve as much as possible in this regard.

Taking advantage of existing topography means using all the interesting features existing on the land in our design. Where nature has not provided interesting contours or other features, we must attempt to match nature's theme and make it appear that only clearing, floating, and planting was required to develop the golf course.

A good golf course is interesting and challenging, but not impossible or unfair, for all types of golfers, including low, middle, and high handicapper and, very importantly, the ladies. This is done mostly by having multiple tee locations, and positioning hazards so that the longer hitter is faced with the need for accuracy, while the others are provided with much more space at their drive landing area. In short, the farther one hits the ball, the more accurate he must be.

The practice fairway should face toward the north, with a southerly direction being the second choice. The first several holes on the first nine should not require hitting toward the rising sun, and the final holes on the back nine should not aim toward the west.

Each individual hole should be a complete picture within itself, with each area of the hole being a unified part of the total effect. Tee design, contouring throughout the entire length of the hole; mowing patterns at tee, fairway, and green; tree types and location; water courses and lakes; and perhaps the most important part of the whole picture, the individual design of each green, together with locations of those seemingly necessary, but oh, so troublesome cart paths; all are part of the picture to be developed.

If possible, each hole should be aimed in a somewhat different direction than the previous hole, to prevent monotony of the view from the several holes as play progresses. If it is necessary at times to have a succession of parallel holes, they should individually be of different lengths and character.

This is only a short summary of some of the items involved in designing and developing a "good" golf course. The profession of Golf Course Architecture, created out of necessity as a result of the development of the game in Scotland, requires a lifetime of study and practice. It overlaps, and requires knowledge of other fields, such as agronomy, hydrology, land surveying, civil engineering, landscape architecture, arboriculture, site planning, golf course maintenance, heavy equipment operation, and others.

The education process never ends.

— Arthur Jack Snyder
　Former President
　Golf Course Architects Association

Guide Notes

The royal and ancient game of golf is the leading participatory sport in the United States. According to the National Golf Foundation, there are more than 20 million golfers in America. Until now there has not been a comprehensive guide to this nation's public golf courses.

In this Guide we strive to acquaint you with over 8,000 public courses. Of necessity their descriptions are chip shot descriptions: that is, very brief, just enough to give you the basics and tempt you into a pleasant yet challenging round. The listed green and cart fees are based on current information supplied to us by the course's staff. Naturally, prices are always subject to change, and fees often vary with season and time of day, so be sure to confirm policies and prices when you telephone to book your tee time. Many courses have less play in the afternoon, and you're more likely to be at the top of the starter's list if you're willing to tee off later in the day. Also, high handicappers will feel less pressure starting a round after mid-day. You can enjoy a more leisurely game without the long hitters breathing down your back.

Consider the pro shop personnel your best friends. They will help you with rentals, replenish your tee supply and advise you of fast greens and unmarked hazards. And if you don't have a partner ask the fellow at the pro shop to arrange a game when he gives you a starting time. We've found it to be a fantastic way to make new friends. If you prefer a caddie to a cart, ask if they're available when you make your initial inquiries. Most public courses don't offer caddie services, but often the pro can round up one if he has adequate advance notice.

We hope you enjoy using this Guide. If we've missed any of your favorite courses, please send us their names and addresses on our Reader Comment form in the back of the Guide. We welcome your input, and we would like to hear from you.

Straight shooting!

— J. C. Wright
 Berkeley
 January, 1993

How This Guide Is Organized

This guide is organized alphabetically by state, and within each state, alphabetically by city or town. Featured courses appear in the front of the Guide. There are additional public courses in our supplementary list at the back of the Guide.

Reservations

Each listing includes reservation policy information. We strongly recommend that you call ahead to reserve a tee time. If the course is in a popular resort area, or is highly touted, consider an advance telephone call to confirm your arrangements.

USGA Rating

Most of the listed courses show the USGA rating for the course at the men's white tees.

Restaurant, Bar and Pro Shop

We note these amenities, knowing that golfers enjoy relaxing at the 19th hole.

Green Fees and Rates

The prices shown are intended to give you an idea of the cost of play for one golfer. Prices are always subject to change, and should be verified when you book your tee time. Cart rentals generally refer to the whole cart. The fee can then be split between you and your partner.

Name
Address
Phone

Name of City
or Town

This course has a restaurant/bar or pro shop

———————————— ANY CITY ————————————

Any Golf Course   Yards: 5555, Holes: 55   Restaurant/Bar/Proshop
Any Street, ZIP Code   Par: 55, USGA: 55.5   **GF:** Green Fees
Ph: 555-555-5555   RP: Reservation Policy   **Carts:** $5.55
Elevated greens, two lakes and a creek running full length of course offers a challenge to all golfers.

Abbreviations:
TC = Tennis Club
RC = Racquet Club
GC = Golf Club
CC = Country Club
PC = Public Course
GL = Golf Links
GR = Golf Resort

USGA: United States Golf Association official course rating.

GF: w/day: weekday cost of green fees to nearest $. w/end: weekend cost to nearest $.

Description given about the characteristics of the golf course.

VOTE!

For Your Choice of
GOLF RESORT OF THE YEAR

Did you find your stay at a Golf Resort particularly enjoyable? Use the form in the back of the book or just drop us a note and we'll add your vote for the "Golf Resort of the Year."

The winning entry will be featured in the next edition of **Golf Resorts, The Complete Guide.**™

Please base your decision on:

- Helpfulness of Staff
- Quality of Service
- Cleanliness
- Amenities
- Food
- Decor
- Course

Look for the winning Resort in the next Updated & Revised edition of **Golf Resorts, The Complete Guide.**™

GOLF COURSES
Listings by State/City

ALABAMA

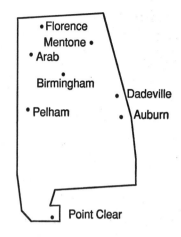

• Florence
Mentone •
• Arab
•
Birmingham
•\Dadeville
• Pelham   •\Auburn

•| Point Clear

―――――――――――――― ARAB ――――――――――――――

Twin Lakes GC   Yards: 6800, Holes: 18   Restaurant/Proshop
201 13th Ave. N.E., 35016 Par: 72, USGA: 69.3   **GF:** w/day $9
Ph: 205-586-3269   RP: Reserve on   **Carts:** $14.00
                           weekends only

Twin Lakes features tree lined fairways, small greens, and nine lakes placed to compliment each hole. Our eleventh hole is a short par 3 with water from tee to green. It will reward good play but will penalize irreverent shots.

―――――――――――――― AUBURN ――――――――――――――

Pine Oaks GC   Yards: 6208, Holes: 18   Restaurant/Bar/Proshop
P.O. Box 1792, I-85/US 29 Par: 72, USGA: 72.0   **GF:** w/day $10
So., 36830   RP: Starting time not   **Carts:** $8.00
Ph: 205-821-0893   required

Fairways lined with pine and oak trees with rolling fairways. Front side championship with lots of dogleg holes. Crossing lake on 3 holes. Back side fun, short and challenging. Lots of doglegs. All four 5 pars great holes.

―――――――――――――― BIRMINGHAM ――――――――――――――

North Birmingham   Yards: 5383, Holes: 9   Proshop
Muni GC   Par: 70, USGA: 65.4   **GF:** w/day $6
2120 36th Ave. N, 35207   **Carts:** $6.00
Ph: 205-326-2445

Our course is the oldest in Birmingham with a beautiful overview of downtown from our #2 & #3 holes. We have nine greens with front nine and back nine tee boxes making our course play like the toughest 18 hole course in the southeast. Play here well means you can play anywhere.

―――――――――――――― DADEVILLE ――――――――――――――

Still Waters GC   Yards: 5903, Holes: 18   Restaurant/Bar/Proshop
1000 Still Waters Dr.,   Par: 72, USGA: 69.1   **GF:** w/day $20
36853   **Carts:** $8.00
Ph: 205-825-7887

Birdies abound at our 6,500-yard course. Not because famed golf architect George Cobb designed it to be overly easy, but because he created it to be very fair. What's more, Cobb, who has seen more than his share of woods, calls those at Still Waters among the most beautiful he's ever seen.

─────────────── FLORENCE ───────────────

McFarland Park GC Yards: 6660, Holes: 18 Proshop
200 McFarland Dr., 35630 Par: 72, USGA: 69.7 **GF:** w/day $8
Ph: 205-760-6428 RP: Call for weekend **Carts:** $12.00
& holidays

Located on the banks of the Tennessee River you will find 18 challenging holes with pine trees lining the fairways. As you approach the greens be prepared to bring those short-game skills into play because you'll need a special touch around the 18 elevated greens.

─────────────── FLORENCE ───────────────

New Sky Park GC Yards: 5900, Holes: 9 Proshop
Rt. 7, Box 327, 35630 Par: 72, USGA: 69.5 **GF:** w/day $3
Ph: 205-757-4911 **Carts:** $8.00

This sporty 9 hole course plays from two sets of tees for greater variety. Rolling fairways and small lush greens demand a variety of shots to score well.

─────────────── MENTONE ───────────────

Saddle Rock GC Yards: 2181, Holes: 9 Restaurant/Bar/Proshop
Cloudmont Resort, P.O. Par: 31 **GF:** w/day $6, w/end $8
Box 435, 35984 RP: Call for tee times **Carts:** $8.00
Ph: 205-634-4344

Our first tee is located on top of a thirty foot rock. While up there you can see across the entire course. Executive length course with rolling greens, lakes, tight fairways and an all round challenge.

─────────────── PELHAM ───────────────

Oak Mountain State Yards: 6423, Holes: 18 Restaurant/Bar/Proshop
Park GC Par: 72, USGA: 68.9 **GF:** w/day $8, w/end $10
P.O. Box 278, 35124 RP: Earliest is 6 days **Carts:** $10.00
Ph: 205-663-6731 in advance

Scenic view—this course sets in the valley of Oak Mountain and Double Oak Mountains. Flat fairways with some elevated greens. Long par 3's and dogleg par 4's and 5's.

─────────────── POINT CLEAR ───────────────

Lakewood GC Yards: 6676, Holes: 18 **GF:** w/day $37
Scenic Highway 98, Par: 71, USGA: 70.5 **Carts:** $11.00
36564 RP: Must be guest of
Ph: 205-928-9201 hotel

Golf here is unhurried on two fine 18 hole layouts which zigzag through white pines and sleepy lagoons. Home of the Women's Western Amateur Championship. What was more mosquito-ridden swampland, and later a confederate cemetery is today 36 holes of championship pleasure with majestic tree-lined fairways.

Plan ahead! Reserve tee time well in advance, and while you're doing so, confirm rates and services.

ALASKA

Anchorage

Soldotna

ANCHORAGE

Anchorage GC
3651 O'Malley Rd., 99516
Ph: 907-522-3322

Yards: 6115, Holes: 18
Par: 72, USGA: 69.2
RP: One week ahead

Restaurant/Bar/Proshop
GF: w/day $21, w/end $21
Carts: $20.00

You start out with a spectacular view of Anchorage and Mt. McKinley in the background. The front is very tight with a little water. A back nine of rolling fairways and mountain view.

SOLDOTNA

Birch Ridge GC
Box 828, 99669
Ph: 907-262-5270

Yards: 3106, Holes: 9
Par: 35

Restaurant/Bar/Proshop
GF: w/day $7
Carts: $1.00

Not a long course, but tree-lined on all fairways with small elevated greens. You will enjoy the mountain views and perhaps the local wildlife, because around here "Moose and other wild critters have the right-of-way."

ARIZONA

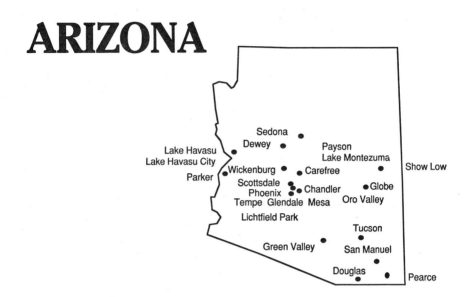

Sedona
Dewey
Payson
Lake Havasu
Lake Montezuma
Lake Havasu City
Wickenburg • Carefree
Show Low
Parker
Scottsdale
Phoenix • Chandler • Globe
Tempe Glendale Mesa Oro Valley
Lichtfield Park
Tucson
Green Valley
San Manuel
Douglas
Pearce

─────────── CAREFREE ───────────

Boulders GC | Yards: 6926, Holes: 36 | Restaurant/Bar
34631 N. Tom | Par: 71, USGA: 72.6 | **GF:** w/day $52
Darlington, 85377 | RP: Resort and Private | **Carts:** Included
Ph: 602-488-9028 | Club

South #18 is a post-card scenic par 5, 583 yard gem which requires over a 200 yard carry to the fairway from the back tees. Your second shot has to favor the left and the approach shot, if played from the left will keep you out of the lake. This is assuming you didn't slice into the 300 year old saguaro near the tee and lose your ball.

─────────── CHANDLER ───────────

Ocotillo GC | Yards: 6729, Holes: 27 | Restaurant
3751 South Clubhouse | Par: 72, USGA: 70.6 | **GF:** w/day $29
Dr., 85248 | | **Carts:** Included
Ph: 602-275-4355

As you initiate yiur takeaway, envision the ball strategically sailing over a waterfall, and watch out for the bunkers on the fairways and green. Lakes cover 90 acres, with 14 miles of shoreline, lush, sloping fairways and spectacular watwerfalls.

─────────── CHANDLER ───────────

San Marcos GC | Yards: 6117, Holes: 18 | Restaurant/Bar/Proshop
100 N. Dakota St., 85224 | Par: 72, USGA: 67.5 | **GF:** w/day $23
Ph: 602-963-3358 | RP: Three days in | **Carts:** $10.00
| advance

Golf has been a tradition at the San Marcos since 1913. Today, those traditions are being renewed, and we invite you to play golf on our historic PGA championship course. Lined by stately palms, eucalyptus and tamarisk, the 6,500 yards of finely manicured fairways have been renewed from tee to green.

──────────────── CHANDLER ────────────────

Sunbird Golf   Yards: 4131, Holes: 18   Bar/Proshop
Community   Par: 65, USGA: 58.7   **GF:** w/day $16
1661 East Riggs Rd.,   **Carts:** $7.00
85249
Ph: 602-732-1000

You start out on the short, but tight and well bunkered front nine, with five shimmering lakes. The tough back nine overlooks the San Tan Mountains, where the par 5 16th has six bunkers strategically placed with a huge lake bordering the right side.

──────────────── DEWEY ────────────────

Prescott CC   Yards: 6420, Holes: 18   Restaurant/Bar/Proshop
1030 Prescott Country   Par: 72, USGA: 69.6   **GF:** w/day $15
Club Rd., 86327   RP: 3 days in advance   **Carts:** $8.00 ea.
Ph: 602-772-8984

Prescott Country Club is surrounded by the beautiful rolling hills, and clear blue skies of Northern Arizona. The course is set for an excellent test of golf. From the elevated tees to the slick bent greens, a round you'll want to remember, Prescott Country Club!!!

──────────────── DOUGLAS ────────────────

Douglas GC   Yards: 3093, Holes: 9   Bar/Proshop
N 7/10 Mi Leslie, P.O.   Par: 35, USGA: 67.5   **GF:** w/day $6, w/end $9
Box 1220, 85608   **Carts:** $9.00
Ph: 602-364-3722

The course is a beautiful desert scene surrounded by mountains. Golf is played the year around. We are in the process of expanding our RV park to accommodate 48 full hook-ups with TV. Within the next two years we plan to expand the course to a full 18 holes.

──────────────── GLENDALE ────────────────

Arrowhead CC   Yards: 7001, Holes: 18   Restaurant/Bar
19888 North 73rd Ave.,   Par: 72, USGA: 73.3   **GF:** w/day $50
85308   **Carts:** Included
Ph: 602-561-9625

We asked Arnold Palmer to design the golf course of his dreams. This is it. It will also be the golf course of your dreams, with its breathtaking vistas and challenges for the most experienced pros as well as the most basic beginners.

──────────────── GLOBE ────────────────

Cobre Valley CC   Yards: 3320, Holes: 9   Restaurant/Bar/Proshop
Box 2629, Apache Trail,   Par: 36, USGA: 69.9   **GF:** w/day $15
85502   **Carts:** $12.60
Ph: 602-473-2542

Lush greens enhance the enjoyment of our fine golf course but watch out for the subtle breaks and slopes or there may be a few three putts.

Subscribe to our free newsletter, "Great Golf Gazette" and hear about the latest special golf vacation values.

─────────────── GREEN VALLEY ───────────────

Canoa Hills GC
1401 W. Calle Urbano,
85614
Ph: 602-648-1880

Yards: 6077, Holes: 18
Par: 72, USGA: 68.2
RP: Two days in
advance

Restaurant/Bar/Proshop
GF: w/day $26
Carts: Included

Canoa Hills is a beautiful, well manicured desert golf course set in the Santa Cruz Valley offering large undulating bent grass greens, rolling fairways and panoramic tees. Course has tight fairways with natural desert surroundings making your game at Canoa Hills truly a memorable experience.

─────────────── LAKE HAVASU ───────────────

Nautical Inn GC
1000 McCulloch Blvd.,
86403
Ph: 602-855-2131

Yards: 4012, Holes: 18
Par: 61, USGA: 57.4
RP: 24 hrs. in advance

Restaurant/Bar/Proshop
GF: w/day $18
Carts: $12.00

Our two most famous holes are No.'s 14-15. Both par 3's, #14 is 170 yards from the men's tee and #15 is 190 yards. Both holes require a carry over part of beautiful Lake Havasu. The lake view from both holes is breathtaking.

─────────────── LAKE HAVASU ───────────────

Queens Bay GC
1480 Queens Bay, 86403
Ph: 602-855-4777

Yards: 1560, Holes: 9
Par: 27, USGA: 52.2
RP: 1 week in advance

Bar/Proshop
GF: w/day $8
Carts: $5.00

Erratic tee shots on any of our nine holes could produce high numbers on your score card. The course was built on the natural terrain of the desert, which engulfs all fairways.

─────────────── LAKE MONTEZUMA ───────────────

Beaver Creek Golf Resort
Montezuma &
Lakeshore, 86342
Ph: 602-567-4487

Yards: 6054, Holes: 18
Par: 71, USGA: 68.0
RP: 48 hours in
advance

Restaurant/Bar/Proshop
GF: w/day $18, w/end $18
Carts: $7.00 ea

Rushing waters of Beaver Creek echo softly against craggy cliffs that cradle the lush fairways and bent grass greens of Beaver Creek Golf Resort. Many an Arizonan has claimed Beaver Creek Golf Resort as their personal retreat. We welcome you to one of Arizona's best kept secrets.

─────────────── LITCHFIELD PARK ───────────────

Wigwam Golf & CC
451 N. Litchfield Rd.,
85340
Ph: 602-935-9414

Yards: 6504, Holes: 18
Par: 72, USGA: 71.7

Restaurant/Bar/Proshop
GF: w/day $75
Carts: Included

The Gold Course is the Wigwam's premier challenge of golf. A championship Robert Trent Jones design, elevated greens and meandering fairways are dotted by 97 bunkers. The golfer must hit every club in his bag as he winds his way through palm and pine trees. Making the turn you're faced with the 600 yard double dogleg tenth with its green protected by a lake left and two yawning bunkers.

Subscribe to our free newsletter, "Great Golf Gazette" and hear about the latest special golf vacation values.

———————————— MESA ————————————

Arizona GR
425 South Power Rd.,
85206
Ph: 602-832-1661

Yards: 6574, Holes: 18
Par: 71, USGA: 71.1
RP: Call for availability

Restaurant/Bar/Proshop
GF: w/day $20
Carts: $10.00

Arizona Golf Resort is unique, in that it is easy for the high handicapper and challenging for the low handicapper. There is out of bounds on both sides of every hole.

———————————— MESA ————————————

Red Mountain Ranch CC
6425 East Teton, 85205
Ph: 602-985-0285

Yards: 6797, Holes: 18
Par: 72, USGA: 74.1
RP: 3 days maximum
in advance

Restaurant/Bar/Proshop
GF: w/day $79, w/end $89
Carts: Included

Red Mountain Ranch Country Club is located in the beautiful desert foothills of North East Mesa, Arizona. This Pete Dye designed championship course is a classic desert target design. Impeccably maintained, hand mown bentgrass greens have the reputation of being some of the finest!

———————————— MESA ————————————

Superstition Springs GC
6542 E. Baseline Rd.,
85206
Ph: 602-890-9009

Yards: 7005, Holes: 18
Par: 72, USGA: 74.1
RP: Three days in
advance

Restaurant/Bar/Proshop
GF: w/day $29, w/end $29
Carts: Included

Nominated by Golf Digest magazine as one of the best new public courses in the country, Superstition Springs Golf Club features spectacular water holes and large white sand bunkers. Selected as a site for the 1992 and 1993 PGA Tour regional qualifying competition.

———————————— ORO VALLEY ————————————

El Conquistador CC
10555 N La Canada,
85704
Ph: 602-742-6500

Yards: 6178, Holes: 36
Par: 72, USGA: 69.0
RP: Required

GF: w/day $25
Carts: $15.00

The course measures 6,715 from the blue tees, so it gives you plenty of room to really let your long ball fly. Hole #6 is a par 5573 yards from blue tee and 540 from the white. The hole has a slight dogleg and can keep you on your toes!

———————————— PARKER ————————————

Emerald Canyon GC
72 Emerald Canyon Dr.,
85344
Ph: 602-667-3366

Yards: 6421, Holes: 18
Par: 72, USGA: 66.6
RP: Up to one week in
advance

Proshop
GF: w/day $16
Carts: $15.00

Located along the beautiful Colorado River, the course is nestled in the hills and canyons next to the river. Spectacular views are throughout the course. Our favorite hole is #5. A short par 3, 150 yards from an elevated tee, the ball must be hit across the canyon to a green carved out of a mountain. A breathtaking hole!!

Plan ahead! Reserve tee time well in advance, and while you're doing so, confirm rates and services.

8 Arizona

Payson GC, Inc.
1504 West Country Club
Dr., 85541
Ph: 602-474-2273

Yards: 5854, Holes: 18
Par: 71, USGA: 66.1
RP: Up to 1 week in
advance

Restaurant/Bar/Proshop
GF: w/day $22, w/end $25
Carts: $14.00

You can wander on the front nine but you better have it under control when you go to the backside. Never a dull moment!

Arizona Sunsites CC
Box 384, 85625
Ph: 602-826-3412

Yards: 6600, Holes: 27
Par: 72, USGA: 68.9
RP: Please call

Restaurant/Bar/Proshop
GF: w/day $10
Carts: $5.00

Not crowded. Basically an average course. Suited for average player.

Anasazi GC
4435 East Paradise
Village, 85032
Ph: 602-953-9110

Yards: 7113, Holes: 18
Par: 72, USGA: 70.1H

This Scottish Links course was designed for the utmost in golfing pleasure. You'll take pleasure in the lush, emerald-green fairways and meticulously-maintained greens with just the right balance of hazards—all enhanced by a beautiful mountain view.

Arizona Biltmore CC
24th St. & Missouri,
85016
Ph: 602-955-9655

Yards: 6400, Holes: 18
Par: 71, USGA: 72.2
RP: Up to 7 days with
credit card

Restaurant/Bar
GF: w/day $53
Carts: Included

Golfers will want to play one or both of the PGA-rated championship courses. Try flat Adobe, built in 1930 with 6900 yards of tree-lined fairways, streams and lakes. Or play the long, narrow Links, with its unusual rolling terrain, five lakes and scenic views of the resort. #15, a par 3, is straight downhill with a clear shot of Phoenix.

Cave Creek GC PC
15202 North 19th Ave.,
85023
Ph: 602-866-8076

Yards: 6290, Holes: 18
Par: 72, USGA: 68.8
RP: 2 days in advance

Restaurant/Bar/Proshop
GF: w/day $18
Carts: $12.80

Cave Creek wash works its way through the middle of the course. It is deep and wide. After three easy starting holes the wash comes into play on holes 4, 5, 6, 7, 8, 9, 11, 12 & 18. On holes 11 and 18 the drive must carry the wash. Pick your direction angle carefully!

El Caro GC
2222 West Royal Palm
Rd., 85021
Ph: 602-995-3664

Yards: 3400, Holes: 18
Par: 60, USGA: 54.7

Restaurant/Bar
GF: w/day $8
Carts: $13.00

An executive style course right in Phoenix. The course abounds with doglegs, with a particularly good one on #18 for a really challenge of a finish!

─────────────────── PHOENIX ───────────────────

Papago GC   Yards: 7053, Holes: 18   Restaurant/Proshop
5595 E. Moreland Ave.,   Par: 72, USGA: 70.8   **GF:** w/day $18
85008   RP: 2 days in advance   **Carts:** $15.00
Ph: 602-275-8428

Site of the 1971 National Publinks Championship. Features large mature trees rolling fairways and undulating greens in a natural desert setting. Many sand traps and water hazards—ranked in the top 75 public golf courses by Golf Digest.

─────────────────── PHOENIX ───────────────────

The Pointe on S.   Yards: 6400, Holes: 18   Restaurant/Bar/Proshop
Mountain   Par: 72, USGA: 69.9   **GF:** w/day $13
7777 South Pointe   RP: 2 days in advance   **Carts:** $12
Pkwy., 85044
Ph: 602-438-9000

This unique course offers pristine Sonoran desert terrain, rolling arroyos filled with saguaros and blossoming palo verde trees, with islands of manicured greens and tees—all placed before a spectacular backdrop of rugged mountains. Number 10 tee rises 210 feet above the hole below!

─────────────────── PHOENIX ───────────────────

Valley Club of Royal   Yards: 2300, Holes: 9   Restaurant/Bar/Proshop
Palms Inn   Par: 36, USGA: 62.1   **GF:** w/day $8
5200 East Camelback   **Carts:** $12.00
Rd., 85018
Ph: 602-840-3610

A delightful nine hole (regulation nine) par 36 at the south slope of Camelback Mountain. Registered guests have complimentary golf.

─────────────────── SAN MANUEL ───────────────────

San Manuel GC   Yards: 3220, Holes: 9   Restaurant/Bar
Box 59, 85631   Par: 36, USGA: 69.7
Ph: 602-385-2224

Often the panoramic view of the surrounding mountains is quickly forgotten as one is astounded by the most treacherous bent grass greens in the Southwest. It is frequently said if you can chip and putt San Manuel, you can chip and putt the PGA Tour.

─────────────────── SCOTTSDALE ───────────────────

Camelback GC   Yards: 6486, Holes: 18   Restaurant/Bar
7847 N. Mockingbird   Par: 72, USGA: 70.9   **GF:** w/day $65
Ln., 85253   RP: Outside res. on   **Carts:** Included
Ph: 602-948-6770   space avail

The long and open Indian Bend Course lies within a verdant natural wash basin. Its links-type layout provides the golfer with stretches of gently-rolling terrain and incredible mountain vistas. The Padre course is short but tight. There's plenty of challenge here. Sweeping eucalyptus and stately palms line the well-manicured fairways.

Plan ahead! Reserve tee time well in advance, and while you're doing so, confirm rates and services.

───────────────── SCOTTSDALE ─────────────────

Gainey Ranch GC   Yards: 6818, Holes: 27   Restaurant/Bar
7600 Gainey Club Dr.,   Par: 72, USGA: 70.0   **GF:** w/day $64
85285   RP: Hyatt Regency   **Carts:** Included
Ph: 602-951-0022   guest can play

Three 9 holes courses make up a 27 hole championship course. Dunes is charac-
terized by sand dunes amidst rolling greens. Golfers will find five lakes cropping
up on the next nine, called the Lakes. The most difficult of the three is Arroyo,
with a winding dry river bed and two lakes. It's three finishing holes were
designed to be particularly challenging.

───────────────── SCOTTSDALE ─────────────────

McCormick Ranch GC   Yards: 7021, Holes: 18   Restaurant/Bar/Proshop
7505 McCormick Pkwy.,   Par: 72, USGA: 68.8   **GF:** w/day $18
85258   RP: 2 days in advance   **Carts:** $10.00
Ph: 602-948-0260

Home of the Arizona Open, the annual Arizona State University Golf Tourna-
ment, the Ping World Pro-Am. Surrounded by Scottsdale's most prominent hotels.

───────────────── SCOTTSDALE ─────────────────

Orange Tree GC PC   Yards: 6762, Holes: 18   Restaurant/Bar/Proshop
10601 North 56th St.,   Par: 72, USGA: 69.6   **GF:** w/day $49
85254   **Carts:** Included
Ph: 602-948-3730

Among the hazards on these tree-lined links are four lakes and 70 sand bunkers.
The 403-yard par 4 finishing hole is a bogey-maker with water on the left and a
green trapped with front-side bunkers. It's been featured by the USGA Golf Jour-
nal and ABC TV Sports.

───────────────── SCOTTSDALE ─────────────────

TCP Scottsdale   Yards: 6992, Holes: 18   Restaurant/Bar
17020 North Hayden   Par: 71, USGA: 68.9   **GF:** w/day $25
Rd., 85255   RP: 7 days in advance   **Carts:** $10.00
Ph: 602-585-3600

The Stadium course was built specifically to be the host of the PGA Tour Phoenix
open. The most dramatic hole on the Stadium course is number 15—the island
green. A reachable par 5 with a lake on the left side of the fairway leading up to
an island green. The Desert course is a Scottsdale Municipal course which has
bent grass greens just as the Stadium course. A little less challenging than the
Stadium course, the Desert course does have desert areas lining the fairways
instead of the huge stadium mounds.

───────────────── SEDONA ─────────────────

Oakcreek CC   Yards: 6880, Holes: 18   Restaurant/Bar/Proshop
690 Bell Rock Blvd.,   Par: 72, USGA: 69.9   **GF:** w/day $45, w/end $45
86336   RP: 6 days in advance   **Carts:** Included
Ph: 602-284-1660

Oakcreek Country Club is located in Arizona's red rock country. Oakcreek for a
number of years has been declared one of the ten courses to play while visiting
Arizona. If you're looking for championship golf, breath-taking vistas, Sedona is
for you.

─────────────── SHOW LOW ───────────────

Show Low CC   Yards: 5702, Holes: 18   Bar/Proshop
860 N. 36th Dr., 85901   Par: 71, USGA: 65.0   **GF:** w/day $14
Ph: 602-537-4564   RP: 1 week in advance   **Carts:** $15.00

The front side was designed with accuracy in mind when cut out of beautiful ponderosa pines. No. 5 is a short and exacting par 4 that yields few birdies. The back is relatively open. Our course offers two different playing conditions; one is sure to please you!

─────────────── TEMPE ───────────────

Shalimar GC   Yards: 2134, Holes: 9   Restaurant/Bar/Proshop
2032 East Golf Ave.,   Par: 33, USGA: 60.0   **GF:** w/day $10, w/end $11
85282   RP: 2 days in advance   **Carts:** $5.00 ea
Ph: 602-838-0488

Shalimar is a challenging par 33 9 hole golf course, featuring 6 par 4's and 3 par 3's. The 5th (100 yard par 3) and 9th (330 yard par 4) are the most memorable holes as the greens are virtually surrounded by water.

─────────────── TEMPE ───────────────

Tempe Rolling Hills GC Yards: 3594, Holes: 18   Restaurant/Bar/Proshop
1415 North Mill Ave.,   Par: 62, USGA: 56.3   **GF:** w/day $5, w/end $9
85281   RP: 2 days in advance   **Carts:** $6.00
Ph: 602-350-5275

Two executive nines flow over hilly terrain amid the Papago Buttes. Challenging par 3's demand accuracy. Par 4's are mild in distance. #8 on south, a par 3 of 172 yards, compares to the best in the golf world.

─────────────── TUCSON ───────────────

El Conquistador PC   Yards: 7073, Holes: 18   Restaurant/Bar
10000 N. Oracle, 85737   Par: 72, USGA: 73.6   **GF:** w/day $53
Ph: 602-297-0404   RP: 7 days in advance   **Carts:** Included

45 holes await the golfer staying at El Conquistador. Nine holes are at the resort itself. These are desert courses, with a spectacular backdrop of jagged mountain peaks and seemingly cloudless azure skies, gullies, dry washes, and a variety of cacti.

─────────────── TUCSON ───────────────

La Paloma CC   Yards: 7088, Holes: 27   Restaurant/Bar/Proshop
3660 East Sunrise Dr.,   Par: 72, USGA: 71.8   **GF:** w/day $75
85718   RP: Hotel guests or   **Carts:** Included
Ph: 602-742-6100   members

LaPaloma is a target golf course using about one-half the amount of grass as a traditional course with native, low water using vegetation used to frame the fairways. The most picturesque par 3 at LaPaloma is ridge #4. You must hit across the edge of a canyon floor 30 to 40 feet below the green. Elevated tee offers unobstructed view of all of downtown Tucson.

─────────────── TUCSON ───────────────

Randolph Muni GC   Yards: 6501, Holes: 18   Restaurant/Bar
600 S. Alveron Way,   Par: 72, USGA: 70.0   **GF:** w/day $14
85711   **Carts:** $12.00
Ph: 602-325-2811

The course features water hazards on six holes, long fairways, and sports three rearranged holes that were reconstructed according to PGA recommendations to enhance the course and make it more challenging for the pros.

12 Arizona

Silverbell
3600 N. Silverbell Rd.,
85745
Ph: 602-743-7284

Yards: 6500, Holes: 18
Par: 72, USGA: 69.4
RP: Can be made 7
days in advance

Restaurant/Bar
GF: w/day $13
Carts: $12.00

Silverbell Golf Course is built along the west bank of the Santa Cruz River. The course features nine lakes, but also offers spacious and grassy fairways and ample size greens. The course terrain is for the most part flat in nature.

Sun City Vistoso GC
1495A E. Rancho
Vistoso Blvd., 85737
Ph: 602-297-2033

Yards: 6759, Holes: 18
Par: 72, USGA: 68.9
RP: Up to 3 days in
advance

Restaurant/Bar/Proshop
GF: w/day $24
Carts: $8.00

Rolling desert course in the foothills of the Catalina Mountains. Many spectacular mountain views.

Tucson National Resort
2727 W. Club Dr., 85741
Ph: 800-528-4856

Yards: 6550, Holes: 27
Par: 73, USGA: 71.0
RP: 30 days in advance

Restaurant/Bar/Proshop
GF: w/day $66, w/end $66
Carts: $14.00

A park like setting with lots of trees and water. Tucson National is rated one of the top 75 resort golf courses in America by Golf Digest. Home of the Northern Telecom Open. A PGA Tour event.

Ventana GC
6200 N. Clubhouse Ln.,
85715
Ph: 602-577-1400

Yards: 6818, Holes: 18
Par: 72, USGA: 74.0
RP: 5 days in advance

Restaurant/Bar
GF: w/day $75
Carts: Included

The PGA Resort course leads pros and novices through rocky canyons, stony washes and crevasses of the foothills. The eighteenth hole is a smashing finish. This par 5 is a real challenge, with water to the right and behind the big green. Beware the Ventana Wash guarding the green in front. It must be carried for par.

Silver Creek GC
P.O. Box 965, Silver Lake
Blvd., 85912
Ph: 602-537-2744

Yards: 6813, Holes: 18
Par: 71, USGA: 70.0
RP: One day in
advance

Restaurant/Bar/Proshop
GF: w/day $25
Carts: $16.00

Teeing up on #17 is always a thrill for me. A tight driving hole for the long hitter, this straight away par four has everything imaginable including beauty. An approach shot that misses the undulating bent grass green will find water right and sand bunkers left. Make a par here and you'll know you're a player.

Los Caballeros GC PC
P.O. Box QQ, Vulture
Mine Rd., 85358
Ph: 602-684-2704

Yards: 6959, Holes: 18
Par: 72, USGA: 73.2
RP: Recommended

Restaurant/Bar/Proshop
GF: w/day $50
Carts: Included

Recently voted one on Top 75 Resort Courses in the U.S. (Golf Digest) Los Caballeros Golf Course offers many vista tees yet virtually every approach shot is uphill. Over 7000 yards from the back tees the course will give you all the golf you'll ever want.

Cherokee Village

• Rogers   • Blytheville

• Harrison

Siloam Springs •

Oscola •

• Forrest City

•
Benton

ARKANSAS

BENTON

Longhills GC
Old Little Rock
Hwy–Hwy 5, 72015
Ph: 501-794-9907

Yards: 6300, Holes: 18
Par: 72, USGA: 68.9

Restaurant/Proshop
GF: w/day $7, w/end $10
Carts: $12.00

Interesting layout. Not too difficult. Minutes from Interstate 30.

BLYTHEVILLE

Blytheville Muni GC
1205 North Second,
72315
Ph: 501-762-5949

Yards: 6022, Holes: 9
Par: 72, USGA: 67.1

GF: w/day $5, w/end $6
Carts: $10.00

Water can be reached from almost every tee box. A very deceptive course that requires accuracy. No. 6 will be an island by summer of 89. A fun course to play.

CHEROKEE VILLAGE

Cherokee Village GC
P.O. Box 840, 72525
Ph: 501-257-2555

Yards: 6515, Holes: 18
Par: 72, USGA: 70.0

Restaurant/Bar/Proshop

Offers two spectacular golf courses. The South Course is a whopping 7,086 yards from the blue tees. All holes over well bunkered greens, and though you can really let 'er fly at times your shotmaking is very important too!

FORREST CITY

Forrest City CC
922 E. Cross St., 72335
Ph: 501-633-3380

Yards: 5697, Holes: 18
Par: 70, USGA: 65.5

Restaurant/Bar/Proshop
GF: w/day $10
Carts: $15.00

Located on Crowleys Ridge, the front nine is relatively open on rolling fairways with greens protected with sand and two water holes. The back nine is cut from timber land, fairways are narrow, tee shots must be controlled to score well. One favorite hole is No. 3, drive uphill, second shot to green downhill over water that fronts the green, a challenge.

────────────────── HARRISON ──────────────────

Harrison CC
P.O. Box 113, 72602
Ph: 501-741-2443

Yards: 5964, Holes: 18
Par: 70, USGA: 69.0

Restaurant/Bar/Proshop
GF: w/day $10
Carts: $12.00

Our course is relatively open but great for the beginners as well as for a good golfer. You also want to lean back and let her fly.

────────────────── HOLIDAY ISLAND ──────────────────

Table Rock GC
95 Woodsdale Dr., 72632
Ph: 501-253-7733

Holes: 27H

Duffers and scratch players alike have a field day on our 18-hole course. Tree-lined fairways and impeccable greens challenge every shot. There is also a nine-hole executive golf course.

────────────────── OSCEOLA ──────────────────

Riverlawn CC
140 West, 72370
Ph: 501-563-1221

Yards: 6370, Holes: 9
Par: 72, USGA: 70.5
RP: In advance

Restaurant/Bar/Proshop
GF: w/day $8, w/end $10
Carts: $12.00

Hackers beware, this course is loaded with sand traps and water lurking on the 1st and 2nd holes.

────────────────── ROGERS ──────────────────

Prairie Creek CC
P.O. Box 828, Hwy 12
East, 72757
Ph: 501-925-2414

Yards: 6574, Holes: 18
Par: 72, USGA: 72.9

Restaurant/Proshop
GF: w/day $10
Carts: $13.40

Prairie Creek Country Club is a beautiful championship course located in the Ozarks four miles from Rogers, Arkansas near Beaver Lake. It is a stiff challenge with tree lined fairways, and a springfed creek comes into play on 8 holes of the second 9. Open all year.

────────────────── SILOAM SPRINGS ──────────────────

Dawn Hill GC
P.O. Box 296, Dawn Hill
Rd., 72761
Ph: 501-524-9321

Yards: 6768, Holes: 18
Par: 72, USGA: 70.7
RP: Call in advance

Restaurant/Bar/Proshop
GF: w/day $15
Carts: $15.00

Set in the rustic Ozarks, the golf course is set in a valley surrounded by colorful oaks and maples. Course is not tough, but demands accurate approach shots to relatively small greens. A big hitter will score well here. Dawn Hill features a beautiful meandering creek throughout the property.

Please mention "Golf Courses—The Complete Guide" when you reserve your tee time. Our goal is to provide as complete a listing of golf courses open to the public as possible. If you know of a course we don't list, please send us the name and address on the form at the back of this guide.

CALIFORNIA

—————— AGOURA ——————

Lake Lindero CC
5719 Lake Lindero Dr.,
91301
Ph: 818-889-1158

Yards: 3338, Holes: 9
Par: 58, USGA: 56.5
RP: 1 week in advance

Bar/Proshop
GF: w/day $7, w/end $9

Difficult executive golf course. Rolling hills. Great for mid irons. Narrow fairways with two tough par 4's. Greens are small and tough to hit.

──────────── ANAHEIM ────────────

Anaheim Hills CC
6501 Nohl Ranch Rd.,
92807
Ph: 714-748-8900

Yards: 5966, Holes: 18
Par: 71, USGA: 68.4
RP: 1 week in advance

Restaurant/Bar/Proshop
GF: w/day $13, w/end $16
Carts: $17.00

This challenging 18-hole championship course rests in the enchanting natural terrain of the Santa Ana Canyons, full of valleys, slopes and stands of ancient sycamores and oaks. Enjoy the country club atmosphere complete with modern clubhouse, pro shop and "The Hills," an outstanding restaurant and lounge complete with banquet facilities.

──────────── ANAHEIM ────────────

H. G. "Dad" Miller Muni GC
430 N. Gilbert St., 92804
Ph: 714-991-5530

Yards: 5811, Holes: 18
Par: 71, USGA: 66.2
RP: 1 week in advance

Restaurant/Bar/Proshop
GF: w/day $9, w/end $13
Carts: $14.00

This exceptionally well-kept course features a natural lake with lovely old trees surrounding the fairways. The course is perfect for individual or tournament play and offers the convenience of fine snack bar, restaurant and cocktail lounge complete with banquet facilities.

──────────── ARNOLD ────────────

Meadowmont GC
Hwy 4 & Country Club
Dr., 95223
Ph: 209-795-1313

Yards: 2931, Holes: 9
Par: 36, USGA: 66.2
RP: Starting times
accepted

Restaurant/Bar/Proshop
GF: w/day $12
Carts: $15.00

Located in the Sierra Nevada mountains, our picturesque setting includes Raes Creek which meanders thru the course and comes into play on 7 of the 9 holes. This combined with the beautiful pine and poplar trees, makes for narrow fairways and a challenging test of golf.

──────────── ARVIN ────────────

Sycamore Canyon GC
Kenmar Ln., 93203
Ph: 805-854-3163

Yards: 6644, Holes: 18
Par: 72, USGA: 70.9
RP: 7 days in advance

Restaurant/Bar/Proshop
GF: w/day $8, w/end $10
Carts: $15.00

Nestled among ancient sycamore groves this beautiful setting offers a challenge to all levels of golfing.

──────────── AVILA BEACH ────────────

San Luis Bay Club
Box 129; Box 487, 93424
Ph: 805-595-2307

Yards: 6544, Holes: 18
Par: 71, USGA: 68.4

Restaurant/Bar/Proshop
GF: w/day $13, w/end $17
Carts: $16.00

The front nine has blind doglegs, elevated trees, ponds and creek with excessive sloping greens. The back nine is wide open, next to creek.

──────────── BAKERSFIELD ────────────

Rio Bravo GC
11200 Lake Ming Rd.,
93306
Ph: 805-872-5000

Yards: 6960, Holes: 18
Par: 72, USGA: 70.1

Restaurant/Bar
GF: w/day $39
Carts: Included

The front nine is flat and the back nine is hilly. The greens are big and undulating. #11 is a 600 yard par 5 uphill with a slope to the right fairway and the green is difficult.

━━━━━━━━━━━━━━━━ BANNING ━━━━━━━━━━━━━━━━

Sun Lakes CC
850 South Country Club
Dr., 92220
Ph: 714-845-2135

Yards: 6997, Holes: 18
Par: 72, USGA: 70.4
RP: 4 days in advance

Restaurant/Bar/Proshop
GF: w/day $40, w/end $50
Carts: Included

The golf course appears innocent enough looking at it from the clubhouse, but the seven lakes, 111 sand traps, and small subtle greens affords only the golfer that hits accurate shots either to the pin or to a position that might allow a chip and a one putt.

━━━━━━━━━━━━━━━━ BERKELEY ━━━━━━━━━━━━━━━━

Tilden Park GC
Gizzly Peak and Shasta
Rd., 94708
Ph: 415-848-7373

Yards: 7000, Holes: 18
Par: 70, USGA: 67.7

GF: w/day $9, w/end $18
Carts: $9.00

The scenic course it set in the Berkeley hills. Wildlife abounds amid the parklike setting. A hilly course that doesn't let you get by with many mistakes. The greens are a real challenge, so you'd better practice on your putting.

━━━━━━━━━━━━━━━━ BODEGA BAY ━━━━━━━━━━━━━━━━

Bodega Harbour GC
21301 Heron Dr., 94923
Ph: 707-875-3538

Yards: 6220, Holes: 18
Par: 70, USGA: 71.9
RP: Can book 60 days
in advance

Restaurant/Bar/Proshop
GF: w/day $35, w/end $53
Carts: $12.00 ea

West of Scotland—north of Pebble Beach, Bodega Harbour Golf Links provides one of the finest golfing experiences in northern California. Sculpted along the rugged Sonoma coast, this Scottish links style course by Robert Trent Jones, Jr. provides breathtaking ocean views from every hole. The 3 finishing holes 16, 17, 18 play down to the water's edge—a must for every golfer!

━━━━━━━━━━━━━━━━ BONITA ━━━━━━━━━━━━━━━━

Bonita GC
5540 Sweetwater Rd.,
92002
Ph: 619-267-1103

Yards: 6287, Holes: 18
Par: 71, USGA: 67.0
RP: 1 week in advance

Restaurant/Bar/Proshop
GF: w/day $14, w/end $20
Carts: $16.00

The course plays to a 4 hour average and all the holes are fair to all levels of skill. We are located in a river valley so most holes are flat, very nice course to walk and enjoy our coastal breeze!

━━━━━━━━━━━━━━━━ BORREGO SPRINGS ━━━━━━━━━━━━━━━━

Rams Hill CC
1881 Rams Hill Rd., 92004
Ph: 619-767-5124

Yards: 7076, Holes: 18
Par: 72, USGA: 69.9
RP: 5 days—hotel
guest at res.rm.

Restaurant
GF: w/day $50
Carts: Included

A championship is the magnificent Anza-Borrego Desert State Park area. You can really let her fly on this one, 7,076 yards from the long tees. But watch out for the 52 traps and 4,000 trees along the way.

━━━━━━━━━━━━━━━━ BOULDER CREEK ━━━━━━━━━━━━━━━━

Boulder Creek GC
16901 Big Basin Hwy.,
95006
Ph: 408-338-2121

Yards: 4279, Holes: 18
Par: 65, USGA: 61.2
RP: Up to one week in
advance

Restaurant/Bar/Proshop
GF: w/day $16, w/end $26
Carts: $16.00

This scenic course, set among the redwoods, lakes and creeks, offers golfers a challenging and memorable golf experience in an absolutely beautiful setting.

─────────────── BUELLTON ───────────────

Zaca Creek GC
223 Shadow Mountain
Dr., 93427
Ph: 805-688-2575

Yards: 1544, Holes: 9
Par: 29, USGA: 50.0
RP: 1 week in advance

Restaurant/Proshop
GF: w/day $5
Carts: $1.50

9 hole executive course where par is a challenge. Often narrow, with short, medium and long par 3s. The greens offer the biggest challenge, being fairly quick and undulating.

─────────────── CARLSBAD ───────────────

La Costa Resort GC & Spa
Costa Del Mar Rd., 92009
Ph: 619-438-9111

Yards: 6888, Holes: 36
Par: 72, USGA: 72.6
RP: Must be guest of hotel

Restaurant/Bar/Proshop
GF: w/day $75, w/end $75
Carts: $40.00

A tee shot on the North Course's picturesque 16th, 181-yard par three, involves a lake that edges into play from the left and leads to a large, undulating green, well protected by bunkers and backed by a beautiful waterfall. The South Course features the famed par 5, 546 yard 17th hole, a true test of driving skill and shot-making at every stroke.

─────────────── CARMEL ───────────────

Carmel Valley Ranch Resort GC
One Old Ranch Rd., 93923
Ph: 408-626-2510

Yards: 6005, Holes: 18
Par: 70, USGA: 69.6
RP: 10 days in adv. for guests

Restaurant/Bar
GF: w/day $85, w/end $85
Carts: Included

Test your prowess on some of Dye's trademarks here—a layout dappled with numerous deep sand and grass bunkers, undulating greens, and railroad ties and telephone pole bulkheading. Five of the holes climb the mountainside affording some incredible views of the valley and the cooling fog banks that hover over the coast.

─────────────── CARMEL ───────────────

The Golf Club at Quail Lodge
8000 Valley Greens Dr., 93923
Ph: 408-624-2770

Yards: 6515, Holes: 18
Par: 71, USGA: 70.8
RP: Members and Lodge guests only

Restaurant/Bar/Proshop
GF: w/day $95
Carts: Included

The beautiful golf club at Quail Lodge, one of the very few Mobil Five-Star properties in the United States, is situated 3.5 miles from Highway One in sunny Carmel Valley. Each year this well manicured course with 10 lakes hosts the Women's California State Amateur Championships.

─────────────── CATHEDRAL CITY ───────────────

Desert Princess CC
28-555 Landau Blvd., 92234
Ph: 619-322-2280

Yards: 5719, Holes: 27
Par: 72, USGA: 69.6
RP: Only if staying at hotel

Restaurant/Bar/Proshop
GF: w/day $50, w/end $60
Carts: Included

Truly a unique combination of luxury hotel and golf club. Just two hours from the beach. Lake dotted 27-hole championship offers a range of playing challenges. Designed with a view in mind, every turn captures the spectacular theme of the desert's painted hills and purple mountains.

─────────────── CATHEDRAL CITY ───────────────

Lawrence Welk's   Yards: 3196, Holes: 27   **GF:** w/day $60, w/end $60
Desert Oasis   Par: 72, USGA: 71.6   **Carts:** Included
34567 Cathedral Canyon
Dr., 92234
Ph: 619-321-9000

One of the valley's hardest and best kept golf courses. The greens are well guarded by bunkers, trees and water hazards, 23 lakes and over 90 bunkers. #16 best par 4 course in desert by golf pros, #14 voted best in desert by Palm Springs Life.

─────────────── CHINO ───────────────

Los Serranos GC CC   Yards: 6121, Holes: 18   Restaurant/Bar/Proshop
15656 Yorba Ave., 91709   Par: 71, USGA: 69.0   **GF:** w/day $14, w/end $16
Ph: 714-597-1711   RP: One week in   **Carts:** $16.00
advance

Host to California State Open, L.A. Open Qualifying, So. Calif. Qualifying for State Amateur Championship. One of the favorite holes on the North Course is #15, a short 4-par, 329 yards, with a large lake in front of the green and 2 sand traps. On the South Course, probably the most beautiful hole is #17, par-3, 149 yards, with a tennis racket shaped lake in front of the green.

─────────────── CITY OF INDUSTRY ───────────────

Industry Hill GC   Yards: 6270, Holes: 18   Restaurant
1 Industry Hills Pkwy.,   Par: 72, USGA: 70.9   **GF:** w/day $42, w/end $57
91744   RP: Required   **Carts:** Included
Ph: 818-965-0861

You can play the Babe Zaharias Course or the adjacent Eisenhower Course. The Eisenhower is a long, wide open course featuring high rough and plenty of hills. #2 is a par 4. You tee off on top of a hill, and by the time you're on the green, you've dropped a hundred feet. The test is avoiding the waterfall next to the green.

─────────────── CONCORD ───────────────

Diablo Creek GC   Yards: 6344, Holes: 18   Restaurant/Bar/Proshop
4050 Port Chicago Hwy.,   Par: 72, USGA: 69.5   **GF:** w/day $10, w/end $12
94520   RP: Call in advance   **Carts:** $16.00
Ph: 415-686-6262

Course has an excellent view of Mt. Diablo, our tallest mountain in the area. The front nine starts out easy until we meet the third hole. 598 yards from white tees, 660 yards from blue tees. Hole is dogleg left with two large lakes in front and to left of teeing area requiring 200 yard carry from blue tees. The prevailing wind is normally into players face making this hole exceedingly long.

─────────────── CORONADO ───────────────

City of Coronado Muni Yards: 6446, Holes: 18   Restaurant/Bar/Proshop
GC   Par: 72, USGA: 69.9   **GF:** w/day $13
2000 Visalia Row, 92118   RP: 2 days in advance   **Carts:** $15.00
Ph: 619-435-3121

Built along the shoreline of San Diego Bay, offering views of the Coronado Bay Bridge, downtown San Diego with the bay coming into play on several holes. A challenging course especially in p.m. when off shore breezes impact shotmaking on the back 9.

———————————— DEATH VALLEY ————————————

Furnace Creek GC   Yards: 5759, Holes: 18   Restaurant/Bar
Furnace Creek Box 1,   Par: 70, USGA: 66.3   **GF:** w/day $25
92328   RP: Weekends   **Carts:** $18.00H
Ph: 619-786-2301

———————————— DOWNEY ————————————

Rio Hondo CC   Yards: 6003, Holes: 18   Restaurant/Bar/Proshop
10627 Old River School   Par: 70, USGA: 67.3   **GF:** w/day $9, w/end $12
Rd., 90241   RP: One week in   **Carts:** $14.00
Ph: 213-927-2420   advance

Although a short golf course it is well lined with trees on all holes. Greens are on the small side and well bunkered par 3's toughest holes on course. Short game important to score well on our course.

———————————— EL CAJON ————————————

Singing Hills CC   Yards: 6600, Holes: 18   Restaurant/Bar/Proshop
3007 Dehesa Rd., 92019   Par: 72   **GF:** w/day $25, w/end $30
Ph: 619-442-3425   RP: 1 week in advance   **Carts:** $18.00

Favorite hole #5 Oak Glen Course, 395 yards—drive across river to narrow, rolling fairway sloping to river; mid iron into very long, narrow 3 level green protected on left by bunker and lateral water hazard; deep pit bunker fronts right entry to green—one of best holes in San Diego County.

———————————— ESCONDIDO ————————————

Castle Creek CC   Yards: 6410, Holes: 18   Restaurant/Bar/Proshop
8797 Circle R Dr., 92026   Par: 72, USGA: 70.4   **GF:** w/day $18, w/end $25
Ph: 619-749-2422   RP: 7 days in advance   **Carts:** $20.00

No. 14, 350 and 340 long, you must carry your tee shot over Castle Creek, which is 170 yards away if you're dead straight, and close to 200 if you should fade your shot. Then you still have a demanding iron over lake that fronts green.

———————————— ESCONDIDO ————————————

Lawrence Welk Resort   Yards: 4002, Holes: 18   Restaurant/Bar/Proshop
Fountains   Par: 62, USGA: 54.6   **GF:** w/day $18, w/end $22
8860 Lawrence Welk Dr.,   RP: Resort guests any   **Carts:** $20.00
92026   time—1 week
Ph: 619-749-3225

Southern California's 1,000 acre Lawrence Welk Resort is the home of the beautiful 4,002 yard Fountains Executive Golf Course. Four spring-fed lakes are strategically located among the 10 par 3 and 8 par 4 holes, adding beauty and difficulty to an already superb golf layout.

———————————— FALLBROOK ————————————

Fallbrook GC   Yards: 6205, Holes: 18   Restaurant/Bar/Proshop
Box 2167, 2757 Gird Rd.,   Par: 72, USGA: 69.1   **GF:** w/day $22, w/end $30
92088   RP: 10 days in advance   **Carts:** $18.00
Ph: 619-728-8334

Although our course is relatively short, golfers are still challenged by the natural hazards presented by Live Oak Creek (which runs the length of the course) and our beautiful, native live oak trees.

──────────────── FULLERTON ────────────────

Fullerton GC
2700 North Harbor
Blvd., 92635
Ph: 714-871-5141

Yards: 5380, Holes: 18
Par: 67, USGA: 63.8
RP: 1 week in advance

Restaurant/Bar/Proshop
GF: w/day $9, w/end $13
Carts: $15.00

The course is nestled in a valley with a creek winding through 14 holes. The area is surrounded by a nice residential area in the heart of the Orange County, only 7 miles from Disneyland.

──────────────── GALT ────────────────

Dry Creek Ranch GC
809 Crystal Way, 95632
Ph: 209-745-2330

Yards: 6502, Holes: 18
Par: 72, USGA: 71.3
RP: 2 weeks in
advance, Slope 126

Restaurant/Bar/Proshop
GF: w/day $16, w/end $26
Carts: $18.00

We are one of the best public courses in Northern California with beautiful and towering oak trees and lakes and creeks in the play. Slope 126 (White).

──────────────── GOLETA ────────────────

Sandpiper GC
7925 Hollister Ave., 93117
Ph: 805-968-1541

Yards: 7035, Holes: 18
Par: 72, USGA: 72.5
RP: 7 Days in advance

Restaurant/Bar/Proshop
GF: w/day $45, w/end $65
Carts: $22.00

Sandpiper Golf Course presently ranks in the top 25 public golf courses in America. It is a championship public course situated in a spectacular coastal setting near scenic Santa Barbara. Its large sweeping fairways and spacious greens are designed to meet the requirements of major PGA and LPGA tournament competition.

──────────────── GOLETA ────────────────

Twin Lakes GC
6034 Hollister Ave., 93117
Ph: 805-964-1414

Yards: 1400, Holes: 9
Par: 29, USGA: 49.0
RP: 1 week in advance

Restaurant/Bar/Proshop
GF: w/day $6

This course is a sleeper, with well bunkered, fast, sloping bent grass greens, Twin Lakes offers a challenge to all players. The par 4 360 yard 7th hole is as tight a driving hole as you will ever find. Tree line up on the right, O.B. left and a water hazard fronting the green the hole gives up birdies very rarely.

──────────────── GRAEAGLE ────────────────

Graeagle Meadows GC
P.O. Box 68, 96103
Ph: 916-836-2323

Yards: 6655, Holes: 18
Par: 72, USGA: 70.7
RP: Call in advance

Restaurant/Bar/Proshop
GF: w/day $20
Carts: $18.00

Located in the Sierra's one hour north of Lake Tahoe Graeagle Meadows is built along the banks of the Feather River. The three pars are relatively short with longer four pars. The 6th hole is noted as one of the most picturesque in California.

──────────────── HALF MOON BAY ────────────────

**Half Moon Bay GC &
GL**
2000 Fairway Dr., 94019
Ph: 415-726-4438

Yards: 7166, Holes: 18
Par: 72, USGA: 74.5

GF: w/day $68, w/end $88
Carts: Included

This beautiful 7116 yards of golf links designed by Francis Duane with Arnold Palmer as consultant capitalized on the picturesque setting of seascape and mountains. Here is a delightful test of golf—water holes, barrancas, and bluffs, plus the fabulous 18th hole on the ocean.

────────────── HOLTVILLE ──────────────

Barbara Worth CC and | Yards: 6239, Holes: 18 | Restaurant/Bar/Proshop
Inn | Par: 71, USGA: 68.6 | **GF:** w/day $14, w/end $16
2050 Country Club Dr., | RP: Reservations a | **Carts:** $16.00
92250 | must
Ph: 619-356-2806

Huge tamarack (50-80 feet tall) close in most fairways—lots of water in our desert setting—lots of tall palm trees. Completely surrounded by vegetable fields—course completely manicured.

────────────── INDIAN WELLS ──────────────

Indian Wells Golf | Yards: 6686, Holes: 18 | Restaurant/Bar/Proshop
Resort | Par: 72, USGA: 71.6 | **GF:** w/day $**, w/end $**
44-500 Indian Wells Ln., | RP: 2 days in advance | **Carts:** Included
92210
Ph: 619-346-4653

The Resort's East and West golf courses offer beautiful greens, wide rolling fairways, splashes of water and fantastic panoramic views of the Santa Rosa Mountains. The courses feature an island green, an island fairway and a world class golfing environment provides an enjoyable, yet demanding, test of golf.

────────────── KERMAN ──────────────

Fresno West GC | Yards: 6959, Holes: 18 | Restaurant/Bar/Proshop
23986 W. Whitebridge | Par: 72, USGA: 70.1 | **GF:** w/day $10, w/end $12
Rd., 93630 | RP: Call in advance | **Carts:** $16.00
Ph: 209-846-8655

Our course is long and wide open, with big greens, plus seven lakes, our eighth hole the par 3 174 yard was regarded as one of the toughest 18 holes in the San Joaquin Valley according to Bruce Farris of the Fresno Bee. It's a green that is surrounded by two traps and water in back and side of the sloping green!

────────────── LA QUINTA ──────────────

La Quinta Hotel GC | Yards: 5775, Holes: 18 | Restaurant/Bar
50-200 Ave. Vista Bonita, | Par: 72, USGA: 68.7 | **GF:** w/day $35, w/end $75
92253 | RP: 1 week in advance | **Carts:** Included
Ph: 619-346-2904

Look for typical Dye touches such as railroad ties, big waste bunkers, elevation changes, and mirror-smooth water hazards. #17 is one of the toughest 18 holes in America according to pros. The acclaimed course hosted the 1985 World Cup Pro-Am, the PGA Tour Qualifying in 1985 and 1988, and the 1986 and 1987 PGA Club Professional Championship.

────────────── LAGUNA BEACH ──────────────

Aliso Creek GC | Yards: 2200, Holes: 9 | Restaurant/Bar
31106 S. Coast Hwy., | USGA: 69.4 | **GF:** w/day $11, w/end $18
92677 | RP: 7 days in advance | **Carts:** $8.00
Ph: 714-499-2271

The course is in a canyon setting, with a creek running down the middle, rolling hills and sea breeze. There are 19 sand traps. The course is very narrow and very challenging. Golf instruction, seminar and banquet facilities.

Enter your favorite resort in our "Golf Resort of The Year" contest (entry form is in the back of the book).

─────────────── LANCASTER ───────────────

Rancho Sierra GC   Yards: 2431, Holes: 9   **GF:** w/day $8
47205 60th Street East,   Par: 35, USGA: 62.2
93535
Ph: 805-946-1080

Relatively short and flat course. Water comes into play on 7 of the 9 holes. Narrow fairways reward precise shot making. Bent grass greens hold exceptionally and putt true.

─────────────── LIVERMORE ───────────────

Las Positas GC   Yards: 6540, Holes: 18   Bar/Proshop
909 Clubhouse Dr., 94550 Par: 72, USGA: 69.4   **GF:** w/day $9, w/end $15
Ph: 415-443-3122   RP: One week in   **Carts:** $14.00
advance

Each of the 18-holes has its own strategy (green placement, water, tree lines and traps). There are nine lakes on the course with a stream running through the course. The golf course offers an executive nine holes at a par 31. The facility offers a complete golf shop with a large turf driving range.

─────────────── LOMPOC ───────────────

La Purisma GC   Yards: 7105, Holes: 18   Restaurant/Proshop
3455 State Hwy. 246,   Par: 72, USGA: 72.8   **GF:** w/day $35, w/end $45
93436   RP: 7 days in advance   **Carts:** $22.00
Ph: 805-735-8395

La Purisima Golf Course is a championship public golf course situated on 300 acres of gently rolling hills bordering the beautiful Lompoc Valley in Santa Barbara County. Fairways and greens are surrounded by large stands of majestic oak trees.

─────────────── MARYSVILLE ───────────────

Plumas Lake GC   Yards: 6500, Holes: 18   Restaurant/Bar/Proshop
1551 Country Club Ave.,   Par: 71, USGA: 71.0   **GF:** w/day $12, w/end $15
95901   RP: 1 weeks in advance **Carts:** $16.00
Ph: 916-742-3201

The course is level, small and tight fairways with small greens. There are a few parallel holes and plenty of oaks. #14 is a challenging, tight hole.

─────────────── McKINLEYVILLE ───────────────

Beau Pre GC   Yards: 5762, Holes: 18   Restaurant/Bar/Proshop
1777 Norton Rd., P.O.   Par: 71, USGA: 67.6   **GF:** w/day $11, w/end $15
Box 2278, 95521   **Carts:** $14.00
Ph: 707-839-2342

Pine and spruce trees line most of the fairways on both the mountainous and meadow portions of this course requiring precision placement shots. Water comes into play on nine holes and the sand traps are strategically placed. The views of the ponds, lush fairways and Pacific Ocean from the elevated golf holes make Beau Pre an esthetically pleasing course to play in addition to testing your golf game.

Please mention "Golf Courses—The Complete Guide" when you reserve your tee time. Our goal is to provide as complete a listing of golf courses open to the public as possible. If you know of a course we don't list, please send us the name and address on the form at the back of this guide.

―――――――――― MIDDLETOWN ――――――――――

Hidden Valley Lake   Yards: 6237, Holes: 18   Proshop
G&CC   Par: 71, USGA: 69.5   **GF:** w/day $10, w/end $17
P.O. Box 5130, #1   **Carts:** $10.00
Hartman Rd., 95461
Ph: 707-987-3035

The front nine is long with 3 Par 4's over 400 yds. Although flat and open, the front 9 is challenging. The back 9 is very different.

―――――――――― MONTEREY ――――――――――

Old Del Monte GC   Yards: 6278, Holes: 18   **GF:** w/day $40, w/end $45
300 Sylvan Rd., 93940   Par: 72, USGA: 70.0   **Carts:** $12.00
Ph: 408-373-2436   RP: 60 days in advance

The oldest golf course still in operation west of the Mississippi. Wide fairways bounded by strategically placed bunkers; greens are small and well-placed. Many large trees line the fairways. The course served as the site of California's first golf championship.

―――――――――― MORRO BAY ――――――――――

Morro Bay GC   Yards: 6116, Holes: 18   Restaurant/Bar/Proshop
State Park Rd., 93442   Par: 71, USGA: 68.2   **GF:** w/day $10, w/end $12
Ph: 805-772-4341   RP: 1-3 days ahead   **Carts:** $15.00

Morro Bay Golf Course is situated high up on the knoll of Morro Bay State Park. Beautiful views of the ocean can be seen from almost every tee. The course proves to be an interesting challenge for every golfer as the fairways and greens slope every which way. A challenge it may, or may not be for you, but the beauty of the place you will never forget.

―――――――――― MURRIETA ――――――――――

Rancho California CC   Yards: 6900, Holes: 18   Restaurant/Proshop
38275 Murrieta Hot   Par: 72, USGA: 71.4   **GF:** w/day $35, w/end $50
Springs, 92362   RP: 7 days in advance   **Carts:** Included
Ph: 714-677-7446

Rancho California is Robert Trent Jones Sr. masterpiece. It's built on 190 acres of sprawling terrain. The 3rd hole is, as my 8 year old son says, a rad hole. Elevated tee to fairway lined with trees with a pond fronting the green. The view from the tee is breathtaking.

―――――――――― NAPA ――――――――――

Napa Municipal GC   Yards: 6730, Holes: 18   Restaurant/Bar/Proshop
2295 Streblow Dr., 94558   Par: 72, USGA: 70.7   **GF:** w/day $11, w/end $15
Ph: 707-255-4333   RP: 7 days prior   **Carts:** $15.00

This is a champion golf course that will play to over 7,000 yards with water hazards in play on 14 of the 18 holes.

―――――――――― NAPA ――――――――――

Silverado GC   Yards: 6620, Holes: 36   Restaurant/Bar
1600 Atlas Peak Rd.,   Par: 72, USGA: 73.9   **GF:** w/day $55
94558   RP: 2 days non guest   **Carts:** Included
Ph: 707-257-5460

The South Course is a nicely contoured design with deceiving side-hill lies and over a dozen water crossings. The North Course stretches to 6700 yards and is occasionally more forgiving. Beautifully maintained, have been honored by the National Groundskeepers Association.

─────────────────── OAKHURST ───────────────────

Sierra Sky Ranch GC   Yards: 5944, Holes: 9   Restaurant/Bar/Proshop
50556 Rd. 632, 93644   Par: 36, USGA: 68.0   **GF:** w/day $6
Ph: 209-683-7433   RP: 1 day in advance   **Carts:** $7.00

*Our challenging regulation 9 hole golf course is surrounded by the serene beauty
of the Sierras. Our climate affords year-round golfing with over 300 days of play.*

─────────────────── OAKLAND ───────────────────

Lew Galbraith GC   Yards: 6298, Holes: 18   Proshop
10505 Doolittle Dr., 94603 Par: 72, USGA: 69.9   **GF:** w/day $8, w/end $10
Ph: 415-569-9411   **Carts:** $14.00

*Lew F. Galbraith Golf course is essentially flat. You can really let 'er fly here
because you have plenty of length. Holes #5 and 16 are particularly challenging
par-4s.*

─────────────────── OJAI ───────────────────

Ojai Valley Inn and CC Yards: 6252, Holes: 18   Restaurant/Bar/Proshop
Country Club Rd., 93023   Par: 70, USGA: 70.6   **GF:** w/day $76, w/end $76
Ph: 805-646-5511   RP: Guests 90 days,   **Carts:** $14.00 ea
                            outside 1 day

*The inn has a truly classic course that is the host to the PGA Senior Tour GTE
Classic. It offers a variety of terrain through mature stands of California oaks. It is
definitely a shotmaker's golf course requiring careful placement from tee to
green. It is always in fine condition with outstanding greens.*

─────────────────── PALM DESERT ───────────────────

Marriott's Desert   Yards: 6679, Holes: 36   Restaurant/Bar/Proshop
Springs GC   Par: 72, USGA: 68.5   **GF:** w/day $90
74-855 Country Club Dr.,   RP: Resort guest 30   **Carts:** Included
92260   days
Ph: 619-341-1756

*Palms Course—Signature course by Ted Robinson "King of the Waterscape";
6800 yards of water, sand and breathtaking views. Valley Course—nominated
best course/resort category by Golf Digest 1988. Tight fairways and small greens
make the Valley Course a challenge for all handicaps.*

─────────────────── PALM DESERT ───────────────────

Oasis CC   Yards: 3700, Holes: 18   Restaurant/Bar/Proshop
42-330 Casbah Way,   Par: 60, USGA: 54.0   **GF:** w/day $23
92260   RP: 3 days in advance   **Carts:** $20.00
Ph: 619-345-2715

*One of the finest executive course challenges in golf. Featuring 22 lakes to
entertain the golfer while testing your ability upon our superbly manicured fairways and greens. The 18th hole par 4 dogleg back to the clubhouse offers a
majestic view of Mt. San Jacinto.*

─────────────────── PALM DESERT ───────────────────

Suncrest CC   Yards: 4886, Holes: 9   Restaurant/Bar/Proshop
73-450 Country Club Dr.,   Par: 33, USGA: 60.0   **GF:** w/day $30
92260   RP: 2 days in advance   **Carts:** $1/2 cart
Ph: 619-340-2467

*Best 9 hole course in desert which boast almost 100 courses. Sits on elevated
knoll with panoramic view of desert area. Very challenging for a 9-hole executive course.*

──────────────── PALM DESERT ────────────────

Woodhaven CC Yards: 5644, Holes: 18 Restaurant/Bar/Proshop
41-555 Woodhaven Dr. Par: 70, USGA: 66.1 **GF:** w/day $50
E., 92260 RP: one day in advance **Carts:** Included
Ph: 619-345-7513

Woodhaven has gently rolling hills and narrow fairways all of which are bunkered. Once you get the ball in play you are faced with a shot into a small and well bunkered green. It is a fun and challenging 5644 yards.

──────────────── PALO ALTO ────────────────

Palo Alto Muni GC Yards: 6525, Holes: 18 Restaurant/Bar/Proshop
1875 Embarcadero Rd., Par: 72, USGA: 70.1 **GF:** w/day $10, w/end $14
94303 RP: Weekdays–1 week **Carts:** $16.00
Ph: 415-856-0881 in advance

#14 long par 3 usually against the wind. A right to left wind is most prevalent. Bunker placed to right of green. 216 yards from white tee and 232 from blue tee, requires a real solid wood shot from most players.

──────────────── PARADISE ────────────────

Tall Pines GC Yards: 4209, Holes: 9 Restaurant/Bar/Proshop
5325 Clark Rd., 95969 Par: 68, USGA: 62.2 **GF:** w/day $10
Ph: 916-877-5816 RP: On weekends **Carts:** $16.00

At 1600 feet elevation Tall Pines is positioned above central valley fog below the snow line of the Sierra Nevada foothills affording it playability year round. One of the most challenging holes #1 at 340 yards, is a dogleg par 4 approaching an elevated green nestled among beautiful but treacherous Ponderosa Pines native to the region.

──────────────── PEBBLE BEACH ────────────────

Links at Spanish Bay Yards: 6195, Holes: 18 Restaurant/Bar
17-Mile Dr., 93953 Par: 72, USGA: 72.7 **GF:** w/day $75, w/end $90
Ph: 408-647-4500 RP: May be made with **Carts:** $30.00
hotel res.

A true seaside links course. A unique challenge of sand and soil, sea and foggy weather. The 13th, which turns the player back toward the Pacific and into the dunes, a 130-yard par 3 patterned after the "Postage Stamp" at Scotland's Royal Troon; Jones calls it his "Christmas Seal because it's a gift when you get on."

──────────────── PEBBLE BEACH ────────────────

Pebble Beach GL Yards: 6357, Holes: 72 Restaurant/Bar
17-Mile Dr., 93953 Par: 72, USGA: 72.7 **GF:** w/day $125, w/end
Ph: 408-624-3811 RP: Call Golf Central $135
408-624-6611 **Carts:** Included

A round of golf here is special because its unusual for tournament-class courses to be available to the public. Pebble Beach course starts out along the ocean, then swings back and forth along the coast for holes 4 through 10. 11 through 16 are inland, and 17 and 18 return to the rugged shoreline are second to none as a finish.

Enter your favorite resort in our "Golf Resort of The Year" contest (entry form is in the back of the book).

─────────────── PEBBLE BEACH ───────────────

Poppy Hills GC   Yards: 6213, Holes: 18   Restaurant/Bar/Proshop
3200 Lopez Rd., 93953   Par: 72, USGA: 72.4   **GF:** w/day $30
Ph: 408-625-2035   RP: 1 month in   **Carts:** $20.00
                        advance

The first course fully owned and operated by a regional golf association, the Northern California Golf Association. Poppy Hills requires both accuracy and length off the tee along with a proficient putting ability . . . a true test of golf.

─────────────── PEBBLE BEACH ───────────────

Spyglass Hill GC   Yards: 6810, Holes: 18   **GF:** w/day $95
Spyglass Hill Rd. &   Par: 72, USGA: 73.1   **Carts:** Included
Stevenson, 93953   RP: Call Golf Central
Ph: 408-624-3811   408-624-3811

The course swings back and forth along the coast for holes 4 through 10, moves inland for the 11th through 16th, and returns to the rugged shoreline for the 17th and 18th. The 18th green is a strip of land running between the main building of the Lodge and the bay.

─────────────── RANCHO MIRAGE ───────────────

Westin Mission Hills   Yards: 6707, Holes: 18   Restaurant/Bar
Resort GC   Par: 70, USGA: 73.5   **GF:** w/day $45
71-501 Dinah Shore Dr.,   RP: 2 days   **Carts:** Included
92270
Ph: 619-328-3198

Guests have preferred tee times at the Westin Mission Hills Resort Course. A gently rolling, tough layout designed by Pete Dye with his trademarks of large lakes on five holes. Rancho Mirage offers some tremendous views of the nearby San Jacinto Mountains.

─────────────── RANCHO MURIETA ───────────────

Rancho Murietta GC   Yards: 6371, Holes: 36   **GF:** w/day $75
14813 Jackson Rd., 95683   Par: 72, USGA: 71.1   **Carts:** $22.00
Ph: 916-985-7200   RP: Reciprocal play—3
                           days in adv

With 36 holes nestled among the oaks, Rancho Murieta is one of northern California's most challenging golf courses. Accurate drives, and approach shots are a must. My favorite hole is the 3rd, a par 5 that requires three well placed shots for a slippery putt for birdie.

─────────────── RANCHO SANTA FE ───────────────

Rancho Santa Fe   Yards: 6497, Holes: 18   Restaurant
P.O. Box 869, 92067   Par: 72, USGA: 71.3   **GF:** w/day $50
Ph: 619-765-3094   RP: 5 daysin advance   **Carts:** $25.00
                        through Inn

Inn guests play at private Rancho Santa Fe Golf Club, a rolling, wooded, challenge. The par 72 design claims #13 as its most noteworthy—no doubt due to a couple of small lakes to be carried.

Our listings—supplied by the management—are as complete as possible. Many of the courses have more features than we list. Be sure to inquire when you book your tee time.

─── REDDING ───

Gold Hills CC
1950 Gold Hills Dr., 96003
Ph: 916-246-7867

Yards: 6603, Holes: 18
Par: 72, USGA: 69.5
RP: Call in advance

Restaurant/Bar/Proshop
GF: w/day $16, w/end $20
Carts: $16.00

A tree lined shot maker's course with small greens that are always smooth and fast. Several creeks and lakes add to the natural beauty. During the round, views of both Mt. Shasta and Mt. Lasson abound.

─── RODEO ───

Franklin Canyon GC
Hwy 4, 94572
Ph: 415-799-6191

Yards: 6202, Holes: 18
Par: 72, USGA: 69.3
RP: 7 days in advance

Restaurant/Bar/Proshop
GF: w/day $13, w/end $19
Carts: $16.00

The course is quite challenging due to the canyon which you must cross seven times. Both the ninth and eighteenth finishing holes are par fives with water in front of the greens. You may go for it or lay up depending on how brave you are.

─── SAN CLEMENTE ───

Shorecliffs GC
501 Avenida Vaquero, 92672
Ph: 714-492-1177

Yards: 6097, Holes: 18
Par: 71, USGA: 67.9
RP: One week in advance

Restaurant/Bar/Proshop
GF: w/day $10, w/end $17
Carts: $16.00

It may be a short course but its very narrow and demanding. No. 11 is a tough par 5. We straddle the freeway. Ocean on one side, (foggy maybe misty); on the landward side sunshine and 80 degrees, it's like 2 different courses.

─── SAN DIEGO ───

Rancho Bernardo Inn GC
17550 Bernardo Oaks Dr., 92128
Ph: 619-487-1611

Yards: 6388, Holes: 18
Par: 72, USGA: 69.1
RP: 3 days in advance or room reg.

Restaurant/Bar/Proshop
GF: w/day $44, w/end $54
Carts: $11.00 ea

The West Course unrolls from north to south down the valley like a great green ribbon . . . stunning yet surprisingly deceptive. For here are 6700 yards that must be played with almost rifle like accuracy. Throughout are two lakes, a stream, doglegs, some 60 bunkers. Clumps of olive trees, eucalyptus, sycamore and pine add to the setting and the game.

─── SAN DIMAS ───

San Dimas Canyon GC
2100 Terrebonne Ave., 91773
Ph: 714-599-2313

Yards: 6315, Holes: 18
Par: 72, USGA: 67.9
RP: 7 days in advance

Restaurant/Bar/Proshop
GF: w/day $13, w/end $20
Carts: $19.00

San Dimas is a classic foothill golf course. Fairways are generous on some holes, and stingy on others. The short length is deceptive because it is not wise to hit a driver everywhere. Beautiful panorama of mountains, sky and water blend to create a private club atmosphere with the best greens in Southern California.

─── SANTA ANA ───

River View GC
1800 West 22nd St., 92706
Ph: 714-543-1115

Yards: 5600, Holes: 18
Par: 70, USGA: 66.1
RP: Recommended

Restaurant/Proshop
GF: w/day $10
Carts: $14.00

A sanctuary just minutes from Disneyland and Anaheim Stadium, located in the heart of Orange County, River View Golf offers a relaxing respite to the frenzied tourist. We proudly boast of our flawless putting greens, tight challenging fairways and excellent practice facilities.

──────────── SANTA BARBARA ────────────

Santa Barbara Yards: 6009, Holes: 18 Restaurant/Bar/Proshop
Community GC Par: 70, USGA: 67.2 **GF:** w/day $18, w/end $20
3500 McCaw Ave., 93105 RP: Required **Carts:** $18.00
Ph: 805-687-7087

Extremely scenic view of mountain range along with a beautifully manicured golf course. Best hole on course is #12, a slight dogleg right 455 yards long with out of bounds on left and large trees on the right. A great par 4.

──────────── SANTA CRUZ ────────────

Pasatiempo GC Yards: 6483, Holes: 18 Restaurant/Bar/Proshop
18 Clubhouse Rd., 95060 Par: 71, USGA: 70.9 **GF:** w/day $45, w/end $55
Ph: 408-426-3622 RP: Seven days in **Carts:** $20.00
advance

Each hole on this classic course requires shotmaking accuracy. After 18 holes here you'll find you've had to use every club in the bag. Watch out for the beautiful 16th hole with triple level green and tiny landing area.

──────────── SANTA ROSA ────────────

Fountaingrove CC Yards: 6800, Holes: 18 Restaurant/Bar
3555 Round Barn, 95403 Par: 72, USGA: 72.9 **GF:** w/day $32, w/end $55
Ph: 707-523-7555 **Carts:** Included

The course makes good use of a wooded, hilly site. Challenging topography. Our favorite hole is #17, 218 yard par 3 over water.

──────────── SCOTTS VALLEY ────────────

Valley Gardens GC Yards: 3666, Holes: 9 **GF:** w/day $8, w/end $9
263 Mt. Hermon Rd., Par: 62, USGA: 54.1 **Carts:** $1.50 ea
95066 RP: 1 week in advance
Ph: 408-438-3058

This is a challenging 9 hole course nestled in the Santa Cruz Mountains. Water comes into play on several holes, especially the 175 yard par 3 8th hole. The gentle slope of the course makes it a perfect course to walk. It's ideal for the avid golfer, or beginner.

──────────── SIMI VALLEY ────────────

Simi Hills GC Yards: 6509, Holes: 18 Restaurant/Bar/Proshop
5031 Alamo St., 93063 Par: 71, USGA: 67.9 **GF:** w/day $10, w/end $16
Ph: 805-522-0803 RP: For weekends **Carts:** $16.00

Course is a good public course in excellent condition with a friendly atmosphere.

──────────── SO. SAN FRANCISCO ────────────

California GC Yards: 6675, Holes: 18 Restaurant/Bar/Proshop
844 W. Orange Ave., Par: 72, USGA: 72.0 **GF:** w/day $50, w/end $50
94080 **Carts:** $10.00
Ph: 415-589-0144

The California Club has been the site of several major qualifying tournaments for the U.S. Open, U.S. Amateur. California's greens are fast and the golf course is always in excellent shape.

Subscribe to our free newsletter, "Great Golf Gazette" and hear about the latest special golf vacation values.

────────────────── SOLVANG ──────────────────

Alisal Guest Ranch GC   Yards: 6286, Holes: 18   Restaurant/Bar
1054 Alisal Rd., 93463   Par: 72, USGA: 67.9   **GF:** w/day $24
Ph: 805-688-6411   RP: Recommended   **Carts:** $16.00

The Alisal blends ideally into the natural surroundings of the rolling terrain, dotted by 300 year old oak, sycamore and eucalyptus trees. The course, home of the 1986 South California Seniors, meanders along a seasonal creek and affords plenty of variety.

────────────────── SOUTH LAGUNA ──────────────────

Aliso Creek GC   Yards: 2200, Holes: 9   Restaurant/Bar
31106 S. Coast Hwy.,   USGA: 69.4   **GF:** w/day $11, w/end $18
92677   RP: 7 days in advance   **Carts:** $8.00
Ph: 714-499-2271

The course is in a canyon setting, with a creek running down the middle, rolling hills and sea breeze. There are 19 sand traps. The course is very narrow and very challenging. Golf instruction, seminar and banquet facilities.

────────────────── ST. HELENA ──────────────────

Meadowood Resort GC   Yards: 4130, Holes: 9   Restaurant/Bar
900 Meadowood Ln.,   Par: 62, USGA: 61.0   **GF:** w/day $20
94574   RP: 1 day in advance
Ph: 707-963-3646

A nine-hole executive course. The layout winds around California Live Oak lined fairways which are tight, but demand accuracy. Players of all levels, genders and ages await the Century Pro-Am, a scratch best-ball 18-hole event in which the combined ages of partners must be at least 100 years.

────────────────── TEMECULA ──────────────────

Temecula Creek Inn GC   Yards: 6380, Holes: 18   Restaurant/Bar
44-501 Rainbow Canyon   Par: 72, USGA: 69.4   **GF:** w/day $16, w/end $21
Rd., 92390   **Carts:** $15.00
Ph: 714-676-5631

The course has played host to the U.S. Open Qualifying, U.S. Public Links Qualifying, and Golden State Tour events. There are rolling hills and tree lined fairways. The 13th hole has an elevated green with crosswind over the green.

────────────────── TRUCKEE ──────────────────

Northstar GC   Yards: 6897, Holes: 18   Restaurant/Bar/Proshop
Hwy. 267 & Northstar.   Par: 72, USGA: 67.4   **GF:** w/day $35
P.O. Box 12, 95734   **Carts:** $10.00
Ph: 916-562-1010

This scenic mountain course offers views of the rugged Sierra Nevada and Martis Valley and a challenging 18 holes with water hazards on 14 of the holes, including the new lake on hole number 6. The front nine is fairly wide open and the back nine is tree-lined.

────────────────── WALNUT CREEK ──────────────────

Boundary Oak GC   Yards: 6788, Holes: 18   Restaurant/Bar/Proshop
3800 Valley Vista Rd.,   Par: 72, USGA: 70.2   **GF:** w/day $10, w/end $14
94598   RP: Required   **Carts:** $18.00
Ph: 415-934-6212

One of the more challenging municipal courses in Northern California.

─────────────── WATSONVILLE ───────────────

Pajaro Valley GC, Inc. Yards: 6234, Holes: 18   Restaurant/Bar/Proshop
967 Salinas Rd., 95076   Par: 72, USGA: 68.2   **GF:** w/day $32, w/end $35
Ph: 408-724-3851   RP: Wknd 1 week;   **Carts:** $21.00
   wkdy 1 month

Pajaro Valley Golf Club opened in 1926. It is a beautiful, well maintained golf course designed for an enjoyable golfing experience with both pleasurable landscaping as well as a challenging layout. Pajaro Valley Golf Club regularly hosts the Little Helpers Golf Tournament.

─────────────── WEED ───────────────

Lake Shastina GC Yards: 6317, Holes: 18   Restaurant/Bar/Proshop
5925 Country Club Dr., Par: 72, USGA: 69.5   **GF:** w/day $32
96094   **Carts:** $12.00
Ph: 916-938-3201

Four sets of strategically placed tees leading to broad fairways sculptured from native shrubland and pine forests, large undulating greens, well placed sand traps, a generous display of lakes and water hazards, are a tribute to Mr. Jones' ingenuity. Dominating the presence of nearly every hole is the splendid sentinel. . .majestic 14,162 foot Mount Shasta.

─────────────── WILLOW CREEK ───────────────

Big Foot GC & CC Yards: 5007, Holes: 9   Restaurant/Bar/Proshop
P.O. Box 836, 95573   Par: 70, USGA: 63.9   **GF:** w/day $12, w/end $14
Ph: 916-629-2977   RP: Call for weekends   **Carts:** $14.00
   & holidays

The golf course is a true "gem." Surrounded by tree covered mountains. Warm to hot weather April thru September. Open year round.

─────────────── YUCCA VALLEY ───────────────

Blue Skies CC Yards: 6660, Holes: 18   Restaurant/Bar/Proshop
55-100 Martinez Trail, Par: 71, USGA: 68.4   **GF:** w/day $15
92284   **Carts:** $15.00
Ph: 619-365-7694

Back east beauty in a high desert setting over 400 hardwood trees make this course exceptional for play and for relaxing beauty. The course plays at 80 degrees when lower desert courses around Palm Springs are over 100 degrees—yet only 20 minutes away.

COLORADO

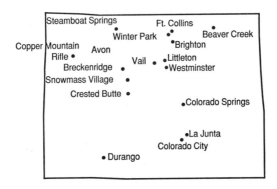

Steamboat Springs • Ft. Collins •
Winter Park •• Beaver Creek
Copper Mountain Avon • Brighton
Rifle • • Littleton
Breckenridge • Vail • • Westminster
Snowmass Village •
Crested Butte •
• Colorado Springs
• La Junta
Colorado City
• Durango

AVON

Eagle Vail GC PC
Box 5660, 81620
Ph: 303-949-5267

Yards: 6819, Holes: 18
Par: 72, USGA: 68.4

Restaurant/Bar
GF: w/day $40
Carts: $20.00

Water come into play on 10 holes, so you'd better be a good shotmaker or bring your wading boots! Also plenty of trees just to keep it interesting. A very scenic course.

BEAVER CREEK

Beaver Creek GC
103 Offerson Rd., 81620
Ph: 303-949-7123

Yards: 6464, Holes: 18
Par: 70, USGA: 69.2
RP: 48 hours in
advance

Restaurant/Bar
GF: w/day $50
Carts: $10.00

Beaver Creek is a world renowned Robert Trent Jones II course. A true mountain course with undulating fairways. Creeks run through the course.

BRECKENRIDGE

Breckenridge GC PC
200 Clubhouse Dr. P.O.
Box 7965, 80424
Ph: 303-453-9104

Yards: 7279, Holes: 18
Par: 72, USGA: 66.4
RP: Two days in
advance

Restaurant/Bar/Proshop
GF: w/day $40
Carts: $10.00

Jack Nicklaus designed, the course plays through mountains, valleys, forests and streams. Almost 7300 yards from the championship tees and approximately 6600 yards from the men's tee. The length of the golf course is shortened by the 9300 plus feet of elevation. Because of the thin air a golf ball will fly as much as 15% further than at sea level.

BRIGHTON

Riverdale GC PC
13300 Riverdale Rd.,
80601
Ph: 303-659-6700

Yards: 7027, Holes: 18
Par: 72, USGA: 66.3
RP: 1 day in advance

Restaurant/Bar/Proshop
GF: w/day $23
Carts: $17.00

Scottish design, only Pete Dye public course west of Mississippi, so bigger landing areas than normal. Hole #5 429 yards from back tee, par 4 with big green, level, surrounded by grass swails and big depression undulating, can't see flag from it.

─────────────── COLORADO CITY ───────────────

Hollydot GC
#1 North Park Rd., 81019
Ph: 303-676-3341

Yards: 7010, Holes: 27
Par: 72, USGA: 68.4

Restaurant/Bar/Proshop
GF: w/day $7, w/end $10
Carts: $18.00

On this 27 hole championship course each 9 is unique. The first 9 is lush meadows with long par 4's, the Links nine is named appropriately as it links the 2 former 9 hole courses together in a Scottish style. The old course is tight with rolling fairways, a creek, and large trees.

─────────────── COLORADO SPRINGS ───────────────

**Country Club of
Colorado PC**
125 E. Clubhouse Dr.,
80906
Ph: 719-576-5560

Yards: 6978, Holes: 18
Par: 71, USGA: 69.5
RP: Guest at Cheyenne
Mt. Resort

Restaurant/Bar/Proshop
GF: w/day $67
Carts: Included

The first nine holes (Mountain nine) present a great test of golf with large undulating greens and requiring exceptional putting skills. The back nine (Lake nine) revolves around a 35 acre lake filled with trophy sized trout. The views of the Cheyenne Mountain Range offers spectacular views. A great golf course.

─────────────── COLORADO SPRINGS ───────────────

Pine Creek GC
9850 Divot Trail, 80920
Ph: 719-594-9999

Yards: 6980, Holes: 18
Par: 72, USGA: 72.1
RP: 3 days in advance

GF: w/day $16
Carts: $16.00

Generous fairways landing areas with subtle breaking greens ensure playability for all skill levels. Bunkers, trees, creeks and lakes, combined with elevation differences of the course are important features that create superb shot values, and strategic opportunities for each golfer to play.

─────────────── COPPER MOUNTAIN ───────────────

Copper Creek GC
170 and JNC. 91, P.O.
Box 3415, 80443
Ph: 303-968-2339

Yards: 6129, Holes: 18
Par: 70, USGA: 67.2
RP: 30 days resort
gst,4 otherwise

Restaurant/Bar/Proshop
GF: w/day $45
Carts: Included

Magnificent panoramas of the snow-capped 13,000 foot peaks surround you while golfing at Copper Creek Golf Course. Copper Mountain's championship course, at an elevation of 9,700 feet, is the highest 18 hole golf course in America. The course is another stunning example of the design talents of Pete and Perry Dye.

─────────────── CRESTED BUTTE ───────────────

Skyland Resort & CC
P.O. Box 879, 81225
Ph: 303-349-6131

Yards: 6635, Holes: 18
Par: 72, USGA: 68.8

Restaurant/Bar/Proshop
GF: w/day $45
Carts: Included

Skyland Resort and Country Club earned top marks from the national press from the day it opened and was rated in the top one percent of all new golf courses in the country. The spectacular mountain backdrop offers a breathtaking distraction just in case the challenging course leaves you in need of consolation.

Subscribe to our free newsletter, "Great Golf Gazette" and hear about the latest special golf vacation values.

──────────── DURANGO ────────────

Tamarron Resort GC
40292 U.S. Hwy 550 N.,
81301
Ph: 303-259-2000

Yards: 6885, Holes: 18
Par: 72, USGA: 69.9
RP: 1 day, if not on
package

Restaurant
GF: w/day $45
Carts: Included

Number 10 is one of Tamarron's more interesting holes. Try for about 210 yards on your drive. Any more and the ball and you will be in the rough of a steep embankment that drops far below the fairway's upper level. Although the green is large, it's almost totally surrounded by monstrous sand traps, plus water to the left rear.

──────────── FT. COLLINS ────────────

Collindale GC PC
1441 E. Horsetooth Rd.,
80525
Ph: 303-221-6651

Yards: 7011, Holes: 18
Par: 71, USGA: 68.8
RP: Day before

Restaurant/Bar/Proshop
GF: w/day $12, w/end $12
Carts: $15.00

Easy walking course in very good shape. Tight fairways with fast-soft greens. #6 is par 5 with beautiful view of Rocky Mountains in background.

──────────── HIGHLANDS RANCH ────────────

**The Links at
Highlands Ranch**
5815 E. Gleneagles
Village Park, 80126
Ph: 303-470-9292

Yards: 4780, Holes: 18
Par: 62, USGA: 60.9
RP: 1 week in advance

Restaurant/Bar/Proshop
GF: w/day $16, w/end $16
Carts: $14.00

Standing on the first tee you have a panoramic view of the Rocky Mountains. Looking straight west on the first tee is a view of Mt. Evans. Although we are considered an executive golf course—each hole presents its own special challenge. With pride we think our course is manicured like a country club. Open to the public

──────────── LA JUNTA ────────────

La Junta GC PC
27696 Harris Rd., 81050
Ph: 719-384-7133

Yards: 6374, Holes: 18
Par: 71, USGA: 69.0

Restaurant/Bar/Proshop
GF: w/day $8, w/end $10
Carts: $12.00

The course is relatively flat—no water holes. Blue grass fairways, bent grass greens. Very difficult rough. Tree lines fairways, small greens, narrow fairways. Tougher than it first appears.

──────────── LITTLETON ────────────

Arrowhead GC PC
10850 W. Sundown Trail,
80125
Ph: 303-973-4076

Yards: 6682, Holes: 18
Par: 70, USGA: 68.7
RP: 7 days in advance

Restaurant/Bar/Proshop
GF: w/day $45
Carts: Included

Very mountainous with some shots thru rock formations. There are 300 foot high rocks in fairway. There are elevated tees and fairways lined with pine, aspen and oak trees.

Please mention "Golf Courses—The Complete Guide" when you reserve your tee time. Our goal is to provide as complete a listing of golf courses open to the public as possible. If you know of a course we don't list, please send us the name and address on the form at the back of this guide.

--------------------- RIFLE ---------------------

Rifle Creek GC PC
3004 State Hwy. 325,
81650
Ph: 303-625-1093

Yards: 6250, Holes: 18
Par: 72, USGA: 67.0
RP: No more than 7
days in advance

Restaurant/Bar/Proshop
GF: w/day $13, w/end $16
Carts: $16.00

You will enjoy the greatly contrasting nines—the front nine winding through the canyons and sandstone rock cliffs, the back nine meanders through the meadows and along the banks of sparkling clear Rifle Creek—both have a fabulous view of the Rocky Mountains.

--------------------- SNOWMASS VILLAGE ---------------------

Snowmass GC
P.O. Drawer G-2, 81615
Ph: 303-923-5600

Yards: 6900, Holes: 18
Par: 71, USGA: 70.4

Restaurant/Bar/Proshop
GF: w/day $52
Carts: Included

Snowmass Golf Links is situated at the base of the valley, very Scottish links in appearance. It has nice elevation changes, and a substantial amount of water. Has hosted the Snowmass Club Invitational Pro-Am 1984-1987.

--------------------- STEAMBOAT SPRINGS ---------------------

Sheraton Steamboat GC
P.O. Box 774808, 80477
Ph: 303-879-2220

Yards: 6906, Holes: 18
Par: 72, USGA: 71.7
RP: Given with room
reservation

Restaurant/Bar/Proshop
GF: w/day $50, w/end $70
Carts: $12.00

The course is characterized by some great water holes, large greens. Greens are bentgrass while fairways and tees are bluegrass. #10 is a par 5, requiring length and accuracy off the tee to reach the green in two. Lay up shot is generally recommended, as a clear Colorado stream protects the green.

--------------------- VAIL ---------------------

Vail GC
1778 Vail Valley Dr.,
81657
Ph: 303-479-2260

Yards: 6282, Holes: 18
Par: 71, USGA: 68.0
RP: 48 hours in
advance

GF: w/day $65, w/end $40
Carts: $14.00 ea

The Vail Golf Club is an experience beyond description. The 7,100 yard championship course offers spectacular views of the magnificent Gore Range & is host to the annual Jerry Ford Invitational Golf Tournament. The par 71 course follows the meandering Gore Creek past numerous ponds.

--------------------- WESTMINSTER ---------------------

Hyland Hills GC
9650 N. Sheridan Blvd.,
80030
Ph: 303-428-6526

Yards: 7200, Holes: 18
Par: 72, USGA: 68.7
RP: Required

Restaurant/Bar/Proshop
GF: w/day $14
Carts: $16.00

The busiest course in Colorado. A tight hilly course with bent grass and big lakes. #7 is uphill 1st, par 4, downhill shot to a creek. #8 has an island green.

--------------------- WINTER PARK ---------------------

Pole Creek GC PC
P.O. Box 3348, 80482
Ph: 303-726-8847

Yards: 6882, Holes: 18
Par: 72, USGA: 69.6
RP: Up to 5 days ahead

Restaurant/Bar
GF: w/day $40, w/end $45
Carts: $22.00

Voted best new public course of 1985 by Golf Digest. The flowing Pole Creek comes into play many times as it meanders through the course. Its four lakes, sand, elevated tees and greens makes each hole a unique and different experience.

CONNECTICUT

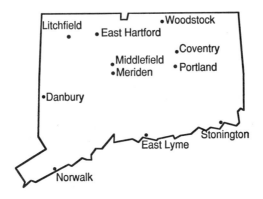

COVENTRY

Skungamaug River GC
104 Folly La., 06238
Ph: 203-742-9348

Yards: 6034, Holes: 18
Par: 70, USGA: 68.6
RP: One week in
advance

Restaurant/Bar/Proshop
GF: w/day $15
Carts: $16.00

Very sporty course, not too long, but narrow, heavily wooded fairways and undulating greens make it a challenge for all handicaps. The course is named after the beautiful trout stream that comes into play on four holes.

DANBURY

Richter Park GC
100 Aunt Hack Rd., 06811
Ph: 203-792-2552

Yards: 6741, Holes: 18
Par: 72, USGA: 71.1

Restaurant/Bar/Proshop
GF: w/day $40, w/end $40
Carts: $22.00

13 holes have water. The front 9 has West Lake, back nine has forest of maple, oak, birch and dogwoods. #14 overlooks city with highest elevation.

EAST HARTFORD

East Hartford GC
130 Long Hill St., 06108
Ph: 203-528-5082

Yards: 6076, Holes: 18
Par: 71, USGA: 68.6
RP: On weekends &
holidays

Restaurant/Bar/Proshop
GF: w/day $14, w/end $15
Carts: $8.50 ea.

"Looks are deceiving." Don't let yardage fool you. Course poses a challenge for everyone from beginner to club champion. One of the most heavily played golf courses in northeast.

EAST LYME

Cedar Ridge GC
18 Drabik Rd., 06333
Ph: 203-739-8439

Yards: 2959, Holes: 18
Par: 54

Proshop
GF: w/day $10, w/end $13

The finest par 3 layout in Connecticut with rolling hills and water hazards makes this course a challenge for the serious and a pleasant 2-2½ hours for the amateur. Ideal location for travelers and vacationers.

─────────────── LITCHFIELD ───────────────

Stonybrook GC   Yards: 5454, Holes: 9   Restaurant/Bar/Proshop
263 Milton Rd., 06759   Par: 68, USGA: 66.2   **GF:** w/day $11, w/end $15
Ph: 203-567-9977   RP: Call for starting   **Carts:** $11.00
                           times

Demanding 9 hole course with small, undulating greens and rolling contour mowed fairways. Accuracy off the tee is a must and putting skills are tested.

─────────────── MERIDEN ───────────────

Hunter GC   Yards: 6400, Holes: 18   Restaurant/Bar/Proshop
680 Westfield Rd., 06450   Par: 71, USGA: 71.3   **GF:** w/day $12
Ph: 203-634-3366   RP: Call in advance   **Carts:** $16.00

National Arbor Society recognizes the oak tree on 5th hole as oldest in state of Connecticut. The logo for golf course, also 610 yard par 5 10th hole longest in state of Connecticut. All new renovated in 1987 clubhouse and golf course outstanding test of golf on championship course.

─────────────── NORWALK ───────────────

Oak Hills GC   Yards: 6400, Holes: 18   Restaurant/Bar/Proshop
165 Fillow St., 06850   Par: 71, USGA: 68.0   **GF:** w/day $16
Ph: 203-838-0303   RP: Walk in or 1 week   **Carts:** $18.00
                           in advance

The first 7 holes are tight and hilly, while the remaining 11 holes appear to be more open and longer. The course in general is aesthetically pleasing and with the wooded area and random trees there's a feeling of being far removed from urban life.

─────────────── PORTLAND ───────────────

Portland GC West   Yards: 4012, Holes: 18   Restaurant/Bar/Proshop
Gospel Ln. (Rt 17), 06480 Par: 60, USGA: 60.4   **GF:** w/day $18, w/end $20
Ph: 203-342-4043   RP: Only needed for   **Carts:** $17.00
                           weekends

18 hole par 60. A true test for any type of golfer.

─────────────── STONINGTON ───────────────

Pequot GC   Yards: 5903, Holes: 18   Restaurant/Bar/Proshop
Wheeler Rd., Box 139A,   Par: 70, USGA: 67.2   **GF:** w/day $11, w/end $15
06378   RP: Tee times on   **Carts:** $18.00
Ph: 203-535-1898   weekends

Pequot's par 70, 18 hole course is laid out over gently rolling terrain in a beautiful Connecticut country setting. A favorite golfing spot for summer visitors as well as year round residents.

─────────────── WOODSTOCK ───────────────

Harrisville GC   Yards: 3019, Holes: 9   Proshop
Harrisville Rd., 06281   Par: 36   **GF:** w/day $7, w/end $10
Ph: 203-928-6098   **Carts:** $7.50

The uphill battle of the 610 yard par 5 6th hole has been the making or breaking of many a round of play at Harrisville.

DELAWARE

Smyrna

MIDDLEFIELD

Lyman Meadow GC
Route 157, 06455
Ph: 203-349-8055

Yards: 7011, Holes: 18
Par: 72, USGA: 73.5
RP: Required

Restaurant/Bar/Proshop
GF: w/day $18, w/end $23
Carts: $20.00

The front nine is more tree lined than the back. The back nine has water on 8 out of the 9 holes. The 12th hole is a great dogleg left par 5 with the gambler trying to cut off as much of the dogleg as possible. There is water on the left and right of the fairway along with a brook behind the green.

SMYRNA

Garrisons Lake GC
101 Fairways Circle,
19977
Ph: 302-653-6349

Yards: 7028, Holes: 18
Par: 72
RP: Members only Sat
& Sun

Restaurant/Bar/Proshop
GF: w/day $15, w/end $21
Carts: $9.00 ea

The course is a tree lined championship course. Holes 5 and 8 were chosen as 2 of the best holes in Delaware. The back nine has 5 water holes. The course has been chosen by Golf Digest as one of the five best in the state and it has been the site of the Delaware amateur and open championships on several occasions.

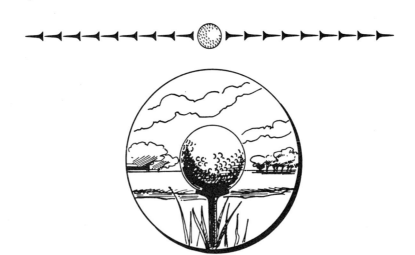

Niceville
Pensacola
Destin
Port St. Joe
Sunny Hills
Gulf Breeze
Fort Walton Beach
Tallahassee
Bonifay
Deland
Crystal River
Inverness
Middleburg
Amelia Island
Ponte Vedra Beach
St. Augustine
Ocala
Crescent City
Grenelefe
Winter Springs
Orlando
Zephyrhills
Wesley Chapel
Tarpon Springs
Valrico
St. Petersburg
Longboat Key
Venice
Punta Gorda
Captiva
Sarasota
Cape Coral
Bonita Springs
Naples
Hutchinson Island
Marathon
Taveres
Kissimee
Hernando
Dunedin
Lake Placid
Winter Haven
Sebring
N. Fort Myers
Ft. Myers
Lehigh
Cocoa Beach
Melbourne
Titusville
Palm Beach
Stuart
Palm Beach Gardens
Boynton Beach
Boca Raton
Vero Beach
Pompano Beach
Ft. Lauderdale
Tamarac
Miami
Hollywood-By-The-Sea
Royal Palm Beach
Howey-in-the-Hills
Key Biscayne

FLORIDA

AMELIA ISLAND

Amelia Island Plantation
Highway A1A South, 32034
Ph: 904-261-6161

Yards: 6740, Holes: 45
Par: 72, USGA: 72.5
RP: Must be guest

Restaurant/Bar
GF: w/day $50
Carts: $22.00

Amelia Links is a Pete Dye 27-hole masterpiece. Long, winding fairways are framed by vivid moss-draped forests. Holes 4, 5 and 6 hug the Atlantic to keep you on your tees. Long Point beckons with unusual natural hazards, highly elevated fairways, large bodies of water and more marshland and beachside play.

BOCA RATON

Boca Raton Resort & Club
501 E. Camino Real, 33432
Ph: 407-395-3000

Yards: 6154, Holes: 36
Par: 71, USGA: 71.7
RP: Must be hotel guest or member

Restaurant/Bar/Proshop
GF: w/day $45
Carts: $13.50

You step out of your room to 18 hole Joe Lee, championship course. A 2nd 18 holes, our Country Club course, a short 6 miles west of us.

BOCA RATON

Camino Del Mar CC
22689 Camino Del Mar Dr., 33433
Ph: 407-392-7992

Yards: 6609, Holes: 18
Par: 71, USGA: 69.1
RP: Public 2 days in advance

Proshop
GF: w/day $32, w/end $32
Carts: $12.00 ea

Offers the golfer an opportunity to test his/her strength, skill, and ingenuity on 18 holes of varying difficulty and complexity. Some holes are relatively simple, while others (like the 12th) will serve as barometers of one's ability to deal with dogleg holes, water, and embankment.

──────────────── BONIFAY ────────────────

Dogwood's CC Yards: 6583, Holes: 18 Restaurant/Bar/Proshop
Rt. 3, Box 954, 32425 Par: 72, USGA: 71.4 **GF:** w/day $9
Ph: 904-547-9381 **Carts:** $12.00

The Dogwood's is a gently rolling, tight fairways, water comes into play on 6 holes and all greens are well trapped. The Dogwood's is a beautiful setting and country club style. Very challenging well laidout course, the best kept secret in the panhandle of Florida.

──────────────── BONITA SPRINGS ────────────────

Pelican's Nest Yards: 6908, Holes: 18 Restaurant/Bar/Proshop
4450 Bay Creek Dr., Par: 72, USGA: 70.8 **GF:** w/day $35
33923 RP: 2 days in advance **Carts:** Included
Ph: 813-947-4600

Designed for beauty, bordered by picturesques spring creek with venerable cypress and oak with views of forest. There are also pines, palm, meadow bushes and tropical swamp. #9 a par 5 is challenging with trees as obstacle, long shot into green over canyon with creek.

──────────────── BOYNTON BEACH ────────────────

Boynton Beach Muni GC Yards: 6032, Holes: 27 Restaurant/Bar/Proshop
8020 Jog Rd. 33437 Par: 71, USGA: 68.5 **GF:** w/day $8
Ph: 407-969-2200 RP: Call in advance **Carts:** $6.00

Surrounded on three sides by major canals, and a farm to the west, this 156 acre 27 hole golf complex provides an isolated spot to play golf and commune with nature. Noted for its rolling terrain, numerous trees, and eight lakes, Boynton Beach Municipal Golf Course is unique to Florida and run only by P.G.A. professionals.

──────────────── BOYNTON BEACH ────────────────

Cypress Creek CC Yards: 6369, Holes: 18 Restaurant/Bar/Proshop
9400 Military Trail, 33436 Par: 72, USGA: 70.0 **GF:** w/day $17
Ph: 407-732-4202 RP: Required 24 hours **Carts:** Included
  in advance

A relatively open golf course with water on 13 holes, not all of which come into play. The small greens have many interesting breaks for some different putting situations. Wide variety of par threes from 120 to 210 yards.

──────────────── CAPE CORAL ────────────────

Cape Coral G & RC Yards: 6771, Holes: 18 Restaurant/Bar/Proshop
4003 Palm Tree Blvd., Par: 72, USGA: 69.3 **GF:** w/day $7
33904 RP: 48 hour **Carts:** $10.50
Ph: 813-542-7879 cancellation

Features 113 sand traps and has water come into play on nine of the eighteen holes. Number nine, a par 5, is our character hole; the golfer starts out with trees and bunkers to the right and out of bounds to the left coming out of the shoot. From that point on, the remaining fairway is guarded both left and right by lakes and sand traps and the golfer finds himself hitting into a well bunkered green.

──────────────── CAPTIVA ────────────────

South Seas Plantation GC Yards: 3300, Holes: 9 Restaurant/Bar
P.O.Box 194 33924 Par: 36 **GF:** w/day $14
Ph: 813-472-5111 RP: 1 day in advance

The course is flat with a couple of lakes and a pretty stretch of fairway bordering the beach. This is the site of the annual South Seas Plantation Golf Traditional Tournament benefitting the Big Brothers/Sisters of Lee County.

─────────── COCOA BEACH ───────────

Cocoa Beach GC
Tom Warriner Blvd.,
POB 320280, 32932
Ph: 407-868-3351

Yards: 6600, Holes: 18
Par: 72, USGA: 70.7
RP: Weekends and
holidays

Restaurant/Bar/Proshop
GF: w/day $14
Carts: $14.00

The front nine plays 1-2 shots easier than the back on this long open course set by the Banana River. The back nine can be particularly brutal when winds come up each afternoon. Being only 2 miles from the ocean provides comfortable weather year round.

─────────── CRESCENT CITY ───────────

Live Oak G&CC
SR 309, Star Route 2
Box 452, 32012
Ph: 904-467-2512

Yards: 2800, Holes: 9
Par: 35, USGA: 33.5

Rolling contour elevated green, giant oaks, lush tropical foliage and blue waters of Clearwater Bay. Water comes into play on most holes.

─────────── CRYSTAL RIVER ───────────

Plantation Inn & GR
P.O. Box 1116, 32629
Ph: 904-795-4211

Yards: 6644, Holes: 27
Par: 72

Restaurant/Bar/Proshop

Home of the Florida Women's Open. Tropical vegetation, many natural lakes and ponds, and strategically placed traps and bunkers offer a real test of your game. We also have a marked driving range.

─────────── DELAND ───────────

Southridge GC
800 E Euclid Ave., 32724
Ph: 904-736-0560

Yards: 5855, Holes: 18
Par: 72, USGA: 67.4
RP: 2 days in advance

Bar/Proshop
GF: w/day $11
Carts: $18.00

Southridge is an interesting, well maintained, 18 hole course, built on rolling hills with lots of trees. A favorite of many people in Central Florida. People come here year after year. Once you play it, you'll see why.

─────────── DESTIN ───────────

Sandestin GC
Emerald Coast Pkwy.,
32541
Ph: 904-267-8248

Yards: 5565, Holes: 18
Par: 72, USGA: 66.1
RP: Up to 24 hours in
advance

Restaurant/Bar/Proshop
GF: w/day $25, w/end $39
Carts: $21.00

45 beautifully scenic holes—from the Links side course where 15 holes play around and through canals and levy to Baytowne where you can choose between The Dunes, The Harbor and The Troon 9's. Some of the most beautiful in Florida.

─────────── DESTIN ───────────

Santa Rosa GC & BC
Rt 1, Box 3950, 32459
Ph: 904-267-2229

Yards: 6608, Holes: 18
Par: 72, USGA: 66.1
RP: 3 days in advance

Restaurant/Bar/Proshop
Carts: $20.00

Four sets of tees allow visiting players the opportunity to challenge their own abilities. The golf course plays through a mature seaside forest out to a scenic view of the Gulf of Mexico. Every club will be used in attempt to subdue and enjoy a course of six hard, six soft, and six medium holes.

─────────────────── DUNEDIN ───────────────────

Dunedin CC
1050 Palm Blvd., 34698
Ph: 813-733-7836

Yards: 6245, Holes: 18
Par: 72, USGA: 69.0
RP: Must stay in/live
in Dunedin

Restaurant/Bar/Proshop
GF: w/day $31
Carts: Included

Formerly PGA National Golf Course from 1945 to 1962.

─────────────────── FORT LAUDERDALE ───────────────────

Bonaventure Hotel GC
250 Racquet Club Rd.,
33326
Ph: 305-389-3300

Yards: 6557, Holes: 18
Par: 72, USGA: 71.0

Restaurant/Bar
GF: w/day $26
Carts: Included

Plenty of trees, water and bunkers on this course to make true shotmaking very important. The East Course at 7,011 from the blue tees, also give you plenty of opportunities to really cut loose. The 3rd hole of the East Course is a waterfall hole which is often photographed.

─────────────────── FORT MYERS ───────────────────

River's Edge Yacht & CC
14700 Portsmouth Blvd.
33908
Ph: 813-433-4211

Yards: 6896, Holes: 18
Par: 72, USGA: 67.9
RP: Two days in
advance

Proshop
GF: w/day $35
Carts: Included

To warm up, the customer uses our beautiful aqua driving range. Our course is bordered by the beautiful Calooshatchee River in S.W. Fort Myers. Our golf course offers 4 sets of tees to accommodate all level of players.

─────────────────── FORT WALTON BEACH ───────────────────

**Fort Walton Beach
Muni GC**
Louis Turner Blvd,
P.O. Box 4090, 32549
Ph: 904-862-3314

Yards: 6083, Holes: 18
Par: 72, USGA: 67.7
RP: 2 days in advance

Restaurant/Proshop
GF: w/day $13
Carts: $10.00

There are four water holes, the tees are long, the greens large and the wide fairways are bordered by huge pines and live oaks. There are occasional fairway bunkers, but they are not too hard to avoid. The course is heavily played but is well handled by starters and well maintained by the grounds staff.

─────────────────── GRENELEFE ───────────────────

Grenelefe Resort
3200 St. Rd. 546, 33844
Ph: 813-422-7511

Yards: 7325, Holes: 18
Par: 72
RP: Private Resort—
Resv. available

Restaurant/Bar
GF: w/day $28, w/end $33
Carts: $13.50 ea

54 holes of championship golf on 3 courses. The West Course has long, tight fairways lined with tall pines and monstrous bunkers. The East Course is much shorter and tighter. The South Course incorporates a variety of length, terrain and hazards. Site of the 1991 PGA Tour Qualifying School finals.

─────────────────── GULF BREEZE ───────────────────

Tiger Point CC
1255 Country Club Dr.,
32561
Ph: 904-932-1333

Yards: 7033, Holes: 18
Par: 72, USGA: 69.8
RP: 2 days in advance

Restaurant/Bar/Proshop
GF: w/day $40
Carts: $18.00

The natural beauty and seaside scenery of the Tiger Point East and West course is a golfer's delight—offering memorable challenges in a picturesque setting. Pine trees and waterways line links type fairways. My favorite hole is the 4th hole on Tiger Point East, it is a challenging par 4 with an island green.

──────────────── HERNANDO ────────────────

Citrus Hills G & CC   Yards: 6418, Holes: 36   Restaurant/Bar/Proshop
500 E. Hartford St., 32642   Par: 70, USGA: 66.3   **GF:** w/day $18
Ph: 904-746-4425   RP: 2 days in advance   **Carts:** $10.00

Citrus Hills offers a bit of New England in sunny Florida. The tree lined fairways traipse across gentle rolling hills. Water and sand bunkers around aplenty.

──────────────── HOLLYWOOD-BY-THE-SEA ────────────────

Diplomat CC   Yards: 6625, Holes: 18   Restaurant/Bar
3515 S. Ocean Dr., 33019   Par: 72, USGA: 70.6   **GF:** w/day $15
Ph: 305-457-8111   **Carts:** Included

The Diplomat is a flat course with plenty of water hazards and bunkers.

──────────────── HOWEY-IN-THE-HILLS ────────────────

Mission Inn Golf &   Yards: 6770, Holes: 36   Restaurant/Bar/Proshop
Tennis Resort   Par: 72, USGA: 70.9   **GF:** w/day $37
10400 CR 48, 34737   RP: 1 week   **Carts:** Included
Ph: 904-324-3101

Mission Inn's picturesque 18 hole championship golf course boasts 85 foot elevation differences from tee to green, 13 holes with water, Scottish berms, well-placed traps, island greens and tree-lined fairways. New clubhouse & 2nd. 18-hole championship course designed by Gary Koch.

──────────────── HUTCHINSON ISLAND ────────────────

Indian River   Yards: 4042, Holes: 18   Restaurant/Bar
Plantation GC   Par: 61, USGA: 56.9   **GF:** w/day $22
385 NE Plantation Rd.,   RP: 1 day in advance   **Carts:** $24.00
33996
Ph: 407-225-3700

The River Course, and Plantation Course are both relatively flat (everything is in these parts), have terrific bunkering, undulating greens, ocean breezes, and seem to have water everywhere.

──────────────── INVERNESS ────────────────

Point O' Woods GC   Yards: 1836, Holes: 9   Restaurant/Bar/Proshop
Gospel Island Rd., 32650   Par: 30, USGA: 29.5   **GF:** w/day $8
Ph: 904-726-3113   **Carts:** $10.00

Easy walking executive 9 hole course, reasonable rates—friendly atmosphere.

──────────────── KEY BISCAYNE ────────────────

Key Biscayne GC   Yards: 7070, Holes: 18   Restaurant/Bar/Proshop
6700 Crandon Blvd.,   Par: 72, USGA: 71.0   **GF:** w/day $10, w/end $12
33149   RP: 2 days in advance   **Carts:** $22.0
Ph: 305-361-9129

Only course on an island, it's surrounded by mangrove swamps. On Biscayne Bay, palm trees, alligators and birds abound. #3 in Golf Magazine in U.S. public courses.

Subscribe to our free newsletter, "Great Golf Gazette" and hear about the latest special golf vacation values.

---------------------------------- KISSIMMEE ----------------------------------

Poinciana GC
500 E. Cypress Pkwy.,
32759
Ph: 407-933-5300

Yards: 6700, Holes: 18
Par: 72, USGA: 69.1
RP: 7 days in advance

Restaurant/Bar/Proshop
GF: w/day $8, w/end $12
Carts: $14.00

Poinciana combines water on 13 holes, 69 bunkers and carves it's way through a cypress forest. The result is one of Florida's top rated and best kept secrets. Hole #7 is challenging, fun and beautiful. Your tee shot must carry the lake that also runs down the left side and guards the front of green. To the right is the cypress forest. Please don't feed the alligators.

---------------------------------- LAKE PLACID ----------------------------------

Placid Lakes Inn CC
3601 Jefferson Ave.,
33852
Ph: 813-465-4333

Yards: 6632, Holes: 18
Par: 72, USGA: 69.9
RP: 1 day in advance

Restaurant/Bar/Proshop
GF: w/day $14
Carts: $10.00

Our toughest hole is #18. This long, straightaway par four measures 405 yards with water guarding both sides of the landing area. A tough finishing hole which usually plays into the wind.

---------------------------------- LEHIGH ----------------------------------

Lehigh CC
225 East Joel Blvd.,
33936
Ph: 813-369-2121

Yards: 6115, Holes: 18
Par: 72, USGA: 68.8
RP: 24 hours before

Restaurant/Bar/Proshop
GF: w/day $20
Carts: $20.00

Number 9 on the North Course is the pro's favorite hole. The hole offers a dogleg right requiring an extremely long tee shot and a pin point accurate second shot onto a well bunkered green. The yardage on #5 at our South Course speaks for itself; a 249 par 3, over water and into a very well bunkered green.

---------------------------------- LONGBOAT KEY ----------------------------------

Longboat Key GC
301 Gulf of Mexico Dr.,
34228
Ph: 813-383-8821

Yards: 6890, Holes: 45
Par: 72, USGA: 74.2
RP: Hotel guest—2½
days advance

Restaurant/Bar
GF: w/day $100.00
Carts: Included

Islandside, the "watery challenge" is an acknowledged 18-hole test of accuracy with long fairways threaded throughout lakes and lagoons. Harbourside is a longer 27-hole layout. The course is wrapped around Sarasota Bay and cuts through a lush sub-tropical jungle. Sixty bunkers await the golfer who also has to negotiate lagoons, canals and the bay itself.

---------------------------------- MARATHON ----------------------------------

Sombrero CC
33050
Ph: 305-743-3433

Yards: 6303, Holes: 18
Par: 71, USGA: 68.0

Fabulous golfing awaits you at the Sombrero Country Club. Water abounds, affecting at least 12 holes. The 18th hole is a bang up finishing hole: 2 water hazards, one for you to teeoff over and the other guarding the green.

Enter your favorite resort in our "Golf Resort of The Year" contest (entry form is in the back of the book).

───────── MELBOURNE ─────────

Palm Gardens GC
2630 Minton Rd., 32904
Ph: 407-723-3182

Yards: 1600, Holes: 9
Par: 31, USGA: 55.5

Restaurant/Bar/Proshop
GF: w/day $5
Carts: $5.19

Palm Gardens is a challenging nine hole executive golf course. It is an attractive course laid out with minimum alterations to the beautiful Florida landscape. Tees and greens are elevated, with water and traps in play often. You have to hit them straight!

───────── MIAMI ─────────

Doral Hotel GC
4400 NW 87th Ave., 33178
Ph: 305-592-2000

Yards: 6597, Holes: 99
Par: 72, USGA: 70.4
RP: When you make hotel res.

Restaurant/Bar
GF: w/day $72, w/end $72
Carts: Included

The resort offers 99 holes of golf, including a par 3 executive course. The Blue Monster is a watery, sandy long expanse. The 18th hole here has been consistently ranked as one of the toughest on the PGA tour, a par 4 unless you're bunkering it or al lago.

───────── MIAMI ─────────

Kings Bay Resort CC
14401 SW 62nd Ave.,
33158
Ph: 305-235-7161

Yards: 6556, Holes: 18
Par: 73, USGA: 69.1

Restaurant/Bar
GF: w/day $15
Carts: $12.00

The rolling fairways, well-trapped greens and water hazards of the front nine contrast beautifully with the bayside back nine where both land and sea blend to provide the ultimate challenge.

───────── MIAMI ─────────

Miami Lakes GC
7601 NW Miami Lakes
Dr., 33014
Ph: 305-821-1150

Yards: 6512, Holes: 18
Par: 72, USGA: 70.5
RP: 24 hours

Restaurant/Bar
GF: w/day $15
Carts: $24.00

Beautiful course in a natural setting with tree lined fairways and wandering lakes. Our favorite is the 427 yard, par 4, 18th hole dogleg left over one of the largest lakes on the course.

───────── MIAMI ─────────

Turnberry Isle CC
19735 Turnbury Way,
33180
Ph: 305-932-6200

Yards: 6985, Holes: 36
Par: 72, USGA: 72.9

Restaurant/Bar
GF: w/day $22
Carts: $22.00

Two of Robert Trent Jones' creations provide 36 challenging hole, featuring the largest triple green in the world. The South course has been the site of the Elizabeth Arden Classic and the PGA Senior Championship, as well as numerous celebrity and private tournaments.

───────── MIDDLEBURG ─────────

Ravines Golf & CC
2932 Ravines Rd., 32068
Ph: 904-282-7800

Yards: 6132, Holes: 18
Par: 72, USGA: 72.2
RP: 2 days in advance

Restaurant/Bar/Proshop
GF: w/day $15
Carts: $10.00 ea

Ravines Golf Course is without reservation or close competition the most dramatic natural course in Florida. More than 50 varieties of hardwood trees, rolling terrain, and deep ravines make it similar in character to the highland courses found in North Carolina.

─────────────── NAPLES ───────────────

Naples Beach Hotel GC Yards: 6101, Holes: 18   Restaurant/Bar
851 Gulf Shore Blvd.,   Par: 72   **GF:** w/day $31
33940
Ph: 813-261-2222

Our golf course is a golfer's delight. Undulating greens, manicured fairways. . .a superb layout where doglegs, water and sand combine to challenge every player's skill.

─────────────── NAPLES ───────────────

Palm River CC   Yards: 6426, Holes: 18   Restaurant/Bar/Proshop
Palm River Blvd., 33942   Par: 72, USGA: 71.3   **GF:** w/day $14
Ph: 813-597-3554   RP: 48 hours in   **Carts:** $11.00 ea
   advance

One of Naples' oldest golf courses that proves challenging and enjoyable to golfers of all ability levels.

─────────────── NICEVILLE ───────────────

Country Club at Blue   Yards: 6888, Holes: 27   Restaurant/Bar
Water Bay   Par: 72, USGA: 70.4
P.O. Box 247, 32578
Ph: 904-897-3613

Golf on any combination of our three championship 9 hole Fazio designed courses is a beautiful, challenging experience. The heavily wooded course is enhanced by water, marsh and rolling terrain. The course is ranked among the top courses in the state and number one in Northwest Florida.

─────────────── NORTH FORT MYERS ───────────────

Del Tura CC   Yards: 4102, Holes: 27   Restaurant/Bar/Proshop
18621 N. Tamiami Tr.,   Par: 61, USGA: 59.3   **GF:** w/day $15
33903   RP: 1 day in advance   **Carts:** $10.00
Ph: 813-731-5400

Don't let the term "executive" steer you clear of this golf course. The course record stands at 6 under par and this is through over 10 professional tournaments. This little tiger is very fair but no pussycat.

─────────────── NORTH FORT MYERS ───────────────

El Rio GC PC   Yards: 2923, Holes: 18   Restaurant/Bar/Proshop
1801 Skyline Dr., 33903   Par: 60, USGA: 52.9   **GF:** w/day $9
Ph: 813-995-2204   RP: May be made 7   **Carts:** $4.50 ea
   days in advance

El Rio is a sporty executive course where shot placement is more important than distance. Sand traps, lakes and trees blend to create a picturesque setting and add a challenging angle to the game.

─────────────── NORTH FORT MYERS ───────────────

Lochmoor CC   Yards: 6940, Holes: 18   Restaurant/Bar/Proshop
3911 Orange Grove   Par: 72, USGA: 70.6   **GF:** w/day $13
Blvd., 33903   RP: Two days in   **Carts:** $8.00 ea
Ph: 813-995-0501   advance

Hundreds of existing and majestic Pines and Palms dot and shape the fairways and blend naturally with picturesque lakes as if they had been there for many years. Several lakes come directly into play, but are fairly situated so as to add to Lochmoor's competitive spirit.

──────────────── OCALA ────────────────

Pine Oaks GC
2201 NW 21st St, 32675
Ph: 904-622-8558

Yards: 5762, Holes: 27
Par: 72, USGA: 67.5
RP: 2 days in advance

Restaurant/Bar/Proshop
GF: w/day $11
Carts: $6.00

The North nine begins with a short but tight par 4. Then opens up to give you a little breathing room. The last four holes are long and narrow with smaller greens. The East nine is very narrow with many large oak trees well placed. Overall the greens are very small requiring accurate approach shots.

──────────────── ORLANDO ────────────────

Alhambra G & TC
4700 S. Texas Ave., 32809
Ph: 407-851-6250

Yards: 6400, Holes: 18
Par: 72
RP: Jan-Mar everyday

Restaurant/Bar/Proshop
GF: w/day $8
Carts: $10.00 ea

The golf course is mainly wide open but challenging to all caliber of golfers. Our fully stocked prop shop and friendly golf pros can assist you with all aspects of your game.

──────────────── ORLANDO ────────────────

Bay Hill GC & Lodge
9000 Bay Hill Blvd., 32819
Ph: 407-876-2429

Yards: 7114, Holes: 27
Par: 72, USGA: 71.8
RP: Lodge guests &
members only

Restaurant/Bar/Proshop
GF: w/day $100,
w/end $100
Carts: $12.00 ea

Length is a must with some very demanding approach shots to greens. All eighteen greens were recently redesigned and renovated by Arnold Palmer, we are home to the Nestle Invitational and the 18th hole has been considered one of the toughest holes in the country. Arnold Palmer owns Bay Hill and makes his home here at Bay Hill.

──────────────── ORLANDO ────────────────

Grand Cypress GC
1 N. Jacaranda, 32819
Ph: 407-239-4700

Yards: 7024, Holes: 45
Par: 72, USGA: 73.9
RP: 60 days in advance

Restaurant/Bar/Proshop
GF: w/day $100
Carts: Included

Jack Nicklaus has created courses characterized by meandering grassy dunes, natural brush-like hazards, pot bunkers, wildflowers and trees. The "New Course" pays tribute to the St. Andrews "Old Course." Uundulating double greens, bridges, walls and burns are Scottish style. The Grand Cypress North-South Course was host to the 1990 World Cup of Golf by Kraft General Foods November 21-24.

──────────────── ORLANDO ────────────────

Marriott's Orlando
World Center
One World Center Dr.,
32821
Ph: 407-239-5659

Yards: 6290, Holes: 18
Par: 71, USGA: 67.9
RP: One week in
advance

Restaurant/Bar/Proshop
GF: w/day $70, w/end $70
Carts: Included

Although this Joe Lee designed course is not long, water and sand make bogies out of errant shots. Our breathtaking hotel is in clear view from every hole. A prevailing wind from the east and elevated greens makes our 18th a difficult par.

Our listings—supplied by the management—are as complete as possible. Many of the courses have more features than we list. Be sure to inquire when you book your tee time.

─────────────── ORLANDO ───────────────

Wedgefield GC CC   Yards: 6738, Holes: 18   Restaurant/Bar/Proshop
20550 Maxim Pkwy.,   Par: 72, USGA: 70.5   **GF:** w/day $21, w/end $28
32820   RP: 3 days in advance
Ph: 407-568-2116

An interesting blend of short and long holes. Short holes placing a premium on accurate shotmaking. A very well manicured layout. The closing holes of Wedgefield are the makers or breakers of champions.

─────────────── PALM BEACH ───────────────

Breakers Hotel GC   Yards: 7101, Holes: 36   Restaurant/Bar
South County Rd., 33480   Par: 71, USGA: 70.1   **GF:** w/day $24
Ph: 305-659-8470   RP: 2 days in advance   **Carts:** $22.00

The Ocean Course is short with tight fairways and small, elevated greens. #14, a figure "S" hole uphill, has deep bunkers and small elevated green. The Breakers West's re-designed #9 has a distinct dog leg requiring a second water shot onto the new three-tiered green.

─────────────── PALM BEACH GARDENS ───────────────

PGA National Golf Club   Yards: 7022, Holes: 90   Restaurant/Bar
1000 Ave. of the   Par: 72, USGA: 74.4   **GF:** w/day $65
Champions, 33418   RP: 1 year designated   **Carts:** $16.00
Ph: 407-627-1800

There are five championship courses, including Jack Nicklaus redesigned Champion: host to P.G.A. Seniors' Championships, 1987 P.G.A. Championship, and 1983 Ryder Cup Matches. Health & Raquet Club w/ 19 Tennis Courts, Nautilus, Racquetball, Swiming Pools. Croquet, Spa de Mer, and Golf Schools.

─────────────── PENSACOLA ───────────────

Carriage Hills GC   Yards: 5530, Holes: 18   Restaurant/Bar/Proshop
2355 W. Michigan Ave.,   Par: 72, USGA: 65.3   **GF:** w/day $18
32506   RP: 2 days in advance   **Carts:** $14.00
Ph: 904-944-5497

Scenic course with creek running the entire length of the course. On several holes you have to make the decision of whether or not to lay up or "go for it". A real test of nerves.

─────────────── PLANTATION ───────────────

Jacaranda GC   Yards: 6790, Holes: 36   Restaurant/Bar/Proshop
9200 W. Broward Blvd.,   Par: 72, USGA: 70.3   **GF:** w/day $60, w/end $65
33324   RP: 7 days in   **Carts:** Included
Ph: 305-472-5836   advance—resort

Both golf courses are aesthetically appeling, providing a great challenge. Our East Course is open, comparatively speaking, to the West. Narrow fairways and small rolling greens on the West. The East Course stretches to 7400 yards and the West 6700 yards.

─────────────── POMPANO BEACH ───────────────

Crystal Lake CC   Yards: 6600, Holes: 18   Restaurant/Bar/Proshop
3800 Crystal Lake Dr.,   Par: 72, USGA: 72.0   **GF:** w/day $11, w/end $18
33064   RP: 2 days in advance   **Carts:** $12.00
Ph: 305-943-2902

Amen corner holes 4-5-6 are really good tests of golf. #18 on back requires 3 good shots just to reach the green. Plays 590 from back tees.

─────────────── POMPANO BEACH ───────────────

Palm Aire Spa Resort
2601 Palm Aire Dr. N.,
33069
Ph: 305-972-3300

Yards: 6371, Holes: 58
Par: 72, USGA: 70.1
RP: 3 days in advance

Restaurant/Bar
GF: w/day $36, w/end $36
Carts: $11.00

This destination Resort has won the "Best of the South" award from Southern Links Magazine, as well as, the Mobil Four Star and AAA Four Diamond Awards; it features two challenging 18-Hole Championship Courses - "the Palms" and "the Pines" and a 22-Hole Executive Course-"the Sabals".

─────────────── PONTE VEDRA BEACH ───────────────

Marriott at Sawgrass-TCP Stadium
P.O. Box 600, 32082
Ph: 904-285-7777

Yards: 5761, Holes: 99
Par: 72, USGA: 70.6
RP: May be made with room resv.

Restaurant/Bar
GF: w/day $80
Carts: $15.00

There are 99 holes of championship golf, including the famous par 3, 17th floating hole of the PGA TPC Stadium course. The new TPC Valley Course is rated as one of the all-time great courses. There's also Marsh Landing Course, Oceanside Course, plus Oak Bridge. This short and narrow course is the most forgiving.

─────────────── PORT ST. JOE ───────────────

St. Joseph's Bay CC
Route C-30 South, P.O.
Box 993, 32456
Ph: 904-227-1751

Yards: 6473, Holes: 18
Par: 72, USGA: 70.7

Restaurant/Bar/Proshop
GF: w/day $12
Carts: $6.50 ea

Warm up on our first five holes, then get ready for a challenge. Sixteen ponds plus natural rough will test your ability. The par 3 twelfth hole is 180 yards plus with a very narrow fairway. Green is guarded by a pond on the right and a dense woods on the left.

─────────────── PUNTA GORDA ───────────────

Marina GC at Burnt Store
3150 Matecumbe Key Rd., 33955
Ph: 813-637-1577

Yards: 5809, Holes: 18
Par: 60, USGA: 59.3
RP: Call for tee times

Restaurant/Bar
GF: w/day $10
Carts: $7.50

An 18 hole par 60 executive course, it is a flat layout with plenty of water. A second nine, par 29, was designed by Mark McCumber, also credited with Dunes Country Club on neighboring Sanibel Island.

─────────────── ROCKLEDGE ───────────────

Turtle Creek GC
1278 Admiralty Blvd.,
32955
Ph: 407-632-2520

Yards: 6709, Holes: 18
Par: 72, USGA: 70.1
RP: 7 days in adv.,
Slope 129

Restaurant/Bar/Proshop
GF: w/day $37, w/end $37
Carts: Included

Blending the natural beauty of the terrain with the insight of the Arnold Palmer Golf Management Company, the course features wooded fairways, meandering creeks and strategic bunkers resulting in a splendid challenge for golfers of all levels. Experience legendary excellence at Turtle Creek Golf Club.

Enter your favorite resort in our "Golf Resort of The Year" contest (entry form is in the back of the book).

———————————————— ROYAL PALM BEACH ————————————————

Royal Palm Beach CC Yards: 7067, Holes: 18 Restaurant/Bar/Proshop
900 Royal Palm Beach Par: 72, USGA: 72.5 **GF:** w/day $18
Blvd., 33411 **Carts:** Included
Ph: 407-798-6430

*Old style Florida course featuring wide fairways bordered by impressive banyan
trees. Well trapped with a moderate number of water hazards. Large, easily-
accessible greens. Very fair for the average golfer using the white tees and an
excellent challenge from the blue tees for the low handicapper.*

———————————————————— SARASOTA ————————————————————

Bobby Jones Golf Yards: 6468, Holes: 45 Restaurant/Bar/Proshop
Complex Par: 72, USGA: 69.2 **GF:** w/day $8, w/end $8
1000 Azinger Way, 34232 RP: First come, first **Carts:** $8.00 ea
Ph: 813-955-8041 serve

*This fine municipal facility was opened by Bobby Jones playing the inaugural
match in 1927. Since that time many golf inmortals such as Tommy Armour,
Gene Saragen, Walter Hogen, Helen Hicks and Patty Berg have frequented the
course. Facility is dotted with majestic Oaks and several lakes.*

———————————————————— SARASOTA ————————————————————

Foxfire GC Yards: 6000, Holes: 27 Restaurant/Proshop
7200 Proctor Rd., 34241 Par: 72, USGA: 69.1
Ph: 813-921-7757 RP: 2 days in advance

*Pretty course out in country. Pine 9—lots of trees, small well trapped greens. Pine
9—fairly open, links style, a bit longer than other 2 nines. Oak 9—pretty narrow,
lots of trees, a bit of water, small, well trapped greens. Overall all three nines are
fun and challenging to play for all skill levels.*

———————————————————— SEBRING ————————————————————

Harder Hall GC Yards: 6300, Holes: 18 Restaurant/Bar/Proshop
3600 Golfview Dr., 33872 Par: 72, USGA: 68.8 **GF:** w/day $6, w/end $6
Ph: 813-382-0500 RP: 1 day in advance **Carts:** $10.00 ea

*A charming course with character of the 50's. Carved in a southern slash pine
forest, the course is especially a favorite with senior players, as it is very forgiving.*

———————————————————— SEBRING ————————————————————

Spring Lake Golf & Yards: 6600, Holes: 18 Restaurant/Bar/Proshop
Tennis Resort Par: 72, USGA: 69.5 **GF:** w/day $14
100 Clubhouse Lane, RP: Public 48 hours in **Carts:** $16.00
33870 advance
Ph: 813-665-0101

*Florida golfing at its classic best - come play and enjoy a game on a course
designed by Bob Solomon. Nearby is Spring Lake Villas Hotel.*

———————————————————— SEBRING ————————————————————

Sun'n Lake GC Yards: 7024, Holes: 18 Restaurant/Bar/Proshop
4101 Sun 'n Lake Blvd., Par: 72, USGA: 72.1 **GF:** w/day $10
33872 RP: At time of room **Carts:** $13.00
Ph: 813-385-4830 reservation

*Long, with very tough rough. Holes 6 through 12 are very demanding and 18 is
one of the longest par 5 holes in Central Florida.*

─────────── SEVEN SPRINGS ───────────

Seven Springs CC
7000 Country Club
Blvd., 33553
Ph: 813-376-0035

Yards: 6500, Holes: 18
Par: 72, USGA: 69.2
RP: Semi-private
May-Dec, Call

Restaurant/Bar/Proshop
GF: w/day $25
Carts: $12.50

The courses place a premium on shot placement. Water comes into play on 16 of 18 holes on the championship course. The front nine offers opportunities for the long hitter but the back is tight and tricky.

─────────── SPRING HILL ───────────

Quail Ridge G&CC
1600 Shady Hills Rd.,
34610
Ph: 813-856-6064

Yards: 5600, Holes: 18
Par: 70, USGA: 69.0
RP: 2 days in advance

Restaurant/Bar/Proshop
Carts: $24.00

Opens up with straightaway par 4 in preparation for interesting double dogleg par five with water down left side of fairway to just left of green. Second shot requires pinpoint accuracy and correct club selection.

─────────── ST. AUGUSTINE ───────────

Ponce De Leon GC
4000 US 1 North, P.O.
Box 98, 32085
Ph: 904-829-5314

Yards: 6698, Holes: 18
Par: 71, USGA: 69.3

Restaurant/Bar
GF: w/day $22
Carts: $10.00

A Scottish link course. Very windy on certain fairways, marshlands do come into play. The 14th hole, the "cyclops" named for the one eyed monster, with four sets of tees offers all levels of golfers a challenge yet is a "playable" hole.

─────────── ST. PETERSBURG ───────────

Mangrove Bay GC
875 62nd Ave. N.E., 33702
Ph: 813-893-7797

Yards: 6113, Holes: 18
Par: 72, USGA: 68.4
RP: 7 days in advance
by Phone

Restaurant/Proshop
GF: w/day $18, w/end $18
Carts: $18.00

One of the Top 50 Municipal golf courses in the United States, Golf Digest 1981. Tee time Pro Shop phone: 813-893-7800.

─────────── STUART ───────────

Golden Marsh at Harbour Ridge
P.O. Box 2451, 33495
Ph: 407-336-1800

Yards: 6785, Holes: 18
Par: 72

Restaurant/Bar

Every hole at Golden Marsh offers spectacular views of the lush surroundings. From atop the elevated tees you look out on expanses of magnolia, myrtle, fresh-water lakes and pine, to say nothing of the manicured fairways and speedy putting greens.

─────────── SUN CITY CENTER ───────────

Sun City Center GC
South Pebble Beach Dr.,
33573
Ph: 813-634-3377

Holes: 99
USGA: 70.0
RP: Resident of Sun
City only

Restaurant/Bar/Proshop
GF: w/day $20, w/end $22
Carts: $10.00

Approximately one-third of Sun City Center's residents are active golfers, taking daily advantage of the 108 holes of play available in the community. The golf courses available to Sun City Center residents only, designed to be equally challenging to golfers of all skill levels.

─────────────────── SUNNY HILLS ───────────────────

Sunny Hills CC
1150 Country Club
Blvd., 32428
Ph: 904-773-3619

Yards: 6888, Holes: 18
Par: 72, USGA: 70.3
RP: 2 days in advance

Restaurant/Bar/Proshop
GF: w/day $7
Carts: $12.00

Sunny Hills has a slightly rolling terrain with wide, well maintained fairways. Greens are bermuda in summer and rye in winter. The course is well trapped but has only one hole with water. A good challenge for expert and beginner alike.

─────────────────── TALLAHASSEE ───────────────────

Hilaman Park GC
2737 Blairstone Rd.,
32301
Ph: 904-878-5830

Yards: 6364, Holes: 18
Par: 72, USGA: 68.5
RP: Weekends one
week in advance

Restaurant/Bar/Proshop
GF: w/day $8
Carts: $6.60

Although the course is short, it requires accuracy due to some tight fairways. The entire back 9 can be seen from the 18th green.

─────────────────── TALLAHASSEE ───────────────────

Killfarn Inn and CC
100 Tyron Circle, 32308
Ph: 904-893-2144

Yards: 6412, Holes: 27
Par: 72, USGA: 71.1
RP: Inn guests only or
with member

GF: w/day $25, w/end $30
Carts: $20.00

This 27-hole championship golf course in Tallahassee, Florida, is the home of the PGA Central Classic. The fairways are lined with beautiful, mature trees, and add to the beauty as well as the hazards.

─────────────────── TAMARAC ───────────────────

Colony West CC
6800 NW 88th Ave., 33321
Ph: 305-726-8430

Yards: 7271, Holes: 18
Par: 71, USGA: 71.8
RP: 3 days in advance

Restaurant/Bar/Proshop
GF: w/day $22, w/end $27
Carts: $15.00

The course is level with fast greens. There are trees on every hill and 14 holes have water. #12, a 452 yard par 4, is in a cypress forest. 2nd rated in Florida.

─────────────────── TARPON SPRINGS ───────────────────

**Innisbrook Resort &
GC PC**
US 19 (P.O. Drawer
1088), 34688
Ph: 813-942-2000

Yards: 6570, Holes: 63
Par: 72, USGA: 71.3
RP: Golf plan, up to
one year

Restaurant/Bar/Proshop
GF: w/day $45
Carts: $12.00

The Copperhead, Florida's #1 ranked course, blends rolling terrain with tall pines. The Island, like the Copperhead ranked among the countries top 59 resort courses, blends from cypress-swamps, to unusual elevations, to citrus trees over its 6999 yards. The Sandpiper, Innisbrook's shortest course, features plenty of water and sand which makes it challenging for both the experienced and novice golfers.

─────────────────── TAVERES ───────────────────

Village Green GC
Shirley Shores Rd., POB
1226, 32778
Ph: 904-343-7770

Yards: 2620, Holes: 18
Par: 56

Proshop
GF: w/day $7
Carts: $1.00

A very challenging executive, easy to walk course available to the public all day, every day. Family owned and operated, impeccably maintained. Back nine overlooks beautiful lake. Quiet location out in the country.

————————————— TITUSVILLE —————————————

Royal Oak GC	Yards: 6709, Holes: 18	Restaurant/Bar/Proshop
2150 Country Club Dr.,	Par: 71, USGA: 70.1	**GF:** w/day $11 to $35
32780	RP: 24 hours in	seasonal
Ph: 407-269-4500	advance	**Carts:** $10.00 to $12.50

Owned and operated by the Canadian P.G.A., our beautiful 18 hole champion-ship course is carved from rolling terrain, sprinkled with crystal clear lakes which provide a lot of water hazards and is considered a challenging test for all levels of ability.

————————————— VALRICO —————————————

Bloomingdale Golfers	Yards: 7165, Holes: 18	Restaurant/Bar/Proshop
Club	Par: 72, USGA: 70.2	**GF:** w/day $50
1802 Nature's Way Blvd.,	RP: 9 days in advance	**Carts:** Included
33594		
Ph: 813-685-4105		

Our Golfers Only Club plays thru a setting of 100 year old oaks, towering pines, a marsh preserve and shimmering ponds. At the Golfers Club those around you, whether hacks, scratch golfers or visiting tour pros share your love of the game. Rated 11th best in Florida by Golfweek Magazine.

————————————— VENICE —————————————

Lake Venice GC	Yards: 6862, Holes: 18	Restaurant/Proshop
Harbor Dr. (P.O. Box	Par: 72, USGA: 70.7	**GF:** w/day $15
1385), 34285		**Carts:** $15.00
Ph: 813-488-3948		

4 of the most difficult finishing holes.

————————————— VENICE —————————————

Plantation GC	Yards: 6128, Holes: 18	Restaurant/Bar/Proshop
500 Rockley Blvd., 34293	Par: 72, USGA: 69.0	**GF:** w/day $35
Ph: 813-493-2000	RP: Off season	**Carts:** $10.00

Both courses are Scottish Links courses. They contain many hills with consider-able elevation changes. The courses are a blend of rolling fairways guarded by lakes and pot bunkers with small but rolling greens. The 2nd hole on Bobcat course is a par 4 playing 422 yards from the tee. The tee shot is played to a tiered fairway. The second shot is a medium to long iron to a green surrounded by a wall on 3 sides.

————————————— VERO BEACH —————————————

Vista Royale GC	Yards: 3000, Holes: 9	Restaurant/Bar/Proshop
100 Vista Royale Blvd.,	Par: 35, USGA: 33.4	**GF:** w/day $17
32962	RP: 2 days in advance	**Carts:** $16.00
Ph: 407-562-8110		

A challenging par 70 golf course featuring the preservation of the flora of the property.

————————————— WESLEY CHAPEL —————————————

Saddlebrook GC	Yards: 6603, Holes: 18	Restaurant/Bar
5700 Saddlebrook Way,	Par: 70, USGA: 69.3	**GF:** w/day $72, w/end $72
33543	RP: 1 week in advance	**Carts:** $18.00 ea
Ph: 813-973-1111		

The Saddlebrook Course features water on 13 holes, the greens are large, with open approaches and more than enough pine and cypress trees. The Palmer Course, completed in 1985, has undulating terrain; level lies are a rarity.

─────────── WINTER HAVEN ───────────

Willowbrook GC
4200 Hwy. 544 N, 33881
Ph: 813-299-7889

Yards: 6328, Holes: 18
Par: 72
RP: 6 days in advance

Restaurant/Bar/Proshop
GF: w/day $9
Carts: $7.98

Willowbrook Golf Course is one of the finest municipal courses in central Florida. The course is challenging yet very playable, plenty of trees and water!!! Our most challenging and rewarding hole is our par 5 #17, water comes into play with every shot, place your shots properly and you're in position for birdie, if not, double boogie!

─────────── WINTER SPRINGS ───────────

Winter Springs GC
900 State Rd. 434, 32708
Ph: 407-699-1833

Yards: 6551, Holes: 18
Par: 71, USGA: 70.4
RP: 2 days in advance

Restaurant/Bar/Proshop
GF: w/day $19, w/end $23
Carts: $18.00

Course meanders through a scenic nature preserve featuring sparkling lakes and 2500-year-old cypress trees. You will face a challenging mixture of tree-lined fairways, such as the 583-yard sixth, and shots over and around water at Devil's Elbow, which includes #15, #16, #17.

─────────── ZEPHYRHILLS ───────────

Valle Oaks GC PC
6716 Old Wire Rd., 34248
Ph: 813-788-4112

Yards: 5500, Holes: 18
Par: 70, USGA: 68.0
RP: 1 day in advance

Bar/Proshop
GF: w/day $10
Carts: $9.54

Open, rolling front 9 with minor hazards. Back 9 tight through giant live oaks with water on 5 holes. #10 #1 hole with water, trees and out of bounds. Great hole.

Chatsworth   Blairsville
Rocky Face   Helen
          Cedartown
Acworth   Commerce
Villa Rica   Decatur   Cleveland
     Douglasville   Greensboro

Stone Mountain

• Pine Mountain
• Midland
      • Milledgeville
   • Macon   Savannah

Americus
•   Sea Island
         Valdosta   • St. Simons Island
              • Fargo   • Jekyll Island
           Lake Park

GEORGIA

─────────────── ACWORTH ───────────────

Centennial GC	Holes: 18	Restaurant/Bar/Proshop
5225 Woodstock Rd.,	Par: 72	**GF:** w/day $21, w/end $31
30101		**Carts:** $11.50
Ph: 404-974-8313		

One of the finest championship public courses in the South. From the back tees, the course is over 7,000 yards long. By the time you reach the 440 yard, par 4, 13th hole, you had better have your game in shape. #18 is a 450 yard, par 4 with the 2nd shot over water. The Centennial also has a large driving range and is the future home of the Georgia State Golf Association.

─────────────── AMERICUS ───────────────

Brickyard Plantation	Yards: 6114, Holes: 18	Restaurant/Bar/Proshop
GC	Par: 72, USGA: 69.1	**GF:** w/day $12
Hwy 280 E Rt 4, Box 360,		**Carts:** $12.00
31709		
Ph: 912-874-1234		

An intimidating par 3 is number 5. It is 205 yards all across water. The water is a large 8 acre lake and when the winds blow, especially in your face, this par 3 plays like 250 yards with no escape.

─────────────── BLAIRSVILLE ───────────────

Butternut Creek GC	Yards: 5862, Holes: 9	Proshop
P.O. Box 771, 30512	Par: 72, USGA: 67.8	**GF:** w/day $7, w/end $8
Ph: 404-745-4744		**Carts:** $5.50

The 1st tee looks out on a panoramic view of the Tuylog Mountains. It is an easy par 4 if you can negotiate Butternut Creek, downhill and about a 180 yard carry. Water comes into play on 16 holes. The course is quite short if you can hit it straight.

─────────────── BRASELTON ───────────────

Chateau Elan GC	Yards: 7030, Holes: 18	Restaurant/Bar/Proshop
6060 Golf Club Dr., 30517	Par: 71, USGA: 73.5	**GF:** w/day $35, w/end $35
Ph: 404-339-9838	RP: 3 days in advance	**Carts:** $10.00 ea

The Chateau Elan Golf Club is a regional site for the Golf Digest Instructional Schools and has been nominated as the "Best New Public Course" for 1990 by Golf Digest. The course has two creeks, three lakes and 87 well placed bunkers.

─────────────── CEDARTOWN ───────────────

Cedar Valley CC Yards: 6006, Holes: 9 Restaurant/Proshop
Hiway 27 South, 30125 Par: 72, USGA: 68.5 **GF:** w/day $5, w/end $7
Ph: 404-748-9671 RP: Call **Carts:** $7.00 ea

The #9 hole is a par 5. The green sits on a hill overlooking the fairway, the clubhouse has a view of the entire hole. Cedar Valley is in a valley of cedars. The course is really Cedar Valley.

─────────────── CEDARTOWN ───────────────

Meadow Lakes GC Yards: 5987, Holes: 18 Restaurant/Proshop
Adams Rd., 30161 Par: 72, USGA: 69.4 **GF:** w/day $15
Ph: 404-748-4942 RP: Weekends only **Carts:** $16.00

Meadow Lakes has twelve lakes and a winding creek, all of which comes into play on ten holes. Also has large, very undulated greens which may be the best putting surface in this area. Course is short enough to gamble, but tight enough where gambling can really hurt.

─────────────── CHATSWORTH ───────────────

Magnolia Ridge GC Yards: 6213, Holes: 18 Restaurant/Bar/Proshop
Route 6, Box 6181, 30705 Par: 71, USGA: 69.8 **GF:** w/day $12, w/end $17
Ph: 404-695-9300 RP: Call for weekend **Carts:** $8.00 ea
 times

The course is located on 170 acres with lakes and mountains forming a picturesque backdrop. The 18-hole championship course covers 6213 yards and is a par 71. It has 5 lakes and lots of Georgia pines. A full view of the Blue Ridge Mountains offers golfers a breathtaking view.

─────────────── CLEVELAND ───────────────

Skitt Mountain GC Yards: 6020, Holes: 18 Restaurant/Proshop
Route 2, Box 2131, 30528 Par: 70, USGA: 67.4 **GF:** w/day $9, w/end $12
Ph: 404-865-2277 RP: Weekends & **Carts:** $14.00
 holidays

This beautifully maintained golf course is surrounded by mountains and running streams. You can find delight in any season, but particularly our fall season where you are tempted by the changing leaves. Also tempting, is the 17th hole, long par 4, with Georgia pines and water penalties.

─────────────── COLUMBUS ───────────────

Bull Creek GC Yards: 6840, Holes: 36 Restaurant/Proshop
7333 Lynch, 31802 Par: 72, USGA: 71.3 **GF:** w/day $10, w/end $12
Ph: 706-561-1614 RP: Weekends & **Carts:** $16.00
 holidays

A scenic course with duck ponds, new red nine. Landscaping and upkeep great.

─────────────── COMMERCE ───────────────

Deer Trail CC Yards: 6380, Holes: 9 Proshop
Hwy 15, 30529 Par: 72, USGA: 69.1 **GF:** w/day $9
Ph: 404-335-3987 RP: On weekends **Carts:** $6.50

Our best hole is #9 425 yards uphill.

Our listings—supplied by the management—are as complete as possible. Many of the courses have more features than we list. Be sure to inquire when you book your tee time.

─────────────── DOUGLASVILLE ───────────────

West Pines GC   Yards: 6300, Holes: 18   Restaurant/Bar/Proshop
6606 Selman Dr., 30134   Par: 71, USGA: 69.4   **GF:** w/day $12, w/end $18
Ph: 404-949-7428   RP: Weekends   **Carts:** $7.00 ea

A scenic, hilly and sporty layout. Located one mile off Interstate 20, fifteen minutes west of downtown Atlanta.

─────────────── FARGO ───────────────

Fargo Recreation   Yards: 6300, Holes: 9   **GF:** w/day $10
Center   Par: 73, USGA: 69.8   **Carts:** $8.00
P.O. Box 218, Highway
441, 31631
Ph: 912-637-5218

Course is located on banks of the Sawannee River and edge of the Okefenokee Swamp. Camp Stephen Foster (Fargo entrance to Okefenokee) is nearby with full camping facilities.

─────────────── GREENSBORO ───────────────

Port Armor Club   Yards: 6924, Holes: 18   Restaurant/Bar/Proshop
One Port Armor Dr.,   Par: 72, USGA: 73.6   **GF:** w/day $35
30642   RP: Guest of mem.,or   **Carts:** $10.00
Ph: 404-453-4561   stay at Inn

Port Armor offers a tremendous challenge for golfers of any ability. On the front nine, hole #4 and #5 offer breathtaking views of Lake Oconee and both greens are situated right next to the Lake. Port Armor was recently ranked 2nd in the State of Georgia behind The Augusta National as stated in Golf Reporter Magazine.

─────────────── HELEN ───────────────

Innsbruck Golf Club   Yards: 6220, Holes: 18   Restaurant/Bar/Proshop
of Helen   Par: 72, USGA: 70.0   **GF:** w/day $35, w/end $40
P.O. Box 580, 30545   **Carts:** Included
Ph: 404-878-2100

A mountain course built for playability—spectacular views. 150 foot drop par three is a challenge for professional—fun for everyone. Rated 16th best in Georgia (Golf Digest).

─────────────── JEKYLL ISLAND ───────────────

Jekyll Island GC   Yards: 6596, Holes: 18   Restaurant/Bar/Proshop
Capt. Wylly Rd., 31520   Par: 72, USGA: 69.3   **GF:** w/day $17
Ph: 912-635-2368   RP: Call in advance   **Carts:** $19.00

Jekyll Island is Georgia's largest and leading public golf resort. Four courses with 63 holes have all the challenges you could want as you play along rolling fairways among stately oaks and pines. Winds from the nearby Atlantic provide an extra challenge, especially on the par 36, nine-hole Oceanside, Georgia's oldest golf course.

─────────────── LAKE LANIER ISLAND ───────────────

Stouffer Pine Isle   Yards: 6003, Holes: 18   Restaurant/Bar
Resort   Par: 72, USGA: 69.8   **GF:** w/day $32
Holiday Rd., 30518   RP: Non-hotel guest—7   **Carts:** $12.50
Ph: 404-945-8921   days

This course is very tight, with 8 holes calling for drives across sections of Lake Lanier. Hilly, rolling and pine-scented, with elevated tees. #5 is similar in design to Pebble Beach's 18th—a long drive over water, and the second shot is anywhere from a 160-250 yard shot with an inlet guarding the front part of the green.

────────────── LAKE LANIER ISLANDS ──────────────

Lake Lanier Islands Yards: 6254, Holes: 18 Restaurant/Bar/Proshop
Hotel & GC Par: 72 **GF:** w/day $24
7000 Holiday Rd., 30518 RP: 1 week in advance **Carts:** $10.00
Ph: 404-945-8787

Thirteen holes are on the banks of Lake Lanier. There are 85 bunkers. There are bent grass greens and no parallel fairways. You are challenged as a golfer, while you are tantalized by the views, the trees, and the rolling fairways.

────────────── LAKE PARK ──────────────

Francis Lake Golf & CC Yards: 6200, Holes: 18 Restaurant/Bar/Proshop
340 Golf Dr. South, 31636 Par: 72, USGA: 67.5 **GF:** w/day $8, w/end $11
Ph: 912-559-7961 RP: First come, first **Carts:** $12.00
served

Stay and play and shop!!! Over 100 manufacturers outlet stores within a 9 iron shot of the back nine on this beautiful 18 holes par 72 championship length course. No. 11 a 523 yard par 5 monster requires pinpoint accuracy between the tight Georgia pines and beach white sand bunkers. Golf packages available.

────────────── LITHONIA ──────────────

Metropolitan GC TC Yards: 6930, Holes: 18 Restaurant/Bar/Proshop
3000 Fairington Pkwy., Par: 72, USGA: 70.5 **GF:** w/day $20, w/end $30
30038 RP: 2 days in advance **Carts:** $11.00 ea
Ph: 404-981-5325

The Metropolitan Club has a championship golf course, which requires length off the tee and accuracy. It is a fair course which is enjoyable for all levels of players and is maintained in championship condition throughout the year.

────────────── MACON ──────────────

Oak Haven G & CC Yards: 6205, Holes: 18 Restaurant/Bar/Proshop
Rt 2 - Thomaston Rd., Par: 71, USGA: 67.2 **GF:** w/day $12, w/end $15
31210 RP: Weekend & **Carts:** $8.00 ea
Ph: 912-474-8080 holiday - 48 hours

Number three is a great 205 yard par 3—downhill to a well bunkered green, out of bounds right—heavy woods left. Rated one of best par 3 holes in Georgia by USGA. Walk away with 3 and feel lucky.

────────────── ROCKY FACE ──────────────

The Farm GC Yards: 6900, Holes: 18 Restaurant/Bar/Proshop
1000 Millcreek Rd., 30740 Par: 72, USGA: 73.5 **GF:** w/day $75, w/end $75
Ph: 404-673-4716 RP: Must be **Carts:** $13.75 ea
accompanied by
member

Designed by Tom Fazio this course is nestled in the mountains of northern Georgia. It's scenic beauty alone makes for an enjoyable and memorable round, but it also offers a considerable challenge. The course offers a unique blend of Scottish and mountain characteristics with steep face bunkers, mounds and undulating greens.

Subscribe to our free newsletter, "Great Golf Gazette" and hear about the latest special golf vacation values.

──────────────── SAVANNAH ────────────────

Hunter GC	Yards: 6866, Holes: 18	Proshop
Hunter Army Airfield,	Par: 72, USGA: 72.1	**GF:** w/day $10, w/end $15
31409	RP: 3 days in advance,	**Carts:** $12.00
Ph: 912-925-5622	military	

An excellent front nine with heavy trees and water on 5 holes. Picturesque and challenging even to top players. Second nine will compliment in kind. Considered one of the best layouts in the area; but limited to who can play. Military and their guests.

──────────────── SAVANNAH ────────────────

Sheraton Savannah	Yards: 7000, Holes: 18	Restaurant/Bar/Proshop
Resort & GC	Par: 72, USGA: 70.3	**GF:** w/day $28
612 Wilmington Island	RP: Strongly	**Carts:** $10.00 ea
Rd., 31410	recommended	
Ph: 912-897-1612		

Four artificial lakes, a winding stream, live oaks, pine trees, and palm trees add to the scenic beauty of this exceptional island course. The course provides a very fine, fair test of golf; not overly difficult, but a real challenge. Contoured fairways and raised undulating greens planted in Tifton Bermuda grass are enhanced by strategic placement of 81 bunkers and 10 water holes.

──────────────── SAVANNAH ────────────────

Southbridge GC	Yards: 6990, Holes: 18	Restaurant/Bar/Proshop
415 Southbridge Bvld.,	Par: 72, USGA: 73.3	**GF:** w/day $17, w/end $23
31405	RP: Required	**Carts:** $10.00
Ph: 912-651-5455		

The golf course is extremely well trapped off the tee as well as near the greens. Each hole is like a private hole all to yourself. You don't see other golfers because of all the Georgia pines that cover both sides of the fairways.

──────────────── ST. SIMONS ISLAND ────────────────

Sea Island GC	Yards: 3185, Holes: 18	Restaurant/Bar
100 Retreat Ave., 31522	Par: 36, USGA: 34.7	**GF:** w/day $75
Ph: 912-638-3611	RP: No more than 3	**Carts:** $13.00
	tee times adv.	

All four nines include the beauty of moss draped oak trees, beautiful marches and the Atlantic Ocean. "Seaside will leave you challenged and breathtaken. The seventh hole is 425 yds. long which includes a 185 yd. carry over an inland creek to a narrow elevated green.

──────────────── ST. SIMONS ISLAND ────────────────

Sea Island GC	Yards: 6322, Holes: 36	Restaurant/Bar/Proshop
100 Retreat Avenue,	Par: 72, USGA: 39.7	**GF:** w/day $45
31522	RP: 24 hour advance	**Carts:** $13.00 ea
Ph: 912-638-5118	suggested	

Seaside Nine's #7, at 424 yards requires a powerful carry from the tee across 200 yards of tidal creek and marshes, then a tremendous bunker blocks a shorter drive to require a dogleg. Plantation Nine is characterized by sweeping fairways and the lagoon that lurks around 4 holes. Retreat Nine emphasizes huge lakes and the Atlantic itself. Marshside Nine was created to be wholly different. The name tells you a lot about the layout.

——————————— ST. SIMONS ISLAND ———————————

Sea Palms GC Yards: 6672, Holes: 27 Restaurant
5445 Frederica Rd., 31522 Par: 72, USGA: 69.8 **GF:** w/day $35, w/end $35
Ph: 912-638-3351 **Carts:** $13.00 ea

The championship Sea Palms golf course winds its way through the live oaks and sparking ponds of the island landscape. The East Course is famous as the site of the Georgia PGA and Challenge Matches, and is ranked among the state's top 10 golf courses.

——————————— STONE MOUNTAIN ———————————

Hidden Hills CC Yards: 6338, Holes: 18 Restaurant/Bar/Proshop
5001 Biffle Rd., 30088 Par: 72, USGA: 70.3 **GF:** w/day $31
Ph: 404-981-6781 RP: Guest with **Carts:** $9.00
   member only

Fairways are lined with Georgia pine trees, bent grass greens. Our favorite hole is the 4th a pretty hole from the tee, requires good placement drive over a creek must carry 180 yards. Second shot to elevated green with three sand traps and a large pond on the right side. If you play this hole smart you may have a good round today.

——————————— STONE MOUNTAIN ———————————

Southland GC, The Yards: 6717, Holes: 18 Restaurant/Bar/Proshop
5726 Southland Dr., Par: 72, USGA: 70.0 **GF:** w/day $28, w/end $35
30088 RP: Weekend times **Carts:** $8.50 ea
Ph: 404-469-2816 taken Wednesday

You stand on the 18th tee and have a glorious view of Georgia's "Stone Mountain." A beautiful 25 acre lake borders the entire right side of this challenging hole.

——————————— STONE MOUNTAIN ———————————

Stone Mountain Park Yards: 6875, Holes: 18 Restaurant/Bar/Proshop
P.O. Box 778, 30086 Par: 72, USGA: 69.9 **GF:** w/day $26, w/end $28
Ph: 404-498-5715 RP: Weekend and **Carts:** Included
   holidays

A hilly course with Bermuda grass fairways and bent grass greens. Most tees are elevated. Course is heavily wooded with pines and maples, very narrow. No holes are parallel. #11 has water, long and narrow par 4, 420 yards.

——————————— VALDOSTA ———————————

Northlake Golf & CC Yards: 4650, Holes: 18 Restaurant/Bar/Proshop
131 Northlake Dr., 31602 Par: 66, USGA: 63.5 **GF:** w/day $7
Ph: 912-247-8986 RP: Weekends **Carts:** $10.00

Northlake is an executive length course. The front 9 holes are lighted for night play. The back nine is very challenging with water coming into play on 8 of the 9 holes. We have a driving range which is lighted, tennis courts, pool and fishing for our guests.

——————————— VILLA RICA ———————————

Plantation CC Yards: 6193, Holes: 18 Restaurant/Bar/Proshop
Fairfield Pl, 1053 Par: 72, USGA: 68.4 **GF:** w/day $20
Monticello, 30180 RP: 7 days in advance **Carts:** $10.00
Ph: 404-834-7781

Tree lined fairways, rolling terrain with no parallel fairways to 6612 yards from the championship tees offer a tremendous challenge to the high handicapper as well as the professional. Forty-eight bunkers and lateral water hazards on five holes increase the challenge. Large double terraced bent grass greens also require a deft touch.

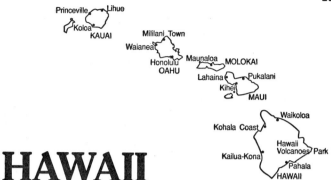

HAWAII

───────────── HAWAII VOLANCOES PARK ─────────────

Volcano GC
Hwy. 11, P.O. Box 46,
96718
Ph: 808-967-7331

Yards: 5965, Holes: 18
Par: 72, USGA: 68.6
RP: Call for
reservations

Restaurant/Bar/Proshop
GF: w/day $50, w/end $50
Carts: Included

The most picturesque and challenging hole is the 15th, which is a dogleg left measuring 375 yards from the middle tees. During the winter months, both our majestic mountains, MaunaLoa and Mauna Kea seem to await your approach shot to an elevated green. Throughout the entire course, which was designed by "Arthur Jack Snyder", the rare Nene goose (state bird) flock freely, making this one of the most peaceful and serene there is!!

───────────── KAILUA-KONA ─────────────

Keauhou GC
78-7000 Alii Dr., 96740
Ph: 808-322-2595

Yards: 6800, Holes: 27
Par: 72

Proshop

27 holes of championship golf designed to call for every club in your bag. Play over and through ancient, rugged lava flows, on lush fairways, large manicured greens that are fast and rolling and true.

───────────── KAPALUA ─────────────

Kapalua GC
300 Kapalua Dr.,
Kapalua, 96761
Ph: 808-669-8044

Yards: 6600, Holes: 18
Par: 72, USGA: 73.0
RP: One week in
advance

Restaurant/Bar
GF: w/day $**, w/end $**
Carts: Included

The Bay course's fifth is Kapalua's signature hole. The hole will vary in length depending on the tee used. While carrying the Pacific is first order of business, the green is well bunkered and offers varying pin placements. The Village Course climbs higher in the hills then plunges dramatically into deep green valleys. Big, bold and beautiful describes our newest 18-hole championship course, The Plantation. The Plantation Course is the new venue for the annual Kapalua International in November.

───────────── KIHEI ─────────────

Makena GC
5415 Makena Alanui,
96753
Ph: 808-879-3344

Yards: 6739, Holes: 18
Par: 72, USGA: 71.9
RP: Prior reservations
accepted

Restaurant/Bar/Proshop
GF: w/day $80
Carts: $20.00

Many have considered the 10th hole truly outstanding; a picture perfect "postcard" hole. The tee-shot heads straight downhill from the clubhouse toward the ocean falling from over 50 feet to a fairway bordered by water to its right. The entire green is fronted by another water hazard with two bunkers.

———————————————— KOHALA COAST ————————————————

Francis H. I'l Brown GC Yards: 6813, Holes: 18   Restaurant/Bar/Proshop
P.O. Box 4959, 97743   Par: 72, USGA: 70.5   **GF:** w/day $80, w/end $80
Ph: 808-885-6655   RP: 1 day in advance   **Carts:** Included

South Course . . . Fairways sculpted in ancient lava flows with ocean & mountain views & famous 15th hole crashing ocean surf. North Course. . .Built on lava bed much older than the Kaniku flow on which the South Course lies. Characterized by rolling terrain & Kiawe forest. Each hole on both courses offers an experience like no other.

———————————————— KOHALA COAST ————————————————

Waikoloa Village GC   Yards: 6687, Holes: 18   Restaurant/Bar/Proshop
P.O. Box 3008, 96756   Par: 72, USGA: 69.7   **GF:** w/day $40
Ph: 808-883-9621   RP: 2 days in advance   **Carts:** $12.00

A golf challenge for all levels of golfing expertise. The pro's believe this to be one of the 5 most challenging golf courses in Hawaii from the blue tees. Unsurpassed views of the Pacific Ocean and Mauna Kea from all fairways. The 18th is perhaps the most challenging par 5 on the Big Island of Hawaii.

———————————————— KOHALA COAST, HAWAII ————————————————

Mauna Kea Beach GC   Yards: 7114, Holes: 18   Restaurant/Bar/Proshop
P.O. Box 218, 96743   Par: 72, USGA: 70.6   **GF:** w/day $60, w/end $60
Ph: 808-882-7222   RP: 1 day in advance   **Carts:** $40.00

It is love at first sight. When they created Mauna Kea, they combined a multitude of elements and built a course and a resort that is simply a pleasure to visit. Mauna Kea is ranked among "America's 100 Greatest" golf courses and as "Hawaii's Finest" by Golf Digest and more recently voted in the Top 12 of America's finest golf resorts.

———————————————— KOLOA ————————————————

Kiahuna GC   Yards: 6353, Holes: 18   Restaurant/Bar/Proshop
2545 Kiahuna Plantation   Par: 70, USGA: 66.5   **GF:** w/day $75, w/end $75
Dr., 96756   RP: Two weeks in   **Carts:** Included
Ph: 808-742-9595   advance

Rolling fairways and undulating greens are a trademark at the Kiahuna Golf Club. Built in 1983 by world renowned golf course architect Robert Trent Jones Jr., Kiahuna lies on an ancient Hawaiian settlement with the lava rock walls and houses left as an integral part of the golf course.

———————————————— LAHAINA ————————————————

Royal Kaanapali GC   Yards: 6305, Holes: 18   Restaurant/Bar
Kaanapali Beach   Par: 72, USGA: 70.0   **GF:** w/day $70
Resorts, 96767   RP: 2 days in advance   **Carts:** Included
Ph: 808-661-3691

The North Course has undulating elevated greens, and generous bunkers, difficult to par—but easy to boggie. The South Course can be even trickier, with narrow fairways and small greens.

Plan ahead! Reserve tee time well in advance, and while you're doing so, confirm rates and services.

──────────── LIHUE ────────────

Kauai Lagoons GC   Yards: 6942, Holes: 18   Restaurant/Bar/Proshop
Kalapaki Beach, 96766   Par: 72
Ph: 808-245-5063

The course, with its generous and gently rolling fairways, sandy waste areas, native grasses, and well contoured greens, is reminiscent of traditional Scottish links-type golf courses. A course where the players have plenty of room to hit the ball, and still find some exciting and fun-filled golf.

──────────── LIHUE ────────────

Westin Kauai   Yards: 6164, Holes: 36   Restaurant/Bar
Kalapaki Beach, 96766   Par: 72   **GF:** w/day $**
Ph: 808-246-5061   RP: Guests up to a   **Carts:** Included
                            month in adv.

The Dunes is a Scottish style links course with treacherous pot bunkers, extensive mounding, grass traps and fairways full of swales and ripples. There's also Cypress Course by Pete and P.B. Dye. There's still another nine, the fabulous Fazio holes. All 45 holes are in excellent shape.

──────────── MAUNALOA, MOLOKAI ────────────

Kaluakoi GC   Yards: 6564, Holes: 18   Restaurant/Bar/Proshop
P.O. Box 26, 96770   Par: 72, USGA: 70.4   **GF:** w/day $45
Ph: 808-552-2739   RP: 1 month in   **Carts:** $15.00
                            advance

We have five holes along the ocean and you can see the ocean from every hole, very scenic. Unspoiled beauty. The real Hawaii.

──────────── MILILANI TOWN ────────────

Mililani GC   Yards: 6360, Holes: 18   Restaurant/Bar/Proshop
95-176 Kuahelani Ave.,   Par: 72, USGA: 70.4   **GF:** w/day $80, w/end $85
96789   RP: 3 months in   **Carts:** Included
Ph: 808-623-2222   advance

Mililani Golf Club is located in central Oahu. It is flanked by mountain ranges on both sides. The golf course has numerous trees and water to make your play challenging.

──────────── PAHALA ────────────

Seamountain GC at   Yards: 6300, Holes: 18   Restaurant/Bar/Proshop
Punaluu   Par: 72, USGA: 69.7   **GF:** w/day $30
Hwy. 11, P.O. Box 85,   **Carts:** $11.50
96777
Ph: 808-928-6222

The golf course layout starts from sea level and eventually travels to 600 feet above sea level. Our signature hole is #17 with four lagoons and numerous monkey pod trees. Sea Mountain is known as the "Secret Golf Heaven" and is the home of the Rip Collins Golf Schools.

Please mention "Golf Courses—The Complete Guide" when you reserve your tee time. Our goal is to provide as complete a listing of golf courses open to the public as possible. If you know of a course we don't list, please send us the name and address on the form at the back of this guide.

64 Hawaii

--------------------------------- PRINCEVILLE ---------------------------------

Princeville Makai GC
P.O. Box 3040, 96722
Ph: 808-826-3580

Yards: 6778, Holes: 27
Par: 72, USGA: 72.3
RP: Up to 1 year in
advance

Restaurant/Bar
GF: w/day $70, w/end $70
Carts: Included

Number 3 on the Ocean Course, a par 3, is world-renowned. Only 125 yards with dense grass on the left, a placid lake in front and a canyon beyond. Lake Course boasts ocean views and plenty of water. 16 years rated in America's 100 Greatest Golf Courses by Golf Digest. The Prince offers the most challenging course in Hawaii with natural waterfalls, jungle, ancient mango trees and other natural vegetation. Rated Best New Resort Course in 1990 by Golf Digest.

--------------------------------- PUKALANI ---------------------------------

Pukalani GC
360 Pukalani St., 96768
Ph: 808-572-1314

Yards: 6494, Holes: 18
Par: 72, USGA: 70.6
RP: 3 days in advance

Restaurant/Bar/Proshop
GF: w/day $30
Carts: $20.00

Set in the rolling hillsides of "upcountry" Maui, Pukalani Country Club actually has 19 holes (two greens on our 3rd hole - par 3). One green is across a gully and the other straight down.

--------------------------------- WAIANAE ---------------------------------

Makaha Valley CC
84-627 Makaha Valley
Rd., 96792
Ph: 808-695-7111

Yards: 6091, Holes: 18
Par: 71, USGA: 67.6
RP: Recommended tee
times

Restaurant/Bar/Proshop
GF: w/day $50, w/end $50
Carts: Included

Sporty, well conditioned golf course in resort area. Great par 3s and tough finishing holes.

--------------------------------- WAIANAE ---------------------------------

**Sheraton Makaha
Resort**
84-626 Makaha Valley
Rd. Waianae, 96792
Ph: 808-695-9544

Yards: 7091, Holes: 18
Par: 72, USGA: 74.3
RP: 3 days in advance

Restaurant/Bar/Proshop
GF: w/day $75, w/end $75
Carts: Included

Our favorite hole is #18. Although not difficult in length it requires accuracy. Guarding the fairway are two bunkers and two ponds. Right of the fairway is best for all approaching shots. The green (like all of our greens) slopes towards the ocean. There are an additional three bunkers guarding the green.

--------------------------------- WAIKOLOA ---------------------------------

**Waikoloa GC - Kings'
Golf Course**
HCO2 Box 5575, 96743
Ph: 808-885-4647

Yards: 7074, Holes: 18
Par: 72, USGA: 75.0
RP: 1 day in advance

Restaurant/Bar/Proshop
GF: w/day $80, w/end $80
Carts: Included

The Kings' Course was designed by Tom Weiskopf and Jay Morrish. In Morrish's words, "The variety in the green design, the sophisticated bunker strategy, and the multiple tee placements all work together to create a course that can challenge the great players of the world, or be fun for those less skilled."

Our listings—supplied by the management—are as complete as possible. Many of the courses have more features than we list. Be sure to inquire when you book your tee time.

Sandpoint

Sun Valley

New Meadows

IDAHO

NEW MEADOWS

Kimberland Meadows Resort
PO Drawer C, Hwy 95, 83654
Ph: 208-347-2164

Yards: 6927, Holes: 18
Par: 72, USGA: 69.8
RP: 1 week for tee times

Restaurant/Bar/Proshop
GF: w/day $15, w/end $18
Carts: $8.00

The course is set among mountains and pine trees. It's a demanding course from the championship tees and play fair from the whites. The fairways are treelined and tight, the view in all directions is spectacular. Snow peaked mountains, etc. Highest rating in the state of Idaho.

SANDPOINT

Hidden Lakes CC
8838 Lower Pack River, 83864
Ph: 208-263-1642

Yards: 6155, Holes: 18
Par: 71, USGA: 69.1
RP: 1 week in advance

Restaurant/Bar/Proshop
GF: w/day $20, w/end $24
Carts: $20.00

Water, water, water. Truly a Florida golf course among the beautiful northwest evergreens. Water comes into play on 17 of the 18 holes. . .82 sand bunkers. Set in the Pack River Valley with the Pack River wandering through the golf course. Very scenic. Course record 70.

SUN VALLEY

Elkhorn GC
P.O. Box 6009, 83354
Ph: 208-622-4511

Yards: 6575, Holes: 18
Par: 72, USGA: 73.2
RP: May be made with reservations

Restaurant/Bar
GF: w/day $40
Carts: Included

This lengthy scenic treat nestled under majestic snow-capped peaks. Top rated course in Idaho. A very hilly course with a lot of water, antelope, fox, hare, and deer.

SUN VALLEY

Sun Valley Resort GC
Sun Valley Rd., 83353
Ph: 208-622-4111

Yards: 6057, Holes: 18
Par: 71, USGA: 71.1
RP: 7 days in advance

Restaurant/Bar
GF: w/day $32
Carts: $21.00

This is one of the west's truly beautiful mountain settings, and has hosted the Idaho Governor's Cup, Danny Thompson Memorial Celebrity Golf Tournament, and numerous others. The fifteenth hole, a 244 yard par 3 is singled out as a challenger.

Thomson Huntley Marengo St. Charles Vernon Hills
Hanover Mt Carroll Richmond Fox Lake Itasca Mt. Prospect Downers Grove
Galena •Byron Elgin •Palatine Great Lakes Lincolnshire Woodridge
Port Byron Morrison • Rochelle Sandwich • Rosemont Glencoe
Aledo Sterling • N. Aurora • Glen Ellyn Hawthorn Woods
Morris Lemont Arlington Hts.
Sheffield • Peru St. Anne
East Moline •Knoxville
Quincy
Biggsville Galesburg
Alton • Washington •
Macomb • Pekin •
Bloomington •Danville
Mahomet •
•Taylorville
• Matteon
• Lebanon
• Carlyle
Whittington

ILLINOIS

ALEDO

Hawthorn Ridge GC
RR 2, SR-94, 61231
Ph: 309-582-5641

Yards: 6670, Holes: 18
Par: 72, USGA: 69.9
RP: Recommended

Restaurant/Proshop
GF: w/day $12
Carts: $15.50

Natural wooded setting, features plush watered fairways, large rolling greens and a very quiet setting abounding with wildlife, large oaks, ponds and streams. The par 4, #12 hole, with a fairway lined with huge oaks offers a striking shot across a pond to a green guarded by another large oak and a heart shaped trap.

ALTON

Spencer T. Olin Community GC
4701 College Ave., Box 1093, 62002
Ph: 618-465-3111

Yards: 6945, Holes: 18
Par: 72, USGA: 70.3
RP: One week in advance

Restaurant/Bar/Proshop
GF: w/day $34, w/end $40
Carts: Included

This Arnold Palmer designed and managed facility is first class from the word go!! Already recognized as the finest public facility in the mid-west. Renowned for the standards of excellence exampled in the golf course and the service of its staff. A truly spectacular facility. Designed to accommodate all levels of play.

ARLINGTON HTS.

Arlington Lakes GC
1211 S. New Wilke Rd., 60005
Ph: 312-577-3030

Yards: 5331, Holes: 18
Par: 68, USGA: 64.6
RP: 5 days in advance

Restaurant/Bar/Proshop
GF: w/day $14, w/end $16
Carts: $17.00

The course abounds with water hazards. And if that isn't enough the greens are well guarded by innumerable bunkers!

BIGGSVILLE

Hend-Co Hills CC
RR 1, 61418
Ph: 309-627-2779

Yards: 3235, Holes: 9
Par: 37, USGA: 70.6
RP: Weekends

Restaurant/Bar/Proshop
GF: w/day $6
Carts: $6.00

Hend-Co has golf, swimming pool, campgrounds, fishing. Golf lessons, driving range. This is pretty wide open course with 2 par threes one over water, the other with an uphill green 3 par 5's which are all over 500 yards.

───────────── BLOOMINGTON ─────────────

Lakeside CC
1201 E. Croxton, 61701
Ph: 309-827-5402

Yards: 2900, Holes: 9
Par: 64, USGA: 62.9
RP: Call—usually can
walk on

Restaurant/Bar/Proshop
GF: w/day $12, w/end $12
Carts: $13.00

Don't let the yardage fool you, this is an exceptionally challenging course. The greens are small and undulating. The fairways are extremely narrow and the long par 3's are mind boggling. My favorite hole is #6, only 290 yard par 4 but packed with excitement.

───────────── BOURBONNAIS ─────────────

Bon Vivant CC
Career Center Road, PO
Box 67, 60914
Ph: 815-935-0403

Yards: 7400, Holes: 18
Par: 72, USGA: 75.8
RP: No more than 7
days in advance

Restaurant/Bar/Proshop
GF: w/day $12, w/end $18
Carts: $14.00

The course is known for its elevated trees, length, large greens, and pesky water hazards.

───────────── BYRON ─────────────

Prairie View GC
7993 River Rd., 61010
Ph: 815-234-GOLF

Yards: 6990, Holes: 18
Par: 72

Bar/Proshop
GF: w/day $14, w/end $17
Carts: $10.00

Newest public course with unusual aesthetic additions of natural prairie, five tees per hole with challenging greens, traps and bunkers. Natural dolomite prairie with 600 acre Tonest Preserve adjacent to facility.

───────────── CARLYLE ─────────────

Carlyle Lake GC
Rt. 127 South, 62231
Ph: 618-594-8812

Yards: 3295, Holes: 9
Par: 36, USGA: 35.5

Bar/Proshop
GF: w/day $5, w/end $6
Carts: $14.00

Challenging 9 holes of golf. Course features multiple tees to challenge players of any level. Bermuda tees add to players enjoyment.

───────────── DANVILLE ─────────────

Harrison Park GC
W. Voorhees, 61832
Ph: 217-431-2266

Yards: 6066, Holes: 18
Par: 73, USGA: 69.0

Restaurant/Bar/Proshop
GF: w/day $8, w/end $9
Carts: $14.00

You will enjoy newly watered fairways on this mature layout. Tree marred hills surround the course offering a beautiful backdrop sure to test your concentration. Keep focused on your golf shots and the opportunities will be there—most cannot.

───────────── DOWNERS GROVE ─────────────

Downers Grove GC
2420 Haddow St., 60515
Ph: 312-963-1306

Yards: 2900, Holes: 9
Par: 34, USGA: 33.4
RP: Weekends &
holidays

Restaurant
GF: w/day $8, w/end $9
Carts: $9.00

Site of 1st 18 holes in USA now 9 holes. #7 Par 4, 375 yards tight fairway gradual rise to small tight green.

Plan ahead! Reserve tee time well in advance, and while you're doing so, confirm rates and services.

―――――――――――――― EAST MOLINE ――――――――――――――

Golfmohr GC
16724 Hubbard Rd.,
61244
Ph: 309-496-2434

Yards: 6543, Holes: 18
Par: 72, USGA: 69.8
RP: Recommended

Restaurant/Bar/Proshop
GF: w/day $10
Carts: $15.00

The course is surrounded by woods and a nature preserve Lakes or ponds come into play on several holes, including the #2, par 4 hole, that in spite of its beauty claims 20,000 balls each year! Golfer survey rates Golfmohr #1 public course in the Quad Cities!

―――――――――――――――――― ELGIN ――――――――――――――――――

Rolling Knolls GC
RR 1 Box 319, Rohrssen
Rd., 60120
Ph: 312-888-2888

Yards: 4300, Holes: 18
Par: 68
RP: Recommended

Bar/Proshop
GF: w/day $15
Carts: $16.00

An extremely challenging executive 18 hole golf course with fairways the width of airport runways and tees lining both sides. If the trees don't get you our water and traps will. A course you'll want to play again and again.

―――――――――――――――― FOX LAKE ――――――――――――――――

Fox Lake CC
7220 State Park Rd.,
60020
Ph: 312-587-6411

Yards: 6347, Holes: 18
Par: 72, USGA: 70.5
RP: Recommended

Restaurant/Bar/Proshop
GF: w/day $20, w/end $25
Carts: $20.00

Fox Lake Country Club presents blind approach shots, difficult sidehill, downhill lies and deceptively fast greens. There is a fully stocked pro shop, driving range and snack shop. Banquet facility for up to 180 people. Golf outings welcome. Fox Lake Country Club is one of northern Illinois' hidden jewels.

―――――――――――――――――― GALENA ――――――――――――――――――

**Eagle Ridge Inn &
Resort**
Box 777, 61036
Ph: 815-777-2444

Yards: 6836, Holes: 45
Par: 72, USGA: 73.4

Restaurant/Bar/Proshop
GF: w/day $68, w/end $68
Carts: $22.00

Eagle Ridge has 45 holes set in the hills of the Mississippi River Valley.The North Course cuts through the highlands. It has many elevated tees and approach shots with spectacular views of the country side. The South Course is set in a valley and has many creeks winding throughout the course, posing threats on 10 of the 18 holes.

―――――――――――――――― GALESBURG ――――――――――――――――

Bunker Links GKC
Lincoln Park, 61401
Ph: 309-344-1818

Yards: 6083, Holes: 18
Par: 71, USGA: 67.5
RP: Weekends &
holidays

Restaurant/Proshop
GF: w/day $6, w/end $7
Carts: $13.00

#15 is a short par 3 picturesque hole guarded in front of green by a pond—sandtrap to left of green. Automatic water system on tees, greens, and fairways.

―――――――――――――――― GLEN ELLYN ――――――――――――――――

**Village Links of Glen
Ellyn**
485 Winchell Way, 60137
Ph: 708-469-8180

Yards: 6933, Holes: 27
Par: 71, USGA: 72.8
RP: 7 days in advance

Restaurant/Proshop
GF: w/day $25, w/end $28
Carts: $20.00

Well placed drives and crisp iron shots will help avoid the 96 sand traps and 21 lakes strategically placed throughout the golf course. Every club in the bag will be used to successfully negotiate this championship layout. Quality golf is the hallmark of the "Village Links experience."

─────────────────── GLEN ELLYN ───────────────────

Western Acres GC
21 W. 680 Butterfield
Rd., 60148
Ph: 312-469-6768

Yards: 3018, Holes: 9
Par: 35, USGA: 69.1
RP: Weekends only

Restaurant/Bar/Proshop
GF: w/day $6, w/end $7
Carts: $6.50

No. 3 a 215 yard, par 3—The green is so near yet so far. You must clear the water and avoid the bunkers on each side. There is out of bounds on the left and a tree nursery on the right.

─────────────────── GLENCOE ───────────────────

Glencoe GC
621 Westley Rd., 60022
Ph: 312-835-0981

Yards: 6233, Holes: 18
Par: 72, USGA: 68.9
RP: Must be made in person

Restaurant/Proshop
GF: w/day $15, w/end $17
Carts: $18.00

Glencoe Golf Club is a very beautiful older golf course. We have 3 sets of tees to challenge the average or advanced golfer. Over 18 holes run through the woods and next to the Chicago Botanic Gardens. Our golf club is rated one of the top public golf courses in the Chicago land area.

─────────────────── GREAT LAKES ───────────────────

Great Lakes GC
Bldg. 160, 60088
Ph: 312-688-4593

Yards: 6449, Holes: 18
Par: 72, USGA: 69.5
RP: Required on weekends

Restaurant/Bar/Proshop
GF: w/day $8, w/end $10
Carts: $13.00

The course is relatively open with a gentle rolling terrain. Scoring is tough due to small greens and narrow fairways. Favorite hole is #17 which is 385 yards normally playing into a head wind. It doglegs right over a creek and a well bunkered double tier green.

─────────────────── HANOVER ───────────────────

Storybrook CC
2124 W. Storybrook Rd.,
61041
Ph: 815-591-2210

Yards: 3318, Holes: 9
Par: 36, USGA: 34.3
RP: 1 day ahead

Restaurant/Bar/Proshop
GF: w/day $11
Carts: $12.00

Story Brook is a fine 9 hole course site in the beautiful Jo Davies County of Illinois. A course where you cross water on every hole. The most spectacular view from the 5th tee box overlooks the whole course plus a large surrounding area.

─────────────────── HAWTHORN WOODS ───────────────────

Kemper Lakes GC
Old McHenry Rd., 60047
Ph: 312-540-3450

Yards: 7217, Holes: 18
Par: 72, USGA: 71.7
RP: 1 week in advance

Restaurant/Bar/Proshop
GF: w/day $75
Carts: Included

Heavily wooded course with lakes everywhere, #17 has an island green. Golf Shop Magazine rated the pro shop in the best 100 in the country.

─────────────────── HUNTLEY ───────────────────

Pinecrest Golf & CC
11220 Algonquin Rd.,
60142
Ph: 312-669-3111

Yards: 6636, Holes: 18
Par: 72, USGA: 68.7
RP: 1 week in advance

Restaurant/Bar/Proshop
GF: w/day $15, w/end $20
Carts: $20.00

Relatively open and gently rolling this public course is manicured like a private club to give the average golfer the best chance for a low score. A favorite hole is number 11, 161 yards over water to a peninsula green! It can make or break your back nine.

─────────────── ITASCA ───────────────

Nordic Hills GC Yards: 5897, Holes: 18 Restaurant/Bar/Proshop
Rohlwing & Nordic Par: 71, USGA: 68.9
Rds., 60143
Ph: 312-773-3510

Recreation at Nordic Hills begins with a challenging 18-hole golf course, originally designed as a private country club by Scandinavian businessmen over 60 years ago. There is rolling terrain and century-old oaks.

─────────────── KNOXVILLE ───────────────

Laurel Greens GC Yards: 3100, Holes: 9 Restaurant/Bar/Proshop
RR 1 Box 115, 61448 Par: 36 **GF:** w/day $7
Ph: 309-289-4146 **Carts:** $12.00

A beautiful country setting with an outstanding 9 hole layout, manicured to perfect, 3100 yards, par 36. The additional new 9 holes is under construction. Keeping with the rustic setting, the clubhouse has been renovated from an old barn, lending to a unique atmosphere.

─────────────── LEBANON ───────────────

Locust Hills GC Yards: 6005, Holes: 18 Restaurant/Bar/Proshop
1015 Belleville St., 62254 Par: 71, USGA: 67.2 **GF:** w/day $9, w/end $11
Ph: 618-537-4590 RP: Weekends & **Carts:** $15.00
holidays

Located 20 minutes from downtown St. Louis—Locust Hills is an interesting course with the accent on accuracy. Water and trees abound the front nine with bunkers and rolling hills on the back nine. Area's finest greens! A true test of golf for beginner and low handicapper.

─────────────── LEMONT ───────────────

Cog Hill Golf & CC Yards: 6219, Holes: 72 Restaurant/Bar/Proshop
12294 Archer Ave., 60439 Par: 71, USGA: 68.7 **Carts:** $24.00
Ph: 708-257-5872 RP: Required, 6 days
in advance

With four different 18-hole courses, Cog Hill offers a quality round of golf to players of all handicaps. Courses 1 and 3 are medium length and medium difficulty. #2 is par 72 sporty, rolling and wooded, #4 is championship calibre, rated "Greatest 100" by Golf Digest magazine.

─────────────── LINCOLNSHIRE ───────────────

Marriott's Lincolnshire Yards: 6300, Holes: 18 Restaurant/Bar
Resort Par: 70, USGA: 69.8 **GF:** w/day $44, w/end $48
1 Marriott Dr., 60015 RP: Hotel, 6 mos., **Carts:** Included
Ph: 312-634-1179 outside 1 week

Superlative, 18-hole course designed by George Fazio. Tee off and travel down pristine fairways edged by woodlands, around the shores of five shimmering lakes, over bunkers and onto immaculately-maintained greens. An inviting course bordered by the Des Plaines River.

─────────────── LOCKPORT ───────────────

Big Run GC Yards: 6850, Holes: 18 Restaurant/Bar/Proshop
135th St., 60441 Par: 72, USGA: 73.1 **GF:** w/day $30, w/end $30
Ph: 815-838-1057 RP: 1 week in advance **Carts:** $12.00 ea

Oak tress, hilly, exceptional par 5's and par 3's. Beautiful layout. 708-972-1652

─────────── MACOMB ───────────

Western Illinois Univ. Yards: 3200, Holes: 9   Proshop
GC   Par: 36, USGA: 69.0   **GF:** w/day $7, w/end $8
1215 Tower Rd., 61455   RP: 1 day in advance   **Carts:** $6.00
Ph: 309-837-3675

Designed by Kilian and Nugent (Kemper Lakes), this 9 hole course is one of the best 9 hole facilities in Illinois. The rural setting and affordable price offers the avid golfer a different twist. The 196 yard par 3 8th hole will be one you won't forget.

─────────── MAHOMET ───────────

Lake of the Woods GC   Yards: 6503, Holes: 18   Restaurant/Bar/Proshop
Box 669 (1 mile N. of   Par: 72, USGA: 69.8   **GF:** w/day $11
Mahomet), 61853   RP: Call Monday for   **Carts:** $13.00
Ph: 217-586-2183   weekend

A rolling tree lined course with water on seven of the eighteen holes. Accuracy is rewarded more than length.

─────────── MARENGO ───────────

Marengo Ridge CC   Yards: 6500, Holes: 18   Restaurant/Bar/Proshop
9508 Harmony Hill Rd.,   Par: 72, USGA: 70.8   **GF:** w/day $14
60152   RP: Required on   **Carts:** $16.00
Ph: 815-923-2332   weekends

Marengo Ridge is gently rolling and rewards precision rather than power. Although 6800 yards from our championship tees, a golfer who uses his/her mind will outscore those who rely on muscle alone. Holes 6 and 15 reward the golfer with panoramic views and #18 is a strong finishing hole which requires distance and precision to win the match.

─────────── MATTOON ───────────

Buck Grove Indian   Yards: 3250, Holes: 9   Restaurant/Proshop
Trails GC   Par: 36   **GF:** w/day $7
RR #3 Box 283A, 61938   RP: Up to 1 wk.   **Carts:** $7.00
Ph: 217-258-PUTT   advance

9 holes are to open to open July 1991, then all 18 holes will be open by July 1992. Big mounds, deep bunkers make the course very unique for this area.

─────────── MORRIS ───────────

Morris CC   Yards: 6000, Holes: 18   Restaurant/Bar/Proshop
Rt 6 West, 60450   Par: 71, USGA: 68.5   **GF:** w/day $20
Ph: 815-942-3628   RP: Must play with   **Carts:** $14.00
member

A good test of golf with many hills and "blind" shots. The yardage does not indicate the difficulty of the course.

─────────── MORRISON ───────────

Morrison CC   Yards: 6100, Holes: 9   Restaurant/Bar/Proshop
915 W. Morris St., 61270   Par: 72, USGA: 69.8   **GF:** w/day $7
Ph: 815-772-7708   RP: 1 days in advance   **Carts:** $7.00

Tree-lined fairways are the rule, added to very small greens makes this course a very good challenge. Out-of-bounds to the right on 10 holes, plus 1 creek and 2 lakes. Watered tees, fairways, and greens make for good conditions. The 4th hole could possibly be among the toughest par 4's in the country and the 17th hole is an equally tough par 3.

72 Illinois

──────────────── MT. CARROLL ────────────────

Oakville CC
RR 2, 61053
Ph: 815-684-5295

Yards: 3111, Holes: 9
Par: 36, USGA: 69.7
RP: Weekends &
holidays

Restaurant/Bar/Proshop
GF: w/day $9, w/end $12
Carts: $13.00

A gently rolling course with many old trees with tight fairways. Water can come into play on 6 of the 9 holes. Greens are moderate to severely sloped making putting difficult. Hole #5 is the favorite hole, a short 114 yard par 3 going over a stream 4 times.

──────────────── MT. PROSPECT ────────────────

Old Orchard CC
700 W. Rand Rd., 60056
Ph: 312-255-2025

Yards: 6010, Holes: 18
Par: 71, USGA: 68.3
RP: 7 days in advance

Restaurant/Bar/Proshop
GF: w/day $23, w/end $25
Carts: $20.00

Old Orchard is one of the finest kept courses in the Chicago land area. The last 4 holes are a great chance to test your skills. The 17th hole is 230 yard par 3, all carry. It is the best par 3 in this whole area.

──────────────── N. AURORA ────────────────

Valley Green GC
314 Kingswood Dr., 60542
Ph: 312-897-3000

Yards: 3831, Holes: 18
Par: 60, USGA: 60.1
RP: Carts avail. by
appointment

Restaurant/Proshop
GF: w/day $9, w/end $11
Carts: $12.00

This course is a very challenging "executive style" layout which puts more emphasis on accuracy than length off the tees. It is popular with both young and old as well as the novice and the low handicapper.

──────────────── ORLAND PARK ────────────────

Silver Lake CC
147th & 82nd Ave., 60462
Ph: 708-349-6940

Yards: 6485, Holes: 45
Par: 72, USGA: 70.4
RP: Can be made 14
days in advance

Restaurant/Bar/Proshop
GF: w/day $21, w/end $25
Carts: $22.00

Our favorite hole is the 8th on the South Course. An accurate and lengthy drive into a prevailing wind is required for a chance to reach the green in two. The second shot must carry over an expansive marsh to a steeply sloped elevated green.

──────────────── PALATINE ────────────────

Palatine Hills GC
512 W. NW Hwy., 250 E.
Wood St., 60067
Ph: 312-359-4020

Yards: 6500, Holes: 18
Par: 72, USGA: 70.6
RP: 1 week in adv.
weekend, else 2

Restaurant/Bar/Proshop
GF: w/day $19
Carts: $17.50

Our golf course is a combination of hills and flat surfaces. Water comes into play on several holes, both on the front nine and the back nine. Our golf course will test the skills of all golfers, especially our three finishing holes which confuse distance, water and precise shots.

──────────────── PEKIN ────────────────

Lick Creek GC
2210 Pkwy. Dr., 61554
Ph: 309-346-0077

Yards: 6906, Holes: 18
Par: 72, USGA: 71.1
RP: 1 week in advance

Restaurant/Proshop
GF: w/day $8, w/end $11
Carts: $13.50

Very hilly course with tree-lined fairways. Front nine is the toughest. #6 is best hole in Central Illinois, par 5, 533 yards. Big ravine 130 yards off tee. Tree-lined fairway which drops 20 feet down.

───────────────── PERU ─────────────────

South Bluff CC   Yards: 2978, Holes: 9   Restaurant/Bar/Proshop
R.R. 1, 61354   Par: 36   **GF:** w/day $6, w/end $7
Ph: 815-223-0603   **Carts:** $7.50

Sporty nine holes in the bluff overlooking LaSalle-Peru area.

───────────────── RICHMOND ─────────────────

Hunter CC   Yards: 6405, Holes: 18   Restaurant/Bar/Proshop
5419 Kenosha St., 60071   Par: 72, USGA: 71.2   **GF:** w/day $15
Ph: 815-678-2631   RP: 1 week in advance   **Carts:** $16.00

Favorite hole is the 415 yard 9th. Your drive must be carefully positioned between out of bounds left and a creek that runs along the right side of the fairway and cuts across the fairway about 220 yards out. An exceptional drive can carry the creek.

───────────────── ROCHELLE ─────────────────

Rochelle CC   Yards: 4650, Holes: 18   Restaurant/Bar
US-251 S, P.O. Box 419,   Par: 66, USGA: 62.0   **GF:** w/day $10, w/end $15
61068   **Carts:** $12.00
Ph: 815-562-7279

While the front is longer than the back the last nine holes can be extremely tough due to the large oak trees that line each fairway. #13 is a deadly dogleg left, hit your 1st shot too long or too short and you can forget the green.

───────────────── ROSEMONT ─────────────────

Ramada Htl O'Hare 9   Yards: 650, Holes: 9   Restaurant/Bar
Hole Par 3   Par: 27   **GF:** w/day $5
6600 N. Mannheim Rd.,   RP: First come first
60018   serve
Ph: 312-827-5131

Our Course is perfect for the beginner yet tricky enough to challenge the best of players. Perhaps the most unique part about our par 3 nine hole is that we are lighted for night play.

───────────────── ROUND LAKE BEACH ─────────────────

Renwood CC   Yards: 6000, Holes: 18   Restaurant/Bar/Proshop
1413 Hainesville Rd.,   Par: 72, USGA: 68.6   **GF:** w/day $13, w/end $16
60073   RP: Weekends &   **Carts:** $18.00
Ph: 708-546-8242   holidays only

Although the course is not overly long, some small greens and a roving creek keep play very interesting.

───────────────── SANDWICH ─────────────────

Edgebrook CC   Yards: 6076, Holes: 18   Restaurant/Bar/Proshop
RR 1 Box 1A, 60548   Par: 72, USGA: 68.4   **GF:** w/day $18, w/end $20
Ph: 815-786-3058   RP: Weekends &   **Carts:** $9.50 ea
                           holidays

The back nine is a little more wide open with undulating greens. The front nine is shorter but requires a little more planning. The fifth hole will tempt all golfers at all levels with water right and out of bounds left. Edge Brook also has a nice range to hit balls from.

───────────────── SHEFFIELD ─────────────────

Hidden Lake CC
R.F.D. 1, 61361
Ph: 815-454-2660

Yards: 2904, Holes: 9
Par: 36, USGA: 34.5
RP: Recommended

Restaurant/Bar/Proshop
GF: w/day $10
Carts: $6.00

Country setting in a very private atmosphere. Wild game abounding everywhere and you may bring your fishing gear for some nice bass fishing.
Illinois

───────────────── ST. ANNE ─────────────────

Shamrock GC
R #6 Box 255, 60964
Ph: 815-937-9355

Yards: 3600, Holes: 18
Par: 60, USGA: 60.0

Proshop
GF: w/day $8
Carts: $9.50

Shamrock is known as an executive course. We have only four par 4's—all the rest are par 3. The course is tight and calls for control. There are lots of trees and almost everyone is able to walk, which is what golfing is supposed to be all about.

───────────────── ST. CHARLES ─────────────────

Pheasant Run GC
4051 East Main St., 60174
Ph: 708-584-6300

Yards: 6100, Holes: 18
Par: 71, USGA: 70.0
RP: Recommended

Restaurant/Bar/Proshop
GF: w/day $25
Carts: $23.00

Our par 5's are our most thought provoking holes. Each is done so you may get home in two. However—failure is severe and keeping them 3 shot holes may be the smart thing to do.

───────────────── STERLING ─────────────────

Lake View CC
23319 Hazel, 61081
Ph: 815-626-2886

Yards: 3010, Holes: 18
Par: 70, USGA: 68.7

Restaurant/Bar/Proshop
GF: w/day $9, w/end $11
Carts: $14.00

In playing the back nine a player must cross water 6 times.

───────────────── TAYLORVILLE ─────────────────

Lake Shore GC
316 N. Shumway, P.O.
Box 263, 62568
Ph: 217-824-5521

Yards: 6813, Holes: 18
Par: 72, USGA: 71.5
RP: 2 days in advance

Restaurant/Bar/Proshop
GF: w/day $11
Carts: $14.00

Bring every club in your bag! Good mixture of long and short holes—open and tight fairways. Good character—with trees, water and bunkers. Medium fast, gently rolling greens challenge the best putter. Lake Taylorville runs alongside 5 holes.

───────────────── THOMSON ─────────────────

Lynnwood Lynks
RR #1 Box 78, 61285
Ph: 815-259-8278

Yards: 2860, Holes: 9
Par: 36, USGA: 34.5
RP: Weekends &
holidays

Restaurant/Bar/Proshop
GF: w/day $6, w/end $7
Carts: $7.00

A beautiful 9 hole completely watered fairways Plenty of sandtraps. Beautiful pine trees line the fairways along with extraordinary houses. Our #9 is a long par 5 with a rolling green, that is sure to get even with the best putter.

Subscribe to our free newsletter, "Great Golf Gazette" and hear about the latest special golf vacation values.

──────────── VERNON HILLS ────────────

Vernon Hills GC Yards: 2828, Holes: 9 Bar/Proshop
291 Evergreen Dr., 60061 Par: 34, USGA: 32.3 **GF:** w/day $7
Ph: 312-680-9310 RP: Weekends & **Carts:** $8.00
  holidays

While the course is not long by most standards, water comes into play on 7 holes requiring all but the longest players to lay up, leaving longer irons into well protected greens. The fact the course record is 33 indicates the difficulty of the course.

──────────── WASHINGTON ────────────

Pine Lakes GC Yards: 6132, Holes: 18 Bar/Proshop
RR # Schuck Rd., 61571 Par: 71, USGA: 68.8 **GF:** w/day $9, w/end $10
Ph: 309-745-9344 RP: 1 day in advance **Carts:** $12.00

Front nine is totally different from back nine. Front has only one lake and is generally flat and open. Back nine has more rolling hills with three water holes, 16, 17 and 18. Number 10 is very scenic, yet difficult — 413 yards. Tight.

──────────── WHITTINGTON ────────────

Rend Lake GC Yards: 6426, Holes: 18 Restaurant/Bar/Proshop
RR 1, 62897 Par: 72, USGA: 69.2 **GF:** w/day $13, w/end $13
Ph: 618-629-2353 RP: Anytime in **Carts:** $16.00
  advance

Championship course 6851 from blue tee but fun for players of all caliber from 6400 yard white tees. Large greens with combination of open holes and tree lined overlooking beautiful Rend Lake.

──────────── WOODRIDGE ────────────

Village Greens of Yards: 6290, Holes: 18 Restaurant/Bar/Proshop
Woodridge GC Par: 72, USGA: 68.5 **GF:** w/day $20
1575 W. 75th St., 60517 **Carts:** $18.00
Ph: 312-985-8366

Visit a spacious and colorful golf shop, that has been rated by Golf Digest *as being one of the top 100 golf shops of America. The 18 hole 6800 yard championship golf course occupies 116 acres of rolling greens and fairways with mature trees surrounding quiet lakes and challenging sand traps.*

──────────── PORT BYRON ────────────

Byron Hills GC Yards: 6017, Holes: 18 Bar/Proshop
23316 94th Ave. North, Par: 71, USGA: 69.1 **GF:** w/day $9
61275 RP: Weekends, **Carts:** $14.00
Ph: 309-523-2664 weekday if large grp

A course blending old with new and a rolling terrain and a number of level lies make this a course where all your clubs are used. My favorite hole is the 14th. A dogleg par 4, you have a choice, over out of bounds or play safe.

Plan ahead! Reserve tee time well in advance, and while you're doing so, confirm rates and services.

INDIANA

———————————— BLOOMINGTON ————————————

Pointe GR
2250 E. Pointe Rd., 47401
Ph: 812-824-4040

Yards: 6707, Holes: 18
Par: 71, USGA: 70.8
RP: 30 days in advance

Restaurant/Bar/Proshop
GF: w/day $27, w/end $36
Carts: Included

Large greens, very well bunkered, long par threes, a very demanding and fun resort golf course. Golf packages available.

———————————— COLUMBUS ————————————

Otter Creek GC
11522 E. 50 North, 47203
Ph: 812-579-5227

Yards: 7258, Holes: 18
Par: 72
RP: Weekdays as far
ahead as like

Restaurant/Bar/Proshop
GF: w/day $35, w/end $44
Carts: $22.00

214 acres of rolling terrain bisected by creek. 2,000 ornamental trees, dogwood, crabapple, red bud, cherry. #11 is our most famous hole: Tee off a hill, 60 foot drop and over creek. 2nd shot over pond and 2 bunkers.

———————————— FRENCH LICK ————————————

French Lick Springs CC
Hwy 56, 47432
Ph: 812-935-9381

Yards: 6629, Holes: 36
Par: 70, USGA: 70.0
RP: Up to 6 months in
advance

Restaurant/Bar
GF: w/day $30, w/end $30
Carts: $11.00 ea

The Country Club Course is a Donald Ross design constructed in 1920. It was the site of the 1924 P.G.A. championship won by Walter Hagen. Two L.P.G.A. championship tournaments were held in the late 1950's. The Valley Course offers a milder challenge.

———————————— INDIANAPOLIS ————————————

Eagle Creek GC
8802 W. 56th St., 46234
Ph: 317-297-3366

Yards: 7154, Holes: 27
Par: 72, USGA: 73.4
RP: Required on
weekends

Restaurant/Bar/Proshop
GF: w/day $12
Carts: $21.00

Secluded course in a preserve like setting, with 2 ponds, blue grass and bent grass greens and tees. Very hilly with elevated tees and no parallel holes. #16 is a challenging par 4 split through 2 huge trees, drive onto a plateau, very elevated green downwind, and 2 big shots to reach it.

LEBANON

GC of Indiana
6905 South 525 East,
46052
Ph: 317-769-6388

Yards: 7222, Holes: 18
Par: 72, USGA: 73.2
RP: at least 1 week in
advance

Restaurant/Bar/Proshop
GF: w/day $30, w/end $35
Carts: Included

Level course on a farm. There are 75 bunkers and 15 holes have water, little ponds and curving stream. Also bent grass, trees and very big greens. #12 a par 5 reached in two with creek and pond to carry on left.

SANTA CLAUS

Christmas Lake GC
Hwy. 245, 47579
Ph: 812-544-2271

Yards: 6515, Holes: 18
Par: 72, USGA: 71.4
RP: 7 days in advance

Restaurant/Bar/Proshop
GF: w/day $13, w/end $19
Carts: $8.00 ea

A player must decide to play the regular tees or challenge the championship tees at 7383 yards. Except for the first couple of holes, the front nine is relatively open. The back nine holes provide breathtaking scenery with doglegs carved through hilly forests.

TERRE HAUTE

Hulman GC
Rt 32 Box 315, 47803
Ph: 812-877-2096

Yards: 7225, Holes: 18
Par: 72, USGA: 71.4
RP: 3 days in advance

Restaurant/Bar/Proshop
GF: w/day $15, w/end $20
Carts: $16.00

Like Florida on front and Michigan on back. There are 130 sandtraps and bent grass greens. #18 has 2 ponds with a double dogleg par 5, 40 yards wide and U shaped sandtrap called "The Tunnel."

Enter your favorite resort in our "Golf Resort of The Year" contest (entry form is in the back of the book).

IOWA

Milford
Spirit Lake
Garner • Clear Lake
Primghar •Webster City
Ankeny
Boone •
• Indianola
• Atlantic
• Panora
Milford
• Clarksville
Peosta
Dubuque
Iowa City • North Liberty
Clinton
Wilton

ANKENY

Otter Creek GC
2388 NE 110th Ave.,
50021
Ph: 515-964-1729

Yards: 6479, Holes: 18
Par: 72, USGA: 70.0
RP: 1 week in advance

Restaurant/Bar/Proshop
GF: w/day $9, w/end $10
Carts: $15.00

One of two public courses in central Iowa having watered fairways, fast but grass greens and a beautiful clubhouse.

ATLANTIC

Atlantic Golf & CC
Box 363, 102 W. 29th St.,
50022
Ph: 712-243-3656

Yards: 5930, Holes: 18
Par: 69, USGA: 75.0

Restaurant/Bar/Proshop
GF: w/day $10, w/end $12
Carts: $16.00

Accuracy is important from the starting tee. Large oak trees surround every fairway on the older front nine before moving to an entirely different look on the back. The newer back nine is more open, lots of sand, with large, undulating greens.

BOONE

Boone Golf & CC
P.O. Box 573, South
Cedar St., 50036
Ph: 515-432-6002

Yards: 3243, Holes: 9
Par: 36, USGA: 70.1

Restaurant/Bar/Proshop
GF: w/day $9, w/end $15
Carts: $18.00

Gently rolling, fully irrigated bluegrass fairways, lush bent grass greens, and tall, graceful trees make this a beautiful garden in which to play.

CLARKSVILLE

C.A.R.D. Inc.
Box 752, RR 1, 50619
Ph: 319-278-4787

Yards: 3126, Holes: 9
Par: 36

Bar/Proshop
GF: w/day $5, w/end $7
Carts: $7.00

This quiet rural Iowa course offers a golfer some unexpected difficulties. For example our No. 6 hole, a par 4, 392 yards, has a pond that juts into the fairway on the right, out of bounds bordering the left, and a hungry creek cutting diagonally through the middle. This hole demands an accurate drive.

CLEAR LAKE

All Vets GC
2000 N. Shore Dr., P.O.
Box 3, 50428
Ph: 515-357-4457

Yards: 3061, Holes: 9
Par: 36, USGA: 66.4
RP: Weekends

Restaurant/Bar/Proshop
GF: w/day $6, w/end $9
Carts: $7.50

Challenging nine hole layout. Rolling terrain with manicured irrigated fairways. Well maintained course with a pleasant atmosphere. On the north shore of beautiful Clear Lake.

─────────────────── CLINTON ───────────────────

Valley Oaks GC Yards: 6363, Holes: 18 Bar/Proshop
3330 Harts Mill Road, Par: 72, USGA: 70.4 **GF:** w/day $8, w/end $11
52732 RP: In advance **Carts:** $7.5
Ph: 319-242-7221

Beautiful challenging 18 hole course with lots of water and oak trees, two lakes on front 9, two lakes on back 9, with a creek winding through the course that comes into play on several holes.

─────────────────── DUBUQUE ───────────────────

Bunker Hill GC Yards: 5316, Holes: 18 Proshop
2200 Bunker Hill Rd., Par: 69, USGA: 65.0 **GF:** w/day $9, w/end $9
52001 RP: 1 week in advance **Carts:** $16.80
Ph: 319-589-4261

You may think the course looks short and easy, but the terrain is non-other like you have seen. Set in the rolling hills of the northern Mississippi River valley, it gives you the opportunity to hit every type of lie imaginable.

─────────────────── GARNER ───────────────────

Garner GC Yards: 3015, Holes: 9 Restaurant/Bar/Proshop
205 Country Club Dr, Par: 36, USGA: 68.9 **GF:** w/day $9, w/end $11
50438 **Carts:** $12.00
Ph: 515-923-2819

With big greens, lots of traps and water, Garner Golf Club sets itself apart from many courses in north Iowa. Though the trees are young, they are becoming more of a hazard each year. Voted 9 hole course of the year in Iowa for 1987.

─────────────────── INDIANOLA ───────────────────

Indianola CC Yards: 2922, Holes: 9 Bar/Proshop
Country Club Rd., 50125 Par: 35, USGA: 66.9 **GF:** w/day $12
Ph: 515-961-3303 **Carts:** $10.00

Hilly with tree lined fairways, two ponds, creek bisects course opening hole par 5, 594 yards with creek coming into play on opening drive.

─────────────────── IOWA CITY ───────────────────

Elks Golf & CC Yards: 5400, Holes: 9 Restaurant/Bar/Proshop
637 Foster Rd., 52240 Par: 70, USGA: 65.3 **GF:** w/day $9, w/end $9
Ph: 319-351-3700 RP: Must be guest of **Carts:** $9.00
member

Although short by today's standards, its narrow fairways and rolling terrain put a premium on accuracy. The putting surfaces are some of the truest in the midwest. The setting of this country club is on one of the highest settings in Iowa City, providing a dramatic view of the surrounding area.

─────────────────── IOWA CITY ───────────────────

Finkbine GC Yards: 6850, Holes: 18 Proshop
W. Melrose Ave., Univ. Par: 72, USGA: 72.1 **GF:** w/day $15
of Iowa, 52242 RP: 7 days in advance **Carts:** $17.00
Ph: 319-335-9556

Hole #13, 160 yards, par 3—from elevated tee to green surrounded by water.

──────────── MILFORD ────────────

Woodlyn Hills GC
RR 1 Box 169, 51351
Ph: 712-338-9898

Yards: 2660, Holes: 9
Par: 35

Restaurant
GF: w/day $5
Carts: $7.00

My favorite hole is #7, a par 3. The wind plays an important part at this hole as you must shoot across the water to reach it. People enjoy this course as it is not flat, yet can be walked with ease.

──────────── NORTH LIBERTY ────────────

Quail Creek GC
Highway 965, 52317
Ph: 319-626-2281

Yards: 3520, Holes: 9
Par: 36, USGA: 36.1

Restaurant/Bar/Proshop
GF: w/day $9, w/end $10
Carts: $18.00

Quail Creek opens with 5 interesting and challenging holes: two par 5's, two par 4's and a par 3. If a low score is what you seek, you need to have it by the fifth green, for up next is our "Amen" corner. Holes 6 through 9 are all long.

──────────── PANORA ────────────

Lake Panorama
National GC
East Lake Panorama,
PO Box 625, 50216
Ph: 515-755-2024

Yards: 7001, Holes: 18
Par: 72, USGA: 71.2
RP: Tee times 1 week
in advance

Bar/Proshop
GF: w/day $20, w/end $30
Carts: $10.00

The front 9 is long and interesting to play. Most scenic hole is number 3 with a view of the course and lake. The back 9 is tight with #12 always the toughest. Beware of the big oak tree! Come and enjoy! Toll free #: 800-766-7013.

──────────── PEOSTA ────────────

Timberline GC
19804 E. Pleasant Grove
Rd., 52068
Ph: 319-876-3210

Yards: 6543, Holes: 18
Par: 72, USGA: 70.9
RP: Required - 5 days
in advance

Restaurant/Bar/Proshop
GF: w/day $10
Carts: $15.00

Carved out of native hardwood timber in the heartland of Iowa, Timberline offers a course that's "fun for all ages." #18, 368 yards downhill to a green completely fronted by a large pond, 4 lakes and a creek. Fall colors are fantastic! Come and enjoy.

──────────── PRIMGHAR ────────────

Primghar GC CC
2nd St. N.E., 51245
Ph: 712-757-6781

Yards: 3250, Holes: 9
Par: 36, USGA: 34.6
RP: First come first
served

Restaurant/Bar/Proshop
GF: w/day $6
Carts: $6.00

It's hard to pick a favorite hole because they all offer a good challenge along with being aesthetically pleasing. A beautiful stream that winds its way through the course and two ponds bring water into play on five of the nine holes.

──────────── WEBSTER CITY ────────────

Briggs Woods GC
RR #1, Box 7, Hwy. 17
South, 50595
Ph: 515-832-2536

Yards: 6400, Holes: 18
Par: 71, USGA: 69.6
RP: Weekends and
holidays

Restaurant/Bar/Proshop
GF: w/day $7, w/end $9
Carts: $7.50

The golf course is situated on rolling terrain with a beautiful view of a 70 acre lake and park. A new back 9 opened August 10, 1991, with a new clubhouse. Water, woods, sand traps and beautiful scenery enhances the golf outing.

KANSAS

Manhattan
Junction City •
Council Grove •
• Garden City
Andover •
Bonner Springs
Lawrence
• Newton
• Wichita
•Wellington

ANDOVER

Terradyne CC
1400 Teradyne, 67002
Ph: 316-733-5851

Yards: 6215, Holes: 18
Par: 71, USGA: 71.6
RP: Required

Restaurant/Bar/Proshop
GF: w/day $25
Carts: $15.00

Terradyne is a unique Scottish style facility that must be seen to believe. Terradyne was nominated in 1988, by Golf Digest, for private newcomer of the year.

BONNER SPRINGS

Sunflower Hills GC
122nd & Riverview, 66012
Ph: 913-721-2727

Yards: 7001, Holes: 18
Par: 72, USGA: 73.3
RP: 2 days in advance

Restaurant/Bar/Proshop
GF: w/day $12, w/end $12
Carts: $18.00

Generally acknowledged as the best public golf course in the greater Kansas City area, Sunflower Hills best holes begin at #12 and finish on #17. If anyone shoots par on these holes they should end up with a great score!

COUNCIL GROVE

Council Grove CC
830 Hays St., 66846
Ph: 316-767-5516

Yards: 2875, Holes: 9
Par: 36, USGA: 32.7

Proshop
GF: w/day $6, w/end $10

A short but challenging course lying in the Flint Hills on the Santa Fe Trail. Challenge lies in negotiating the hilly terrain, blind shots and tricky greens. A large lake and meandering creek put water in play on seven holes.

GARDEN CITY

Buffalo Dunes GC
So. Star Route 83, Box
415, 67846
Ph: 316-275-1727

Yards: 6443, Holes: 18
Par: 72, USGA: 71.8
RP: 1 week in advance

Restaurant/Bar/Proshop
GF: w/day $7, w/end $9
Carts: $14.00

Buffalo Dunes was nominated to be considered for the Top 100 Public Courses by Golf Digest. Home of Kansas' biggest and richest golf tournament—The Southwest Kansas Pro-Am. You will enjoy excellent blue grass fairways and will be challenged by the native rough—course located in sand dunes of southwest Kansas.

JUNCTION CITY

Junction City CC
W Hwy 18, 66441
Ph: 913-238-1161

Yards: 6250, Holes: 9
Par: 72, USGA: 69.5
RP: Members/guest
only

Restaurant/Bar/Proshop
GF: w/day $20
Carts: $12.00

The golf course is located right outside the city limits. The hilly terrain surrounding the golf course provides a great view along with a great challenge, local knowledge is necessary to deal with both elevation contrasts from the tee to green and especially on the large greens.

───────────── LAWRENCE ─────────────

Alvamar GC   Yards: 7096, Holes: 18   Restaurant/Bar
1800 Crossgate Dr., 66047 Par: 72, USGA: 71.7   **GF:** w/day $15, w/end $18
Ph: 913-842-1907   RP: 4 days in advance   **Carts:** $20.00

The course is very hilly and has steep and long for par 3's. There are cotton-
woods, sweet-gums, walnuts, pines and silver maples lining the course. #14 has
trees, creek, dogleg left, right and left again, a par 4.

───────────── MANHATTAN ─────────────

Stagg Hill GC   Yards: 6427, Holes: 18   Restaurant/Proshop
4441 Ft. Riley Blvd.,   Par: 72, USGA: 70.3   **GF:** w/day $11
66502   RP: Weekends   **Carts:** $14.00
Ph: 913-539-1041

Keeping your drives in play on tree lined fairways and accurate irons to small
greens will determine how well you score here. The par 3, 167 yard, 14th hole
across water to a small, elevated green is a beautiful challenging hole.

───────────── NEWTON ─────────────

Newton Public GC   Yards: 5662, Holes: 18   Bar/Proshop
622 E. 6th St., Jct I135 & Par: 70, USGA: 66.4   **GF:** w/day $6, w/end $7
K15, 67114   RP: Accepted   **Carts:** $13.00
Ph: 313-283-4168

Elevated greens, two lakes and a creek running full length of course offers a
challenge to all golfers. Two par threes back to back, #6 and #7 are said to be
the toughest around. Our favorite is the 4th a long par 5 with a lake to carry and
double dogleg.

───────────── WELLINGTON ─────────────

Wellington GC   Yards: 6201, Holes: 18   Restaurant/Bar/Proshop
1500 W. Harvey, P.O.   Par: 70, USGA: 66.6   **GF:** w/day $8, w/end $9
Box 117, 67152   RP: 1 week in advance   **Carts:** $14.00
Ph: 316-326-7904

The Wellington Golf Club is a par 70 course, 6201 yards long, and has an
average green size of 4,000 square feet. The hundreds of cedar, pine, oak, and
elm trees, along with smallish greens will challenge most any golfer's game.

───────────── WICHITA ─────────────

Tallgrass Club   Yards: 6758, Holes: 18   Restaurant/Bar/Proshop
2400 Tallgrass P.S., 67226 Par: 71, USGA: 71.3   **GF:** w/day $25, w/end $40
Ph: 316-684-5663   **Carts:** $15.00

Annual site of LPGA Tour Q-school. A tough course with plush bluegrass fair-
ways. Greens are well bunkered, with a lot of undulation. Rough is thick and
wiry, a tribute to the name of the course. Definitely one of the best in the Midwest.

KENTUCKY

- Frankfort
- Lexington
- Springfield
Cadiz
Burnside

──────── BURNSIDE ────────

General Burnside State Park GC
P.O. Box 488, 42519
Ph: 606-561-4104

Yards: 5905, Holes: 18
Par: 71, USGA: 67.5

Proshop
GF: w/day $10
Carts: $15.75

Scenic gently rolling course on the shores of Lake Cumberland. Five holes run along the shores of the lake.

──────── CADIZ ────────

Lake Barkley State Resort Park
P.O. Box 790, 42211
Ph: 502-924-1131

Yards: 6417, Holes: 18
Par: 72, USGA: 70.1

Restaurant
GF: w/day $10
Carts: $15.75

Level 18 holes with a winding creek in a valley between the hills, the big blue spring that supplies water for the course and winds twice across the 18th fairway.

──────── FRANKFORT ────────

Juniper Hills GC
800 Louisville Rd., 40601
Ph: 502-875-8559

Yards: 6100, Holes: 18
Par: 70, USGA: 66.7
RP: Starters times 1st of week

Proshop
GF: w/day $8, w/end $8
Carts: $15.00

The course offers rolling fairways, small greens, tree lined fairways. Favorite hole #13 with new lake and bridge is always in great shape with very courteous personnel.

──────── LEXINGTON ────────

Marriott's Griffin Gate Resort
1720 Newtown Pike, 40511
Ph: 606-254-4101

Yards: 6300, Holes: 18
Par: 72, USGA: 71.5
RP: Required

Restaurant/Bar
GF: w/day $42, w/end $47
Carts: Included

A rambling, tree-lined layout with large rolling greens, long bluegrass fairways, more than 65 sand bunkers and water coming into play on twelve holes. Home for seven years of the Senior PGA Bank One Classic.

──────── SPRINGFIELD ────────

Lincoln Homestead St. Park GC
Rt. 1 Hwy. 528, 40069
Ph: 606-336-7461

Yards: 6359, Holes: 18
Par: 71
RP: Weekends

Proshop
GF: w/day $10
Carts: $15.00

Setting in a lovely wooded area. #15 is a particularly challenging par 5 with 2 large bunkers guarding either side of the fairway and 2 additional bunkers toward the front of the green, accuracy is a must.

LOUISIANA

---------- GRETNA ----------

Plantation G & CC
1001 Behrman Hwy.,
70053
Ph: 504-392-3363

Yards: 5780, Holes: 18
Par: 69
RP: 1 day ahead

Bar/Proshop
GF: w/day $5, w/end $6
Carts: $10.00

The golf course is not too long but it is difficult to par the course. Course is not too crowded, you can always get a starting time. Due to small greens, the course is great to test your short game. Available for outings.

---------- SLIDELL ----------

Royal GC
201 Royal Dr., 70460
Ph: 504-643-3000

Yards: 6800, Holes: 18
Par: 72, USGA: 71.3
RP: Needed weekends
& holidays

Bar/Proshop
GF: w/day $10, w/end $12
Carts: $15.00

We are located 45 minutes off Interstate Drive from downtown New Orleans. We have Tiff Dwarf greens, 419 Bermuda fairways and tees. Plenty of hardwoods, pines, and cypress.

---------- W. MONROE ----------

Riverside Golf & CC
100 Arkansas Rd., 71291
Ph: 318-322-0696

Yards: 6389, Holes: 9
Par: 72, USGA: 70.5

Restaurant/Bar/Proshop
GF: w/day $7, w/end $8
Carts: $7.00

Enjoy the easy 108 yard par 3 #8—if you hit the green; if not, good luck! Water in front of green and three sand traps to front, right and left side can spell trouble for the weekend golfer.

MAINE

Island Falls •

• Moose River
•
Carrabasset Valley

Carmel •

Bangor
Brooks • •
•Bethel • Rockport
• Rockland Trenton
Leeds Camden

Cumberland
Westbrook Hollis

BANGOR

Bangor Muni GC   Yards: 6400, Holes: 18   Restaurant/Proshop
278 Webster Ave., 04401   Par: 71   **GF:** w/day $11
Ph: 207-945-9226   **Carts:** $12.00

1980 Golf Digest Top 50 Public.

BETHEL

Bethel Inn & CC   Yards: 6663, Holes: 18   Restaurant/Bar/Proshop
Village Common, 04217   Par: 72   **GF:** w/day $22, w/end $27
Ph: 207-824-2175   **Carts:** $22.00

A classic New England resort offering traditional inn and luxury townhouse accommodations, fine dining, health center, and lake house. Geoffrey Cornish designed championship layout offers mountain vistas and a challenge for golfers of all levels. 70 miles from Portland, 13 miles from the New Hampshire border.

BROOKS

Country View GC   Yards: 2950, Holes: 9   Restaurant/Proshop
Rt. 7, 04921   Par: 36   **GF:** w/day $12, w/end $12
Ph: 207-722-3161   **Carts:** $16.00

This beautiful 9 hole layout is very unique as it sets on top of a hill with spectacular views from nearly every hole. No. 9 features a shot from the tee like you have never seen before.

CAMDEN

Goose River GC   Yards: 2910, Holes: 9   Restaurant/Bar/Proshop
Simonton Rd., Box 4820,   Par: 36, USGA: 34.0   **GF:** w/day $10
04843   **Carts:** $14.00
Ph: 207-236-8488

Tough par 5 to begin with hazard and woods on left off tee. Playing to right forces long carry over river with river again in play left of green. Goose River in play on 5 holes. Separate tees give entirely different look on back 9.

---------------------- CARMEL ----------------------

Carmel Valley GC
Rt. 2 Main Rd., P.O. Box
133, 04419
Ph: 207-848-5237

Yards: 2416, Holes: 9
Par: 27, USGA: 55.7

Proshop
GF: w/day $5, w/end $6
Carts: $8.00

Carmel Valley Golf Course is a true championship course for any level golfer. Each hole has its own character. The rewards can be enjoyed by all. The most interesting hole would be #6 miss and take six, 143 yards can give you a very unexpected surprise with its small pond in front of the green and rolling green.

---------------------- CARRABASSETT VALLEY ----------------------

Sugarloaf GC
RR 1 Box 5000, 04947
Ph: 207-237-2000

Yards: 6902, Holes: 18
Par: 72
RP: 5 days in advance

Restaurant/Bar/Proshop
GF: w/day $32, w/end $40
Carts: $13.00 ea

Sugarloaf Golf Course is truly a wilderness course with spectacular vistas, picturesque views and abundant wildlife. Six holes on the back 9 play along or over the Carrabassett River, with the favorite being the 222 yard, par 3 eleventh. This hole tees off 125 feet above the green with water, sand and trees to negotiate.

---------------------- CUMBERLAND ----------------------

Val Halla GC
Val Halla Rd., 04021
Ph: 207-829-2225

Yards: 6324, Holes: 18
Par: 72, USGA: 70.6

Restaurant/Bar/Proshop
GF: w/day $12, w/end $15
Carts: $18.00

Our first nine is relatively open, conducive to good scoring but the back nine is carved out of woods and requires accurate tee shots. Our favorite hole would be the 18th, 398 yard dogleg right with out of bounds on the left and the green is fronted by a water hazard.

---------------------- HOLLIS ----------------------

Salmon Falls Resort
Salmon Falls Rd. - off Rt.
202, 04042
Ph: 207-929-5233

Yards: 6000, Holes: 18
Par: 72, USGA: 70.0
RP: Weekends &
holidays

Restaurant/Bar/Proshop
GF: w/day $15, w/end $15
Carts: $18.00

Salmon Falls Country Club, restaurant, motel and golf course has a beautifully manicured course situated along the Saco River in Maine. It's subtle beauty is accentuated by Maine's scenic wonders that have made Maine one of the leading recreational spots in the USA.

---------------------- ISLAND FALLS ----------------------

Va-Jo-Wa GC
142 Walker Rd., 04747
Ph: 207-463-2128

Yards: 6203, Holes: 18
Par: 72
RP: Walk on—call for
res. times

Restaurant/Bar/Proshop
GF: w/day $15, w/end $15
Carts: $18.00

The course features small greens which are well guarded by trees, traps and water. Approaches with accuracy are a must. The front nine is located in a valley on the shores of Pleasant Lake. The back nine, on a plateau, has panoramic views of Mt. Katahdin and the surrounding countryside. Well groomed, challenging, with several elevation changes.

Plan ahead! Reserve tee time well in advance, and while you're doing so, confirm rates and services.

---------------------------- LEEDS ----------------------------

Springbrook GC Yards: 6408, Holes: 18 Restaurant/Bar/Proshop
RR1, Box 2030, 04263 Par: 71, USGA: 71.2 **GF:** w/day $12
Ph: 207-946-5900 RP: Recommended **Carts:** $16.00

Converted in 1966 from a farm, Springbrook offers a challenging championship course which has hosted the Maine Open in recent years. Known for excellent putting greens, Springbrook also offers a friendly, relaxing atmosphere in our unique clubhouse "barn"! Come visit us.

------------------- MOOSE RIVER/JACKMAN -------------------

Moose River GC Yards: 1976, Holes: 9 **GF:** w/day $7
04945 Par: 31
Ph: 207-668-5331

We have 4 par 4 and 5 par 3. One water hole but very small greens. Open May 15, until November 1, or until snow flies. We also have a cemetery between #1 fairway and #3 hole.

-------------------------- ROCKLAND --------------------------

Rockland GC, Inc. Yards: 6010, Holes: 18 Restaurant/Bar/Proshop
Old County Rd., 04841 Par: 70, USGA: 69.0 **GF:** w/day $15
Ph: 207-594-9322 RP: Recommended **Carts:** $18.00

Near Maine's beautiful coast, and a view of Chickawaukee Lake from the back nine. A wide open course, with few hazards, but wayward shots present many problems. The 595 yard par 5, 15th hole is a test for any golfer.

-------------------------- ROCKPORT --------------------------

Samoset Resort GC Yards: 6362, Holes: 18 Restaurant/Bar/Proshop
On the Ocean, 04856 Par: 70, USGA: 68.9 **GF:** w/day $25, w/end $25
Ph: 207-594-2511 RP: Tee times **Carts:** $22.00
 recommended

The Samoset Resort Golf Club has been described as "the Pebble Beach of the East." With seven holes bordering the ocean and thirteen holes having ocean vistas the perfectly maintained golf course and beautiful gardens will make this a unique golfing experience.

-------------------------- TRENTON --------------------------

Bar Harbor GC Yards: 6621, Holes: 18 Restaurant/Bar/Proshop
Jct. Rts. 3 & 204, 04605 Par: 71, USGA: 69.5 **GF:** w/day $15
Ph: 207-667-7505 **Carts:** $18.00

Playing alongside the Jordan River with the majestic mountains of Acadia National Park in the background, this course is one of the most picturesque in Maine. Save some strength for the 18th—no one has ever reached the green in two shots on the 620 yard monster.

-------------------------- WESTBROOK --------------------------

River Meadow GC Holes: 9 Restaurant/Proshop
216 Lincoln St., Box Par: 70 **GF:** w/day $8
1201, 04092 RP: No tee times **Carts:** $7.00
Ph: 207-854-1625

We have 9 holes not very long but interesting. It is easy to walk, follows close to the river with small streams running through the holes. #9 is a par 5 teeing from an island tee dogleg left out of the woods; small greens. We have land for 9 more holes in 2 years.

MARYLAND

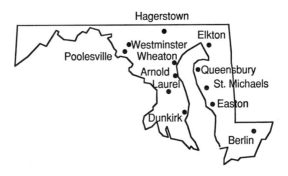

ARNOLD

Bay Hills GC
545 Bay Hills Dr., 21012
Ph: 301-974-0669

Yards: 6057, Holes: 18
Par: 70, USGA: 68.5

Restaurant/Bar/Proshop
GF: w/day $20, w/end $25
Carts: $9.00

The character of this scenic course lies in the natural beauty of its wooded and gently rolling terrain. Six doglegs, fifty plus bunkers, and water coming into play on nine of the holes, all combine to place a premium on strategy and shot placement.

BERLIN

Pine Shore GC
11285 Beauchamp Rd.,
21811
Ph: 301-641-5100

Yards: 3380, Holes: 27
Par: 60, USGA: 52.7

Restaurant/Bar/Proshop
GF: w/day $9
Carts: $12.10

There are three nine hole courses which rotate daily, so that you would get a different 18 every three days. The Dogwood is tight (wooded). The Pines and Willow have plenty of water. The greens and tees are regulation size so each hole could stand on its own at any golf course.

DUNKIRK

Twin Shields GC
2425 Roarty Rd., 20754
Ph: 301-855-8228

Yards: 6284, Holes: 18
Par: 70, USGA: 68.0

Restaurant/Bar/Proshop
GF: w/day $15, w/end $18
Carts: $18.00

Enjoy the beauty and personality of one of Southern Maryland's most scenic courses. Gently rolling terrain and large undulating greens present a challenge for even the most experienced golfers.

EASTON

Hog Neck GC
Old Cordova Rd., 21601
Ph: 301-822-6079

Yards: 7018, Holes: 27
Par: 72, USGA: 71.2
RP: 1 week in advance

Restaurant/Proshop
GF: w/day $18
Carts: $17.00

Front nine wide open with sand and water 7 of 9 holes. The back nine is longer and more scenic with pine trees.

---------------------------- ELKTON ----------------------------

Brantwood GC | Yards: 6222, Holes: 18 | Restaurant/Bar/Proshop
1190 Augustine Herman | Par: 70, USGA: 68.9 | **GF:** w/day $13, w/end $16
Hwy., 21921 | RP: 1 week in advance | **Carts:** $16.00
Ph: 301-398-8848

Brantwood Golf Club is a fairly short track, but don't let that fool you, with water coming into play on eight holes and trees capturing many errant shots, the course is pleasantly surprising. It's easy to walk and not too crowded on weekdays.

---------------------------- HAGERSTOWN ----------------------------

Beaver Creek CC | Yards: 6388, Holes: 18 | Restaurant/Bar/Proshop
Route 9, Box 368 B, 21740 | Par: 72, USGA: 70.2 | **GF:** w/day $16, w/end $20
Ph: 301-733-5152 | RP: Must call for | **Carts:** $16.00
 | starting time |

It's the kind of golf course you never get tired of playing. You always think you should have done better. It has a good variety of holes. Fair but challenging. "Form follows function."

---------------------------- LAUREL ----------------------------

Patuxent Greens GC | Yards: 6207, Holes: 18 | Restaurant/Bar/Proshop
14415 Greenview Dr., | Par: 71, USGA: 69.1 | **GF:** w/day $12, w/end $18
20708 | RP: Weekend | **Carts:** $18.00
Ph: 301-776-5533

A huge clubhouse for a public course with fine dining and banquet rooms. The golf course has a definite "Myrtle Beach" style with 16 water holes and many tall trees, and bunkers. Back nine is very scenic.

---------------------------- POOLESVILLE ----------------------------

Poolesville GC | Yards: 6757, Holes: 18 | Restaurant/Bar/Proshop
16601 West Willard | Par: 71, USGA: 72.3 | **GF:** w/day $15, w/end $17
Rd.,POB 146, 20837 | RP: Weekends & | **Carts:** $20.00
Ph: 301-428-8143 | holidays $17.00 |

The front nine is rather long but most trouble is left. The back nine is shorter and has more water in play. The greens are excellent and relatively small. The course is generally rolling. You will need to ride because of distance between green's and tees.

---------------------------- QUEENSTOWN ----------------------------

Queenstown Harbor GL | Yards: 7110, Holes: 27 | Restaurant/Bar/Proshop
Rt 2 Box 54, 21658 | Par: 72 | **GF:** w/day $25, w/end $36
Ph: 301-827-6611 | RP: One week in | **Carts:** $6.00 ea
 | advance |

All 3 combinations of championship golf wander through woods and wetlands. Our 9 man made ponds and over 2 miles of shoreline, along with spectacles of wild geese and deer make Queenstown Harbor an exciting experience. Our plush bent grass fairways are unsurpassed.

Subscribe to our free newsletter, "Great Golf Gazette" and hear about the latest special golf vacation values.

---------- ST. MICHAELS ----------

Harbourtowne GR
Miles River at
Chesapeake Bay, 21663
Ph: 301-745-9066

Holes: 18
Par: 70, USGA: 68.5
RP: Hotel guest &
guests of pro

Restaurant/Bar/Proshop
GF: w/day $35

The Harbourtowne Course has been described as three courses in one. The first nine holes are right by the Eastern Bay, open to blue sky and soft bay breezes. Number 10 starts a stretch of five holes that are tight—reminiscent of the pine woods courses of the Carolinas. The four finishing holes are open, playing back into westerly breezes off the bay.

---------- WESTMINSTER ----------

Wakefield Valley GC
1000 Fenby Farm Rd.,
21157
Ph: 301-876-6662

Yards: 6650, Holes: 27
Par: 72, USGA: 71.4

Restaurant/Bar/Proshop
GF: w/day $18, w/end $20
Carts: $20.00

27 holes featuring beautiful Carroll County rolling countryside. All holes feature plenty of water and challenging shots from (4) sets of tees—best conditioned course in area.

---------- WHEATON ----------

Northwest Park GC
15711 Layhill Rd., 20906
Ph: 301-598-6100

Yards: 7185, Holes: 27
Par: 72, USGA: 71.9
RP: 6 days in advance

Restaurant/Proshop
GF: w/day $14, w/end $18
Carts: $17.00

Northwest Park Golf Course is one of the longest courses you will play. Off the blue tees you could play as long a 7,500 yards with par fours averaging 430 yards. Creeks border the course on the front and back nines as lateral water hazards. Wooded back nine will test the nerve of your driver.

Enter your favorite resort in our "Golf Resort of The Year" contest (entry form is in the back of the book).

MASSACHUSETTS

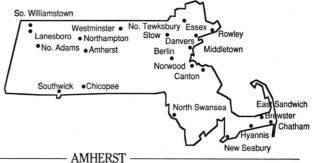

So. Williamstown
Westminster • No. Tewksbury Essex
Lanesboro • Northampton Stow • Danvers Rowley
• No. Adams • Amherst Berlin • Middletown
• Norwood •
Canton
Southwick • Chicopee
North Swansea East Sandwich
Brewster
Chatham
Hyannis
New Seabury

─────────────── AMHERST ───────────────

Hickory Ridge CC	Yards: 6794, Holes: 18	Restaurant/Bar/Proshop
West Pomeroy Ln., 01002	Par: 72, USGA: 68.8	GF: w/day $20, w/end $25
Ph: 413-253-9320	RP: 1 day in advance	Carts: $18.00

Our favorite hole is the 18th, a 440 yard par four, a good drive from the elevated tee will leave you a solid iron to a large bunkered green, with the clubhouse as a background. Turn it loose!

─────────────── BERLIN ───────────────

Berlin CC	Yards: 2313, Holes: 9	Restaurant/Bar/Proshop
25 Carr Rd., 01503	Par: 33, USGA: 62.9	GF: w/day $8
Ph: 508-838-2733		

Berlin Country Club provides a scenic view of the New England countryside. Although nestled in the small town of Berlin, it is only minutes away from major highways located in central Massachusetts.

─────────────── BREWSTER ───────────────

Captains (The)	Yards: 6794, Holes: 18	Restaurant/Bar/Proshop
1000 Free Man's Way, 02631	Par: 72, USGA: 69.4	GF: w/day $25
Ph: 508-896-5100	RP: 2 months in advance	Carts: $21.00

Course is very gently sloping with lots of pine and oak trees. #13 is a par 4, 448 yard hole with tight drive into wind, lake and pond near 14, golf over it and lay up on 2nd shot.

─────────────── BREWSTER ───────────────

Ocean Edge GC	Holes: 18	Restaurant/Bar
Route 6A, 02631		
Ph: 800-221-1837		

Our course is a true test of strategy and finesse. You'll tee off over a ravine, then over a cranberry bog. You'll chip over deep blue ponds and out of Scottish-style pot bunkers on your way to the sharply contoured greens.

─────────────── CANTON ───────────────

Brookmeadow CC	Yards: 6750, Holes: 18	Bar/Proshop
100 Everendon Rd., 02021	Par: 72, USGA: 69.4	GF: w/day $15, w/end $18
Ph: 617-828-4444		Carts: $20.00

A full championship layout cut in wooded undulating land, large greens, lush fairways, lined with trees, water holes and bunker hazards.

─────────────── CHATHAM ───────────────

Chatham Bars Inn
Shore Rd., 02633
Ph: 508-945-0096

Yards: 2325, Holes: 9
Par: 34, USGA: 61.8

Restaurant/Bar
GF: w/day $6
Carts: $2.00

Definitely short but quite challenging as the course winds through rolling terrain, with views of the harbor and ocean from the 7th and 8th holes.

─────────────── CHICOPEE ───────────────

Chicopee C
1290 Burnett Rd., 01020
Ph: 413-592-4156

Yards: 7010, Holes: 18
Par: 72, USGA: 70.4
RP: Weekends

Restaurant/Bar/Proshop
GF: w/day $10
Carts: $15.00

Our golf course is tree lined with pine and oak and is considered a golf course for golfers who can hook the ball. It's tight and we have on the front nine a double green for #2 and #5 holes, the 2nd is a par 5 and the 5th holes is a very narrow difficult par 4, our number 1 difficult hole. Each hole you have to play a different club.

─────────────── DANVERS ───────────────

Tara Ferncroft GC
50 Ferncroft Rd., 01923
Ph: 617-777-2500

Holes: 18
Par: 72

Restaurant/Bar

Championship golf course, lots of mature trees, bunkers and water. Home of the LPGA Boston Five Classic July 1987.

─────────────── EAST SANDWICH ───────────────

Round Hill CC
Round Hill Rd., 02537
Ph: 508-888-3384

Yards: 6525, Holes: 18
Par: 72
RP: 1 day in advance

Restaurant/Bar/Proshop
GF: w/day $20, w/end $22
Carts: $20.00

Round Hill Country offers a unique setting with rolling fairways and a scenic view of Cape Cod on the south side. The back 9 holes display a spectacular view of Cape Cod Bay. Round Hill offers a challenge and the beauty of Cape Cod.

─────────────── ESSEX ───────────────

Cape Ann GC
John Wise Ave (Rte.
133), 01929
Ph: 508-768-7544

Yards: 2950, Holes: 9
Par: 35, USGA: 70.0

Restaurant/Bar/Proshop
GF: w/day $8, w/end $10
Carts: $9/00

Most scenic course north of Boston. Panoramic view of salt marshes and beaches from 3rd hole to top of 4th tee.

─────────────── HYANNIS ───────────────

Tara Hyannis GC
West End Circel, 02601
Ph: 508-775-7775

Yards: 2600, Holes: 27
Par: 9
RP: 1 day in advance

Restaurant/Bar/Proshop
GF: w/day $15

Eight water holes, well bunkered, tree lined, excellent greens. Third hole, a difficult par 3 of 165 yards uphill, steep drop down the left side, right side guarded by a long bunker.

─────────────── LANESBORO ───────────────

Skyline CC
Rt 7 405 South Main St.,
01257
Ph: 413-445-5584

Yards: 6517, Holes: 9
Par: 72, USGA: 70.4
RP: Weekends

Restaurant/Bar/Proshop
GF: w/day $9, w/end $12
Carts: $15.00

The fourth tee provides one of the best views in Berkshire County. You will be able to see Mt. Greylock, Pontoosie Lake and almost over the mountains into New York.

———————————————— MIDDLETON ————————————————

Middleton GC   Yards: 3215, Holes: 18   Restaurant/Bar/Proshop
Route 114, 01949   Par: 54   **GF:** w/day $20, w/end $20
Ph: 508-774-4075

*Recognized as one of New England's finest par 3's. Middleton has holes that
vary in length from 115 to 240 yards, with large modern tees and greens, and
gently rolling fairways. The New England PGA annually plays a Pro-Lady
Invitational on this meticulously maintained layout.*

———————————————— NEW SEABURY ————————————————

Challenger   Yards: 5900, Holes: 18   Restaurant/Bar/Proshop
New Seabury Cape Cod, Par: 70, USGA: 67.2   **GF:** w/day $20
P.O. Box B, 02649   RP: 1 day in advance   **Carts:** $12.00 ea
Ph: 508-477-9111

*New England's premier resort/residential community boasts the Blue Champion-
ship course, rated among the best in the nation. Together with the classic Green
Challenger course, golfers are led past 36 holes of seascapes, salt marshes
splashed with Ragosa roses.*

———————————————— NEW SEABURY ————————————————

New Seabury Cape   Yards: 6900, Holes: 18   Restaurant/Bar/Proshop
Cod GC   Par: 72, USGA: 70.8   **Carts:** $12.00 ea
P.O. Box B, 02649   RP: 1 day in advance
Ph: 508-477-9110

*New Seabury, New England's premier resort/residential community, boasts the
magnificent Blue Championship course, rated among the best in the nation.
Together with the classic Green Challenger course, golfers are led past 36 holes
of dramatic seascapes, salt marshes splashed with Ragosa roses, and exquisite
greens.*

———————————————— NO. ADAMS ————————————————

North Adams CC   Yards: 5440, Holes: 9   Restaurant/Bar/Proshop
P.O. Box 241, 01247   Par: 72, USGA: 69.5   **GF:** w/day $7
Ph: 413-664-9011   **Carts:** $7.50

*Old country course is popular, and in excellent condition. Some narrow fair-
ways are a continuous challenge. Par 3, second hole may be reached in one, but
is guarded ingeniously by traps! Par 5, ninth needs a might wallop to get over
pond—birdies here are a real test of skill!*

———————————————— NO. TEWKSBURY ————————————————

Trull Brook GC   Yards: 6320, Holes: 18   Restaurant/Proshop
170 River Rd., 01876   Par: 72, USGA: 68.2   **GF:** w/day $20
Ph: 508-851-6731   RP: Recommended   **Carts:** $18.00

*Our 15th hole—a 195 yard par 3—has been featured in Golf Digest for being a
beautiful example of New England golf architecture. From a hilltop tee carved
out of the rocks, you hit to a large green, surrounded by 4 large bunkers, and the
Merrimack River in the back and meandering Trull Brook in the front. It is a
pretty sight, but a difficult hole when the wind kicks up!*

*Plan ahead! Reserve tee time well in advance, and while you're
doing so, confirm rates and services.*

---------------------------------- NORTH SWANSEA ----------------------------------

Wampanoag GC Yards: 3240, Holes: 9 Restaurant/Bar/Proshop
168 Old Providence Rd., Par: 35, USGA: 67.6 **GF:** w/day $7, w/end $9
02777 **Carts:** $14.00
Ph: 508-379-9881

Located on Palmer River—Wampanoag Indians fought settlers here—8th hole par 3, 185-215 yards. Brook in front of green, well trapped. Least number of pars on this hole, cool breeze always.

---------------------------------- NORTHAMPTON ----------------------------------

Pine Grove GC Yards: 6115, Holes: 18 Restaurant/Bar/Proshop
254 Wilson Rd., 01060 Par: 72, USGA: 70.6 **GF:** w/day $10, w/end $11
Ph: 413-584-4570 RP: Weekends **Carts:** $14.00

A sporty and challenging picturesque 18 hole course, in a beautiful New England setting, if you stay in Northampton for business or pleasure, make your stay even more enjoyable, take time to play a round of golf, located just minutes from where you are staying.

---------------------------------- NORWOOD ----------------------------------

Norwood CC & Resort Yards: 5942, Holes: 18 Restaurant/Bar/Proshop
400 Providence Par: 70, USGA: 67.6 **GF:** w/day $14, w/end $17
Highway, 02062 **Carts:** $20.00
Ph: 617-769-5880

The only hotel golf resort within greater Boston area. The course is flat, not long, but demands accuracy due to trees and water hazards. Hotel, tennis, 2 swimming pools, driving range are on the golf course. Lush fairways.

---------------------------------- ROWLEY ----------------------------------

Rowley CC Yards: 3055, Holes: 9 Restaurant/Bar/Proshop
Dodge Rd., 01969 Par: 36 **GF:** w/day $9, w/end $12
Ph: 508-948-2731 RP: Weekends & **Carts:** $9.00
holidays

Cross a covered bridge to the first green, view the many ponds that magnify the beauty of this tight course. The 8th hole a long downhill par 5 meets a pond crossing the fairway. Score well and you are playing good golf.

---------------------------------- SOUTH WILLIAMSTOWN ----------------------------------

Waubeeka GL Yards: 6296, Holes: 18 Restaurant/Bar/Proshop
137 New Ashford Rd., Par: 71, USGA: 69.5 **GF:** w/day $13, w/end $16
P.O. Box 511, 01267 **Carts:** $18.00
Ph: 413-458-8355

View from the third tee is outstanding, looking down the tight fairway the tee shot must be well-placed. This should put you in position for a second shot overlooking the green which is well-trapped behind and a small pond in front. Very interesting.

---------------------------------- SOUTHWICK ----------------------------------

Southwick CC Yards: 6281, Holes: 18 Restaurant/Bar/Proshop
739 College Highway, Par: 71, USGA: 67.0 **GF:** w/day $15
01077 RP: Call for tee times **Carts:** $17.00
Ph: 413-569-0136

First hole, a par 4, is the toughest starting hole in Western Massachusetts.

──────── STOW ────────

Stow Acres CC Yards: 6907, Holes: 36 Restaurant/Bar/Proshop
58 Randall Rd., 01775 Par: 72, USGA: 72.4 **GF:** w/day $23, w/end $30
Ph: 508-568-1100 RP: Call up to 5 days **Carts:** $20.00
 in advance

Stow acres offers the golfer 36 well maintained holes in a quiet, rural setting. The North Course, rated in the top 50 by Golf Digest, wanders through cathedral pines. A true test for those who like to be challenged. The South features rolling hills, many dogleg holes and outstanding views. Stow Acres was voted Best of Boston by Boston magazine.

──────── WESTMINSTER ────────

Westminster CC Yards: 6223, Holes: 18 Restaurant/Bar/Proshop
51 Ellis Rd., 01473 Par: 71, USGA: 69.5 **GF:** w/day $20, w/end $25
Ph: 508-874-5938 RP: Call in advance **Carts:** $20.00

The first ten holes are the warm up area of the golf course. The eleventh thru the sixteenth hole are the challenge. Length and accuracy are required to score these holes. Do that well, and you will be playing good golf.

Please mention "Golf Courses—The Complete Guide" when you reserve your tee time. Our goal is to provide as complete a listing of golf courses open to the public as possible. If you know of a course we don't list, please send us the name and address on the form at the back of this guide.

MICHIGAN

ADRIAN

Lenawee CC
4110 Country Club Rd.,
49221
Ph: 517-265-8227

Yards: 6300, Holes: 18
Par: 71, USGA: 69.1
RP: Private club,
members only

Restaurant/Bar/Proshop
GF: w/day $25
Carts: $20.00

Well manicured hilly course with 83 bunkers. Out of bounds left on 9 holes. Only one water hazard. Greens are small but always in near perfect condition. Fun course with no two holes alike.

ADRIAN

Woodlawn GC
4634 Treat Hwy., 49221
Ph: 517-263-3288

Yards: 6064, Holes: 18
Par: 71, USGA: 69.2
RP: 7 days in advance

Restaurant/Bar/Proshop
GF: w/day $11, w/end $15
Carts: $18.00

Gently rolling fairways lined with a variety of mature trees. Sand traps and water hazards also enhance the scenic beauty. Small to medium sized contoured greens make shot-making necessary, especially the par 3's which are definite "skill testers". "Country Club Conditioning—Daily Fee Rates"!

ALTO

Tyler Creek GC
13495 92nd St., SE, 49302
Ph: 616-868-6751

Yards: 6055, Holes: 18
Par: 70, USGA: 68.4
RP: 1 week in advance

Restaurant/Proshop
GF: w/day $12, w/end $12
Carts: $16.00

Creek winds through rolling hills amidst beautiful pine and hardwood forests. Water hazards, deep bunkers, and elevated greens will challenge you. Spectacular vacation packages. Campground and chalet available. Enjoy swimming, fishing and tubing. Weekly specials. Week, month and season memberships offered.

ATTICA

Arcadia Hills GC
3801 Haines Rd., 48412
Ph: 313-724-6967

Yards: 2703, Holes: 9
Par: 36

Bar/Proshop
GF: w/day $5, w/end $6
Carts: $7.00

Arcadia Hills is a short course good for beginners. But is also a challenge for the more avid golfer. The course is set in the middle of a wooded area. It makes for a good one-day get away.

─────────────────── AUGUSTA ───────────────────

Gull Lake View GC
7417 N. 38th St., 49012
Ph: 616-731-4148

Yards: 6262, Holes: 18
Par: 71, USGA: 69.0
RP: Required

Restaurant/Bar/Proshop
GF: w/day $17, w/end $19
Carts: $17.00

The East Course, rated among Michigan's top ten public golf courses in 1986, is not long, but its par 70 is seldom matched. Bedford Valley has long holes, many well-placed bunkers, woods and big greens. Stonehedge, the newest course, is shaped out of rolling wooded terrain.

─────────────────── BATTLE CREEK ───────────────────

Cedar Creek GC
14000 Renton Rd., 49017
Ph: 616-965-6423

Yards: 6225, Holes: 18
Par: 72, USGA: 69.9
RP: Required

Bar/Proshop
GF: w/day $9
Carts: $15.00

Water comes into play on six holes. The third hole a par 5 550 yard hole is especially difficult with two ponds across the fairway. Accuracy is a definite must or you're in trouble.

─────────────────── BAY CITY ───────────────────

Bay Valley Inn GC
2470 Old Bridge Rd.,
48706
Ph: 517-686-3500

Yards: 6610, Holes: 18
Par: 71, USGA: 71.9

Restaurant/Bar/Proshop

Begin with a few rounds of golf on the magnificent championship course designed by Desmond Muirhead and Jack Nicklaus. The challenge of the "Heather Hole" and the thirteen water holes awaits you!

─────────────────── BELLAIRE ───────────────────

Shanty Creek-Schuss Mt. Resort
Box 355, 49615
Ph: 616-533-6076

Yards: 6394, Holes: 18
Par: 72, USGA: 71.5
RP: 2 months in
advance

Restaurant/Bar
GF: w/day $60
Carts: Included

Arnold Palmer joined with his partner Ed Seay to create the outstanding "Legend," one of his star creations. Playing the course is like walking solo in the north woods. There are no parallel holes, and each fairway is framed by mature pine and birch.

─────────────────── BELMONT ───────────────────

Grand Island Golf Ranch Inc.
6266 West River Dr.,
49306
Ph: 616-363-1262

Yards: 6266, Holes: 18
Par: 72, USGA: 69.5
RP: Weekends &
holidays

Restaurant/Proshop
GF: w/day $10
Carts: $14.00

You ease off the first two par 4 holes with water behind the first green and water in front of the 2nd tee. Than the fun begins by crossing a meandering creek on #3, 4, 5 and 8 holes with a river behind #5 and 7 greens. The back 9 is long with elevated greens.

Please mention "Golf Courses—The Complete Guide" when you reserve your tee time. Our goal is to provide as complete a listing of golf courses open to the public as possible. If you know of a course we don't list, please send us the name and address on the form at the back of this guide.

─────────────────── BIG RAPIDS ───────────────────

Katke GC
Ferris State University,
M-20, 49307
Ph: 616-592-3765

Yards: 6683, Holes: 18
Par: 72, USGA: 69.6
RP: Two weeks in
advance

Restaurant/Bar/Proshop
GF: w/day $16, w/end $16
Carts: $18.00

Located in the rolling hills of west central Michigan, Katke is one of the most scenic and well-conditioned university courses in the country with large greens and 5 par 5's and 5 par 3's. There is variety for everyone. Enjoy a view of the whole course and surrounding area from the pro shop and adjacent hotel.

─────────────────── BRIDGMAN ───────────────────

Pebblewood CC
9794 Jericho Rd., 49106
Ph: 616-465-5611

Yards: 5576, Holes: 18
Par: 68, USGA: 62.0
RP: Weekends

Restaurant/Bar/Proshop
GF: w/day $11, w/end $13
Carts: $12.00

Pebblewood is the oldest course in the area. This course has all new bent grass fairways, and trees. 3 new lakes, 100 new trees, the entire course has been rebuilt. Also, all new restaurant and lounge with an all glass view of the course. Best food in the area.

─────────────────── BRIGHTON ───────────────────

Huron Meadows
Metropark
8765 Hammel Rd., 48116
Ph: 313-227-2757

Yards: 6647, Holes: 18
Par: 72, USGA: 70.0
RP: 1 week in advance

Restaurant/Proshop
GF: w/day $11, w/end $13
Carts: $15.00

Beautiful, wide, lush green fairways with a front nine spread over 200 acres. It's almost like playing your very own private course on each and every hole, with just enough challenge to bring you back again and again.

─────────────────── BUCHANAN ───────────────────

Brookwood GC
1339 Rynearson Rd.,
49107
Ph: 616-695-7818

Yards: 6540, Holes: 18
Par: 72, USGA: 72.0
RP: Weekends &
holidays

Restaurant/Bar/Proshop
GF: w/day $12, w/end $16
Carts: $17.00

Brookwood's front nine calls upon your attention from the opening tee shot. The demand is shot placement off the tee to position your game for par numbers. Don't get greedy on this front nine that shares 7 out of 9 holes as blind shots from the teeing ground.

─────────────────── CADILLAC ───────────────────

Lakewood on Green
GC
128 Lakewood Dr., 49601
Ph: 616-775-4763

Yards: 2931, Holes: 9
Par: 35, USGA: 75.0
RP: Required June,
July, August

Restaurant/Proshop
GF: w/day $7, w/end $8

Scenic and relaxing to play—good test of golf—picked by N.G.F. as one of five golf courses in Michigan as most scenic and playable. Most favorite hole is #6. Placement of drive very important.

─────────────────── CADILLAC ───────────────────

Mc Guire's Evergreen
7800 Mackinaw Trail,
49601
Ph: 616-775-9947

Yards: 6601, Holes: 27
Par: 71, USGA: 69.2

Restaurant/Bar

27 holes of superb golf, but watch out for all those trees. #14 on the Spruce Course is a par 4, 352 yard straightaway where you can really cut loose, if you're a shotmaker you'll stay out of the water guarding the large green.

-------------------------------- CARLETON --------------------------------

Carleton Glen GC, Inc. Yards: 6307, Holes: 18 Restaurant/Bar/Proshop
13470 Grafton Rd., 48117 Par: 71, USGA: 71.0 **GF:** w/day $15
Ph: 313-654-6201 RP: Required **Carts:** $16.00

Eighteen holes of scenic delight and challenging golf, is the best way to describe Carleton Glen Golf Course. Every hole is completely different in yardage and scenery. Bring all your golf clubs. The variety of shots are a golfers pleasure.

-------------------------------- CEDAR --------------------------------

Sugar Loaf Resort GC Yards: 6901, Holes: 18 Restaurant/Bar/Proshop
RTE 1, 49621 Par: 72, USGA: 70.1 **GF:** w/day $50, w/end $50
Ph: 616-228-5461 RP: Required **Carts:** Included

Golfers of all abilities will enjoy the challenge and the beauty of our 18-hole championship golf course. Jan Stephenson, LPGA, has chosen Sugar Loaf Resort to call home while visiting the Grand Traverse area. Please reserve tee-times in advance.

-------------------------------- CLARKSTON --------------------------------

Indian Springs Yards: 6703, Holes: 18 Proshop
Metropark Par: 72, USGA: 70.4 **GF:** w/day $11, w/end $13
5100 Indian Trail, 48016 RP: 1 week in advance **Carts:** $15.00
Ph: 313-625-7870

The front nine of this new course is open enough that the "everyday" golfer can warm up and enjoy the round. Beware—the back nine! The 13th hole is all of 600 yards and the 16th very short but treacherously surrounded by sand.

-------------------------------- COLDWATER --------------------------------

Coldwater CC Yards: 6363, Holes: 18 Restaurant/Bar/Proshop
42 Narrows Rd., Box 69, Par: 72, USGA: 70.4 **GF:** w/day $19
49036 RP: 3 days advance **Carts:** $18.00
Ph: 517-278-4892 for non-members

Front nine is longer and relatively open, while the back nine features tight and rolling fairways. All situated on beautiful Morrison Lake.

-------------------------------- DOWAGIAC --------------------------------

Hampshire CC Yards: 7030, Holes: 18 Restaurant/Bar/Proshop
29592 Pokagon Hwy., Par: 72, USGA: 71.0 **GF:** w/day $11, w/end $14
49047 RP: Weekends & **Carts:** $14.00
Ph: 616-782-7476 holidays - 1 week

Just when you think you have mastered the front nine which is quite open, and you can spray the ball, and there are only 2 water holes—then you reach the back nine with its narrow, wooded fairways—a very different nine. Holes No 4 and 14 are two great par 4's loved by many—dreaded by most.

-------------------------------- EMPIRE --------------------------------

Dunes GC Yards: 3277, Holes: 9 Proshop
M-72, 49630 Par: 36 **GF:** w/day $7
Ph: 616-326-5390 **Carts:** $7.00

The unique features are the roughs, have been left to nature but not hard to play out of. The favorite 5th hole par 5 has a hill in the center of the fairway, with a good roll to the right. A long straight drive off of tee is required. Following shots going to the left for a roll downhill to the green.

──────────── FRANKENMUTH ────────────

Frankenmuth GC CC   Yards: 2960, Holes: 9   Restaurant/Bar/Proshop
950 Flint St., Box 304,   Par: 35, USGA: 68.5   **GF:** w/day $14, w/end $15
48734   RP: Recommended   **Carts:** $9.00
Ph: 517-652-9229

The key holes are 6, 7, and 8. Hole #6 is a 130-160 yard par 5 island hole to a small green. Hole #7 is 560 yards, par 5 uphill and #8 is 435 yard par 4 uphill. If you can putt the fast sloping greens you'll do well! Frankenmuth is the number 1 tourist attraction in Michigan, featuring German Chicken dinners and Christmas decorations.

──────────── GAYLORD ────────────

Hidden Valley GC   Yards: 6305, Holes: 18   Restaurant/Bar/Proshop
P.O. Box 556, 49735   Par: 71
Ph: 517-732-4653

Hidden Valley Classic is acclaimed for impeccable maintenance and casually elegant setting. Carpet like fairways and perfect but tough undulating greens combined with character-building tee shots out of the woods place demands on both accuracy and nerve.

──────────── GAYLORD ────────────

Michaywe Hills GC   Yards: 6835, Holes: 36   Restaurant/Bar/Proshop
1535 Opal Lake Rd.,   Par: 72, USGA: 71.4   **GF:** w/day $40, w/end $40
49735   RP: Begin taking tee   **Carts:** $10.00
Ph: 517-939-8911   times in Jan.

All holes on the Pines Course are framed by large northern Michigan white pines and birches with large greens and strategic bunkering. The Lake Course features six "alpine" style holes, six holes of "Scottish" design, and six lakeside holes. Beat grass greens, tees and fairways throughout.

──────────── GAYLORD ────────────

Treetops Sylvan Resort Yards: 6399, Holes: 18   Restaurant/Bar/Proshop
GC   Par: 71, USGA: 72.6   **GF:** w/day $68
3962 Wilkinson Rd.,   RP: Call in advance   **Carts:** Included
49731
Ph: 517-732-6711

The Robert Trent Jones masterpiece covers over 400 glacier carved acres through the densely wooded Pigeon River valley. Treetops is bold but fair, the spectacular terrain offers you a variety of design features and breathtaking vistas, also new for 92—the Tom Fazio design.

──────────── GAYLORD ────────────

Wilderness Valley GC   Yards: 6985, Holes: 18   Restaurant/Bar/Proshop
7519 Mancelona Rd.,   Par: 71, USGA: 68.4   **GF:** w/day $18, w/end $23
49735   RP: Recommended on   **Carts:** $12.00 ea
Ph: 800-423-5949   weekends

The Valley Course is carved from the forest. The front nine demands accurate tee shots over the water hazards and between the dense woods that border each fairway. The back nine is slightly more forgiving off the tee and provides a pleasant challenge over superbly maintained fairways and greens. Our new course, the Black Forest Course has spectacular bunkering and strategic holes reminiscent of Alister MacKenzie as its trademarks.

----------------------------- GRAND HAVEN -----------------------------

Grand Haven GC Yards: 6789, Holes: 18 Restaurant/Bar/Proshop
17000 Lincoln, 49417 Par: 72, USGA: 69.2 **GF:** w/day $26, w/end $28
Ph: 616-842-4040 RP: 1 week in advance **Carts:** $20.00
for weekends

Set in gentle hills, narrow and tight with no parallel holes. There are heavy pines and sand dunes with no water to carry. The course is oval in shape with no fairway bunkers.

----------------------------- GRAND RAPIDS -----------------------------

Gracewil CC Yards: 5025, Holes: 18 Restaurant/Bar/Proshop
2597 Four Mile Rd NW, Par: 72, USGA: 67.9 **GF:** w/day $9, w/end $9
49504 RP: Weekends & **Carts:** $14.00
Ph: 616-784-2455 holidays

Family owned/run business for 60 years. Carved thru an old apple orchard out in the country atmosphere minutes from Grand Rapids. We offer two 18 hole courses to choose from. Something for everyone.

----------------------------- GRAND TRAVERSE VILLAGE -----------------------------

Grand Traverse Resort Yards: 440, Holes: 36 Restaurant/Bar
Village Par: 72, USGA: 75.8 **GF:** w/day $45
Box 404, 49610 RP: Guests - 2 weeks **Carts:** $10.00 ea
Ph: 616-938-1620 in advance

The Bear is demanding #3, rated as one of the best holes in the state, is a picturesque par 5 at 529 yards. No two holes are similar. The Resort Course offers challenging versatility on a gently rolling landscape.

----------------------------- GREENBUSH -----------------------------

Greenbush GC Yards: 3005, Holes: 9 Restaurant/Bar/Proshop
1981 US-23, 48738 Par: 35 **GF:** w/day $5
Ph: 517-724-6356 **Carts:** $8.00

We have redesigned 3 new holes for more interesting and testing play. The course overlooks beautiful Lake Huron and we call it the world's only air conditioned golf course.

----------------------------- HALE -----------------------------

Wicker Hills GC Yards: 2975, Holes: 9 Restaurant/Bar/Proshop
7287 Wickert Rd., 48739 Par: 36, USGA: 33.8 **GF:** w/day $6
Ph: 517-728-9971 **Carts:** $4.00 ea

Scenic, hilly, situated and surrounded by the Huron National Forest in Northeast Lower Michigan.

----------------------------- HARBOR SPRINGS -----------------------------

Boyne Highlands GC Yards: 7210, Holes: 18 Restaurant/Bar/Proshop
49740 Par: 72, USGA: 74.0 **GF:** w/day $80, w/end $80
Ph: 800-GO-BOYNE RP: May be made with **Carts:** Included
room res.

The Heather course's greens are vast 7,000 to 10,000 sq. ft. It's heavily wooded with marshes & ponds dotting your scorecard. This is a toughie to par. The Moor plays a little longer with rather wide landing areas and fairways. New Donald Ross Mem. course duplicates most famous holes—Seminole & Oakland Hills.

──────────────── HOLLAND ────────────────

Holland CC   Yards: 5953, Holes: 18   Proshop
51 Country Club Rd.,   Par: 70, USGA: 66.6   **GF:** w/day $15, w/end $17
49423   RP: 4 days in advance   **Carts:** $15.00
Ph: 616-392-1844

This relatively short course will surprise you. Narrow tree lined fairways, small greens and the Macatawa River add to the beauty and the challenge of the beautiful course. Our favorite hole is the uphill 15th with the river, two ponds and two traps to test you.

──────────────── HOUGHTON ────────────────

Portage Lake GC   Yards: 6300, Holes: 18   Restaurant/Proshop
US 41, 49931   Par: 72, USGA: 69.7   **GF:** w/day $10
Ph: 906-487-2641   **Carts:** $13.00

Scenic course borders the Pilgrim River and water comes into play on 5 holes. The most difficult is the 527 yard par 5 11th hole which has your tee shot over water, and bunkers to left front of green and one to the right—lots of luck.

──────────────── HUDSONVILLE ────────────────

Summergreen GC   Yards: 1947, Holes: 9   Proshop
3441 New Holland, 49426 Par: 30   **GF:** w/day $4, w/end $5
Ph: 616-669-0950   **Carts:** $5.00

Our favorite hole is No. 4, a 347 yard par 4 with a deep ditch directly in front of the tee, 2 more ditches crossing the fairway. Condominiums lining the right rough, and dense trees lining the left rough.

──────────────── JACKSON ────────────────

Cascades GC   Yards: 6614, Holes: 18   Restaurant/Proshop
1992 Warren, 49203   Par: 72, USGA: 70.8   **GF:** w/day $11
Ph: 517-788-4323   RP: Weekends &   **Carts:** $16.00
                        holidays

Cascades is challenging, long by most standards, and features water and beautiful scenery. Number 17 is one hole golfers should take note of. It is one of the state's best according to the Michigan Travel Bureau. The Cascades has been nominated as one of the top 75 public courses in America by Golf Digest.

──────────────── LANSING ────────────────

Royal Scot GC   Yards: 6606, Holes: 18   Restaurant/Bar/Proshop
4722 W. Grand River,   Par: 71, USGA: 68.9   **GF:** w/day $14, w/end $18
48906   RP: Call for tee times   **Carts:** $20.00
Ph: 517-321-GOLF

Lansing's Michigan Capital Choice golf course. Scottish link golf course with undulating greens. Our favorite hole—so many to choose from. . .you come out and let us know!

──────────────── LEXINGTON ────────────────

Lakeview Hills CC   Yards: 6206, Holes: 18   Restaurant/Bar/Proshop
6560 E. Peck Rd., 48450 Par: 72, USGA: 69.3   **GF:** w/day $15
Ph: 313-359-7333   RP: Required   **Carts:** $18.00

Lakeview Hills challenging course and scenic views of Lake Huron. From narrow tree lined fairways, to small carefully guarded greens. To a more generous fairway with spacious greens inviting you to hit away. A course that requires a variety of skills and guarantees to offer a fair and challenging round to golfers of all levels of ability.

──────────────── MACKINAC ISLAND ────────────────

Grand Hotel GC   Yards: 2335, Holes: 9   Restaurant/Bar
49757   Par: 33   **GF:** w/day $12
Ph: 906-847-3331   RP: Requested   **Carts:** $10.00

A renovation program has made the nine-hole links more challenging, and much more enjoyable to play. The number seven green has been rebuilt as a peninsula out in the lake. Bunkers and sand traps have been added and/or enlarged to make shot placement more exacting.

──────────────── MACKINAC ISLAND ────────────────

Wawashkamo GC   Yards: 3019, Holes: 9   Proshop
British Landing Rd.,   Par: 36   **GF:** w/day $12
49757   RP: Recommended   **Carts:** $10.00
Ph: 906-847-3871

This course is a trip back in time. The Scottish links style 9 hole course was designed by Scot, Alex Smith in 1898 and remains basically unchanged. Tall heathery rough, hidden pot bunkers and beautiful wild flowers await you. Wawashkamo is rich in history.

──────────────── MARNE ────────────────

Li'l Acres GC   Yards: 1835, Holes: 9   Proshop
1831 Johnson Rd., 49435 Par: 30   **GF:** w/day $3, w/end $4
Ph: 616-677-3379   RP: Tee times may be
                        reserved

Short challenging course, excellent for beginners and senior citizens.

──────────────── MARNE ────────────────

Western Greens GC   Yards: 6400, Holes: 18   Restaurant/Bar/Proshop
2475 Johnson, 49435   Par: 71, USGA: 68.5   **GF:** w/day $10
Ph: 616-677-3677   RP: Preferred   **Carts:** $14.00

Being the highest point in Ottawa County the wind is always a factor. Course is rolling but not hilly. There now are 1500 trees but well placed.

──────────────── MASON ────────────────

Branson Bay GC   Yards: 6111, Holes: 18   Restaurant/Bar/Proshop
215 Branson Bay Dr.,   Par: 72, USGA: 69.8   **GF:** w/day $12, w/end $13
48854   RP: Not more than 1   **Carts:** $14.50
Ph: 517-663-4144   week adv.

#1 and #12 are ranked in the 18 most challenging holes in the Lansing golf market of over 40 courses. The back nine was carved out of mixed pines and hardwoods, with hills and ponds adding beauty and more concentration.

──────────────── MILFORD ────────────────

Kensington Metropark Yards: 6436, Holes: 18 Proshop
2240 W. Buno Rd., 48042 Par: 71, USGA: 70.8   **GF:** w/day $11, w/end $13
Ph: 313-685-9332   RP: Recommended   **Carts:** $15.00

Our well-manicured layout provides challenge for all golfers. However, the 382 yard 11th hole has both difficulty and beauty. An elevated, panoramic view of beautiful, sailboat-laden Kent Lake requires a precise tee shot if both the scenery and your score are to be enjoyed.

Plan ahead! Reserve tee time well in advance, and while you're doing so, confirm rates and services.

─────────────── MONROE ───────────────

Raisin River GC Yards: 6876, Holes: 18 Restaurant/Bar/Proshop
1500 N. Dixie Hwy, 48161 Par: 71, USGA: 70.2 **GF:** w/day $12, w/end $14
Ph: 313-289-3700 RP: 1 week in advance **Carts:** $14.00

Two championship layouts. The East Course has mammoth greens, wooded holes, lots of water and gently sloping watered fairways. The West Course is a compact beautifully designed course which demands expert shot placement. All greens trapped and water comes into play on five holes. You will use every club in your bag.

─────────────── MT. CLEMENS ───────────────

Bello Woods GC Yards: 6141, Holes: 18 Restaurant/Bar/Proshop
23650 32 Mile Rd., 48045 Par: 72, USGA: 68.4 **GF:** w/day $11
Ph: 313-949-1200 RP: Recommended **Carts:** $15.00

Our Red Course has six holes that water comes in play. Our White Course has water on four holes and some tricky greens. The Gold, our newest nine is cut through a beautiful woods with narrow fairways.

─────────────── MT. CLEMENS ───────────────

Partridge Creek GC Yards: 6405, Holes: 18 Restaurant/Bar/Proshop
43843 Romeo Plank Rd., Par: 72, USGA: 70.2 **GF:** w/day $12, w/end $13
48044 RP: Required **Carts:** $17.00
Ph: 313-286-9822 weekends & holidays

Although there are no sand traps 2 meandering creeks and tree lined fairways make all 3 courses interesting and challenging.

─────────────── NEW BUFFALO ───────────────

Whittaker Woods GC Holes: 18
& CC
Wittaker Rd., 49117
Ph: 616-469-1313

Whittaker Woods Golf and Country Club in New Buffalo, Michigan is presently under construction, designed by Ken Killian and developed by O'Brien Development Company. Plans include single family homes and maintenance free townhouses along with complete amenities, making this one of Harbor Countries most complete and pleasant golf communities.

─────────────── NEW HAVEN ───────────────

Oak Ridge GC Yards: 6811, Holes: 18 Restaurant/Bar/Proshop
35035 26 Mile Rd., 48048 Par: 72, USGA: 71.2 **GF:** w/day $12, w/end $15
Ph: 313-749-5151 RP: 2 weeks for **Carts:** $17.00
  weekends

Beautiful tree lined fairways make you want to play the course as soon as you see it. Service is number 1 at Oak Ridge, specializing in golf outing packages.

─────────────── NUNICA ───────────────

Crockery Hills GC, Inc. Yards: 6032, Holes: 18 Restaurant/Bar/Proshop
11741 Leonard Rd., 49448 Par: 70 **GF:** w/day $8, w/end $9
Ph: 616-837-8249 **Carts:** $14.00

If you like a challenge, if you like water, in a beautiful setting, you'll enjoy your round at Crockery. Top it off at our bar for refreshments—and enjoy dinner at one of West Michigan's newest and finest restaurants—"Terra Verde."

---------------------------- ONTONAGON ----------------------------

Ontonagon GC   Yards: 2676, Holes: 9   Bar/Proshop
Parker Ave., P.O. Box   Par: 35   **GF:** w/day $7
236, 49953
Ph: 906-884-4130

We have trees, left and right doglegs, two holes for the long ball hitters, a blind approach to a green, and our famous numbers 8 and 9 with elevated tees, creeks, and elevated greens. Beautiful, challenging 9 hole course just 1 mile from Lake Superior.

---------------------------- PIERSON ----------------------------

Whitefish Lake GC   Yards: 2200, Holes: 9   Proshop
2241 Bass Lake Rd. N.W.,   Par: 34   **GF:** w/day $5, w/end $6
49339   RP: Recommended   **Carts:** $6.00
Ph: 616-636-5260

You have to be accurate. It's a tight, challenging 9 holes. The greens are elevated so you don't want to be over. Our #3 is tough. It's a dogleg left par 4. You have to get the ball up quick and have distance to be over the trees or play it safe down the fairway.

---------------------------- PLAINWELL ----------------------------

Lake Doster GC   Yards: 6570, Holes: 18   Restaurant/Bar/Proshop
136 Country Club Blvd.,   Par: 72, USGA: 72.6   **GF:** w/day $17, w/end $20
49080   **Carts:** $10.00 ea
Ph: 616-685-5308

Lake Doster is ranked as one of the top 25 courses in the state of Michigan. It is also the home of the PGA Super Seniors Pro-Am Golf outing. The number three hole is called the Little Monster—100 yards, green directly downhill surrounded completely by sand and water.

---------------------------- PLYMOUTH ----------------------------

Fox Hills GC   Yards: 3200, Holes: 9   Restaurant/Bar/Proshop
8768 N. Territorial Rd.,   Par: 35   **GF:** w/day $10, w/end $11
48170   RP: Weekends only, 7   **Carts:** $10.00
Ph: 313-453-7272   days in adv

Our favorite hole is #2 on the Lakes Course. A deceiving par 3, protected by four large bunkers. Hit your ball in these bunkers and you're history! If you do make the green, you're still not safe! It's just a great little hole. Try it!

---------------------------- PONTIAC ----------------------------

White Lake Oaks GC   Yards: 5572, Holes: 18   Restaurant/Bar/Proshop
991 Williams Lake Rd.,   Par: 70, USGA: 67.0   **GF:** w/day $13, w/end $16
48386   RP: Weekends &   **Carts:** $15.00
Ph: 313-698-2700   holidays

Built on fairly flat terrain, this gently rolling 18 holes is popular with every type of golfer. Easy to walk, relatively short, but challenging. Our favorite hole is the 13th, a tough par 4, dogleg right with the second shot over a pond to a slightly elevated green tucked in the woods.

─────────── PONTIAC ───────────

White Lake Oaks GC
991 S. Williams Lake
Rd., 48054
Ph: 313-698-2700

Yards: 5572, Holes: 18
Par: 70, USGA: 65.9
RP: Weekends &
holidays

Restaurant/Bar/Proshop
GF: w/day $11, w/end $13
Carts: $15.00

Built on fairly flat terrain, this gently rolling 18 holes is popular with every type of golfer. Easy to walk, relatively short, but challenging. Our favorite hole is the 13th, a tough par 4, dogleg right with the second shot over a pond to a slightly elevated green tucked in the woods.

─────────── RIVERVIEW ───────────

Riverview Highlands GC
15015 Sibley Rd., 48192
Ph: 313-479-2266

Yards: 6800, Holes: 27
Par: 72, USGA: 71.0
RP: Daily May thru
October

Restaurant/Bar/Proshop
GF: w/day $13
Carts: $15.00

The Gold 9 offers a good challenge to the novice as well as the low handicapper. The Red 9 features a number of water hazards along with numerous tree lots. The Blue 9, probably the most challenging of the 3 courses, is a links style course designed by famous golf course architect Arthur Hills.

─────────── ROMEO ───────────

Pine Valley GC
16801 31 Mile Rd., 48065
Ph: 313-752-9633

Yards: 6485, Holes: 27
Par: 72, USGA: 70.1
RP: 1 week in advance

Restaurant/Bar/Proshop
GF: w/day $16
Carts: $18.00

From an elevated 1st tee with water left and right, the challenging front nine offers 6 blind shots and tests your skill on the 470 yard par 4 ninth. The 13th, our signature hole, can be played several ways, any of which can result in a big score. The rolling, well bunkered layout features water on 10 holes.

─────────── ROSCOMMON ───────────

Ye Olde CC
904 W. Sunset, 48653
Ph: 517-275-5582

Yards: 3003, Holes: 9
Par: 35
RP: Recommended

Proshop
GF: w/day $8
Carts: $8.00

Challenging 9 holes that are beautifully maintained. The friendly staff and surroundings will make you glad you stopped. Watch the greens—they are small and tricky! We are five minutes away from beautiful Higgins Lake and the famous Au Sable River.

─────────── SAUGATUCK ───────────

Clearbrook GC
135th Ave. at 65th, P.O.
Box 66, 49453
Ph: 616-857-2000

Yards: 6439, Holes: 18
Par: 72, USGA: 69.8
RP: Recommended

Restaurant/Bar/Proshop
GF: w/day $16, w/end $20
Carts: $16.00

Meandering across eight of the eighteen holes is the "clear brook" of the course's name and when combined with the small target size greens a stiff challenge to every golfer is provided. In addition, this fabulous golf course features rolling terrain, mature plantings, and narrow tree-lined fairways. Clearbrook will be the site of the 1989 Michigan PGA Assistant's Championship.

Enter your favorite resort in our "Golf Resort of The Year" contest (entry form is in the back of the book).

─────────────── SHELBY ───────────────

Benona Shores GC
3410 Scenic Dr., 49455
Ph: 616-861-2098

Yards: 4200, Holes: 18
Par: 60, USGA: 58.2
RP: Required, July &
August

Proshop
GF: w/day $7
Carts: $12.00

A rolling 18 hole course which winds through hard woods, pines and fruit orchards.

─────────────── ST. CLAIR ───────────────

Rattle Run
7163 St. Clair Hwy., 48079
Ph: 313-329-2070

Yards: 6891, Holes: 18
Par: 72, USGA: 73.4
RP: 1 week in advance

Restaurant/Bar/Proshop
GF: w/day $15, w/end $40
Carts: $10.00 ea

Rolling tree-lined fairways, many elevated tees and 95 sandtraps. #6 requires complete control of drive. From blue tees 418 yards, cross river twice. Shot up a hill elevated 20 feet.

─────────────── ST. HELEN ───────────────

De Carlo's Birch Pointe CC
7071 Artesia Beach Rd., 48656
Ph: 517-389-7009

Yards: 3200, Holes: 9
Par: 36
RP: Holiday weekends

Restaurant/Bar/Proshop
GF: w/day $7
Carts: $7.00

A true North Michigan layout. We offer rolling wooded fairways. Every hole features trees that come into play if your shot is not true. Our par 5 #7 hole has two water hazards plus woods on both sides, a real challenge and beauty. If you're lucky, you might even spot a deer or two!

─────────────── THOMPSONVILLE ───────────────

Crystal Mountain GC
M-115 @ Lindy Rd., 49683
Ph: 616-378-2911

Yards: 6404, Holes: 18
Par: 72, USGA: 66.6

Restaurant/Bar/Proshop
GF: w/day $28
Carts: $20

This course was carved out of a hardwood and pine forest with very few fairways adjoining each other. In designing the course, great attention was given to preserving the natural landscape. Add to this the 13 ponds found on the back nine and you have a golf course which well represents the natural beauty found in Northern Michigan.

─────────────── WASHINGTON ───────────────

Stoney Creek GC
5140 Main Pkwy., 48094
Ph: 313-781-9166

Yards: 6884, Holes: 18
Par: 72, USGA: 71.3
RP: 3 days in advance

Restaurant/Proshop
GF: w/day $12, w/end $14
Carts: $16.00

This golf course is 15 miles from any major road. It's very quiet and nature is all around us. The course itself is very different from most others combining water, sand and out of bounds throughout the course.

─────────────── WEBBERVILLE ───────────────

Oak Lane GC
4875 N. Main, 48892
Ph: 517-521-3900

Yards: 6000, Holes: 18
Par: 70, USGA: 67.8
RP: Recommended

Restaurant/Bar/Proshop
GF: w/day $10, w/end $11
Carts: $15.00

Water on course on 8, 10, and 11. Quiet surroundings and rolling and above average in trees but wide fairways. Good course for all players.

MINNESOTA

Warroad •

Staples Ely •

Pine River Longville •Virginia
Pequot Lakes⎰East Grand Forks Garrison
Glyndon ⎰ •Erskine •⁚• Cloquet •
Detroit Lakes •Hawley
Glenwood Eagle Bend •Brainerd •Onamia Paynesville
Elbow Lake •Little Falls •Deerwood
Henning Fergus Falls • •Alexandria Coon Rapids Maplewood Pine City
Annandale •• Circle Pines Golden Valley Woodbury
Melrose Eagan • Richfield Hamel St. Paul
• • Watertown
Tyler Minneota Shakopee Rushford
Fairfax • • • Rochester
Fairmont •• Rochester
Albert Lea Austin
Mankato

ALBERT LEA

Green Lea GC
101 Richway Dr., 56007
Ph: 507-373-1061

Yards: 6157, Holes: 18
Par: 73, USGA: 67.8
RP: Weekends

Restaurant/Bar/Proshop
GF: w/day $11
Carts: $14.00

Our favorite hole is the par 3 #6. It's a short 127 yards but accuracy is essential. Completely surrounded by tall oak trees except for a narrow opening in front, the elevated green and prevailing winds taunt every golfer to land one on the slick dance floor.

ALEXANDRIA

Lake Miltona GC
Hwy. 29N & Cty. Rd.5,
Box 207, 56308
Ph: 612-852-7078

Yards: 3102, Holes: 9
Par: 36, USGA: 33.7
RP: Recommended

Restaurant/Bar/Proshop
GF: w/day $9
Carts: $10.00

The first hole starts out through a chute of beautiful oaks and maples; with a dogleg left it opens to gently rolling terrain with a view of Lake Miltona. The ninth hole brings you back through the trees with a double dogleg par 5 where a double eagle is possible but a double bogie more likely.

ANNANDALE

Whispering Pines GC
County Rd. 6, P.O. Box
179, 55302
Ph: 612-274-8721

Yards: 3100, Holes: 9
Par: 35, USGA: 68.8
RP: Weekends

Restaurant/Bar/Proshop
GF: w/day $7
Carts: $8.00

Slightly rolling course with part of course with many mature trees. Large greens, some with two levels. #9 hole 210 par three 150 feet top to bottom greens with 2 levels great finishing hole. Has two holes with sharp dogleg right.

AUSTIN

Ramsey GC
R.R. 1, 55912
Ph: 507-433-9098

Yards: 6034, Holes: 18
Par: 71, USGA: 68.2

Restaurant/Bar/Proshop
GF: w/day $9
Carts: $7.42

Our front nine is very sporty, back nine longer and more wide open. Play our tough par 3's well and you'll score well. Outstanding hole is No. 15 which measures 595 yards, one of the longest holes in state. Friendly atmosphere.

─────────────── BRAINERD ───────────────

Grand View Lodge PC Yards: 2300, Holes: 9 Restaurant/Bar/Proshop
Rt. 6 Box 22, 56401 Par: 35, USGA: 64.0
Ph: 218-963-2234

In the Minnesota Northwoods, our course is called by many the most beautiful course in the state. Thousands of flowers encircle the tree boxes while birch, oak, aspen and Norway Pines line the fairways.

─────────────── BRAINERD ───────────────

Madden's Pine Beach Yards: 5900, Holes: 45 Restaurant/Bar/Proshop
8001 Pine Beach, Box Par: 72, USGA: 67.2 **Carts:** $20.00
387, 56401 RP: 1 day in advance
Ph: 218-829-2811

Maddens offers what no other midwest resort can, the challenge and beauty of 45 holes of on premise golf. There are two 18 hole courses. Pine Beach East (with a par 6, 618 yard hole) and Pine Beach West. Maddens also has a par 3 executive 9 hole course, perfect for pure relaxation. Plus, a driving range, P.G.A. pro, two pro shops and more.

─────────────── CIRCLE PINES ───────────────

KateHaven GC Yards: 1663, Holes: 9 Restaurant/Proshop
8791 Lexington Ave., Par: 30 **GF:** w/day $7, w/end $8
N.E., 55014 RP: Required **Carts:** $9.00
Ph: 612-786-2945

A challenging par 30 course with multiple tees which give choices to cross water or not. When standing on the par 4, 262 yard tee for the 5th hole you can barely see the flag and the creek is over the hill and out of sight.

─────────────── CLOQUET ───────────────

Big Lake GC Yards: 1565, Holes: 9 Restaurant/Bar/Proshop
18 Cary Rd., 55720 Par: 27, USGA: 79.0 **GF:** w/day $7
Ph: 218-879-4221 RP: Call **Carts:** $10.00

The toughest par 3 in Minnesota. In 20 years and a couple of million rounds of golf, has only been pared a couple of dozen times.

─────────────── COON RAPIDS ───────────────

Bunker Hills GC Yards: 7030, Holes: 18 Restaurant/Bar/Proshop
12800 Bunker Prarie Rd., Par: 72, USGA: 71.9 **GF:** w/day $16
55433 RP: 3 days in advance **Carts:** $19.00
Ph: 601-755-4140

A level course that is heavily wooded with pines and oaks. 3 lakes abut 7 of the holes. #15 (best 15th hole in state) is challenging with a narrow, tree-lined fairway.

Our listings—supplied by the management—are as complete as possible. Many of the courses have more features than we list. Be sure to inquire when you book your tee time.

─────────────── COON RAPIDS ───────────────

Coon Rapids-Bunker Hills GC
P.O. Box 33081, 55433
Ph: 612-755-4140

Yards: 7300, Holes: 27
Par: 72, USGA: 71.9
RP: 3 days in advance

Restaurant/Bar/Proshop
GF: w/day $16
Carts: $20.00

Site of 1976 USGA National Publinks Champ—Golf Digest Top 50 Public Courses. Annual site of National Open Championship.

─────────────── DEERWOOD ───────────────

Ruttgers Championship Lakes Course
Rt. 2, P.O. Box 400, 56444
Ph: 218-678-2885

Yards: 6485, Holes: 18
Par: 72, USGA: 71.0
RP: Call for tee times

Restaurant/Bar/Proshop
GF: w/day $22, w/end $25
Carts: $22.50

Ruttger's Championship Lakes Course is distinguished by a spectacular design skillfully meshed with the area's natural beauty. Hole lengths range from 130 to 550 yards. Natural hazards abound as the placid waters of Goose & Bass Lakes come into play on 10 holes.

─────────────── DETROIT LAKES ───────────────

Detroit CC
Rt 5, 56501
Ph: 218-847-5790

Yards: 5970, Holes: 36
Par: 71, USGA: 67.5
RP: 1 day in advance

Restaurant/Bar/Proshop
GF: w/day $16
Carts: $16.00

Hills, trees, sand, water and fast greens test all your golf skills. Home of the nationally known Pine to Palm amateur golf tournament.

─────────────── EAGAN ───────────────

Parkview GC PC
1310 Cliff Rd., 55123
Ph: 612-454-9884

Yards: 4568, Holes: 18
Par: 63, USGA: 60.8
RP: Recommended - up to 1 week

Restaurant/Bar/Proshop
GF: w/day $11
Carts: $15.00

An 18-hole executive golf course (par 63) that requires the use of all clubs. Can be played in close to three hours. A challenge to golfers of all skills. Many beautiful gardens, three fountains, bridge over rock causeway—all bring responses of great care, love, and beauty.

─────────────── EAGLE BEND ───────────────

Double Eagle GC PC
Cty Rd. #3, 56446
Ph: 218-738-5155

Yards: 6873, Holes: 18
Par: 73, USGA: 71.1

Restaurant/Bar/Proshop
GF: w/day $16
Carts: $15.00

Rated by M.G.A. as toughest 9 hole course in state. Lots of water and woods. Only Reversible golf course in U.S. Wrote up in June 1987 issue Golf Digest. 18 sets of tee boxes, reverses direction every other day.

─────────────── EAST GRAND FORKS ───────────────

Valley GC
1800 21st St. NW, 56721
Ph: 218-773-1207

Yards: 6001, Holes: 18
Par: 72, USGA: 68.9
RP: Weekends & holidays

Bar/Proshop
GF: w/day $10
Carts: $14.00

Narrow fairways, lots of trees, several doglegs, water on 7 holes, several elevated greens requiring lofted approach. Very scenic with several holes along the Rod River of the North.

―――――――――――― ELBOW LAKE ――――――――――――

Tipsinah Mounds CC Yards: 3055, Holes: 9 Restaurant/Proshop
Grant County Rd. #24, Par: 35, USGA: 68.8 **GF:** w/day $7, w/end $8
56531 **Carts:** $7.00
Ph: 218-685-4271

Course built around Indian mounds used for hazards. Several mounds are formed in the shape of snakes to line edges of fairways, other animals for hazards and several peaks or mounds to protect greens. Holes 6 and 7 center around water and create a great challenge.

―――――――――――――――― ELY ――――――――――――――――

Ely GC Yards: 4692, Holes: 9 Proshop
901 S. Central Ave., Box Par: 36, USGA: 61.2 **GF:** w/day $6
507, 55731 **Carts:** $7.00
Ph: 218-365-5932

Our course is a challenge—some hills and trees on most fairway borders. As we are under a large change now, I don't know which hole will be special. It was #8 below a hill and #9 across a valley.

―――――――――――――― ERSKINE ――――――――――――――

Win-E-Mac GC PC Yards: 2620, Holes: 9 **GF:** w/day $8
Junction of Hwy. 2 & 59, Par: 35, USGA: 32.3 **Carts:** $8
56535 RP: Only on weekends
Ph: 218-687-4653

A nice little 9 hole grass green country golf course, not very busy, rolling hills, fun to play. Watch out for moose strolling through the course.

―――――――――――――― FAIRFAX ――――――――――――――

Fort Ridgely GC Yards: 2772, Holes: 9 **GF:** w/day $5, w/end $7
Rt 1, Box 65, 55332 Par: 35
Ph: 507-426-7840

This 60 year old course, located in Fort Ridgely State Park, features narrow, mature hardwood lined fairways and Mod-Sod artificial grass greens. The park also offers 39 campsites, hiking trails, and an historic site for non-golfing family members.

―――――――――――――― FAIRMONT ――――――――――――――

Rose Lake GC, Inc. Yards: 6249, Holes: 18 Restaurant/Bar/Proshop
RR 2 Box 264-A, 56031 Par: 71, USGA: 69.4 **GF:** w/day $15, w/end $15
Ph: 507-235-9332 RP: Recommended **Carts:** $14.00

This natural setting with a lake, two large ponds, and a stream makes for a most picturesque and challenging golf course for any caliber golfer. We sincerely hope your experience here fulfills your desire to enjoy this game in the spirit intended.

―――――――――――――― FERGUS FALLS ――――――――――――――

Pebble Lake GC, Inc. Yards: 6342, Holes: 18 Restaurant/Bar/Proshop
P.O. Box 772, 56537 Par: 72, USGA: 69.6 **GF:** w/day $14
Ph: 218-736-7404 RP: Call for tee times **Carts:** $17.00

Front nine is wide open but there are fairway bunkers which come into play for the better than average golfer. The back nine is a hookers nightmare with some water and bunkers. An excellent course bordering Minnesota's lake country. Hole #16 is one you will remember.

──────────────── GARRISON ────────────────

Mille Lacs Lake GC   Yards: 5968, Holes: 18   Restaurant/Bar/Proshop
Star Route, 56450   Par: 71, USGA: 67.6   **GF:** w/day $16, w/end $20
Ph: 612-682-4325   **Carts:** $18.00

The course is located on the shores of Mille Lacs Lake and will delight you with its secluded, tree-lined fairways, and small beautifully maintained greens.

──────────────── GLENWOOD ────────────────

Minnewaska GC   Yards: 6212, Holes: 18   Bar/Proshop
Box 110, Golf Course   Par: 72, USGA: 69.8   **GF:** w/day $8, w/end $11
Rd., 56334   RP: 2 days in advance   **Carts:** $11.00
Ph: 612-634-3680

Layed out on a bluff overlooking huge Lake Minnewaska, golfers are often hard pressed to keep their mind on the game because of the views. But don't be fooled! Gently rolling terrain seldom leaves you a flat lie and many greens break toward the lake in defiance of what you see. Each hole is a challenge!

──────────────── GLENWOOD ────────────────

Pezhekee National GC   Yards: 3000, Holes: 9   Restaurant/Bar/Proshop
Peters Sunset Beach   Par: 35, USGA: 68.5   **GF:** w/day $11, w/end $15
RR2 Box 118, 56334   RP: Resort guests   **Carts:** $9.50
Ph: 612-634-4501   have priority

Heavily wooded 9 hole course requires accuracy more than distance except for the par 4 #7 hole. It requires a 190 yard drive to fly the creek. However, big hitters still must use a long iron to hit the long sloping green in regulation.

──────────────── GLYNDON ────────────────

Ponderosa GC   Yards: 3073, Holes: 9   Restaurant/Proshop
RR #2, 56547   Par: 36, USGA: 72.0   **GF:** w/day $5, w/end $6
Ph: 218-498-2201   **Carts:** $7.50

First three holes are long and wide. #4 nice par 5, 255 to clear river elevated green, woods on all sides. No fairways running alongside one another. Lots of trees, river, water and sand traps. Lots of deer and small animals.

──────────────── GOLDEN VALLEY ────────────────

Brookview GC PC   Yards: 6369, Holes: 18   Restaurant/Proshop
200 Brookview Parkway,   Par: 72, USGA: 69.0   **GF:** w/day $17, w/end $17
55426   RP: 2 days in advance   **Carts:** $19.00
Ph: 612-544-8446

An exciting challenge with water coming into play on 13 out of 18 holes. 18 newly reconstructed greens are challenging target, with rolling hills and trees throughout the course. The 9th and 18th holes are challenging par 4's with water and traps surrounding redesigned undulating greens.

──────────────── HAMEL ────────────────

Shamrock GC   Yards: 6388, Holes: 18   Restaurant/Proshop
19625 Lakin Rd., 55340   Par: 72, USGA: 68.1   **GF:** w/day $14, w/end $16
Ph: 612-478-9977   RP: Recommended   **Carts:** $18.00

An easy course to walk, Shamrock is fairly flat. Fairways are spacious, with very few sand traps, so it's a great ego builder. Acres of rough separate fairways, making it a safe course too.

──────────────── HENNING ────────────────

Oakwood GC, Inc.   Yards: 2840, Holes: 9   Restaurant/Bar/Proshop
RR #1. Box 262 A, 56551 Par: 36, USGA: 32.9   **GF:** w/day $7
Ph: 218-583-2127   **Carts:** $8.00

A short but demanding course requiring driving accuracy and the small undulating greens require patience and skill. Rolling terrain, beautifully wooded with 100 year old white and red oak trees.

──────────────── LITTLE FALLS ────────────────

Little Falls GC   Yards: 6051, Holes: 18   Restaurant/Bar/Proshop
Golf Rd., 56345   Par: 72, USGA: 68.4   **GF:** w/day $11
Ph: 612-632-3584   RP: Suggested on   **Carts:** $12.00
                         weekends

The Little Falls Golf Course has 18 holes carved out of mature oaks and pines. The final three holes are situated along the Mississippi River. Par the 16th and 17th holes and you have a round to remember!

──────────────── LONGVILLE ────────────────

Erwin Hills GC   Yards: 3006, Holes: 9   Restaurant/Proshop
Route 1 Box 240, 56655   Par: 36, USGA: 37.2   **GF:** w/day $8
Ph: 218-363-2552   RP: Call for tee time   **Carts:** $10.00

Designed with beauty and challenge in mind, Erwin Hills meanders through 128 acres of rolling, northern Minnesota woods and lakes. Towering hardwoods lend an air of maturity to this new and exciting course. A 70-yard water carry of the 5th tee is but one of the surprises that await you at Erwin Hills.

──────────────── MANKATO ────────────────

Terrace View GC   Yards: 3093, Holes: 9   Restaurant/Proshop
Highway 22 South, P.O.   Par: 36, USGA: 33.6   **GF:** w/day $7, w/end $8
Box 1203, 56001   **Carts:** $8.00
Ph: 507-387-2192

We have a challenging regulation nine hole course and a par 3 nine hole course across the driveway. We also have a driving range and practice green. We host numerous group events and tournaments. We have an extensive lesson program.

──────────────── MAPLEWOOD ────────────────

Goodrich GC   Yards: 6007, Holes: 18   Restaurant/Bar/Proshop
1820 N Van Dyke Ave.,   Par: 70, USGA: 67.8   **GF:** w/day $12
55109   RP: 4 days in advance   **Carts:** $17.00
Ph: 612-777-7355

Fairly open course except for oak woods surrounding holes 4, 5 and 6. Popular course for seniors who are able to walk entire 18 holes. Noted for its exceptionally fine greens and manicured fairways.

──────────────── MELROSE ────────────────

Meadowlark CC   Yards: 3135, Holes: 9   Bar/Proshop
837 S. 3rd Ave. W, 56352 Par: 36, USGA: 34.8   **GF:** w/day $8, w/end $9
Ph: 612-256-4989   RP: Weekends and   **Carts:** $10.00
                         holidays

Hole 8, 475 yard par 5, fairway traps. Water to left and right of green, narrow approach to green. Trees on right side of fairway, trap in left rough.

───────────────── MINNEOTA ─────────────────

Country Side GC Yards: 3340, Holes: 9   Bar/Proshop
E. Lyon St., 56264   Par: 36, USGA: 34.9   **GF:** w/day $6, w/end $9
Ph: 507-872-9925   RP: None   **Carts:** $6.00

Hole #8 is our favorite. It's only 345 yards but has tight out of bounds and water. Must hit tee shot 240 to be safe.

───────────────── NISSWA ─────────────────

Birch Bay GC   Yards: 2900, Holes: 9   Restaurant/Proshop
1771 Birch Dr. West, Par: 36, USGA: 65.4   **GF:** w/day $11, w/end $11
56468   RP: First come, first **Carts:** $12.00
Ph: 218-963-4488   served

At Birch Bay we offer a fun time for all levels of golfer. Open fairways lure even timid golfers back again and again. Scratch golfers are excited about our perfectly manicured trees, shrubs, and lush fairways. Our greens are the best in the area.

───────────────── ONAMIA ─────────────────

Izatys GC   Yards: 6300, Holes: 18 Restaurant/Bar/Proshop
1 Izatys Rd., 56359 Par: 71, USGA: 68.5   **GF:** w/day $20
Ph: 612-532-3101   RP: Required 2 days in **Carts:** $20.00
                     advance

Nestled amongst central Minnesota's scenic woodlands, Izatys' demands precise shot-making and course strategy to overcome its numerous challenges which include sharp doglegs, pot bunkers, railroad ties, countless water hazards, and maybe its biggest challenge of all—severe undulating greens. Good putters beware!

───────────────── PAYNESVILLE ─────────────────

Koronis Hills GC   Yards: 2990, Holes: 9   Restaurant/Proshop
Highway 23, P.O. Box 55,   Par: 36, USGA: 33.5   **GF:** w/day $6, w/end $7
56362   RP: Required   **Carts:** $8.00
Ph: 612-243-4111

An old style course, with hundreds of oak trees. Position on drives more important than distance, not many flat areas on this tough little course. Our favorite hole is #9, lined with huge oaks to an elevated green 179 yards away, requires steady nerves.

───────────────── PEQUOT LAKES ─────────────────

Whitefish GC   Yards: 6407, Holes: 18 Restaurant/Bar/Proshop
Rt. 1 Box 111-B, 56472 Par: 72, USGA: 68.9   **GF:** w/day $13
Ph: 218-543-4900   RP: 1 day in advance   **Carts:** $16.00

Whitefish Golf Course has been cut out of the north woods. It is surrounded by birch, oak and pine with a few attractive waterholes to add to its beauty.

───────────────── PINE CITY ─────────────────

Pine City CC PC   Yards: 6348, Holes: 9
55063   Par: 36, USGA: 68.3H
Ph: 612-629-3848

Water covers 11 of the 18 holes. Many of the holes are cut through mighty oak trees that are characteristic of majestic oaks. Greens are very undulating and well protected by deep bunkers. The Minnesota Professional Golfers Association has their headquarters located at Majestic Oaks.

──────────────── PINE RIVER ────────────────

Irish Hills GC at Piney Ridge
Rt. 1 Box 315, 56474
Ph: 218-587-2296

Yards: 3231, Holes: 9
Par: 36, USGA: 70.8

Restaurant/Bar/Proshop
GF: w/day $9
Carts: $9.00

Considered one of the finest new courses in Minnesota. Nationally featured in Golf Digest as well as Golf Traveller magazines. Carved out of a pine forest, Irish Hills rolls from ridge to ridge snuggling up against ponds, valleys and nature's beautiful lake country scenery.

──────────────── RAMSEY ────────────────

Rum River Hills GC PC
16659 ST. Frances Blvd., 55303
Ph: 612-753-3339

Yards: 6100, Holes: 18
Par: 71, USGA: 68.7
RP: 3 days in advance

Restaurant/Bar/Proshop
GF: w/day $13, w/end $16
Carts: $20.00

Scenic views with water on 12 holes, the English/Scottish influence is evident on the course.

──────────────── RICHFIELD ────────────────

Rich Acres GC PC
2201 East 66th St., 55423
Ph: 612-861-7145

Yards: 6606, Holes: 27
Par: 71, USGA: 69.2
RP: One day in advance

Restaurant/Bar/Proshop
GF: w/day $12, w/end $13
Carts: $16.00

On the regulation course you will find 120 acres of beautiful undulating terrain. On the par-3 course there is an interesting variety of water hazards and sand traps set among the large rolling greens.

──────────────── ROCHESTER ────────────────

Maple Valley G&CC
RR 3, Box 165, 55904
Ph: 507-285-9100

Yards: 6106, Holes: 18
Par: 71, USGA: 67.4
RP: Tee Times

Restaurant/Bar
GF: w/day $14
Carts: $15.00

Located on Root River in hardwood forest of S.E. Minnesota. 18 hole scenic challenging. Open to public 7 days a week.

──────────────── RUSHFORD ────────────────

Ferndale CC
Hwy 16, 55971
Ph: 507-864-7626

Yards: 3228, Holes: 9
Par: 36, USGA: 69.8
RP: 1 week in advance

Bar/Proshop
GF: w/day $11, w/end $12
Carts: $12.00

Situated in S.E. Minnesota's hardwood forest area just 2 miles from Rushford. The entire course can be viewed from the clubhouse area. A challenging and very beautiful 9-hole club where par is seldom broken.

──────────────── SHAKOPEE ────────────────

Stonebrooke GC
2693 Cty Rd 79, 55379
Ph: 612-496-3171

Yards: 6600, Holes: 18
Par: 71, USGA: 69.2
RP: 3 days in advance

Restaurant/Bar/Proshop
GF: w/day $21, w/end $24
Carts: $20.00

Elevation changes and mature stands of native hardwoods allow for spectacular views and adventurous golf at Stonebrooke. Challenge the 13 great water holes and don't forget the relaxing ferry ride to your second shot on the famous par 4 8th hole.

116 Minnesota

───────────────── ST. PAUL ─────────────────

Keller GC
2166 Maplewood Dr.,
55109
Ph: 612-484-3011

Yards: 6524, Holes: 18
Par: 72, USGA: 69.8
RP: 4 days in advance

Restaurant/Bar/Proshop
GF: w/day $16, w/end $16
Carts: $19.00

Very scenic, gently rolling terrain, that requires you to use all the clubs in your bag. Very interesting and challenging. Home of the St. Paul open 1930-1968, the National Pub-Links 1931, the National P.G.A. Championship 1932, 1954, the Western Open 1949, the Patty Berg Golf Classic 1973-1980.

───────────────── TYLER ─────────────────

Tyler Community GC
56178
Ph: 507-247-3242

Yards: 3184, Holes: 9
Par: 36, USGA: 67.8

Restaurant/Bar/Proshop
GF: w/day $7, w/end $9
Carts: $7.00

Just a nine hole watered fairway course. Small greens, no sand, no water—but a real challenge.

───────────────── VIRGINIA ─────────────────

Virginia Muni GC
9th Ave. North, 55792
Ph: 218-741-4366

Yards: 6131, Holes: 18
Par: 71, USGA: 68.7

Restaurant/Proshop
GF: w/day $9
Carts: $14.00

Course is situated on undulating hills dotted with mature pines. A challenging course!

───────────────── WARROAD ─────────────────

WarRoad Estates GC
HCO-2 Box 30, 56763
Ph: 218-386-2025

Yards: 7101, Holes: 18
Par: 72, USGA: 70.7

Restaurant/Bar/Proshop
GF: w/day $11
Carts: $14.50

One of Minnesota's most challenging golf courses located near Canada, has an international flavor, on beautiful Lake of Woods known for its excellent fishing. Course has 11 holes of water hazards coming into play and several well-treed holes.

───────────────── WATERTOWN ─────────────────

Timber Creek GC
9750 Co. Rd. 24, 55388
Ph: 612-446-1415

Yards: 6800, Holes: 18
Par: 72, USGA: 69.2
RP: Weekends

Restaurant/Proshop
GF: w/day $12
Carts: $16.00

Timber Creek is located in a beautiful rural setting; with two creeks, ponds, sandtraps and rolling wooded acres. The back tees challenge the low handicap golfer by locating many hazards in areas that will reward only the best of shots but the average golfer is not penalized.

───────────────── WOODBURY ─────────────────

Wedgewood GC
9555 Wedgewood Dr.,
55125
Ph: 612-731-4779

Yards: 6790, Holes: 18
Par: 72, USGA: 70.0
RP: 1 day in advance

Restaurant/Proshop
GF: w/day $17, w/end $25
Carts: $18.00

The golf course is a part of a residential golf community. The golf course features large bent grass greens and tees with several panoramic views over gently rolling fairways. Water comes into play on ten holes. The course is fun to play regardless of your golfing ability.

Pontotoc •
• Greenville

• Silver City

MISSISSIPPI

• Natchez

Ocean Springs
Biloxi • •
Bay St. Louis

BAY ST. LOUIS

Diamondhead CC
7600 Country Club
Circle, 39520
Ph: 601-255-2525

Yards: 6086, Holes: 18
Par: 72

The Cardinal Course demands accuracy on its tight fairways flanked by deep woods and features large, fast Tiftdorf green, ideal for winter play. The layout of the Pine Course is wider fairways and smaller, slower greens.

BILOXI

Broadwater Beach
39533
Ph: 601-388-2211

Yards: 6001, Holes: 18
Par: 71, USGA: 69.0
RP: Guests 6-8 mos.,
others 2 days

Restaurant/Bar

The Sea Course is a flat, tight layout on the Gulf. The Sun Course is more open, but word has it that the pros quietly agree to play the middle tees so they can save face. Fourteen of its holes traverse water.

GREENVILLE

**Greenville Municipal
GC**
Airbase Rd., 28755
Ph: 601-332-4079

Yards: 6439, Holes: 18
Par: 72

Restaurant/Bar/Proshop
GF: w/day $5, w/end $7
Carts: $12.00

Beautiful well designed course. Water involved on 10 of 18 holes. Former United States Air Force golf course now owned by City of Greenville. #3 one of toughest short par 3's anywhere. Out of bounds directly behind green. Deer Creek meanders almost to edge of putting surface.

NATCHEZ

Duncan Park GC
c/o Duncan Park, 39120
Ph: 601-442-5955

Yards: 6058, Holes: 9
Par: 72, USGA: 68.4

Proshop
GF: w/day $6
Carts: $7.00

Duncan Park Golf Course is a very tricky old course built in 1925 on part of the grounds of the Antebellum Home Auburn. It is nestled among gigantic live oaks and pine trees, and it located almost in the heart of Natchez, the oldest city on the Mississippi River.

───────────── OCEAN SPRINGS ─────────────

Pine Island GC   Yards: 6001, Holes: 18   Restaurant/Bar/Proshop
Gulf Park Estates, P.O.   Par: 71, USGA: 69.0   **GF:** w/day $14
Box 843, 39564   RP: Weekends   **Carts:** $16.00
Ph: 601-875-1674

This course is built on 3 islands, beautiful serene setting, full of wildlife. Each hole has its own name, et al: "The Secret Garden" all titles of books.

───────────── OCEAN SPRINGS ─────────────

Royal Gulf Hills Resort Holes: 18   Restaurant
13701 Paso Rd., 39564   Par: 71
Ph: 800-638-4902

Legendary Golfing — Country Inn setting. 65 years of tradition. Challenging, undulating greens. Must tee to appreciate.

───────────── PONTOTOC ─────────────

Pontotoc CC   Yards: 6400, Holes: 18   Restaurant/Proshop
P.O. Box 390, 38863   Par: 72, USGA: 68.5   **GF:** w/day $15
Ph: 601-489-1962   RP: Call for tee times   **Carts:** $14.00

You get introduced with a relatively open front nine with rolling fairways overlooking the Natchez Trace State Park 2,100 acre lake. The back nine offers the golfer with challenging demanding shots with a 170 yard island par three which is one of the most scenic holes in Mississippi.

───────────── SILVER CITY ─────────────

Humphreys County CC   Yards: 6335, Holes: 9   Restaurant/Bar/Proshop
P.O. Box 35, 39166   Par: 72, USGA: 68.9   **GF:** w/day $7, w/end $10
Ph: 601-247-3294   **Carts:** $7.00

Best layout and most character of any course in the Mississippi delta. Requires length or accuracy on every tee shot, sometimes both. Don't let the levee intimidate you.

MISSOURI

Excelsior Springs
Sullivan •
Lake Ozark •
• Osage Beach

Dexter •

DEXTER

Hidden Trails CC
W. Grant St., P.O. Box
355, 63841
Ph: 314-624-3638

Yards: 6439, Holes: 18
Par: 72, USGA: 69.2
RP: Call for reservation

Restaurant/Bar/Proshop
GF: w/day $12, w/end $12
Carts: $13.00

A rolling course built atop Crowley Ridge. The front nine is relatively open and conducive to scoring. The back side is tight as it winds through a scenic subdivision of huge new homes. Straight tee shots are a premium.

EXCELSIOR SPRINGS

Excelsior Springs GC
1201 E. Golf Hill, P.O.
Box 417, 64024
Ph: 816-637-3731

Yards: 6464, Holes: 18
Par: 72, USGA: 70.3
RP: Required
weekends & holidays

Restaurant/Bar/Proshop
GF: w/day $9, w/end $10
Carts: $16.00

Designed by world-fames architect, Tom Bendelow, often referred to as an "English-type: course, it is unique in that is has no bunkers, traps or other unpopular characteristics of the English course. The course is highly rated by top professionals.

LAKE OZARK

**Lodge of Four Seasons
GC**
P.O. Box 215, 65049
Ph: 314-365-8544

Yards: 6416, Holes: 45
Par: 72, USGA: 71.4
RP: Members/Lodge
Guest Only

Restaurant
GF: w/day $55, w/end $60
Carts: Included

Seasons Ridge Golf Club, a public championship golf course, is the Lodge Of Four Seasons newest addition to the existing 27-hole resort golf facilities. The 6416 par 72 course is one of the finest new golf facilities in the Midwest. Winding through hills & valleys & over 180 ft. elevation change, Seasons Ridge golf course views & vistas are breathtaking.

--- OSAGE BEACH ---

Best Western
Dogwood Hills GC
Route 1, Box 1300, 65065
Ph: 314-348-3153

Yards: 6200, Holes: 18   Restaurant/Bar
Par: 71

One of the most picturesque holes is #17, a 357-yard hole dogleg right; you play uphill, past a lake and through the colorful trees. The fairways are wide with rolling hills, and the greens are undulated with smooth bent grass putting surfaces.

--- OSAGE BEACH ---

Marriotts Tan-Tar-A
The Oaks
State Route KK, 65065
Ph: 314-348-4163

Yards: 6465, Holes: 18   Restaurant/Bar/Proshop
Par: 71, USGA: 72.1   **GF:** w/day $40
RP: 7 days guests–1   **Carts:** $12.00 ea
day non

The Oaks plays 6465 yards from the blue tees. Small and well bunkered greens demand proper placement of tee shots as well as approach shots. Water comes into play on 11 of the 18 holes which are carved out of the natural oaks surroundings found in the hilly terrain of the Ozarks. Marriott's Tan-Tar-A Golf Shop selected as one of the "Best 20 Resort Shops in the Country" in 1988 and 1990.

--- SULLIVAN ---

Sullivan CC
E. Vine St., 63080
Ph: 314-468-5803

Yards: 3115, Holes: 9   Restaurant/Proshop
Par: 36, USGA: 68.4   **GF:** w/day $12, w/end $12
RP: Out-of-towners   **Carts:** $12.00
only on weekend

Our 9-hole course is fun and very well manicured. Big oak trees scattered around course is our trademark. Keeping down the middle is a must to score well.

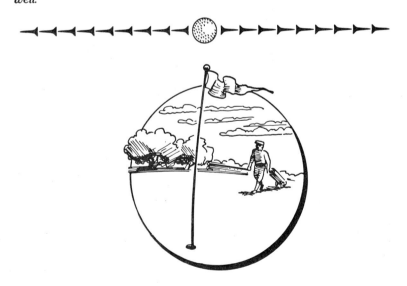

Subscribe to our free newsletter, "Great Golf Gazette" and hear about the latest special golf vacation values.

MONTANA

BIG SKY

Big Sky GC　Yards: 6115, Holes: 18　Restaurant/Bar
P.O. Box 1, 59716　Par: 72　**GF:** w/day $22
Ph: 406-995-4211　**Carts:** $16.00

The course sits in an alpine meadow at 6,500 feet. This is a relatively flat course, where you can't help but get the feeling of wide open spaces. The course meanders around the West Fork of the Gallitin River, with water coming into play on six holes.

BIG TIMBER

Overland GC　Yards: 6776, Holes: 9　Proshop
P.O. Box 1091, 59011　Par: 36, USGA: 69.9　**GF:** w/day $6, w/end $7
Ph: 406-932-4297　RP: Weekends　**Carts:** $7.00

A beautifully maintained course with a spectacular view of the Yellowstone Valley and the Crazy Mountains. Play in a totally relaxed atmosphere, where it is not unusual to see deer on the course. The nine holes meander between babbling brooks and several ponds, yet offer plenty of open space for play. You will enjoy this one.

BIGFORK

Eagle Bend GC　Yards: 6237, Holes: 18　Restaurant/Bar/Proshop
279 Eagle Bend Dr., PO　Par: 72, USGA: 69.6　**GF:** w/day $35, w/end $35
Box 960, 59911　**Carts:** $10.00 ea
Ph: 406-837-7300

Rated the #1 course in Montana and among America's top 50 public courses by Golf Digest. Located at the scenic north end of Flathead Lake. Meticulously manicured fairways and greens is complemented by the incomparable mountain and lake vistas typical of the Flathead Valley. Delights golfers of all levels.

COLUMBIA FALLS

Meadow Lake GC　Yards: 6574, Holes: 18　Restaurant/Bar/Proshop
1415 Tamarack Ln., 59912　Par: 71, USGA: 69.4　**GF:** w/day $15
Ph: 406-892-7601　RP: 2 days in advance　**Carts:** $16.00

The course combines the best of Rocky Mountain golf—spectacular grandeur, lakes, streams and trees. A back nine that meanders among tall pines gives one a feeling of solitude and peacefulness.

─────────────── FORSYTH ───────────────

Forsyth CC, Inc.
Box 191, 59327
Ph: 406-356-7710

Yards: 6140, Holes: 18
Par: 71, USGA: 67.9
RP: Weekends &
holidays

Restaurant/Bar/Proshop
GF: w/day $7
Carts: $7.00

You tee off on #1 to a elevated green which is trapped raising more than 40 feet from the tee. The #2 hole sits on a needle requiring a well placed shot to hold the green. The #3 hole is a long 560 yard hole as is #4 to be followed by a 235 yard par 3 with the water to the right and fronted with grass bunkers. Holes #6 and #7 are short par four and three respectively. You finish high above the clubhouse on a par 5 and a 165 yard over the water approach to #9.

─────────────── GLENDIVE ───────────────

Cottonwood CC
P.O. Box 317, 59330
Ph: 406-365-8797

Yards: 3130, Holes: 9
Par: 36, USGA: 69.5

Restaurant/Bar/Proshop
GF: w/day $8, w/end $10
Carts: $6.00

Good test for all playing levels, 9 holes with creeks, trees and sandtraps and shrubs for hazards. Excellent small greens to challenge everyone. Friendly, clean, new clubhouse with bar and proshop.

─────────────── KALISPELL ───────────────

Buffalo Hill GC
N Main, P.O. Box 1116,
59903
Ph: 406-755-5902

Yards: 6247, Holes: 27
Par: 72, USGA: 70.2
RP: 2 days in advance

Restaurant/Bar/Proshop
GF: w/day $17
Carts: $16.00

Montana's #1 ranked public golf course, redesigned in 1978 by Robert Muir Graves, 27 holes of sheer pleasure. A shotmakers delight requiring a premium on accuracy rather than power, until you get to #13, a demanding par 4 with water, out of bounds, fairway trees and length. A true joy to play.

─────────────── MISSOULA ───────────────

Larchmont GC
3200 Old Fort Rd., 59801
Ph: 406-721-4416

Yards: 7118, Holes: 18
Par: 72, USGA: 69.8
RP: 1 day in advance

Restaurant/Bar/Proshop
GF: w/day $12, w/end $14
Carts: $16.00

This course is one of the longest in the area, but fairly wide open. Known for its exemplary maintenance, the greens are fast, smooth, and firm, and surrounded by deep Scottish style bunkers. Surrounded by the majestic Bitterroot Mountain range, Larchmont is the perfect site for the annual Montana open.

─────────────── THREE FORKS ───────────────

Headwaters GC
7th Ave. E, 59752
Ph: 406-285-3700

Yards: 3158, Holes: 9
Par: 36, USGA: 67.1
RP: Preferred

Restaurant/Bar/Proshop
GF: w/day $7
Carts: $7.00

You will have many options to play the ball safe however, there are water hazards on 6 of our 9 holes. As our name implies, Three Forks is located at the headwaters of the Missouri River. A superb vacation area.

If a golfing vacation is in your travel plans, order a copy of **Golf Resorts** *or* **Golf Resorts International.** *See order form in back of the Guide.*

───────────── WEST GLACIER ─────────────

Glacier View GC   Yards: 5105, Holes: 18   Restaurant/Bar/Proshop
Box 185, 59936   Par: 68, USGA: 63.9   **GF:** w/day $15
Ph: 406-888-5471   RP: Weekends   **Carts:** $14.00

Glacier View Golf Club features unsurpassed views of Glacier National Park from all 18 holes. Visitors are pleased to find a pro shop, bar and fine restaurant all within the open beam ceilings of the clubhouse. The frequently seen wildlife, an on-site availability of RV hook-ups make Glacier View Golf Club even more unique.

───────────── WHITEFISH ─────────────

Whitefish Lake GC   Yards: 6302, Holes: 27   Restaurant/Bar/Proshop
Hwy 93 N–Box 666,   Par: 72, USGA: 68.7   **GF:** w/day $16
59937   RP: 2 days in advance   **Carts:** $16.00
Ph: 406-862-4000

Whether you're looking towards the big mountain ski resort or out over Whitefish Lake, the course has complete beauty offering you lakes, sand and large pines surrounding each hole. You will use every club in your bag over the 17-hole layout.

Subscribe to our free newsletter, "Great Golf Gazette" and hear about the latest special golf vacation values.

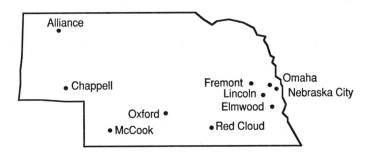

NEBRASKA

ALLIANCE

Skyview GC
RR 2, 69301
Ph: 308-762-1446

Yards: 6449, Holes: 18
Par: 72, USGA: 68.8

Bar/Proshop
GF: w/day $7, w/end $9
Carts: $12.00

The 2nd hole is protected by two bunkers, one strategically placed midway on this par 3, 485 yard hole. The other bunker guards the green at the front right. Accuracy is everything!

CHAPPELL

Chappell GC
I-80 Exit, 69129
Ph: 308-874-9973

Yards: 6630, Holes: 9
Par: 72, USGA: 69.8
RP: Recommended

Proshop
GF: w/day $8
Carts: $10.00

You will not find better fairways and greens anywhere. User friendly course, not a lot of hazards, five small traps, water on two holes, flat and easy to walk if you desire.

ELMWOOD

Grandpa's Woods CC
Box 245, 68349
Ph: 402-994-3415

Yards: 1802, Holes: 9
Par: 31

GF: w/day $2

Grandpa's woods is a beautiful, challenging nine hole golf course located in a remote wooded area.

FREMONT

Valley View GC
Box 344, Rt. 2, 68025
Ph: 402-721-7772

Yards: 5232, Holes: 9
Par: 70, USGA: 64.1

Bar/Proshop
GF: w/day $8, w/end $11
Carts: $8.50

The top nine offers a spectacular view of Fremont and the Platte River Valley. Back nine is more challenging with longer fairways and water. Hole #10 offers a huge elevation drop through a canyon.

Enter your favorite resort in our "Golf Resort of The Year" contest (entry form is in the back of the book).

─────────────────── LINCOLN ───────────────────

Mahoney GC   Yards: 6450, Holes: 18   Proshop
7900 Adams, 68507   Par: 71, USGA: 66.9   **GF:** w/day $7, w/end $8
Ph: 402-464-7542   RP: 1 week in advance   **Carts:** $15.00

Flexibility of yardage is the greatest virtue of the golf course. The 6450 yards consist of undulating greens, rolling fairways and difficult roughs. 8th hole, slight dogleg left, 2nd shot across lake aiming at a small targeted 2 tiered green, resulting in one of the toughest par 4's in Nebraska.

─────────────────── McCOOK ───────────────────

Heritage Hills GC   Yards: 6715, Holes: 18   **GF:** w/day $12, w/end $14
108 West D St., 69001   Par: 72, USGA: 68.3   **Carts:** $14.00
Ph: 308-345-5032

A great course on undulating fairways. One of Golf Digest's *Top 75 Public Golf Courses in America.*

─────────────────── NEBRASKA CITY ───────────────────

Wildwood Muni GC   Yards: 2831, Holes: 9   Proshop
Steinhart Park, Highway   Par: 36, USGA: 67.3   **GF:** w/day $5, w/end $6
2 W., 68410
Ph: 402-873-3661

Enjoy this beautiful course adjacent to 2 major parks in Nebraska City which is also home of Arbor Day. This course is loaded with trees. Our fifth hole is on the Omaha World Herald's hall of fame by being surrounded by oaks and green itself being surrounded by 2 bunkers and many beautiful crabapple trees in flower in spring.

─────────────────── OMAHA ───────────────────

Miracle Hill Golf &   Yards: 6412, Holes: 18   Proshop
Tennis Center   Par: 70, USGA: 70.0   **GF:** w/day $9, w/end $10
1401 North 120th, 68154   RP: 7 days in advance   **Carts:** $16.00
Ph: 402-498-0220

Miracle Hill holds the site of the Guiness Book of World Records for the Longest Straight Hole in One. Achieved by Bob Mitera on October 7, 1965 at age 21, his 444 yard ace on the par 4 #10 has yet to have been out done.

─────────────────── OXFORD ───────────────────

Oxford CC   Holes: 9   Restaurant/Bar
101 Golf Course Rd.,   Par: 36   **GF:** w/day $10
68967
Ph: 308-824-3296

Beautiful course winding around a creek in the rolling hills of southern Nebraska. The Republican River Valley lies just to the south. The course is known for the tough greens. You had better look twice when setting up a putt.

─────────────────── RED CLOUD ───────────────────

Red Cloud CC   Yards: 3132, Holes: 9   Bar/Proshop
Rt. 2 Box 17A, 68970   Par: 36, USGA: 69.6   **GF:** w/day $6
Ph: 402-746-2567   **Carts:** $7.00

Accuracy a must with our narrow-rolling fairways. Precision iron shots when approaching the small elevated greens will give you a good shot at a birdie, but if you miss, just getting on and staying on is the next challenge.

NEVADA

Incline Village • Reno
Stateline
Ely

• Mesquite

Pahrump • Las Vegas
Henderson

ELY

White Pine GC	Yards: 6489, Holes: 9	Restaurant/Bar/Proshop
1 Burch Dr., 89301	Par: 72, USGA: 69.2	**GF:** w/day $8
Ph: 702-289-4095		**Carts:** $15.00

9 hole golf course with two sets of tees, flat terrain with small greens and very narrow fairways. Our favorite hole is #3, 441 yards dogleg left well bunkered both fairway and around the green. Small green to hit to and tough to putt.

HENDERSON

Indian Wells CC	Yards: 6917, Holes: 18	Restaurant/Bar/Proshop
1 Showboat Country	Par: 71, USGA: 72.4	**GF:** w/day $50, w/end $50
Club Dr., 89014	RP: 1 week, weekends	**Carts:** Included
Ph: 702-451-2106	2 days	

The Indian Wells Country Club is a championship golf course on semi-flat desert terrain. The second hole is a 609 yard double dogleg par 5 that demands 3 good shots. The last 2 holes can either make or break a good round with length, out of bounds and water. Lots of big numbers are possible here.

INCLINE VILLAGE

Incline Village	Yards: 7138, Holes: 36	Restaurant/Bar/Proshop
Championship	Par: 72, USGA: 70.5	**GF:** w/day $75, w/end $75
955 Fairway Blvd., Box	RP: May call in May	**Carts:** Included
7590, 89450	for season	
Ph: 702-832-1144		

The championship course has recently been rated as one of the Top 50 public golf courses in the U.S. by Golf Digest. And the executive course has long been considered one of the Top 5 of its kind in the country. Both are a blend of beauty and difficulty to be enjoyed by all.

LAS VEGAS

Desert Inn CC	Yards: 7111, Holes: 18	Restaurant/Bar/Proshop
3145 Las Vegas Blvd.	Par: 72, USGA: 73.0	**GF:** w/day $90
South, 89109	RP: Sat.-Sun. guests &	**Carts:** $10.00 ea
Ph: 702-733-4444	member only	

The Desert Inn has a rich golf history, staring in 1953-1966 as the original home of PGA Tours "Tournament of Champions" and over the years played host to several LPGA Tour events. Presently the home of the "General Tire Las Vegas Classic," a PGA Senior Tour event and, also one of three courses used to conduct the regular PGA tours "Las Vegas Invitational."

──────────── MESQUITE ────────────

Peppermill Palms GC
P.O. Box 360, 89024
Ph: 800-621-0187

Yards: 6096, Holes: 18
Par: 72, USGA: 70.9
RP: Hotel guest-1
month; else 1 wk

Restaurant/Bar/Proshop
GF: w/day $23, w/end $28
Carts: $12.00 ea

The front nine is a typical resort type layout featuring numerous bunkers and palm trees as well as 26 acres of water. The back nine is a desert type course with several elevation changes. Number fourteen is an exacting par three of 210 yards from the back tees over a canyon. Number fifteen is the most scenic view as the tee sits 150 feet above the fairway of this 548 yard par 5.

──────────── RENO ────────────

Northgate GC
1111 Clubhouse Dr.,
89523
Ph: 702-747-7577

Yards: 6966, Holes: 18
Par: 72, USGA: 67.5
RP: 7 days in advance

Restaurant/Bar/Proshop
GF: w/day $20
Carts: $12.00

We have 37 sand bunkers and 144 grass bunkers. There are no holes that parallel one another. This is probably one of the finest 18 hole layouts without any trees. Hole #16 par 3, 216 yards from tiger tees. This hole is all carry from a slightly elevated tee to a green with grass bunkers on the right side and a huge sand bunker on the left.

──────────── RENO ────────────

Wildcreek GC
3500 Sullivan Ln., 89431
Ph: 702-673-3100

Yards: 6200, Holes: 27
Par: 72, USGA: 69.1
RP: Taken one week in
advance

Restaurant/Bar/Proshop
GF: w/day $32
Carts: Included

The course is on a rolling piece of ground, with a creek coming into play on 7 holes. There also are 9 lakes in play on several holes. Outstanding hole #17, 211 from gold tees—guarded on left by creek and in front by a lake. 9 hole par 3 course also.

──────────── STATELINE ────────────

Edgewood Tahoe GC
Hwy. 50 and Lake Pkwy.,
89449
Ph: 702-588-3566

Yards: 7491, Holes: 18
Par: 72, USGA: 69.6
RP: Two weeks in
advance

Restaurant/Bar/Proshop
GF: w/day $100, w/end
$100
Carts: Included

Course is on scenic Lake Tahoe. One champion was quoted as saying: "If I played this course always, I'd either be ready for an institution or I'd be one good golfer."

Our listings—supplied by the management—are as complete as possible. Many of the courses have more features than we list. Be sure to inquire when you book your tee time.

NEW HAMPSHIRE

Dixville Notch •

Jackson
Hanover • Lisbon
Woodstock • Bretton Woods
Waterville Valley
Ashland
• Meredith
Grantham
• North Sutton
Contoocook
Francestown •
Keene • • North Hampton
Nashua

──────────────── ASHLAND ────────────────

White Mountain CC	Yards: 6400, Holes: 18	Restaurant/Bar/Proshop
N. Ashland Rd., P.O. Box	Par: 71, USGA: 68.6	**GF:** w/day $16, w/end $18
83, 03217	RP: Weekends	**Carts:** $18.00
Ph: 603-536-2227		

The first hole starts you off with a spectacular view of Stinson Mountain and the Pemi-Baker River Valley. A solid front nine is a must because the back nine is where every club in the bag comes out. With its narrow fairways and two of the toughest finishing holes in the area. Break 80 and you've played quality golf!

──────────────── BRETTON WOODS ────────────────

Mt. Washington CC	Yards: 6638, Holes: 18	Restaurant/Bar
Rt. 302, 03575	Par: 71, USGA: 70.1	**GF:** w/day $17
Ph: 603-278-1000	RP: 1 day in advance	**Carts:** $18.00

Holes #2 and #18 require a drive across the Ammonoosuc River, and local rules dictate a one stroke penalty should you blow it. The course winds around a fairly flat front nine, with a hillier finish. Who knows, maybe you'll find one of Thomas Edison's or Babe Ruth's balls.

──────────────── CONTOOCOOK ────────────────

Duston CC	Yards: 2109, Holes: 9	Bar/Proshop
Rte. 3, Box 400, 03229	Par: 32, USGA: 59.5	**GF:** w/day $7, w/end $10
Ph: 603-746-4234	RP: Weekends only	**Carts:** $8.00

Duston Country Club is a relatively short course, with four par threes and five par fours. Duston requires a premium on shotmaking, rather than a long ball, because of its postage stamp size greens.

──────────────── DIXVILLE NOTCH ────────────────

Balsams Grand Resort	Yards: 6804, Holes: 27	Restaurant/Bar/Proshop
Hotel	Par: 72, USGA: 71.4	**GF:** w/day $30
Rte 26, 03576	RP: 24 hour notice—no	**Carts:** $22.00
Ph: 603-255-4961	chg htl.gst	

The Panorama Course is a spectacular Donald Ross layout built high on the side of Keyser Mountain. From the first tee scan a 30 mile horizon overlooking Vermont and Canada. This classic course is rated "toughest" in the state because of mountainside lies, deceptively positioned greens, and prevailing alpine winds.

---------------------------------- FRANCESTOWN ----------------------------------

Tory Pines GC　　Yards: 5818, Holes: 18　Restaurant/Bar/Proshop
RTE 47, 03043　　　Par: 71　　　　　　**GF:** w/day $10, w/end $12
Ph: 603-588-2923

Tory Pines' Hall of Fame Golf Course is patterned after 18 great holes from across the world. Beautiful mountain vistas and numerous flower gardens will enhance your golfing pleasure. Careful placement and a keen putting touch is necessary to excel on this beautiful layout.

---------------------------------- GRANTHAM ----------------------------------

Eastman Golf Links　Yards: 6338, Holes: 18　Restaurant/Bar/Proshop
Clubhouse Ln., 03753　Par: 71, USGA: 71.5　**GF:** w/day $27
Ph: 603-863-4500　　RP: 2 days in advance **Carts:** $24.00

Rated by Golf Digest as one of top courses in New Hampshire. Each hole cut through forests of pine and birch. No parallel fairways. 9th hole is long uphill par 4. The green is guarded by three traps. Rated most difficult on course.

---------------------------------- HANOVER ----------------------------------

Hanover CC　　　Yards: 6015, Holes: 18　Restaurant/Bar/Proshop
Rope Ferry Rd., 03755　Par: 70, USGA: 67.2　**GF:** w/day $25, w/end $25
Ph: 603-646-2000　　RP: 4 days in advance **Carts:** $20.00

A lush New England antique in process of being updated by Nicklaus "Golforce" group. Home of Dartmouth Men's and Women's Collegiate Golf Teams.

---------------------------------- JACKSON ----------------------------------

Wentworth Resort GC　Yards: 5360, Holes: 18　Restaurant/Bar/Proshop
Rte 16A, 03846　　　Par: 69, USGA: 64.5　**GF:** w/day $16, w/end $18
Ph: 603-383-9700　　RP: One week in　**Carts:** $18.00
　　　　　　　　　advance

The course is surrounded by the breathtaking mountains and forests of the White Mountain National Forest.

---------------------------------- KEENE ----------------------------------

Bretwood GC　　　Yards: 6852, Holes: 27　Restaurant/Proshop
E. Surry Rd., 03431　Par: 72, USGA: 71.6　**GF:** w/day $20, w/end $22
Ph: 603-352-7626　　RP: Weekends only　**Carts:** $18.00

Rated one of the finest 18-hole courses in New Hampshire by Golf Digest. Our gentle, rolling, irrigated fairways are always plush and green. The large Penncross greens are guarded by interesting bunkers and mounds. Water hazards include several ponds, a brook and the Ashuelot River that winds its way through the golf course.

---------------------------------- LISBON ----------------------------------

Lisbon Village CC　Yards: 6000, Holes: 9　Restaurant/Bar/Proshop
P.O. Box 3 Bishop Rd.,　Par: 72　　　　　**GF:** w/day $8, w/end $10
03585　　　　　　　　　　　　　　　**Carts:** $10.00
Ph: 603-838-6004

Play begins on lower portion of course with five holes along the Ammonoosuc River. An extremely challenging fifth (par 3, 212) brings play to a tight shotmakers upper four. These include breathtaking views of Mt. Lafayette in the Franconia Range. A true test, spectacular during fall foliage.

─────────────── MEREDITH ───────────────

Waukewan GC
P.O. Box 403, 03253
Ph: 603-279-6661

Yards: 5735, Holes: 18
Par: 71, USGA: 67.0
RP: Open time

Restaurant/Bar/Proshop
GF: w/day $20
Carts: $20.00

18 individual holes in natural setting of New Hampshire terrain. Spectacular panoramic view of White Mountains. Shotmaking is the premium, yet enough length exists to challenge the long hitter. Golf cars available, but not mandatory.

─────────────── NASHUA ───────────────

Nashua CC
Fairway St., 03060
Ph: 603-888-9858

Yards: 6131, Holes: 18
Par: 71, USGA: 68.8
RP: Must play with
member

Restaurant/Bar/Proshop
GF: w/day $35, w/end $45
Carts: $20.00

Home of LPGA professional, Pat Bradley. Undulating, #5 green responsible for 4 putts.

─────────────── NORTH HAMPTON ───────────────

Sagamore-Hampton GC
101 North Rd., 03862
Ph: 603-964-5341

Yards: 6511, Holes: 18
Par: 71, USGA: 67.1
RP: Call ahead

Restaurant/Bar/Proshop
GF: w/day $18

Two courses in one with the first nine a wide open par 35 (blue rating 34.2) with a minimum of hazards, while the back nine is a longer, narrower par 36 (blue rating 36.3) requiring the use of all 14 clubs and a fair share of strategy.

─────────────── NORTH SUTTON ───────────────

**Country Club New
Hampshire**
P.O. Box 142, 03026
Ph: 603-927-4246

Yards: 6727, Holes: 18
Par: 72, USGA: 69.6
RP: Taken 1 week in
advance

Proshop
GF: w/day $20, w/end $22
Carts: $20.00

The course is backed up against the Kearsarge Mountains. Very hilly and heavily wooded with pines and birch. Back side has narrow fairways. Many holes are parallel, many elevated tees.

─────────────── WATERVILLE VALLEY ───────────────

Waterville Valley GC
Rte 49, 03223
Ph: 603-236-8666

Yards: 2407, Holes: 9
Par: 32

Restaurant/Bar
GF: w/day $10
Carts: $10.00

Located on the valley floor of the resort, surrounded by mountain peaks. The 7th hole, par 4, is elevated. Very small green, over the road.

─────────────── WOODSTOCK ───────────────

Jack O'Lantern
Rte. 3, 03293
Ph: 603-745-8121

Yards: 5820, Holes: 18
Par: 70, USGA: 68.2
RP: Required until 1
p.m.

Restaurant/Bar/Proshop
GF: w/day $20
Carts: $19.00

Surrounded by the White Mountain National Forest and bordered for over a mile by the Pemigewasset River, this testing layout lies on gently rolling valley terrain in a virtually undisturbed setting. The golf course is very good; the experience is unforgettable.

NEW JERSEY

ABSECON

Marriott CC
Route Nine, 08201
Ph: 609-652-1800

Yards: 6417, Holes: 36
Par: 71, USGA: 70.9
RP: Guests 7 days in advance

Restaurant/Bar
GF: w/day $40
Carts: $13.00

The Bay Course features windswept bunkers and panoramic seaside views. As with most layouts subjected to buffeting winds, it is relatively short in yardage. The newer, more demanding Pines course, lined with 100 year old pines, oaks and plays over and around of bunkers. Greens are lightning quick and undulating.

FARMINGDALE

Howell Park GC
Preventarium Rd., 07727
Ph: 201-938-4771

Yards: 6869, Holes: 18
Par: 72, USGA: 70.0
RP: First come, first serve

Restaurant/Proshop
GF: w/day $21
Carts: $20.00

Level course which circles around. Fairways wide open and lined with trees and little meandering creeks. #7 cuts off the corner and has a big trap.

FLANDERS VALLEY

Flanders Valley GC
Pleasant Hill Rd., 07836
Ph: 201-584-8964

Yards: 6765, Holes: 18
Par: 72, USGA: 71.4

Restaurant/Bar/Proshop
GF: w/day $14, w/end $20
Carts: $20.00

On the White Course #5 has water on left, tree-lined par 4, dogleg right. Course has lots of traps. On the Blue #5 is a dogleg left around water, longer, elevated green. The Blue Course is more challenging with more doglegs, only 3 straight holes.

McAFEE

Great Gorge CC
Route 517, P.O. Box 1140, 07428
Ph: 201-827-5757

Yards: 6819, Holes: 27
Par: 71, USGA: 73.3
RP: 1 month in advance

Restaurant/Bar/Proshop
GF: w/day $34, w/end $50
Carts: $14.00

The golf course is located in an area which is unlike anything in New Jersey. It sits in a valley between the tallest mountains in the state northwest corner. The views combine with 3 different nines here make this one of NJ's best public/resort courses.

—————————————— MOUNT LAUREL ——————————————

Ramblewood CC
Country Club Pkwy.,
08054
Ph: 609-235-2119

Yards: 6498, Holes: 27
Par: 72, USGA: 71.1

Restaurant/Bar/Proshop
GF: w/day $20, w/end $25
Carts: $20.00

Our golf course is very playable! For low handicappers as well as high handicappers. There are many super holes on this golf course.

—————————————— NESHANIC STATION ——————————————

Hillsborough GC CC
Wertsville Rd., P.O. Box
365, 08853
Ph: 201-369-3322

Yards: 6100, Holes: 18
Par: 70, USGA: 68.7
RP: Weekends

Restaurant/Bar/Proshop
GF: w/day $15, w/end $20
Carts: $20.00

Arguably the nicest view in the state. Front side relatively open, our back side tight and hilly. Favorite hole #8, 190 yard par 3 tight left, traps right, narrow green. Good luck!

—————————————— PISCATAWAY ——————————————

Rutgers University GC
777 Hoes Ln., 08854
Ph: 201-932-2631

Yards: 5890, Holes: 18
Par: 71, USGA: 68.2
RP: Weekends &
holidays

Proshop

All of our holes are named after trees. Our favorite is the Sour Gum at hole #11 which is delight to see especially during the fall when the colors are red, gold, and yellow and the curving branches give it character.

—————————————— TUCKERTON ——————————————

Atlantis GC
Country Club Rd., 08087
Ph: 609-296-2444

Yards: 6313, Holes: 18
Par: 72, USGA: 69.7H

One of the most beautiful and challenging courses in Southern New Jersey. Fairways are well maintained to ensure a good lie to your ball. Greens receive tender loving care and your first putt will show the difference.

—————————————— WASHINGTON ——————————————

Fairway Valley GC
Box 219A, Minehill Rd.,
07882
Ph: 201-689-1530

Yards: 3006, Holes: 9
Par: 70, USGA: 69.9

Restaurant/Bar/Proshop
GF: w/day $7, w/end $8
Carts: $17.00

Located in the "Valley of the Hawk", lies Fairway Valley Golf Club. Known for its beauty in all seasons, the club boasts a track to challenge the low handicapper and novice alike, in a setting where nature and wildlife galley for pleasure.

—————————————— WOODBURY ——————————————

Westwood GC
850 Kings Highway,
08096
Ph: 609-845-2000

Yards: 5931, Holes: 18
Par: 71, USGA: 67.9
RP: Suggested on
weekends

Restaurant/Bar/Proshop
GF: w/day $14, w/end $18
Carts: $20.00

Our par 3, 11th hole is definitely a challenge with a "slight" northern downhill slope to it.

NEW
MEXICO

● Los Alamos

●Cochiti Lake

●Albuquerque

●Mescalero
● Cloudcroft

Deming ● ●Las Cruces

──────────── ALBUQUERQUE ────────────

University of New Yards: 6480, Holes: 36 Restaurant/Proshop
Mexico GC Par: 72, USGA: 70.8 **GF:** w/day $14
Univ. Blvd. SE., 87131 RP: 3 players to **Carts:** $16.00
Ph: 505-277-4546 reserve weekend

University of New Mexico South is one of Golf Digest's Top 25 public courses in America. The course features rolling fairways and desert terrain which present many challenging shots into large, undulating, well-bunkered greens, and panoramic views of Albuquerque and the Rio Grande Valley.

──────────── CLOUDCROFT ────────────

Lodge GC Yards: 2451, Holes: 9 Restaurant/Bar/Proshop
Corona Ave., P.O. Box Par: 34, USGA: 63.0 **GF:** w/day $9, w/end $12
182, 88317 RP: 7 days ahead with **Carts:** $10.00
Ph: 505-682-2098 credit card

Established in 1899 near it's present location. For many years this was the highest golf course in the world at 9200 feet. Our double tee and double pin layout makes for an interesting 18 hole game. Rolling mountain greens that break away from beautiful pine forests add to the excitement. Number 1 drops 200 feet in 250 yards.

──────────── COCHITI LAKE ────────────

Cochiti Lake GC Yards: 6450, Holes: 18 Restaurant/Proshop
Box 125, 87083 Par: 72, USGA: 68.5 **GF:** w/day $16, w/end $18
Ph: 505-465-2239 RP: 7 days in advance **Carts:** $18.00

A Robert Trent Jones design at the foot of Jemez Mountains. Tree-lined with a mix of cedar and ponderosa pines. Hole #13 one of top 50 holes in country. Rated as one of top 25 Public courses in America.

──────────── DEMING ────────────

Rio Mimbres GC Yards: 6188, Holes: 9 Restaurant/Bar/Proshop
Rt. 2, P.O. Box 110, 88030 Par: 71, USGA: 68.6 **GF:** w/day $10, w/end $11
Ph: 505-546-9481 **Carts:** $11.00

Our golf course is flat and relatively short. The strength of Rio Mimbres Country Club is the greens. They're small, undulated and difficult to approach to and putt on.

─────────────── LAS CRUCES ───────────────

Picacho Hills CC Yards: 6970, Holes: 18 **GF:** w/day $30, w/end $35
6861 Via Campestre, Par: 72, USGA: 70.9 **Carts:** $15.00
88005
Ph: 505-523-2556

A rolling desert golf course with a total elevation change of 200 feet, overlooks the historic Mesilla Valley and the Rio Grande. From the bluegrass fairways you can view the mighty Organ Mountains while negotiating a fine test of golf with 9 lakes.

─────────────── LOS ALAMOS ───────────────

Los Alamos GC Yards: 6440, Holes: 18 Restaurant/Bar/Proshop
4250 Diamond Dr., 87544 Par: 71, USGA: 69.8 **GF:** w/day $10, w/end $12
Ph: 505-662-8139 RP: Weekends & **Carts:** $14.50
holidays

Beautiful mountain setting 7500 feet altitude, 35 miles north of Santa Fe. Tree lined fairways, ponderosa pines and cottonwoods. Average playing season April through November.

─────────────── MESCALERO ───────────────

Inn of the Mountain Yards: 6819, Holes: 18 Restaurant/Bar/Proshop
Gods Par: 72, USGA: 70.1 **GF:** w/day $32, w/end $32
Box 269, Rt. 4 Carrizzo **Carts:** $20.00
Rd., 88340
Ph: 505-257-5141

The Inn of the Mountain Gods resort course is rated as the top course in New Mexico and in the top 25 in America. The 18 hole-championship course is situated at the foothills of Sierra Blanca, flanked by beautiful Lake Mescalero. Every hole offers a different challenge, par 5 14th offering a remarkable reverse S double-dogleg.

NEW YORK

Loon Lake
Lake Placid
Clayton
East Amhearst
Ellicottville
LeRoy • Rochester
Lima Shortsville
• Locke
• Clymer
Catskill New Paltz
South Fallsburg Ellenville • Accord Greenport
Kiamesha Lake Brewster
Montgomery Montauk
Suffern
Middle Island
Hauppauge
Long Island

---------------------------- ACCORD ----------------------------

Rondout CC | Yards: 7035, Holes: 9 | Restaurant/Bar/Proshop
P.O. Box 194, Whitfield | Par: 35, USGA: 68.5 | **GF:** w/day $6
Rd., 12404 | | **Carts:** $9.00
Ph: 914-626-2513

No trick holes with yardage markers every 25 yards from 200 yards out from the center of the greens. Our reputation for excellent greens and also being very quick is consistent year after year. Our favorite hole is one of our shortest par 4s with water and sand all around the wedge shot must be sweet.

---------------------------- BREWSTER ----------------------------

Vails Grove GC | Yards: 4300, Holes: 9 | Proshop
RFD #2, Peach Lake, | Par: 66, USGA: 58.5 | **GF:** w/day $15, w/end $15
10509 | | **Carts:** $18.00
Ph: 914-669-5721

Picturesque, challenging. Friendly atmosphere.

---------------------------- CATSKILL ----------------------------

Catskill GC | Yards: 6286, Holes: 9 | Restaurant/Bar/Proshop
27 Brooks Ln., 12414 | Par: 72, USGA: 69.5 | **GF:** w/day $15
Ph: 518-943-2390 | | **Carts:** $18.00

Fairly wide fairways with tiny greens. 7 different tees on back nine completely change 7 of the 9 holes. Totally irrigated and always in top condition. Par 5 3rd hole, at 560 yards, with water fronting the green is a classic, natural beauty requiring length, accuracy with a deft putting touch on a large, severely sloped green.

---------------------------- CLAYTON ----------------------------

C-Way GC | Yards: 6102, Holes: 18 | Restaurant/Bar/Proshop
RD #1 Box 271, 13624 | Par: 72, USGA: 68.0 | **GF:** w/day $12, w/end $13
Ph: 315-686-3084 | RP: 1 day in advance | **Carts:** $16.00

C-Way Golf Club is in the heart of the 1000 islands. The course stretches over acres of scenic hills and valleys. Partially wooded course complete with sand traps and water hazards to test your skills.

──────────── CLYMER ────────────

Peek'n Peak GC
Ye Olde Rd., 14724
Ph: 716-355-4141

Yards: 6260, Holes: 18
Par: 72, USGA: 69.8
RP: Call anytime for
starting time

Restaurant/Bar
GF: w/day $18, w/end $25
Carts: $20.00

Ponds and streams interspersed within tree-lined fairways create an unparalleled golfing experience. Roland Stafford School at Peek's Peak provides intense personalized golf training. Additional 9-hole openning Spring '93 — offering distinctly different terrain.

──────────── EAST AMHEARST ────────────

Glen Oak
711 Smith, 14051
Ph: 716-688-5454

Yards: 6730, Holes: 18
Par: 72, USGA: 71.9
RP: 3 days in advance

Restaurant/Bar/Proshop
GF: w/day $21, w/end $30
Carts: Included

Course is level with small rolling hills and many creeks and ponds. Many elevated tees with oaks and evergreens lining the fairways. #18 choose easy or hard route; tough one over a pond.

──────────── ELLENVILLE ────────────

Fallsview Hotel & CC
12428
Ph: 914-647-5100

Yards: 3173, Holes: 9
Par: 35, USGA: 70.4
RP: One day in
advance

Restaurant/Bar/Proshop
GF: w/day $9, w/end $11
Carts: $11.00

Best 9 holes course in the area.

──────────── ELLENVILLE ────────────

The Nevele GC
12428
Ph: 914-647-6000

Yards: 6500, Holes: 18
Par: 70, USGA: 69.4
RP: Guests 2 weeks;
non guest 1 wk

Restaurant/Bar/Proshop
GF: w/day $20
Carts: $20.00

The entire course is fair yet quite challenging for all caliber of golfers. Keep plenty of balls around for the devilish 16th hole. A carry across water to a green almost surrounded by water makes for some exciting shotmaking.

──────────── ELLICOTTVILLE ────────────

Holiday Valley Resort
PO Box 370, Holiday
Valley Rd., 14731
Ph: 716-699-2346

Yards: 6555, Holes: 18
Par: 72, USGA: 70.9

Restaurant/Bar/Proshop
GF: w/day $22, w/end $22
Carts: $20.00

Holiday Valley Resort is best known as a great ski area. The ponds used for snowmaking provide watery graves for many golf balls and the tree lined ski slopes produce tight fairways. Hit it straight and score well.

──────────── ELMA ────────────

Elma Meadows GC
1711 Girdle Rd., 14059
Ph: 716-652-2022

Yards: 6415, Holes: 18
Par: 70, USGA: 70.0
RP: First come, first
serve

Restaurant/Proshop
GF: w/day $8, w/end $10
Carts: $16.00

18 holes with rolling fairways which are almost all treelined. 1st tee shot off a huge hill is just a start of 18 uniquely different golf holes.

Subscribe to our free newsletter, "Great Golf Gazette" and hear about the latest special golf vacation values.

──────────────── GOLTON LANDING ────────────────

The Sagamore GC   Yards: 6810, Holes: 18   Restaurant/Bar
On Lake George, 12814   Par: 70, USGA: 71.5
Ph: 518-644-9400   RP: With Reservation

The thirteenth hole is considered by many to be the most breathtaking, but also the most difficult. It's a very tight driving hole with water right and in front of the green. The second shot is uphill to "one undulating mass."

──────────────── GREENPORT ────────────────

Island's End Golf & CC   Yards: 6639, Holes: 18   Restaurant/Bar/Proshop
Box 39 Rte 25, 11944   Par: 72, USGA: 68.9   **GF:** w/day $10, w/end $25
Ph: 516-477-9457   RP: Recommended   **Carts:** $20.00

Relatively flat. 700' Long Island Sound selected one of the top 18 holes in metropolitan area in 1968. Hole #16 par 3, 220 yards over a ravine and out of bounds to Sound side.

──────────────── HAUPPAUGE ────────────────

Hauppauge CC   Yards: 6280, Holes: 18   Restaurant/Bar/Proshop
Veterans Memorial   Par: 72, USGA: 70.4   **GF:** w/day $20
Hwy, Box 237, 11788   **Carts:** $22.00
Ph: 516-724-7500

A very challenging course where water comes into play on seven of the eighteen holes. The 17th hole is a 370 yard par 4 with a large pond guarding the front of the green and three bunkers nestled at the rear of green. Accuracy is a must or you're in real trouble!

──────────────── HAUPPAUGE ────────────────

Marriott's GC at   Yards: 6405, Holes: 18   Restaurant/Bar/Proshop
Windwatch   Par: 71   **GF:** w/day $46, w/end $52
1717 Vanderbilt Motor   RP: Hotel guests 7   **Carts:** $13.00 ea
Pkwy., 11788   days; public 3
Ph: 516-232-9850

Perhaps Gene Sazazan says it best, "Joe Lee, course architect has a graceful ability to combine the pleasures of a golf course for the average player with the strategy concept of a championship test without getting out of a balance in either direction."

──────────────── KIAMESHA LAKE ────────────────

Concord Hotel GC   Yards: 7205, Holes: 45   Restaurant/Bar
12751   Par: 72, USGA: 76.0   **GF:** w/day $60
Ph: 914-794-4000   RP: 7 months in   **Carts:** Included
advance

Concord's 45 holes include its infamous "Monster," a 6,793 yard by Joe Finger, wizard of Cedar Ridge in Oklahoma. This par 72 heavily wooded rolling course has hosted many tournaments.

──────────────── LAKE PLACID ────────────────

Whiteface Inn Resort   Yards: 6490, Holes: 18   Restaurant/Bar/Proshop
& CC   Par: 72, USGA: 70.6   **GF:** w/day $19
Whiteface Inn Rd., 12946   RP: Required for all   **Carts:** $24.00
Ph: 518-523-2551   play

One of golf's great par 3's is the 14th hole at White Face. Over 200 yards in length, the tee shot over a pond with trees bordering closely on each side must be well struck to land on the tiered green, bordered by huge bunkers.

────────────────── LE ROY ──────────────────

Le Roy CC
7759 East Main Road,
14482
Ph: 716-768-7330

Yards: 6400, Holes: 18
Par: 71, USGA: 67.6
RP: Starting times 24
hrs in adv

Restaurant/Bar/Proshop
GF: w/day $11, w/end $13
Carts: $18.00

Front fairly short—gives the golfer a chance to warm up before playing a much longer back nine which includes from the blues, a 555 yard part 5, 470 yard par 4 and a 227 yard par 3.

────────────────── LIMA ──────────────────

Lima Golf & CC
2681 Plank Rd., 14485
Ph: 716-624-1490

Yards: 6372, Holes: 18
Par: 72, USGA: 72.3
RP: Required
weekends

Restaurant/Bar/Proshop
GF: w/day $12, w/end $14
Carts: $16.00

Play some of the finest greens anywhere. Our fast greens hold well. Eighteen, a good finishing hole, where you lay up short of pond with a 200 yard tee shot. Them hit a middle iron to a two-tiered green, trapped on left.

────────────────── LOCKE ──────────────────

Fillmore GC
RD 1 Box 409, 13092
Ph: 315-497-3145

Yards: 5523, Holes: 18
Par: 71, USGA: 67.1

Restaurant/Bar/Proshop
GF: w/day $8, w/end $9
Carts: $14.00

This 18 hole course, named in honor of the 13th President of the USA, sets on a hill overlooking the beautiful Owasco Lake and valley. The front nine is designed for the amateur golfer while the back nine offers a challenge to the more ardent golfer.

────────────────── LOON LAKE ──────────────────

Loon Lake GC
12968
Ph: 518-891-3249

Yards: 5400, Holes: 18
Par: 70

Restaurant/Bar/Proshop
GF: w/day $8
Carts: $12.00

If you want to see what America's earliest courses looked like, Loon Lake is worth the stop. The holes are short; the greens, especially on the front nine, tiny. You'll need you ace wedge game. The back nine, built in 1894, is treed and curvy, but a neat test.

────────────────── MIDDLE ISLAND ──────────────────

Spring Lake GC
Bartlett Rd., Rt.25, 11953
Ph: 516-924-5115

Yards: 7048, Holes: 27
Par: 72, USGA: 71.0

Restaurant/Bar/Proshop
GF: w/day $17, w/end $20
Carts: $23.00

With 27 holes available, you can play a picturesque 9 hole course on the shore of Spring Lake or the tree lined, manicured, 18 hole championship course. Hosts of the 1989 Met Public Links Championship which plays from 5732 yards to 7048 yards.

────────────────── MONTAUK ──────────────────

Montauk Downs GC
P.O. Box 735 off
Westlake Dr., 11954
Ph: 516-668-5000

Yards: 6762, Holes: 18
Par: 72, USGA: 70.5
RP: None

Restaurant/Bar/Proshop
GF: w/day $14, w/end $16
Carts: $20.00

75 percent of the fairways are narrow, first few are parallel. Course is wooded with rolling hills, big ponds and lakes. #18 is a challenging par 4, 417 yard hole.

――――――――――――― MONTGOMERY ―――――――――――――

Stony Ford GC
Rd #3, Box 100, Rt. 416,
12549
Ph: 914-457-3000

Yards: 6200, Holes: 18
Par: 72, USGA: 69.2
RP: One no more than
1 week ahead

Restaurant/Bar/Proshop
GF: w/day $10, w/end $20
Carts: $15.00

A scenic, well-landscaped course with hilly terrain, numerous water hazards, and wooded fringe. The front nine requires good positioning due to the many hazards and doglegs on five of the holes. On the back nine, the par 4 15th offers the challenging blend of distance and an unforgiving green.

――――――――――――― NEW PALTZ ―――――――――――――

New Paltz GC
215 Huguenot St., 12561
Ph: 914-255-8282

Yards: 3610, Holes: 9
Par: 36, USGA: 70.0
RP: None

Restaurant/Bar/Proshop
GF: w/day $6, w/end $8
Carts: $8.00

Clearly one of New York's finest 9 hole layouts. Tee shots that drift can find water on 5 of the well designed 9 holes. Throughout the challenge there is a feeling of peacefulness when playing this course. The contrast of the thick woods, marshes, water or the view of the mountains is what gives the golfer a sense of fulfillment.

――――――――――――― ROCHESTER ―――――――――――――

Durand Eastman GC
1200 Kings Hwy. North,
14617
Ph: 716-266-8364

Yards: 6089, Holes: 18
Par: 70, USGA: 68.8
RP: First come

Proshop
GF: w/day $8, w/end $9
Carts: $16.00

My favorite hole is the 17th, 146 yards, rolling fairway that look over Lake Ontario. It is often called the mountain goat course and is said to be one of the sportiest, if not the sportiest and most scenic in the land.

――――――――――――― SHORTSVILLE ―――――――――――――

Winged Pheasant GL
1475 Sand Hill Rd., 14548
Ph: 716-289-8846

Yards: 6345, Holes: 18
Par: 70, USGA: 69.0

Restaurant/Bar/Proshop
GF: w/day $13, w/end $15
Carts: $14.00

Opening hole is a dog right par 5. The course on the front nine demands a careful positioning of shots and water must be contended with. Our par threes are rated 3.2. The course has several holes that are outlined with trees.

――――――――――――― SOUTH FALLSBURG ―――――――――――――

Tarry Brae GC
Pleasant Valley Rd.,
12779
Ph: 914-434-9782

Yards: 6800, Holes: 18
Par: 72, USGA: 70.0
RP: Only taken for
afternoon

Restaurant/Bar/Proshop
GF: w/day $13
Carts: $20.00

Tarry Brae is a hilly course with many tree lined fairways. There are several panoramic views of mountains and valleys. There are several excellent courses in the Catskill Mountains and Tarry Brae is one of them.

――――――――――――― SUFFERN ―――――――――――――

Spook Rock GC
Spook Rock Rd., 10952
Ph: 914-357-6466

Yards: 6894, Holes: 18
Par: 72, USGA: 70.9
RP: Required

Restaurant/Bar/Proshop
GF: w/day $20, w/end $27
Carts: $19.00

All fairways are narrow and tree-lined. The course is heavily wooded with maple and pine and water on 5 holes. The tees are elevated.

NORTH CAROLINA

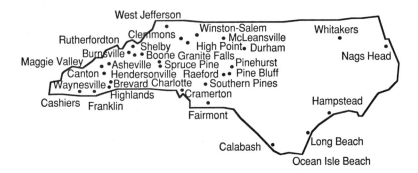

West Jefferson
Rutherfordton Clemmons Winston-Salem Whitakers
Shelby High Point McLeansville
Burnsville Boone Granite Falls Durham
Maggie Valley Asheville Spruce Pine Pinehurst Nags Head
Canton Hendersonville Raeford Pine Bluff
Waynesville Brevard Charlotte Southern Pines
Highlands Cramerton
Cashiers Franklin Hampstead
Fairmont
Calabash Long Beach
Ocean Isle Beach

ASHEVILLE

Great Smokies Hilton Yards: 5263, Holes: 18 Restaurant/Proshop
One Hilton Inn Dr., 28806 Par: 70, USGA: 65.6 **GF:** w/day $18
Ph: 704-253-5874 RP: Tee times required **Carts:** $12.00 ea

Great Smokies Hilton is a championship mountain golf course. Scratch golfers and hackers alike find the tight course and winding creeks a real challenge.

BOONE

Hanging Rock Golf & Yards: 6153, Holes: 18 Restaurant/Bar/Proshop
CC Par: 71, USGA: 67.0 **GF:** w/day $24
P.O. Box 628 DTS, 28607
Ph: 704-963-6565

Our fairways wind themselves through the many cuts, runs, and ridges that are common to mountain terrain. And around every turn is a strategically placed green, manicured and groomed to our high standards, with a variety of hazards to make your game interesting.

BREVARD

Sherwood Forest GC Yards: 2260, Holes: 18 Restaurant/Proshop
Box 156, Hwy 276 South, Par: 54 **GF:** w/day $12, w/end $13
28712
Ph: 704-884-7825

"Birdy"! That is golf at Sherwood Forest! Your accurate shots will reward you. It would be hard to single out any one hole; they are all challenging! And if that "bird" eludes you on the green, listen to them in the tranquility of our beautiful forest.

BURNSVILLE

Mount Mitchell GC Yards: 6475, Holes: 18 Restaurant/Proshop
7590 Highway 80 South, Par: 72, USGA: 68.0 **GF:** w/day $25
28714 RP: 1 week in advance **Carts:** $10.00 ea
Ph: 704-675-5454

This mountain course lies in a valley at 3000 feet elevation with 15 flat holes. The back nine follows the Southtoe River which comes into play on 2 holes. The par 4, 450 yard 14th hole requires a second shot over the river to a well bunkered green.

──────────────── CALABASH ────────────────

Marsh Harbour GL
P.O. Box 65, North
Mrytle Beach, 29597
Ph: 803-249-3449

Yards: 6970, Holes: 18
Par: 71, USGA: 70.1
RP: 9 months in
advance

Restaurant/Bar/Proshop
GF: w/day $47
Carts: Included

The course has a lot of marsh grass and sand with big shady oak trees every-where. 7 closing holes are by the marsh. #18 has logo tree; #17, par 5, has 3 island landing areas.

──────────────── CALABASH ────────────────

Pearl Golf Links
Route 8, Sunset Lakes
Blvd., 28459
Ph: 919-579-8132

Yards: 6749, Holes: 18
Par: 72
RP: Call for starting
times

Restaurant/Bar/Proshop
GF: w/day $39
Carts: $11.00

Start off on a Scottish links, then play into a Pinehurst look, then finish along the scenic coastal marsh land. Extensive manicuring and landscaping, magnificent clubhouse facility, this world class masterpiece awaits you with a warm wel-come, and southern hospitality at its best.

──────────────── CANTON ────────────────

Springdale CC
Rt.2 Box 271, 28716
Ph: 800-553-3027

Yards: 6437, Holes: 18
Par: 72, USGA: 70.7
RP: Recommended

Restaurant/Proshop
GF: w/day $21, w/end $21
Carts: $13.00 ea

Despite unusually large penncross bent greens, Springdale places a premium on accuracy. The front nine is long, hilly and well trapped. And there's a mountain stream you'll get to know. The back nine is shorter and flatter with wider fair-ways. It's a course you'll come back to play again.

──────────────── CASHIERS ────────────────

**High Hampton Inn &
CC**
P.O. Box 338, Hwy. 107,
South, 28717
Ph: 704-743-2411

Yards: 6012, Holes: 18
Par: 71
RP: 1 day in advance

Restaurant/Proshop
GF: w/day $29
Carts: $21.00

High Hampton Inn & Country Club is a golfer's mecca. The par 3, 137-yard famed 8th hole (upon which Golf Digest bestowed the title "One of America's Great Golf Holes") is rivaled by 17 others, each one equally beautiful and equally challenging.

──────────────── CHARLOTTE ────────────────

Pawtuckett GC
1 Pauwtuckett Rd., 28214
Ph: 704-394-5890

Yards: 6510, Holes: 18
Par: 70, USGA: 68.5
RP: 1 day in advance

Restaurant/Bar/Proshop
GF: w/day $19, w/end $24
Carts: $5.00

The rolling hills and beautiful countryside setting will make Pawtuckett a golf course you will love to play.

──────────────── CLEMMONS ────────────────

Tanglewood Park GC
Tanglewood Park, 27012
Ph: 919-766-0591

Yards: 6710, Holes: 18
Par: 72, USGA: 68.5
RP: 2 weeks in advance

Restaurant/Bar/Proshop
GF: w/day $20
Carts: $10.00

Two courses as different as night and day, both bent greens and bermudas. #5 Champ, par 4, 435 yards across water, 200 yard carry, fairway slope. #18 Rey, very hilly, 430 yards uphill, lake with sandtrap 30 yards from landing area.

——————————————— CRAMERTON ———————————————

Lakewood GL Yards: 5907, Holes: 18   Proshop
25 Lakewood Rd., 28032   Par: 71, USGA: 67.1   **GF:** w/day $8
Ph: 704-825-2852   RP: Weekends only   **Carts:** $6.00

Front 9 wide open with small bent grass greens. Back 9 tight, #15 long par 4 dogleg right!

——————————————— DURHAM ———————————————

Duke University GC   Yards: 7003, Holes: 18   Restaurant/Bar/Proshop
Route 751 & Science Dr.,   Par: 72, USGA: 70.3   **GF:** w/day $13, w/end $18
27706   **Carts:** $18.00
Ph: 919-684-2817

Opened in 1957, this typically outstanding Jones creation will offer you a memorable golf outing. On the course, we feature hole after hole of lush bermuda fairways and fast bent grass greens. To top off your golf experience, enjoy our unique expansive practice facilities.

——————————————— DURHAM ———————————————

Hillandale GC   Yards: 6350, Holes: 18   Proshop
P.O. Box 2786,   Par: 71, USGA: 69.5   **GF:** w/day $12, w/end $13
Hillandale Rd., 27705   RP: For   **Carts:** $15.00
Ph: 919-286-4211   weekends—7-14 days
adv.

Located in the heart of Durham, Hillandale encompasses a variety of situations. The front side is relatively flat terrain with the Ellerbee Creek meandering through 7 of the nine holes. The back side becomes rolling and entails three holes with double greens, a rarity among golf courses.

——————————————— DURHAM ———————————————

Lakeshore GC   Yards: 5829, Holes: 18   Proshop
4621 Lumley Rd., 27703   Par: 71, USGA: 67.3   **GF:** w/day $8, w/end $11
Ph: 919-596-2401   RP: Weekends   **Carts:** $14.00

This course is laid out around a 25 acre lake and it is very picturesque.

——————————————— FAIRMONT ———————————————

Flag Tree GC   Yards: 6183, Holes: 18   Bar/Proshop
Golf Course Rd., 28340   Par: 72, USGA: 69.5   **GF:** w/day $8, w/end $10
Ph: 919-628-9933   RP: Weekends   **Carts:** $8.00 ea

Enjoy a fairly open front nine in preparation for the Flat Tree "Amen Corner." The 12th through the 15th wrap around a series of old irrigation ponds requiring a number of challenging shots. It's quality golf in a serene country setting.

——————————————— FRANKLIN ———————————————

Holly Springs GR   Yards: 6000, Holes: 18   Restaurant/Bar/Proshop
110 Holly Springs Golf   Par: 72   **GF:** w/day $12
Village, 28734   **Carts:** $16.00
Ph: 704-524-7561

A beautiful mountain challenge with 13 water hazard holes. You experience unsurpassed mountain views from every fairway and tee. Hole #1 is a ninety yard chip across a lake. From the elevated tee #14 you can view mountain ranges 10 to 15 miles away while stroking for the green 300 feet below and 235 yards away.

―――――――――――― GRANITE FALLS ――――――――――――

Tri-County GC, Inc. Yards: 6094, Holes: 18 Bar/Proshop
Rt. 2, Box 281, 28630 Par: 72 **GF:** w/day $9, w/end $12
Ph: 704-728-3560 RP: Required **Carts:** $9.00
  weekends & holidays

Set in the foothills of the Appalachian Mountains, the rolling terrain gives golfers a true test of golf skills. The front nine offers a wide variety of golf shots, while the back nine reward you if you deserve it.

―――――――――――― HAMPSTEAD ――――――――――――

Belvedere Plantation Yards: 6500, Holes: 18 Bar/Proshop
Box 999, 28443 Par: 72
Ph: 919-270-2703

Elevated greens on most holes, surrounded by steeply sloping mounds which can severely penalize the errant approach shot. Getting the ball up and down demands shotmaking at its best. If your game is hitting the ball not very far but always just where you aim it, this is a great place to take that big-driving friend of yours for a day of getting even.

―――――――――――― HENDERSONVILLE ――――――――――――

Etowah Valley Yards: 6880, Holes: 27 **GF:** w/day $25
P.O. Box 2150, 28793 Par: 72, USGA: 70.0 **Carts:** $12.00 ea
Ph: 704-891-7022 RP: 2 days in advance

The bent grass greens are probably some of the largest in the south—some as large as 9,000 feet, as the course winds through rolling valleys. The course is designed to eliminate ball crossover from one fairway to another, insuring uninterrupted play.

―――――――――――― HIGH POINT ――――――――――――

Blair Park GC Yards: 6449, Holes: 18 Restaurant/Proshop
1901 S. Main St., 27260 Par: 72, USGA: 67.4 **GF:** w/day $6
Ph: 919-883-3497 RP: Weekends & **Carts:** $8.00
  holidays

Newly renovated bent grass greens are relatively small. There are few bunkers, many tall pine trees and a creek that runs throughout the course which comes into play on 10 holes. Hole #14 is 400 yards; 2nd shot is 175 yards, downhill lie, carry over rock-walled creek.

―――――――――――― HIGH POINT ――――――――――――

Oak Hollow GC Yards: 6429, Holes: 18 Restaurant/Proshop
1400 Oakview Rd., 27260 Par: 72, USGA: 67.9 **GF:** w/day $10, w/end $13
Ph: 919-869-4014 RP: 2 days in advance **Carts:** $16.00

This Pete Dye designed course, which follows the shoreline of the lake to a large extent, has bermuda fairways and bent grass greens. Some of Dye's design features include sand bunkers lined with pilings, an island tee, fairways shored up with railroad ties, grass traps and a green situated on a peninsula. Rated in Top 25 public courses in USA.

―――――――――――― HIGHLANDS ――――――――――――

Highlands Falls CC Yards: 6111, Holes: 18 Restaurant/Bar/Proshop
PO Box 1800, 1 Club Dr., Par: 70, USGA: 67.5 **GF:** w/day $50, w/end $50
28741 RP: Play w/member, **Carts:** $10.00
Ph: 704-526-4101 or rent condo

Nestled in the high Blue Ridge Mountains. Course features rolling fairways and elevated tees with our spectacular par 3 15th waterfall hole. This was rebuilt in 1987 by the Director of Golf, Frank Montgomery and Superintendent, David Hassel.

─────────────── LONG BEACH ───────────────

Oak Island GC CC Yards: 6608, Holes: 18 Restaurant/Bar/Proshop
P.O. Box 789, 28465 Par: 72, USGA: 69.6 **GF:** w/day $20
Ph: 919-278-5275 RP: 1 week in advance **Carts:** $10.00 ea

#18 par 5—The fairway is lined with gnarled oak trees from a steady ocean wind. You are hitting 2 good shots into the ocean wind, which will leave you 150 yards carry over water that sometimes has alligators in it.

─────────────── MAGGIE VALLEY ───────────────

Maggie Valley Resort Yards: 6284, Holes: 18 Restaurant/Bar/Proshop
P.O. Box 99, 340 Country Par: 71, USGA: 68.5 **GF:** w/day $25, w/end $25
Club Rd., 27851 RP: Call for tee time **Carts:** $12.50 ea
Ph: 800-438-3861 same day

Maggie's 18-hole, par 71 championship course is scenically beautiful, with the mountain setting of Blue Ridge and Smokies, the front nine begins in the valley with the back nine built into the mountains. The elevation changes gradually from 2,600 to 3,500 feet.

─────────────── MCLEANSVILLE ───────────────

Cedar Crest GC Yards: 5682, Holes: 18 Proshop
340 Birch Creek Rd., Par: 70, USGA: 66.0 **GF:** w/day $8
27301 **Carts:** $7.50 ea
Ph: 919-697-8251

The course is relatively short by some standards, rolling with the land, yet designed for pleasure. Our favorite hole is No. 3 with short par 5 and all uphill. The penalty is the large oak tree in the center of the fairway at 210 yards. We have special retiree rates all year.

─────────────── NAGS HEAD ───────────────

Nags Head Golf Links Yards: 6240, Holes: 18 Restaurant/Bar/Proshop
P.O. Box 1719, Hwy. Par: 71, USGA: 68.9 **GF:** w/day $40, w/end $40
158,Mi Ps 15, 27959 RP: Reserve through **Carts:** $10.00
Ph: 919-441-8073 year

A visit to Scottish golf lies here on the Outer Banks of North Carolina. Sandy lies, love grass and sea oats await the errant shot with prevailing winds always a factor. Selected to "Top 50 in the Southeast" by Golf Week Magazine.

─────────────── OCEAN ISLE BEACH ───────────────

Brick Landing Yards: 6482, Holes: 18 Restaurant/Bar/Proshop
Plantation GC Par: 72, USGA: 69.4 **GF:** w/day $22, w/end $35
Route 2, 28459 **Carts:** $10.00 ea
Ph: 919-754-4373

Once again Brick Landing has been selected by Golfweek magazine as one of the Top 50 resort developments in the Southeast. "The Amateur," a new national men's amateur tournament is contested here every July. "The Amateur" brings 120 top players together to test their playing ability.

Our listings—supplied by the management—are as complete as possible. Many of the courses have more features than we list. Be sure to inquire when you book your tee time.

─────────── PINEBLUFF ───────────

Pines Golf Resort
US Hwy. 1 S., P.O. Box
427, 28373
Ph: 919-281-3165

Yards: 6610, Holes: 18
Par: 72, USGA: 68.5
RP: Call for tee times

Restaurant/Bar/Proshop
GF: w/day $10
Carts: $10.00 ea

The Pines Golf Resort course is situated on 250 acres in the beautiful sandhills (Pinehurst) area. The course is on rolling terrain through stands of longleaf and lollolly pine and is punctuated by several lakes. A challenging and fun course for golfers of every level.

─────────── PINEHURST ───────────

Foxfire Resort & CC
P.O. Box 711, 28374
Ph: 919-295-5555

Yards: 6286, Holes: 18
Par: 72, USGA: 69.7

Restaurant/Bar/Proshop
GF: w/day $40, w/end $40
Carts: $14.00 ea

The original West Course follows the gentle slopes along the shores of Lake Mackenzie and the large Foxfire ponds. The newer East Course winds through the hillier section surrounding wide Lake Forest.

─────────── PINEHURST ───────────

Pinehurst Hotel CC
P.O. Box 4000, 28374
Ph: 919-295-6811

Yards: 7020, Holes: 18
Par: 72, USGA: 73.5
RP: Hotel/resort guests

Restaurant/Bar/Proshop
GF: w/day $50, w/end $50
Carts: $13.00

It's impossible to describe one hole at Pinehurst. With seven championship courses, Pinehurst is affectionately known as the "Golf Capital of the World." The world renowned #2 Course is considered Donald Ross's great masterpiece; here you are able to use every club in your bag. Pinehurst #7, a Rees Jones creation, is a delightful challenge and, along with #2, ranked among the best in the country.

─────────── PINEHURST ───────────

Pit, The
P.O. Box 3006 Macintire
Sta., 28374
Ph: 919-944-1600

Yards: 6455, Holes: 18
Par: 71, USGA: 69.3

Restaurant/Bar/Proshop
GF: w/day $42
Carts: Included

#8 is in the top 50 U.S. holes! (public), a par 5 elevated tee, sand ridges with fairway lateral to it, bushes and trees line it. #15 is a par 5, very tight, S-shaped downhill, very hilly, like sand dunes.

─────────── RAEFORD ───────────

Arabia GC
Rt 2 Box 151, Golf
Course Rd., 28376
Ph: 919-875-3524

Yards: 6013, Holes: 27
Par: 71, USGA: 68.8
RP: 1 day in advance

Proshop
GF: w/day $12, w/end $21
Carts: Included

Family oriented semi-private course about 30 miles from Pinehurt. Our favorite hole is the No. 2, par 3. Water from tee to green splashing over a dam demands deep concentration to avoid penalties.

─────────── RUTHERFORDTON ───────────

Cleghorn Plantation GC
Rt 4 Box 69 Cleghorn
Mill Rd., 28139
Ph: 704-286-9117

Yards: 6313, Holes: 18
Par: 72, USGA: 70.5
RP: 1 week in advance

Restaurant/Proshop
GF: w/day $8, w/end $15
Carts: $10.00 ea

Truly great George Cobb design. Rolling hills and flowing streams. Bent grass greens, laid out around Civil War battlegrounds and burial grounds. Very historic.

────────────── RUTHERFORDTON ──────────────

Meadowbrook GC
Rt. 4, Box 185-B, 28139
Ph: 704-863-2690

Yards: 6348, Holes: 18
Par: 72, USGA: 69.4

Proshop
GF: w/day $11
Carts: $14.00

Nice rolling terrain with bent grass greens, water on six holes.

────────────── SHELBY ──────────────

Challenger 3 GC
1650 N. Post Rd., 28150
Ph: 704-482-5061

Yards: 2600, Holes: 18
Par: 54

Proshop
GF: w/day $5

We think this is the south's finest par 3 golf course. We have bent greens, excellent lighting for night play. Holes up to 160 yards. Greens average 3400 square feet.

────────────── SOUTHERN PINES ──────────────

Mid Pines Resort
1010 Midland Rd., 28387
Ph: 919-692-2114

Yards: 6500, Holes: 18
Par: 72, USGA: 71.4
RP: Advised to book
well ahead

Restaurant
GF: w/day $40, w/end $40
Carts: $14.00 ea

A narrow, tree-lined course with small undulating greens. Mid Pines isn't particularly long or strenuous, but often the subtle undulations are difficult to read. The course has played host to several national championships, including the 1988 Women's Eastern Amateur. A Donald Ross original design opened for play in 1921. Toll free # 800-323-2114.

────────────── SOUTHERN PINES ──────────────

Pine Needles Resort
P.O. Box 88, 28387
Ph: 919-692-7111

Yards: 6235, Holes: 18
Par: 71
RP: Resort guests only

Restaurant/Bar/Proshop
GF: w/day $25
Carts: $20.00

As our name suggests, our course is surrounded by thousands of long leaf pines. The many changes in elevation make each hole unique. The third hole of our golf course is one of the most photographed holes. We look forward to seeing you on our challenging course!

────────────── SOUTHERN PINES ──────────────

Southern Pines CC
Country Club Dr., P.O.
Box 1180, 28387
Ph: 919-692-6551

Yards: 6250, Holes: 27
Par: 71, USGA: 70.0
RP: May be made
anytime

Restaurant/Bar/Proshop
GF: w/day $18
Carts: $12.00

Southern Pines Country Club is a classic 80 year old Donald Ross course. No 2 holes are similar, with many doglegs, hills and beautiful surroundings of dogwood and pine trees. A great test for the low handicapper and most enjoyable for the high.

────────────── SPRUCE PINE ──────────────

Grassy Creek G&CC
101 Golf Course Rd.,
28777
Ph: 704-765-7436

Yards: 6277, Holes: 18
Par: 72, USGA: 70.0
RP: Tee times are
required

Restaurant/Proshop
GF: w/day $20
Carts: $10.00 ea

Cool mountain weather, a chance to escape the heat of the lowlands. #15 is a 514 yard par 5, the drive will take a 200 yard carry over a creek to a small landing area. Then you are uphill the rest of the way to a small tucked away green.

————————————— WAYNESVILLE —————————————

Lake Junaluska GC   Yards: 2872, Holes: 9   Restaurant/Proshop
19 Golf Course Rd., 28786   Par: 35, USGA: 34.7   **GF:** w/day $8
Ph: 704-456-5777   RP: Call for tee times   **Carts:** $16.00

Lake Junaluska is a beautiful nine hole course set in the Smokey Mountains of North Carolina. The lake itself is a beautiful background for the second hole. Number six is our strongest hole requiring a very accurate drive with out of bounds on the left and taking a long iron into a small elevated green.

————————————— WAYNESVILLE —————————————

Waynesville CC Inn   Yards: 6080, Holes: 27   Restaurant/Proshop
Box 390, 28786   Par: 70   **GF:** w/day $23
Ph: 704-456-3551   RP: Tee times required   **Carts:** $12.00 ea

The 18-hole course has certain subtleties that demand a well placed shot. No matter what hole you're playing, you'll find the bent grass greens painstakingly perfect, the fairways lush and quiet and the views unparalleled.

————————————— WEST JEFFERSON —————————————

Mountain Aire GC   Yards: 3240, Holes: 9   Proshop
Rt. 3, Golf Course Rd.,   Par: 36, USGA: 68.0   **GF:** w/day $5, w/end $10
28694   RP: Call for tee time   **Carts:** $10.00
Ph: 919-877-4716

A beautiful course in an unsurpassed setting in the Blue Ridge Mountains. Spectacular views from holes 2, 4, 8 and 9. 3500 feet elevation. A second nine holes are under construction.

————————————— WHITAKERS —————————————

Hickory Meadows GC   Yards: 6440, Holes: 18   Restaurant/Proshop
Rt. 1, Box 88, 27891   Par: 72, USGA: 68.4   **GF:** w/day $6, w/end $8
Ph: 919-437-0591   RP: First come, first   **Carts:** $6.50
                         serve

The only public course in North Carolina on I-95, Exit 150. You'll find the fairways lined with tall Carolina pines. Water, sand traps, or trees come into play on every hole. Excellent greens, along with Southern hospitality, makes Hickory Meadows a must for golfers.

————————————— WILLOW SPRINGS —————————————

Hidden Valley GC   Yards: 6174, Holes: 18   Restaurant/Proshop
Rt. 2 Box 7900, 27592   Par: 72, USGA: 69.0   **GF:** w/day $8, w/end $11
Ph: 919-639-4071   RP: Taken on   **Carts:** $8.00
                           weekends only

The course is wide open on most holes on the front side, with very few sand traps. But the most treacherous thing about the course is the greens. They are small bentgrass greens with a lot of funny breaks to them. My favorite hole is a 490 yard par 5 on the back side, number 16. The second shot is over a small creek.

————————————— WINSTON-SALEM —————————————

Heather Hills GC   Yards: 3700, Holes: 18   **GF:** w/day $7, w/end $9
3801 Heathrow Dr., 27117 Par: 62, USGA: 62.0   **Carts:** $7.00
Ph: 919-788-5785

A short but tight course with well bunkered (grass) greens. Greens are bent. Located only 2 miles from shopping and business areas.

NORTH DAKOTA

Grand Forks •

• Hazen   • Bismarck
Bowman

──────────────── BISMARCK ────────────────

Riverwood | Yards: 6900, Holes: 18 | Restaurant/Proshop
Box 2063, 58501 | Par: 72, USGA: 69.8 | **GF:** w/day $9
Ph: 701-223-9915 | RP: 1 day in advance | **Carts:** $13.00

Riverwood is a tree lined golf course. The 60 foot cottonwood trees also create an ideal habitat for much wildlife: deer, wild turkey, wild ducks. So while you enjoy your round of golf you can also enjoy the wildlife.

──────────────── BOWMAN ────────────────

Sweetwater GC | Yards: 2985, Holes: 9 | Bar/Proshop
P.O. Box 1182, Highway | Par: 36, USGA: 64.8 | **GF:** w/day $8
85 S, 58623 | | **Carts:** $10.00
Ph: 701-523-5800

This short but difficult par nine golf course features water hazards on six of the nine holes. The conservative golfer who concentrates on shot placement will walk away with bragging rights while the ego busting type of golfer might very well hang his head after the round is completed.

──────────────── GRAND FORKS ────────────────

Ray Richards GC | Yards: 3165, Holes: 9 | Proshop
De Mers W, Box 8275 | Par: 36, USGA: 34.6 | **GF:** w/day $5, w/end $5
Univ. Sta., 58202 | | **Carts:** $6.50
Ph: 701-777-4340

A young course with a bright future. Located next to the University of North Dakota within the city of Grand Forks. Our favorite hole is the 9th, a par 4 with water on the left and an elevated green protected by a large bunker in the front.

──────────────── HAZEN ────────────────

Hazen GC | Yards: 2664, Holes: 9 | Restaurant/Bar/Proshop
Highway 200, east ½ | Par: 35, USGA: 64.0 | **GF:** w/day $6, w/end $8
mile, 58545 | | **Carts:** $7.50
Ph: 701-748-2011

The most challenging hole is the 5th, a medium to long par 3, playing from 180 to 230 yards. With out of bounds right, trees left, water in front, and an elevated green, it has often been called "the shortest par 5 in North Dakota."

Findlay •
Clyde • •Sandusky • Warren
Upper Sandusky •Hinckley
• •Caledonia
Van Wert • Dellroy •
Canton

OHIO

•Middletown
•Cincinnati

BOARDMAN

Mill Creek Park GC
West Golf Dr., 44512
Ph: 216-740-7112

Yards: 6302, Holes: 36
Par: 70, USGA: 70.8
RP: Weekends &
holidays only

Proshop

The par 70 North Course is played on gently rolling terrain through majestic trees. The South Course, also par 70, is laid out on nearly level land with tree lined fairways. Numerous sand bunkers and occasional creeks on both courses challenge one's golfing skills.

CALEDONIA

Whetstone GC
5211 Marion Mt. Gilead
Rd., 43314
Ph: 614-389-4343

Yards: 6371, Holes: 18
Par: 72, USGA: 69.5
RP: Weekends

Restaurant/Bar/Proshop
GF: w/day $10
Carts: $14.00

Whetstone offers a challenge to all golfers with water, sand and tight greens in a rural country setting.

CANTON

Tam O'Shanter GC PC
5055 Hills and Dales Rd.
NW, 44708
Ph: 800-462-9964

Yards: 6249, Holes: 36
Par: 70, USGA: 107
RP: Anytime with
major credit card

Restaurant/Bar/Proshop
GF: w/day $18, w/end $20
Carts: $18.00

Designed in the 1920's by a disciple of Donald Ross, both Tam O'Shanter courses are traditional layouts shaped by glaciers, not bulldozers. Rolling terrain, mature trees, lush fairways, wall-to-wall irrigation; an atmosphere reminiscent of a first-class private club. Five minutes from Pro football Hall of Fame.

CORTLAND

Tamer Win G&CC
2940 Niles Cortland Rd.
N.E., 44410
Ph: 216-637-2881

Yards: 6260, Holes: 18
Par: 71, USGA: 68.8
RP: W/end needed,
Call for daily.

Restaurant/Proshop
GF: w/day $13, w/end $14
Carts: $15.00

A family owned golf course, we take pride in our condition of the course. It will challenge you and give you a great feel of the out doors.

────────────────── CLYDE ──────────────────

Green Hills GC Yards: 5800, Holes: 27 Restaurant/Bar/Proshop
1959 S. Main St., 43410 Par: 70, USGA: 65.6 **GF:** w/day $10
Ph: 419-547-9996 RP: 1 week in advance **Carts:** $15.00

This 18 hole golf course is one you will never tire of playing. Each hole is a totally different hole, with hills, trees, traps, lakes, and creeks. A course you will want to play again and again.

────────────────── CONCORD ──────────────────

Quail Hollow GC Holes: 18 Restaurant/Bar/Proshop
11080 Concord- Par: 72, USGA: 71.6 **GF:** w/day $33, w/end $38
Hambden Rd., 44077 **Carts:** $12.69 ea
Ph: 216-352-6201

In the warmer months, enjoy the challenging 18-hole, par 72 golf course designed and planned by Bruce Devlin and Robert Von Hagge. Also a driving range and putting green.

────────────────── DELLROY ──────────────────

Atwood Resort GC Yards: 6057, Holes: 18 Restaurant
2650 Lodge Rd., 44620 Par: 70, USGA: 68.0 **GF:** w/day $12, w/end $13
Ph: 216-735-2630 RP: Tee times 1 year **Carts:** $19.00
  in advance

The 18-hole golf course is challenging, playable and always meticulously maintained. The lighted par-three is in top shape for quick rounds or casual family golf and to polish your game, a practice range.

────────────────── FINDLAY ──────────────────

Findlay Hillcrest GC Yards: 6981, Holes: 18 Restaurant/Bar/Proshop
800 W. Bigelow, 45840 Par: 72, USGA: 69.4 **GF:** w/day $11, w/end $12
Ph: 419-423-7211 **Carts:** $19.00

Plenty of length. The front nine is fairly tight. Lots of trees. Back is more open but longer than the front. Two lakes on each nine. Favorite hole #16. You hit through a chute of large oak trees out of bounds left.

────────────────── HINCKLEY ──────────────────

Hinckley Hills GC Yards: 6248, Holes: 18 Restaurant/Bar/Proshop
300 State Rd., 44233 Par: 72, USGA: 70.9 **GF:** w/day $16
Ph: 216-278-4861 RP: Weekends **Carts:** $16.00

This scenic 18 holes of golf offers the ultimate in golf. With its long, rolling and challenge it offers a beautiful view of the area. One of the nicest in our area.

────────────────── HINCKLEY ──────────────────

Pine Hills GC Yards: 6300, Holes: 18 Restaurant/Bar/Proshop
433 W. 130th St., 44233 Par: 72 **GF:** w/day $15
Ph: 216-225-4477 RP: Necessary on **Carts:** $15.00
  weekends

Pine Hills is hilly, filled with traps, trees and doglegs, and water, not to mention slick greens. It has a par of 72, slope rating 124. It plays tough, but it's fair. Gather your courage and play—you may even spot one of Hinckley's famous buzzards.

Plan ahead! Reserve tee time well in advance, and while you're doing so, confirm rates and services.

─────────── KINGS ISLAND ───────────

Jack Nicklaus Sports Center
3565 Kings Mill Rd., 45034
Ph: 513-398-5200

Yards: 6250, Holes: 18
Par: 71, USGA: 69.6
RP: Seven days in advance

Restaurant/Bar/Proshop
GF: w/day $21, w/end $27
Carts: $8.75

The most challenging hole on our course is the par 5 18th, the "Grizzly". Don't let the length of 546 yards scare you, there's also out of bounds left and a creek down the right. The green is well guarded by a lake and 3 sand traps. To hit this green in two requires a second shot of 250 yards over water to a small green.

─────────── MEDINA ───────────

Bunker Hill GC
3060 Pearl Rd., 44256
Ph: 216-722-4174

Yards: 5805, Holes: 18
Par: 70, USGA: 67.1
RP: Tee times weekends & holidays

Bar/Proshop
GF: w/day $14, w/end $17
Carts: $17.00

Bunker Hill is the oldest and most beautiful course in Medina County, Ohio. Featuring rolling hills, elevated tees and greens on several holes, this is a testy and scenic joy for most any level of golfer. Our favorite hole is #18. Only 379 yards but it runs down a tree lined fairway, crosses two creeks to a large elevated green.

─────────── MIDDLETOWN ───────────

Weatherwax
5401 Mosiman, 45042
Ph: 513-425-7886

Yards: 7174, Holes: 36
Par: 72, USGA: 71.0
RP: Weekends & holidays

Restaurant/Bar
GF: w/day $10
Carts: $16.00

4 sets of 9 holes, making 6 combinations possible for your play. Water runs along side of most holes, hills and big mature woods line courses. 2 long ones, wider open, more parallel and other 2 shorter with lots of sand and tighter.

─────────── SANDUSKY ───────────

Woussickett GC
6311 Mason Rd., 44870
Ph: 419-359-1141

Yards: 5963, Holes: 18
Par: 70, USGA: 67.0
RP: Daily tee times

Restaurant/Bar/Proshop
GF: w/day $10
Carts: $15.00

The 18th hole is one of the most scenic and demanding holes in the area. The creek splits the fairway that runs in front of this large double green with trees on both sides. A beautiful view from the clubhouse.

─────────── UPPER SANDUSKY ───────────

Lincoln Hills GC
5377 U.S. 30, 43351
Ph: 419-294-3037

Yards: 3084, Holes: 9
Par: 36, USGA: 68.3

Restaurant/Bar/Proshop
GF: w/day $9
Carts: $14.00

Postage stamp greens and hilly terrain make Lincoln Hills unique in Northwest Ohio.

─────────── VAN WERT ───────────

The Woods GC
12083 SR 127 S, 45891
Ph: 419-238-0441

Yards: 6775, Holes: 18
Par: 72, USGA: 69.5
RP: Weekends & holidays

Restaurant/Bar/Proshop
GF: w/day $9, w/end $10
Carts: $14.00

Water hazards on 10 of the 18 holes provide some rough going. #4 is a toughy, par 3 160 yards almost completely over water! #11 is a sharp dogleg par 4 that should really keep you on your toes.

OKLAHOMA

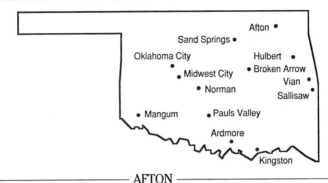

--------------------------- AFTON ---------------------------

Shangri-La GC
Rte 3, Highway 125, 74331
Ph: 918-257-4204

Yards: 6500, Holes: 18
Par: 72, USGA: 70.3
RP: In advance

GF: w/day $35
Carts: Included

36 holes of challenging golf with lush fairways, polished bent-grass greens and tree-studded roughs in a one-of-a-kind natural landscape. This home course of touring pro Bruce Lietzke includes a practice tee and driving range, a putting green.

--------------------------- ARDMORE ---------------------------

Ardmore Muni GC
3905 N. Commerce, P.O.
Box 249, 73402
Ph: 405-223-4260

Yards: 6367, Holes: 18
Par: 70, USGA: 68.0
RP: 1 day in advance
for weekends

Restaurant/Proshop
GF: w/day $7
Carts: $13.00

The golf course meanders through rolling hills, and pine trees with Lake Meadow bordering several holes on each nine. The short but challenging layout provides fun for all levels of ability.

--------------------------- BROKEN ARROW ---------------------------

Forest Ridge GC
7501 E. Kenosha, 74014
Ph: 918-357-2787

Yards: 7069, Holes: 18
Par: 71, USGA: 74.0
RP: 7 days with card,
else 4 days

Restaurant/Bar/Proshop
GF: w/day $50
Carts: Included

Each hole has it's own individual personality and playing characteristics. The signature hole is the sixteenth which typifies the uniqueness and beauty of Forest Ridge. The drive from elevated tees must carry a native area with a creek to the fairway landing area. The approach shot to the green must carry another creek and native area. The green which is nestled in a grove of trees is surrounded by bunkers and grass depressions.

--------------------------- HULBERT ---------------------------

Sequoyah State Park GC
Western Hills Rt 1-Box 201, 74441

Yards: 5860, Holes: 18
Par: 70

GF: w/day $7
Carts: $13.00

#9 is our favorite hole. It looks easy. Pine trees line both sides of the fairway; it dogleg's to the right. There is an open slot in trees on right side, encouraging an attempt to cut dogleg but, very difficult to make it back into fairway. Results are a hard shot from underneath trees.

———————————————— KINGSTON ————————————————

Lake Texoma GC   Yards: 6128, Holes: 18   Restaurant/Bar/Proshop
5 miles east of   Par: 71, USGA: 67.8   **GF:** w/day $7
Kingston, 73439   **Carts:** $13.00
Ph: 405-564-3333

Low undulating fairways with large bent grass greens, long open front nine and shorter tight back nine. #12, 475 yard par 5, 230 yards to 90 degree dog leg right between tree lines, 30 yard fairway, 225 yards to green with tree hazard to left and trees in center fairway 80 yards from green, sand trap right and left front of green.

———————————————— MANGUM ————————————————

Mangum Muni GC   Yards: 5558, Holes: 9   Proshop
West of Intersect Hwy   Par: 70, USGA: 32.0   **GF:** w/day $5, w/end $6
9-Hwy 34, 73554   **Carts:** $6.00
Ph: 405-782-3676

One of the best bent grass greens in the State of Oklahoma. Irrigated fairways and sand traps on all par 3's. Driving range and tee markers that show the layout of the hole with hazards. Very unusual to catch a day when the wind doesn't blow, makes for an interesting game on any given day.

———————————————— MIDWEST CITY ————————————————

John Conrad GC   Yards: 6854, Holes: 18   Restaurant/Proshop
711 S. Douglas Blvd.,   Par: 36, USGA: 70.1   **GF:** w/day $9
73130   RP: 24 hrs. weekday-7   **Carts:** $13.91
Ph: 405-732-2209   day weekend

Heavily treed, winding fairways with particularly demanding par threes. The last four holes, 15, 16, 17 and 18, provides a challenge to the best of players.

———————————————— MIDWEST CITY ————————————————

Midwest City GC   Yards: 1937, Holes: 9   Bar/Proshop
3210 Belaire Dr., 73110   Par: 30, USGA: 29.0   **GF:** w/day $4
Ph: 405-732-9021   **Carts:** $6.42

Midwest City Golf Club has the distinction of being the only executive course in the state of Oklahoma. Our scenic course offers fairways lined with a variety of beautiful trees. With a par of thirty, the course has 6 par threes and 3 par fours.

———————————————— NORMAN ————————————————

Univ. of Oklahoma GC   Yards: 6251, Holes: 18   Restaurant/Proshop
One Par Dr., 73019   Par: 72, USGA: 69.0   **GF:** w/day $9
Ph: 405-325-6716   RP: Required on   **Carts:** $14.00
    weekends

A typical Maxwell design with small greens and rolling fairways. "Dog Out" Creek provides an extra challenge on 10 holes. Front nine open and long, back nine short and tight.

———————————————— NORMAN ————————————————

Westwood Park GC   Yards: 6015, Holes: 18   Restaurant/Bar/Proshop
2400 Westport Dr., 73069   Par: 70, USGA: 66.4   **GF:** w/day $10
Ph: 405-321-0433   RP: Weekends &   **Carts:** $15.00
    holidays

My favorite hole is the 14th a short par 4 demanding an accurate tee shot, hookers go home!, and a delicate approach to a postage stamp unforgiving green.

154 Oklahoma

Earlywine Park GC Yards: 6295, Holes: 18 Restaurant/Proshop
115 & So. Portland, P.O. Par: 71, USGA: 69.1 **GF:** w/day $10
Box 2086, 73156 RP: Recommended **Carts:** $15.00
Ph: 405-691-1727

Cohansy bent grass. The first putting surface presented by Jim Broughton, C.G.C.S. From the first hole past Howard's tree to the sun-setting backdrop of the eighteenth green, golfers of all levels enjoy the game of golf.

Lake Hefner GC Yards: 6305, Holes: 18 Restaurant/Proshop
4491 S. Lake Hefner Dr., Par: 70, USGA: 67.0 **GF:** w/day $10, w/end $10
73132 RP: Weekends-1 week; **Carts:** $15.00
Ph: 405-843-1565 else 1 day

South course is diverse with doglegs, rolling terrain and ending with one of the greatest finishing holes. North course places a premium on the shot into the green as well as a bonus of a view of Lake Hefner throughout your round.

Pauls Valley GC Yards: 3177, Holes: 9 Proshop
Airport Rd.. P.O. Box Par: 36, USGA: 68.5 **GF:** w/day $6, w/end $8
578, 73035 **Carts:** $6.00
Ph: 405-238-7462

We're proud to offer golfers a clean, quiet "Country" golf course. Nothing fancy— just small town friendliness. Greens small and elevated, bent grass.

Shadow Creek CC Yards: 5655, Holes: 18 Proshop
27 Club View, 74955 Par: 71 **GF:** w/day $8, w/end $10
Ph: 918-775-6997 **Carts:** $14.00

The course lays flat with 2 meandering creeks, beautifully green with lots of trees. Distance is no great accomplishment, but accuracy and ball control is a must for good scores. All holes are different and very interesting. Greens are probably the best in 3 states.

Sand Springs GC Yards: 6113, Holes: 18 Restaurant/Proshop
1801 N. McKinley, 74063 Par: 71, USGA: 66.8 **GF:** w/day $7, w/end $8
Ph: 918-245-7551 RP: Weekends & **Carts:** $14.00
holidays

Narrow fairways, doglegs, and uphill or downhill lies make the course play longer than the card reads. The breathtaking view of the Tulsa skyline from the 185 foot drop-off of the par 3 12th tee will leave a lasting impression in any golfers memory and bring them back to play this course many times.

East Lake Hill Golf & Yards: 7444, Holes: 18 Restaurant/Bar/Proshop
CC Par: 72, USGA: 71.1 **GF:** w/day $10, w/end $12
Rt 1-Box 182, Hwy 82-N, **Carts:** $14.00
74962
Ph: 918-773-8436

You warm up on a relatively open front nine, but don't become too over confident #6 will cause you trouble if not long off the tee. #18 if played well you should, your score should reflect you are playing good golf.

OREGON

Gerhart
Gleneden Beach Portland Wilsonville
Waldport McMinnville Weiches
Newport Warm Springs
Neskowin Redmond
Eugene Sunriver
Springfield Blue River
Creswell Cottage Grove

Medford
Gold Hill Klamath Falls

BLACK BUTTE RANCH

Lodge at Black Butte Ranch-Glaze 97759
Ph: 503-595-6689

Yards: 6600, Holes: 36
Par: 72, USGA: 68.0
RP: Call for starting time

GF: w/day $28
Carts: $10.00

Golfers love it here—no outside events are held on the two 18 hole course, Big Meadow and Glaze Meadow. They're gently rolling as they zigzag through tall pines, and aspen, and across water. You'll have ample time to gaze upward for a glimpse of geese in flight and some awesome views of the Sisters.

BLUE RIVER

Tokatee GC 97413
Ph: 503-882-3220

Yards: 6817, Holes: 18
Par: 72, USGA: 69.7
RP: 2 weeks in advance

Restaurant/Bar/Proshop
GF: w/day $22
Carts: $18.00

The course blends with area, looks like nature made it. Offers a great view of the 3 Sisters in the Cascades. Very secluded, with 5 lakes and no parallel holes. Firs line the fairways.

COTTAGE GROVE

Hidden Valley GC
775 N. River Rd., 97424
Ph: 503-942-3046

Yards: 5644, Holes: 9
Par: 70

Restaurant/Bar/Proshop
GF: w/day $7
Carts: $7.00

Tucked away in the northwest hills of Cottage Grove, you'll find a delightful old fashioned Scottish style golf course with oak lined fairways.

CRESWELL

Emerald Valley GC
83293 Dale Kuni Rd., 97426
Ph: 503-484-6354

Yards: 6873, Holes: 18
Par: 72, USGA: 71.4
RP: 1 week in advance

Restaurant/Bar/Proshop
GF: w/day $18, w/end $20
Carts: $15.00

Setting just 10 miles south of Eugene just off Interstate 5 along the coast fork of the Willamette River, Emerald Valley is a championship golf course that is always in excellent condition. Year-round golf, driving range, RV park, and residential homes all at Emerald Valley.

─────────────── GEARHART ───────────────

Gearhart GL
N. Marion, POB 2758,
97138
Ph: 503-738-3538

Yards: 6089, Holes: 18
Par: 72, USGA: 68.5

Restaurant/Bar
GF: w/day $20, w/end $20
Carts: $20.00

Gearhart Golf Links, oldest golf course in Oregon or Washington. Established 1892, located by the ocean 12 miles south of Astoria which is the oldest settlement in Oregon. Originally 9 holes, extended to 18 holes in 1913.

─────────────── GLENEDEN BEACH ───────────────

Salishan Lodge GL
Hwy. 101, 97388
Ph: 503-764-3632

Yards: 6439, Holes: 18
Par: 72, USGA: 71.5
RP: 2 weeks in advance

Restaurant
GF: w/day $36, w/end $36
Carts: $26.00

Players who prefer to carry their clubs love to play here, carts aren't mandatory. Number 13, a 402 yard par 4, will take a straight drive between the troublesome dunes on both right and left. The green is guarded by a gargantuan H-shaped trap, and should you hook it, you'll be in Siletz Bay with the seals.

─────────────── GOLD HILL ───────────────

Laurel Hill GC
9450 Old Stage Rd., P.O.
Box 167, 97525
Ph: 503-855-7965

Yards: 1905, Holes: 9
Par: 31
RP: Recommended on
weekends

Restaurant/Bar/Proshop
GF: w/day $4, w/end $5

The course meanders through a dense forest of oak, fir, and madrone trees, some of them several hundred years old. The dogleg par-fours and narrow (avg. 40 yards) fairways make this a highly challenging irons course despite its modest length.

─────────────── KLAMATH FALLS ───────────────

Round Lake GC
4000 Round Lake Rd.,
97601
Ph: 503-884-2520

Yards: 1554, Holes: 9
Par: 29

GF: w/day $5

We also have a mobile home park and welcome R.V.'s. Complete hook-up and showers available. Reduced golf rates and swimming pool for tenants only.

─────────────── MEDFORD ───────────────

Cedar Links GC
3155 Cedar Links Dr.,
97504
Ph: 503-773-4373

Yards: 5893, Holes: 18
Par: 70, USGA: 67.7
RP: 1 week in advance

Restaurant/Bar/Proshop
GF: w/day $16, w/end $17
Carts: $18.00

The front nine at Cedar Links is rolling with four water hazards and some smaller greens with breaking putts. From the back nine, which is newer, you have a beautiful view of the Rogue Valley, with larger less contoured greens. Number 7 hole is the toughest par 4 in southern Oregon.

─────────────── NESKOWIN ───────────────

Neskowin Beach GC
#1 Hawk Ave., P.O. Box
839, 97149
Ph: 503-392-3377

Yards: 2616, Holes: 9
Par: 35, USGA: 65.3
RP: Recommended

Restaurant/Bar/Proshop
GF: w/day $8
Carts: $8.00

Very relaxing golf course as it is very flat but built on lush turf with two streams wandering through most holes. Small but beautiful greens and many trees add to difficulty. Number 7 hole will bring you back!

─────────────── NEWPORT ───────────────

Agate Beach GC | Yards: 3002, Holes: 9 | Restaurant/Bar/Proshop
4100 N Coast Hwy., 97365 Par: 36, USGA: 65.8 | **GF:** w/day $16
Ph: 503-265-7331 | **Carts:** $16.00

Beautiful, well-kept golf course, somewhat rolling but easy to walk. Enjoyable and relaxing. Influenced by the breezes off the Pacific Ocean but always in great shape with manicured greens which putt moderately and very true. Trees are a major factor on the last five holes.

─────────────── PORTLAND ───────────────

Eastmoreland GC | Yards: 6508, Holes: 18 | Restaurant/Bar/Proshop
2425 SE Bybee Blvd., | Par: 72, USGA: 69.8 | **GF:** w/day $11, w/end $13
97202 | RP: 6 days in advance | **Carts:** $18.00
Ph: 503-775-2900

A level course, very green and beautiful with many flowers around every hole. Wide creek winds through a couple of times. #13 is a long par 5 with canyon to go over.

─────────────── REDMOND ───────────────

Juniper GC | Yards: 6525, Holes: 18 | Restaurant/Bar/Proshop
139 S. E. Sisters Ave., | Par: 72, USGA: 69.8 | **GF:** w/day $18
97756 | RP: Call for tee times | **Carts:** $15.00
Ph: 503-548-3121

Course wanders through lava rocks and juniper trees to give one a true central Oregon high desert experience. Small greens, four ponds, and difficult roughs make for a fine challenge of golf.

─────────────── SPRINGFIELD ───────────────

McKenzie River GC | Yards: 2800, Holes: 9 | Bar/Proshop
41723 Madrone, 97478 | Par: 35, USGA: 64.8 | **GF:** w/day $8
Ph: 503-896-3454 | RP: 1 week out | **Carts:** $8.00

Immaculately groomed course that is nestled right on the beautiful McKenzie River. Parts of five holes nudge right along the river. The par 3 uphill 9th at 137 yards requires accuracy as a huge maple guards the left, with a creek and steep bank in front.

─────────────── SUNRIVER ───────────────

Sunriver Lodge & | Yards: 6880, Holes: 18 | Restaurant/Bar/Proshop
Resort | Par: 72, USGA: 70.2 | **GF:** w/day $50, w/end $50
P.O. Box 3609, 97707 | RP: 7 day in advance | **Carts:** $25.00
Ph: 503-593-1221

The South Course offers wonderful views of Mt. Bachelor, particularly the 16th hole which is a 192 yard par-3 playing directly toward the mountain. Designed by Robert Trent Jones, II, the North Course offers golfers of any caliber a fun and challenging golf experience. The course is the site of the annual Sunriver Oregon Open and was chosen by Golf Digest as one of the top 25 resort courses in the nation.

─────────────── WALDPORT ───────────────

Crestview Hills GC | Yards: 2800, Holes: 9 | Restaurant/Proshop
1680 Crestline Dr., 97394 | Par: 36 | **GF:** w/day $6
Ph: 503-563-3020 | | **Carts:** $6.00

This beautiful hilltop golf course offers rolling hills and the sound of the ocean. Due to our location of 1.5 miles from the ocean, you can enjoy a view of the ocean from the 8th fairway yet escape the wind and fog.

────────────── WARM SPRINGS ──────────────

Kah-Nee-Ta Resort   Yards: 6288, Holes: 18   Restaurant/Proshop
P.O. Box K, 97761   Par: 72, USGA: 69.7   **GF:** w/day $21
Ph: 503-553-1112   RP: 2 week notice   **Carts:** $20.00

Kah-Nee-Ta offers exciting adventures on a golf course, set upon an ancient natural Indian reservation. The golfer has a chance to test his or her skills by attempting to cross the Warm Springs River on the 17th hole. Kah-Nee-Ta also challenges the golfer's putting skills on the longest greens in the Pacific Northwest.

────────────── WEICHES ──────────────

Rippling River GC   Holes: 27   Restaurant/Bar/Proshop
68010 E. Fairway Ave.,   Par: 72, USGA: 70.0   **GF:** w/day $22, w/end $25
97067 Ph: 503-622-3151   **Carts:** $20.00

Rippling River Resort is located 60 miles east of Portland at the foot of Mt. Hood. We have 27 holes of golf that play through big fir trees and along the Salmon River. We're nestled in a big valley. The #8 hole West is ranked as one of the most difficult par 4s in Oregon.

────────────── WILSONVILLE ──────────────

Charbonneau GC   Yards: 2200, Holes: 27   Restaurant/Bar/Proshop
32020 Charbonneau Dr.,   Par: 31, USGA: 59.3   **GF:** w/day $12, w/end $14
97070   **Carts:** $15.00
Ph: 503-694-1246

This course is in the executive class, even though it has difficult par 3's, 150-250 yards scoring par 4's for the long hitters (good driving targets) a strong test for low handicap players (but high handicap players can play 18 holes in 3 hours). A very good design.

PENNSYLVANIA

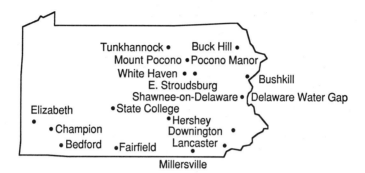

Tunkhannock •   Buck Hill •
Mount Pocono • Pocono Manor
White Haven • •
E. Stroudsburg   Bushkill
Shawnee-on-Delaware • Delaware Water Gap
Elizabeth   •State College
•   •Hershey
• Champion   Downington •
• Bedford •Fairfield Lancaster •
Millersville

---------------------------- BEDFORD ----------------------------

Bedford Springs Hotel   Yards: 7000, Holes: 18   Restaurant
GC   Par: 74
15522
Ph: 814-623-6121

7000 yards of golf course! Lost of problems with water as a creek meanders through the course, and there's also a pond. Long hitters have the advantage until you get to the bunkers guarding the greens.

---------------------------- BUCK HILL ----------------------------

Buck Hill GC   Holes: 27   Restaurant/Bar/Proshop
18323
Ph: 717-595-7441

The brooks and woodlands make this one of the most scenic courses imaginable. Postage-stamp greens, narrow fairways, seven holes with water coming into play, and each hole's personality demanding thought on the part of the player, makes for exciting golf.

---------------------------- BUSHKILL ----------------------------

Fernwood GC   Yards: 6208, Holes: 18   Restaurant/Bar/Proshop
PO Box 447, 18324   Par: 72
Ph: 717-588-6661

On our 600 yard sixth hole, you'll need a cannon, but on the next twelve holes you'll need all your golfing finesse. Two lakes and many streams wind through the back nine holes. The tenth hole doglegs to the left; crosses Fawn Lake to a small terraced green 135 yards up the mountain.

---------------------------- CHAMPION ----------------------------

Seven Springs   Yards: 6360, Holes: 18   Restaurant/Bar/Proshop
Mountain Resort   Par: 71, USGA: 69.5   **GF:** w/day $35, w/end $36
RD. 1, 15622   RP: Required   **Carts:** $12.72
Ph: 814-352-7777

The course sits amid breathtaking scenery of the Laurel Highland Mountains of Western Pennsylvania. While the front nine offers the opportunity to score well, the back nine features rolling hills elevated tees and more yardage. . . beware of #11!

──────────────── DELAWARE WATER GAP ────────────────

Water Gap CC Yards: 6186, Holes: 18 Restaurant/Bar/Proshop
Mountain Rd., P.O. Box Par: 72, USGA: 68.7 **GF:** w/day $16, w/end $20
188, 18327 RP: 5 days in advance **Carts:** $28.00
Ph: 717-476-0200

The championship layout offers a rare challenge to the golfer. . .capitalizing on the natural features of some of the Pocono's most picturesque terrain to present a truly challenging course. The course today is the same well-groomed test that confronted golf greats, Walter Hagen and Johnny Farrell during the Golden Era of Sports.

──────────────── DOWNINGTON ────────────────

Downingtown CC Yards: 6585, Holes: 18 Restaurant/Bar/Proshop
19335 Par: 72, USGA: 69.6
Ph: 215-269-2000

You can really let 'er fly on #11, 425 yards, but be careful of the bunkers to the right of the fairway and guarding the green, not to mention the out of bounds at the rear of the green!

──────────────── EAST STROUDSBURG ────────────────

Skytop GC Yards: 6220, Holes: 18 Restaurant/Bar
RTE 390, 18357 USGA: 69.1 **GF:** w/day $20
Ph: 717-595-7401 **Carts:** $20.00

The course is relatively flat, water in play on two hole, and the greens are small. #18 has narrow landing area, with water coming in play before an elevated green.

──────────────── ELIZABETH ────────────────

Butler's GC Yards: 6398, Holes: 27 Restaurant/Bar/Proshop
800 Rock Run Rd., 15037 Par: 72, USGA: 69.2 **GF:** w/day $15, w/end $17
Ph: 412-751-9121 RP: Reserved times on **Carts:** $9.00
18 hole crse

Butler's is one of the oldest public courses in western Pennsylvania. It is challenging yet still fun to play. Probably the most scenic hole is #13. From it's elevated tee there is an outstanding view of the Youghiogheny River and valley.

──────────────── FAIRFIELD ────────────────

Carrol Valley GC Yards: 6425, Holes: 36 Restaurant/Bar/Proshop
Rt 116, Sanders Rd., P.O. Par: 71, USGA: 70.4 **GF:** w/day $15, w/end $19
Box T, 17320 RP: Mandatory, 7 days **Carts:** $19.00
Ph: 717-642-8211 in advance

Eight holes have water hazards to cross which can cause extreme trouble. Number 4 is a par 5 measuring 580 yards. The area is very scenic with mountain ranges surrounding the golf course. The back nine is the more demanding to shoot par due to being par 35.

──────────────── HERSHEY ────────────────

Hershey CC Yards: 6480, Holes: 36 Restaurant
1000 E. Derry Rd., 17033 Par: 73, USGA: 71.7 **GF:** w/day $50
Ph: 717-533-2360 RP: Must be guest of **Carts:** $13.50 ea
Hershey Hotel

Play a game of golf on the historic West Course which dates back to 1930, for years listed as one of America's top 100 courses, or the new East Course which is dotted with three man-made lakes and 100 traps.

──────────── HERSHEY ────────────

Hershey Parkview Yards: 6146, Holes: 18 Restaurant/Bar/Proshop
600 West Derry Rd., Par: 71, USGA: 68.6 **GF:** w/day $13, w/end $16
17033 RP: Times taken on **Carts:** $9.50 ea.
Ph: 717-534-3450 weekends

*There are only 2 parallel holes here and 1/2 elevated tees. Course is pretty hilly
with lots of obstacles and hazards: meandering creek runs through. There are
many blind shots and the fairways are narrow and lined with dogwood, oak and
pines.*

──────────── LANCASTER ────────────

Sheraton Host Golf Yards: 6859, Holes: 27 Restaurant/Bar/Proshop
Resort Par: 72 **GF:** w/day $28, w/end $28
2300 Lincoln Hwy. E., **Carts:** $23.00
17602
Ph: 717-397-7756

*Gently rolling slopes with water holes surrounded by weeping willow trees. The
course's most famous aspects are the challenging water holes with mature willow trees and surrounding rolling countryside.*

──────────── MILLERSVILLE ────────────

Crossgate CC Yards: 6200, Holes: 18 Restaurant/Bar/Proshop
17551 Par: 70
Ph: 717-872-7415

*The course is under development with a residential community. When com-
pleted, there will be 6 holes along the creek. The 11th. tee is perched to make
you hope you've held up so you can enjoy the view. This course will ensure that
you will use every club in your bag.*

──────────── MOUNT POCONO ────────────

Mount Airy/Pocono Yards: 7200, Holes: 18 Restaurant/Bar/Proshop
Garden Par: 72
18344
Ph: 717-839-8811

*The name to the golf Course is "18 Best." The original design came from Sports
Illustrated's 18 best holes some years ago. Water comes into play on 10 holes and
there are 95 sandtraps to keep the game interesting. The high handicapper can
score decently if he uses his head.*

──────────── POCONO MANOR ────────────

Pocono Manor GC Yards: 6675, Holes: 36 Restaurant/Bar/Proshop
18349 Par: 72, USGA: 71.0
Ph: 717-839-7111

*With two championship courses to conquer, you can spend a day playing golf
and never play the same hole twice. The West Course has plenty of length and if
you're a long hitter you can really cut loose!*

──────────── SHAWNEE-ON-DELAWARE ────────────

Shawnee Inn CC Yards: 6636, Holes: 27 Restaurant/Bar
18356 Par: 72, USGA: 72.4 **GF:** w/day $20, w/end $40
Ph: 717-421-1500 RP: 7 days in advance **Carts:** $15.00

*#7 of the blue nine is a 152 yard par 3 stretch—you tee off from the island to a
green across the river. As you try to stay clear of the water and bunkers, bear in
mind that it was here that many avid golfers chipped and probably prayed to
carry the same river.*

─────────── STATE COLLEGE ───────────

Toftrees Lodge GC
1 Country Club Ln.,
16803
Ph: 814-238-7600

Yards: 7018, Holes: 18
Par: 72, USGA: 71.6

Restaurant
GF: w/day $48, w/end $54
Carts: Included

Enjoy pampered greens and perfectly manicured bent-grass fairways that gently weave through magnificently wooded hillsides. The course stretches a challenging 7,018 yards from back tees. Site of the annual Pennsylvania PGA Golf Tournament, Toftrees receives raves from professionals across the country.

─────────── TUNKHANNOCK ───────────

Shadow Brook GC
RTE. 6, 18657
Ph: 717-836-2151

Yards: 6104, Holes: 18
Par: 72

Restaurant/Bar/Proshop

Out of bounds, creek and ponds, not to mention trees and bunkers, are sure to make careful shotmaking the most important aspect of your round. #7 540 yard dogleg with a pond looming over the green is a terrific hole.

─────────── WHITE HAVEN ───────────

Mountain Laurel GC
I-80 At PA Turnpike NE
Ext., 18661
Ph: 717-443-7424

Yards: 6122, Holes: 18
Par: 72, USGA: 69.3

Restaurant/Bar/Proshop

On our course you will tackle 5 man-made lakes and a unique island green.

RHODE ISLAND

Cranston
•
Harmony

Davisville •

• Wyoming

CRANSTON

Cranston CC   Yards: 6710, Holes: 18   Restaurant/Bar/Proshop
69 Burlingame Rd., 02921   Par: 72, USGA: 71.4   **GF:** w/day $14, w/end $18
Ph: 401-826-1683   RP: Recommended   **Carts:** $18.00

Each hole is challenging in a different way. You will use every club in your bag. The greens are large and kept in excellent condition. The country location is home to many kinds of wildlife and wildflowers. It is really beautiful.

DAVISVILLE

North Kingstown Muni   Yards: 3196, Holes: 18   Restaurant/Bar/Proshop
GC   Par: 70, USGA: 67.4   **GF:** w/day $12, w/end $15
Bldg. D.S. 69, 02854   RP: First come, first   **Carts:** $16.00
Ph: 401-294-4051   served

This scenic former military course is fun to play. The course is not long, includes 5 par 3s, but is a good test of golf. The ever present wind and the tough back nine down by Narragansett Bay make this course one of the most scenic public courses in the state.

HARMONY

Melody Hill CC   Yards: 6185, Holes: 18   Restaurant/Bar/Proshop
off Sawmill Rd., P.O. Box   Par: 71, USGA: 69.0   **GF:** w/day $8, w/end $9
1171, 02829   **Carts:** $9.00
Ph: 401-949-9851

Course is laid out for the average golfer. You cannot take out your driver on all of the long holes. A placement course. Back 9 all doglegs but 2 short holes.

WYOMING

Meadow Brook GC   Yards: 6075, Holes: 18   Proshop
Rte. 138, 02898   Par: 71   **GF:** w/day $12, w/end $15
Ph: 401-539-8491   **Carts:** $15.00

Most of the course winds through large white pine and oak woods. The 18th hole is a 140 yard par 3 over a pond and the small green has sand traps on either side. A well placed tee shot makes this an easy hole but it causes many to have a lot of trouble.

SOUTH CAROLINA

AYNOR

Rolling Hills GC
Hwy. 501 West, P.O. Box
607, 29511
Ph: 800-633-2380

Yards: 6255, Holes: 18
Par: 72, USGA: 68.6
RP: Call toll free for
tee times

Restaurant/Bar/Proshop
GF: w/day $12
Carts: $8.00

The front 9 has an appearance of openness with many links type holes, while the back 9 holes are justly being recognized as 9 of the best holes in Holly County. Come play "OUR" Amen corner and our famed hole number 13.

BEAUFORT

Golf Professional's Club
93 Francis Marion
Circle, 29902
Ph: 803-524-3635

Yards: 6700, Holes: 36
Par: 72, USGA: 71.4
RP: 1 day in advance

Restaurant/Bar/Proshop
GF: w/day $14, w/end $14
Carts: $22.00

The course meanders through majestic oaks, peaceful lakes, saltwater lagoons, and placid marsh lands all filled with an abundance of wildlife. The huge lightning fast greens are well protected by 57 bunkers and make the course exciting to golfers of all levels of ability.

COLUMBIA

Northwoods GC
201 Powell Rd., 29203
Ph: 803-786-9242

Yards: 6800, Holes: 18
Par: 72, USGA: 70.4
RP: One week ahead

Restaurant/Bar/Proshop
GF: w/day $19, w/end $24
Carts: $10.50

Our favorite hole is the 14th, a short 313 yard par 4 that plays along a large lake. The hole features the famous Dye railroad ties and a variety of tees, mounds, and bunkers. It's a gamblers delight, go for the green or play it smart and dry!

EASLEY

Rolling Green GC
Rt. 2 Box 449, 29640
Ph: 803-859-7716

Yards: 6102, Holes: 18
Par: 72, USGA: 69.9
RP: Weekends

Restaurant/Proshop
GF: w/day $10, w/end $12
Carts: $6.00 ea

Rolling Green Golf Club is named after the large rolling, bent grass greens which challenge even the best putters.

──────────────── EDISTO ISLAND ────────────────

Fairfield's CC at Edisto
1 King Cotton Rd., Box
27, 29438
Ph: 803-869-2561

Yards: 6300, Holes: 18
Par: 71, USGA: 69.5
RP: 24 hours in
advance

Restaurant/Bar/Proshop
GF: w/day $29
Carts: Included

Our championship 18-hole course is fully equipped with 59 sand traps, water on 14 holes, and wildlife spectators (among them a resident alligator).

──────────────── FOUNTAIN INN ────────────────

Carolina Springs G&CC
1680 Scuffletown Rd.
29644
Ph: 803-862-3551

Yards: 7036, Holes: 27
Par: 72
RP: Required

Restaurant/Bar/Proshop
GF: w/day $12, w/end $17
Carts: $10.00 ea

Carolina Springs is a semi private 27 hole facility with bent grass greens, masi IV irrigation system, 5 sets of tees, driving range, fully stocked pro shop and snack bar. Hole #3 on the Cedars 9 is outstanding, closely resembling Augusta National.

──────────────── GEORGETOWN ────────────────

Wedgefield Plantation & CC
100 Manor Dr., 29440
Ph: 803-546-8585

Yards: 7077, Holes: 18
Par: 72, USGA: 70.0

Restaurant/Bar/Proshop
Carts: $12.00

Ranked the 15th best in S.C. and among the top 50 in the S.E. by "Golfweek." Set within natural vistas, massive 400 year old moss covered oaks and magnolias provide a suitable backdrop for "Gone With The Wind" and are part of the character and charm. A true challenge to put one skills to test in a spectacular "Old South" setting.

──────────────── GRAMLING ────────────────

Village Greens CC
P.O. Box 76, 29348
Ph: 803-472-2411

Yards: 6372, Holes: 18
Par: 72, USGA: 69.0
RP: Weekends/holidays

Proshop
GF: w/day $9, w/end $12
Carts: $6.00

Lots of water problems as there are ten holes with water hazards. And added to this there are also 46 bunkers to contend with!

──────────────── HARTSVILLE ────────────────

Hartsville CC
116 Golf Course Rd.,
29550
Ph: 803-332-1441

Yards: 6200, Holes: 18
Par: 72

Restaurant/Bar/Proshop
GF: w/day $15
Carts: $7.35

Holes 5-7 represent our "Amen Corner." 3 of the 4 par 3s on the course are over 185 yards long, they are difficult. The greens are very difficult to read. The members of the club play the hole as it lies from June through September, it is in that good of shape.

──────────────── HILTON HEAD ISLAND ────────────────

Harbour Town GL
11 Lighthouse Ln., P.O.
Box 7000, 29938
Ph: 803-671-2446

Yards: 5824, Holes: 18
Par: 71, USGA: 70.0
RP: Sea Pines guest 90
days,14 day

Restaurant/Bar/Proshop
GF: w/day $65
Carts: $11.00

The legendary Harbour Town Golf Links, one of the top 25 courses in America is home of the MCI Heritage Classic. In 1989, Harbour Town will host the Nabisco Championships, the richest event in the history of the PGA. Harbour Town's set of par 3's rank among the finest in the world, and the par 4, 18th hole is one of the most feared finishing holes in golf.

———————————— HILTON HEAD ISLAND ————————————

Palmetto Dunes   Yards: 6122, Holes: 18   Restaurant/Bar
P.O. Box 5606, 29938   Par: 72, USGA: 69.3   **GF:** w/day $67
Ph: 803-785-1138   RP: 2 months in   **Carts:** $12.00 ea
                           advance

The Robert Trent Jones's #10 is a long par 5, with green sitting on the Atlantic's edge. The George Fazio course's 16th hole features a few of the course's yawning fairways and greenside bunkers. The Arthur Hills course is characterized by palmettos, dramatic elevation changes, continuous lines of dunes and some stiff ocean breezes.

———————————— HILTON HEAD ISLAND ————————————

Sea Pines Plantation   Yards: 5824, Holes: 18   Restaurant
P.O. Box 7000, 29938   Par: 71, USGA: 70.0   **GF:** w/day $65
Ph: 803-671-2446   RP: 1-14 days   **Carts:** $10.00 ea
                           depending on season

The Harbour Town Links's course rating is a walloping 74 from the championship tees, certainly one of the highest anywhere. Highly touted by tour pros, this toughie is a shot makers course—not long, but very demanding—a real pond-lovers dream, with smallish fast greens.

———————————— HILTON HEAD ISLAND ————————————

Shipyard GC   Yards: 3035, Holes: 9   Restaurant/Bar
130 Shipyard Dr., 29928   Par: 36, USGA: 34.5   **GF:** w/day $54
Ph: 803-785-2402   RP: 2 weeks in advance   **Carts:** Included

Shipyard Golf Club is the home of the Hilton Head Seniors International, and numerous Senior PGA events. It's a narrow 27 hole course with water hazards on 25 holes. You'll wander through tall pines, magnolias and moss-draped oaks, and over lagoons and ponds which must be avoided to match par.

———————————— HILTON HEAD ISLAND ————————————

Westin Resort   Yards: 6038, Holes: 54   Restaurant/Bar
135 S. Port Royal Dr.,   Par: 72, USGA: 68.7   **GF:** w/day $50
29928   RP: Recommended   **Carts:** $29.60
Ph: 803-681-3671

Barony has small greens that are well-protected by deep bunkers, lagoons and Bermuda rough that require accurate approach shots. Robber's Course is on the marsh side atop what was once Civil War Grounds. Planter's Row, host of the 1985 Hilton Head Seniors International. Greens are large, undulating and sometimes treacherous.

———————————— ISLE OF PALMS ————————————

Wild Dunes GC   Yards: 6108, Holes: 18   Proshop
5757 Palm Blvd., 29402   Par: 72, USGA: 70.3   **GF:** w/day $58
Ph: 803-886-6000   RP: Required-limited   **Carts:** $12.00
                           public access

Links Course—Finishing holes on the beach some of the best in the world. Harbor Course—beautiful, along the intercoastal waterway.

———————————— JOHNSONVILLE ————————————

Wellman Club GC   Yards: 7028, Holes: 18   Restaurant/Bar/Proshop
P.O. Drawer 188, 29555   Par: 72, USGA: 70.2   **GF:** w/day $12
Ph: 803-386-2521   RP: 2 days in advance   **Carts:** $8.50 ea

The Wellman Club is set amid gentle rolling hills and in a relaxed country setting. Opened in 1967, it has quickly become one of the state's finest island golf courses. A lot of fun to play, but definitely not a pushover by any means.

─────────────── LITTLE RIVER ───────────────

River Hills Golf & CC	Yards: 6873, Holes: 18	Restaurant/Bar/Proshop
P.O. Box 1049, 29566	Par: 72, USGA: 70.6	**GF:** w/day $18
Ph: 803-249-8833	RP: Required	**Carts:** $11.00 ea

18 hole championship, signature course designed by Tom Jackson. Non-parallel fairways, designed to challenge golfers at all levels of skill. Four sets of tees on each hole allow you to play according to your own ability. 13 character holes (beautiful, unique and challenging) with lots of water and bermuda grass on the fairways and greens.

─────────────── McCORMICK ───────────────

Hickory Knob State	Yards: 6560, Holes: 18	Restaurant/Bar/Proshop
Park GC	Par: 72	**GF:** w/day $10, w/end $12
Route 1 Box 199-B, 29835	RP: Required	**Carts:** $8.00 ea
Ph: 803-443-2151		

Our championship 18-hole course challenges even the experts with a 72.1 PGA rating. The course is unique for its placement among woodlands, water, dogwoods and azaleas. A full-service pro shop and clubhouse adds the final touch to your pleasant golfing convenience.

─────────────── MT. PLEASANT ───────────────

Patriot's Point Links	Yards: 6575, Holes: 18	Bar/Proshop
P.O. Box 438, 29464	Par: 72, USGA: 71.6	**GF:** w/day $17, w/end $19
Ph: 803-881-0042	RP: Call for	**Carts:** $9.50
	reservations	

Our course is located on the Charleston Harbor and it has a great view of ocean and coastal waters. 5 holes play along ocean water.

─────────────── MYRTLE BEACH ───────────────

Arcadian Shores GC	Yards: 5974, Holes: 18	Restaurant
701 Hilton Rd., 29577	Par: 72, USGA: 68.8	**GF:** w/day $37
Ph: 803-449-5217	RP: Up to 1 year ahead	**Carts:** $11.00

Natural lakes weaving in and out of the fairways, sixty-four white sand bunkers, a variety of trees, and the salty breezes off the Atlantic offer plenty of challenge. When you make your reservation, you'll be able to choose from a slew of nearby courses, and golf package rates.

─────────────── MYRTLE BEACH ───────────────

Cane Patch Par 3 GC	Yards: 2023, Holes: 27	Proshop
72nd Ave. N. & Old	Par: 81	**GF:** w/day $7
Kings Hwy., 29577		
Ph: 803-449-6085		

Enjoy 27 holes of par 3 golf amidst the splendor of tall pines and oaks on rolling acreage situated just two blocks from the Atlantic Ocean. An abundance of flowering dogwood, azaleas, magnolias, and crape myrtles dot the landscape in spring. Open year around.

─────────────── MYRTLE BEACH ───────────────

Island Green CC	Yards: 3047, Holes: 27	Restaurant/Bar/Proshop
P.O. Box 14747, 29587	Par: 36, USGA: 66.3	
Ph: 803-650-2186		

Design of the course carefully utilizes the landscape with its rolling terrain, streams of spring water, native white dogwoods, wild flowers, and stately old oaks. A string of lakes are strewn throughout the ravines and are brought into play on many of our holes.

168   South Carolina

Marsh Harbour GL Yards: 6695, Holes: 18   Restaurant/Bar/Proshop
P.O. Box 65, Sunset   Par: 70, USGA: 70.2   **GF:** w/day $25
Beach, 29597   RP: 9 months in   **Carts:** $12.00
Ph: 803-249-3449   advance

Surrounded by water and greens made out of oyster shells. A tight course with narrow fairways. #13 is "picture hole," short and challenging.

─────────────── PAWLEYS ISLAND ───────────────

Litchfield CC   Yards: 6320, Holes: 36
P.O. Box 320, 29585 Par: 72, USGA: 69.9
Ph: 803-237-3411

Litchfield Country Club and River Club are recognized as two of the Carolinas' top courses, with exquisite Southern Plantation surroundings, brilliant design, meticulous grooming, offers superb golf every season of the year.

──────────────────── SALUDA ────────────────────

Persimmon Hill GC Yards: 6405, Holes: 18   Restaurant/Bar/Proshop
Rt 3 Box 364, 29138   Par: 72, USGA: 70.2   **GF:** w/day $15
Ph: 803-275-3522   RP: Required   **Carts:** $9.00
                       weekends & holidays

Persimmon Hill Golf Course is rated among the top golf facilities in South Carolina by Golf Digest. The large undulating greens, sand bunkers, 8 water hazards and tree lined fairways will add to the challenge and aesthetic appeal of the course. Fully irrigated fairways and greens assure lush playing conditions throughout the year.

──────────────────── ST. STEPHEN ────────────────────

St. Stephen GC   Yards: 3198, Holes: 9   Restaurant/Proshop
River Rd., P.O. Box 1382, Par: 36, USGA: 68.9   **GF:** w/day $4
29479   **Carts:** $4.00
Ph: 803-567-3263

You can start by hitting some practice shots on a nice practice area, and then take off for a fun but challenging nine holes carved out of a natural habitat, consisting of water, sand and trees, wildlife abounds here and lends to a good golf challenge, and a scenic day.

──────────────────── TEGA CAY ────────────────────

Tega Cay CC   Yards: 6352, Holes: 18   Restaurant/Bar/Proshop
One Molokai Dr., 29715   Par: 72, USGA: 69.1   **GF:** w/day $14, w/end $18
Ph: 803-548-2918   RP: 5 days in adv. for **Carts:** $8.00 ea
                             weekends

Rolling hills and valleys encompass the entire layout. Tega Cay requires premium accuracy but rewards good shot placement. Our favorite hole is the par four fifth. The long tee shot is not needed at this hole, but the second shot is one of the most difficult offered to the long sloping green. A four here is a hard earned par.

SOUTH DAKOTA

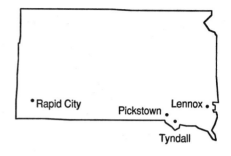

•Rapid City   Pickstown •   Lennox •

Tyndall

―――――――――――――――― LENNOX ――――――――――――――――

Lenkota CC
W. Hwy 44, 57064
Ph: 605-647-5335

Yards: 3113, Holes: 9
Par: 36, USGA: 33.2

Restaurant/Bar/Proshop
GF: w/day $6
Carts: $6.00

An open course with relatively few hazards and a creek which winds its way across four of the nine holes. Number nine offers the men the choice of threading it through the opening in the cottonwoods 80 yards away or blasting it over the top.

―――――――――――――――― PICKSTOWN ――――――――――――――――

Randall Hills CC
57367
Ph: 605-487-7884

Yards: 6550, Holes: 18
Par: 72, USGA: 67.9

Restaurant/Bar/Proshop
GF: w/day $6, w/end $12
Carts: $10.00

The golf course is located just 1/2 mile from the Missouri River and the Fort Randall Dam and the beautiful Lake Francis Case. Both fishing and water sports abound both above and below the dam. There are lovely, modern camping sites also above and below the dam.

―――――――――――――――― RAPID CITY ――――――――――――――――

Meadowbrook GC
3625 Jackson Blvd.,
57702
Ph: 605-394-4191

Yards: 7054, Holes: 18
Par: 72, USGA: 70.7
RP: One day in
advance

Restaurant/Bar/Proshop
GF: w/day $15, w/end $17
Carts: $15.90

Meadowbrook is a very challenging public golf course currently ranked in the top 50 in Golf Digest's America's Best Public Golf Courses.

―――――――――――――――― TYNDALL ――――――――――――――――

Bon Homme CC
Hwy 50, 57066
Ph: 605-589-3186

Yards: 2930, Holes: 9
Par: 36, USGA: 33.3

Restaurant/Bar/Proshop
GF: w/day $7, w/end $8
Carts: $6.00

Course has a creek running through the entire course. It comes into play 8 of 9 holes.

―――――――――――――――― YANKTON ――――――――――――――――

Hillcrest G&CC
2206 Mulberry, 57078
Ph: 605-665-4621

Yards: 6530, Holes: 18
Par: 72, USGA: 70.6
RP: 1 week in advance

Restaurant/Bar/Proshop
GF: w/day $20, w/end $20
Carts: $16.00

Beautifully manicured fairways and greens that are well guarded by strategically placed trees and bunkers. The third ranked course in the state of South Dakota. "If you can par the 8th or 17th hole, you can par any hole."

TENNESSEE

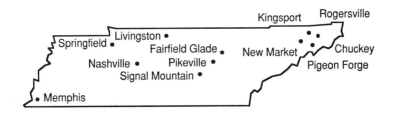

CHUCKEY

Graysburg Hills GC
Rt 1, Box 1415, 37641
Ph: 615-234-8061

Yards: 6341, Holes: 18
Par: 72, USGA: 70.4
RP: Required

Restaurant/Bar/Proshop
GF: w/day $13, w/end $15
Carts: $8.00 ea

Nationally known course designer Rees Jones, combined the site's beautiful topography with strategic design to create a challenging, yet enjoyable, course suited to all playing skills.

FAIRFIELD GLADE

Stonehenge GC
Fairfield Blvd. P.O. Box
1500, 38555
Ph: 615-484-7521

Yards: 6549, Holes: 18
Par: 72, USGA: 71.8
RP: Must be staying at
resort

Restaurant/Bar/Proshop
GF: w/day $46
Carts: Included

Stonehenge is the only course in Tennessee with bent grass tees, greens, and fairways. It is the home of the Tennessee State Open Championship, and was Golf Digest's best new resort course in American in 1985. It is listed by Golf Digest in the top 75 resort courses in America.

GREENEVILLE

Andrew Johnson GC
Rt.2 Box 9A Lick Hollow
Rd., 37743
Ph: 615-636-1476

Yards: 6103, Holes: 18
Par: 70, USGA: 66.1
RP: Tee times
recommended

Restaurant/Proshop
GF: w/day $10, w/end $15
Carts: $8.00 ea

The opening 9 holes are picturesque and tough. The front and back nines are different enough to be two different courses. My favorite hole is the thirteenth— the last and toughest par 3 on the course. The 176 yard tee shot is all over water but do not fly to the right where two large sand traps protect the green.

KINGSPORT

Warriors Path St. Pk.
P.O. Box 5026, 37663
Ph: 615-323-4990

Yards: 6581, Holes: 18
Par: 72, USGA: 68.6
RP: Required
weekends & holidays

Bar/Proshop
GF: w/day $12
Carts: $14.00

Northeast Tennessee offers this scenic bluegrass course. Its rolling hills and well trapped bent grass greens offer an interesting challenge. Especially enjoyable is the downhill 5th, a short par 4 whose tee overlooks Patrick Henry Lake and miles of Tennessee countryside.

──────────────── LIVINGSTON ────────────────

Hidden Valley CC   Yards: 3186, Holes: 9   Bar/Proshop
Hidden Valley Rd., 38570   Par: 36   **GF:** w/day $6
Ph: 615-823-1313   RP: Open to public   **Carts:** $6.00
   Mon-Fri

The trees are such as to be a problem in this course, as they are the main hazards!

──────────────── MEMPHIS ────────────────

Audubon GC   Yards: 6345, Holes: 18   Restaurant/Proshop
4160 Park Ave., 38117   Par: 70, USGA: 69.8   **GF:** w/day $9
Ph: 901-683-6941   RP: 2 days in adv. for   **Carts:** $14.00
   weekend

Locally referred to as Sawgrass North, our favorite hole is the 434 yard par 4 fourth. Trees lining the right and wasteland left demand an accurate tee shot. Into the prevailing wind, a long iron second to a small green hidden behind a giant oak make par scores a true accomplishment.

──────────────── MEMPHIS ────────────────

T.O. Fuller State Park   Yards: 5986, Holes: 18   Restaurant/Proshop
3269 Boxtown Rd., 38109   Par: 71   **GF:** w/day $7, w/end $12
Ph: 901-785-7260   RP: Call for tee times   **Carts:** $14.00

The most difficult hole on the front is the number four hole, located on a plateau with only a 5800 square foot green to reach on this 196 yard par three. If you miss the green to either side you have to go back up hill with a blind shot. Behind the green is heavy rough, very difficult for recovery.

──────────────── MILLINGTON ────────────────

Orgill Park GC   Yards: 6400, Holes: 18   Restaurant/Proshop
9080 Bethuel Rd., 38053   Par: 71, USGA: 66.8   **GF:** w/day $11
Ph: 901-872-3610   RP: 2 days in advance   **Carts:** $7.50 ea
   for weekends

Rolling hills around 82 acre lake, listed in Golf Digest *as public course to play in Tennessee, best fairways in mid-south, Bermuda greens.*

──────────────── NASHVILLE ────────────────

Nashboro Village GC   Yards: 6784, Holes: 18   Restaurant/Bar/Proshop
2250 Murfreesboro Rd.,   Par: 72, USGA: 71.0   **GF:** w/day $15
37217   RP: Make in   **Carts:** $8.00
Ph: 615-367-2311   advance—recommended

The ninth hole is particularly beautiful when viewed from the elevated tee with a tight landing area. This 370 yard par four dogleg right has water hazards left and right the entire length of the hole. A creek in front of the green and a water hazard behind the green makes proper club selection for the approach shot mandatory.

──────────────── NEW MARKET ────────────────

Lost Creek GC   Yards: 5523, Holes: 18   Restaurant/Bar/Proshop
Rt #3, 37820   Par: 71, USGA: 65.4   **GF:** w/day $5, w/end $7
Ph: 615-475-9661   **Carts:** $14.00

Front nine surrounds course—fairly rolling—heavily wooded, large bent grass greens. Back nine less rolling but can still cause trouble. Considered sporty course.

─────────────────── PIGEON FORGE ───────────────────

Gatlinburg CC
Dollywood Ln., P.O. Box
1170, 37863
Ph: 615-453-3912

Yards: 6235, Holes: 18
Par: 72, USGA: 69.9

Restaurant/Bar/Proshop
GF: w/day $20
Carts: $24.00

The course, designed by William Langford, is set in a tranquil wooded setting surrounded by breathtaking panoramic views of nearby mountains. Gatlinburg's hole number 12, affectionately known as "Sky Hi," is one of the most dramatic in the country.

─────────────────── PIKEVILLE ───────────────────

Fall Creek Falls GC
St. Hwy. 30 RT. 3, 37367
Ph: 615-881-3706

Yards: 6706, Holes: 18
Par: 72, USGA: 70.8
RP: Recommended

Restaurant/Proshop
GF: w/day $12
Carts: $14.00

Level, narrow fairways lined with oak, hickory and pines. There are over 70 sand traps but no water to carry. #15 curves to left and is surrounded by trees.

─────────────────── ROGERSVILLE ───────────────────

Camelot GC
Rt 9 Box 376 Hwy 94,
37857
Ph: 615-272-7499

Yards: 6844, Holes: 18
Par: 73, USGA: 69.7
RP: Suggested

Restaurant/Proshop
GF: w/day $10
Carts: $7.00

Camelot Golf Course is nestled in a beautiful valley with a historical background. It was the home of Pressman's Union for 50 years. The front nine challenges the golfer in length par 37 3,640 yards while the back nine takes advantage of mountainous terrain with No. 17 tee 120 feet above the fairway and gives s breathtaking view of the valley.

─────────────────── SIGNAL MOUNTAIN ───────────────────

Signal Mountain Golf & CC
809 James Blvd., 37377
Ph: 615-886-2557

Yards: 5822, Holes: 18
Par: 71

Restaurant/Bar/Proshop
GF: w/day $19
Carts: $7.50 ea

This is a typical mountain golf course with elevated tees and greens, narrow fairways, and small sloping greens. Putting becomes an art in its own on these greens. Several holes offer blind tee shots. Bent grass greens and a mixture of bermuda and winter rye in the fairways.

─────────────────── SPRINGFIELD ───────────────────

Springfield CC
Ruth St., Box 129, 37172
Ph: 615-384-7346

Yards: 5830, Holes: 9
Par: 72, USGA: 67.7

Restaurant/Bar/Proshop
GF: w/day $10
Carts: $12.00

Our nine hole course with bent grass and bermuda fairways in the class for its size in the middle Tennessee area. Although not long, it is very hilly and requires many refined shots to score effectively. Practically no flat lies. Greens unsurpassed!!

TEXAS

Pottsboro
• •Irving
Aledo Carrollton
Fort Worth •• Plano
DFW Airport• • Ennis
Grand Prairie
Comanche •   • Montgomery
Woodlands • •   • Spring
Austin •   Houston •
Winberly   • Boerne   Tomball
•
San Antonio

Brownsville

ALEDO

Lost Creek GC
4101 Lost Creek Blvd.,
76008
Ph: 817-244-3312

Yards: 6388, Holes: 18
Par: 71, USGA: 69.2
RP: Two days in
advance

Restaurant/Bar/Proshop
GF: w/day $15, w/end $22
Carts: $18.00

The peaceful countryside atmosphere will test even the best of golfers. An accurate iron and wood play as well as good club selection is a must.

AUSTIN

Morris Williams GC
4305 Manor Rd., 78723
Ph: 512-926-1298

Yards: 6249, Holes: 18
Par: 72, USGA: 69.3
RP: 4 somes only—1
day in advanc

Restaurant/Bar/Proshop
GF: w/day $9
Carts: $14.00

A tree lined course that is rolling and has target greens. Site of two intercollegiate tournaments sponsored by the University of Texas.

BOERNE

Tapatio Springs Resort & CC
P.O.Box 550 78006
Ph: 512-537-4197

Yards: 6472, Holes: 27
Par: 72, USGA: 67.6

Restaurant/Bar

10 of our holes offer water hazards on the 18-hole course and 5 holes of water on our 9-hole course. #2 is a par 4 with water along the left of fairway with a dogleg right before the green. Over shoot the green and you're in water, under shoot it and you might be in sand.

BROWNSVILLE

Rancho Viejo Resort & GC
P.O. Box 3918, 78520
Ph: 512-350-4000

Yards: 6003, Holes: 18
Par: 70, USGA: 68.8
RP: Resort guests &
members only

Restaurant/Bar/Proshop
GF: w/day $30, w/end $30
Carts: $20.00

Swing into action on one of our two 18 hole championship courses. The palm-lined 70's are designed to challenge the most ardent golfer. El Angel's #4, par 4, 367 yard hole is a dogleg with difficult fairway bunkers on the right and well guarded with both bunkers and trees.

───────────────── CARROLLTON ─────────────────

Indian Creek GC Yards: 7234, Holes: 18 Restaurant/Proshop
1650 Frankford Rd., Par: 72, USGA: 74.7 **GF:** w/day $12, w/end $16
75011 RP: 3 days in advance **Carts:** $14.00
Ph: 214-492-3620

The Creeks Course built in 1984, travels in and around the Trinity River and Indian Creek itself. Beautiful wooded fairways and bermuda greens are mostly bunkered to create a very challenging and light course. The Lakes Course with bent grass greens presents numerous challenges to all levels of golfing.

───────────────── COMANCHE ─────────────────

Par Country GC Yards: 6068, Holes: 18 Restaurant/Bar/Proshop
Rt. 1, P.O. Box 12, 76442 Par: 72, USGA: 67.9 **GF:** w/day $8, w/end $15
Ph: 817-879-2296 **Carts:** $12.00

Located on Lake Procter.

───────────────── DFW AIRPORT ─────────────────

Hyatt Bear Creek GC Yards: 6677, Holes: 36 Restaurant/Bar
P.O. Box 619014, 75261 Par: 72, USGA: 72.7 **GF:** w/day $32, w/end $42
Ph: 214-615-6800 **Carts:** $11.00 ea

Two 18-hole golf courses, driving range and 2 putting greens. #5 East Course is a picturesque par-4 that's not long, but requires 2 perfectly placed shots over water to reach the bentgrass green.

───────────────── ENNIS ─────────────────

Summit at Eagle's Yards: 6801, Holes: 18 Proshop
View GC Par: 72, USGA: 71.7 **GF:** w/day $10, w/end $15
102 Crescent View, 75119 RP: Three days in **Carts:** $16.00
Ph: 214-875-9756 advance

Native foliage, meandering creeks, and bent grass greens join to accent the summit at Eagle's View. Combining six links style holes, an island par three and a variety of contemporary golf holes, the Summit is without question a championship layout to be enjoyed by all golfers.

───────────────── FORT WORTH ─────────────────

Timber View GC Yards: 6345, Holes: 18 Proshop
4508 E. Enon Rd., 76140 Par: 71, USGA: 69.7 **GF:** w/day $6, w/end $9
Ph: 817-478-3601 RP: Do not accept tee **Carts:** $14.00
times at all

The course is a relatively flat open layout, but with a generous supply of large trees strategically located particularly around several of the greens. A significant number of small ponds add up to a real challenge for any golfer.

───────────────── GRAND PRAIRIE ─────────────────

Riverside GC Yards: 7025, Holes: 18 Proshop
3000 Riverside Pkwy., Par: 72, USGA: 69.2 **GF:** w/day $22, w/end $32
75050 RP: 4 days in advance **Carts:** $22.00
Ph: 817-640-7800 for weekends

Rated in the top 20 public courses in Texas, Riverside offers golfers of all abilities a challenge on every hole. Our motto is "Just rip it."

If a golfing vacation is in your travel plans, order a copy of Golf Resorts or Golf Resorts International. See order form in back of the Guide.

─────────────── HORSESHOE BAY ───────────────

Horseshoe Bay CC   Yards: 6839, Holes: 54   Restaurant/Bar
Resort   Par: 72, USGA: 72.0   **GF:** w/day $40
Box 7766, 78654   RP: 7 days in advance   **Carts:** $17.00
Ph: 512-598-2511

54 holes of golf! Slick Rock has water coming into play on seven holes. Ram Rock plays through brooks, waterfalls and rock gardens, small greens, and much sand. The 150 yard par 3 12th plays across the lake to a green protected by bunkers in front and on both sides, oaks behind.

─────────────── HOUSTON ───────────────

Bear Creek Golf World   Yards: 7048, Holes: 18   Restaurant/Bar/Proshop
16001 Clay Rd., 77084   Par: 72, USGA: 71.7   **GF:** w/day $20
Ph: 713-859-8188   RP: 7 days in advance   **Carts:** $17.00

The Masters course is rated in the top 50 public courses in the country and especially the 18th will prove why. No. 18 is among the top 5 finishing holes within country just behind Pebble Beach's #18.

─────────────── HOUSTON ───────────────

Melrose GC   Yards: 2187, Holes: 18   Proshop
401 Canino Rd., 77076   Par: 57, USGA: 59.2   **GF:** w/day $6, w/end $7
Ph: 713-847-1214   RP: Weekends only

Melrose is centrally located to both the downtown business center and intercontinental airport. We feature Houston's finest 18 hole par 3 golf course and practice facility, with nine holes completely lighted for play after dark! Rental clubs available. Fun for the whole family.

─────────────── HOUSTON ───────────────

Pasadena Muni GC   Yards: 6235, Holes: 18   Proshop
1000 Duffer Ln., 77034   Par: 72, USGA: 69.7   **GF:** w/day $6, w/end $9
Ph: 713-481-0834   RP: Weekends   **Carts:** $13.00

You start out on a relatively easy par 5. As you look out over the course you get the feeling that it is wide open. But as you find out on #1 water comes into play on all but one hole. And we never say anything about the wind, which always blows (hard).

─────────────── IRVING ───────────────

TPC at Las Colinas   Yards: 6767, Holes: 18   Restaurant/Bar/Proshop
4150 N. MacArthur   Par: 70, USGA: 69.5   **GF:** w/day $70
Blvd., 75038   RP: Resort Guests   **Carts:** $12.00 ea
Ph: 214-717-0700

TPC #13—it's a long hole, but it demands a very accurate tee shot to the left center of the fairway and a dangerous approach shot over water which is guarded by a tree that stands guard only a few yards from the front of the putting surface.

─────────────── MONTGOMERY ───────────────

April Sound Resort &   Yards: 6189, Holes: 18   Restaurant/Bar/Proshop
CC   Par: 71, USGA: 67.7   **GF:** w/day $20, w/end $25
1000 April Sound Blvd.,   RP: Guests of resort   **Carts:** $18.00
77356
Ph: 409-588-1101

April Sound's Lakeview Course has been rated in Club Corporation of American's Top 10 Maintained Courses by member in 5 of last 7 years. The four finishing holes are as good a test of golf as any amateur would want to find; combining length, water, trees and traps into a true golf challenge.

176 Texas

———————————— MONTGOMERY ————————————

Del Lago Resort GC   Yards: 6825, Holes: 18   Restaurant/Bar/Proshop
500 La Costa Dr., 77356   Par: 71, USGA: 69.1   **GF:** w/day $20, w/end $25
Ph: 409-582-6100   RP: 1 week in advance   **Carts:** $20.00

Most of the fairways are tree lined and the greens well bunkered. Water comes into play on 11 holes. Hole #9 requires a long and accurate tee shot. Your second shot will be with a long iron to a long narrow green that has water on left and 3 large bunkers on the right. Five is a good score on this par 4.

———————————— MONTGOMERY ————————————

Walden on Lake   Yards: 6146, Holes: 18   Restaurant/Bar
Conroe   Par: 72   **GF:** w/day $30
14001 Walden Rd., 77356   RP: 1 week in advance   **Carts:** $20.00
Ph: 409-582-6441

Course winds through Texas timberland where everything seems to be bigger than life. #11 is a monster where double-digit scores are common—a double dogleg par 5 that winds its way up to a peninsula bordered by Lake Conroe.

———————————— PLANO ————————————

Plano Muni GC   Yards: 6879, Holes: 18   Proshop
4501 E.14th, 75074   Par: 72, USGA: 70.1   **GF:** w/day $10, w/end $12
Ph: 214-423-5444   RP: required for   **Carts:** $14.00
    weekends

Plano Municipal is an enjoyable yet challenging golf course for all levels of golfers. From the 6900 yard blue tees to the 550 yard red tees, this pecan, tree lined course is scenic and fun. Our final three finishing holes are our trademark as they reach 450 yards each from the championship tees.

———————————— POTTSBORO ————————————

Tanglewood Texoma   Yards: 7332, Holes: 18   Restaurant/Bar
GC   Par: 72, USGA: 67.0   **GF:** w/day $18, w/end $23
P.O. Box 265, 75076   **Carts:** $7.50
Ph: 214-786-2968

Relatively open with grass and sand bunkers, 3 water holes, bent grass greens. #18 is a dogleg right, par 5 with water two-thirds of the way down on right side. Good change in elevations from tee to green.

———————————— SAN ANTONIO ————————————

Historic Brackenridge   Yards: 6400, Holes: 18   Restaurant/Proshop
Park GC   Par: 72, USGA: 67.0   **GF:** w/day $8, w/end $9
2315 Ave. B, 78215   RP: 1 day notice in   **Carts:** $8.75
Ph: 512-226-5612   person

Several world records are held here—Mike Souchek's 27 under par in 1955 Texas Open. The PGA Tour started here in 1922. Very old oak and pecan trees line the fairways. One is 93 feet tall. The famous San Antonio River runs through the entire course. Large cathedral style clubhouse built for the public in 1923 with 2 foot thick walls.

Our listings—supplied by the management—are as complete as possible. Many of the courses have more features than we list. Be sure to inquire when you book your tee time.

─────────────────────── SAN ANTONIO ───────────────────────

Pecan Valley
4700 Pecan Valley Dr.,
78223
Ph: 512-333-9018

Yards: 7163, Holes: 18
Par: 72, USGA: 71.0
RP: Weekdays 1 week
in advance

Restaurant/Bar/Proshop
GF: w/day $17, w/end $22
Carts: $18.00

All Bermuda grass and level course with many layup shots. Narrow fairways are lined with oaks and pecans. #18 par 5, carry 240 yards to clear creek. In 1968 P.G.A. Championship, Arnold Palmer missed 1st birdie putt.

─────────────────────── SPRING ───────────────────────

Cypresswood GC
21602 Cypresswood Dr.,
77373
Ph: 713-821-6300

Yards: 6906, Holes: 18
Par: 72, USGA: 69.2
RP: Required on
weekends & holiday

Restaurant/Bar/Proshop
GF: w/day $15
Carts: $17.00

Cypresswood Golf Club, Houston's finest 36 hole public golf facility, features rolling terrain, meandering creeks carved from a heavily wooded tract. Cypresswood employs PGA golf professionals to teach individuals by appointment on its 17 acre driving range.

─────────────────────── THE WOODLANDS ───────────────────────

The Woodlands Inn & CC
2301 North Millbend
Rd., 77380
Ph: 713-367-1100

Yards: 6387, Holes: 54
Par: 72
RP: Resort guests
have priority

Restaurant/Bar/Proshop
GF: w/day $60
Carts: Included

The highlight of the resort is the championship TPC Course, one of eight currently used in the United States, and open to the public. #17 is a stickler with a lake guarding the green. North Course is open for Inn guests.

─────────────────────── TOMBALL ───────────────────────

Treeline GC, Inc.
17505 N. Eldridge Pkwy.,
77375
Ph: 713-376-1542

Yards: 5400, Holes: 18
Par: 68, USGA: 66.1
RP: 7 days in advance

Restaurant/Bar/Proshop
GF: w/day $10
Carts: $7.50

This golf course is well liked by all ages and calibers. Senior play is plentiful because of length and design. Seven par 3's make for a challenge for anyone's iron play. Located in the heavily populated area of North Houston. Piney woods and a lot of water.

─────────────────────── WINBERLEY ───────────────────────

Woodcreek Resort
1 Pro. Ln., 78676
Ph: 512-847-9700

Yards: 5973, Holes: 18
Par: 72, USGA: 68.8
RP: Recommended

Restaurant/Proshop
GF: w/day $16
Carts: $16.00

Located in Wimberley, heart of the Texas hill country, Woodcreek golf course twists and bends through this residential community. Driving accuracy off the tee is a premium where distance is lacking. Undulating greens test any golfers shot-making skills. Ya'll come see us!

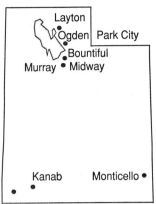

UTAH

---------------------------------- BOUNTIFUL ----------------------------------

Bountiful City GC Yards: 6461, Holes: 18 Restaurant/Proshop
2430 S. Bountiful Blvd., Par: 71, USGA: 67.3 **GF:** w/day $10
84010 RP: 1 day in advance **Carts:** $14.00
Ph: 801-298-6040

Situated on Wasatch Front, the course provides a breathtaking mountain setting as well as a spectacular view of the Salt Lake valley. The course offers long rolling fairways as well as large undulating greens. The open front combined with the tight back nine provide a test for any caliber of player.

---------------------------------- KANAB ----------------------------------

Coral Cliffs GC Yards: 3350, Holes: 9 Proshop
700 East Highway 89, Par: 36, USGA: 69.4 **GF:** w/day $6
84741 RP: 2 weeks in advance **Carts:** $7.00
Ph: 801-644-5005

Unquestionably, the prettiest course in the southern half of Utah. Play this undiscovered gem before they make it a state park! Watch the ball hang against towering red cliffs. So quiet you can hear your shots spin and land on the green. It's the way golf used to be.

---------------------------------- LAYTON ----------------------------------

Valley View GC Yards: 7110, Holes: 18 Restaurant/Bar/Proshop
2501 East Gentile, 84040 Par: 72, USGA: 69.2 **GF:** w/day $10
Ph: 801-546-1630 RP: 1 day in advance **Carts:** $14.00

Mountainous and hilly, unusual terrain with hillside overlooking many elevated tees. 10 ponds and 40 sandtraps. #12 is a par 3 elevated to green bordered by reservoir, bunkered on left side 166 from white tee.

---------------------------------- MIDWAY ----------------------------------

Wasatch Mountain Yards: 6322, Holes: 27 Restaurant/Proshop
State Park GC Par: 72, USGA: 69.2 **GF:** w/day $12
P.O. Box 138, 84049 RP: Recommended **Carts:** $14.00
Ph: 801-654-1901

The entire course is in a beautiful mountain setting with abundant wildlife to break up the monotony of your game. There are streams and lakes and some rolling fairways which will tax your patience yet give you a definite feeling of accomplishment if you complete your game with or without a great score.

─────────────────── MONTICELLO ───────────────────

San Juan GC
549 South Main, 84535
Ph: 801-587-2468

Yards: 5404, Holes: 9
Par: 70, USGA: 63.4

Proshop
GF: w/day $5
Carts: $13.50

The course is located at the foot of the Blue Mountains. At 7,000 foot elevation summer temperature average is about 85 degrees with cool evenings. RV park across the street from the pro shop.

─────────────────── MURRAY ───────────────────

Murray Parkway GC
6345 S. Riverside Dr.,
84123
Ph: 801-262-4653

Yards: 6369, Holes: 18
Par: 72, USGA: 69.2
RP: Call for tee times

Restaurant/Proshop
GF: w/day $12
Carts: $14.00

Nestled at the foot of the Wasatch Mountains Murray Parkway combines rolling fairways, streams and lakes, and over forty bunkers to provide golfers with a scenic and enjoyable test of golf. Score well on key holes throughout the course and Murray Parkway can be mastered.

─────────────────── OGDEN ───────────────────

Schneiters Riverside GC
5460 So. Weber Dr.,
84405
Ph: 801-399-4636

Yards: 6225, Holes: 18
Par: 71, USGA: 66.5
RP: 1 day in advance

Restaurant/Proshop
GF: w/day $10, w/end $12
Carts: $14.00

Beautiful 18 holes situated along the Weber River with a magnificent view of the Wasatch Mountain range. The front 9 framed by large cottonwoods and evergreens. The back 9 more open but water keeps your interest. #17 being the most exciting hole.

─────────────────── PARK CITY ───────────────────

Park City GC
Lower Park Ave., P.O.
Box 2067, 84060
Ph: 801-521-2135

Yards: 6800, Holes: 18
Par: 72, USGA: 69.7
RP: 7 days in advance

Restaurant/Bar/Proshop
GF: w/day $20
Carts: $8.00 ea

We have water on 16 of our holes. Mountain streams and lakes make it exciting getting to the toughest greens in Utah. The course plays short at 7000 feet elevation, but is difficult to score.

─────────────────── WASHINGTON ───────────────────

Green Spring GC
588 North Green Spring
Dr., 84780
Ph: 801-673-7888

Yards: 6717, Holes: 18
Par: 71, USGA: 69.3
RP: Monday for
following, Mon-Sun

Restaurant/Proshop
GF: w/day $20, w/end $20
Carts: $14.00

Nestled in the Red Desert of southern Utah, Green Springs Golf Course is a golfing oasis. This challenging Gene Bates design matches unique surroundings with a magically sculptured layout to form one of the west's most spectacular golfing facilities.

VERMONT

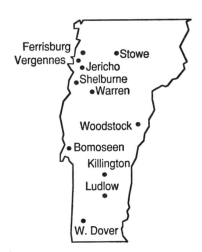

Ferrisburg
Vergennes
•Stowe
•Jericho
•Shelburne
•Warren
Woodstock •
• Bomoseen
Killington
•
Ludlow
•
•
W. Dover

BOMOSEEN

Bomoseen GC
Vt Rt #30, P.O. Box 90,
05732
Ph: 802-468-5581

Yards: 5185, Holes: 9
Par: 35, USGA: 64.0

Restaurant/Bar/Proshop
GF: w/day $11, w/end $13
Carts: $8.00

A resort course on the shore of Lake Bomoseen offering visitors a golf package with meals and lodging.

FERRISBURG

Basin Harbor GC
Basin Harbor Rd., 05456
Ph: 802-475-2311

Yards: 6232, Holes: 18
Par: 72

Restaurant/Bar/Proshop
GF: w/day $16
Carts: $18.00

On the eastern shores of Lake Champlain, Basin Harbor's 6400-yard course is challenging yet enjoyable no matter what your level of play. Also a practice fairway and putting green.

JERICHO

West Bolton GC
P.O. Box 305 West
Bolton, 05465
Ph: 802-434-4321

Yards: 5432, Holes: 18
Par: 69, USGA: 65.6

Bar/Proshop
GF: w/day $11, w/end $13
Carts: $16.00

"One of the prettiest golf courses ever walked by man or deer..." Franklin County Courrier. Early morning golfers can share the course with deer, fox, ducks, and even an occasional moose!

KILLINGTON

Killington GC
Killington Rd., 05751
Ph: 802-422-3333

Yards: 6500, Holes: 18
Par: 72, USGA: 71.5
RP: 2 days in advance

Restaurant/Bar/Proshop
GF: w/day $34, w/end $34
Carts: $26.00

Beautiful mountain course located in Green Mountains of Vermont. Narrow tree lined fairways, large greens, spectacular views.

─────────────── LUDLOW ───────────────

Fox Run GC Yards: 2547, Holes: 9 Restaurant/Bar/Proshop
Fox Ln., RFD #1 Box 123, Par: 36, USGA: 65.6 **GF:** w/day $8
05149 RP: 2 days in advance **Carts:** $10.00
Ph: 802-228-8871

A short but tight golf course. Be careful! It can bring you to your knees.

─────────────── SHELBURNE ───────────────

Kwiniaska GC Yards: 6796, Holes: 18 Restaurant/Bar/Proshop
Spear St., P.O. Box 129, Par: 72, USGA: 71.4 **GF:** w/day $12, w/end $15
05482 **Carts:** $15.00
Ph: 802-985-3672

The front is quite open and flat. The second nine is more rolling with a stream crossing four holes. Beautiful views of the Green Mountains and the Adirondacks.

─────────────── STOWE ───────────────

Stowe GC Yards: 6163, Holes: 18 Restaurant/Bar/Proshop
Cape Cod Rd., 05672 Par: 72, USGA: 68.9 **GF:** w/day $30
Ph: 802-253-4893 RP: Tee times **Carts:** $12.50
requested

Golf course offers spectacular views of the green mountains with enough challenge to satisfy all golfers.

─────────────── STRATTON MT. ───────────────

Stratton Mt. CC Yards: 6400, Holes: 27 Restaurant/Bar/Proshop
05155 Par: 72, USGA: 69.8 **GF:** w/day $50
Ph: 802-297-1880 RP: Public play 1 **Carts:** $26.00
week, 1 day wknd

Stratton Mountain Country Club is a delightful mixture of long and short holes, played at the base of the famous Strattonski resort. Straight, well placed tee shots are required here to avoid the numerous mountain brooks that wander through the course. The large, flat greens offer a good chance for birdies if you reach the greens in regulation.

─────────────── VERGENNES ───────────────

Basin Harbor Club GC Yards: 6513, Holes: 18 Restaurant/Bar/Proshop
RR #3, 05491 Par: 72, USGA: 70.4 **GF:** w/day $26, w/end $26
Ph: 802-475-2309 RP: 2 days in advance **Carts:** $20.00

The front nine require precision, and the long back nine demand concentration. The course is surrounded by native wild areas, with some frontage on Lake Champlain. The Adirondacks and Green Mountains frame the sweeping vistas. Golf in Vermont is a distinct pleasure.

─────────────── WARREN ───────────────

Sugarbush Inn Yards: 6524, Holes: 18 Restaurant/Bar/Proshop
Sugarbush Access Rd., Par: 72, USGA: 71.7 **GF:** w/day $24, w/end $28
05674 RP: Call for availability **Carts:** $22.00
Ph: 802-583-2722

Designed by Rob. Trent Jones, Jr, the course here is dramatic. With mountains that top four thousand feet looming in the background. You won't have a lot of level lies; the old timers will tell you to just play from one landing area to the next.

―――――――――――― WEST DOVER ――――――――――――

Mount Snow CC
Mount Snow Resort,
05356
Ph: 802-464-5642

Yards: 6443, Holes: 18
Par: 72, USGA: 70.3
RP: Required

Restaurant/Bar/Proshop
GF: w/day $28
Carts: $26.00

The par-4 fourth hole, named by Travel Weekly magazine as one of the 100 prettiest holes in North America, features a downhill approach to a green bordered by a marsh and two sand traps. With a spectacular view of the green mountains in the background, it's difficult for golfers to keep their eyes on the ball!

―――――――――――― WOODSTOCK ――――――――――――

Woodstock Inn & Resort
Fourteen the Green,
05091
Ph: 802-457-2114

Yards: 6001, Holes: 18
Par: 69, USGA: 67.0
RP: Same day

Restaurant/Bar/Proshop
GF: w/day $46, w/end $46
Carts: $13.50

Most golfers will find more than enough trouble on this 6001 yard course. The Kedron Brook comes into play on all but six of the eighteen holes coupled with more than eighty bunkers throughout the beautiful Kedron Valley. Golf packages available.

Plan ahead! Reserve tee time well in advance, and while you're doing so, confirm rates and services.

VIRGINIA

BASTIAN

Wolf Creek GC CC Yards: 6079, Holes: 18 Restaurant/Proshop
Rt 1 Box 421, 24314 Par: 71, USGA: 68.7 **GF:** w/day $13, w/end $15
Ph: 703-688-4610 RP: 1 week in advance **Carts:** $15.00

This course has water on 6 of the first 9 holes and all nine on the back. It is surrounded by the beautiful Jefferson National Forest. The 16th hole is a par 3 which has water on three sides and sand in front.

BASYE

Bryce Resort Yards: 6175, Holes: 18 Restaurant/Bar/Proshop
P.O. Box 3, 22810 Par: 71, USGA: 68.7 **GF:** w/day $8, w/end $25
Ph: 703-856-2124 **Carts:** $24.00

The golf course is a relatively flat mountain valley course. A wandering creek, strategically placed bunkers and plentiful trees make every hole a demanding test. Views of the mountains add to the attractiveness of the course. Swimming facilities, grass skiing, lake, horseback riding also available.

CALLAO

Village Green GC Yards: 6000, Holes: 9 Restaurant/Bar/Proshop
P.O. Box 247, 22435 Par: 72, USGA: 68.0 **GF:** w/day $11
Ph: 804-529-6332 **Carts:** $13.00

Enjoy our beautifully landscaped 9 holes in the Old Northern Neck. You won't putt on more lush greens anywhere in Virginia. After a challenging round relax in our restaurant overlooking the 9th hole.

CHARLOTTESVILLE

Birdwood GC Yards: 6821, Holes: 72 Restaurant/Bar
(Univ. of Virginia) Par: 18, USGA: 70.4
Rt. 250 West, P.O. Box
5126, 22905
Ph: 804-293-4653

A really tough course with water on nine holes. #14, a 158 yard par 3 is really something, all carry as the green is on an island in the middle of a pond. You've got to have your shotmaking together for this one!

─────────────── FREDERICKSBURG ───────────────

Shannon Green GC
I-95 & Virginia Rt. 3,
22401
Ph: 703-786-8385

Yards: 7155, Holes: 18
Par: 72, USGA: 72.7
RP: Required

Restaurant/Bar/Proshop
GF: w/day $24
Carts: $22.00

You warm up on a relatively open front nine with a view of the rolling meadows of what used to be dairy farm. Several lakes have to be negotiated to shoot a decent round. The back nine offers a little reprieve for those who stray from the fairway. It is a wooded area with a creek and a lake that come into play on several holes. Our par 5 #13 requires a well placed tee shot and a long hitter may reach it in two if he has confidence in his driver.

─────────────── HERNDON ───────────────

Herndon Centennial GC
909 Ferndale Ave., 22070
Ph: 703-471-5769

Yards: 6445, Holes: 18
Par: 71H

The 27-hole championship course has been called one of New England's best by Golf Digest Magazine. You'll love its spectacular views of mountains, valleys and Stratton Lake as the course challenges you at every turn. A must for every golfer.

─────────────── HOT SPRINGS ───────────────

The Homestead
24445
Ph: 703-839-5500

Yards: 6282, Holes: 54
Par: 70, USGA: 70.0
RP: Required, 1 week
in advance

Restaurant
GF: w/day $75, w/end $75
Carts: $28.00

Considered by many to be the best mountain course, Cascades Upper is hilly and demanding, requiring a variety of shots. Lower Cascades has heavily-trapped large greens and long tees. The Homestead Course claims the oldest first tee in continuous use in the country. It is the shortest of the three, and open year-round.

─────────────── IRVINGTON ───────────────

Golden Eagle GC
Rt. 646, 22480
Ph: 804-438-5501

Yards: 6943, Holes: 27
Par: 72, USGA: 68.2
RP: Hotel guest as far
as wished

Restaurant/Bar/Proshop
GF: w/day $42, w/end $42
Carts: $26.00

The Golden Eagle GC of the Tides Inn has been voted among the top three courses in the state of Virginia. We are rarely crowded and wish to allow our golfing guests a leisurely and unhurried round of golf. Our classy No. 5 hole is one of the many that our guests continue to speak of for years to come.

─────────────── LEESBURG ───────────────

Westpark Hotel & GC
22075
Ph: 703-777-7023

Yards: 6300, Holes: 18
Par: 71, USGA: 71.5

Restaurant/Bar/Proshop

Water on eleven holes, get out your hip boots if your shotmaking goes bad! #7 dogleg, par 4, 417 yards with water running through the fairway and when you get past that there are bunkers on the right and left of the green.

Subscribe to our free newsletter, "Great Golf Gazette" and hear about the latest special golf vacation values.

────────────── NEW MARKET ──────────────

Shenvalee GR   Yards: 6337, Holes: 18   Restaurant/Bar
P.O. Box 930, 22844   Par: 70, USGA: 65.7   **GF:** w/day $17, w/end $19
Ph: 703-740-3181   **Carts:** $18.00

Plenty of course to pull out all the stops on your long ball. Our #17 is a challenging par 5, 507 yard hole with water and sand guarding the green, so get your shotmaking skills ready for this one.

────────────── NEWPORT NEWS ──────────────

Deer Run GC   Yards: 6680, Holes: 36   Restaurant/Proshop
13564 Jefferson Ave.,   Par: 72, USGA: 72.4   **GF:** w/day $8, w/end $10
23603   **Carts:** $13.59
Ph: 804-886-2848

Our scenic 36 holes offer both a bucolic haven and a friendly challenge to golfers of all skill levels. In addition to many outstandingly designed holes, one will see hundreds of deer who make their home in the adjoining woods.

────────────── NORFOLK ──────────────

Lake Wright GC   Yards: 6174, Holes: 18   Restaurant/Bar/Proshop
North Hampton Blvd.,   Par: 70
23502
Ph: 804-461-2246

Silky, smooth putting greens are combined with tough sand traps, water hazards and roughs to challenge even the best golfer on this Lake Wright championship course. The greens are bent grass, and there's also a driving range and two putting greens.

────────────── ROANOKE ──────────────

Countryside GC   Yards: 6861, Holes: 18   Restaurant/Proshop
1 Countryside Rd., 24017   Par: 71, USGA: 68.5   **GF:** w/day $12, w/end $15
Ph: 703-563-0391   RP: 1 day in advance   **Carts:** $18.00

Countryside is located in the beautiful Roanoke Valley surrounded by the Blue Ridge Mountains. The course has four sets of tees. The five par 3 holes are demanding for tee shot. There is a spacious driving range, with practice sand trap, chipping and putting green. The golf shop is the largest in central and southwest Virginia.

────────────── STAUNTON ──────────────

Country Club of   Yards: 6342, Holes: 18   Restaurant/Bar
Staunton   Par: 71, USGA: 71.6   **GF:** w/day $40
P.O. Box3209, 24401   RP: 1 day in advance
Ph: 704-248-6020

The Country Club of Staunton is the home of the 1988 Virginia PGA Championship, and numerous tournaments. Beautiful rolling fairways and classic greens, some sloped, all under the watchful eye of the mountains. Not too much water.

────────────── VIRGINIA BEACH ──────────────

Stumpy Lake GC   Yards: 6347, Holes: 18   Restaurant/Bar/Proshop
4797 E. Indian River Rd.,   Par: 72, USGA: 70.1   **GF:** w/day $11, w/end $12
23456   RP: Required on   **Carts:** $14.00
Ph: 804-467-6119   weekends

Surrounded on three sides by an elegant cypress-filled lake, Stumpy Lake is the quietist golf course in the area. Wildlife from the surrounding woods often add to an 18-hole round. Natural water hazards and strategically placed bunkers intersect the fairways to tantalize your play.

──────────────── WILLIAMSBURG ────────────────

Ford's Colony CC   Yards: 3371, Holes: 27   Restaurant/Bar
240 Ford's Colony Drive, Par: 72, USGA: 72.3   **GF:** w/day $61, w/end $69
23188   RP: 30 days in advance **Carts:** $8.00
Ph: 804-565-4130

The Dan Maples designed golf courses provide challenges for all caliber of golfers. Each hole is distinctive with rolling bermuda grass fairways, speckled with sand and water, and lined with trees. Undulating bentgrass greens provide inviting targets on each hole.

──────────────── WILLIAMSBURG ────────────────

Golden Horseshoe GC Yards: 6750, Holes: 36 Restaurant/Bar/Proshop
Williamsburg Inn,   Par: 71, USGA: 71.0   **GF:** w/day $58, w/end $58
S.England St, 23185   RP: Required   **Carts:** $32.00
Ph: 804-229-1000

One of the top 12 resort golf courses in United States as picked by Golf Magazine in 1988. Narrow fairways, tree lined, lots of water with four of the finest par three holes on any one given golf course. Our sixteenth hole is an island hole of 165 yards from back tees to middle tees at 145 yards.

──────────────── WILLIAMSBURG ────────────────

Kingsmill GC   Yards: 6587, Holes: 36   Restaurant/Bar
100 Golf Club Rd., 23185 Par: 72, USGA: 70.0
Ph: 804-253-3906

Home of the Anheuser-Busch Golf Classic. Kingsmill's 36 holes offer challenge and excitement for golfers at all skill levels. You'll play around lakes, ponds, trees and 350 years of history in a beautiful setting overlooking the James River.

──────────────── WILLIAMSBURG ────────────────

Kingsmill Resort   Yards: 6776, Holes: 36   Restaurant/Bar
1010 Kingsmill Rd., 23105 Par: 71, USGA: 74.5   **GF:** w/day $45
Ph: 809-253-1703   RP: May be made with **Carts:** $13.00
    room resv.

The River Course is home of the PGA Anheuser Bucsh Golf Classic. Plenty of big rolls and swells on the greens. The Plantation Course, around ponds, lakes and river views. The Golf Shop heads the list of "friendliest and most helpful anywhere." Also, new Bray Links Par Three Course opened in 1989.

──────────────── WINTERGREEN ────────────────

Wintergreen GC   Yards: 6500, Holes: 36   Restaurant/Bar
22958   Par: 70
Ph: 804-325-2200

Devils Knob offers magnificent 50-mile views of the Shenandoah Valley, with lush bent grass greens and Kentucky blue grass fairways. The second 18-hole course plays through streams and over Lake Monocan while the surrounding mountains provide a dramatic backdrop.

WASHINGTON

Vancouver   Oroville
Birch Bay • Bellingham • Bridgeport
Sequim • Stanwood • Winthrop
• Spokane
Port Ludlow • Monroe Tacoma
• Fall City North Bend
Orting • Mountlake Terrace
Ocean Shores • Union Spanaway Sumner
Olympia Ellensburg • • Odessa
Tumwater Desert Aire • Warden • Colfax
Longview Richland • Kennewick
Bingen
North Bonneville Goldendale

BELLINGHAM

Lake Padden GC
4004 Samish Way, 98226
Ph: 206-676-6989

Yards: 6406, Holes: 18
Par: 72

Restaurant/Proshop
GF: w/day $10
Carts: $15.00

Recognized as one of the finest municipal golf courses in the Pacific Northwest, the Lake Padden course is carved out of a second growth forest and has the capability of being a 6700 yard championship course.

BELLINGHAM

Sudden Valley GC
399 Sudden Valley, 98226
Ph: 206-734-6435

Yards: 6553, Holes: 18
Par: 72, USGA: 70.0
RP: 7 days in advance

Restaurant/Bar/Proshop
GF: w/day $25, w/end $35
Carts: $23.00

The golf course is located on the shores on Lake Whatcom and is surrounded by the natural beauty of the Pacific northwest. Austin Creek winds its way through the front nine while the tight back nine offers a beautiful view over the lake and the surrounding area.

BINGEN

Museum Hills G & CC
Box 266, 98605
Ph: 509-493-1211

Yards: 2500, Holes: 9
Par: 35, USGA: 67.0
RP: Weekends &
holidays

Restaurant/Bar/Proshop
GF: w/day $11, w/end $18
Carts: $7.00

Museum Hills is nestled between Mt. Hood and Mt. Adams near the Columbia River Gorge. The course is well kept with No. 5 a par 3 the toughest par 3 in the Mid Columbia.

BIRCH BAY

Sea Links GC
7878 Birch Bay Dr., 98230
Ph: 206-371-7933

Yards: 2320, Holes: 18
Par: 54, USGA: 50.7
RP: Required
weekends & holidays

Restaurant/Bar/Proshop
GF: w/day $10
Carts: $13.00

The length and rating of Sea Links is deceiving. Each hole is unique and offers sand bunkers and water for beauty, definition and challenge. The amateur records are 53 for men and 59 for women. Greens are seaside bent and highly rated, terrain is moderate, most holes offer scenic views of snow-capped Mount Baker and The Bay.

---------------------------- BRIDGEPORT ----------------------------

Lake Woods GC
240 State Park Rd., Box
427, 98813
Ph: 509-686-2901

Yards: 5471, Holes: 9
Par: 70, USGA: 63.8

Restaurant/Proshop
GF: w/day $7, w/end $10
Carts: $12.00

Lake Woods golf course is located on the beautiful Columbia River. Fairways are narrow with small fast greens to challenge anyone's ability. For the traveler we have a very nice State Park with full hook ups within walking distance.

---------------------------- BRUSH PRAIRIE ----------------------------

Cedar's GC
15001 NE 181st St., 98606
Ph: 206-687-4322

Yards: 6021, Holes: 18
Par: 72, USGA: 69.2
RP: Desired but not
demanded

Restaurant/Bar/Proshop
GF: w/day $17, w/end $19
Carts: $20.00

A resort course at half the price and half the distance. Only 30 minutes from Downtown Portland. A charming course with Salmon Creek passing through. Lovely cedar trees that make it breathtaking as well as interesting. A must see golf course.

---------------------------- COLFAX ----------------------------

Colfax GC
Rt 1 Box 46A, 99111
Ph: 509-397-2122

Yards: 5476, Holes: 9
Par: 70, USGA: 67.5
RP: Weekends &
holidays

Bar/Proshop
GF: w/day $6, w/end $7
Carts: $15.00

We get a great deal of favorable comments from strangers because of the relatively easy play of the course. It is fairly flat and has two holes on it which are considered birdie holes by the average golfer. Greens superintendent Ron Olson is very conscientious and keeps the course in excellent condition.

---------------------------- DESERT AIRE ----------------------------

Desert Aire GC
3 Club House Way, 99344
Ph: 509-932-4439

Yards: 6223, Holes: 9
Par: 36, USGA: 68.9
RP: Suggested
weekends & holidays

Proshop
GF: w/end $8
Carts: $15.00

Desert Aire Golf Course is located in eastern Washington's desert area on the Columbia River. It offers one of the longest playing seasons in this area, it is a challenging course and very interesting to play.

---------------------------- ELLENSBURG ----------------------------

Ellensburg GC
Route 1 Box 411, Thorp
Rd., 98926
Ph: 509-962-2984

Yards: 6093, Holes: 9
Par: 70, USGA: 68.6
RP: Recommended

Restaurant/Bar/Proshop
GF: w/day $6
Carts: $7.00

This 9 hole golf course plays relatively flat for all 9 holes with the scenic Yakima River coming into play on holes #4 and #5. The wind, which often times blows in our Kittitas Valley, comes out of the northwest and will take many shots out of bounds. Hit it straight and water and wind will not effect your play and you will score well.

---------------------------- FALL CITY ----------------------------

Snoqualmie Falls GC
35109 S.E. Fish Hatchery
Rd., 98024
Ph: 206-222-5244

Yards: 5427, Holes: 18
Par: 71, USGA: 65.2
RP: 6 days in advance

Restaurant/Proshop
GF: w/day $14, w/end $16
Carts: $18.00

Don't slice on holes 1 through 5 and don't hook on holes 10 through 15. Other than that you should have no problems on this well manicured course. The fairly flat terrain is easy to walk and the view of Mt. Si is beautiful.

─────────────────── GOLDENDALE ───────────────────

Goldendale CC Yards: 5610, Holes: 9   Proshop
1901 N. Columbus, 98620 Par: 72, USGA: 66.2   **GF:** w/day $7, w/end $8
Ph: 509-773-4705   **Carts:** $8.00

Looks easy but it pays to think your way around. Both par threes go over Bloodgood Creek. Good views of snow capped mountains. Big hitters can score well here if they are accurate too.

─────────────────── KENNEWICK ───────────────────

Canyon Lakes GC   Yards: 6950, Holes: 18   Restaurant/Proshop
3700 Canyon Lakes Dr., Par: 72, USGA: 69.6   **GF:** w/day $12, w/end $18
99337   RP: Call Tuesdays for   **Carts:** $16.00
Ph: 509-582-3736   following wk

In 1980 Canyon Lakes was rated by Business Week magazine one of the top 50 new courses in the nation. In 1986 Canyon Lakes was rated the best public course in the state of Washington by the Washington Golf Assoc.

─────────────────── LONGVIEW ───────────────────

Mint Valley GC   Yards: 6304, Holes: 18   Restaurant/Proshop
4002 Pennsylvania, 98632 Par: 71, USGA: 67.9   **GF:** w/day $11
Ph: 206-577-3395   **Carts:** $16.00

38 bunkers and water hazards on nine holes! Carefully manicured greens and mature plantings offer visual splendor to match the challenge of Mint Valley's 18 demanding holes. Also a "Pitch 'n Putt" area and a driving range. Open for play throughout the year.

─────────────────── MONROE ───────────────────

Monroe GC   Yards: 4902, Holes: 9   Restaurant/Proshop
22110 Old Owens Rd.,   Par: 33, USGA: 62.2   **GF:** w/day $9, w/end $10
98272   RP: Recommended   **Carts:** $6.00
Ph: 206-794-8498

#6 begins with a check of the fairway ahead through the periscope. You'll see heavy rough and 180 foot firs left and steep slope right. Your 2nd shot is to a narrow green elevated 30 feet and ringed with grass bunkers.

─────────────────── MOUNTLAKE TERRACE ───────────────────

Ballinger Park GC Yards: 2718, Holes: 9   Restaurant/Proshop
23000 Lakeview Dr.,   Par: 34, USGA: 64.6   **GF:** w/day $6, w/end $7
98043   RP: Recommended—1
Ph: 206-775-6467   week in adv.

Easy-walking 9 holes; challenges golfer with Hall's Creek traversing 4 fairways and our famous "lake" hole, a 500 yard par 5, bordered entirely by the north shore of Lake Ballinger.

─────────────────── NORTH BEND ───────────────────

Cascade GC   Yards: 2275, Holes: 9   Restaurant/Proshop
14303 436th Ave SE,   Par: 34, USGA: 60.2   **GF:** w/day $6, w/end $7
98045   **Carts:** $8.65
Ph: 206-888-2044

A flat wooded course surrounded by the beautiful Cascade Mountains and foothills. Located off I-90 at exit 32 with quick easy access. Snoqualmil Pass is 25 miles to the east and Snoqualmil Falls is 6 miles to the west. We take pride in being a friendly, caring owner-run course.

———————————— NORTH BONNEVILLE ————————————

Beacon Rock GC
P.O. Box 162, MP 37,
Hwy 14, 98639
Ph: 509-427-5730

Yards: 5580, Holes: 9
Par: 72, USGA: 67.5
RP: Call for starting
times

Restaurant/Bar/Proshop
GF: w/day $6, w/end $10

The golf course is located in the heart of the Columbia River scenic area and offers the golfers spectacular views to enjoy while playing a tight and tricky 9 hole layout.

———————————— OCEAN SHORES ————————————

Ocean Shores GC
P.O. Box 369, 98569
Ph: 206-289-3357

Yards: 6100, Holes: 18
Par: 71, USGA: 69.0

Restaurant/Bar/Proshop
GF: w/day $15, w/end $20
Carts: $22.00

The front nine is open and close to the ocean while the back nine gets into some large spruce trees. It is a great contrast between nines, with many fine holes on both.

———————————— ODESSA ————————————

Odessa GC
Hwy 28, P.O. Box 621,
99159
Ph: 509-982-0093

Yards: 6300, Holes: 9
Par: 72, USGA: 69.5

Restaurant/Bar/Proshop
GF: w/day $7
Carts: $8.00

Play here on a plush, uncrowded course in a peaceful small town. R.V. spaces available at the course.

———————————— OLYMPIA ————————————

Delphi GC
6340 Neylon Dr. SW,
98502
Ph: 206-357-6437

Yards: 2060, Holes: 9
Par: 32
RP: 1 week in advance

Proshop
GF: w/day $6, w/end $7
Carts: $10.00

Narrow, tree-lined fairways in a residential setting. Don't let the short yardage fool you; small, undulating greens and treacherous pin settings make par an elusive number. Delphi is a serious test of position golf and putting.

———————————— OLYMPIA ————————————

Scott Lake GC
11746 Scott Creek Dr.
S.W., 98506
Ph: 206-352-4838

Yards: 4878, Holes: 9
Par: 70, USGA: 63.4

Restaurant/Proshop
GF: w/day $6, w/end $8
Carts: $9.00

Nine hole course with separate tee boxes. Flat good walking with 2 ponds. Water hazards come into play on 5 holes. Lots of trees with few bunkers. Number 1 borders Scott Lake—#2, tough dogleg left over pond—#6, tee box on island. Grass tees, immaculate greens. Year around play. Beautiful setting.

———————————— OROVILLE ————————————

Oroville GC
Route 1, Box G-20, 98844
Ph: 509-476-2390

Yards: 5880, Holes: 9
Par: 36, USGA: 68.5

Proshop
GF: w/day $10, w/end $13
Carts: $15.00

The first hole is a 458 yard, par 5 to a small green surrounded on three sides by rock outcroppings. A river or canal is in view from most tees but you don't have to shoot over them. A real challenge for the avid golfer.

──────────── ORTING ────────────

High Cedars GC   Yards: 6043, Holes: 18   Restaurant/Proshop
P.O. Box 490, 98360   Par: 72, USGA: 68.5   **GF:** w/day $16
Ph: 206-893-3171   RP: Recommended   **Carts:** $17.00

A very relaxing, well conditioned golf course with a panoramic view of Mt. Rainer. The course has a beautiful creek (Clover Creek) that meanders through the course. Our #13 hole is a great par 5 with a testy shot thru the trees to an elevated green.

──────────── PORT LUDLOW ────────────

Port Ludlow GC   Yards: 6262, Holes: 18   Restaurant/Bar/Proshop
9483 Oak Bay Rd., 98365   Par: 72, USGA: 71.6   **GF:** w/day $20, w/end $25
Ph: 206-437-2222   RP: 1 week unless   **Carts:** $25.00
                             resort guest

Rated in the top 1% in the nation by the Golf Course Architects Society of America, and ranked as one of the 25 best resort courses in the country, Port Ludlow offers the ultimate golf experience.

──────────── RICHLAND ────────────

Meadow Springs GC   Yards: 6926, Holes: 18   Restaurant/Bar/Proshop
700 Country Club Pl.,   Par: 72, USGA: 71.7   **GF:** w/day $30, w/end $30
99352   RP: Guest of member   **Carts:** $18.00
Ph: 509-627-2321

Host course of Washington State Open. One of the top 5 courses in the State of Washington.

──────────── SEQUIM ────────────

Dungeness Golf & CC   Yards: 6400, Holes: 18   Restaurant/Bar/Proshop
491-A Woodcock Rd.,   Par: 72, USGA: 68.8   **GF:** w/day $18, w/end $22
98382   RP: As far ahead as   **Carts:** $20.00
Ph: 206-683-6344   needed

Excellent dry course, our rainfall is only 17 inches per year. Fun course for all types of golfers. Approximately 58 bunkers and scenic water through the whole course. Beautiful view of the mountains from most of the holes.

──────────── SEQUIM ────────────

Sunland Golf & CC   Yards: 6051, Holes: 18   Proshop
109 Hilltop Dr., 98382   Par: 72, USGA: 69.0   **GF:** w/day $14, w/end $18
Ph: 206-683-6800   RP: Required   **Carts:** $18.00

Located in the beautiful Sequim-Dungeness Valley, SunLand is a beautiful, well conditioned and sporty golf course. While the front nine is relatively flat, the back nine is undulating. Although the course is very tight, there are no parallel fairways and offers a variety of shotmaking.

──────────── SPOKANE ────────────

Indian Canyon Muni   Yards: 6296, Holes: 18   Restaurant/Bar/Proshop
GC   Par: 70, USGA: 68.9   **GF:** w/day $18
4304 West Dr., 99204   RP: 1 day in advance
Ph: 509-747-5353

Course has rolling hills and every fairway is lined by evergreen trees. #14 in Sports Illustrated in '82.

─────────────────── STANWOOD ───────────────────

Kayak Point GC   Yards: 6731, Holes: 18   Restaurant/Bar/Proshop
15711 Marine Dr., 98292   Par: 72, USGA: 70.2   **Carts:** $20.00
Ph: 206-652-9676   RP: 1 week in advance

Back Nine magazine lists Kayak Point as the number one public golf course in Washington, number two in the entire region. In addition, Kayak is the only Western Washington course named to Golf Digest's list of America's 75 Best Public Golf Courses. The fairways are tree-lined and shots are made over bunkers to large, tiered greens. Extreme accuracy is required for birdie attempts.

─────────────────── SUMNER ───────────────────

Tapps Island GC   Yards: 2683, Holes: 9   Restaurant/Proshop
20818 Island Pkwy. East,   Par: 35, USGA: 33.0   **GF:** w/day $7, w/end $9
98390   RP: No more than 7
Ph: 206-862-6616   days in advance

In the shadow of the Pacific Northwest's tallest peak, 14,111 foot Mount Rainier, this meticulously maintained course, with narrow contoured fairways, challenging greens, ample white-sand bunkers, and water hazards on seven of nine holes, is more than scenic—Tapps Island is a true test of golf.

─────────────────── TACOMA ───────────────────

Fort Steilacoom GC   Yards: 5000, Holes: 9   Proshop
8202 87th Ave S.W., 98498   Par: 68, USGA: 62.7   **GF:** w/day $6
Ph: 206-588-0613   RP: Required   **Carts:** $6.00
                           weekends & holidays

Very flat easy walking—great for seniors. Despite low course rating course can be difficult to score on due to small greens and numerous out of bounds holes. Favorite hole #7 dogleg left, out of bounds left and fairway tree lined on the right. Requires placement tee shot and if too long can be in tress with no shot to greens.

─────────────────── TUMWATER ───────────────────

Tumwater Valley GC   Yards: 6531, Holes: 18   Restaurant/Bar/Proshop
4611 Tumwater Valley   Par: 72, USGA: 70.5   **GF:** w/day $13, w/end $16
Dr., 98501   RP: Required—can do   **Carts:** $17.00
Ph: 206-943-9500   8 days ahead

Tumwater Valley poses a challenge to good players but is a fair test for golfers of all levels. Players enjoy beautiful views of Mt. Rainier to the east. Another exceptional feature is the player gets a choice on two of the par threes of the hole he wishes to play. Two are short; the other two require a long iron or fairway wood shot over water.

─────────────────── UNION ───────────────────

Alderbrook GC   Yards: 6133, Holes: 18   Restaurant/Bar/Proshop
E 7101 Hwy. 106, 98592   Par: 72, USGA: 69.8   **GF:** w/day $18
Ph: 206-898-2200   **Carts:** $17.00

No fairways border each other and fir trees line each hole. #8 has a double dogleg and par 5. #18 has a view of the Olympic Mountains and Hood Canal.

─────────────────── VANCOUVER ───────────────────

Bowyer's Par 3 GC   Yards: 1020, Holes: 9   Proshop
11608 N. E. 119th, 98662   Par: 27   **GF:** w/day $4
Ph: 206-892-3808

View of Mt. St. Helens (volcano).

---------------------- WARDEN ----------------------

Warden GC Yards: 6772, Holes: 18 Restaurant/Bar/Proshop
Route 1, Box 289, 98857 Par: 72, USGA: 70.3 **GF:** w/day $12
Ph: 509-349-7794 RP: Weekends only **Carts:** $15.00

The openness of the country lends itself to the link style course with wheat grass roughs and great sunsets of the distant Cascade Mountain Range. Our favorite hole is the 606 yard 18th, a long downhill drive through the dogleg to have to lay your second shot on the uphill elevated green is a great challenge of golf skills.

---------------------- WINTHROP ----------------------

Bear Creek GC Yards: 6061, Holes: 9 Restaurant/Proshop
Route 1, Box 275, 98862 Par: 72, USGA: 68.7 **GF:** w/day $10, w/end $12
Ph: 509-996-2284 RP: Required for 3-day **Carts:** $15.00
  holidays

Golf course offers a beautiful view of the North Cascade Mountains. Is a great course for beginner to intermediate golfer with wide lush fairways. This is a nine hole course with 2 sets of tees which drastically change most of the holes for a good variety from front nine to back nine.

Our listings—supplied by the management—are as complete as possible. Many of the courses have more features than we list. Be sure to inquire when you book your tee time.

WEST VIRGINIA

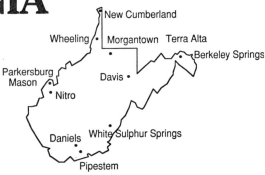

New Cumberland
Wheeling
Morgantown Terra Alta
Berkeley Springs
Parkersburg
Mason
Davis
Nitro
Daniels White Sulphur Springs
Pipestem

───────── BERKELEY SPRINGS ─────────

Cacapon Resort State Park
Rt.1, 25411
Ph: 304-258-1022

Yards: 6940, Holes: 18
Par: 72, USGA: 70.0
RP: Required March thru November

Restaurant/Bar/Proshop
GF: w/day $16
Carts: $16.00

The course is located on a 6,100 acre state park. The front nine plays in a valley with the back nine more in the hills. You will spot many forms of wildlife; deers, squirrels, woodpeckers, etc. as you play the course. Rated as one of the best in West Virginia.

───────── DANIELS ─────────

Glade Springs Resort
Box D, 25832
Ph: 304-763-2000

Yards: 6841, Holes: 18
Par: 72
RP: Required

Restaurant/Bar/Proshop
GF: w/day $22, w/end $27
Carts: $12.50 ea

The course features broad fairways cut through dense oak and spruce with large undulating greens and nine holes with water, #16 green must be reached by hitting through two bodies of water.

───────── DAVIS ─────────

Canaan Valley State Park GC
Rt. 1, Box 330, 26260
Ph: 304-866-4121

Holes: 18

Restaurant/Bar
GF: w/day $20, w/end $20
Carts: $20.00

Canaan Valley Resort's 18 hole championship golf course is relaxing and yet challenging. Surrounded by magnificent mountain vistas and situated in a gently rolling valley.

───────── MASON ─────────

Riverside GC
Rt. 1 Box 35, 25260
Ph: 304-773-9527

Yards: 6022, Holes: 18
Par: 70, USGA: 68.7
RP: Weekends

Restaurant/Proshop
GF: w/day $11
Carts: $8.00 ea

#6 a par 5 of 510 yards number 1 handicap hole. A dogleg right with out of bounds left and hazard right. Large trap in front of green and 3 pot bunkers in rear. A long tee shot over lateral hazards and long second shot may reach green.

─────────────── MORGANTOWN ───────────────

Sheraton Lakeview GC Yards: 6357, Holes: 18 Restaurant/Bar
Rte 6, Box 88A, 26505 Par: 72, USGA: 70.9
Ph: 304-594-1111

The legend and heritage surrounding Lakeview, the original, 18-hole course, is reason enough for professionals and duffers alike to journey to Cheat Lake. Now add the lure of the new Mountainview Golf Course and we think you'll agree that the best way to play is to stay and play the other 18 tomorrow.

─────────────── NEW CUMBERLAND ───────────────

Woodview GC Yards: 6570, Holes: 18 Bar/Proshop
RD 1 Box 6, Ballentyne Par: 71, USGA: 69.0 **GF:** w/day $9
Rd., 26047 RP: 1 day in advance **Carts:** $7.50
Ph: 304-564-5765

Set in majestic West Virginia hills, our course offers greens which are comparable to those of the finest golf courses anywhere. The 190 yard par 3 number 15 leaves no room to escape, with out of bounds behind the green and water short and left.

─────────────── NITRO ───────────────

Scarlet Oaks CC Yards: 6575, Holes: 18 Restaurant/Bar/Proshop
P.O. Box 425, 25143 Par: 72, USGA: 71.7 **GF:** w/day $18
Ph: 304-755-0408 RP: Required **Carts:** $10.00

Set among the hills, Scarlet Oaks offers West Virginia's top rated championship golf course with sculptured greens and multiple tee placements. #17 is one of the most challenging holes. The golfer is faced with a long iron from the tee and a middle iron to a tough putting green surrounded by water.

─────────────── PARKERSBURG ───────────────

Willow Brook GC Yards: 6103, Holes: 18 Restaurant/Bar/Proshop
Gihon Rd., P.O. Box Par: 72, USGA: 69.6 **GF:** w/day $10, w/end $12
3008, 26103 **Carts:** $8.00 ea
Ph: 304-422-8381

Willowbrook golf club is owned and operated by two PGA professionals, who pride themselves, to give the golfer the most challenging, best maintained golf facility in the area. The course is a challenge from the white tees but step back to the blue markers for a true test.

─────────────── PARKERSBURG ───────────────

Worthington GC Yards: 5810, Holes: 18 Restaurant/Bar/Proshop
3414 Roseland Ave., Par: 71, USGA: 67.1 **GF:** w/day $9, w/end $10
26104 **Carts:** $7.00
Ph: 304-428-4297

Flat terrain with creek passing through both nines—lots of trees, but fairways are not generally tight a few sand bunkers.

─────────────── PIPESTEM ───────────────

Pipestem State Park GC Yards: 6884, Holes: 18 Restaurant
25979 Par: 72, USGA: 69.8
Ph: 304-466-1800

An 18-hole championship course carved out of a wooded area. A long 6,884 yard from the blue tees, you'll get plenty of practice with those long shots. There is also a 9-hole par three miniature golf course.

TERRA ALTA

Alpine Lake Resort Yards: 5772, Holes: 18 Restaurant/Bar/Proshop
Rt. 2, Box 99 D-2, 26764 Par: 71, USGA: 67.3 **GF:** w/day $9, w/end $14
Ph: 304-789-2481 RP: Recommended **Carts:** $12.00

Our beautiful and challenging mountain course is sure to provide you with an exhilarating round of golf. Our clean, fresh mountain air is sure to invigorate your spirit. And our greens fees are low enough to be a delight to any golfer's budget.

WHEELING

Speidel GC Yards: 7000, Holes: 18 Restaurant/Bar/Proshop
Oglebay Park, 26003 Par: 71, USGA: 69.0 **GF:** w/day $26
Ph: 304-242-3890 RP: Up to one year **Carts:** $22.00

You begin a front 9 that is very difficult with water holes and tree lined fairways. Landing areas are flat. Back 9 is more open but long. Favorite hole #13 par 3 across a large lake. Course has bent greens, tee and fairway and very lush. Rated top 75 public courses 1988 by Golf Digest. Pro shop rated top 100 in America by Shop Magazine.

WHITE SULPHUR SPRINGS

The Greenbrier Yards: 6311, Holes: 18 Restaurant
24986 Par: 72, USGA: 71.7 **GF:** w/day $75, w/end $75
Ph: 304-536-1110 RP: May be made with **Carts:** $34.00
 hotel

Lakeside opened in 1910. Old White, was next, designed in 1914. Jack Nicklaus redesigned what had been a somewhat flat Greenbrier course in 1976. He added a lake, redid greens so now they're tiered and increased the size of many traps. One course stays open all year, so if you should want to play a round in January, it's yours!

WISCONSIN

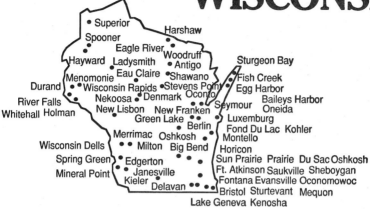

Superior
Spooner
Harshaw
Eagle River
Woodruff
Hayward Ladysmith Antigo
Sturgeon Bay
Menomonie Eau Claire Shawano
Fish Creek
Durand Wisconsin Rapids Stevens Point
Egg Harbor
River Falls Nekoosa Denmark Oconto
Baileys Harbor
Whitehall Holman New Lisbon New Franken Seymour Oneida
Green Lake
Luxemburg
Berlin Fond Du Lac Kohler
Merrimac Oshkosh Montello
Wisconsin Dells Milton Big Bend Horicon
Spring Green Edgerton Sun Prairie Prairie Du Sac Oshkosh
Mineral Point Janesville Ft. Atkinson Saukville Sheboygan
Kieler Fontana Evansville Oconomowoc
Delavan Bristol Sturtevant Mequon
Lake Geneva Kenosha

ANTIGO

Riverview CC & GC
W11817 Highland Rd.,
54409
Ph: 715-623-2663

Yards: 3120, Holes: 9
Par: 36, USGA: 68.9

Restaurant/Bar/Proshop
GF: w/day $7
Carts: $15.00

A scenic and challenging 9 hole layout, which crosses the winding Eau Claire River several times, and features an island green on #4 and a unique par 3 at #8. The 155 yard hole requires a very accurate tee shot over the river to a small, tree guarded green.

BAILEYS HARBOR

Maxwelton Braes GC
Bonnie Brae Rd., 54202
Ph: 414-839-2321

Yards: 6070, Holes: 18
Par: 71, USGA: 68.2

Restaurant/Bar/Proshop
GF: w/day $14
Carts: $14.00

The Scottish brae links are rolling with open fairways dotted with bunkers. Green are bent grass. Club rentals are available.

BERLIN

Mascoutin CC
RTE. 2, P.O. Box 125,
54923
Ph: 414-361-2365

Yards: 6448, Holes: 18
Par: 72, USGA: 70.5
RP: $50.00 1 month
prior tee time

Restaurant/Bar/Proshop
GF: w/day $16, w/end $19
Carts: $19.00

Mascoutin is recognized as one of the top ten courses in the state and is the site of the Gene Edwards Greater Green Lake Pro-Am Tournament. Mascoutin's large, undulating greens, 60 sand traps and water on the 15th, 16th and 17th, and 18th holes offer a challenging but fair test for golf. Several thousand trees planted over the years are maturing.

BIG BEND

Edgewood GC
W240 S10050 Castle Rd.,
53103
Ph: 414-662-2738

Yards: 6424, Holes: 27
Par: 72, USGA: 70.2
RP: 1 week in advance

Restaurant/Bar/Proshop
GF: w/day $16
Carts: $18.00

Rolling fairways meandering between lakes and woods that overlook the Fox River.

――――――――――――― BRISTOL ―――――――――――――

Bristol Oaks CC
16801 75th St., 53104
Ph: 414-857-2302

Yards: 5933, Holes: 18
Par: 72, USGA: 67.8
RP: 2 weeks in advance

Restaurant/Bar/Proshop
GF: w/day $11, w/end $15
Carts: $17.50

Green grass, blue sky, rolling hills and valleys of the beautiful Wisconsin country-side are all part of the experience of golfing at Bristol Oaks Country Club. The scenic course will delight as well as challenge both the professional and novice golfer.

――――――――――――― DELAVAN ―――――――――――――

Lake Lawn Lodge GC
Hwy. 50 E., 53115
Ph: 414-728-5511

Yards: 6173, Holes: 18
Par: 70, USGA: 67.3
RP: Tee times recommended

Restaurant/Bar/Proshop
GF: w/day $38, w/end $38
Carts: $12.00 ea

Scenic course on the shore of Delavan Lake, beautiful mature trees. Number 13, a par 4,301 yard hole where your tee shot is over water, then a fairway bunker on the left side and your shot into the green with trees backing the green.

――――――――――――― DENMARK ―――――――――――――

Twin Oaks CC N
Box 85, Rt. 3, 54208
Ph: 414-863-2716

Yards: 6400, Holes: 18
Par: 72, USGA: 68.4
RP: 7 days in advance

Restaurant/Bar/Proshop
GF: w/day $10, w/end $11
Carts: $15.50

The front nine is relatively open and short with its signature hole being the attractive 140 yard par 3 3rd hole. The back nine is longer so grip it and rip it all you want. The sixteenth is a beautiful 402 yard par 4 with the green nestled amongst the oaks.

――――――――――――― DURAND ―――――――――――――

Durand GC
1324 3rd Ave. West, 54736
Ph: 715-672-8139

Yards: 3274, Holes: 9
Par: 36, USGA: 34.0
RP: 1 days in advance

Restaurant/Bar/Proshop
GF: w/day $7
Carts: $7.00

A member of the CUGS this demanding 9 hole course puts a premium on accuracy. Starting with a very difficult par 3 of 205 yards and.ending with a 400 yard par 4 with out of bounds right and tree lined on the right.

――――――――――――― EAGLE RIVER ―――――――――――――

Eagle River Muni GC
527 McKinley Blvd.,P.O. Box 39, 54521
Ph: 715-479-8111

Yards: 6075, Holes: 18
Par: 70, USGA: 68.0
RP: First come, first serve

Restaurant/Bar/Proshop
GF: w/day $12
Carts: $12.00

Formerly a 9 hole course, our newly redesigned 18 hole golf course features 12 new holes. Holes 1 thru 8 wind through the northwoods forest and hole 9's elevated tee offers a view of Eagle River which connects to a chain of 28 lakes. Holes 10 thru 14 offer a short breather before returning to the forest for the finish.

――――――――――――― EAU CLAIRE ―――――――――――――

Mill Run
3905 Kane Rd., 54703
Ph: 715-834-1766

Yards: 6027, Holes: 18
Par: 71, USGA: 65.1
RP: Recommended

Restaurant/Bar/Proshop
GF: w/day $15, w/end $15
Carts: $14.00

Gently rolling terrain with lush fairways. Five ponds and a cattail filled creek that catches balls that go. A fun course that is landscaped with thousands and thousands of flowers throughout the course. Clubhouse with patio area with outdoor grill; practice area and driving range available.

───────────── EDGERTON ─────────────

Coachman's Inn CC
984 County Trunk A,
53534
Ph: 608-884-8484

Yards: 6184, Holes: 18
Par: 71, USGA: 68.7
RP: Suggested

Restaurant/Bar/Proshop
GF: w/day $11, w/end $12
Carts: $17.00

The longest hole is 503 yards, the shortest 180 yards. Located on gentle rolling land, slightly wooded, with several water hazards, it is a sporty and challenging course for all golfers.

───────────── EGG HARBOR ─────────────

Alpine GC
County Trunk G, P.O.
Box 200, 54209
Ph: 414-868-3232

Yards: 6047, Holes: 27
Par: 70, USGA: 69.4
RP: 1-2 days in
advance

Restaurant/Bar
GF: w/day $13
Carts: $14.00

We have a tram that takes the golfer up a bluff from the white to the blue nine . . . our 9th hole on the Blue nine was written up in Golf Digest *as the most scenic hole in Wisconsin.*

───────────── EVANSVILLE ─────────────

Evansville C
Route 1, Cemetery Rd.,
53536
Ph: 608-882-6524

Yards: 6300, Holes: 9
Par: 36, USGA: 34.5
RP: 1 week in advance

Restaurant/Bar/Proshop
GF: w/day $6, w/end $7
Carts: $8.00

One of the finest 9 hole courses in the midwest. A very picturesque course with water coming in to play on four holes and somewhat rolling terrain throughout the course. Our No. 7 and No. 9 holes have been sources of beautiful pictures for scorecards, newspapers and magazines.

───────────── FISH CREEK ─────────────

Peninsula State Park GC
P.O. Box 218, 54212
Ph: 414-868-5791

Yards: 6211, Holes: 18
Par: 71, USGA: 67.5
RP: 7 days in advance

Restaurant/Proshop
GF: w/day $12
Carts: $16.00

Peninsula's challenging and very wooded 18 holes are interspersed with varying views of the water of Green Bay and outlying islands. A most memorable hole is the big dogleg on number 12 where golfers approach an elevated hillside green. Golfers are rewarded with magnificent views while hitting their last strokes on this 351 yard hole.

───────────── FOND DU LAC ─────────────

Ledgewood GC
W4430 Golf Course Dr.,
54935
Ph: 414-921-8053

Yards: 3094, Holes: 9
Par: 36, USGA: 68.6
RP: 30 days in advance

Restaurant/Bar/Proshop
GF: w/day $6
Carts: $7.50

A sporty nine hole course located on the Ledge called the Niagra escarpment. The course overlooks the city of Fon Du Lac and the Lake Winnebago. Hilly terrain with woods bordering 6 out of 9 holes.

Plan ahead! Reserve tee time well in advance, and while you're doing so, confirm rates and services.

─────────────── FONTANA ───────────────

Abbey Springs GC
Route 1, Box K, So Lake
Dr., 53125
Ph: 414-275-6111

Yards: 6342, Holes: 18
Par: 72, USGA: 69.8
RP: 2 weeks in advance

Restaurant/Bar/Proshop
GF: w/day $28
Carts: $12.00 ea

Scenic beauty with spectacular views of Geneva Lake are the hallmark of this course. Oak woods line many of the fairways making accuracy of shots important as reflected in the 129 slope rating. Beautiful flower plantings and undulating greens are a course signature.

─────────────── FORT ATKINSON ───────────────

Koshkonong Mounds CC
R.R. 3 Koshkonong
Mounds Rd., 53538
Ph: 414-563-2823

Yards: 6259, Holes: 18
Par: 71, USGA: 69.3
RP: Recommended

Restaurant/Bar/Proshop
GF: w/day $13
Carts: $18.0

Between 700 A.D. and 1,000 A.D., Indians built burial grounds around a 10,000 acre natural lake. You will see 23 of these mounds on the course and finish on #18 which overlooks many of these mounds as well as scenic Lake Koshkonong.

─────────────── GREEN LAKE ───────────────

Lawsonia GC
Hwy. 23 RTE. 1, 54941
Ph: 414-294-3320

Yards: 6764, Holes: 36
Par: 72, USGA: 72.8
RP: Starting Jan 1 for
all year

Restaurant/Proshop
GF: w/day $28, w/end $28
Carts: $12.00 ea

Two 18 hole courses to choose from. Links is ranked by Golf Digest as one of the top 75 public courses. Woodlands - wooded contrast features holes such as 165 yard-par 3 bluff next to lake surrounded by woods 65 foot drop to green. Beautiful surrounding area.

─────────────── HARSHAW ───────────────

Pinewood CC
4705 Lakewood Rd.,
54529
Ph: 715-282-5500

Yards: 6085, Holes: 18
Par: 71, USGA: 74.9
RP: Reservations
required

Restaurant/Bar/Proshop
GF: w/day $18, w/end $18
Carts: $18.00H

Shorter and open front nine with Bearskin Creek wandering through the course. The back nine is long, hilly with #15 offering a tough golf hole with pines near the landing area. The back nine is cut right through the woods with no parallel holes.

─────────────── HAYWARD ───────────────

Hayward GC TC
P.O. Box 1079, 54843
Ph: 715-634-2760

Yards: 6550, Holes: 18
Par: 72, USGA: 69.7
RP: Strongly advised

Restaurant/Bar/Proshop
GF: w/day $12, w/end $13
Carts: $8.00

Our golf course features 10 doglegs lined with spruce and Norway pine. The front nine is fairly wide open although well bunkered, while our back nine is noted for smaller greens and tighter fairways.

Please mention "Golf Courses—The Complete Guide" when you reserve your tee time. Our goal is to provide as complete a listing of golf courses open to the public as possible. If you know of a course we don't list, please send us the name and address on the form at the back of this guide.

———————————— HOLMAN ————————————

Drugan's Castle Mound | Yards: 6150, Holes: 18 | Restaurant/Bar/Proshop
GC | Par: 72, USGA: 66.9 | **GF:** w/day $10, w/end $11
W7765 Sylvester Rd., | RP: Suggested | **Carts:** $13.00
54636
Ph: 608-526-3225

The tight front nine challenges even the best golfers, with tree-lined fairways and undulating valleys. Nature surrounds you as you nestle among the "hidden holes." You can "open up" on the lengthier back nine, but caution still lingers as you approach the mounds and sandy bunkers. Bent grass tees and greens.

———————————— HORICON ————————————

Rock River Hills GC | Yards: 5945, Holes: 18 | Restaurant/Bar/Proshop
Main St. Rd., 53032 | Par: 70, USGA: 68.7 | **GF:** w/day $9, w/end $12
Ph: 414-485-4990 | RP: Call for tee times | **Carts:** $15.00

Located on the beautiful Rock River just south of the famous Horicon Marsh Wildlife Area. The panoramic view with migrating geese make for a most enjoyable round of golf. A superb restaurant coupled with a friendly 19th hole tops off the day.

———————————— JANESVILLE ————————————

Riverside GC | Yards: 6322, Holes: 18 | Restaurant/Bar/Proshop
City Route Hwy 14, 53545 | Par: 71 | **GF:** w/day $11, w/end $13
Ph: 608-754-9085 | RP: Weekends | **Carts:** $11.00

Three holes are bordered by the Rock River. The third hole is bordered by a ravine, so you'd better make a good shot or you're in trouble!

———————————— KENOSHA ————————————

Petrifying Springs GC | Yards: 5970, Holes: 18 | Restaurant/Bar/Proshop
4909 7th St., 53142 | Par: 71, USGA: 67.5 | **GF:** w/day $15, w/end $16
Ph: 414-552-9052 | RP: 12 days in advance | **Carts:** $15.00

Very pretty course. Cut out of natural forest. Trees a definite factor on all but two of the holes, accuracy a must.

———————————— KIELER ————————————

Birchwood GC Inc | Yards: 3171, Holes: 9 | Restaurant/Bar/Proshop
P.O. Box 72, 53812 | Par: 36 | **GF:** w/day $7
Ph: 608-748-4743 | | **Carts:** $8.00

The landing areas are narrow and sloped. #2 is a 359 yard par 4 that doglegs to the left, and slopes severely from right to left. Land your drive on the right edge of the fairway and it's likely to bounce down to the left edge of the rough. Because of the seriously sloping landscape, putts have a tendency to break the opposite direction of what you think.

———————————— KOHLER ————————————

Blackwolf Run GC | Yards: 6068, Holes: 36 | Restaurant/Bar/Proshop
111 West Riverside Dr., | Par: 72, USGA: 70.7 | **GF:** w/day $62, w/end $62
53044 | RP: 1 month in | **Carts:** $13.00 ea
Ph: 414-457-4446 | advance

Selected as best new public course for 1988 by Golf Digest magazine. With its Penncross Creeping Bent grass fairways, fescue roughs, prairie grass mounds and wild flowers which border many of the playing areas. It is a course to be played over and over again. Designed by Pete Dye with many water holes and countless acres of sand traps, the golfer is given myriads of opportunities to display his shot-making skills.

──────────────── LADYSMITH ────────────────

Tee-A-Way GC
1401 E. 11th St. No.,
54848
Ph: 715-532-3766

Yards: 2946, Holes: 9
Par: 35, USGA: 67.3
RP: Call ahead

Restaurant/Bar/Proshop
GF: w/day $8
Carts: $8.50

Beautiful rolling course, lots of large trees that come into play, greens are fast and undulating. Number 9 hole is a tough par 4 with the Flambeau River a lateral hazard the entire length of the hole.

──────────────── LAKE GENEVA ────────────────

**Americana Lake
Geneva**
Hwy 50 & U.S. 12, 53147
Ph: 414-248-8811

Yards: 7250, Holes: 18
Par: 72, USGA: 74.5
RP: The earlier, the
better

Restaurant/Bar/Proshop
GF: w/day $38
Carts: $12.50

The Briar Patch is typical Scottish style with small greens, (some double), deep rough, and little rolling hills. The aptly-named Brute, with a rating of 74.5, is a longer course, with water on twelve holes, and typically American in design. With lots of acreage, you won't find parallel fairways or crowds.

──────────────── LUXEMBURG ────────────────

NorthBrook CC
P.O. Box 238, 407 North
Brook Dr., 54217
Ph: 414-845-2383

Yards: 6110, Holes: 18
Par: 71, USGA: 68.3
RP: Required, J.
Proper Golf Pro.

Restaurant/Bar/Proshop
GF: w/day $15, w/end $15
Carts: $18.00

NorthBrook Country Club has become a standard to the Green Bay area and northeast Wisconsin for its excellent golf and fine food since 1970. Our favorite hole is the 10th, a long par 4 with beautiful trees dissected by a picturesque, rock-ledged brook. Truly the best conditioned course in the area!

──────────────── MENOMONIE ────────────────

Rainbow Ridge GC
2200 Crestwood Dr.,
54751
Ph: 715-235-9808

Yards: 3088, Holes: 9
Par: 36, USGA: 33.6

Restaurant/Bar/Proshop
GF: w/day $6, w/end $6
Carts: $7.00

A good test of golf for all skill level players featuring beautifully rolling terrain and mature trees to challenge the golfer. Clubhouse overlooks most of course enabling golfers to relive memorable shots in the cozy comfort of the 19th hole.

──────────────── MEQUON ────────────────

Mee-Kwon Park GC
6333 W. Bonniwell Rd.,
53092
Ph: 414-242-1310

Yards: 6185, Holes: 18
Par: 69, USGA: 69.2
RP: 3 days in advance

Restaurant/Bar/Proshop
GF: w/day $12
Carts: $16.00

Run by the county park system, the course abounds in beautiful trees, which also add to the challenge of the course. #13 has two bunkers guarding the green and a water hazard on the right side of the fairway which extends to the middle of same.

──────────────── MERRIMAC ────────────────

Devil's Head GC
S6330 Bluff Rd., 53561
Ph: 608-493-2251

Yards: 6336, Holes: 18
Par: 73, USGA: 69.8

Restaurant/Bar/Proshop
GF: w/day $20
Carts: $20.00

Devil's Head well manicured greens and sloping fairways will provide any golfer a challenging 18 holes of golf. The course meanders through acres upon acres of lush forest and rolling countryside thriving with oaks, ash and fruit trees.

─────────────── MILTON ───────────────

Oak Ridge GC
1280 Bowers Lake Rd.,
53563
Ph: 608-868-4353

Yards: 5949, Holes: 18
Par: 70, USGA: 68.3
RP: 1 day in advance

Restaurant/Bar/Proshop
GF: w/day $12
Carts: $8.40 ea

Very attractive, sporty, well maintained course with numerous sandtraps and fully watered tees, greens and fairways. Although, a short course, the greens are very challenging with tricky undulations.

─────────────── MINERAL POINT ───────────────

Ludden Lake GC
Rt 3 Box 100, 53565
Ph: 608-987-2888

Yards: 2500, Holes: 9
Par: 34
RP: 1 day in advance
for weekends

Restaurant/Bar/Proshop
GF: w/day $7
Carts: $8.00

Dedicated in the memory of Allen Ludden, popular T.V. game show host of Password. A sporty 9 hole course with rolling terrain and hilltop views of beautiful Ludden Lake.

─────────────── MONTELLO ───────────────

White Lake GR
R.R. 2 Box 274, 53949
Ph: 608-297-2255

Yards: 6516, Holes: 9
Par: 72, USGA: 70.4

Restaurant/Bar/Proshop
GF: w/day $11
Carts: $8.00

Rolling hills, elevated greens and wood lined fairways make this a scenic course and a challenge to the average golfer. Hole #3–152 yards long, you have to shoot over a water hazard to the green which is 35 feet in elevation above the tee.

─────────────── NEKOOSA ───────────────

Lake Arrowhead GC
1195 Apache Ln., 54457
Ph: 715-325-2929

Yards: 6624, Holes: 18
Par: 72, USGA: 70.2
RP: 2 weeks ahead

Restaurant/Bar/Proshop
GF: w/day $20, w/end $24
Carts: $20.00

Course is heavily wooded and bunkered with bent grass all the way. #9 is a par 5 towards clubhouse, bunker of rock wall, water to carry, pond out of bounds down right, green to right.

─────────────── NEW FRANKEN ───────────────

Royal Scot CC
4831 Church Rd., 54229
Ph: 414-866-2356

Yards: 6572, Holes: 18
Par: 72, USGA: 70.0
RP: 5 days in advance

Restaurant/Bar/Proshop
GF: w/day $10, w/end $12
Carts: $16.00

Royal Scot boasts about its huge greens, fast greens, and soft greens. Along with the best greens in northeast Wisconsin Royal Scot has 44 large sand bunkers, and water holes coming into play 10 out of the 18 championship holes. Along with complete practice facilities, locker rooms and restaurant Royal Scot is far above the competition.

─────────────── NEW LISBON ───────────────

Castle Rock GC
W6285 Welch Prairie
Rd., 53950
Ph: 608-847-4658

Yards: 6184, Holes: 18
Par: 72, USGA: 71.1
RP: 1 week in advance

Restaurant/Bar/Proshop
GF: w/day $14, w/end $15
Carts: $18.00

Located 2.5 miles north of Mouston nestled among a well developed forest. The course is tight and very well manicured. Our favorite hole is the 3rd hole. It is a par 5, 485 yards. You tee off over a creek. The hole is a dogleg right with a pond guarding the second shot on the right side and out of bounds over the green.

───────────────── OCONOMOWOC ─────────────────

Olympia Resort GC   Yards: 6567, Holes: 18   Restaurant/Bar
1350 Royale Mile Rd.,   Par: 72, USGA: 71.0   **GF:** w/day $18
53066   RP: Resort guests   **Carts:** $20.00
Ph: 414-567-0311   have priority

This course, most of which is level or gently rolling with many crisscrossing small lakes and streams, plays longer than the yardage indicates. Both nines are very different, with the front characterized by long, narrow holes and rolling tree-lined fairways. The back is more open and flat, but water awaits you on seven holes.

───────────────── OCONTO ─────────────────

Oconto GC   Yards: 3030, Holes: 9   Restaurant/Bar/Proshop
532 Jefferson St., 54153   Par: 36, USGA: 64.1   **GF:** w/day $5, w/end $6
Ph: 414-834-3139   RP: 1st come, 1st   **Carts:** $7.00
    served

If you're a bird lover, the par 4, number 5 is the hole for you. As the crow flies, the 370 yard dogleg left can be shortened if you're not afraid to challenge the three possible water hazards along the left side of the fairway. However the safer route is to travel to the right side of the fairway where the gallery consists of wild geese guarding the wetlands near the waters of Green Bay.

───────────────── ONEIDA ─────────────────

Brown County GC   Yards: 6729, Holes: 18   Restaurant/Bar/Proshop
897 Riverdale Dr., 54155   Par: 72, USGA: 70.2   **GF:** w/day $16, w/end $16
Ph: 414-497-1731   RP: 1 day in advance   **Carts:** $18.00

The course is 5 miles out in the country. Has rolling terrain and is heavily wooded with hickory, oak, elm and pines. It's curvy and tight with creeks and ponds.

───────────────── OSHKOSH ─────────────────

Lake Shore GC   Yards: 6030, Holes: 18   Restaurant/Bar/Proshop
2175 Punhoqua Dr.,   Par: 70, USGA: 66.9   **GF:** w/day $9
54901   RP: One week in   **Carts:** $15.00
Ph: 414-236-5090   advance

The front 9 starts off with a difficult par 4 going to back to back par 5's centered around beautiful Lake Butte des Morts. The back 9 is shorter in length but plays between 100 year old oak trees with tight fairways. The club house is conveniently located for access and overlooks beautiful lake Butte des Morts.

───────────────── PRAIRIE DU SAC ─────────────────

Lake Wisconsin CC   Yards: 5690, Holes: 18   Restaurant/Bar/Proshop
N1076 Golf Rd., 53578   Par: 70, USGA: 67.2   **GF:** w/day $14, w/end $17
Ph: 608-643-2405   RP: 1 day in advance   **Carts:** $15.00

Distances are deceiving, basically a short course with some tight fairways. Back nine plays along both Lake Wisconsin and Wisconsin River. The most unique hole on the course is the twelfth, which play from an island tee.

───────────────── RIVER FALLS ─────────────────

Clifton Hollow GC   Yards: 5950, Holes: 27   Restaurant/Bar/Proshop
Route #3, P.O. Box 260,   Par: 72, USGA: 67.7   **GF:** w/day $10, w/end $14
54022   RP: Recommended on   **Carts:** $14.50
Ph: 715-425-9781   weekends

18 holes of championship golf, a fun par 3 course and a spacious driving range make Clifton Hollow a complete golf experience located in the St. Croix River Valley Clifton Hollow Golf Club is 30 minutes from the Twin Cities Metro area.

─────────────── SAUKVILLE ───────────────

Hawthorne Hills GC   Yards: 6403, Holes: 18   Restaurant/Bar/Proshop
4720 County Trunk I,   Par: 71, USGA: 69.6   **GF:** w/day $12
53080   RP: 3 days in advance **Carts:** $16.00
Ph: 414-692-2151

Fairways are lined with trees with beautiful, mature trees. The first hole, a 357 yard par 3 is a great opening hole. It's a sharp dogleg over water with water behind the green. Accuracy is a must for this one!

─────────────── SEYMOUR ───────────────

Crystal Springs GC   Yards: 6236, Holes: 18   Restaurant/Bar/Proshop
French Rd., P.O. Box   Par: 72, USGA: 68.9   **GF:** w/day $11, w/end $12
185, 54165   RP: 1 week in advance   **Carts:** $16.00
Ph: 414-833-6348   only

Opening and finishing holes on each side are very good par 5's. Hole #10, 560 yards.

─────────────── SHAWANO ───────────────

Shalagoco CC   Yards: 6201, Holes: 18   Restaurant/Bar/Proshop
1233 Lake Dr., 54166   Par: 71, USGA: 67.9   **GF:** w/end $11
Ph: 715-524-4890   **Carts:** $16.00

Both nines very challenging, fairways lined with trees, six water holes, numerous bunkers and elevated greens. A scenic course with each hole different.

─────────────── SISTER BAY ───────────────

Bay Ridge GC   Yards: 2934, Holes: 9   Proshop
1116 Little Sister Rd.,   Par: 35   **GF:** w/day $12, w/end $16
54234   RP: Do not take   **Carts:** $17.00
Ph: 414-854-4085

Very clean, neat and well kept golf course with two different tees for each hole. An abundance of flowers make Bay Ridge a very special place.

─────────────── SPOONER ───────────────

Spooner GC   Yards: 6407, Holes: 18   Restaurant/Bar/Proshop
Rt 1, 54801   Par: 71, USGA: 68.0   **GF:** w/end $11
Ph: 715-635-3580   RP: Call for tee times **Carts:** $15.00

With 36 bunkers, 4 water holes and fast greens, Spooner Golf Club is a links style course developed on rolling farm terrain intermixed with numerous white pine. The 18th hole requires two demanding shots over water and is one of the best finishing holes in the state.

─────────────── SPRING GREEN ───────────────

Springs GC   Yards: 6603, Holes: 18   Restaurant/Bar/Proshop
Route 3 Golf Course   Par: 72, USGA: 68.9   **GF:** w/day $14
Rd., 53588   RP: Can phone at   **Carts:** $15.00
Ph: 608-588-7707   beginning season

Course is a well-kept secret. Magnificently secluded with beautiful oak, birch, poplar and black walnut. Set in a valley shaped like a bow tie, back nine with streams, springs and ponds. Course is level and walkable with lots of water to carry.

--- STEVENS POINT ---

Sentry World GC
601 N. Michigan Ave.,
54481
Ph: 715-345-1600

Yards: 7055, Holes: 18
Par: 72, USGA: 69.8
RP: March 1 beginning
of booking

Restaurant/Bar/Proshop
GF: w/day $55
Carts: Included

A flat course with 35 acres of water, four big lakes. #5 is a challenge with water down the full left side. #16 is our flower hole with 90-100,000 flowers! Multicolored flowers change every year.

--- STURGEON BAY ---

Cherry Hills GC
5905 Dunn Rd., 54235
Ph: 414-743-3240

Yards: 6163, Holes: 18
Par: 72, USGA: 68.6
RP: Pass, 7 days,
Lodge, 1 year

Restaurant/Bar/Proshop
GF: w/day $17, w/end $19
Carts: $19.00

Great view of pastoral Wisconsin farmland vistas. Each nine different—front open and expansive suggestive of a Scottish links course and the back surrounded by native birch and cedar tress combined with Door County rock cliffs.

--- STURTEVANT ---

Ives Grove Golf Links
14101 Washington Ave.,
53177
Ph: 414-878-3714

Yards: 6915, Holes: 18
Par: 72, USGA: 70.3
RP: 1 week in advance

Restaurant/Bar/Proshop
GF: w/day $14
Carts: $14.50

The sweeping winds at Ives Grove provide an ever changing personality to this outstanding public course. Large well trapped greens, watered fairways and our bent grass tees await all golfers. The strategy and skill needed to finish on the 18th will keep you coming back!

--- SUN PRAIRIE ---

Sun Prairie CC
Box 1, Happy Valley Rd.,
53590
Ph: 608-837-6211

Yards: 6487, Holes: 18
Par: 72, USGA: 69.1
RP: Call ahead

Bar/Proshop
GF: w/day $10
Carts: $14.00

The course is known for having some of the largest greens in the state. Enjoy the peaceful country side setting.

--- SUPERIOR ---

Nemadji GC
N. 58th St. & Hill Ave.,
54880
Ph: 715-394-9022

Yards: 6058, Holes: 36
Par: 72, USGA: 71.4
RP: 1 day M-F; Wknds:
prior Wend.

Restaurant/Bar/Proshop
GF: w/day $8, w/end $8
Carts: $7.50

On May 20, 1992 Nemadji Golf Course became a 36-hole facility. The Old Course features open fairways, lush greens, and a level terrain. The New Course plays to rolling hills, large bunkers, undulating greens and 6 lagoons. Challenge, service and variety are what Nemadji offers

--- WHITEHALL ---

Whitehall CC
West & Creamery Sts.,
54773
Ph: 715-538-4800

Yards: 6080, Holes: 9
Par: 70, USGA: 68.4

Restaurant/Bar/Proshop
GF: w/day $5, w/end $7
Carts: $7.00

You start out on #1 (par 4) with a tree lined dogleg right termed the toughest starting hole in the state by CUGA President. The course has rolling terrain which causes many (up, down, and side) hill stances. Our favorite #2 (dogleg right) par 4 to elevated green with newly planted trees to the right.

———————————— WISCONSIN DELLS ————————————

Christmas Mountain Yards: 6589, Holes: 18 Restaurant/Bar/Proshop
Village Par: 71, USGA: 72.1 **GF:** w/day $22, w/end $22
S. 944 Christmas Mt. RP: Requested, Slope **Carts:** $20.00
Rd.,Hwy H, 53965 129
Ph: 608-253-1000

Relax among the rolling fairways flanked by stands of pines and oaks. The front nine is challenging but somewhat forgiving. The back nine, cut from the wooded hills is more than a walk in the park, requiring both accuracy and distance. Our favorite hole is 18 which brings woods, sand and water into play with the green located at the base of Christmas Mountain ski hill.

———————————— WISCONSIN DELLS ————————————

Cold Water Canyon GC Yards: 2444, Holes: 9 Restaurant/Bar/Proshop
4065 River Rd., Box 64, Par: 33, USGA: 63.4 **GF:** w/day $9
53965 RP: Recommended **Carts:** $9.00
Ph: 608-254-8489

With natural hazards, along the famous canyons of the Upper Dells, the beauty of this course far exceeds others in the area. For instance, though relatively short, Coldwater provides challenge to all levels of golfers. Hole #5 is a 296 yard (par 3) down the hill and over a ravine—onto an elevated green.

———————————— WISCONSIN RAPIDS ————————————

Ridges GC Yards: 6322, Holes: 18 Restaurant/Bar/Proshop
2311 Griffith Ave., 54494 Par: 72, USGA: 69.6 **GF:** w/day $14, w/end $18
Ph: 715-424-1111 RP: Suggested **Carts:** $17.00

The golf course is an 18 hole championship caliber layout winding through woods, a river, and hills.

———————————— WOODRUFF ————————————

Trout Lake G & CC Yards: 6175, Holes: 18 Restaurant/Bar/Proshop
AV 3800 Hwy. 51 North, Par: 72, USGA: 69.6 **GF:** w/day $10
54568 RP: Recommended **Carts:** $18.00
Ph: 715-385-2189

This is a challenging, 18-hole course carved out of the beautiful forests of northern Wisconsin. Huge oak, maple, birch, and pine trees line the fairways as the Trout River wends its way through the course and comes into play on many of the hole.

WYOMING

• Jackson Hole

Cheyenne •

———————— CHEYENNE ————————

**Holding's Little
America GC**
P.O. Box 1529, 82003
Ph: 307-634-2771

Yards: 2080, Holes: 9
Par: 30

Restaurant/Bar
GF: w/day $8

Enjoy golf on our 9-hole executive course surrounding the hotel, but look out for sandtraps, lakes, and a stray antelope or two.

———————— JACKSON ————————

Teton Pines CC
3450 Clubhouse Dr.,
83001
Ph: 307-733-1733

Yards: 7401, Holes: 18
Par: 72, USGA: 74.2
RP: Beginning in April
for season

Restaurant/Bar
GF: w/day $75, w/end $75
Carts: $13.00

Water comes into play on nearly every hole of the meadow-type course, which is well-bunkered with contoured greens. Players rave about the par three #12 (221 yards) with its "over the water" tee shot set dramatically at mountain's base.

———————— JACKSON HOLE ————————

Jackson Hole GC
5200 Spring Gulch Rd.,
83001
Ph: 307-733-3111

Yards: 7168, Holes: 18
Par: 72, USGA: 70.3

Restaurant/Bar/Proshop
GF: w/day $28
Carts: $21.00

Scattered lakes and streams provide interesting and challenging hazards. The course is rated among the 65 "Best Designed" golf courses in the country built prior to 1962 by American Society of Golf Course Architects.

MORE
GOLF COURSES

Alexander City Muni GC, Alexander City, 35010, 205-825-9860 *Alabama*
Par: 72, Holes: 18
Alpine Bay Resort GC, Alpine, 35014, 205-268-9411
Par: 72, Holes: 18
Arrowhead GC, Jasper, 35501, 205-384-3065
Holes: 9
Azalea City GC, 1000 Gaillard Dr., Mobile, 36608, 205-342-4221
Holes: 18
CC of Alabama, Eufaula, 36027, 800-446-4917
Par: 72, Holes: 18
Chriswood GC, Athens, 35611, 205-232-9759
Holes: 9
Citronelle Muni GC, Citronelle, 36522, 205-866-7881
Par: 71, Holes: 9
Colonial GC, Huntsville, 35709, 205-828-0431
Par: 72, Holes: 18
Craig GC, Highway 80 E, Selma, 36701
Holes: 9
Crawford Ridge GC, Anniston, 36205, 205-820-4030
Par: 72, Holes: 18
Cullman Muni GC, 4 Mi south of Cullman Courthou, Cullman, 35055
Holes: 18
Dogwood Hills GC, Route 2, Flat Rock, 35966, 205-632-3634
Holes: 9
Don A. Hawkins, 9820 Roebuck Ave., Birmingham, 35215
Driftwood CC, Bayou La Batre, 36509, 205-824-2429
Par: 72, Holes: 18
Evans Barnes GC, Lurleen Wallace State College, Andalusia, 36420,
205-222-6591 Par: 36, Holes: 9
Frank House Municipal, 900 Green Isle Drive, Bessemer, 35023, 205-424-9540
Holes: 18
Goosepond Colony, Hwy 79, South of Scottsboro, Scottsboro, 35768,
205-259-3037 Holes: 18
Green Acres, Decatur, 36303
Holes: 9
Gulf GC, SP HC 79, Mobile, 36542
Gulf Pines GC, 167 Bay Front Dr., Mobile, 36615, 205-431-6413
Holes: 18
Gulf Shores GC, Hwy. 59, Gulf Shores, 36542, 205-968-7366
Par: 72, Holes: 18, Pro: Joe Terry
Hatchett Creek GC, Goodwater, 35072, 205-839-5612
Holes: 9
Headland Country Club, Rte. 3, Headland, 36345, 205-693-2324
Par: 27, Holes: 9
Highland Park, 3300 Highland Avenue, Birmingham, 35205, 205-326-2445
Holes: 18
Indian Pines GC, Auburn, 36830, 205-821-0880
Par: 71, Holes: 18
Isle Dauphine GC, 100 Orleans Dr., Dauphin Island, 36528, 205-861-2433
Par: 72, Holes: 18
Joe Wheeler GC, SP Aiway 29, RT 4, Rogersville, 35652, 205-247-9308
Yards: 7172, Par: 72, USGA: 70.0, Holes: 18, Pro: Bob Butz
Lagoon Park GC, 2855 Lagoon Park Dr., Montgomery, 36109, 205-271-7000
Yards: 6773, Par: 72, USGA: 70.3, Holes: 18, Pro: Nick Gettys
Lake Guntersville GC, SP Star RTE 63, Box 224, Guntersville, 35976,
205-582-2061 Yards: 6286, Par: 72, Holes: 18, Pro: Buddy Moore

Lakepoint State Resort Park GC, Rt.2 Box 94, Eufaula, 36027,　205-687-6676
Yards: 6531, Par: 72, USGA: 70.9, Holes: 18, Pro: Bobby Bowling
Lakeside GC, Route 2, Oakman, 35579
Holes: 9
Lakeview CC, Greensboro, 36744,　205-624-8654
Holes: 9
Lakeview GC, 9530 Clubhouse Drive, Foley, 36535
Holes: 9
LBW GC, Hwy. 84, Andalusia, 36420,　205-222-8400
Yards: 6515, Par: 72, USGA: 71.6, Holes: 9
Linksman GC, Mobile, 36611,　205-661-0018
Par: 72, Holes: 18
Montgomery GC, 4507 Mobile Highway, Montgomery, 36108,　205-288-9662
Northside Par 3 GC, 2002 Max Luther Dr., Huntsville, 35810
Par: 27, Holes: 9
Olympia Resorts, P.O. Box 6108, Dothan, 36302,　205-677-3321
Yards: 6560, Par: 72, USGA: 72.0, Holes: 18, Pro: Doug Warnock
Oxford Lake 3-Par GC, Oxford, 36203
Par: 27, Holes: 9
Paine Tree GC, 5100 Pine Whispars Rd., Birmingham, 35210
Point Mallard Park, 3109 8th St., Decatur, 35601,　205-350-3005
Par: 72, Holes: 18
Prichard Muni GC, 4603 Golfway Dr., Prichard, 36613
Holes: 9
River Run GC, PO Box 17802, Montgomery, 36117
Holes: 18
Roebuck Municipal GC, 8920 Roebuck Rd., Birmingham, 35215,　205-836-1661
Holes: 18
Roland Cooper State Park, Camden, 36726,　205-682-4838
Par: 36, Holes: 9
Selma GC, Highway 80 W, Selma, 36702
Sky Center GC, 10001 James Reord Rd., Huntsville, 35806
Spring Creek GC, Tuscumbia, 35674,　205-381-5460
Holes: 9
Spring Hill College GC, 4307 Old Shell Rd., Mobile, 36608,　205-343-2356
Par: 72, Holes: 18
Stoney Mountain GC, Guntersville, 35976,　205-582-2598
Par: 72, Holes: 18
Stony Brook GC, Jacksonville, 36265,　205-435-3114
Par: 72, Holes: 18
Terri Pines Country Club, Cullman, 35055,　205-739-0720
Holes: 9
Trojan Oaks Golf & Racquet, Troy State University, Troy, 36082,
205-566-3000　Par: 36, Holes: 9
Twin Lakes GC, Route 10, Jasper, 35501,　205-221-3526
Holes: 9
Union Chapel GC, Jasper, 35501,　205-483-6656
Holes: 9
University of Montevallo, Montevallo, 35115,　205-665-8057
Holes: 18
VA Hospital GC, Tuskegee, 36083,　205-727-0550
Holes: 18
West Side Golf Center, 3501 Cleburn Ave. SW, Birmingham, 35221,
205-923-2979　Holes: 9
Woodland GC, Athens, 35611,　205-233-5847
Holes: 9

Chena Bend GC, APVR-FW-PAD, Ft. Wainwright, 99703, 907-353-6749   *Alaska*
Yards: 6648, Par: 36, USGA: 12.8, Holes: 9
Eagle Glen GC, 21CSG/SSRG Bldg 23-100, Elmendof Anchorage, 99506,
907-552-3821 Yards: 6084, Par: 72, USGA: 68.6, Holes: 18, Pro: Al Frey
Fairbanks G&CC, Fairbanks, 99711, 907-479-6555
Par: 35, Holes: 9

500 Club at Adobe Dam, 4707 W. Pinnacle Peak Rd., Phoenix, 85310   *Arizona*
602-492-9500 Yards: 6700, Par: 72, Holes: 18, Pro: Stuart Bruening
5200 E. Camelback Road PC, 5902 West Indian School Road, Phoenix, 85018
Ahwatukee CC, 12432 S. 48th St., Phoenix, 85044, 602-893-1161
Yards: 6652, Par: 72, USGA: 71.5, Holes: 18, Pro: Doug McDonald
Ahwatukee Lakes GC, 13431 South 44th Street, Phoenix, 85044, 602-893-3004
Yards: 4000, Par: 60, USGA: 59.1, Holes: 18, Pro: Doug MacDonald
Ajo CC, P.O. Drawer 400, Ajo, 85321, 602-387-5011
Yards: 3096, Par: 36, USGA: 67.6, Holes: 9, Pro: Sheila Wiman
Alpine GC, 100 Country Club Ln., Alpine, 85920, 602-339-4944
Yards: 5708, Par: 72, USGA: 65.7, Holes: 18
Apache Wells CC, 5601 East Hermosa Vista Drive, Mesa, 85205, 602-830-4725
Yards: 6006, Par: 71, USGA: 66.7, Holes: 18, Pro: Jim McElheney
Arizona City GC, 200 N. Pima, Arizona City, 85223, 602-466-5327
Yards: 6440, Par: 72, USGA: 70.3, Holes: 18, Pro: Mel McIntyre
Arroyo Dunes Golf Course PC, 32nd St. & Avenue "A", Yuma, 85364,
602-726-8350 Yards: 2174, Par: 54, Holes: 18, Pro: Don King
Arthur Pack Desert GC, 9101 N. Thornydale Rd., Tucson, 85704, 602-744-3322
Yards: 6384, Par: 72, USGA: 69.2, Holes: 18, Pro: Steve Porter
Bellair GC, 17233 North 45th Avenue, Glendale, 85308, 602-978-0330
Yards: 3675, Par: 59, USGA: 55.3, Holes: 18, Pro: Bob Phillips
Benson G & CC, 800 E. Country Club Dr., Benson, 85602, 602-586-2323
Yards: 5690, Par: 35, USGA: 64.7, Holes: 9
Bisbee GC, Newell Road, Naco, 85620, 602-432-7233
Yards: 6713, Par: 72, USGA: 69.5, Holes: 18, Pro: Steve Townsend
Camelot GC, 6210 East McKellips, Mesa, 85205, 602-832-0156
Yards: 5600, Par: 70, USGA: 64.6, Holes: 27, Pro: Kenny Pruitt
Canyon Mesa CC, 500 Jacks Canyon Rd., Sedona, 86336, 602-284-2176
Yards: 2950, Par: 56, Holes: 9, Pro: Lou Nichols
Casa Grande GC, 2121 N. Thornton Rd., Casa Grande, 85222, 602-836-9216
Yards: 3223, Par: 72, USGA: 70.5, Holes: 18, Pro: Tony Farmer
Chaparral CC, 1260 East Mohave Drive, Riviera, 86442, 602-758-3939
Yards: 2350, Par: 32, USGA: 60.6, Holes: 9, Pro: Mike Crawford
Cliff Valley Golf Course PC, 5910 North Oracle Rd., Tucson, 85704,
602-887-6161 Yards: 2261, Par: 54, Holes: 18, Pro: Dave Rodger
Cocopah Bend RV Resort, 6800 Strand Ave., Yuma, 85634, 602-343-1663
Yards: 5264, Par: 70, USGA: 63.4, Holes: 18, Pro: Bob Blackwell
Concho Valley CC, HC 30, Box 900, Concho, 85924, 602-337-4644
Yards: 3069, Par: 36, USGA: 67.6, Holes: 9, Pro: Gary Pratt
Continental Golf Course PC, 7920 East Osborn, Scottsdale, 85251,
602-941-1585 Yards: 3766, Par: 60, USGA: 57.4, Holes: 18, Pro: Neil Brown
Coronado Golf Course PC, 2829 North Miller Road, Scottsdale, 85257,
602-947-8364 Yards: 2000, Par: 31, USGA: 56.7, Holes: 9, Pro: Dick Taylor
Country Meadows GC, 8411 North 107th Avenue, Peoria, 85345, 602-972-1364
Yards: 4292, Par: 63, USGA: 59.4, Holes: 18, Pro: Steve Herron
Cypress GC, 10801 E. McDowell Rd., Scottsdale, 85256, 602-946-5155
Yards: 5200, Par: 38, Holes: 18, Pro: Dave Rabuck
Dave White Regional Park, Casa Grande, 85222
Holes: 9

Desert Fairways GC, 813 W. Calle Rosa, Casa Grande, 85222, 602-723-4418
Yards: 2922, Par: 35, USGA: 66.7, Holes: 9
Desert Forest GC, 37207 N. Mule Train Rd., Carefree, 85377
Desert Highlands GC, 10040 E. Happy Valley Rd., Phoenix, 85255
Desert Hills Golf Course PC, 1245 Desert Hills Dr., Yuma, 85364, 602-344-4653
Yards: 6785, Par: 72, USGA: 69.0, Holes: 18, Pro: Don King
Desert Lakes GC, 5701 Desert Lakes Dr., Fort Mohave, 86427, 602-768-1800
Holes: 9
Desert Mountain-Geronimo GC, 38580 N. Desert Mt. Pkwy, Scottsdale, 85262
Holes: 18
Desert Sands GC, 7400 E. Baseline Road, Mesa, 85208, 602-832-0210
Yards: 3900, Par: 65, USGA: 56.5, Holes: 18, Pro: Les Wimp
Dobson Ranch GC, 2155 South Dobson Rd., Mesa, 85202, 602-644-2291
Yards: 6599, Par: 72, USGA: 71.0, Holes: 18, Pro: Glen Harvey
Dorado Golf Course PC, 6601 E. Speedway Blvd., Tucson, 85710, 602-885-6751
Yards: 3965, Par: 62, USGA: 56.9, Holes: 18, Pro: Jim Silvey, Jr.
Dove Valley GC PC, 220 N. Marshall Loop Rd., Somerton, 85350, 602-627-3262
Yards: 2921, Par: 35, USGA: 66.8, Holes: 9, Pro: Chuck Dodd
Dreamland Villa GC, 5641 E. Albany, Mesa, 85205, 602-985-6591
Yards: 1950, Par: 31, USGA: 57.6, Holes: 9, Pro: Gary Humphrey
Eagle Creek GC, 5734 E. Rancho Manana Blvd., Cave Creek, 85331,
602-252-3245 Yards: 6400, Par: 72, USGA: 69.7, Holes: 18, Pro: Ralph Tiffany
El Rio Golf Course PC, 1400 West Speedway, Tucson, 85745, 602-791-4229
Yards: 6000, Par: 70, USGA: 68.6, Holes: 18, Pro: Trini Alvarez
Elden Hills, 2580 N. Oakmont Drive, Flagstaff, 86004, 602-526-3232
Yards: 6500, Holes: 18
Encanto Golf Course PC, 2705 North 15th Ave., Phoenix, 85007, 602-495-0333
Yards: 6195, Par: 70, USGA: 69.0, Holes: 18, Pro: Jim Farkas
Encanto Nine, 2300 North 17th Ave., Phoenix, 85007, 602-262-6870
Yards: 1700, Par: 30, USGA: 55.0, Holes: 9, Pro: Jim Farkas
Estrella Mountain GC, South Bullard Avenue, Goodyear, 85338, 602-932-3714
Yards: 6415, Par: 71, USGA: 69.3, Holes: 18, Pro: Dick Mulvaine
Evergreen Golf Course PC, 10801 E. McDowell, Scottsdale, 85256,
602-946-5155 Yards: 3600, Par: 38, Holes: 9
Fiesta Lakes GC, 1415 S. Westwood, Mesa, 85202, 602-868-0377
Yards: 1500, Par: 29, Holes: 9, Pro: Todd Bartholow
Foothills Golf Course PC, 2201 E. Clubhouse Dr., Phoenix, 85044,
602-460-8337 Yards: 6967, Par: 72, USGA: 72.7, Holes: 18, Pro: Robert Prange
Forty Niner GC, 12000 E. Tanque Verde, Tucson, 85749
Fountain Hills GC, 10440 Indian Wells Drive, Fountain Hills, 85268,
602-837-1173 Yards: 6087, Par: 71, USGA: 68.9, Holes: 18, Pro: Sam Cobb
Fountain of the Sun CC, 8001 East Broadway, Mesa, 85208, 602-986-3128
Yards: 4020, Par: 62, USGA: 58.0, Holes: 18, Pro: Ken Taylor
Francisco Grande GC, 2600 Gila Bend Hwy., Casa Grande, 85222,
602-426-9205 Yards: 6454, Par: 72, USGA: 68.5, Holes: 18, Pro: Kent Chase
Fred Enke Golf Course PC, 8250 E. Irvington Rd., Tucson, 85730,
602-791-2539 Yards: 5800, Par: 72, USGA: 70.5, Holes: 18, Pro: Terry Wilks
Gila River CC, 3831 N. Florence Blvd., Florence, 85232, 602-868-5301
Yards: 1272, Par: 29, Holes: 9, Pro: Russ Norm
Glen Canyon GC, Box 1333, Highway 89, Page, 86040, 602-645-2715
Yards: 3259, Par: 36, USGA: 70.3, Holes: 9, Pro: Nick Neeley
Glen Lakes GC, 5450 W. Northern, Glendale, 85302, 602-939-7541
Yards: 2381, Par: 33, USGA: 60.4, Holes: 9, Pro: Van Johns
Gold Canyon GC, 6100 S. Kings Ranch Rd., Appache Junction, 85219,
602-982-9449 Yards: 6398, Par: 71, USGA: 70.9, Holes: 18, Pro: Phil Green

Happy Trails GC, 17200 West Bell Road, Surprise, 85374, 602-975-5500
Yards: 6652, Par: 72, USGA: 73.8, Holes: 18, Pro: Matt Michaels
Haven GC, 110 North Abregado, Green Valley, 85614, 602-625-4281
Yards: 6829, Par: 72, USGA: 68.9, Holes: 18, Pro: E. Harrington
Hayden GC, Golf Course Rd., Hayden, 85235, 602-356-7801
Yards: 2827, Par: 35, USGA: 66.6, Holes: 9, Pro: Andy Guzman
Hidden Cove Golf Resort, Box 70, Hidden Cove Rd., Holbrook, 86005,
602-524-3097   Yards: 3149, Par: 36, USGA: 66.1, Holes: 9, Pro: Carlyle DeWitt
Hillcrest GC, 20002 Star Ridge Drive, Sun City West, 85375, 602-584-1500
Yards: 6900, Par: 72, USGA: 69.8, Holes: 18, Pro: Gary Balliet
Hohokam CC, H 287-Florence & Coolidge,POB, Coolidge, 85228, 602-723-7192
Yards: 6184, Par: 70, USGA: 67.2, Holes: 18, Pro: Dennis Weadock
Karsten GC at ASU, 1125 E. First St., Tempe, 85281, 602-921-8070
Yards: 7057, Par: 72, USGA: 69.9, Holes: 18, Pro: Gary White
Kearny GC, P.O. Box 927, 301 Airport Rd., Kearny, 85237, 602-363-7441
Yards: 3168, Par: 35, USGA: 69.1, Holes: 9
Ken McDonald Golf Course PC, 800 Divot Drive, Tempe, 85283, 602-730-1767
Yards: 6316, Par: 72, USGA: 68.7, Holes: 18, Pro: Dick Sanders
Kingman GC, 1001 Gates Ave., Kingman, 86401, 602-753-6593
Yards: 3170, Par: 36, USGA: 69.8, Holes: 9, Pro: Paul Mowry
Kino Springs CC, One Kino Spring Drive, Nogales, 85621, 602-287-8701
Yards: 6017, Par: 72, USGA: 67.3, Holes: 18, Pro: Jim Chestnut
La Paz County GC, 72 Emerald Canyon Drive, Parker, 85344, 602-669-6155
Holes: 18
Legend GC, 21025 N. 67th Ave., Glendale, 85308, 602-561-9778
Yards: 7000, Par: 72, USGA: 73.8, Holes: 18, Pro: Jeff Quinn
London Bridge GC—London Brid, 2400 Clubhouse Drive, Lake Havasu,
86403, 602-855-2719   Yards: 6618, Par: 71, USGA: 69.5, Holes: 18, Pro: Van Johns
Maryvale Golf Course PC, 5902 West Indian School Road, Phoenix, 85033,
602-495-0444   Yards: 6191, Par: 72, USGA: 68.2, Holes: 18, Pro: John Martin
Meadow Hills GC, 3425 Country Club Rd., Nogales, 85621, 602-281-0011
Yards: 3441, Par: 36, USGA: 68.9, Holes: 9, Pro: A. Zuniga
Mesa Del Sol, 10583 Camino del Sol, Yuma, 85365, 602-342-1283
Yards: 6765, Par: 72, USGA: 69.1, Holes: 18, Pro: Dick Walters
Mount Graham Country Club PC, P.O. Box 743, Safford, 85548, 602-428-1260
Yards: 6354, Par: 72, USGA: 69.5, Holes: 18, Pro: Burt Watkins
Mountain Shadows Country Club, 5641 East Lincoln Dr., Scottsdale, 85253,
602-948-7111   Yards: 3000, Par: 56, USGA: 51.7, Holes: 18, Pro: Gene Counter
Mountain View GC, 1430 E. University, Mesa, 85203, 602-834-7191
Yards: 1100, Par: 29, Holes: 9
Palo Verde Golf Course PC, 6215 North 15th Ave., Phoenix, 85015,
602-249-9930   Yards: 1820, Par: 30, USGA: 55.3, Holes: 9, Pro: Scott Monroe
Paradise Valley Park Golf Cour, 3505 East Union Hills Drive, Phoenix, 85032,
602-992-7190   Yards: 4000, Par: 61, USGA: 57.0, Holes: 18, Pro: Brian Whitcomb
Pepperwood Golf Course PC, 647 West Baseline Road, Tempe, 85283,
602-831-9457   Yards: 2010, Par: 31, USGA: 56.0, Holes: 9, Pro: Leo Johnson
Riverview GC, 2202 W. 8th St., Mesa, 85201, 602-644-3515
Yards: 3150, Par: 36, USGA: 69.2, Holes: 9, Pro: Jim Mooney
Tubac Valley Counrty Club PC, Box 1358, Otera Rd., Tubac, 85646,
602-398-2211   Yards: 6592, Par: 72, USGA: 70.4, Holes: 18, Pro: Joe Stephens
Phoenician GC, 6000 E. Camelback Rd., Scottsdale, 85251, 602-423-2449
Yards: 6487, Par: 71, USGA: 71.2, Holes: 18, Pro: Doug Hoskins
Pima Golf Resort PC, 7331 North Pima Road, Scottsdale, 85253, 602-948-3370
Yards: 6952, Par: 72, USGA: 69.8, Holes: 18, Pro: Tom Evans
Pine Meadows, Country Club Dr., Overgaard, 85933, 602-535-4220
Yards: 2631, Par: 34, USGA: 64.4, Holes: 9, Pro: Larry Morrison

Pinetop Lakes CC, P.O. Box 1699D, Bucksprings Rd, Pinetop, 85935,
602-369-4531   Yards: 4558, Par: 63, USGA: 60.6, Holes: 18, Pro: Mike Wright
Pinewood CC, P.O. Box 584, Munds Park, 86017,   602-286-1110
Yards: 6434, Par: 72, USGA: 69.2, Holes: 18, Pro: Al Murdock
Pueblo Del Sol Golf Course PC, 2770 St. Andrews Drive, Sierra Vista, 85635,
602-378-6444   Yards: 6599, Par: 72, USGA: 70.0, Holes: 18, Pro: Pat Kelly
Pueblo El Mirage, 11201 North El Mirage Road, El Mirage, 85335,   602-583-0425
Yards: 6521, Par: 72, USGA: 70.0, Holes: 18, Pro: Pat Lynch
Queen Valley CC, 600 Fairway Dr., Appache Junction, 85220,   602-463-2214
Yards: 4459, Par: 66, USGA: 59.9, Holes: 18, Pro: Al Huestis
Ramada Pima Golf Resort, 7330 North Pima Rd., Scottsdale, 85258,
602-948-3800   Yards: 7000, Par: 72, USGA: 69.8, Holes: 18, Pro: Jim Mooney
Scottsdale GC, 7702 E. Shea Blvd., Scottsdale, 85260,   602-948-6911
Yards: 6200, Par: 70, USGA: 69.0, Holes: 27, Pro: Bruce L. Brown
Rancho Del Rey GC, 21515 Rancho Del Rey Blvd., Queen Creek, 85242,
602-987-9059   Yards: 5840, Par: 71, USGA: 67.4, Holes: 18, Pro: Henry Trevino
Resort at Gold Canyon, 6210 S. Kings Ranch Road, Apache Junction, 85220,
602-982-9449   Yards: 6398, Par: 71, USGA: 68.9, Holes: 18, Pro: Phil Green
Rio Rico GC, 1550 Camino a la Posada, Rio Rico, 85621,   602-281-8567
Yards: 6426, Par: 72, USGA: 70.9, Holes: 18
Rio Verde CC, Box 1, Four Peaks Blvd., Rio Verde, 85255,   602-991-3451
Yards: 6554, Par: 72, USGA: 70.8, Holes: 36, Pro: Fred Anschutz
Road Haven GC, 1000 South Idaho, Apache Junction, 85220,   602-982-GOLF
Yards: 1029, Par: 27, USGA: 24.8, Holes: 9, Pro: Steve Hatcher
Royal Palms GC, 1415 E. McKellips, Mesa, 85203,   602-964-1709
Yards: 1501, Par: 30, USGA: 52.2, Holes: 9
Saddlebrooke GC, 64500 E. Saddlebrooke Blvd., Tucson, 85737,   602-825-2505
Yards: 3129, Par: 36, USGA: 69.4, Holes: 9, Pro: Jim Chestnut
San Ignacio GC, 24245 S. Camino del Sol, Green Valley, 85614,   602-648-3468
Yards: 6700, Par: 72, Holes: 18, Pro: Kevin Lewis
Santa Rita CC, 16461 S. Houghton Rd., Tucson, 85747,   602-629-9717
Yards: 6070, Par: 71, USGA: 68.0, Holes: 18, Pro: Darrell Crossan
Snowflake Golf Course PC, Box 1116, Highway 277 West, Snowflake, 85937,
602-536-7233   Yards: 3112, Par: 36, USGA: 68.2, Holes: 9, Pro: Steve Schneider
Stone Bridge GC, 2400 Clubhouse Dr., Lake Havasu, 86403,   602-855-2719
Yards: 6166, Par: 71, USGA: 68.8, Holes: 18, Pro: Jim Tuttle
Stonecreek, The Golf Club, 4435 E Paradise Village Pkwy S, Paradise Valley,
85032,   602-953-9110   Yds: 6839, Par: 71, USGA: 73.5, Holes: 18, Pro: Mike Petty
Sun City Lakes East, 10433 Talisman Road, Sun City, 85351,   602-876-3023
Yards: 3244, Par: 60, USGA: 56.3, Holes: 18, Pro: Joe Lynch
Sun Village PC, 14300 W. Bell Road, Surprise, 85374,   602-584-5774
Yards: 1029, Par: 27, USGA: 46.8, Holes: 9, Pro: Tim Hasbrouck
Sunland Village GC, 725 South Rochester, Mesa, 85206,   602-832-3691
Yards: 3579, Par: 62, USGA: 56.6, Holes: 18, Pro: Sue Barle
Tatum Ranch Golf Course PC, 4410 E. Dixileta Dr., Phoenix, 85024,
602-252-1230   Yards: 6870, Par: 72, USGA: 72.3, Holes: 18, Pro: Michael Ellis
TCP at Starpass, 3645 W. 22nd St., Tucson, 85745,   602-622-6060
Yards: 7010, Par: 72, USGA: 74.9, Holes: 18, Pro: Jeff Reich
Thunderbird Country Club PC, 701 East Thunderbird, Phoenix, 85040,
602-243-1262   Yards: 6169, Par: 72, USGA: 68.9, Holes: 18, Pro: J.D.Thompson
Tierra Grande, 701 Clubhouse Drive, Casa Grande, 85222,   602-723-4418
Yards: 2900, Par: 35, Holes: 9, Pro: Al Heustis
Trail Ridge GC, 21021 N. 151st Ave., Sun City West, 85375,   602-546-0858
Yards: 6605, Par: 72, USGA: 71.2, Holes: 18, Pro: Ed Ekis
Tucson Estates Golf Course PC, 2500 South Western Way, Tucson, 85713,
602-883-0151   Yards: 2584, Par: 57, Holes: 18, Pro: Al Cinquemoni

Twin Lakes Municipal Golf Course, Rex Allen Jr. Rd., Willcox, 85643, 602-384-2720 Yards: 3076, Par: 36, USGA: 64.7, Holes: 9, Pro: Wm. Hamilton
Valle Vista CC, 9686 Concho Drive, Kingman, 86401, 602-757-8744 Yards: 6266, Par: 72, USGA: 67.4, Holes: 18, Pro: Betty Raver
Verde Valley CC, P.O. Box 458, Country Club Rd., Clarkdale, 86324, 602-634-5491 Yards: 3193, Par: 36, USGA: 67.8, Holes: 9, Pro: George Short
Viewpoint R.V. Golf Resort, 8700 East University Drive, Mesa, 85207, 602-373-8715 Yards: 2153, Par: 34, USGA: 58.9, Holes: 9, Pro: Mike Rus
Villa De Paz Golf Course PC, 4220 North 103rd Ave., Phoenix, 85039, 602-877-1171 Yards: 6153, Par: 72, USGA: 67.2, Holes: 18, Pro: P. Schumacher
Villa Monterey Golf Course PC, 8102 E. Camelback, Scottsdale, 85251, 602-990-7100 Yards: 1889, Par: 31, USGA: 56.7, Holes: 9, Pro: Gary Bonesteel
Westbrook Village CC, 19260 N. Westbrook Parkway, Peoria, 85345, 602-933-0174 Yards: 6412, Par: 71, USGA: 69.1, Holes: 18, Pro: Terry Johnson
Wickenburg CC, Country Club Dr., Wickenburg, 85358, 602-684-2011 Yards: 3191, Par: 38, USGA: 69.3, Holes: 9, Pro: Harvey Eckert
Winslow Municipal GC, North Road, Winslow, 86047, 602-289-4915 Yards: 3214, Par: 36, USGA: 68.8, Holes: 9, Pro: Larry Parker

Arkadelphia G&CC, Route 3, Box 312, Arakdelphia, 71923 *Arkansas*
Holes: 9
Bald Knob CC, P.O. Box 789, Bald Knob, 72010
Holes: 9
Batesville CC, Box 2996, Batesville, 72501
Holes: 9
Batesville Muni GC, Batesville, 72501, 501-793-9947
Yards: 2999, Par: 35, Holes: 9
Bay Ridge Boat & GC, Route 2, Dardanelle, 72934, 501-229-4162
Yards: 2984, Par: 36, Holes: 9
Bella Vista CC, Bella Vista, 72712
Holes: 54
Belvedere CC, Route 18 Box 115, Hot Springs, 71901
Holes: 18
Ben Geren Regional Park GC, Box 3609, Fort Smith, 72913, 501-646-5301
Yards: 6702, Par: 72, Holes: 18
Big Lake CC, P.O. Box 599, Manila, 72442, 501-561-9988
Yards: 2952, Par: 36, Holes: 9
Blytheville CC, P.O. Box 265, Hwy 61 N, Blytheville, 72316, 501-763-7821
Yards: 6600, Par: 71, USGA: 67.3, Holes: 18, Pro: Gary Darter
Brinkley CC, Inc., P.O. Box 752, Brinkley, 72021
Holes: 9
Burns Park GC, P.O. Box 973, North Little Rock, 72114, 501-758-5800
Yards: 6354, Par: 71, Holes: 27
Cadron Valley CC, P.O. Box 456, Conway, 72032
Holes: 18
Camden CC, 1915 Washington St., Camden, 71701
Holes: 18
Carroll County CC, P.O. Box 66, Berryville, 72616, 501-423-3230
Yards: 2900, Par: 36, Holes: 9
Cedars CC, P.O. Box 249, Van Buren, 72596, 501-474-2412
Yards: 2857, Par: 36, Holes: 9
Clarksville CC, P.O. Box 396, Clarksville, 72830, 501-754-3026
Yards: 3129, Par: 36, Holes: 9
Conway CC, P.O. Box 669, Conway, 72032
Holes: 18

Cortez GC, Hot Springs Village, 71901
Holes: 18
Country Club of Little Rock, 4200 Country Club, Little Rock, 72207
Holes: 18
Crowley Ridge CC, P.O. Box 595, Wynne, 72396
Holes: 9
Cypress Creek CC, P.O. Box 486, Augusta, 72006
Holes: 9
DeGray State Park Golf Course, Route 3, Box 490, Bismarck, 71929,
501-865-3711   Yards: 6417, Par: 72, USGA: 69.7, Holes: 18
Delta CC, Box 846, McGehee, 71654
Holes: 9
DeQueen G&CC, Inc., P.O. Box 870, DeQueen, 71832
Holes: 9
DeSota GC, Hot Springs Village, 71901
Holes: 36
Diamond Hills CC, Diamond City, 72644,   501-422-7613
Yards: 6311, Par: 69, Holes: 18
Diamondhead G&CC, Box 6053, Hot Springs, 71901,   501-262-3734
Par: 72, Holes: 18
Duffer's Club, P.O. Box 677, North Little Rock, 72115,   501-753-5608
Yards: 2768, Par: 35, Holes: 9
El Dorado G&CC, P.O. Box 1111, El Dorado, 71730
Holes: 18
El Dorado Lions Club GC, P.O. Box 1228, El Dorado, 71730,   501-863-0800
Yards: 6380, Par: 72, Holes: 18
England CC, P.O. Box 223, England, 72046
Holes: 9
Fayetteville CC, Route 8, Fayetteville, 72701
Holes: 18
Fianna Hills CC, P.O. Box 3007, Fort Smith, 72901
Holes: 18
Fordyce GC, Box 633, Fordyce, 71742
Holes: 9
Fort Smith CC, 5500 Midland Blvd., Fort Smith, 72901,   501-783-9308
Yards: 2476, Par: 35, Holes: 9
Fox Hills CC, Route #4 Box 362-B, Paragould, 72450,   501-236-7847
Yards: 2868, Par: 35, Holes: 9
Foxwood CC, 701 Foxwood Drive, Jacksonville, 72076,   501-982-1254
Yards: 6397, Par: 72, Holes: 18
Grand Prairie CC, P.O. Box 459, Hazen, 72064,   501-255-3043
Yards: 6397, Par: 35, Holes: 9
Hardscrabble GC, 5211 S. Cliff Dr., Fort Smith, 72901
Holes: 18
Helena CC, Box 2518, Walden Ridge Drive, West Helena, 72390
Holes: 18
Hindman Park GC, 60 Brookview Drive, Little Rock, 72209,   501-565-6450
Yards: 6501, Par: 72, Holes: 18
Holiday Island CC, Route 3 Box 226, Holiday Island, 72632,   501-253-9511
Yards: 5954, Par: 70, Holes: 27
Hope CC, Box 134, Hope, 71801
Holes: 9
Horseshoe Bend Turkey Mtn. GC, Horseshoe Bend, 72512,   501-670-5252
Par: 73, Holes: 18
Hot Springs CC—Arlington, 3400 Malvern Ave., Hot Springs, 71901,
501-624-2661   Yards: 6646, Par: 72, Holes: 18, Pro: John Endsley

Hot Springs CC- Pineview GC, Hot Springs, 71912, 501-624-2661
Yards: 2717, Par: 34, Holes: 9
Indian Hills CC, P.O.Box 3008, Fairfield Bay, 72038
Holes: 18
Jonesboro CC, P.O.Box 1325, Jonesboro, 72403-1
Holes: 18
Lake Village CC, P.O.Box 627, Lake Village, 71653
Holes: 9
Little Creek Recreation Club, Box 38, Ratcliff, 72951
Holes: 9
Little River Club, Inc., Horation, 71842
Holes: 9
Little Rock GC, 4200 Country Club Blvd., Little Rock, 72207
Magnolia CC, P.O. Box 654, Magnolia, 71753
Holes: 18
Malvern CC, P.O. Box 456, Malvern, 72104
Holes: 9
Marianna CC, 190 Rodgers T., Marianna, 72360
Holes: 9
Maumelle CC, 100 Club Manor Road, Maumelle, 72118
Holes: 18
Meadowbrook CC, Box 339, West Memphis, 72301
Holes: 18
Millwood CC, Route 1 Box 43-F-35, Ashdown, 71822
Holes: 18
Montivrllo CC, P.O. Box 463, Monticello, 71655
Holes: 9
Morrilton G&CC, P.O. Box 381, Morrilton, 72110
Holes: 9
Mountain Ranch GC, P.O. Box 3008, Fairfield Bay, 72088, 501-884-3333
Yards: 6780, Par: 72, Holes: 18
Nashville CC, Route 5 Box 49B, Nashville, 71852
Holes: 18
Newport CC, Inc., P. O. Box 661, Newport, 72112
Holes: 18
North Hills CC, P. O. Box 6084, Sherwood, 72116
Holes: 18
Oakwood Hills CC, P. O. Box 574, DeWitt, 72042
Holes: 9
Ouachita CC, P. O. Box 1165, Mena, 71953
Holes: 9
Ozark Recreation Club, Box 543, Ozark, 72949
Holes: 9
Paradise Valley Athletic Club, P.O. Box 1132, Fayetteville, 72701
Holes: 18
Paragould CC, Route 3, Box 373, Paragould, 72450
Holes: 18
Pine Bluff CC, P. O. Box 6809, Pine Bluff, 71601
Holes: 18
Pine Hills Golf & Tennis Club, P. O. Box 111, Smackover, 71762
Holes: 9
Pines Recreation Assn., P. O. Box 431, Clarendon, 72029
Pleasant Valley GC, 1 Pleasant Valley Dr., Little Rock, 72212
Holes: 27
Prairie CC, P. O. Box 944, Crosset, 71635, 501-364-2456
Holes: 9

Prescott CC, P. O. Box 572, Prescott, 71857
Holes: 9
Razorback Park GC, Fayetteville, 72701, 501-443-5862
Yards: 2872, Par: 35, Holes: 9
Rebsamen Park GC, 210 Poinsetta, Little Rock, 72205, 501-666-7965
Yards: 6271, Par: 71, Holes: 27
Red Apple CC, Iden Isle, Heber Springs, 72543, 501-362-3131
Yards: 6431, Par: 71, Holes: 18
Red Martin CC, P. O. Box 128, Gurdon, 71743
Holes: 9
Ridgecrest Club, Inc., P. O. Box 369, Forrest City, 72335
Holes: 9
Rivercliff GC, Route 1 Box 507, Bull Shoals, 72619
Holes: 9
Riverlawn CC, P. O. Box 134, Osceola, 72370
Holes: 18
Rolling Hills CC, P. O. Box 250, Pocahontas, 72455, 501-892-4931
Yards: 3268, Par: 35, Holes: 9
Rolling Hills CC, P. O. Box 260, Cabot, 72023
Holes: 18
Rosswood GC, 1100 Country Club Ln., P.O.Box, Pine Bluff, 71601
Holes: 18
Russellville CC, P. O. Box 1143, Russellville, 72891
Holes: 18
Searcy CC, Box 52, Searcy, 72149
Holes: 9
Searcy GC, P. O. Box 1004, Searcy, 72143
Holes: 9
Sheridan GC, P. O. Box 144, Sheridan, 72150
Holes: 9
Siloam Springs CC, P. O. Box 74, Siloam Springs, 72761
Holes: 9
South Haven GC, Route 10 Box 201, Texarkana, 75501, 501-474-2412
Yards: 2690, Par: 35, Holes: 9
Springdale CC, P.O. Box 64, Springdale, 72764
Holes: 9
Stuttgart CC, P.O. Box 608, Stuttgart, 72160
Holes: 9
Sugar Creek CC, Clay County Re, P.O. Box 346, Piggott, 72454
Holes: 9
Texarkana CC, Box 513, Texarkana, 75501
Holes: 18
Thunderbird CC, Inc., 2909 Case Ford Road, Heber Springs, 72553, 501-362-5200
Yards: 3000, Par: 36, Holes: 9
Trace Creek CC, Box 242, Benton, 72015
Holes: 9
Trumann CC, P. O. Box 5, Trumann, 72472
Holes: 9
Twin Lakes Golf Assn., Route #4 Box 110A, Mountain Home, 72653
Holes: 18
University Heights GC, Brookland, 72417, 501-932-3253
Par: 36, Holes: 9
Vache Grasse Recreation Center, P. O. Box 411, Greenwood, 72396, 501-996-4191
Yards: 6326, Par: 72, Holes: 18

Village Creek GC, P. O. Box 252, Newport, 72112
Holes: 9
Waldron CC, Waldron, 72958,   501-637-4374
Yards: 3126, Par: 36, Holes: 9
Walnut Lake CC, P. O. Box 121, Pickens, 71662
Holes: 9
War Memorial Munik GC, 5511 West Markham, Little Rock, 72205,
501-663-0854   Yards: 4480, Par: 65, Holes: 18
Warren CC, Route 2, Warren, 71671
Holes: 9
Western Hills CC, 5207 Western Hills Ave., Little Rock, 72204,   501-565-5830
Yards: 5939, Par: 71, Holes: 18
Yarborough Landing, Ashdown, 71822,   501-898-6674
Yards: 6915, Par: 72, Holes: 18

Adams Springs GC, Hwy 175 at Snead Ct, PO Box, Loc Lomond,   *California*
95426, 707-928-9992   Yds: 5182, Par: 70, USGA: 64.7, Holes: 9, Pro: V.S. Doucette
Aetna Springs GC, 1600 Aetna Springs Rd., Pope Valley, 94567,   707-965-2115
Yards: 5372, Par: 70, USGA: 64.7, Holes: 9, Pro: Dale Frandsen
Airways GC, 5440 E. Shields Ave., Fresno, 93727,   209-291-6254
Yards: 5300, Par: 68, USGA: 63.8, Holes: 18, Pro: Art Forrester
Alamanor West GC, 111 Slim Drive, Lake Almanor W, Chester, 96020,
916-259-4555   Yards: 3135, Par: 36, USGA: 34.8, Holes: 9
Alameda GC—Jack Clark Course, One Memorial Dr., Alameda, 94501,
415-522-4321   Yards: 5947, Par: 71, USGA: 69.1, Holes: 18, Pro: Robert Klein, Jr.
Alhambra Municipal GC, 630 So. Almansor St., Alhambra, 91801,   818-570-5059
Yards: 5156, Par: 70, USGA: 62.0, Holes: 18, Pro: Jerry Wisz
Allen's GC, 2780 Sacramento Dr., Redding, 96001,   916-241-5055
Yards: 3412, Par: 62, USGA: 56.5, Holes: 9, Pro: Pat Allen
Allen's Women's GC, 2780 Sacramento Dr., Redding, 96001,   916-241-5055
Yards: 3368, Par: 61, USGA: 58.6, Holes: 9, Pro: Pat Allen
Almaden GC, 6663 Hampton Dr., San Jose, 95120
Alta Sierra G&CC, 144 Tammy Way, Grass Valley, 95949,   916-273-2010
Yards: 6342, Par: 18, USGA: 70.1, Holes: y, Pro: Jeff Chlebourn
Altadena Town & CC, 2290 Country Club Dr., Atadena, 91001,   818-794-5792
Yards: 5828, Par: 72, USGA: 66.3, Holes: 18, Pro: Boyd Glazier
Ancil Hoffman Park GC, 6700 Tarshes Dr., Carmichael, 95608,   916-482-5660
Yards: 6794, Par: 72, USGA: 71.0, Holes: 18, Pro: Steve Price
Anderson-Tucker Oaks GC, P.O. Box 654, Anderson, 96007,   916-365-3350
Yards: 6346, Par: 72, USGA: 68.4, Holes: 9, Pro: Bill De Wildt
Angus Hills GC, 14520 Musso Rd., Auburn, 95603,   916-878-7818
Yards: 2378, Par: 54, USGA: 51.7, Holes: 9, Pro: Fred Strong
Aptos Par-3 GC, 2600 Mar Vista Dr., Aptos, 95003, 408-688-5000
Yards: 2100, Par: 27, Holes: 9, Pro: Howard Menge
Aptos Seascape GC, 610 Clubhouse Dr., Aptos, 95003,   408-688-3212
Yards: 6054, Par: 72, USGA: 69.0, Holes: 18, Pro: Don Elser
Arbuckle GC, POB 975, Hillgate Road, Arbuckle, 95912,   916-476-2470
Yards: 6460, Par: 72, USGA: 69.9, Holes: 18, Pro: Carl Funk
Arrowhead GC, 1901 N. Warner St., Alturas, 96101,   916-233-3404
Yards: 6136, Par: 70, USGA: 67.0, Holes: 9, Pro: Bud Porter
Avondale GC, 75800 Avandale Dr., Palm Desert, 92260,   619-345-2727
Yards: 6465, Par: 72, USGA: 70.4, Holes: 18, Pro: Fred Scherzer
Azusa Greens CC, 919 West Sierra Madre Blvd., Azusa, 91702,   818-969-1727
Yards: 6126, Par: 70, USGA: 67.7, Holes: 18, Pro: Vince Castillo
Bajamar CC, Box 27, San Ysidro, 92073,   016-678-3838
Yards: 5972, Par: 71, USGA: 69.0, Holes: 18, Pro: Rodolfo Perez

Balboa Park CG, Golf Course Dr., San Diego, 92102, 619-239-1632
Yards: 6058, Par: 72, USGA: 68.1, Holes: 18, Pro: Mike Turnbull
Benbow GC, 7000 Benbow Dr., Garberville, 95440, 707-923-2777
Yards: 5098, Par: 70, USGA: 64.1, Holes: 18, Pro: Don Hunt
Bennett Valley GC, 3330 Yulupa Ave., Santa Rosa, 95405, 707-528-3673
Yards: 6221, Par: 71, USGA: 68.6, Holes: 18, Pro: Bob Borowicz
Bethel Island GC, 3303 Gateway Rd., P.O. Box 455, Bethel Island, 94511,
415-684-2654   Yards: 6120, Par: 72, USGA: 68.8, Holes: 18, Pro: Coreen Hornbeak
Bidwell Park GC—El Rancho Ch, Wildwood Ave., P. O. Box 1341, Chico,
95927, 916-891-8417   Yards: 6163, Par: 70, USGA: 68.1, Holes: 18, Pro: Dan Kowall
Bijou GC, South Lake Tahoe, 95705, 916-541-4611
Yards: 2015, Par: 30, Holes: 9
Bing Maloney GC, 6801 Freeport Blvd., P.O. Box, Sacramento, 95823,
916-428-9401   Yards: 6281, Par: 71, USGA: 69.7, Holes: 18, Pro: Tom Doris
Birch Hills GC, Box 1150, 2250 East Birch St., Brea, 92621, 714-990-0201
Yards: 3521, Par: 59, USGA: 54.0, Holes: 18, Pro: Larry Taylor
Bishop CC, POB 1586, Highway 395 South, Bishop, 93514, 619-873-5828
Yards: 6072, Par: 71, USGA: 67.1, Holes: 18
Black Lake GC, 1490 Golf Course Lane, Nipomo, 93444, 805-481-4204
Yards: 6427, Par: 72, USGA: 70.7, Holes: 18, Pro: Al Carlin
Black Oak Women's GC, 2455 Black Oak Rd., Auburn, 95603, 916-885-8315
Yards: 5240, Par: 72, USGA: 69.8, Holes: 9, Pro: Thurm Krater
Black Oak GC, 2455 Black Oak Rd., Auburn, 95603, 916-885-8315
Yards: 5896, Par: 72, USGA: 69.4, Holes: 9, Pro: Thurm Krater
Blackberry Farm GC, 22100 Stevens Creek Blvd., Cupertino, 95014,
408-253-9200   Yards: 3250, Par: 58, USGA: 54.6, Holes: 9, Pro: Jeff Piserchio
Blue Rock Springs, Vallejo, 94589, 707-643-8476
Par: 72, Holes: 18
Blythe GC, Route 1 Box 38A, Blythe, 92226, 619-922-7272
Yards: 6626, Par: 72, USGA: 70.6, Holes: 18, Pro: Willie Getchell
Bolado Park GC, P.O. Box 419, Tres Pinos, 95075, 408-628-9995
Yards: 5879, Par: 70, USGA: 67.5, Holes: 9, Pro: Bob Trevino
Borrego Springs Road Runner Club, 1010 Palm Canyon Drive, Borrego
Springs, 92004, 619-767-5373   Yards: 2445, Par: 36, Holes: 9, Pro: Daniel Slade
Brookside GC, 1133 Rosemont Ave., Pasadena, 91103, 818-796-8151
Yards: 6611, Par: 72, USGA: 70.7, Holes: 18, Pro: John Wells
Brooktrails GC, 24860 Birch St., P.O. Box 1003, Willits, 95490, 707-459-6761
Yards: 2718, Par: 56, USGA: 50.1, Holes: 9, Pro: Bill Runberg
Buchanan Fields GC, 3330 Concord Ave., Concord, 94520, 415-682-1846
Yards: 5164, Par: 68, USGA: 63.0, Holes: 9, Pro: Frank Benicasa
Buckingham G&CC, 2855 Eastlake Drive, Kelseyville, 95454, 707-279-4863
Yards: 6238, Par: 72, USGA: 67.9, Holes: 18
Buena Vista GC, Rt. 1 Box 115-C, Taft, 93268, 805-763-5124
Yards: 6656, Par: 72, USGA: 69.0, Holes: 18, Pro: David James
Buenaventura GC, 5880 Olivas Park Dr., Santa Barbara, 93003
Calimesa CC, 1300 South Third St., Calimesa, 92320, 714-795-2488
Yards: 5513, Par: 70, USGA: 65.5, Holes: 18, Pro: C. L. Simmons
Camarillo Springs GC, 791 Camarillo Springs Rd., Camarillo, 93010,
805-484-1075   Yards: 5876, Par: 71, USGA: 67.0, Holes: 18, Pro: Louie Garcia
Camelot Golf Club, 3430 Camelot Blvd., Mojave, 93501, 805-824-4107
Yards: 6366, Par: 72, USGA: 70.3, Holes: 9, Pro: Pat Simmons
Campus Commons GC, #2 Cadillac Dr., Sacramento, 95825, 916-922-5861
Yards: 3346, Par: 58, USGA: 54.0, Holes: 9, Pro: Mike Fancolli
Canyon GC, 1100 Murray Canyon Dr., Palm Springs, 92264, 619-323-3921
Yards: 6419, Par: 72, USGA: 70.1, Holes: 18, Pro: David Reardon

Canyon Hotel GC, 28-505 S. Palm Canyon Dr., Palm Springs, 92262
Canyon Lakes GC, 640 Bollinger Canyon Way, San Ramon, 94583,
415-867-0600 Yards: 5975, Par: 71, USGA: 68.2, Holes: 18, Pro: Russ Dicks
Canyon South GC, 1097 Murray Canyon Drive, Palm Springs, 92264,
619-327-2019 Yards: 6205, Par: 71, USGA: 68.6, Holes: 18, Pro: Brian Morrison
Carlton Oaks Lodge GC, 9200 Inwood Dr., Santee, 92071, 619-448-8500
Yards: 6233, Par: 72, USGA: 69.2, Holes: 18, Pro: Rex Cole
Carmel Highland GC, 14455 Penasquitos Dr., San Diego, 92129, 619-672-2200
Yards: 6112, Par: 72, USGA: 68.9, Holes: 18, Pro: M. Flannagan
Carmel Mountain Ranch GC, 14151 Carmel Ridge Rd., San Diego, 92128,
619-487-9224 Yards: 6241, Par: 72, USGA: 70.6, Holes: 18, Pro: Gary Glaser
Casserly Par-3 GC, 626 Casserly Road, Watsonville, 95076, 408-724-1654
Yards: 1158, Par: 27, Holes: 9
Casta Del Sol GC, 27601 Casta del Sol Rd., Mission Viejo, 92692, 714-581-0940
Yards: 3868, Par: 60, USGA: 58.8, Holes: 18, Pro: Al Roush
Catalina GC, #1 Country Club Rd., Avalon, 90704, 213-510-0530
Yards: 2100, Par: 32, USGA: 58.0, Holes: 9, Pro: None
Chardonnay GC, POB 3779, 2555 Jameson Canyon, Napa, 94558, 707-257-8950
Yards: 6600, Par: 72, USGA: 69.4, Holes: 27, Pro: C. Williamson
Cherry Hills GC, Box G 26583 Cherry Hills Blvd, Sun City, 92381, 714-679-1182
Yards: 6483, Par: 72, USGA: 71.8, Holes: 18, Pro: Wayne Elliott
Chimney Rock GC, 5320 Silverado Trail, P.O. Box, Napa, 94559, 707-255-3363
Yards: 6772, Par: 72, USGA: 70.7, Holes: 9, Pro: Harrie Thomas
China Lake GC, Box 507 411 Midway Dr., Ridgecrest, 93555, 619-939-2976
Yards: 6533, Par: 72, USGA: 70.7, Holes: 18, Pro: James Cantrell
Chula Vista GC, Box 403 4475 Bonita Rd., Bonita, 92002, 619-479-4141
Yards: 6381, Par: 73, USGA: 69.9, Holes: 18, Pro: John Gonzales
Churn Creek GC, P.O. Box 762, Anderson, 96007, 916-222-6353
Yards: 6203, Par: 72, USGA: 67.6, Holes: 9, Pro: Bill DeWildt
Clear Lake Riviera GC, 10200 Fairway Drive, Kelseyville, 95451, 707-277-7129
Yards: 2819, Par: 36, USGA: 33.8, Holes: 9, Pro: Ed Corrigan
Club Circle GC, Marker Lane & Club Circle, Box, Borrego Springs, 92004,
619-767-5944 Yards: 1150, Holes: 9
Colony CC, 40603 Colony Drive, Murrieta, 92362
Holes: 18
Colusa CC, POB 686, Highway 20 East, Colusa, 95932, 916-458-5577
Yards: 3309, Par: 36, USGA: 34.8, Holes: 9, Pro: Randy Scott
Combat Center GC, Box X-11 Special Services Bld., 29 Palms, 92278,
619-368-6132 Yards: 6487, Par: 72, USGA: 70.4, Holes: 18, Pro: Bill Buckley
Cordova GC, 9425 Jackson Rd., Sacramento, 95826, 916-362-1196
Yards: 4755, Par: 63, USGA: 61.0, Holes: 18, Pro: Jim Marta
Costa Mesa Golf & CC, Box 1829 1701 Golf Course Dr., Costa Mesa, 92626,
714-754-5267 Yards: 6233, Par: 72, USGA: 69.0, Holes: 18, Pro: Steve Hookano
Cottonwood CC, 3121 Willow Glen Rd., El Cajon, 92020, 619-442-9891
Yards: 6645, Par: 73, USGA: 71.3, Holes: 18, Pro: Rick Sprouse
Cresta Verde GC, 1295 Cresta Rd., Corona, 91719, 714-737-2255
Yards: 5390, Par: 71, USGA: 64.9, Holes: 18, Pro: Gene Butler
Crystal Springs BC, Inc., 6650 Golf Course Dr., Burlingame, 94010,
415-342-0603 Yards: 6321, Par: 72, USGA: 69.9, Holes: 18, Pro: Roger GRaves
Cypress Hills GC, 2001 Hillside Blvd., Colma, 94014, 415-922-5155
Yards: 3443, Par: 37, Holes: 9, Pro: Michael Jick
Cypress Point GC, 17 Mile Dr., Pebble Beach, 93953
De Anza Palm Springs CC, 36-200 Date Palm Dr., Cathedral City, 92234,
619-328-1315 Yards: 3085, Par: 58, USGA: 51.4, Holes: 18, Pro: Herb Cleveland
De Laveaga GC, 401 Upper Park Rd., Suite A, Santa Cruz, 95065, 408-423-7212
Yards: 6001, Par: 72, USGA: 69.8, Holes: 18, Pro: Gary Loustalot

Deep Cliff GC, 10700 Clubhouse Ln., Cupertino, 95014,   408-253-5359
Yards: 3365, Par: 60, USGA: 54.4, Holes: 18, Pro: L. Scott Cline
Del Norte GC, 130 Club Drive, Crescent City, 95531,   707-458-3214
Yards: 3000, Par: 36, USGA: 33.4, Holes: 9
Del Rio CC, Box 38 102 East Del Rio Rd., Brawley, 92227,   619-344-0085
Yards: 5890, Par: 70, USGA: 66.7, Holes: 18, Pro: G. St. Germaine
Desert Aire GC, 3620 East Ave. P, Palmdale, 93550,   805-273-7778
Yards: 6195, Par: 72, USGA: 68.1, Holes: 18, Pro: Steve Applegate
Desert Crest Country Club, 16-900 Desert Crest Ave., Desert Hot Springs,
92240, 619-329-8711   Par: 27, Holes: 9
Desert Dunes GC, 19300 Palm Drive, Desert Hot Springs, 92240
Holes: 18
Desert Falls CC, 1111 Desert Falls Parkway, Palm Desert, 92260,   619-340-5646
Yards: 6218, Par: 72, USGA: 70.2, Holes: 18, Pro: Rex Colwell
Diablo Hills GC, 1551 Marchbanks Dr., Walnut Creek, 94598,   415-939-7372
Yards: 4604, Par: 68, USGA: 61.7, Holes: 9, Pro: Hardev Singh
Diamond Oaks GC—Roseville GC, 349 Diamond Oakd Rd., Roseville, 95678,
916-783-4947   Yards: 6200, Par: 72, USGA: 69.0, Holes: 18, Pro: Ed Vasconcellas
Dryden Park GC—Modesto GC, 920 So. Sunset Blvd., Modesto, 95351,
209-577-5359   Yards: 6140, Par: 72, USGA: 68.3, Holes: 18, Pro: Andrew Silva
Eagle Nest GC, 22112 Klamath River Rd., Klamath River, 96050,   916-465-9276
Yards: 3634, Par: 64, USGA: 58.9, Holes: 9, Pro: Nuno Bonno
Echo Hills GC, 545 E. Thornton, Hemet, 92343,   714-652-2203
Yards: 4466, Par: 35, USGA: 60.2, Holes: 9, Pro: Wm. Bennington
El Dorado Hills GC, El Dorado Hills Blvd., El Dorado Hills, 95630,
916-933-6552   Yards: 3920, Par: 61, USGA: 59.0, Holes: 18, Pro: Ted Fitzpatrick
El Dorado GC, Box 15687 2400 Studebaker Rd., Long Beach, 90815,
213-430-5411   Yards: 6321, Par: 72, USGA: 68.9, Holes: 18, Pro: Bob Vogel
El Pardo GC, 6555 Pine Ave., Chino, 91710,   714-597-1753
Yards: 6296, Par: 72, USGA: 69.1, Holes: 18, Pro: Robert Bickford
El Rancho Verde CC, Foot of Country Club Dr., Rialto, 92376,   714-875-5346
Yards: 6844, Par: 72, USGA: 70.2, Holes: 18, Pro: Lee Deitrick
El Rivino CC, Box 3369 5530 El Rivino Rd., Riverside, 92519,   714-684-8905
Yards: 6132, Par: 72, USGA: 68.2, Holes: 18, Pro: Dennis Burdo
Elkins Ranch GC, Box 695 1386 Chambersburg Rd., Fillmore, 93015,
805-524-1440   Yards: 6010, Par: 71, USGA: 68.5, Holes: 18, Pro: Wyatt Detmer
Emerald Hills GC, Wilmington Way, P.O. Box 3, Redwood City, 94061,
415-368-7820   Yards: 2950, Par: 58, USGA: 50.9, Holes: 9, Pro: Bernie Meyer
Emerson Lake GC, 470-835 Wingfield Rd. N, Susanville, 96130,   916-257-6303
Yards: 6348, Par: 72, USGA: 68.4, Holes: 9, Pro: Bob Genasci
Escalon GC, 17051 So. Escalon Bellota Rd., Escalon, 95320,   209-838-1277
Yards: 3040, Par: 62, USGA: 52.6, Holes: 9, Pro: Tom Hagan
Eureka GC, 4750 Fairway Dr., Eureka, 95501,   707-443-4808
Yards: 5589, Par: 70, USGA: 66.5, Holes: 18, Pro: Les Wheeler
Fairchild's Bel-Aire Greens, 1001 S. El Cielo Rd., Palm Springs, 92262,
619-327-0332   Yards: 1670, Par: 32, Holes: 9, Pro: Bill Roberts
Fairmont Park GC, 2681 Dexter Dr., Riverside, 92501,   714-683-9030
Yards: 6165, Par: 72, USGA: 68.5, Holes: 18, Pro: Wm. Capehart
Fall River Valley GCC, Highway 299 E, P.O. Box PAR, Fall River Mills, 96028,
916-336-5555   Yards: 6835, Par: 72, USGA: 72.5, Holes: 18, Pro: Karen Boyer
Feather River GC, Hwy 70, P.O. Box 67, Blairsden, 96103,   916-836-2722
Yards: 5760, Par: 70, USGA: 66.2, Holes: 9, Pro: Mile Conley
Fig Garden GC, 7700 North Van Ness Blvd, Fresno, 93771,   209-439-2928
Yards: 6300, Par: 72, USGA: 69.0, Holes: 18, Pro: Gary Bauer
Fore Bay GC, P.O. Box 311, Los Banos, 93635,   209-826-3637
Yards: 6637, Par: 72, USGA: 69.6, Holes: 9, Pro: Eric Nelson

Forest Lake GC, 2450 E. Woodson Rd., Acampo, 95220, 209-369-5451
Yards: 3675, Par: 60, USGA: 55.1, Holes: 18, Pro: Leroy Silva
Forest Meadows GC, Box 70, Murphys, 95247, 209-728-3439
Yards: 4004, Par: 60, USGA: 57.5, Holes: 18, Pro: Norby Wilson
Fresno Airways GC, 5440 E. Shields Ave., Fresno, 93727, 209-291-6254
Yards: 5182, Par: 68, USGA: 63.8, Holes: 18, Pro: Art Forrester
Gavilan GC, 5055 Santa Teresa Blvd., Gilroy, 95020, 408-848-1363
Yards: 3598, Par: 62, USGA: 54.8, Holes: 9, Pro: Steve Janisch
Gilroy GC, 2695 Hecker Pass Highway, Gilroy, 95020, 408-842-2501
Yards: 5934, Par: 70, USGA: 67.4, Holes: 18, Pro: Don DeLorenzo
Gleneagles International GC, 2100 Sunnydale Ave, San Francisco, 94134,
415-587-2425   Yards: 3211, Par: 36, USGA: 35.5, Holes: 9
Glenn G&CC, R2 Box 172F, Bayliss Blue Gum, Willows, 95988, 916-934-9918
Yards: 3258, Par: 36, USGA: 34.8, Holes: 9, Pro: Tony De Napoli
Golden Gate Park GC, 47th Avenue & Fulton St., San Francisco, 94117,
415-751-8987   Yards: 1357, Par: 27, Holes: 9
Golden Hills G & CC, St.Rt. 2, Box 3289, Tehachapi, 93561, 805-822-9116
Yards: 6284, Par: 72, USGA: 70.6, Holes: 18, Pro: Don Moulton
Golden Valley GC, 19920 First St., PO Box 760, Hilmar, 95324, 209-667-1161
Yards: 3016, Par: 58, USGA: 54.5, Holes: 9, Pro: George Buzzini
Goldmine GC, MCG—45, Box 3592, Big Bear Lake, 92315, 714-585-8002
Yards: 5642, Par: 70, USGA: 65.6, Holes: 18, Pro: S. Wright
Green River GC—Riverside, 5215 Green River Drive, Corona, 91720,
714-970-8411   Yards: 6028, Par: 71, USGA: 67.8, Holes: 18, Pro: Howard Smith
Griffith Park GC, 4730 Crystal Springs Dr., Los Angeles, 90027, 213-664-2255
Yards: 6522, Par: 72, USGA: 69.9, Holes: 18, Pro: Tom Barber
Haggin Oaks GC—South Course, 3645 Fulton Ave., P.O. Box 137, Sacramento,
95853, 916-481-4507   Yds: 6254, Par: 72, USGA: 67.6, Holes: 18, Pro: Ken Morton
Harding Park GC, 15 Morton Dr., Daly City, 94015, 415-664-4690
Yards: 6586, Par: 72, USGA: 71.3, Holes: 27, Pro: Jeff Wilson
Hesperia G & CC, 17970 Bangor Ave., Hesperia, 92345, 619-244-9301
Yards: 6570, Par: 72, USGA: 71.7, Holes: 18, Pro: Alan Arvesen
Hidden Valley Lake G&CC, POB 5130, #1 Hartman Road, Middletown, 95461,
707-987-3035   Yards: 6237, Par: 71, USGA: 69.5, Holes: 18, Pro: Stephen Brown
Hill Country GC, 1590 Foothill Ave., PO Box 999, Morgan Hill, 95037,
408-779-4136   Yards: 3110, Par: 58, USGA: 52.0, Holes: 18, Pro: Jim MacGowan
Hobergs Forest Lake G&CC, POB 235, Hwy 175 & Golf Road, Cobb, 95436,
707-928-5276   Yards: 2246, Par: 33, USGA: 30.1, Holes: 9, Pro: Les Russo
Horse Thief GC, Star RTE 1, Box 2800, Tehachapi, 93561, 805-822-5581
Yards: 6317, Par: 72, USGA: 70.1, Holes: 18, Pro: Joe Haggerty
Imperial GC, 2200 E. Imperial Hwy., Brea, 92621, 714-529-3923
Yards: 5927, Par: 72, USGA: 66.9, Holes: 18, Pro: Bob Breeding
Indian Creek CC, 4487 Barton Rd., PO Box 303, Loomis, 95650, 916-652-5546
Yards: 4140, Par: 64, USGA: 59.9, Holes: 9, Pro: Vic Kulik
Indian Hills CC, 5700 Club House Dr., Riverside, 92509, 714-685-7443
Yards: 6099, Par: 70, USGA: 66.5, Holes: 18, Pro: Don Willis
Indian Palms GC, 47-639 Monroe, Indio, 92201, 619-347-2326
Yards: 6403, Par: 72, USGA: 70.3, Holes: 27, Pro: Dale Shaw
Indian Springs CC, 46080 Jefferson, La Quinta, 92253, 619-347-0651
Yards: 6106, Par: 71, USGA: 67.7, Holes: 18, Pro: Jim Osborn
Indian Valley GC, Stafford Lake-Novato Blvd., PO, Novato, 94948,
415-897-1118   Yards: 5759, Par: 72, USGA: 67.4, Holes: 18, Pro: Ron Hoyt
Indio Municipal GC, 83-040 Ave. 42, Indio, 92202, 619-347-9156
Yards: 3004, Par: 54, USGA: 49.1, Holes: 18, Pro: Marvin Burns
International Golf & CC, Box 681 275 Anza Rd., Calexico, 92231

Ivey Ranch GC, 74580 Varner Rd., Palm Desert, 92276,   619-343-2013
Yards: 2611, Par: 34, USGA: 64.0, Holes: 9, Pro: Jimmy Clarke
Jackson Lakes GC, 14868-18th Ave., Lemoore, 93245,   209-924-2763
Yards: 5787, Par: 71, USGA: 66.5, Holes: 18, Pro: Charles Hudson
Joe Mortara GC, 815 Valle Vista Ave, Vallejo, 94590,   707-642-5146
Yards: 1591, Par: 28, USGA: 27.2, Holes: 9
Jurupa Hills CC, 6161 Moraga Ave., Riverside, 92509,   714-685-7214
Yards: 6029, Par: 70, USGA: 67.4, Holes: 18, Pro: Ron Robinson
Kelly Ridge GL, 36 Royal Oaks Dr., Oroville, 95966,   916-589-0777
Yards: 4207, Par: 66, USGA: 61.8, Holes: 9, Pro: Ron Anderson
Kern River GC, Box 3355, Bakersfield, 93386,   805-872-5128
Yards: 6258, Par: 70, USGA: 68.8, Holes: 18, Pro: Chet Foss
Kern Valley GC & CC, Box 888, Kernville, 93238,   619-376-2828
Yards: 6061, Par: 72, USGA: 67.2, Holes: 18
King City GC, 613 S. Vanderhurst, King City, 93930,   408-385-4546
Yards: 5634, Par: 70, USGA: 66.0, Holes: 9, Pro: Jon Olson
Kings Valley GC, 3030 Lesna Rd., Crescent City, 95531,   707-464-2886
Yards: 2518, Par: 56, USGA: 52.0, Holes: 9, Pro: Keith Fields
La Costa GC, Costa Del Mar Rd., San Diego, 92009
Laguna Seca GC, York Rd., Monterey, 93940,   408-373-3701
Yards: 5758, Par: 71, USGA: 67.3, Holes: 18, Pro: Nick Lombardo
Lake Almanor CC, POB 3323, 951 Clifford Drive, Lake Almanor, 96137,
916-259-2868   Yards: 2937, Par: 35, USGA: 33.5, Holes: 9
Lake Chabot GC, End of Golf Links Rd., Oakland, 94605,   415-351-5812
Yards: 6180, Par: 72, USGA: 67.7, Holes: 27, Pro: Jeff Dennis
Lake Don Pedro G&CC, POB 193, Hayward Road, La Grange, 95329,
209-852-2242   Yards: 6007, Par: 70, USGA: 67.4, Holes: 18, Pro: Ray Claveran
Lake Elizabeth GC, 14700 W. Elizabeth Lake Rd., Lake Elizabeth, 93532,
805-724-1221   Yards: 6318, Par: 72, USGA: 69.8, Holes: 9, Pro: John Snabb
Lake Redding GC, 1795 Benton Dr., Redding, 96003,   916-243-5531
Yards: 3756, Par: 62, USGA: 57.3, Holes: 9, Pro: Bob Divine
Lake San Marcos GC—Executive, 1556 Camino Del Arroyo, Lake San
Marcos, 92069, 714-744-9092   Yards: 2700, Par: 58, Holes: 18, Pro: Randy Olson
Lake San Marcos GC, 1750 San Pablo Dr., Lake San Marcos, 92069,
619-744-1310   Yards: 6214, Par: 72, USGA: 68.8, Holes: 18, Pro: Jim Gilbert
Lake Tahoe CC—South Lake Tah, Hwy 50, South Lake Tahoe, 95702,
916-577-0802   Yards: 6244, Par: 71, USGA: 67.9, Holes: 18, Pro: Bob Billings
Lake Tamarisk GC, Box 316, Desert Center, 92239,   619-227-3203
Yards: 3014, Par: 35, USGA: 66.9, Holes: 9
Lemoore GC, 785 S. Lemoore Ave., Lemoore, 93245,   209-924-9658
Yards: 6338, Par: 72, USGA: 68.9, Holes: 9, Pro: Bill Holloway
Lincoln Park GC, 3139 Clement St., San Francisco, 94121,   415-752-3422
Yards: 5149, Par: 68, USGA: 65.3, Holes: 18, Pro: Steve Hatch
Links at Monarch Beach, The, 23841 Stonehill Dr., Laguna Niguel, 92677,
714-240-8247   Yards: 5600, Par: 70, USGA: 67.2, Holes: 27, Pro: L. Brotherton
Little River Inn GC, POB Drawer B, 7750 N Hwy 1, Little River, 95456,
707-937-5667   Yards: 2725, Par: 36, USGA: 33.0, Holes: 9, Pro: Doug Howe
Lomas Santa Fe Executive GC, 1580 Sun Valley Road, Solana Beach, 92075,
619-755-0195   Yards: 2317, Par: 56, USGA: 56.0, Holes: 18, Pro: Vicki Paul
Lone Tree GC—Antioch GC, 4800 Lone Tree Way, PO Box 986, Antioch,
94509, 415-757-5200   Yards: 5970, Par: 73, USGA: 67.1, Holes: 18, Pro: Pat Cain
Los Alamitos CC, Box 332 4561 Katella Ave., Los Alamitos, 90720,   714-821-5990
Yards: 5070, Par: 66, USGA: 63.4, Holes: 18, Pro: Don Gifford
Los Angeles Royal Vista GC, 20055 East Colima Rd., Walnut, 91789,
818-965-1634   Yards: 6300, Par: 71, USGA: 69.8, Holes: 18, Pro: Tom Mc Hugh

Los Robles GC, 299 S. Moorpark Rd., Thousand Oaks, 91361, 805-495-6471
Yards: 5789, Par: 70, USGA: 66.7, Holes: 18, Pro: Bob Meyer
Los Verdes GC, 7000 W. Los Verdes Dr., Rancho Palos Verdes, 90274,
213-377-7370 Yards: 6273, Par: 71, USGA: 69.0, Holes: 18, Pro: Len Kennett
Mace Meadows GC, 26570 Fairway Drive, Pioneer, 95666, 209-295-7020
Yards: 6054, Par: 72, USGA: 68.4, Holes: 18, Pro: Jack Fox
Mallard Lake GC, 4238 Sawtelle Ave, Yuba City, 95991, 916-674-0475
Yards: 2637, Par: 35, Holes: 9, Pro: Jim Kelley
Manteca GC, 305 N. Union Rd., PO Box 611, Manteca, 95336, 209-823-5945
Yards: 6281, Par: 72, USGA: 69.2, Holes: 18, Pro: Alan Thomas
Marrakesh CC, 47-000 Marrakesh Drive, Palm Desert, 92260, 619-568-2660
Yards: 3595, Par: 60, USGA: 57.2, Holes: 18, Pro: Chris Egan
Marriott's Desert Springs Resort, 74-855 Country Club Dr., Palm Desert,
92260, 619-341-2211 Yards: 6761, Par: 72, USGA: 69.0, Holes: 18, Pro: Tim Skogen
McCloud GC, 1001 Squaw Valley Rd., PO Box, McCloud, 96057, 916-964-2535
Yards: 6010, Par: 72, USGA: 67.6, Holes: 9, Pro: Robert Purdy
Meadow Lake CC, 10333 Meadow Glen Way East, Escondido, 92026,
619-749-1620 Yards: 6521, Par: 72, USGA: 69.6, Holes: 18, Pro: Brad Booth
Meadowlark GC, 16782 Graham St., Huntington Beach, 92647, 714-846-1364
Yards: 5761, Par: 70, USGA: 66.1, Holes: 18, Pro: John Anselmo
Mesquite GC, 2700 E. Mesquite Ave., Palm Springs, 92264, 619-323-9377
Yards: 5944, Par: 72, USGA: 67.9, Holes: 18, Pro: Bruce Conroy
Mile Square GC, 10401 Warner Ave., Fountain Valley, 92708, 714-968-4556
Yards: 6669, Par: 72, USGA: 69.9, Holes: 18, Pro: Steve Seals
Mill Valley GC, 280 Buena Vista Ave., Mill Valley, 94941, 415-388-9982
Yards: 4182, Par: 65, USGA: 60.5, Holes: 9, Pro: Stephen Yuhas
Mission Lakes CC, 8484 Clubhouse Dr., Desert Hot Springs, 92240,
619-329-6481 Yards: 6396, Par: 71, USGA: 70.2, Holes: 18, Pro: Norman Popkin
Mission Trails GC, 7380 Golfcrest Pl., San Diego, 92119, 619-460-5400
Yards: 5780, Par: 71, USGA: 66.7, Holes: 18, Pro: Bert Geisendof
Montclair GC, 2477 Monterey Blvd, Oakland, 94611, 415-482-0422
Yards: 1134, Par: 27, Holes: 9, Pro: Dick Jausch
Montebello GC, Box 34 901 Via San Clemente, Montbello, 90640, 213-723-2971
Yards: 6265, Par: 71, USGA: 68.4, Holes: 18, Pro: Thomas Camacho
Mount St. Helena GC, Napa Couty Fairgrounds, Calistoga, 94515,
707-942-9966 Yards: 5510, Par: 68, USGA: 64.9, Holes: 9, Pro: Mike Kenney
Mount Whitney GC, POB O, Highway 395, Lone Pine, 93545, 619-876-9885
Yards: 3312, Par: 36, USGA: 34.5, Holes: 9, Pro: John Farr
Mountain Meadows GC, 1875 Ganesha Blvd., Pomona, 91768, 714-629-1166
Yards: 6146, Par: 72, USGA: 68.3, Holes: 18, Pro: Dave Cink
Mountain Shadows GC—North Course, 100 Golf Course Dr., Rohnert Park,
94928, 707-584-7766 Yards: 6160, Par: 72, USGA: 68.6, Holes: 18, Pro: Dan Ross
Mountain View CC, 2121 Mountain View Drive, Corona, 91720, 714-633-0282
Yards: 6157, Par: 72, USGA: 69.4, Holes: 18, Pro: S. Cartwright
Mountain View GC, 16799 South Mountain Rd., Santa Paula, 93060,
805-525-1571 Yards: 5231, Par: 69, USGA: 64.9, Holes: 18, Pro: Tony Pawlak
Mountain View CC, 74-580 Varner Rd., Thousand Palms, 91720, 619-343-2013
Par: 33, Holes: 9
Muroc Lake GC, Box 207 Edwards AFB, Edwards, 93253, 805-277-3469
Yards: 6361, Par: 72, USGA: 69.8, Holes: 18, Pro: Paul Chapman
Nevada County CC, 1040 East Main Street, Grass Valley, 95945, 916-273-6436
Yards: 2732, Par: 34, USGA: 32.3, Holes: 9, Pro: Jeff Fish
Newport Beach GC, Box 18426, Irvine, 92714, 714-852-8689
Yards: 3209, Par: 59, USGA: 55.5, Holes: 18, Pro: John Leonard
North Kern GC, Box 80123, Bakersfield, 93380, 805-399-0347
Yards: 6461, Par: 72, USGA: 69.9, Holes: 18, Pro: Bill McKinley

Oak Creek GC, 350 Gilmore Rd., Lot 95, Red Bluff, 96080,   916-529-0674
Yards: 5130, Par: 70, USGA: 62.9, Holes: 9, Pro: Cal Phillian
Oak Ridge GC, 225 Cottle Rd., San Jose, 95123,   408-227-6557
Yards: 5829, Par: 72, USGA: 67.2, Holes: 18, Pro: Dwight Barnett
Oakmont GC—East Course, 7025 Oakmont Dr., Santa Rosa, 95409,
707-538-2454   Yards: 5000, Par: 63, USGA: 58.6, Holes: 18, Pro: Dean James
Oaks North GC, 12602 Oaks North Drive, San Diego, 92128,   619-487-3021
Yards: 3394, Par: 60, Holes: 27, Pro: Craig Clark
Oasis CC, The, 42-330 Casbah Way, Palm Desert, 92260,   619-345-2715
Yards: 3146, Par: 60, USGA: 54.3, Holes: 18, Pro: Brent Garlock
Ocean Meadows GC, 6925 Whittier Dr., Goleta, 93117,   805-968-6814
Yards: 6061, Par: 72, USGA: 67.5, Holes: 18, Pro: Dave Atchison
Oceanside Center City Course, 2323 Green Brier Drive, Oceanside, 92054,
619-433-8590   Yards: 5590, Par: 71, Holes: 9, Pro: Ludwig Keehn
Oceanside GC, 825 Douglas Drive, Oceanside, 92056,   619-433-1360
Yards: 6056, Par: 72, USGA: 67.9, Holes: 18, Pro: Jeanne Wood
Oceanside Municipal GC, Box 321, San Luis Rey, 92068
Olympic Club GC, The, Skyline Blvd., San Fransisco, 94015
Ontario National GC, 2525 Riverside Dr., Ontario, 91764,   714-947-3512
Yards: 6270, Par: 72, USGA: 68.1, Holes: 18, Pro: Dave Ferrell
Pacific Grove Municipal GC, 77 Asilomar Blvd., Pacific Grove, 93950,
408-375-3456   Yards: 5553, Par: 70, USGA: 66.3, Holes: 18, Pro: Peter Vitarisi
Pala Mesa Resort, 2001 Old Hwy 395, Fallbrook, 92028,   619-728-5881
Yards: 6472, Par: 72, USGA: 69.5, Holes: 18, Pro: C. Starkjohann
Palm Desert Resort GC, 40-999 Resorter Blvd., Palm Springs, 92260,
619-345-2781   Yards: 6202, Par: 72, USGA: 69.0, Holes: 18
Palm Desert Resort CC, 77-333 Country Club Dr., Palm Desert, 92260,
619-345-2791   Yards: 6241, Par: 72, USGA: 68.8, Holes: 18, Pro: Tom Bienek
Palm Desert CC, 77-200 California Drive, Palm Desert, 92260,   619-345-2525
Yards: 6273, Par: 72, USGA: 67.9, Holes: 18, Pro: Lew Gilliam
Palm Lakes GC, 5025 E. Dakota, Fresno, 93727,   209-292-1144
Yards: 4262, Par: 62, USGA: 57.9, Holes: 18, Pro: Jim Moore
Palm Royale CC, Fred Waring Dr. & Washington S, La Quinta, 92253,
619-328-1005   Par: 72, USGA: 69.4, Holes: 18, Pro: Tom Marcuzzo
Palm Springs CC, 2500 Whitewater Club Drive, Palm Springs, 92262,
619-323-8625   Yards: 5714, Par: 71, USGA: 66.5, Holes: 18, Pro: Steve Brown
Palm Springs Muni GC, 1885 Gulf Club Dr., Palm Springs, 92264,   619-328-1956
Yards: 6460, Par: 72, USGA: 69.6, Holes: 18, Pro: Mike Carroll
Palo Alto GC, 1875 Embarcadero Road, Palo Alto, 94303, 415-856-0881
Yards: 6525, Par: 72, USGA: 70.1, Holes: 18, Pro: Brad Lozares
Palos Verdes GC, 3301 Via Campesina, Palos Verdes Estates, 90274,
213-375-2759   Yards: 6206, Par: 71, USGA: 70.5, Holes: 18, Pro: Richard Cox
Paradise Pines GC, 13917 S. Park Dr., Magalia, 95954,   916-873-1111
Yards: 5200, Par: 68, USGA: 64.6, Holes: 9, Pro: Chuck Overmyer
Parkway GC, 3400 Stevenson Blvd., Fremont, 94538,   415-656-6862
Yards: 4428, Par: 54, USGA: 49.9, Holes: 18, Pro: Mike Pope
Peacock Gap GC, 333 Biscayne Dr., San Rafael, 94901,   415-453-4940
Yards: 6284, Par: 71, USGA: 67.9, Holes: 18, Pro: Al Hand
Petaluma G&CC, POB 26, 1100 Country Club Dr., Petaluma, 94953,
707-762-7041   Yards: 2805, Par: 35, USGA: 32.8, Holes: 9
Peter Hay GC, POB 658, 17-Mile Drive, Pebble Beach, 93953,   408-624-3811
Yards: 1570, Par: 27, Holes: 9, Pro: Steve McLennan
PGA West GC—Jack Nicklaus Resort, 55-955 PGA Blvd, La Quinta, 92253,
619-564-7170   Yards: 6001, Par: 72, USGA: 69.2, Holes: 18, Pro: Jeff Walser
Phoenix Lake GC, 21448 Paseo De Los Portales, Sonora, 95370,   209-532-0111
Yards: 5421, Par: 70, USGA: 65.8, Holes: 9, Pro: Chris Bitticks

Pine Meadows GC, 451 Vine Hill Way, Martinez, 94453, 415-372-9559
Yards: 2882, Par: 27, Holes: 9
Pine Mountain Lake GC, POB PMLA, Mueller Drive, Groveland, 95321,
209-962-7783 Yards: 6106, Par: 70, USGA: 68.4, Holes: 18, Pro: Steve Caulkins
Pittsburg G&CC, 2222 Golf Club Road, Pittsburg, 94565, 415-439-9766
Yards: 3053, Par: 36, USGA: 39.0, Holes: 9
Pleasant Hill G&CC, 1093 Grayson Road, Pleasant Hill, 94523, 415-932-0276
Yards: 3051, Par: 58, USGA: 52.5, Holes: 18, Pro: Keith Boam
Pleasanton Fairways GC, PO Box 123, Pleasanton, 94566, 415-462-4653
Yards: 5020, Par: 60, USGA: 56.0, Holes: 9, Pro: Rn Curtola
Pleasant Hills GC, 2050 South White Rd., San Jose, 95122, 408-238-3485
Yards: 6503, Par: 72, USGA: 69.6, Holes: 36, Pro: Robbie Robinson
Plumas Pines CC, 402 Poplar Valley Road, Blairsden, 96103, 96103
Yards: 5843, Par: 72, USGA: 70.5, Holes: 18, Pro: Gregg Karterba
Polvadero G&CC, 41605 Sutter Avenue, Coalina, 93210, 209-935-1275
Yards: 3268, Par: 36, USGA: 35.0, Holes: 9
Ponderosa GC, POB 729, 10962 Brockway, Truckee, 95734, 916-587-3501
Yards: 3000, Par: 36, USGA: 33.7, Holes: 9, Pro: Greg Carter
Porterville GC, 702 E. Isham, Porterville, 93257, 209-784-9468
Yards: 5698, Par: 70, USGA: 65.6, Holes: 9, Pro: Arlie Morris
Pruneridge GC, 400 N. Saratoga Ave., Santa Clara, 95050, 408-248-4424
Yards: 3878, Par: 62, USGA: 56.6, Holes: 9, Pro: Wayne Wallick
Quail Ranch Resort & CC, 15960 Gilman Springs, Moreno, 92360,
714-654-2727 Yards: 6868, Par: 72, USGA: 70.4, Holes: 18, Pro: Claude Waymire
Rainbow Canyon GC, 44-501 Rainbow Canyon Rd., Temecula, 92390
Rams Hill GC, 1881 Rams Hill Rd., San Diego, 92004
Rancho Canada GC—West Course, Carmel Valley Rd., Carmel, 93922,
408-624-0111 Yards: 6071, Par: 72, USGA: 69.0, Holes: 18, Pro: Shim Lagoy
Rancho Carlsbad CC, 5200 El Camino Real, Carlsbad, 92008, 619-438-1772
Yards: 2068, Par: 56, USGA: 54.5, Holes: 18, Pro: Craig Hunt
Rancho Del Rey GC, 5250 Green Sands Ave., Atwater, 95301, 209-358-7131
Yards: 6262, Par: 72, USGA: 68.8, Holes: 18, Pro: Bob Riechel
Rancho Las Palmas GC, 42000 Bob Hope Drive, Rancho Mirage, 92270,
619-568-2727 Yards: 5716, Par: 71, Holes: 18
Rancho Maria GC, 1950 Casmalia Rd., Santa Maria, 93455, 805-937-2019
Yards: 6114, Par: 72, USGA: 68.7, Holes: 18, Pro: Jack O'Keefe
Rancho Park GC, 10460 W. Pico Blvd., Los Angeles, 90064, 213-838-7373
Yards: 6216, Par: 71, USGA: 68.9, Holes: 18, Pro: Ron Weiner
Rancho San Diego GC—Ivanhoe, 3121 Willow Glen Rd., El Cajon, 92019,
619-442-9891 Yards: 6649, Par: 73, USGA: 71.3, Holes: 18, Pro: Rick Sprouse
Rancho San Joaquin GC, One Sandburg Way, Irvine, 92715, 714-786-5522
Yards: 6229, Par: 72, USGA: 68.8, Holes: 18, Pro: Buck Page
Rancho Solano GC, 3250 Rancho Solano Parkway, Fairfield, 94533,
707-429-4653 Holes: 18
Red Hill CC, 8358 Red Hill Country Club Dr., Rancho Cucamonga, 91730
Ridgemark GC, 3800 Airline Hwy., Hollister, 95023, 408-637-1010
Yards: 6032, Par: 72, USGA: 69.8, Holes: 36, Pro: Jom Crotz
River Oaks GC, 3441 E. Hatch Rd., Hughson, 95326, 209-537-4653
Yards: 6000, Par: 58, USGA: 52.7, Holes: 18, Pro: Dick Ollis
River Ridge GC, 2401 West Vineyard Ave., Oxnard, 93030, 805-983-1756
Yards: 6111, Par: 72, USGA: 68.7, Holes: 18, Pro: Marc Sipes
Riverbend GC, 500 Douglas St., West Sacramento, 95605, 915-372-0810
Yards: 5521, Par: 70, USGA: 64.8, Holes: 18, Pro: Hap Crockett
Riverside GC, 1011 Orange St., Riverside, 92501, 714-682-3748
Yards: 6252, Par: 72, USGA: 67.3, Holes: 18, Pro: Bob Schwartz

Riverside GC, 7672 N. Josephine Ave., Fresno, 93722, 209-275-5900
Yards: 6505, Par: 72, USGA: 70.8, Holes: 18, Pro: Ray Bouty
Riverside GC, PO Box 13128, Coyote, 95013, 408-463-0622
Yards: 6504, Par: 72, USGA: 69.6, Holes: 18, Pro: Tom Smith
Riviera GC, 1250 Capri Dr., Los Angeles, 90272
Roadrunner Dunes GC, 4733 Desert Knoll Ave., 29 Palms, 92277, 619-367-7610
Yards: 6259, Par: 36, USGA: 68.8, Holes: 9, Pro: Steve Barron
Roseville Rolling Greens GC, 5572 Eureka Rd., Roseville, 95661, 916-797-9986
Yards: 5980, Par: 54, USGA: 53.5, Holes: 9, Pro: Bob Peterson
Salinas Fairways GC, 45 Skyway Blvd., Salinas, 93902, 408-758-7300
Yards: 6347, Par: 72, USGA: 70.7, Holes: 18, Pro: Cotton Kaiser
San Bernardino GC, 1494 S. Waterman Ave., San Bernardino, 92408,
714-885-2414 Yards: 5631, Par: 69, USGA: 66.5, Holes: 18, Pro: Cheryl Thomas
San Clemente GC, 150 East Magdalena, San Clemente, 92672, 714-492-3943
Yards: 6119, Par: 72, USGA: 67.3, Holes: 18, Pro: Dave Cook
San Geronimo Valley GC, POB 130, 5800 S F Drake, San Geronimo, 94963,
415-488-4030 Yds: 6000, Par: 72, USGA: 69.7, Holes: 18, Pro: J. Vanderhoof
San Juan Hills GC, Box 1026 32120 San Juan Creek, San Juan Capistrano,
92675, 714-493-1167 Yds: 5970, Par: 71, USGA: 67.5, Holes: 18, Pro: Arne Dokka
San Luis Rey Downs GC, 5772 Camino Del Rey, Bonsall, 92005, 619-758-9699
Yards: 6610, Par: 72, USGA: 69.6, Holes: 18, Pro: Pinky Stevenson
San Mateo GC, Box 634, San Mateo, 94401, 415-347-1461
Yards: 5496, Par: 70, USGA: 64.7, Holes: 18, Pro: Jake Montes
San Ramon Royal Vista GC, 9430 Fircrest Lane, San Ramon, 94583,
415-828-6100 Yards: 6300, Par: 72, USGA: 69.3, Holes: 18, Pro: Daniel Hornig
San Vincente GC, 24157 San Vincente Rd., Ramona, 92065, 619-789-3477
Yards: 5595, Par: 72, USGA: 66.3, Holes: 18, Pro: Terry Horn
Sands Mobile Home Country Club, 15-500 Bubbling Wells Rd., Desert Hot
Springs, 92240, 619-329-9333 Par: 29, Holes: 9
Santa Clara Golf & Tennis Club, 2501 Talluto Way, Santa Clara, 95054,
408-980-9515 Yards: 6474, Par: 72, USGA: 70.5, Holes: 18, Pro: Tom Hale
Santa Teresa GC, 260 Bernal Rd., San Jose, 95150, 408-225-2650
Yards: 6373, Par: 72, USGA: 69.6, Holes: 18, Pro: Chris Bitticks
Saticoy Regional GC, 1025 South Wells Rd., Saticoy, 93004, 805-647-6678
Yards: 5423, Par: 67, USGA: 64.8, Holes: 18, Pro: Bob Wilshire
Sea Ranch Golf Links, POB 10, Highway 1, Sea Ranch, 95497, 707-785-2468
Yards: 3138, Par: 36, USGA: 34.9, Holes: 9, Pro: Rich Bland
Sebastopol GC, 2881 Scotts Right of Way, Sebastopol, 95472, 707-823-9852
Yards: 3242, Par: 62, USGA: 52.1, Holes: 9, Pro: Lee Farris
Selma Valley GC, 12389 East Rose Ave., Selma, 93662, 209-896-2424
Yards: 5349, Par: 69, USGA: 64.3, Holes: 18, Pro: Walt Short
Seven Hills GC, 1537 South Lyon Ave., Hemet, 92343, 714-925-4815
Yards: 6313, Par: 72, USGA: 67.7, Holes: 18, Pro: Steve Kim
Shandin Hills GC, 3380 Littel Mountain Dr., San Bernadino, 92407,
714-886-0669 Yards: 6600, Par: 72, USGA: 68.9, Holes: 18, Pro: John Neubauer
Sharp Park GC, Sharp Park Hwy. #1, Pacifica, 94044, 415-586-2370
Yards: 6283, Par: 72, USGA: 69.6, Holes: 18, Pro: Jack Gage
Shasta Valley GC, 500 Golf Course Rd., Montague, 96064, 916-842-2302
Yards: 6130, Par: 72, USGA: 67.9, Holes: 9, Pro: Paul Kirchen
Sherwood Forest GC, 79 N. Frankwood Ave., Sanger, 93657, 209-787-2611
Yards: 6160, Par: 71, USGA: 68.4, Holes: 18, Pro: Randy Hansen
Sherwood Greens GC, 1050 N. Main St., Salinas, 93906, 408-758-7333
Yards: 5426, Par: 56, USGA: 50.2, Holes: 9, Pro: G. Stubblefield
Shoreline GC, P.O. Box 1206, Mountain View, 94042, 415-969-2041
Yards: 6235, Par: 72, USGA: 69.0, Holes: 18, Pro: Mike Petty

Sierra GC, 1822 Country Club Dr., Placerville, 95667, 916-622-0760
Yards: 3348, Par: 62, USGA: 56.0, Holes: 9, Pro: Dean Peterson
Sierra la Verne CC, 6300 Country Club Dr., La Verne, 91750
Sierra Pines GC, POB 1013, 23736 S Fork Road, Twain Harte, 95383,
209-586-2118 Yards: 2325, Par: 33, USGA: 31.0, Holes: 9
Sierra View GC of Visalia, 12608 Ave. 264, Visalia, 93277, 209-732-2078
Yards: 6465, Par: 72, USGA: 68.4, Holes: 18, Pro: Ralph Lomeli
Skywest GC, 1401 Golf Course Rd., Hayward, 94541, 415-278-6188
Yards: 6540, Par: 72, USGA: 69.4, Holes: 18, Pro: Cheryl Pastore
Small River Horizon GC, Needles, 92363, 619-326-3931
Par: 70, Holes: 18
Soboba Springs CC, 1020 Soboba Road, San Jacinto, 92383, 714-654-9354
Yards: 6352, Par: 73, USGA: 70.5, Holes: 18, Pro: Mike Karney
Sonoma National GC, 17700 Arnold Dr., Sonoma, 95476, 707-996-0300
Yards: 6391, Par: 72, USGA: 70.9, Holes: 18, Pro: Ron Blum
Soule Park GC, 1033 E. Ojai Ave., Ojai, 93023, 805-646-5633
Yards: 6350, Par: 72, USGA: 68.8, Holes: 18, Pro: 8Jim Allen
Spring Hills GC, 31 Smith Rd., Watsonville, 95076, 408-724-1404
Yards: 6218, Par: 71, USGA: 68.7, Holes: 18, Pro: Hank Schimpler
Spring Valley GC, 3441 E. Calaveras Blvd., Milpitas, 95035, 408-262-1722
Yards: 6185, Par: 71, USGA: 67.2, Holes: 18, Pro: Richard Stewart
Springtown GC, 939 Larkspur Dr., Livermore, 94550, 415-449-9880
Yards: 5468, Par: 70, USGA: 65.4, Holes: 9, Pro: Rudy Eichner
Stardust Hotel GC, 950 N. Hotel Circle, San Diego, 92108, 619-297-4796
Par: 72, Holes: 27, Pro: Cliff Crandall
Summit Point GC, Milpitas, 95035, 408-262-8813
Par: 72, Holes: 18
Sun 'N' Sky GC, 2781 Country Club Dr., Barstow, 92311, 619-253-5201
Yards: 6354, Par: 72, USGA: 69.0, Holes: 18, Pro: Dick Andreasen
Sunken Gardens GC, 1010 South Wolfe Road, Sunnyvale, 94086, 408-739-6588
Yards: 3127, Par: 29, Holes: 9, Pro: Art Wilson
Sunnyvale GC, 605 Macara, Sunnyvale, 94086, 408-738-3666
Yards: 5744, Par: 69, USGA: 67.0, Holes: 18, Pro: Art Wilson
Sunol Valley GC—Palm Course, Interstate 680 at Andrade Road, Sunol,
94586, 415-862-2404 Yds: 6195, Par: 72, USGA: 69.5, Holes: 18, Pro: J. Thormann
Sunset Whitney GC, 4201 Midas Ave., Sacramento, 95677
Swenson Park GC, 6803 Alexandria Pl., Stockton, 95207, 209-477-0774
Yards: 6479, Par: 72, USGA: 70.1, Holes: 18, Pro: Ernie George
Table Mountain GC, P.O. Box 2769, Oroville, 95965, 916-533-3924
Yards: 6472, Par: 72, USGA: 70.1, Holes: 18, Pro: Hal Pritchard
Tayman Park GC, 927 So. Fitch Mtn. Rd., Healdsburg, 95448, 707-433-4275
Yards: 5304, Par: 70, USGA: 64.8, Holes: 9, Pro: Kevin Sullivan
Tahoe City GC, P.O. Box 226, Tahoe City, 95730, 916-583-1516
Yards: 5251, Par: 66, USGA: 63.4, Holes: 9, Pro: Don Hay
Tahoe-Donner GC, Truckee, 95737, 916-587-6046
Yards: 6635, Par: 72, Holes: 18, Pro: Fred Elliott
Tahoe Paradise GC, Hwy 50, Tahoe Paradise, 95709, 916-577-2121
Yards: 4070, Par: 66, USGA: 60.0, Holes: 18, Pro: Dave Beman
Three Rivers GC, P.O. Box 202, Three Rivers, 93271, 209-561-3133
Yards: 4950, Par: 68, USGA: 64.8, Holes: 9, Pro: Greg Carter
Tierra Del Sol GC, 10300 North Loop Blvd., California City, 93505,
619-373-2384 Yards: 6300, Par: 72, USGA: 69.6, Holes: 18, Pro: Carroll Sharp
Tijuana CC, Box 891, San Ysidro, 92073, 861-401-0203
Yards: 6459, USGA: 70.4, Holes: 18, Pro: Carlos Acosta
Tony Lema GC—Marina Course, 13800 Neptune Dr., San Leandro, 94577,
415-895-2162 Yards: 3316, Par: 29, USGA: 55.0, Holes: 9, Pro: Steve Elbe

Torrey Pines GC—South Course, 11480 N. Torrey Pines Rd., San Diego, 92109, 619-453-0380 Yds: 6706, Par: 72, USGA: 72.3, Holes: 18, Pro: O. Vincent
TPC Stadium Course, The, Box 1578 55-900 PGA Blvd., La Quinta, 92253, 619-564-7170 Yards: 6331, Par: 72, USGA: 71.2, Holes: 18, Pro: Jeff Walser
Trinity Alps G&CC, POB 582, 111 Fairway Drive, Weaverville, 96093, 916-623-5411 Yards: 1950, Par: 31, USGA: 29.5, Holes: 9, Pro: Felix Claveran
Tularcitos GCC, 1202 Country Club Dr., Milpitas, 95035, 408-262-8813 Yards: 6048, Par: 72, USGA: 69.0, Holes: 18, Pro: Kim Sandmann
Tulare GC, 5319 S. Laspina St., Tulare, 93274, 209-686-9839 Yards: 6534, Par: 72, USGA: 69.5, Holes: 18, Pro: Dave Vogt
Turlock G&CC, POB X, 10532 N Golf Links Road, Turlock, 95381, 209-634-4976 Yards: 6331, Par: 72, USGA: 69.9, Holes: 18, Pro: Shane Balfour
Tustin Ranch GC, Tustin, 92681 Holes: 18
Twain Harte G&CC, POB 333, 22909 Meadow Lane, Twain Harte, 95383, 209-586-3131 Yards: 1715, Par: 29, USGA: 29.0, Holes: 9, Pro: Tim Huber
Ukiah GC, P.O. Box 707, Ukiah, 95482, 707-462-8857 Yards: 5612, Par: 70, USGA: 66.5, Holes: 18, Pro: Steve Frye
Upland Hills CC, 1231 East 16th St., Upland, 91786, 714-946-4711 Yards: 5700, Par: 70, USGA: 66.0, Holes: 18, Pro: John Scappatura
Green Tree GC, Leisure Town Rd., P.O. Box 105, Vacaville, 95688, 707-448-1420 Yards: 5893, Par: 72, USGA: 67.0, Holes: 27, Pro: Kelly Adams
Valencia GC, 27330 North Tourney Rd., Valencia, 91355, 805-254-6200 Yards: 6311, Par: 72, USGA: 70.6, Holes: 18, Pro: Gregg McHatton
Valle Grande GC, 1119 Watts Dr., Bakersfield, 93307, 805-832-2259 Yards: 5915, Par: 72, USGA: 66.3, Holes: 18, Pro: Roland Reese
Vallejo GC—J. Mortara Fairgrounds, Columbus Parkway, Vallejo, 94591, 707-643-8476   Yards: 3182, Par: 56, USGA: 54.4, Holes: 9, Pro: Ralph Harris
Valley Oaks GC, Inc., 1800 So. Plaza Dr., Visalia, 93277, 209-651-1441 Yards: 6250, Par: 72, USGA: 68.2, Holes: 18, Pro: Mike Roberson
Van Buskirk GC, 1740 Houston Ave., Stockton, 95206, 209-464-5629 Yards: 6541, Par: 72, USGA: 69.2, Holes: 18, Pro: Jose Santiago
Victorville Municipal GC, 14144 Greentree Blvd., Victorville, 92392, 619-245-4860 Yards: 6270, Par: 72, USGA: 69.1, Holes: 18, Pro: Ray Echols, Jr
Village Greens G&CC, Fresno, 93725, 209-255-2786 Par: 30, Holes: 9
Vineyard Knolls GC, 1129 Dealy Ln., Napa, 94558, 707-255-7388 Yards: 4000, Par: 58, USGA: 52.1, Holes: 9, Pro: Cliff Barnweolt
Vista Valencia GC, 24700 Trevino Dr., Valencia, 91355, 805-255-4670 Yards: 4160, Par: 61, USGA: 60.3, Holes: 18, Pro: Richard Smith
Wawona Hotel GC, P.O. Box 214, Bass Lake, 93604, 209-375-6572 Yards: 6006, Par: 70, USGA: 68.3, Holes: 18, Pro: Bill Miller
Weed GC, POB 204, 27730 Old Edgewood Rd, Weed, 96094, 916-938-9971 Yards: 2741, Par: 35, USGA: 32.8, Holes: 9
Westlake Village GC, Box 4216, 4812 Lakeview Canyon, Westlake Village, 91359, 818-889-0770   Yards: 4973, Par: 67, USGA: 62.2, Holes: 18, Pro: Dan Yenny
Whispering Palms GC, 4000 Concha De Golf, Rancho Santa Fe, 92067, 619-756-3255 Yards: 6343, Par: 72, USGA: 69.2, Holes: 27, Pro: Henry Sandler
Wikiup GC, 5001 Carriage Ln., Santa Rosa, 95401, 707-546-8787 Yards: 3254, Par: 58, USGA: 54.0, Holes: 9, Pro: Pete Perelli
William Land Park GC, 1701 Sutterville Rd., Sacramento, 95822, 916-455-5014 Yards: 5100, Par: 68, USGA: 63.5, Holes: 9, Pro: Fred Crockett
Willow Park GC, 17007 Redwood Rd., Castro Valley, 94546, 415-537-4733 Yards: 6070, Par: 71, USGA: 67.2, Holes: 18, Pro: Robert Bruce
Willowwick GC, 3017 West Fifth St., Santa Ana, 92703, 714-554-0672 Yards: 6013, Par: 71, USGA: 67.2, Holes: 18, Pro: Thomas Pulliam

Windsor GC, 6555 Skylane Blvd., Windsor, 95492
Holes: 18
Woodvista GC, POB 1269, 7900 N. Lake Road, Kings Beach, 95719,
916-546-9909   Yards: 3038, Par: 35, USGA: 34.9, Holes: 9, Pro: Brian Eilders

Alamoda GC, 6615 N. River Road, Alamosa, 81101,   303-589-9515   *Colorado*
Holes: 9
Alamosa Golf Club PC, 6615 N. River Road, Alamosa, 81101,   303-589-9515
Yards: 6020, Par: 72, USGA: 68.6, Holes: 18
Appletree CC, 10150 Rolling Ridge Road, Colorado Springs, 80925,
719-382-3518   Holes: 9
Applewood Golf Club PC, 14001 W. 32nd Ave., Golden, 80401,   303-279-3003
Yards: 6054, Par: 71, USGA: 66.4, Holes: 18, Pro: Larry Root
Aspen Golf Course PC, 22475 W. Highway 82, Aspen, 81611,   303-925-2145
Holes: 18
Aurora Hills Golf Club PC, 50 S. Peoria St., Aurora, 80010,   303-364-6111
Holes: 18
Battlement Mesa GC, 73 G. Sipprelle Dr., Battlement Mesa, 81635,
303-285-PAR4   Yards: 7500, Holes: 18
Boulder CC, 7350 Clubhouse Road, Boulder, 80301,   303-530-2226
Broadmoor Golf Club—West, P.O.Box 1439, Colorado Springs, 80901,
719-577-5790   Yards: 6109, Par: 72, USGA: 70.2, Holes: 18, Pro: Dow Finsterwald
Burlington Golf Club PC, 48680 Snead Dr., Burlington, 80807
Yards: 2991, Par: 37, Holes: 9
Cedar Ridges Golf Club PC, 611 S. Stanolind Ave., Rangely, 81648,
303-675-8404   Yards: 6281, Par: 36, Holes: 9, Pro: Hans Parkinson
Centennial Golf Course PC, 861 E. Applewood Ave., Littleton, 80121,
303-794-5838   Holes: 9
Centre Hills GC, 16300 E. Centre Tech Pkwy., Aurora, 80012,   303-343-4935
Cimarron Hills Golf Club PC, 1805 Tuskegee Pl., Colorado Springs, 80915,
303-597-2637   Holes: 9
City Park Municipal Golf Club, 2500 York St., Denver, 80205,   303-295-2095
Holes: 18
City Park Golf Course, 3900 Thatcher, Pueblo, 81005,   303-561-4946
Yards: 6245, Par: 70, USGA: 67.0, Holes: 27, Pro: Larry Brooks
City Park Nine Golf Club PC, 411 S. Bryan St., Ft. Collins, 80521,   303-221-6650
Holes: 9
Collegiate Peaks Golf Club PC, 28775 Fairway Dr., Buena Vista, 81211,
719-395-8189   Yards: 2992, Par: 36, Holes: 9
Colorado City Golf Club PC, 4704 Santa Fe Dr., Colorado City, 81019,
303-676-3340   Holes: 9
Conquistador Muni GC, Cortez, 81321,   303-565-9208
Par: 72, Holes: 36
Cooper Mountain, POB 3001, Cooper Mountain, 80443,   800-458-8386
Yards: 6129, Holes: 18
Cortez Municipal Golf Course Park, 2018 N. Delores Rd. P.O. Box 8, Cortez,
81321,   303-565-9208   Holes: 18
Cottonwood Golf Club PC, 1679 H 75 Rd., Delta, 81416,   303-874-7263
Yards: 6324, Par: 72, USGA: 66.9, Holes: 18
Dos Rios Golf Club PC, HWY 50 W. P.O. Box 86, Gunnison, 81230,
303-641-1482   Yards: 6054, Par: 71, USGA: 72.6, Holes: 18, Pro: G.J. Santelli
Eagle CC, N. Main & 12th St., Broomfield, 80020,   303-466-3322
Eagles Nest Golf Club PC, 305 Golden Eagle Road, Silverton, 80498,
303-468-0681   Holes: 18
Englewood Golf Course PC, 2101 W. Oxford, Englewood, 80110,   303-761-0848
Yards: 6426, Par: 72, USGA: 69.1, Holes: 18, Pro: Mark Kindahl

Estes Park Golf Club, 1080 S. St. Vrain, Estes Park, 80817, 303-586-8146
Yards: 6000, Par: 70, USGA: 67.6, Holes: 18, Pro: Skip Peck
Evergreen Municipal Golf Club, 29614 Upper Bear Creek Rd., Evergreen,
80439, 303-674-5597 Holes: 9
Fairfield Pagosa GC, P.O.Box 4040, Pagosa Springs, 81157, 303-731-4141
Yards: 6282, Par: 71, USGA: 68.9, Holes: 18, Pro: Mark Amberson
Flatirons Country Club PC, 5706 E. Arapahoe Rd., Boulder, 80301,
303-442-7851 Holes: 18
Foothills Golf Club, 3901 S. Carr St., Denver, 80235, 303-989-3901
Holes: 18
Fort Morgan Golf Course PC, Jct. I-76 & Hwy 52, Fort Morgan, 80701,
303-867-5990 Yards: 6416, Par: 73, USGA: 72.9, Holes: 18, Pro: Rich Zulkoski
Fox Hill Country Club PC, P.O. Box 762, Longmont, 80501
Glenwood Springs Golf Course P, P.O. Box 2304, Glenwood Springs, 81602,
303-945-7086 Par: 35, Holes: 9
Grand Lake Golf CoursePC, 1111 Country Rd. 48, Grand Lake, 80447,
303-627-8008 Holes: 18
Grandote G&CC, 127 W. Ryus St., La Veta, 81055, 303-742-3123
Haystack Mountain Golf Course, 5877 Niwot Road, Longmont, 80501,
303-530-1400 Yards: 3250, Par: 32, Holes: 9
Heather Gardens CC, 2888 S. Heather Gardens Way, Aurora, 80014,
303-751-2390
Heather Ridge CC, 13521 E. Iliff Ave.,, Aurora, 80014, 303-755-3350
High Plains Golf Course, 1/4 Mi N.E. of Yuma, Yuma, 80759, 303-848-2813
Yards: 3407, Par: 36, USGA: 69.2, Holes: 9
Highland Hills Golf Club PC, 2200 Clubhouse Dr., Greeley, 80631,
303-330-7327 Yards: 6002, Par: 71, USGA: 72.8, Holes: 18, Pro: Robert McNamee
Hillcrest Golf Club, 40292 HW 550 N., Durango, 81301, 303-247-1499
Yards: 6251, Par: 71, USGA: 68.6, Holes: 18, Pro: Jim Fiala
Holyoke Golf Club PC, 415 E. Carnahan P.O. Box 243, Holyoke, 80734,
303-854-3200 Holes: 18
Indian Tree Golf Club PC, 7555 Wadsworth Blvd., Arvada, 80005,
303-423-3450 Yards: 6645, Par: 71, USGA: 67.5, Holes: 18, Pro: C. "Vic" Kline
Inverness GC, 317 Inverness Way South, Englewood, 80112, 303-790-1581
John F. Kennedy GC, 10500 E. Hampden Ave., Aurora, 80014, 303-755-0105
Holes: 18
Keystone Ranch GC, POB 38, Keystone, 80435, 303-468-4250
Yards: 7090, Holes: 18
Lake Arbor Golf Course PC, 8600 Wadsworth Blvd., Arvada, 80002,
303-423-1650 Par: 70, Holes: 18
Lake Valley Golf Club PC, P.O. Box 1006, Boulder, 80306, 303-444-2114
Yards: 6396, Par: 70, USGA: 66.9, Holes: 18, Pro: Jim Phillips
Las Animas—Bent Co. GC, 220 Country Club Dr., Las Animas, 81054,
719-456-2511 Par: 34, Holes: 9
Lincoln Park Golf Club PC, 14th & Gunnison, Grand Junction, 81501,
303-242-6394 Par: 36, Holes: 9
Link N Greens Golf Course PC, 777 E. Lincoln Ave., Ft. Collins, 80524,
303-221-4818 Yards: 2100, Par: 30, USGA: 57.2, Holes: 9, Pro: Mike Musgrave
Los Animas GC, P.O. Box 431, Los Animas, 81054, 303-456-1339
Holes: 9
Loveland Golf Course PC, 2115 W. 29th St., Loveland, 80538, 303-667-5256
Yards: 6487, Par: 72, USGA: 67.9, Holes: 18, Pro: Don Fox
Mad Russian GC, P.O. Box 301, Milliken, 80534, 303-587-5157
Holes: 18
Meadow Creek Golf Course PC, Colorado City, 81019

Meadow Hills Golf Club PC, 3609 S. Dawson St., Aurora, 80014, 303-690-2500
Par: 70, USGA: 68.9, Holes: 18, Pro: Mickey Byrne
Meadows Golf Club PC, The, 6937 So. Simms, Littleton, 80127,   303-972-8831
Yards: 6543, Par: 72, USGA: 69.2, Holes: 18, Pro: Bill Ramsey
Meeker Golf Club PC, 903 Country Rd. 13, Meeker, 81641,   303-878-5642
Yards: 2613, Par: 34, Holes: 9, Pro: Dan Sommers
MICIT GC, 9432 Motsenbocker Road, Parker, 80134
Holes: 9
Monte Vista Golf Course PC, P.O. Box 505, Monte Vista, 81144,   303-852-9995
Holes: 9
Montrose Golf Course PC, 2060 Birch St., Montrose, 81401,   303-249-8551
Holes: 9
Mountain View Golf Club, 5091 So. Quebeck St., Denver, 80237,   303-694-3012
Holes: 9
Overland Park Municipal Golf Course, 1801 So. Huron St., Denver, 80223,
303-777-7331   Holes: 18
Park Hill Golf Club PC, 4141 E. 35th Ave., Denver, 80207,   303-333-5411
Holes: 18
Patty Jewett Golf Club—9 hole, 990 E. Espanola, Colorado Springs, 80907,
303-578-6826 Yards: 3006, Par: 34, USGA: 67.8, Holes: 9, Pro: Paul Ransom
Prairie Pines G & CC, 28775 Fairway Dr., Buena Vista, 80807,   303-346-8698
Holes: 9
Ptarmigan GC, 5410 So. Lemay, Ft. Collins, 80525,   303-226-6600
Pueblo West Golf Club PC, P.O. Box 7125, Pueblo, 81007,   303-547-2280
Holes: 18
Raccoon Creek Golf Club PC, 7301 W. Bowles Ave., Littleton, 80123,
303-973-4653   Holes: 18
Riverview Golf Club PC, 13064 Country Road 370, Sterling, 80751,
303-522-3035   Par: 71, Holes: 18
Rocky Ford Country Club PC, 91 Play Park Hill, Rocky Ford, 81067,
303-254-7528   Yards: 5679, Par: 70, USGA: 65.6, Holes: 18
Salida Golf Club PC, Crestone Ave., Salida, 81201,   303-539-6373
Holes: 9
Sedgwick Country Golf Course P, Two miles north of Julesburg, Julesburg,
80717, 303-445-2119   Holes: 9
Singletree Golf Club PC, P.O. Box AA, Edwards, 81632,   303-926-3533
Holes: 18
South Suburban Golf Course PC, 7900 So. Colorado Blvd., Littleton, 80122,
303-770-5500   Yards: 6359, Par: 72, USGA: 75.3, Holes: 18, Pro: Don Thompson
Southridge Greens Golf Club PC, 5750 So. Lemay, Ft. Collins, 80525,
303-226-2828   Yards: 5731, Par: 71, USGA: 66.0, Holes: 18, Pro: K. Heusinkveld
Spreading Antlers Golf Club PC, P.O. Box 670, Lamar, 81052,   303-336-5274
Holes: 9
Springhill Golf Course PC, 17979 E. 6th Ave., Aurora, 80011,   303-343-3963
Holes: 18
Steamboat Springs Golf Club PC, Hwy. 40 West, Steamboat Springs, 80477,
303-879-4295   Yards: 2777, Par: 35, USGA: 65.1, Holes: 9, Pro: Dennis Johnson
Sunset Golf Club PC, 1900 Longs Peak Ave., Longmont, 80501,   303-776-3122
Holes: 9
Tamarack Golf Course PC, One-half mile S. of Limon Hwy., Limon, 80828,
303-775-9998   Holes: 9
Tiara Rado Golf Course PC, 2063 S. Broadway, Grand Junction, 81501,
303-245-9979   Par: 71, Holes: 18
Trinidad Muni GC, P.O. Box 812, Trinidad, 81082,   303-846-4015
Par: 36, Holes: 9

Twin Peaks Golf Course PC, 1200 Cornell Dr., Longmont, 80501, 303-772-1722
Yards: 6767, Par: 70, USGA: 68.1, Holes: 18, Pro: Don Corey
Valley Hi GC, 610 S. Chelton Rd., Colorado Springs, 80910, 303-578-6926
Holes: 18
Walsenburg Golf Club PC, Lathrop State Park Hwy. 160, Walsenburg, 81089,
719-738-2730 Yards: 6395, Par: 72, Holes: 18
Washington County Club Golf Club, P.O. Box 221, Arkon, 80702, 303-345-2309
Holes: 9
Wellshire GC, 3333 S. Colorado Blvd., Denver, 80222, 303-757-1352
Yards: 6542, Par: 72, USGA: 68.8, Holes: 18, Pro: Scott Hart
Westbank Ranch Golf Course PC, 1007 Westbank Rd., Glenwood Springs,
81601, 303-945-7032 Yards: 2978, Par: 35, USGA: 68.0, Holes: 9, Pro: Bart Victor
Willis Case Golf Club PC, 4999 Vrain St., Denver, 80212, 303-455-9801
Yards: 6364, Par: 72, USGA: 68.7, Holes: 18
Wray Country Club PC, 36357 Hwy. 385, Wray, 80758, 303-332-5934
Yards: 2987, Par: 35, USGA: 67.1, Holes: 9
Yampa Valley Golf Club PC, S. of Craig on State Hwy. 394, Craig, 81625,
303-824-3673 Yards: 6344, Par: 72, USGA: 66.0, Holes: 18, Pro: Chuck Cobb

---

Airways GC, S. Grand St., Suffield, 06078, 203-668-4973   *Connecticut*
Yards: 5600, Par: 70, Holes: 18
Alling Memorial GC, Eastern St., New Haven, 06513, 203-369-9560
Yards: 5872, Par: 71, Holes: 18
Banner Lodge CC, Banner Rd., Moodus, 06469, 203-873-8652
Yards: 6400, Par: 72, Holes: 18
Bel Compo GC, Route 44, Avon, 06801, 203-678-1358
Yards: 6304, Par: 72, Holes: 18
Blackledge CC, West St., Hebron, 06248, 203-228-0250
Yards: 6801, Par: 72, Holes: 18
Brookfield GC, Sunset Hill Rd., Brookfiled Centre, 06805, 203-775-2464
Pro: John Urkiel
Brooklyn Hill GC, South St., Brooklyn, 06234, 203-774-1591
Yards: 2815, Par: 35, Holes: 9
Bruce GC, 1300 King St., Greenwich, 06831, 203-531-7261
Pro: Nick Roberto
Buena Vista GC, Buena Vista Rd., W. Hartford, 06107, 203-523-1133
Yards: 1832, Par: 31, Holes: 9
Canaan CC, S. Canaan Rd., No. Canaan, 06018, 203-354-9359
Yards: 3007, Par: 35, Holes: 9
Candlewood Valley CC, Route 7, New Milford, 06776, 203-354-9359
Yards: 6045, Par: 70, Holes: 18
Canton GC, Route 44, Canton, 06019, 203-693-8305
Yards: 3107, Par: 36, Holes: 9
Cedar Knob GC, Billings Rd., Somers, 06071, 203-749-3550
Yards: 6734, Par: 72, Holes: 18
Century Hills GC, Cold Spring Rd., Rocky Hill, 06067, 203-563-5200
Yards: 3212, Par: 35, Holes: 9
Chanticlair GC, Old Hebron Rd., Colchester, 06415, 203-537-3223
Yards: 3217, Par: 35, Holes: 9
Copper Hill CC, Griffin Rd., E. Granby, 06238, 203-653-6191
Yards: 3069, Par: 36, Holes: 9
Crestbrook Park GC, Northfield Rd., Watertown, 06795, 203-274-5411
Yards: 6906, Par: 71, Holes: 18
E. Gaynor Bennan GC, 451 Stillwater Rd., Stamford, 06902, 203-324-4185
Yards: 5868, Par: 71, Holes: 18, Pro: Michael Dale

East Mountain GC, E. Mountain Rd., Waterbury, 06708, 203-753-1425
Yards: 5720, Par: 68, Holes: 18
East Woods CC, Torringford W. St., Torrington, 06790, 203-489-2630
Yards: 3105, Par: 36, Holes: 9
Elmridge CC, Elmridge Rd., Pawcatuck, 06781, 203-599-2248
Yards: 6340, Par: 71, Holes: 18
Fairchild Wheeler GC—#1, Eastern Tpke., Bridgeport, 06001, 203-576-8083
Yards: 6402, Par: 71, Holes: 18, Pro: John McGoldrick
Farmingbury Hills CC, East St., Wolcott, 06716, 203-879-9380
Yards: 2757, Par: 36, Holes: 9
Fenwick GC, 580 Maple Ave., Old Saybrook, 06475, 203-388-2516
Yards: 2820, Par: 34, Holes: 9
Goodwin Park GC—#1, Maple Ave., Hartford, 06114, 203-722-6561
Yards: 3005, Par: 35, Holes: 9
Grassmere GC, Town Farm Rd., Hazardville, 06082, 203-749-7740
Yards: 3065, Par: 35, Holes: 9
Great Hill GC, Seymour, 06483
Greenwoods CC, Torringford St., Winsted, 06098, 203-379-8051
Yards: 3235, Par: 35, Holes: 9
H. Smith Richardson GC, 2425 Morehouse Rd., Fairfield, 06430, 203-255-6094
Yards: 6671, Par: 72, Holes: 18, Pro: Michael Homa
Highland GC, P.O. Box 229, Shelton, 06484, 203-734-9754
Pro: R. Culbertson
Highland Greens GC, Cooke Rd., Prospect, 06712, 203-758-4022
Yards: 1398, Par: 27, Holes: 9
Hop Brook CC, N. Church St., Naugatuck, 06770, 203-729-8013
Yards: 2937, Par: 36, Holes: 9
Hotchkiss School GC, Hotchkiss School, Lakeville, 06039, 203-435-9033
Yards: 3118, Par: 35, Holes: 9
Indian Spring GC, Mack Rd., Middlefield, 06455, 203-349-8109
Yards: 3000, Par: 36, Holes: 9
Keney Park GC, Barbour St., Hartford, 06120, 203-722-6548
Yards: 5989, Par: 70, Holes: 18
Laurel View CC, W. Shepard Ave., Hamden, 06514, 203-281-0670
Yards: 6904, Par: 72, Holes: 18
Lisbon CC, Kendall Rd., Lisbon, 06759, 203-376-4325
Yards: 2300, Par: 33, Holes: 9
Longshore Park, S. Compo Rd., Westport, 06880, 203-226-8311
Yards: 5810, Par: 69, Holes: 18
Mill Stone CC, 348 Herbert St., Milford, 06460, 203-874-5900
Yards: 3910, Par: 36, Holes: 9
Millbrook GC, Pigeon Hill Rd., Windsor, 06095, 203-688-2575
Yards: 6427, Par: 71, Holes: 18
Minnechaug GC, Manchester Rd., Glastonbury, 06033, 203-643-9914
Yards: 6527, Par: 71, Holes: 18
Newtown CC, Newtown, 06480, 203-426-9311
Yards: 4841, Par: 67, Holes: 9
Norwich GC, New London Tpke., Norwich, 06360, 203-889-6973
Yards: 6133, Par: 71, Holes: 18
Orange Hills CC, Racebrook Rd., Orange, 06477, 203-795-4161
Yards: 6146, Par: 71, Holes: 18
Patton Brook CC, Pattonwood Dr., Southington, 06489, 203-747-9466
Yards: 4335, Par: 60, Holes: 18
Pilgrims Harbor CC, Harrison Rd., Wallingford, 06492, 203-269-6023
Yards: 3337, Par: 36, Holes: 9

Pine Valley CC, Welch Rd., Southington, 06489, 203-628-0879
Yards: 6071, Par: 71, Holes: 18
Portland GC, Bartlett St., Portland, 06480, 203-342-2833
Yards: 6213, Par: 71, Holes: 18
Raceway GC, Thompson, 06277, 203-923-9591
Yards: 6550, Par: 72, Holes: 18
Ridgefield GC, 545 Ridgebury Rd., P.O. Box 59, Ridgefield, 06877, 203-748-7008
Yards: 5919, Par: 70, USGA: 68.1, Holes: 18, Pro: Vincent Adams
Rockledge CC, S. Main St., W. Hartford, 06107, 203-521-3156
Yards: 6262, Par: 72, Holes: 18
Shennecossett GC, Plant St., Groton, 06340, 203-445-0262
Yards: 6128, Par: 72, Holes: 18
Simsbury Farms GC, Old Farms Rd., Simsbury, 06070, 203-658-6246
Yards: 6524, Par: 71, Holes: 18
Southington CC, Savage St., Southington, 06489, 203-628-7032
Yards: 6008, Par: 70, Holes: 18
Stanley GC—#1, Hartford Rd., New Britain, 06053, 203-827-8144
Yards: 3130, Par: 36, Holes: 9
Sterling Farms GC, 1349 Newfield Ave., Stamford, 06905, 203-329-8171
Yards: 6271, Par: 71, Holes: 18, Pro: Tom Lupinacci
Sunset Hill GC, Sunset Hill Rd., Brookfield Centre, 06805, 203-531-7261
Yards: 2743, Par: 35, Holes: 9, Pro: Ken Burlinson
Tallwood GC, Route 85, Hebron, 06248, 203-646-1151
Yards: 6364, Par: 72, Holes: 18
Tashua Knolls CC, Tashua Rd., Trumbull, 06611, 203-261-5989
Yards: 6760, Par: 72, Holes: 18, Pro: Walt Bogues
Timberlin GC, Southington Rd., Kensington, 06037, 203-828-3228
Yards: 6745, Par: 72, Holes: 18
Trumbull GC, High Rock Rd., Groton, 06340, 203-445-7991
Yards: 2666, Par: 54, Holes: 18
Tunxis Plantation GC #1, Town Farm Rd., Farmington, 06032, 203-677-1367
Yards: 3358, Par: 36, Holes: 9
Twin Hills CC, Route 31, Coventry, 06238, 203-742-9705
Yards: 6200, Par: 71, Holes: 18
Western Hills GC, Park Rd., Waterbury, 06708, 203-755-6828
Yards: 6246, Par: 72, Holes: 18
Westwoods GC, Route 177, Farmington, 06032, 203-677-9192
Yards: 4506, Par: 61, Holes: 18
Whitney Farms GC, 175 Shelton Rd., Monroe, 06468, 203-268-0707
Yards: 6628, Par: 72, Holes: 18, Pro: Paul McQuire
Woodhaven GC, Miller Rd., Bethany, 06801, 203-393-3220
Yards: 3342, Par: 36, Holes: 9

Greenhill GC, Dupont Rd., Wilmington, 19807, 302-571-7745   *Delaware*
Yards: 6200, Par: 70, Holes: 18
Rock Manor GC, Foulk and Weldin Rds., Wilmington, 19803, 302-652-4083
Holes: 18

Aberdeen G & CC, 4965 La Chalet Blvd., Boynton Beach, 33435,   *Florida*
305-734-3035 Holes: 18
Airco GC, 3650 Roosevelt Blvd., Clearwater, 33520, 813-576-1453
Yards: 6088, Par: 72, USGA: 74.6, Holes: 18, Pro: John Bauer
Alden Pines GC, SR 767, P.O. Box 324, Pineland, 33945, 813-283-2179
Yards: 5044, Par: 71, USGA: 64.5, Holes: 18, Pro: Don Stewart
American Golfers Club, 3850 N. Federal Hwy, Fort Lauderdale, 33308,
305-564-8760 Yards: 3000, Par: 58, Holes: 27, Pro: Ron Sharpe

Arcadia GC, US 17, P.O. Box 1423, Arcadia, 33821, 813-494-4223
Yards: 5965, Par: 71, Holes: 18, Pro: Arthur Roe
Arrowhead CC, 8201 SW 24th St., Fort Lauderdale, 33324, 305-475-8200
Yards: 6350, Par: 71, USGA: 68.9, Holes: 18, Pro: Tom Haney
Atlantis Inn GC, 190 Atlantis Blvd., Atlantis, 33462, 305-968-1300
Yards: 6500, Par: 72, USGA: 68.9, Holes: 18, Pro: Jim Simon
Avon Lakes GC, 106 S. Highway 27, Avon Park, 33825, 813-453-4200
Pro: Bob Young
Babe Zaharias GC, 11412 Forest Hills Dr., Tampa, 33612, 813-932-8932
Yards: 6142, Par: 70, Holes: 18, Pro: Bert Stump
Bardmoor CC—North Course, 8000 Bardmoor Blvd., Largo, 33543,
813-397-0483   Yards: 6484, Par: 72, USGA: 71.5, Holes: 18, Pro: Dick Hyland
Bartow GC PC, 150 Idlewood Ave. (P.O. Box 10, Bartow, 33830, 813-533-9183
Yards: 6247, Par: 72, Holes: 18, Pro: Lee Pearson
Bay Beach GC, Estero Blvd., P.O. Box 2459, Fort Myers Beach, 33931,
813-463-2064   Yards: 3520, Par: 61, USGA: 57.2, Holes: 18, Pro: Nancy Lambert
Bay Point, 100 Delwood Beach Road, Panama City, 32407, 904-234-3307
Yards: 6398, Par: 72, USGA: 70.7, Holes: 18, Pro: Randy Cahall
Bay Pointe GC, 9399 Commodore Dr., Seminole, 33542, 813-595-2095
Yards: 3464, Par: 62, Holes: 18, Pro: M. Ciaffone
Bayshore GC, 2301 Alton Rd., Miami Beach, 33139, 305-673-7705
Yards: 6188, Par: 72, Holes: 18, Pro: Don Staton
Belle Glade G & CC, 110 SW Ave. E, Belle Glade, 33430, 407-996-6605
Yards: 3000, Par: 36, USGA: 68.9, Holes: 9, Pro: George Dermott
Belleview Biltmore CC, 25 Belleview Blvd., Clearwater, 34616, 813-442-6171
Yards: 6388, Par: 71, Holes: 36
Bent Oak GC, 4304 London Town Rd. #125, Orlando, 32796
Bent Tree GC, 4700 Bent Tree Blvd., Tampa, 34241
Big Cypress at Royal Palm, Royal Hammock Blvd., Box 1, Naples, 33962,
813-775-9453   Yards: 6120, Par: 71, USGA: 68.9, Holes: 18, Pro: Ken Elsinger
Biltmore GC—Granada GC, 2001 Granada Blvd., Coral Gables, 33134,
305-442-6584   Yards: 3200, Par: 36, USGA: 34.6, Holes: 9
Biltmore GC—Coral Gables Course, 1210 Anastasia, Coral Gables, 33134,
305-442-6584   Yards: 6652, Par: 71, USGA: 69.5, Holes: 18, Pro: Val Macor
Bird Bay Executive GC, 602 Bird Bat Dr. W, Venice, 33595, 813-485-9333
Yards: 2520, Par: 56, Holes: 18, Pro: Steve Nowak
Boby Jones GC, 1000 Circus Blvd, Tampa, 34232
Boca Delray GC, 5483 Boca Delray Blvd., Delray Beach, 33445, 305-499-3100
Par: 60, Holes: 18, Pro: Tony Dunlea
Boca Raton Municipal GC—18 Hole, 8111 205th St. South, Boca Raton, 33428,
305-483-6100   Yards: 6177, Par: 72, Holes: 18, Pro: Dan Fabian
Boca Raton Hotel GC, 501 El Camino Real, W. Palm Beach, 33432
Boca Teeca CC—East Course, 5800 NW 2nd Ave., Boca Raton, 33431,
305-994-0400   Yards: 3044, Par: 35, USGA: 34.3, Holes: 9, Pro: Joe Vileno
Bonita Springs G & CC, 4 Cockleshell Dr., Bonita Springs, 33923,
813-992-6564   Yards: 6210, Par: 72, USGA: 70.5, Holes: 18, Pro: Richard Hayes
Bonita Springs G&CC PC, 10200 Maddox Lane, Bonita Springs, 33923,
813-992-2800   Yards: 6315, Par: 72, USGA: 70.3, Holes: 18, Pro: Bill Robishaw
Breakers GC, The, P. O. Box 910, Palm Beach, 33480, 407-655-6611
Yards: 5956, Par: 70, USGA: 68.0, Holes: 18, Pro: Ronald Martin
Briar Bay GC, 9373 SW 134th St., Miami, 33176, 305-235-6667
Yards: 1983, Par: 31, Holes: 9, Pro: Allan Weitzel
Buenaventura Lakes CC—East, 301 Buenaventura Blvd., Kissimmee, 32743,
407-348-2394   Yards: 1694, Par: 30, USGA: 28.2, Holes: 9, Pro: Buddy Blandford
Buenaventura Lakes CC West, 600 Competition Drive, Kissimmee, 32743
Holes: 9

Buffalo Creek GC, Old Erie Road, Ellington, 34221
Holes: 18
Calusa GC, 9400 SW 130th Ave., Miami, 33186, 305-386-5533
Yards: 7185, Par: 72, USGA: 72.0, Holes: 18, Pro: Ken Szuch
Camino Del Mar GC, 22689 Camino Del Mar Dr., Boca Raton, 33433,
305-392-7992 Yards: 6252, Par: 71, USGA: 69.1, Holes: 18, Pro: Tex Lankford
Cannongate GC, 3645 West Oak Ridge Rd., Orlando, 32809, 305-351-9778
Yards: 3225, Par: 58, Holes: 18, Pro: John Heine
Cape Coral Exec GC, 1006 SW 4th Place, Cape Coral, 33904, 813-574-4454
Yards: 6325, Par: 72, Holes: 18, Pro: Larry Hauner
Cape Coral Municipal GC, P.O. Box 900, Cape Coral, 33910
Holes: 18
Capri Isles GC, 849 Capri Isles, Venice, 33595, 813-485-3371
Yards: 6296, Par: 72, USGA: 68.8, Holes: 18, Pro: Gary Dennis
Casselberry GC, 3000 S. Lake Triplett Dr., Casselberry, 32707, 305-830-8010
Yards: 6000, Par: 70, Holes: 18, Pro: Tom Webb
Caverns GC PC, 2601 Caverns Rd., Marinana, 32446, 904-482-4257
Yards: 3261, Par: 36, Holes: 9, Pro: Frank Powledge
CC at Silver Springs Shores, 565 Silver Rd., Ocala, 32672, 904-687-2828
Yards: 6162, Par: 72, USGA: 68.8, Holes: 18, Pro: Wade Herguth
CC of Miami—East Course, 6801 NW 186th St, P.O. Box 412, Hlaleah, 33015,
305-821-0111 Yards: 6434, Par: 72, Holes: 18, Pro: Van Silver
Century Village GC, 2751 N. Haverhill Rd., West Palm Beach, 33409,
305-686-0948 Yards: 3690, Par: 60, Holes: 18, Pro: John Cownden
Century Village GC, 2060 W. Hillsboro, Deerfield Beach, 33441, 305-428-3880
Yards: 3549, Par: 62, Holes: 18
Cheeca Lodge GC, Islamorada, 33036, 305-664-4651
Par: 54, Holes: 18
Chi Chi Rodriguez Youth Fund GC, 3030 McMullin Booth Road, Clearwater,
34621 Holes: 18
Chiefland G & CC, Rt. 2 Box 386, Chiefland, 32626, 904-493-2375
Yards: 3208, Par: 36, Holes: 9, Pro: Reatha Flecker
Citrus Springs CC, 150 E. Golfview Dr., Citrus Springs, 32630, 904-489-5045
Yards: 6161, Par: 72, Holes: 18, Pro: Chuck Almony
City of Ocala, PO Box 1270, Ocala, 32678
Holes: 18
City of Miami Beach Par 3, 2795 Prairie Ave., Miami Beach, 33139,
305-534-7511 Yards: 1260, Par: 27, Holes: 9
Clearwater CC, 525 N. Betty Lane, Clearwater, 33515, 813-443-5078
Yards: 6014, Par: 72, Holes: 18, Pro: Greg McCimans
Clearwater Golf Park PC, 1875 Airport Dr., Clearwater, 33515, 904-447-5272
Yards: 4357, Par: 63, USGA: 59.0, Holes: 18, Pro: Jean Frank
Clerbrook GC, Rt. 2, Box 107, Clermont, 32711, 904-394-5513
Yards: 6000, Par: 67, Holes: 18, Pro: Warren Moser
Cleveland Heights G&CC PC, 2900 Buckingham, Lakeland, 33803,
813-682-3277 Yards: 3062, Par: 36, USGA: 35.2, Holes: 27, Pro: Walt Newsome
Clewiston GC, 1200 San Luiz, P.O. Box 998, Clewiston, 33440, 813-983-7064
Yards: 6472, Par: 72, USGA: 68.6, Holes: 18, Pro: Bob Rush
Club at Hidden Creek GC, Gulf Breeze, 32561, 904-939-4604
Par: 72, Holes: 18
Club Med Sandpiper, 3500 SE Marningside Blvd., Port St. Lucie, 34952,
407-337-6615 Par: 72, Holes: 18
Colony West CC—#2, 6800 NW 88th Ave., Fort Lauderdale, 33321, 305-721-7710
Yards: 4197, Par: 63, Holes: 18, Pro: Tim Arpasi
Connell Lake GC, 4555 E. Windmill Dr., Inverness, 32650, 904-726-1461
Yards: 6277, Par: 72, USGA: 69.0, Holes: 18, Pro: George Ritch

Continental CC, SR 44, CCC Box 101, Wildwood, 32785,   904-748-2918
Yards: 6013, Par: 72, Holes: 18, Pro: David Hinkley
Cooper Colony CC, 5050 SW 90th Ave., , Cooper City, 33328,   305-434-2181
Yards: 4000, Par: 60, Holes: 18, Pro: Jack Lucas
Countryside Executive GC PC, 2506 Countryside Blvd., Clearwater, 34623,
813-796-1555   Yards: 3362, Par: 58, Holes: 18, Pro: C.Churchward
Countryway GC, 11111 Waters Ave, Tampa, 33615,   813-854-1182
Holes: 18
Cove Cay G&TC, 2612 Cove Cay Dr., Clearwater, 33520,   813-535-1406
Yards: 6100, Par: 70, USGA: 66.8, Holes: 18, Pro: Chris Snider
Cross Creek CC, 1 Cross Creek Blvd., Fort Myers, 33912,   813-768-1922
Yards: 3510, Par: 60, Holes: 18, Pro: Mike Hays
Crystal Brook GC, 2259 East Spacecoast Highway, Kissimmee, 32741,
305-847-8721   Yards: 1430, Par: 27, Holes: 9
Cutter Sound CC, 951 Colorado Ave., Stuart, 33497,   305-286-4303
Par: 69, Holes: 18
Cypress Creek GC, 5353 S. Vineland Rd., Orlando, 32811,   305-351-3151
Yards: 6335, Par: 72, USGA: 70.9, Holes: 18, Pro: Bill Murchison
Cypress Creek, 4830 W. Kennedy Blvd., Tampa, 33609
Holes: 18
Cypress Greens CC, 1000 Kings Blvd., P.O. Box 569, Sun City Center, 33570,
813-634-3038   Yards: 3187, Par: 36, Holes: 9, Pro: Bill DeAngelis
Cypress Pines CC, 11750 Homestead Rd. S., Leigh Acres, 33936,   813-369-8216
Yards: 6398, Par: 72, Holes: 18, Pro: Kevin Bessonen
Dade City Golf, US 301, Dade City, 33525
Daytona Beach G & CC—South Course, 600 Wilder Blvd., Daytona Beach,
32014, 904-255-4517   Yds: 6229, Par: 72, USGA: 68.6, Holes: 18, Pro: Donald Ross
Daytona Beach GC—North Course, 600 Wilder Blvd., Daytona Beach, 32014,
904-255-4517   Yards: 6566, Par: 72, USGA: 69.0, Holes: 18, Pro: Dick Medford
Deep Creek CC, San Christobal Ave, P.O. Box 2, Port Charlotte, 33949,
813-685-6911   Yards: 5630, Par: 70, USGA: 68.0, Holes: 18, Pro: Paul Barone
Deer Creek G&RV Resort, 4200 US 27 N, Davenport, 33837
Holes: 9
Deer Creek GC, 2801 Country Club Blvd., Deerfield Beach, 33442,
305-421-5550   Yards: 6400, Par: 72, USGA: 70.5, Holes: 18, Pro: Steve Roderick
Deer Run CC, 1525 Eagle Circel S, Casselberry, 32707,   407-699-9592
Yards: 6500, Par: 71, Holes: 18, Pro: Rich Vacaro
Deerfield CC, Lem Turner Rd., Callahan, 32011,   904-879-1210
Yards: 6100, Par: 70, Holes: 18
Delray Beach GC, 2200 Highland Ave., Delray Beach, 33445,   305-278-0315
Yards: 6497, Par: 72, USGA: 73.5, Holes: 18
Deltona Hills G&CC, 1120 Elkcam Blvd., Deltona, 32725,   904-789-4911
Yards: 6460, Par: 72, USGA: 72.2, Holes: 18, Pro: Don Farrell
Diamond Hill GC, Sidney Rd., P.O. Box 309, Valrico, 33594,   813-689-7219
Yards: 6231, Par: 72, USGA: 71.1, Holes: 18, Pro: M.G. Orender
Disney Olds Classic GC, 1 Magnolia Palm Dr., Orlando, 32820
Dodger Pines GC, 4600 26th St., Vero Beach, 32960,   305-569-4400
Yards: 6288, Par: 73, USGA: 69.4, Holes: 18, Pro: Roger Bott
Dodgertown GC, 4201 16th St., P.O. Box 2887, Vero Beach, 32961,   305-569-4800
Yards: 3157, Par: 36, Holes: 9, Pro: Roger Bott
Doral Park Silver GC, 4825 NW 104th Ave., Miami, 33178,   305-594-0954
Yards: 6016, Par: 72, Holes: 18, Pro: Dick Guardiola
Dubsdread CC, 549 W. Par Ave., Orlando, 32804,   305-843-7311
Yards: 5903, Par: 71, USGA: 68.0, Holes: 18, Pro: Harold Rayborn
Dunes CC, 949 Sand Castle Rd., Sanibel Island, 33957,   813-472-2535
Yards: 4875, Par: 66, USGA: 65.9, Holes: 18, Pro: Pat Flinn

Dunes GC, 11751 McCormick Rd., P.O. Box, Jacksonville, 32211, 904-641-8444
Yards: 6100, Par: 72, USGA: 70.5, Holes: 18, Pro: Richard Kent
Eagles GC (The)—18 Hole, 16101 Nine Eagles Dr., Odessa, 33556, 813-920-2805
Yards: 6616, Par: 72, USGA: 71.6, Holes: 18, Pro: Chuck Peters
East Bay GC, 702 Country Club Dr., Largo, 33541, 813-581-3333
Yards: 6272, Par: 72, USGA: 70.0, Holes: 18, Pro: John Brott
Eco GC, 1451 Taft St., Hollywood, 33020, 305-923-4111
Yards: 2000, Par: 31, Holes: 9, Pro: Dan Childers
Emerald Dunes GC, 6565 Okeechobee Blvd, West Palm Beach, 33411,
407-684-5902 Holes: 18
Errol CC, 1355 Errol Pkwy., Apopka, 32712, 407-886-5000 Yards: 6689, Par: 72,
USGA: 71.3, Holes: 27, Pro: Wally Kuchar
Fairgreen GC, 35 Fairgreen Ave., P.O.Box 120, New Smyrna Beach, 32069,
904-427-4138 Yards: 3991, Par: 62, Holes: 18, Pro: Keith Parker
Fairways CC, 14205 E. Colonial Drive, Orlando, 32817, 305-273-9815
Yards: 5414, Par: 70, Holes: 18, Pro: Craig Craver
Falling Waters CC, Hwy 277 So,Falling Waters, POB, Chipley, 32428,
904-638-7398 Yards: 3200, Par: 36, Holes: 9, Pro: Buddy Hartzog
Fernandina Beach GC—North Course, 2800 Bill Melton Rd., Fernandina
Beach, 32034, 904-261-7804 Yards: 3037, Par: 35, Holes: 9, Pro: Mike Phelan
Forest Hills GC, 3332 Forest Hill Blvd., West Palm Beach, 33463, 305-965-2332
Yards: 2569, Par: 57, Holes: 18, Pro: Jean Noah
Forest Hills GC PC, 1518 US 19, Holiday, 33590, 813-934-7317
Yards: 2856, Par: 35, Holes: 9, Pro: Randall Dreher
Forest Lakes GC, 2401 Beneva Rd., Sarasota, 33580, 813-922-1312
Yards: 6050, Par: 71, USGA: 69.5, Holes: 18, Pro: Carl Lundquist
Fort George Island GC, SR A1A, P.O. Box 197, Jacksonville, 32226,
904-251-3132 Yards: 6298, Par: 72, Holes: 18, Pro: Jim Kuhn
Fort Myers CC, 1445 Hill Ave., Fort Myers, 33901, 813-936-2457
Yards: 5950, Par: 71, USGA: 68.0, Holes: 18, Pro: Rich Lamb
Fountainbleau CC—East Course, 9603 Fountainbleau Blvd., Miami, 33172,
305-221-5181 Yards: 6107, Par: 72, Holes: 18, Pro: Sal Monte
Foxwood of Crestview GC, Rt. 2 Box 317, Crestview, 32536, 904-682-2012
Par: 72, Holes: 18, Pro: Buddy Hartzog
Gadsden CC, US 252, P.O. Box 1078, Quincy, 32351, 904-627-9631
Yards: 6289, Par: 72, Holes: 18, Pro: Ben Franklin
Gasparilla Inn Gc, 5th and Palm, Fort Myers, 33921
George Snyder (Champion), Mintz Rd., P.O. Box 87, Cantonment, 32533,
904-968-9325 Yards: 5997, Par: 70, Holes: 18, Pro: Ed Norton
Glades CC—#1, 210 Teryl Rd., Naples, 33962, 813-774-1443
Yards: 5074, Par: 70, Holes: 18, Pro: Bob Lutz
Glen Abbey GC, 391 North Pine Meadow Dr., DeBary, 32713, 305-668-4209
Yards: 6034, Par: 72, USGA: 69.7, Holes: 18, Pro: Lee Sayre
Glen Oaks CC PC, 1345 Court St., Clearwater, 33516, 813-446-5821
Yards: 2014, Par: 54, Holes: 18, Pro: Peter Konefal
Golden Gate GC, 4100 Golden Gate Pkwy., Naples, 33999, 813-455-1010
Yards: 6181, Par: 72, USGA: 69.3, Holes: 18, Pro: Michael Wortis
High Point CC, 1100 High Point Dr., Naples, 33940, 813-261-4442
Yards: 1185, Par: 27, Holes: 9, Pro: Don Jorgenson
Golf & Sea Club, 801 Golf and Sea Blvd., Apollo Beach, 33570, 813-645-6212
Yards: 6435, Par: 72, USGA: 71.0, Holes: 18, Pro: Tom Doozan
Golf Club of Delray, 14800 Cumberland Dr., Delray Beach, 33446,
305-499-2424 Yards: 3700, Par: 62, USGA: 56.4, Holes: 18, Pro: Bob Frier
Golf Club of Jacksonville, 10440 Tournament Lane, Jacksonville, 32222
Holes: 18

Golf Hammock CC, 2222 Golf Hammock Dr., Sebring, 33870, 813-382-2151
Yards: 6226, Par: 72, USGA: 70.0, Holes: 18, Pro: Jimmy Wohl
Grand Palms G&CC, Pembroke Pines, 33024, 305-431-8800
Par: 72, Holes: 36
Great Oaks GC, Rt 7 Box 158 US Hwy 90, Marianna, 32446
Holes: 9
Green Meadows Par Three, 2500 W. Michigan, Pensacola, 32506,
904-453-9325 Par: 27, Holes: 9, Pro: Randy Crooks
Green Valley GC, 14414 Alternate US 98, Panama City Beach, 32407,
904-234-9289 Par: 27, Holes: 9
Green Valley CC PC, Between Clermont & Groveland-H, Clermont, 32711,
904-394-2133 Yards: 6391, Par: 72, Holes: 9
Greynolds Park GC, 17530 West Dixie Highway, North Miami Beach, 33162,
305-949-1741 Yards: 3133, Par: 36, Holes: 9, Pro: Joe Pantaleo
Gulf Gate GC—Blue Course, 2550 Bispham Rd., Sarasota, 33581, 813-921-5515
Yards: 1300, Par: 29, Holes: 9, Pro: Pat Wright
Hammock Dunes Links GC, One Corporate Drive, Palm Coast, 32051,
800-633-3095 Yards: 6820, Par: 72, Holes: 18
Hamptons GC, 13146 Lyons Road, Boca Raton, 33434, 305-483-1305
Yards: 5950, Par: 71, Holes: 18, Pro: Jim Custer
Harbor City GC, 2750 Lake W. Washington, Melbourne, 32936, 407-254-5484
Yards: 6405, Par: 72, USGA: 69.1, Holes: 18, Pro: Adolph Popp
Harbor Palms GC PC, 701 Oak Leaf Blvd., Oldsmar, 33557, 813-855-1720
Yards: 1749, Par: 31, Holes: 9
Haulover Beach GCD, 10800 Collins Ave., Miami Beach, 33154, 305-940-6719
Yards: 810, Par: 27, Holes: 9
Heather GC, 7394 St. Andrews Blvd., Brooksville, 33512, 904-596-2019
Yards: 2427, Par: 33, Holes: 9, Pro: James Neeley
Heather Hills GC, 101 Cortez Rd. West, Bradenton, 33507, 813-755-8888
Yards: 3521, Par: 61, Holes: 18, Pro: Al Kosilla
Hendry Isles GC, Moore Haven, 33471, 813-983-8070
Par: 36, Holes: 9
Heritage Ridge GC, 6510 SE Heritage Blvd., Hobe Sound, 33455, 305-546-2800
Yards: 5700, Par: 68, USGA: 67.2, Holes: 18, Pro: Tom Cioffi
Hidden Valley at Boca Raton CC, 7601 Country Club Blvd., Boca Raton,
33431, 305-997-9410 Yards: 3198, Par: 62, Holes: 18, Pro: Jim Werre
Hillsboro CC, 23211 SR 7, Boca Raton, 33433, 305-482-3060
Yards: 4812, Par: 60, Holes: 18, Pro: N. Nicolayson
Holiday CC, 1827 NW Pine Lake Dr., Stuart, 33494, 305-692-0346
Yards: 4300, Par: 63, Holes: 18, Pro. Art Young
Holiday CC, 7367 N Military Trail, Lake Park, 33404, 305-842-5927
Yards: 4812, Par 60, Holes: 18, Pro: Linda Bernstrom
Holiday GC, Panama City, 33401, 904-234-1800
Par: 72, Holes: 18
Holiday Springs GC, 3300 Holiday Springs Blvd., Margate, 33063,
305-753-4000 Yards: 6324, Par: 72, USGA: 69.9, Holes: 18, Pro: Steve Mullen
Hollywood Beach Golf & CC, 1650 Johnson Street, Hollywood, 33020,
305-927-1751 Yards: 6506, Par: 70, Holes: 18, Pro: Joe Gerlak
Hollywood Lakes CC—West Lake, 14800 Hollywood Blvd, Hollywood, 33026,
305-431-8800 Yards: 6160, Par: 72, Holes: 18, Pro: Mary Dagraedt
Hombre GC, PO Box 9820, Panama City Beach, 32407
Holes: 18
Hyde Park G & CC, 6439 Hyde Grove Ave., Jacksonville, 32210, 904-786-5410
Yards. 6357, Par: 72, Holes. 18, Pro: Billy Maxwell
Indian Bayou G & CC, Country Club Road, P.O. Box 30, Destin, 32541,
904-837-6191 Yards 6186, Par 72, USGA: 69.7, Holes: 18, Pro: Jim Ryan

Island Golf center, P.O. Box 72, Destin, 32541,   904-244-1612
Holes: 9, Pro: Bob Bonezzi
Indian Creek GC, 1800 Central Blvd., Jupiter, 33458,   305-747-6962
Yards: 5505, Par: 70, Holes: 18, Pro: Bobby Dobson
Indian Hills G&CC, 1600 S 3rd St., P.O. Box 546, Fort Pierce, 33450,
305-461-9620   Yards: 5900, Par: 72, USGA: 68.7, Holes: 18, Pro: Al Griffith
Indian Lake Estate G&CC—18 Hole, DeSoto Avenue, P.O. Box 381, Indian
Lakes Estates, 33855,   813-692-1514
Yards: 6228, Par: 72, USGA: 68.9, Holes: 18, Pro: Chris Campbell
Indian Pines GC, 5700 Indian Pines Blvd., Fort Pierce, 33450,   305-464-7018
Yards: 6030, Par: 70, USGA: 70.2, Holes: 18, Pro: Jeff Hower
Indian Rocks GC PC, 12500 131st St. North, Largo, 33540,   813-595-3133
Yards: 3570, Par: 62, Holes: 18, Pro: Tom Hay
Indian Trail GC CC, 122 Country Club Rd., Royal Palm Beach, 33411,
305-793-1400   Yards: 6303, Par: 72, Holes: 18, Pro: Richard Rizzo
Indianwood G & CC, Golf Club Drive, P.O. Box 396, Indiantown, 33456,
305-597-3794   Yards: 3900, Par: 34, Holes: 9, Pro: S. Sirbaugh
Indigo Lakes GC, 312 Indigo Dr., Jacksonville, 32020
Inverness G & CC, Floral City Rd., P.O. Box 547, Inverness, 32651,
904-637-2526   Yards: 6098, Par: 72, Holes: 18, Pro: P.H. Buckley
Ironwood GC, 2100 NE 39th Ave., Gainesville, 32601,   904-378-5240
Yards: 6204, Par: 72, USGA: 69.4, Holes: 18, Pro: Jeff Evans
Isla Del Sol GC, 6000 Sun Blvd., St. Petersburg, 33715,   813-864-2417
Yards: 6127, Par: 72, Holes: 18, Pro: Patrick Walsh
Jacaranda West CC, 601 Jararanda Blvd.], Venice, 33595,   813-493-2664
Yards: 6193, Par: 72, Holes: 18, Pro: G. Witchousky
Jacksonville Beach GC, 605 S. Penman Rd., Jacksonville Beach, 32250,
904-249-8600   Yards: 6278, Par: 70, USGA: 71.6, Holes: 18, Pro: Boots Farley
Jacksonville Par 3 GC, 10700 Beach Blvd., Jacksonville, 33216,   904-641-2686
Yards: 2400, Par: 54, Holes: 18, Pro: Floyd Smith
Jake Gaither GC, 912 Myers Park, Tallahassee, 32304, 904-576-1418
Yards: 2876, Par: 35, Holes: 9
Jefferson CC PC, SR 149 (P.O. Box 487), Monticello, 32344,   904-997-5484
Yards: 3124, Par: 36, USGA: 68.1, Holes: 9, Pro: Scooter Walker
Jendale Lakes West, 15101 N. Kendall Dr., Miami, 33196,   305-361-9129
Yards: 3700, Par: 60, Holes: 18, Pro: Whitey Eastham
Jupiter Dunes GC, 411 N A1A, Jupiter, 33458,   305-746-6654
Yards: 1853, Par: 54, Holes: 18, Pro: Bob Erickson
Jupiter West CC, Mack Dairy & Colony, P.O. Box, Tequesta, 33458,
305-747-4211   Yards: 6254, Par: 72, USGA: 68.8, Holes: 18, Pro: Randy Feather
Kendale Lakes G & CC—Emerald, 6401 Kendale Lakes Dr., Miami, 33183,
305-382-3935   Yards: 3190, Par: 36, Holes: 9, Pro: Tom Gibson
Key West Resort GC (The), 5600 W. Junior College Rd., Key West, 33040,
305-294-5232   Yards: 6046, Par: 70, USGA: 68.7, Holes: 18, Pro: James Penzell
Key West GC, 6450 Jr. College Rd., Miami, 33040
Keystone Heights G & CC, Highway 21 S, P.O. Box 245, Keystone Heights,
32656, 904-473-4540   Yards: 3001, Par: 35, Holes: 9, Pro: Terry Catlett
King's Point Par 3 GC, 7000 Atlantic Ave., Delray Beach, 33445,   305-499-0140
Yards: 2723, Par: 54, Holes: 18, Pro: Norm Bennett
Kings Point Executive GC, 6561 Flanders Waye, Delray Beach, 33445,
305-499-7840   Yards: 3241, Par: 60, Holes: 18, Pro: Norm Bennett
Kissimmee GC, Kissimmee, 32741,   407-847-2816
Par: 72, Holes: 18
Lagoon Legend GC, 100 Delwood Beach Rd., Panama City, 32407,
904-234-3307   Yards: 6079, Par: 72, USGA: 70.7, Holes: 18, Pro: Randy Cahall

Lake Buena Vista Club, 7500 Exchange Drive, Orlando, 32809, 305-828-3741
Yards: 6354, Par: 72, USGA: 71.5, Holes: 18, Pro: Rina Ritson
Lake City CC, Rt. 13, Box 436, Lake City, 32055, 904-752-2266
Yards: 6411, Par: 72, USGA: 70.2, Holes: 18, Pro: Chris Pottle
Lake Fairways CC, US 41 N, P.O. Box 3494, N. Fort Myers, 33903, 813-997-7781
Yards: 3005, Par: 60, USGA: 53.5, Holes: 18, Pro: Frank D. Wright
Lake Okeechobee GC, Lake Okeechobee, 33803, 813-763-0231
Par: 33, Holes: 9
Lake Worth Municipal GC, 1 Seventh Ave. N, Lake Worth, 33460,
305-582-9713   Yards: 5700, Par: 70, USGA: 66.2, Holes: 18, Pro: Merrill Hubbard
Lakeland Par 3 GC, 1740 George Jenkins Blvd., Lakeland, 33801, 813-686-0613
Yards: 1835, Par: 54, Holes: 18, Pro: Jeff Schmucker
Lakeview GC, 2000 Dover Rd., Delray Beach, 33445, 305-498-5486
Yards: 3700, Par: 60, Holes: 18, Pro: Jimmy Ferrell
Largo Muni GC, Largo, 33542, 813-595-3133 Par: 62, Holes: 18
Lauderhill GC, 4141 NW 16th St., Lauderhill, 33313, 305-735-2256
Yards: 1201, Par: 30, Holes: 9
Leisure Lakes G & RC, Rt. 1, Box 199, Lake June Rd., Lake Placid, 33852,
813-465-2888   Yards: 1384, Par: 27, Holes: 9, Pro: Pat Cotroneo
Lely G & CC, 400 Forest Hills Blvd., Naples, 33962, 813-774-3559
Yards: 5080, Par: 72, Holes: 18, Pro: R.J.Fitzek, Jr.
Lely Resort - Flamingo Is. Club, 12665 Tamiami Trail East, Naples, 33962,
813-774-5333 Holes: 18
Lemon Bay Beach & CC, 5800 Placida Rd., Englewood, 33533, 813-697-4190
Yards: 6020, Par: 72, Holes: 18, Pro: Ted Neff
Lexington GC, The, 3515 S. Ocean Dr., Miami, 33022
Lily Lake G&RV Resort, Frostproof, 33843, 813-635-2676
Par: 32, Holes: 9
Links of Beacon Woods East, 8700 Pavillion Drive, Hudson, 34667
Holes: 18
Links of Lake Bernadette, 111 Links Lane, Zephyrhills, 34248, 813-788-GOLF
Yards: 6007, Par: 71, USGA: 70.0, Holes: 18, Pro: Dean Refram
Little Cypress G & CC, Route 3 Hwy 64 West, Wauchula, 33873, 813-735-1333
Yards: 3292, Par: 36, Holes: 9, Pro: Bruce Thompson
Lone Pine GC, 6251 N Military Trail, W Palm Beach, 33407, 305-842-0965
Yards: 4500, Par: 62, Holes: 18, Pro: Bob Fronio
Lucerne Lakes GC, 144 Lucerne Lakes Blvd, Lake Worth, 33463, 305-967-6810
Yards: 5812, Par: 72, Holes: 18, Pro: Karl Schmidt
Lucerne Park Par 3 GC, SR544, Winter Haven, 33881, 813-294-5573
Yards: 1663, Par: 54, Holes: 18, Pro: Pat Perry
Magnolia Valley G&CC—18 Hole, 2102 Moon Lake Rd., New Port Richey,
33552, 813-842-7602   Yards: 6011, Par: 70, Holes: 18, Pro: D. McAllister
Mainlands GC, 4500 Monterey Dr., Tamarac Lakes, 33319, 305-731-6710
Yards: 4000, Par: 62, Holes: 18, Pro: Tony Esposito
Mainlands GC, 9445 Mainlands Blvd. West, Pinellas Park, 33565, 813-577-4847
Yards: 4065, Par: 63, Holes: 18, Pro: Alice Bauer
Majette Dunes G&CC, 1229 Capri Drive, Panama City, 32405
Holes: 18
Manatee County GC, 5290 66th St. W., Bradenton, 33507, 813-792-6773
Yards: 6219, Par: 72, USGA: 69.0, Holes: 18, Pro: Carl Hunter
Maple Leaf Estates GC, 2001 Kings Highway, Box 111,Pa, Port Charlotte,
33952, 813-629-1666   Yds: 3810, Par: 62, USGA: 58.8, Holes: 18, Pro: G. Johnides
Marco Shores GC, 1450 Mainsail Blvd., Fort Myers, 33937
Marion Oaks CC, 4260 SW 162nd St., Ocala, 32673, 904-245-5626
Yards: 6469, Par: 72, USGA: 70.6, Holes: 18, Pro: Dudley Dunn

Martin County G & CC, 2000 SE St Luci Blvd, Stuart, 33494, 305-287-3747
Yards: 6164, Par: 72, Holes: 18, Pro: J. Williams
Matanzas GC, 398 Lakeview Blvd., Palm Coast, 32051, 904-445-1903
Yards: 6278, Par: 72, Holes: 18, Pro: Bob Kendra
Mayfair CC, Rt 46A & Country Club, P.O.Box, Lake Mary, 32746, 305-322-2531
Yards: 6400, Par: 72, USGA: 68.7, Holes: 18, Pro: Red Addison
Meadow Oaks GC, 327½ Jasmine Blvd West, Port Richey, 33568, 813-856-2878
Par: 63, Holes: 18, Pro: Ron Burnham
Meadow Woods GC, Orlando, 32862, 407-859-9778
Par: 36, Holes: 18
Meadowbrook GC, Gainesville, 32602, 904-332-0577
Par: 70, Holes: 18
Meadows CC PC, The, 3101 Longmeadow, Sarasota, 34235, 813-378-6650
Yards: 6150, Par: 72, USGA: 69.7, Holes: 18, Pro: Mike Clayton
Melbourne GC, 475 W New Haven Ave., Melbourne, 32901, 305-723-3565
Yards: 5587, Par: 71, Holes: 18, Pro: Steve Opperman
Melreese CC, 1802 NW 37th Ave., Miami, 33125, 305-635-6770
Yards: 6374, Par: 72, Holes: 18, Pro: Charles DeLucca
Miami Springs GC, 650 Curtiss Parkway, Miami Springs, 33166, 305-888-2377
Yards: 6655, Par: 70, Holes: 18, Pro: Tommy Parks
Miramar CC, 3700 Douglas Rd., Miramar, 33025, 305-431-3800
Yards: 6032, Par: 72, USGA: 68.4, Holes: 18, Pro: Frank Clark
Mirror Lakes CC, Milwaukee Ave., Lehigh, 33936, 813-995-0501
Yards: 6722, Par: 72, Holes: 18, Pro: Tom O'Brien
Mt. Dora GC, 1100 S. Highland, Mount Dora, 32757, 904-383-3954
Yards: 5854, Par: 70, USGA: 67.0, Holes: 18, Pro: Ernie Tardiff
Mt. Plymouth GC, 249 Pine Valley Dr., sorrento, 32776, 904-383-4821
Yards: 6003, Par: 70, USGA: 68.2, Holes: 18, Pro: Tom Hampton
Muirfield Village GC, 14525 SW 67th Avenue, Ocala, 32673
Holes: 18
Myakka Pines GC—Blue Course, South River Road, P. O. Box 12, Englewood,
33533, 813-474-1745   Yards: 3076, Par: 36, Holes: 9, Pro: B. Cioffoletti
New Smyrna Beach GC, PO Box 123, New Smyrna Beach, 32068,
904-427-3437 Yards: 6345, Par: 72, Holes: 18, Pro: Marvin Harvey
Normandy Shores GC, 2401 Biarritz Dr. Miami Beach, Miami Springs, 33141,
305-868-6502   Yards: 6055, Par: 71, Holes: 18, Pro: Jim Longo
North Palm Beach CC, 901 US 1, North Palm Beach, 33408, 305-626-4344
Yards: 5341, Par: 72, Holes: 18, Pro: Pete Finlayson
Northdale GC, 4417 Northdale Blvd., Tampa, 33624, 813-962-0428
Yards: 6274, Par: 72, USGA: 70.1, Holes: 18, Pro: Chuck Winship
Northport CC, US 41, 701 Greenwood Ave, North Port, 33596, 813-426-2804
Yards: 6250, Par: 72, USGA: 68.8, Holes: 18, Pro: Bubba Clark
Oak Ford GC, 1552 Palm View Road, Sarasota, 34240, 813-371-3680
Holes: 18
Oak Hills GC, 2811 Northcliff Blvd., Spring Hill, 33526, 904-683-2261
Yards: 6331, Par: 72, Holes: 18, Pro: Chuck Almony
Oak Ridge GC PC, 120 Palm Blvd. (620 Palm Blvd), Dunedin, 33528,
813-733-5061 Yards: 2129, Par: 54, Holes: 18, Pro: Bill Hook
Oak Ridge GC, 3490 Griffin Rd., Fort Lauderdale, 33312, 305-987-5552
Yards: 6517, Par: 72, USGA: 70.0, Holes: 18, Pro: G.Vanlandingham
Oakland Hills CC, 100 Rotunda Circle, Rotunda West, 33947, 813-697-2414
Yards: 6381, Par: 72, Holes: 18, Pro: Ray LaGoy, Jr.
Oaks—Blue Heron Course, 748 N. Tamiami Trail, Osprey, 33559, 813-966-2191
Par: 72, USGA: 70.0, Holes: 18, Pro: Mark McLain
Oaks—Eagle Course, 748 N. Tamiami Trail, Osprey, 33559, 813-966-2191
Par: 72, Holes: 18, Pro: Mark McLain

Ocala Municipal GC, 3130 E Silver Springs Blvd. , Ocala, 32670, 904-622-8681
Yards: 6340, Par: 72, Holes: 18, Pro: Jim Yancey
Ocean Palm GC, 3600 Central Ave. , South, Flagler Beach, 32036, 904-439-2477
Yards: 2760, Par: 33, Holes: 9, Pro: Craig Shankland
Okeechobee GC, 405 N.E. 131st Ln. , Okeechobee, 33472, 813-763-6228
Yards: 3295, Par: 36, USGA: 71.6, Holes: 9, Pro: Ken Burnette
Orange Brook GC—East, 400 Entrada Dr. , Hollywood, 33021, 305-921-3415
Yards: 6200, Par: 72, Holes: 18, Pro: Bill Entwhistle
Orange Lake GC, 8505 W. Irio Bronson Memorial, Kissimmee, 32741,
305-239-1050   Yards: 6176, Par: 72, USGA: 70.4, Holes: 27, Pro: Dick Farley
Oriole G & TC of Margate—Executive Course, 8000 W. Margate Blvd. ,
Margate, 33063, 305-972-8140   Par: 30, Holes: 9, Pro: Skip Guss
Oriole GC of Delray, Delray Beach, 33444, 407-395-5969
Par: 62, Holes: 18
Osceola Municipal GC, 300 Tonawanda Trail, Pensacola, 32506, 904-456-2761
Yards: 6043, Par: 72, USGA: 69.0, Holes: 18, Pro: Jack Montgomery
Osteen GC, PO Drawer 100, Osteen, 32764, 305-322-9627
Yards: 2000, Par: 33, Holes: 9, Pro: Walter Johnson
Overoaks GC, Kissimmee, 32741, 407-847-3773
Par: 72, Holes: 18
Oxbow GC, 1 Oxbow Dr. , Port LaBelle, 33935, 813-675-4411
Yards: 6688, Par: 72, USGA: 73.2, Holes: 18, Pro: Bob Shields
Palatka Municipal GC, 1715 Moseley Ave. , Palatka, 32077, 904-329-0141
Yards: 5957, Par: 70, USGA: 68.5, Holes: 18, Pro: John Baas
Palm-Aire GC—Pine Course, 2501 Palm-Aire Dr. North, Pompano, 33069,
305-973-8463   Yards: 6610, Par: 72, USGA: 69.7, Holes: 18, Pro: Tom Malone
Palm Beach Par 3 GC, South A1A, Palm Beach, 33480, 305-582-4462
Yards: 2640, Par: 54, Holes: 18, Pro: Rick Dytrych
Palm Beach National GC, 7500 St. Andrews Road, Lake Worth, 33463,
305-965-3381   Yards: 6332, Par: 72, Holes: 18, Pro: Pat Heslin
Palm Beach GC, 11830 Pablo Club Rd. , W. Palm Beach, 33414
Palm Beach Lakes GC, 1100 N. Congress Ave. , W. Palm Beach, 33409,
305-683-2700   Yards: 5421, Par: 68, USGA: 62.9, Holes: 18, Pro: Tony Bryant, Jr
Palm Beach Polo & CC—Dunes, 13198 Forest Hill Blvd. , W. Palm Beach,
33414, 407-798-7000   Yards: 5516, USGA: 73.4, Holes: 45
Palm Breeze GC PC, SR 19 N (P.O. Box 699), Eustis, 32726, 904-357-9449
Yards: 1061, Par: 27, Holes: 9, Pro: Donald Carlson
Palm Harbor GC, Ext. Casper Drivve, Palm Coast, 32037, 904-445-3431
Yards: 6013, Par: 72, USGA: 68.1, Holes: 18, Pro: Bud Burkley
Palm Hill CC, 401 8th Ave. SW, P. O. Box 44, Largo, 33540, 813-581-1710
Yards: 1332, Par: 30, Holes: 9, Pro: Johnny Roberts
Palm Lake Executive GC, 7590 W. Atlantic Blvd. , Margate, 33063,
305-973-7674   Yards: 1059, Par: 28, Holes: 9, Pro: Brad Sage
Palm View Hills GC, 5712 18th Ave. E, Palmetto, 33561, 813-722-2392
Yards: 3869, Par: 63, Holes: 18, Pro: Gary Hamilton
Palma Sola GC, 3807 75th St. W, Bradenton, 33529, 813-792-7476
Yards: 6241, Par: 72, Holes: 18, Pro: Bob Skelton
Palmetto GC, 9300 SW 152nd St. , Perrine, 33157, 305-238-2922
Yards: 6552, Par: 71, USGA: 69.3, Holes: 18, Pro: Ronald Frazier
Palmetto Pines GC—East Course, Rt. 1, Parrish, 33564, 813-776-1375
Yards: 6435, Par: 73, Holes: 18, Pro: Dave Bates
Par 3 GC, 2500 Volusia Ave. , Daytona Beach, 32014, 904-252-3983
Yards: 2129, Par: 54, Holes: 18, Pro: Cliff Seaver
Paradise Island G&TC PC, 10315 Paradise Blvd. , Treasure Island, 33706,
000-360-6062   Yards: 935, Par: 27, Holes: 9

Pasadena GC, 1600 Royal Palm Drive South, St. Petersburg, 33707,
813-345-9329 Yards: 6208, Par: 72, Holes: 18, Pro: Bucky Thornbury
Pat Schwab's Pine Lakes GC, 153 Northside Dr. S, Jacksonville, 32218,
904-757-0318 Yards: 6508, Par: 72, USGA: 70.0, Holes: 18, Pro: Pat Schwab
Pebble Creek GC, 19001 SR 581, Lutz, 33549, 813-973-3870
Yards: 6716, Par: 72, USGA: 70.3, Holes: 18, Pro: Chris Kelley
Pelican Bay South G&CC, 350 Pelican Bay Drive, Daytona Beach, 32014,
904-788-6496 Yards: 6496, Par: 72, Holes: 18, Pro: Keith Hardeman
Pelican CC, 1501 Indian Rock Road, Clearwater, 33516, 813-581-5498
Yards: 6131, Par: 72, USGA: 70.5, Holes: 18, Pro: Ralph Hood
Pembroke Lakes GC, 10500 Taft St., Pembroke Pines, 33026, 305-431-4144
Yards: 6307, Par: 72, Holes: 18, Pro: Jeff Nelson
Perdido Bay GC, 1 Doug Ford Dr., Pensacola, 32507, 904-492-1223
Yards: 7154, Par: 72, Holes: 18, Pro: Bud Cooper
Perry CC, P.O.Box 809, Perry, 32347, 904-584-3590
Yards: 2935, Par: 35, Holes: 9, Pro: Fred Carlton
PGA National GC, 1000 Ave of Champions, W. Palm Beach, 33480
Pine Lakes GC, 400 Pine Lakes Pkwy., Palm Coast, 32037, 904-445-0852
Yards: 6200, Par: 72, USGA: 69.7, Holes: 18, Pro: Ken Van Leuven
Pine Ridge GC, 1005 Elkcam Blvd., Beverly Hills, 32665, 904-746-6177
Yards: 3015, Par: 36, Holes: 9
Pinecrest GC, 1200 8th Ave., SW, Largo, 33540, 813-584-6497
Yards: 2666, Par: 58, Holes: 18, Pro: Hal Shaw
Pinecrest on Lotela GC, 2250 South Little Lake Bonnett, Avon Park, 33825,
813-453-7555 Yards: 6404, Par: 72, USGA: 70.4, Holes: 18, Pro: E.B. Smith
Pines Par 3 GC, 315 SW 62nd Ave., Hollywood, 33023, 305-989-9288
Yards: 800, Par: 27, Holes: 9
Pineview G & CC, Hwy 23A North, P.O. Box 617, Macclenny, 32063,
904-259-3447 Yards: 5738, Par: 72, USGA: 70.8, Holes: 18, Pro: Ray Odom
Placid Lakes Inn GC, 111 Club Rd. Circle NW, Lake Placid, 33852,
813-465-4333 Yards: 6332, Par: 72, USGA: 71.5, Holes: 18
Plant City G & CC, 3102 Coronet Rd., Plant City, 33566, 813-752-1524
Yards: 6288, Par: 72, Holes: 18, Pro: Clyde Huether
Plantation PC, The, 500 Rockley Blvd., Venice, 33595
Plantation at Leesburg, 252 US Highway 27, Leesburg, 34748
Holes: 9
Plantation GC, 7050 W. Broward Blvd., Plantation, 33317, 305-583-5341
Yards: 6424, Par: 72, USGA: 70.4, Holes: 18, Pro: Betty Lumsden
Plantation Inn GC, West Fort Island Trail, Crystal River, 32629, 904-795-4211
Yards: 5711, Par: 72, USGA: 66.9, Holes: 27, Pro: Jim Brennan
Pompano Beach CC—Palms Course, 1101 N. Federal Hwy., Pompano Beach,
33062, 305-781-0426 Yds: 6348, Par: 71, USGA: 68.4, Holes: 18, Pro: R. Kennedy
Ponte Vedra Inn & GC—Lagoon, Ponte Vedra Beach, 32082, 904-285-1111
Yards: 5261, Par: 70, USGA: 64.9, Holes: 18
Ponte Vedra Inn & CC-Ocean Sou, Ponte Vedra Beach, 32082, 904-285-1111
Yards: 6069, Par: 72, USGA: 68.8, Holes: 18
Port Charlotte CC, 22400 Gleneagles Terrace, Port Charlotte, 33952,
813-625-4109 Yards: 6354, Par: 72, USGA: 70.0, Holes: 18, Pro: Jeff Russell
Prairie Oaks CC, P.O. Box 3354, Sebring, 33870, 813-382-3500
Yards: 3272, Par: 36, Holes: 9, Pro: Cliff Lawson
Punta Gorda CC, 3701 Duncan Rd., P.O. Box 1716, Punta Gorda, 33951,
813-639-1494 Yards: 5613, Par: 72, Holes: 18, Pro: Don Williams
Quail Heights CC, Rt.5 Box 1073, Lake City, 32055, 904-752-3339
Yards: 6120, Par: 72, USGA: 68.8, Holes: 18, Pro: C. Ste Marie
Quail Hollow G&CC, 100 Pasco Road, Zephyrhills, 34249, 813-973-0097
Yards: 6161, Par: 72, USGA: 68.0, Holes: 18, Pro: Bob Cleaves

Rainbow Springs CC, US 41 North, P.O. Box 99, Dunnellon, 32630,
904-489-3566   Yards: 6428, Par: 72, Holes: 18, Pro: John Dyal
Raintree GC, 1600 S. Hiatus Rd., Pembroke Pines, 33024,   305-432-1500
Yards: 6201, Par: 72, Holes: 18, Pro: John LaPonzina
Red Reef Municipal GC, 1111 N Ocean Drive, Boca Raton, 33432,
305-391-5014   Yards: 1628, Par: 30, Holes: 9, Pro: Dan Fabian
Redlands G & CC, 24451 SW 177th Ave, P.O. Box 1, Homestead, 33090,
305-247-8503   Yards: 6696, Par: 72, Holes: 18, Pro: Charlie Griggs
Reservation (The), 4000 SR 37 North, Mulberry, 33860,   813-425-3818
Yards: 4565, Par: 35, Holes: 9, Pro: Randy Cayson
Reynolds Park GC, US 16, Green Cove Springs, Keystone Heights, 32043,
904-284-3502   Yards: 3310, Par: 36, Holes: 9, Pro: Dave Kennett
River Greens South GC, 47 Lake Damon Dr., Avon Park, 33825,   813-453-5210
Yards: 5825, Par: 72, USGA: 67.1, Holes: 18, Pro: Wallace Lowery
Riverbend GC, 6270 Walter Hagen Ct., N. Fort Myers, 33903,   813-656-1922
Yards: 3150, Par: 60, Holes: 18, Pro: Mike Hays
Riviera CC, 500 Calle Grande Ave., Ormond Beach, 32074,   904-677-2464
Yards: 6302, Par: 71, USGA: 69.5, Holes: 18, Pro: Mike Boss
Riviera GC of Naples PC, 48 Marseille Dr., Naples, 33962,   813-774-1081
Yards: 4100, Par: 62, Holes: 18
Rocky Bayou CC, Country Club Dr., P.O. Box 577, Niceville, 32578,
904-678-3271   Yards: 6238, Par: 72, USGA: 68.5, Holes: 18, Pro: Al Fulle
Rocky Point GC, 4151 Dana Shores Dr., Tampa, 33614,   813-884-5141
Yards: 6116, Par: 71, Holes: 18, Pro: Bob Arnot
Rogers Park GC, 7910 N 30th St., Tampa, 33610,   813-234-1911
Yards: 6855, Par: 72, Holes: 18, Pro: Mike Cooper
Rolling Green GC PC, 4501 Tuttle Ave., Sarasota, 33580,   813-355-7621
Yards: 6061, Par: 72, Holes: 18, Pro: Joe Mann
Rolling Greens Exec CC, 1815 Gleneagles Rd., Ocala, 32672,   904-694-4688
Yards: 2271, Par: 58, Holes: 18, Pro: Thelma King
Rolling Hills Golf Resort, 3501 W. Rolling Hills Circle, Fort Lauderdale, 33328,
305-475-0400   Yards: 6306, Par: 72, USGA: 69.8, Holes: 27, Pro: Jerry Sehlke
Rolling Hills G&CC, Rt. 2 Box 180, Wildwood, 32785,   904-748-4200
Yards: 6143, Par: 72, Holes: 18, Pro: Chas.Bisignano
Rosemont GC, 4224 Clubhouse Rd., Orlando, 32804,   305-298-1230
Yards: 6190, Par: 72, USGA: 69.5, Holes: 18, Pro: Jeb Boyle
Sabal Palms GC, 5101 W. Commercial Blvd., Tamarac, 33319,   305-731-2600
Yards: 6469, Par: 72, Holes: 18, Pro: Peter Dennis
Sabal Point CC, 2662 Sabal Point, P. O. Box 30, Longwood, 32779,
305-869-1692   Yards: 6400, Par: 72, Holes: 18, Pro: Alan Howell
Sam Snead Executive GC, US 1, Box 147, Sharpes, 32959,   305-632-2890
Yards: 2889, Par: 56, Holes: 18, Pro: P.J. Wilson
San Carlos G & CC, 7420 Constitution Cir SW, Fort Myers, 33912,   813-481-5121
Yards: 6127, Par: 71, USGA: 68.9, Holes: 18, Pro: Jim Beatty
Sandalfoot Cove G&CC—Executive Course, 1400 Country Club Drive, Boca
Raton, 33432, 305-382-8100   Yards: 1627, Par: 27, Holes: 9, Pro: Bob Crissy
Sandestin GC, Highway 98 E, Destin, 32541
Holes: 9
Sandy Creek CC, Hwy. 2297, P.O. Box 1866, Panama City, 32401,   904-871-2673
Yards: 2632, Par: 34, USGA: 32.3, Holes: 9, Pro: Howell Fraser
Sarasotsa GC, 7280 N. Leewynn Dr., Sarasota, 34240,   813-371-2431
Yards: 6231, Par: 72, Holes: 18, Pro: David Tyree
Savanna Club, 9710 S US 1, Port St. Lucie, 33452,   305-876-2380
Par: 61, Holes: 18, Pro: Harry Otterbein
Seascape Resort & Conference C, 100 Seascape Dr., Destin, 32541,
904-837-9181   Yards: 6077, Par: 72, USGA: 69.2, Holes: 18, Pro: Norm Tums

Sebastian Municipal GC, 101 E. Airport Rd., P.O. Box 1, Sebastian, 32958, 305-589-6800   Par: 72, Holes: 18, Pro: Zeno Rowley
Sebring G & CC, 3129 Golfview Rd., Sebring, 33870,   813-385-0889
Yards: 6246, Par: 72, Holes: 18, Pro: Bob Parker
Sebring Shores CC, 603 Lake Sebring Dr., Sebring, 33870,   813-385-1923
Yards: 2028, Par: 27, Holes: 9
Seminole CC, 1750 E. Williamson Road, Longwood, 32779,   305-862-9267
Yards: 3032, Par: 36, Holes: 9, Pro: Bob Jones
Seminole GC, 2550 Pottsdamer Rd., Tallahassee, 32304,   904-644-2582
Yards: 6475, Par: 72, USGA: 70.4, Holes: 18, Pro: Rance Pearson
Shalimar Pointe GC, 2 Country Club Rd., P.O. Box 5, Shalimar, 32579,
904-651-1416   Yards: 6205, Par: 72, Holes: 18, Pro: Ham Carothers
Sherbrooke G&CC, 6151 Lyons Rd., Lake Worth, 33463,   305-964-6011
Yards: 6307, Par: 72, Holes: 18, Pro: Doug Ford, Jr.
Sherwoos Park GC, 14857 Forest Rd., Delray Beach, 33445,   305-499-3559
Yards: 3860, Par: 62, Holes: 18, Pro: Jim Merman
Signal Hill CC, 9515 Thomas Dr., Panama City, 32407,   904-234-5051
Yards: 5459, Par: 70, Holes: 18
Silver Oaks G&CC, Zephyrhills, 34248,   813-788-1225
Par: 72, Holes: 18
Silver Pines GC, 5701 Golf Club Pkwy., Pine Hills, 32808,   305-298-0480
Yards: 2365, Par: 33, Holes: 9, Pro: Joe Rouse
Skyview G&CC, 1100 Skyview Blvd., Lakeland, 33801,   813-665-4008
Yards: 5250, Par: 71, Holes: 18, Pro: Bud Socia
Sorrento Par 3 GC PC, 1910 Bayshore Rd., Nokomis, 33555,   813-966-4884
Yards: 557, Par: 27, Holes: 9, Pro: Stewart Bennett
Spessard Holland GC, 2374 Oak St., Melbourne Beach, 32951,   305-723-1690
Yards: 4550, Par: 67, USGA: 60.8, Holes: 18, Pro: Mike Skovran
Sportsman's Links, 5850 Belvedere Rd, West Palm Beach, 33406,   305-683-4544
Yards: 2775, Par: 56, Holes: 18, Pro: Marc White
Spring Hill G & CC, 12079 Coronado Drive, Spring Hill, 33526,   904-683-2261
Yards: 6397, Par: 72, USGA: 69.4, Holes: 18, Pro: Glenn Gabriel
Spring Lake G & CC, 10350 Duane Palmer Blvd., Sebring, 33870,   813-655-1276
Yards: 6225, Par: 72, USGA: 69.3, Holes: 18, Pro: Richard Cormier
Springer's Gulf Harbor GC PC, 385 Flormar Terrace, New Port Richey,
33552, 813-849-7675   Yards: 3090, Par: 60, USGA: 57.0, Holes: 18
Springtree CC, 8350 Springtree Dr., Fort Lauderdale, 33321,   305-741-8000
Yards: 6155, Par: 72, Holes: 18, Pro: Stan Mack
Spruce Creek GC, 1900 Country Club Dr., Daytona Beach, 32014,   904-767-2241
Yards: 6354, Par: 72, Holes: 18, Pro: Gary Wintz
St. Augustine Shores CC, 295 Shores Blvd., St. Augustine, 32086,   904-794-0303
Yards: 3387, Par: 60, Holes: 18, Pro: Bill Moore
St. Johns GC, 4900 Cypress Land, Elkton, 32084
Holes: 9
St. Leo Abbey GC PC, Hwy 52 (P.O. Box 2168), St. Leo, 33574,   904-588-2016
Yards: 6050, Par: 70, Holes: 18, Pro: Jim Baker
Starke GC, SR 230 East, Rt. 1, Box 869, Starke, 32091,   904-964-5441
Yards: 3196, Par: 36, Holes: 9, Pro: Bill Adams
Sugar Mill CC—Blue Course, 100 Clubhouse Circle, New Smyrna Beach,
32069, 904-428-9011   Yards: 3223, Par: 36, Holes: 9, Pro: Ted Carlson
Summertime GC, 4249 Paradise Point Way, New Port Richey, 33553,
813-856-3502   Yards: 4818, Par: 34, Holes: 9, Pro: Butch White
Sun 'n Lake G&CC, Lake Placid, 33852,   813-465-5303
Par: 63, Holes: 18
Sun Air CC, Rt. 1, Watkins Road, Haines City, 33844,   813-439-4958
Yards: 6750, Par: 71, USGA: 68.6, Holes: 18, Pro: Chas. Priester

Suncet GC, 2727 Johnson, Hollywood, 33020, 305-923-2008
Yards: 3100, Par: 35, Holes: 9, Pro: Bobby Goodman
Sunnybreeze Palms GC, Rt. 3 Box 573B, Arcadia, 33821, 813-494-2521
Yards: 3200, Par: 71, USGA: 68.0, Holes: 27, Pro: Rick Knox
Sunrise CC, 7400 NW 24th Place, Sunrise, 33313, 305-742-4333
Yards: 6155, Par: 72, Holes: 18, Pro: WPS Smith
Sunrise CC, 5710 Clark Road, Sarasota, 33583, 813-924-1402
Yards: 6098, Par: 72, Holes: 18, Pro: Bill Berg
Sunset GC, 600 Snell Isle Blvd NE, St. Petersburg, 33704, 813-895-8429
Yards: 5443, Par: 70, USGA: 68.8, Holes: 18, Pro: Jack Haley
Suwanee CC, Rt. 3, Box 132, Live Oak, 32060, 904-362-1147
Yards: 3096, Par: 36, USGA: 68.0, Holes: 9, Pro: Walter Smith
Suwanee River Valley CC, Route 2 Box 127, Jasper, 32052, 904-792-1990
Yards: 3084, Par: 35, Holes: 9, Pro: Ken Dewey
Sweetwater Golf & Tennis Club, 364 W. Melbourne Drive, Haines City, 33844
Holes: 9
Tall Pines GC, 7511 Blommingdale Dr., New Port Richey, 33552, 813-847-4762
Yards: 3100, Par: 64, Holes: 18, Pro: Royce Hewitt
Tanglewood G&CC, Hwuy 192, P. O. Box 725, Milton, 32570, 904-623-6176
Yards: 3350, Par: 36, USGA: 34.7, Holes: 9, Pro: Hwy. 192
Tara G&CC, 6602 Drewry's Bluff, Bradenton, 34203
Holes: 18
Tarpon Lakes Village CC, 2500 Village Center Drive, Palm Harbor, 33563,
813-784-7333   Yards: 6120, Par: 72, USGA: 70.0, Holes: 18, Pro: C. Malchaski
Tarpon Springs GC PC, 1310 S. Pinellas Ave.(P.O. Box, Tarpon Springs, 33590,
813-937-6906   Yards: 6211, Par: 72, Holes: 18, Pro: Joe Wilkie
Tarpon Woods G&CC PC, 1100 Tarpon Woods Blvd., Palm Harbor, 33563,
813-784-7606   Yards: 6423, Par: 72, USGA: 68.4, Holes: 18, Pro: Dean Wilson
Tatum Ridge Golf Links, 421 N. Tatum Road, Sarasota, 34240
Holes: 18
Tides CC, 11832 66th Ave North, Seminole, 33542, 813-393-8483
Yards: 6285, Par: 72, USGA: 69.7, Holes: 18, Pro: Sonny Mszanski
Timber Creek CC, 6611 Cortez Rd. W, Bradenton, 33507, 813-792-3498
Yards: 1721, Par: 30, Holes: 9, Pro: John McKinney
Timber Oaks GC, 2213 Ponderosa Dr., Port Richey, 33568, 813-863-1072
Yards: 3558, Par: 60, USGA: 58.1, Holes: 18, Pro: Rick Bell
Timber Pines CC, 6872 Timber Pines Blvd., Spring Hill, 33526, 904-683-8439
Yards: 3282, Par: 60, Holes: 18, Pro: Don Bliss
Tomoka Oaks G&CC, 20 Tomoka Blvd., Ormond Beach, 32074, 904-677-7117
Yards: 6448, Par: 72, USGA: 71.0, Holes: 18, Pro: Barney Thompson
Town & Country RV Resort & GC, Dade City, 34297, 904-567-6622
Par: 72, Holes: 18
TPC at Eagle Trace GC, 1111 Eagle Trace Blvd., Miami, 33071
TPC at Sawgrass GC, 112 TPC Blvd., Jacksonville, 32082
Tuscawilla GC, 1500 Winter Springs Blvd., Winter Springs, 32708,
407-365-3259   Yards: 6220, Par: 72, USGA: 69.5, Holes: 18, Pro: John Donohue
Twin Brooks GC, 3800 22nd Ave., S St. Petersburg, 33711, 813-893-7445
Yards: 2000, Par: 54, Holes: 18, Pro: Jack Haley
Univ. of Florida BC, 2800 SW 2nd Ave., Gainesville, 32607, 904-392-0689
Yards: 6053, Par: 70, USGA: 69.7, Holes: 18, Pro: Jeff O'Malley
University of S. Fla GC, 4202 Fowler Ave., Tampa, 33620, 813-974-2071
Yards: 6243, Par: 72, USGA: 69.8, Holes: 18, Pro: Bob Shiver
Venice East GC PC, 107 Venice East Blvd., Venice, 34293, 813-493-0005
Yards: 2781, Par: 57, Holes: 18
Ventura CC, 3201 Woodgate Blvd., Orlando, 32822, 305-277-2640
Yards: 5423, Par: 70, USGA: 62.4, Holes: 18, Pro: John Snuckel

Villa Del Ray GC, 6200 Villa Del Ray, Delray Beach, 33445,   305-498-1444
Yards: 5840, Par: 71, Holes: 18, Pro: Sherry Zimet
Village Green GC, 3500 Pembrook Dr., Sarasota, 33579,   813-922-9500
Yards: 2809, Par: 58, Holes: 18, Pro: J. Bindwanger
Village Green GC, 1401 Village Green Parkway, Bradenton, 33529,
813-792-7171   Yards: 2900, Par: 58, Holes: 18, Pro: Jack Watson
Vista Plantation GC, 47-206 Plantation Dr., Vero Beach, 32960,   305-569-6946
Par: 62, Holes: 18, Pro: Zeno Rowley
Vizcaya CC, 1200 NW 207th St., Miami, 33169,   305-653-9969
Water Oak GC, 1 Water Oak Drive, Lady Lake, 32659,   904-753-3905
Yards: 5759, Par: 72, USGA: 66.2, Holes: 18, Pro: Lee Grimes
Waterford GC, 1454 Glen Eagles Drive, Venice, 34292
Holes: 18
West End GC, Newberry Rd. (POB 14524 Univ.S, Gainesville, 32604,
904-332-2721   Yards: 3682, Par: 60, USGA: 58.0, Holes: 18, Pro: Scott Dombek
West Meadows GC, 11400 W. Meadows Dr., Jacksonville, 32221,   904-781-4834
Yards: 5843, Par: 72, USGA: 70.0, Holes: 18, Pro: Sam Caruso
West Palm Beach GC, 7001 Parker Ave., West Palm Beach, 33405,
305-582-2019   Yards: 6789, Par: 72, USGA: 71.2, Holes: 18, Pro: Dub Pagan
Whispering Oaks CC, 35000 Whispering Oaks Blvd., Ridge Manor, 33525,
904-583-4020   Yards: 6118, Par: 71, Holes: 18, Pro: Tim Kuhlman
Wildflower CC, 3120 Gasparilla Pines Blvd,POB, Englewood, 33533,
813-697-1200   Yards: 3718, Par: 62, USGA: 54.6, Holes: 18, Pro: Jeff Russell
Williston Highlands CC, Rt. 2 Box 1590, Williston, 32696,   904-528-2520
Yards: 6304, Par: 72, USGA: 69.5, Holes: 18, Pro: Bob Kramer
Willow Lakes G & CC—Lakewood, 7300 Blanding Blvd., Jacksonville, 32244,
904-771-6656   Yards: 2723, Par: 36, Holes: 9, Pro: Frank Sansone
Windermere CC, Windermere, 32786,   407-876-4410
Par: 72, Holes: 18
Windsor Parke GC, 4747 Hodges Blvd, Jacksonville, 32224,   904-223-4653
Holes: 18
Winter Park CC, 761 Old England Ave., Winter Park, 32789,   305-644-8195
Yards: 2800, Par: 35, Holes: 9, Pro: Les Moore
Winter Pines CC, 950 S Ranger Blvd., Winter Park, 32792,   305-671-3172
Yards: 5402, Par: 67, Holes: 18, Pro: John Pohira
Zellwood Station CC, 2126 Spillman Dr., Zellwood, 32798,   407-886-3303
Yards: 6044, Par: 72, USGA: 69.4, Holes: 18, Pro: Mike Callahan
Zephyrhills G&CC, 2302 B Avenue, Zephyrhills, 33599,   813-782-9424
Yards: 5769, Par: 71, USGA: 65.0, Holes: 18, Pro: Bill Rinaldo

---

Alfred Tup Holmes GC, 2300 Wilson Dr., Atlanta, 30311,   404-753-6158 *Georgia*
Yards: 5980, Par: 72, USGA: 69.1, Holes: 18
American Legion GC, 107 Philema Road, Albany, 31701,   912-432-6016
Par: 72, USGA: 67.4, Holes: 18, Pro: Buddy Clanton
Americus CC, Route 2 South Lee Street, Americus, 31709,   912-924-9360
USGA: 69.3, Pro: Frank Hines
Ansley GC, 196 Montgomery Ferry Drive, Atlanta, 30309,   404-875-1687
USGA: 69.9, Pro: Art Kraft
Appling CC, Route 7 Box 990, Baxley, 31513,   912-367-3582
USGA: 71.0, Pro: Bill Baker
Arrowhead CC, Box 131, Jasper, 30143,   404-692-5634
USGA: 70.6, Pro: Teddy Duncan
Athens CC, 2700 Jefferson Road, Athens, 30607,   404-354-7111
USGA: 69.9, Pro: Ed Hoard
Atlanta CC, 500 Atlanta Country Club Drive, Marietta, 30067,   404-953-1211
USGA: 69.1, Pro: John Gerring

Atlanta National GC, 310 Tournament Players Drive, Alpharetta, 30201,
404-442-8801 USGA: 70.0, Pro: Mike Fiddelke
Atlantia Athletic Club, Athletic Club Drive, Duluth, 30136, 404-448-8552
USGA: 70.9, Pro: Jack Lewis
Augusta CC, P.O. Box 3166, Augusta, 30904, 404-736-5322
USGA: 70.2, Pro: Mike Reynolds
B.E.A.A., P.O. Box 85, Lindale, 30147, 404-234-8010
Pro: Ron Hyde
Bacon Park GC, Shorty Cooper Dr., P.O. Box 31, Savannah, 31406,
912-354-2625
Bainbridge CC, P.O. Box 445, Bainbridge, 31717, 912-246-4979
USGA: 69.1, Pro: George Herring
Battlefield GC, P.O. Box 5316, Ft. Oglethorpe, 30742, 404-866-1363
USGA: 70.0, Pro: Harry Shoemaker
Beaver Lake G & CC, Route 1, Box 46, Gay, 30218, 404-524-6640
Pro: William Redwine
Belle Meade CC, Route 3 Box 390 Washington Rd., Thomson, 30824,
404-595-4511 USGA: 67.5, Pro: Barbara Bryant
Bent Tree CC, Bent Tree Drive, Jasper, 30143, 404-893-2626
USGA: 69.0, Pro: Rick Frye
Berkeley Hills CC, P.O. Box 956488, Duluth, 30136, 404-448-4661
USGA: 69.3, Pro: Craig Martin
Bobby Jones GC, 384 Woodward Way, N.W., Atlanta, 30305, 404-658-7879
USGA: 67.3, Pro: Liz Duncan
Bremen Links GC, Route 1 Cash Town Road, Bremen, 30110, 404-537-4172
USGA: 64.7, Pro: Van B. Fitts, Jr
Briar Creek CC, P.O. Box 537, Sylvania, 30567, 912-863-4161
USGA: 69.7, Pro: Mike Mobley
Brookfield West CC, 100 Willow Run Road, Roswell, 30075, 404-993-0695
USGA: 69.7, Pro: Butch Hansen
Brookstone G & CC, 5705 Brookstone Drive, Acworth, 30101, 404-953-1225
Pro: Greg Bachaun
Browns Mill GC, 483 Cleveland Ave, Atlanta, 30354, 404-366-3573
USGA: 69.8, Pro: Carl Seldon
Brunswick CC, P.O. Box 2\1741, Brunswick, 31520, 912-264-0331
USGA: 69.9, Pro: Dan Carter
Cabin Creek GC, 1374 North 2nd Street, Griffin, 30223, 404-227-9794
USGA: 69.1, Pro: Ralph Dougherty
Calhoun Elks CC, 143 Craig Town Road, N. E., Calhoun, 30701, 404-629-4091
USGA: 67.1, Pro: Daryll Speegle
Callier Springs cC, 2637 Callier Springs Rd., Rome, 30161, 404-234-1691
USGA: 67.3, Pro: Rick Miller
Canongate GC I, P.O. Box 309, Palmetto, 30268, 404-463-3342
USGA: 69.3, Pro: Emory Lee
Canongate-On-White Oak, 141 Clubview Dr., Newnan, 30265, 404-681-0555
USGA: 70.4, Pro: Mike Lee
Canton GC, P.O. Box 736, Canton, 30114, 404-479-2772
USGA: 69.3, Pro: Jessie Cantrell
Capital City Club, 53 West Brookhaven Drive, Atlanta, 30319, 404-233-2121
USGA: 69.7, Pro: Rich Gaffoglio
Cario CC, P.O. Box 664, Cairo, 31728, 912-377-4506
USGA: 71.0, Pro: Mike Malone
Carroll County GC, Carrollton, 30117, 404-854-5940
Par: 36, Holes: 9
Cartersville CC, P.O. Box 343, Cartersville, 30120, 404-382-1611
USGA: 70.5, Pro:

Cedar Creek C & CC, Rt 4, Box 96, Buena Vista, 31803, 404-649-3381
Par: 36, USGA: 71.0, Holes: 9, Pro: Joe Nagy
Cedar Lake GC, P.O. Box 1169, Snellville, 30278, 404-466-4043
USGA: 68.4, Pro: Robert Johnson
Cedars/Pines Golf Club, Rt 1, Box 385, Zebulon, 30298, 404-299-5659
USGA: 69.1, Pro: Kerwin Roberts
Charles L. Bowden Golf Course, 3111 Millerfield Rd., Macon, 31201,
912-742-9296   Yards: 6500, Par: 72, USGA: 69.0, Holes: 18, Pro: Kieth Brady
Chattahoochee GC, 301 Tommy Aaron Drive SW, Gainesville, 30506,
404-532-0066   USGA: 69.0, Pro: Don Q. Williams
Cherokee G & CC, P.O. Box 145, Cedartown, 30125, 404-748-2800
USGA: 68.6, Pro: Dornan Gresley
Cherokee Rose CC, 225 Cherokee Trail, Hinesville, 31313, 912-876-5503
Pro: Jim Rowe
Cherokee Town & CC, 665 Hightower Trail, Dunwoody, 30338, 404-993-4401
USGA: 70.3, Pro: Dan P. Murphy
Circlestone CC, Rt 1, Box 269, Adel, 31620, 912-896-3893
USGA: 69.8, Pro: Ken Saunders
Clayton Municipal GC, Box 702, Clayton, 30525, 404-782-4512
Holes: 9
Coosa CC, P.O. Box 46, Rome, 30161, 404-234-2200
USGA: 69.0, Pro: Bert Seagraves
Country Club of Columbus, P.O. Box 1046, Columbus, 31902, 404-322-6869
USGA: 70.1, Pro: Bubba Patrick
Country Club of the South, 4100 Old Alabama Road, Alpharetta, 30201,
404-475-1803   USGA: 69.3, Pro: Doug Grove
Country Oaks GC, Rt 7, Box 245, Thomasville, 31792, 912-226-7466
USGA: 68.1, Pro: Ted Scott
Cumberland Creek CC, 2250 Callaway Road, S.W., Marietta, 30060,
404-422-3822   Par: 70, USGA: 67.2, Holes: 18, Pro: Mike Connelly
Dalton G & CC, P.O. Box 892, Dalton, 30720, 404-259-5911
USGA: 67.4, Pro: Lowell Fritz
Dawson CC, Box 407 Graves Road, Dawson, 31742, 912-995-2255
USGA: 69.8, Pro: Warren Brinson
Deer Trail CC, 122 Houston Street, Barnesville, 30204, 404-358-0349
USGA: 66.5, Pro: Lorie Mangham
Dodge County GC, P.O. Box 510, Eastman, 31023, 912-374-3616
USGA: 67.0, Pro: Bobby Slye
Dogwood G & CC, 4207 Flint Hill Road, Austell, 30001, 404-941-2202
USGA: 69.1, Pro: Carolyn Manning
Donalsonville CC, P.O. Box 614, Donalsonville, 31745, 912-524-2955
USGA: 68.9, Pro: Paul Stout
Doublegate CC, 3800 Old Dawson Road, Albany, 31707, 912-436-6503
USGA: 70.0, Pro: Ed Everett
Douglas G & CC, P.O. Box 1007, Douglas, 31533, 912-384-4707
USGA: 69.0, Pro: Larry Hinson
Druid Hills GC, 740 Clifton Road NE, Atlanta, 30307, 404-377-1758
USGA: 69.4, Pro: Randall Couch
Dublin CC, Rt 7 Country Club Drive, Dublin, 31021, 912-272-1549
USGA: 69.6, Pro: Tommy Birdsong
Dunwoody CC, 1600 Dunwoody Club Drive, Dunwoody, 30338, 404-394-1928
USGA: 69.5, Pro: Darrel Knicely
Eagle Watch, 3055 Eagle Watch Drive, Woodstock, 30188
Holes: 18
East Lake CC, 2575 Alston Drive SW, Atlanta, 30317, 404-373-5764
USGA: 70.7, Pro: Herb Rust

Elberton CC, P.O. Box 356, Elberton, 30635, 404-283-5921
USGA: 68.4, Pro: Bert Barger
Evans Heights GC, P.O. Box 276, Claxton, 30417, 912-739-3003
Pro: Steve Collins
Fairfield Plantation GC, RT 1 Montecello, Atlanta, 30180
Fieldstone GC, 2720 Salem Road, S.E., Conyers, 30208, 404-483-4372
USGA: 68.0, Pro: Bill Leathers
Fitzgerald CC, P.O. Box 888, Fitzgerald, 31750, 912-423-3560
USGA: 67.6, Pro: Francis Luke
Flat Creek GC, P.O. Box 2027, Peachtree City, 30269, 404-487-8140
USGA: 70.8, Pro: Boyd Booker
Follow Me GC, P.O. Box 2186, Fort Benning, 31905, 404-687-1940
USGA: 70.2, Pro: George Cliff
Forest Heights CC, P.O. Box 995, Statesboro, 30458, 912-764-3084
USGA: 70.0, Pro: Mike Perpich
Fort McPherson GC, Building 650, Fort McPherson, 30330, 404-752-2620
USGA: 69.6, Pro: Jay Foster
Fort Stewart GC, Gulick Street Building 2150, Fort Stewart, 31314, 912-767-2135
USGA: 68.2, Pro: Doug Graves
Four Seasons GC, P.O. Box 397, Wrens, 30833, 404-547-2816
Pro: Miller Weeks
Fox Creek GC, 1501 Cherokee Road, Smyrna, 30080, 404-435-1000
USGA: 57.2, Pro: Jeff Jerrel
General Electric Athletic Assn, P.O. Box 2342, Rome, 30161, 404-291-2406
USGA: 67.7, Pro: T. Armstrong
Gilmer County GC, Ellijay, 30540, 404-276-3080
Holes: 18
Glen Arven CC, Old Monticello Road—Box 93, Thomasville, 31792,
912-226-1780   USGA: 69.2, Pro: Kerry Miller
Gordon Lakes GC, Range Road Building 537, Fort Gordon, 30905,
404-791-2433   USGA: 71.6, Pro: Mike LaFrante
Goshen Plantation CC, Goshen Clubhouse Drive, Augusta, 30906,
404-793-6295   USGA: 69.0, Pro: Mike Evinger
Green Acres Golf & Recreation, Route 1, Dexter, 31019, 404-875-3110
USGA: 70.0, Pro: Ed Collins
Green Hills CC, Route 3 Barnett Shoals Road, Athens, 30605, 404-548-6032
USGA: 69.0, Pro: Rick Nelson
Green Island CC, P.O. Box 4480, Columbus, 31904, 404-324-3706
USGA: 69.9, Pro: R. Crawford
Green Meadows GC, P.O. Box 5127, Augusta, 30906, 404-798-1533
USGA: 69.3, Pro: Betty Wiggins
Green Valley GC, P.O. Box 596, McDonough, 30253, 404-957-3235
USGA: 68.4, Pro: J. Schwendinger
Greene County CC, Route 1, Union Point, 30669, 404-486-4513
USGA: 70.1, Pro: Lee J. Wade Jr.
Greens Club, 1771 Elizabeth Court, Conyers, 30208, 404-922-5719
Pro: Steve Knight
Griffin CC, 430 Club Drive, Griffin, 30223, 404-228-4744
USGA: 71.0, Pro: Clint Brady
Griffin-Spalding GC, P.O. Box 940, City Park, Griffin, 30224, 404-227-3627
USGA: 69.7, Pro: Gary Burns
Hampton Club, PO Box 286, St. Simons Island, 31522
Holes: 18
Hartwell GC, Rt 1, P.O. Box 189, Hartwell, 30643, 404-376-8161
Par: 71, USGA: 65.4, Holes: 18, Pro: Shelia Tucker

Heritage GC, P.O. Box 805, Clarkesville, 30523, 404-778-4101
USGA: 63.5, Pro: Randy Lovell
Hickory Hill GC, Jackson, 30233, 404-775-2433
Par: 71, Holes: 18
Highland CC, P.O. Box 1366, LaGrange, 30240, 404-884-1727
USGA: 69.4, Pro: David Cook
Highland GC, P.O. Box 1498, Conyers, 30207, 404-483-4235
USGA: 70.3, Pro: Doug Holsback
Holiday Hills GC, P.O. Box 360, Gordon, 31031, 912-628-5150
USGA: 67.0, Pro: Bob Watson
Honey Creek CC, 635 Clubhouse Drive, Conyers, 30208, 404-483-6343
USGA: 67.2, Pro: R. Havenstrite
Horseshoe Bend CC, 2100 Steeplechase Lane, Roswell, 30076, 404-992-1818
USGA: 70.6, Pro: Tom C. Smith
Houston Lake CC, P.O. Box 282, Perry, 31069, 912-987-3243
USGA: 70.0, Pro: Ren Morris
Hunter Pope CC, Route 1, Box 317, Monticello, 31064, 404-468-6222
USGA: 66.5, Pro: James Harrell
Idle Hour G & CC, P.O. Box 4484, Macon, 31208, 912-477-2092
USGA: 66.6, Pro: Dan Nyimicz
Indian Hills CC, 4001 Clubland Drive, Marietta, 30067, 404-971-7663
USGA: 70.0, Pro: Tim Farrell
Jeff Davis G & CC, P.O. Box 807, Hazelhurst, 31539, 912-275-9035
USGA: 69.3, Pro: John Turner
Jennings Mill CC, 1341 Y Camp Road, Bogart, 30622, 404-548-3266
USGA: 70.4, Pro: Bo Haggstrom
Jones Creek GC, 4101 Hammond's Ferry, Augusta, 30809, 404-860-4228
Par: 72, USGA: 70.0, Holes: 18, Pro: Brooks Simmons
Kraftsmen's Club, P.O. Box 1551, Rome, 30161, 404-235-9377
USGA: 67.2, Pro: Curt Summerlin
LaFayette GC, P.O. Box 711, LaFayette, 30728, 404-638-9095
Par: 34, USGA: 66.1, Holes: 9, Pro: Byron Chapman
Lake Arrowhead CC, P.O. Station 20, Cherokee Driv, Waleska, 30181,
404-479-5505   USGA: 68.8, Pro: Bob Frongillo
Lake Spivey CC, 8255 Clubhouse Way, Jonesboro, 30226, 404-477-9836
Par: 72, USGA: 68.1, Holes: 27, Pro: Charles Sorrell
Lakeside CC, 3600 Old Fallburn Road SW, Atlanta, 30331, 404-344-3629
USGA: 71.6, Pro: Leon Butler
Lakeview GC, P.O. Box 432, College Avenue E, Blackshear, 31516, 912-449-3064
USGA: 69.7, Pro: Barry Jacobson
Landings GC, 309 Statham's Way, Warner Robins, 31088
USGA: 69.7, Pro: Alan White
Lanier GC, P.O. Box 639, Cumming, 30130, 404-887-6114
Pro: James Williams
LaVida CC, 525 Windsor Road, Savannah, 31419, 912-925-2440
USGA: 68.4, Pro: Wanda Melton
Magnolia CC, P.O. Box 689, Millen, 30442, 912-982-5717
USGA: 65.9, Pro: J. D. Kent
Marietta CC, 510 Powder Springs Street, Marietta, 30060, 404-422-3400
USGA: 66.6, Pro: Charles Cox, S
Marshwood at the Landings, 1 Palmer Draw, Savannah, 31416, 912-598-1832
USGA: 70.0, Pro: Roger VanDyke
Mary Calder GC, P.O. Box 570, Savannah, 31402, 912-238-7985
USGA: 70.0, Pro: John Nelson
McKenzie Memorial GC, Route 1, Montezuma, 31063, 912-472-6126

Meadow Lakes GC, Rt 6, Box 337, Statesboro, 30458, 912-839-3191
USGA: 69.6, Pro: Mary Cartee
Milledgeville CC, P.O. Box 1191, Milledgeville, 31061, 912-452-3220
USGA: 67.8, Pro: Mike McCollum
Monroe G & CC, Box 286, Jersey Road, Monroe, 30655, 404-267-3110
USGA: 68.7, Pro: Tommy Carlton
Mystery Valley Golf Association, 6094 Shadow Rock Drive, Lithonia, 30058,
404-469-6913 USGA: 69.0, Pro: Randy Davidson
Newnan CC, P.O. Box 309, Newnan, 30263, 404-253-3675
USGA: 70.0, Pro: Dan Mullins
Nob North GC, 298 Nob North Drive, Cohutta, 30710, 404-694-8505
USGA: 69.0, Pro: Al Foster
North Fulton GC, 216 West Wieuca Road, Atlanta, 30342, 404-255-0723
USGA: 69.8, Pro: Jack Duncan
Northwood CC, 3157 Club Drive, Lawrenceville, 30245, 404-923-2991
USGA: 70.0, Pro: John Kirk
Ocilla CC, P.O. Box 107, Ocilla, 31774, 912-468-7512
Yards: 6472, Par: 72, USGA: 70.6, Holes: 9
Okefenokee GC, 201 Riveroak Drive, Blackshear, 31516, 912-283-7235
USGA: 70.4, Pro: Ed Causey
Pebble Creek GC, 9350 Thomas Road, Jonesboro, 30246, 404-477-7256
USGA: 65.7, Pro: Tom Bloodworth
Pebblebrook GC, Route 2, Woodberry, 30293, 404-846-3809
Par: 36, USGA: 70.9, Holes: 9, Pro: Dave Najdowski
Perry CC, P.O. Box 124, Perry, 31069, 912-987-1033
USGA: 70.1, Pro: Ray Wells
Pine Forest CC, P.O. Box 295, Jesup, 31545, 912-427-6505
USGA: 69.4, Pro: Bill Morris
Pine Hills CC, P.O. Box 206, 307 Oak Avenue, Cordele, 31015, 912-273-7587
USGA: 67.6, Pro: Gloria Reed
Pine Hills GC, Highway 29, Winder, 30680, 404-867-3150
USGA: 68.5, Pro: Wayne Crow
Pine Needles CC, P.O. Box 260, Fort Valley, 31030, 912-825-3816
USGA: 67.9, Pro: Floyd Doss
Pinecrest CC, Rt 1, Camilla Highway, Pelham, 31779, 912-294-8525
USGA: 70.4, Pro: Harry Daughtry
Pineknoll CC, Route 1 Box 64, Sylvester, 31791, 912-776-3455
USGA: 71.4, Pro: Ray Bridges
Pinetree CC, 3400 McCollum Parkway, Kennesaw, 30144, 404-428-0553
USGA: 68.4, Pro: Ras Allen
Plantation Club, P.O. Box 13727, Savannah, 31416, 912-598-1917
Pro: Archie Lemon
Polo Fields G & CC, 622 Polo Club Drive, Cumming, 30130, 404-688-7656
Pro: Butch Hansen
Rabun County GC, P.O. Box 394, Clayton, 30525, 404-782-5500
USGA: 65.7, Pro: Nan Short
Radium CC, 310 Skywater Blvd., Albany, 31705, 912-883-2685
USGA: 69.0, Pro: Billy Smith
Reynolds Plantation, 100 Linger Longer Road, Greensboro, 30642,
404-431-4040 Pro: Paul Bergen
River North CC, P.O. Box 7687, Macon, 31297, 912-743-1495
Pro: Jim Hickman
River's Edge Plantation, 300 North Bridge Road, Fayetteville, 30214
Holes: 18
Rivermont G & CC, 3130 Rivermont Parkway, Alpharetta, 30201, 404-993-1779
Pro: Tommy Lyman

Riverview Park GC, P.O. Box 726, Dublin, 31040, 912-272-1620
USGA: 66.1, Pro: Chas. Grinstead
Royal Lakes CC, Georgia Highway 53, Chestnut Mountain, 30501
Holes: 18
Royal Oaks GC, 253 Summit Ridge Drive, S.E., Cartersville, 30120,
404-382-3999 USGA: 68.0, Pro: Robert Phipps
Saint Andrews CC, P.O. Drawer 491, Winston, 30187, 404-949-3859
USGA: 71.2, Pro: Kirk Parker
Savannah GC, P.O. Box 3536, Savannah, 31404, 912-232-2156 .
USGA: 68.9, Pro: John M. Browne
Sconti GC, Big Canoe, 30143, 404-522-8437
Pro: Sam Adams
Sea Island GC, P.O. Box 423, St. Simons Island, 31522, 912-638-5118
Pro: John M. Popa
Settindown Creek GC, 1911 Cox Road, Woodstock, 30188
Pro: Tom Losinger
Sky Valley GC, Dillard, 30537, 404-746-5301
Pro: James D. Mason
Snapfinger Woods GC, 4601 Snapfinger Woods Drive, Decatur, 30035,
404-981-1400 USGA: 70.1, Pro: Joe Rullan
Spring Hill CC, P.O. Box 872, Tifton, 31794, 912-382-3144
USGA: 69.3, Pro: Stan Moore
Springbrook CC, 585 Camp Perrin Road, Lawrenceville, 30245, 404-963-0966
USGA: 67.2, Pro: Stan Czerno
St. Ives Country Club, 10265 Medlock Bridge Road, Duluth, 30136,
404-497-8121 Pro: S. Carmichael
St. Mary's GC, P.O. Box 31558, St. Mary's, 31558, 912-882-4647
USGA: 69.2, Pro: Hilda Munford
St. Simon Island Club, 100 Kings Way, St. Simons Island, 31522, 912-638-5309
USGA: 69.9, Pro: Ray S. Cutright
Standard Club, 6230 Abbotts Bridge Road, Duluth, 30136, 404-497-0055
USGA: 71.1, Pro: Scott Gould
Sugar Creek GC, 3042 Hudson Court, Decatur, 30033, 404-241-7671
USGA: 70.2, Pro: Bo Dotson
Summit Chase CC, P.O. Box 492, Snellville, 30278, 404-972-6772
USGA: 70.6, Pro: David Epps
Sunset CC, P.O. Box 336, Moultrie, 31768, 912-985-9646
USGA: 70.2, Pro: Herring Cole
Sunset Hills CC, Club Drive, Carrollton, 30117, 404-834-6656
USGA: 67.8, Pro: Chris Wyant
Swainsboro CC, P.O. Box 676, Swainsboro, 30401, 912-237-6116
USGA: 68.4, Pro: Carl Barker
Tallapoosa City Golf Course, 593 Golf Course Road, Tallapoosa, 30176,
404-574-7834 Pro: Jane Simpson
Thomaston CC, P.O. Box 622, Thomaston, 30286, 404-648-6910
USGA: 68.0, Pro: Tommy Johnson
Thomson CC, P.O. Box 506, Thomson, 30824, 404-595-2727
Par: 36, USGA: 67.4, Holes: 9, Pro: Ann Cartledge
Toccoa GC, P.O. Box 214, Toccoa, 30577, 404-886-6545
USGA: 68.5, Pro: Allan Campbell
Town and Country Club, P.O. Box 491, Blakely, 31723, 912-723-4737
USGA: 68.7, Pro: Ward Holman
Trion GC, Club Road, Trion, 30753, 404-723-2311
USGA: 69.0, Pro: Willis Smith
Turtle Cove CC, Route 1, Monticello, 31064, 404-468-8805
USGA: 58.6, Pro: Edie Lusk

Twin City CC, P.O. Box 1077, Sandersville, 31082, 912-552-7894
USGA: 68.8, Pro: Ralph Brannin
Uncle Remus GC, Milledgeville Road, Eatonton, 31024, 404-485-6850
USGA: 69.4, Pro: Buster Whitman
University of Georgia GC, Riverbend Road, Athens, 30605, 404-542-1401
USGA: 70.8, Pro: Dave Cousart
Valdosta CC, Old U.S. Hwy. 41 North, Valdosta, 31601, 912-242-4646
USGA: 71.0, Pro: Bo Bowden
Victoria Bryant State Park GC, Royston, 30662, 404-245-6770
Par: 36, Holes: 9
Vidalia CC, P.O. Box 642, Vidalia, 30474, 912-537-3531
USGA: 70.0, Pro: Andy Pittman
Wallace Adams GC, 750 Walker Lane, McRae, 31055, 912-868-6651
Par: 72, USGA: 70.2, Holes: 18, Pro: Ray Gentry
Willow Lake CC, P.O. Box 302, Metter, 30439, 912-685-2724
USGA: 68.3, Pro: Gregg Wolff
Wanee Lake CC, P.O. Box 621, Ashburn, 31714, 912-567-2727
Par: 36, USGA: 69.3, Holes: 9, Pro: Grady Poole
Washington-Wilkes CC, Thomson Highway, Washington, 30673, 404-678-2046
USGA: 70.2, Pro: Romulus Long
Waynesboro CC, P.O. Box 645, Waynesboro, 30830, 404-554-2262
USGA: 70.0, Pro: Wayne Cochran
West Lake CC, 3556 West Lake Drive, Augusta, 30907, 404-863-4642
USGA: 70.4, Pro: Mark E. Darnell
Whispering Pines, P.O. Box 315, Colbert, 30628, 404-788-2720
Par: 72, USGA: 68.4, Holes: 18, Pro: Jim McLuen
Whitepath Men's Golf Associati, Route 5, Box 29-J, Ellijay, 30540,
404-276-3080 USGA: 67.8, Pro: Steve Johnson
Whitewater Creek Golf & Athlet, 165 Birkdale Drive, Fayetteville, 30214,
404-461-6312 USGA: 68.4, Pro: Steve Johnson
Willow Springs CC, 2300 Roxburgh Drive, Roswell, 30076, 404-475-7815
USGA: 69.3, Pro: John Miller
Willowpeg GC, PO Box 1188, Rincon, 31326
Holes: 18

Ala Wai GC, 404 Kapahulu Ave., Honolulu, 96815, 808-732-7741 *Hawaii*
Barbers Point GC, NAS, Barbers Point, 96862, 808-682-3088
Cavendish GC, P.O.Box 862, Lanai City, 96763
Club Waikoloa Village GC, The, P.O. Box 3008, Waikoloa, 96743, 808-883-9621
Country Club, Hilo, 96720, 808-935-7388
Discovery Harbour Golf & CC, Waiohinu, 96786, 808-929-7353
Hamakua CC, P.O. Box 751, Honokaa, 96727, 808-775-7244
Hawaii CC, P. O. Box 966, Wahiawa, 96786, 808-621-5654
Hawaii Kai GC, 8902 Kalanianaole Hwy., Honolulu, 96825, 808-395-2358
Hickam 18 Hole GC, Bldg. 3572, Hickam AFM, 96853
Hilo Municipla Golf Course, 340 Haihai St., Hilo, 96720, 808-959-7711
Yards: 5034, Par: 71, USGA: 68.8, Holes: 18, Pro: William J. DeSa
Honolulu CC, 1690 Ala Puumalu St., Honolulu, 96818, 808-833-4543
Kahuku GC, P.O. Box 143, Kahuku, 96731, 808-293-5842
Kalakaua GC, Schofield Barracks, 96857, 808-655-9833
Kalua Koi GC, R. Maunaloa, Molokai, 96770
Kaneohe Klipper GC, MCAS Kaneohe, Kaneohe, 96744, 808-254-2107
Kona GC, 78-6740 Alii Dr., Hawaii, 96740
Kukuiolono GC, Paplina Rd., Kalaheo, 96741, 808-332-9151
Leilehua GC, Schofield Barracks, 96857, 808-622-1776
Maui CC, Paia, 96779, 808-877-0616

Mid-Pacific CC, 266 Kaelepulu Dr., Oahu, 96734
Moanalua GC, 1250 Ala Aolani Street, Honolulu, 96819, 808-839-2411
Navy Marine GC, Bldg. 43 Valkenburgh St., Honolulu, 96818, 808-471-0142
Oahu CC, 150 Country Club Rd., Honolulu, 96817, 808-595-3256
Olomana Golf Links, 41-1801 Kalanianaole Hwy., Waimanalo, 96795, 808-259-7926
Pali GC, 45-050 Kemehameha Hwy., Kaneohe, 96744, 808-261-9784
Mauna Lani GC, P.O.Box 4959, Kawaihae, 96743, 808-885-6655
Pearl GC, 98-535 Kaonohi St., Aiea, 96701, 808-487-3802
Silversword GC, P.O.Box 1099, Kihei, 96753, 808-874-0777
Ted Makalena GC, Waipio Point Access Road, Waipahu, 96797, 808-671-6488
Turtle Bay Hilton & CC, Kahuku, 96731, 808-293-8811
Waialae CC, 4997 Kahala Ave., Honolulu, 96816, 808-732-1457
Waiehu Muni GC, Waiehu, 96793, 808-244-5433
Waikoloa (Kings Course), Waikoloa Road, Waikoloa, 96743 Holes: 18
Wailea GC—Blue Course, 120 Kaukahi St., Wailea, Kihei, Maui, 96753,
808-879-2966 Yards: 6152, Par: 72, USGA: 68.6, Holes: 18, Pro: Rick Castillo
Wailua Muni GC, 4444 Rice St. Rm. 230, Lihue, 96766, 808-245-2163
Yards: 6585, Par: 72, USGA: 71.9, Holes: 18, Pro: Larry Lee, Sr.
Walter Nagorski GC, Bldg. 716, Fort Shafter, 96858, 808-438-9587
Westin Mauna Kea GC, P.O. Box 218, Kamuela, 96743, 808-882-7222
Yards: 6365, Par: 72, USGA: 70.6, Holes: 18, Pro: J.D.Ebersberger

---

Aspen Acres GC, Ashton, 83420, 208-652-3524   *Idaho*
Par: 60, Holes: 18
Bear Lake West GC, Pro Shop, Fish Haven, 83287, 208-945-2222
Par: 33, USGA: 62.0, Holes: 9, Pro: Jeff Willmore
Bigwood GC, Sun Valley, 83353, 208-726-4024
Par: 36, Holes: 9
Canyon Springs GC, Twin Falls, 83301, 208-734-7609
Par: 72, Holes: 18
Crane Creek GC, 500 W. Curling Dr., Boise, 83702
Hillcrest CC, 4610 Hillcrest Dr., Boise, 83705
Idaho Falls GC, 11611 Country Club Dr., Idaho Falls, 83402
Kellogg G&CC, Pinehurts, 83850, 208-682-2013
Par: 36, Holes: 9
Kimberland Meadows Resort, New Meadows, 83654, 208-347-2164
Par: 72, Holes: 18
Montpelier GC, Montpelier, 83254, 208-847-1981
Par: 36, Holes: 9
Moscow Elks GC, Moscow, 83843, 208-882-3015
Par: 35, Holes: 9
Pinecrest GC, 701 E. Elva St., Idaho Falls, 83401, 208-529-1485
Yards: 6394, Par: 70, USGA: 69.5, Holes: 18, Pro: Tim D. Reinke
Priest Lake GC, Priest Lake, 83822, 208-443-2525
Par: 36, Holes: 9
Ranch Club GC, Priest River, 83856, 208-448-1731
Par: 33, Holes: 9
Rexburg Muni GC, Rexburg, 83440, 208-359-3037
Par: 35, Holes: 9
Salmon Valley GC, Salmon, 83467, 208-756-4734
Par: 36, Holes: 9
Scotch Pines GC, Payette, 83661, 208-642-9981
Par: 72, Holes: 18
St. Maries GC, St. Maries, 83861, 208-245-3842
Par: 35, Holes: 9

Terrace Lakes Recreation Ranch, Garden Valley, 83622, 208-462-3250
Par: 72, Holes: 18
Twin Lakes Village GC, Rathdrum, 83858, 208-687-1311
Par: 72, Holes: 18
University of Idaho GC, Moscow, 83843, 208-885-6171
Par: 72, Holes: 18

Addison GC, Army Trail Mills Rds., Addison, 60101, 312-628-9713   *Illinois*
Yards: 1711, Par: 27, Holes: 9
Alton Muni GC, Golf Rd., Alton, 62002, 618-465-9861
Yards: 3003, Par: 35, Holes: 9
American Legion GC, 308 S. 8th, Marshall, 62441, 217-826-2713
Yards: 2842, Par: 35, Holes: 9
American Legion GC, St. Louis Rd., Edwardsville, 62025, 618-656-9774
Yards: 4500, Par: 35, Holes: 9
Anderson Field GC, RR 4, Streator, 61364, 815-672-3702
Yards: 2682, Par: 35, Holes: 9
Anets GC, 180 Anets Dr., Northbrook, 60065, 312-272-0770
Yards: 1200, Par: 28, Holes: 9
Apple Canyon Lake GC, 14 A 57 Canyon Club Dr., Apple River, 61001,
815-492-2182   Yards: 3169, Par: 36, USGA: 35.8, Holes: 9
Apple Orchard GC, 696 Stearns Rd., Bartlett, 60103, 312-837-5292
Yards: 2729, Par: 27, Holes: 9
Arrowhead CC, 1100 Pruitt Rd., Chillicothe, 61523, 309-274-4675
Yards: 6380, Par: 72, USGA: 68.9, Holes: 18
Arrowhead GC—#1, 26 W. 151 Butterfield Rd., Wheaton, 60187, 312-653-5800
Yards: 3240, Par: 35, USGA: 68.4, Holes: 9, Pro: Pete Drogof
Arrowhead Heights GC, RR 2, Camp Point, 62320, 217-593-6619
Yards: 3000, Par: 36, USGA: 33.3, Holes: 9
Atwood GC, 8990 Old River Rd., Rockford, 61103, 815-623-9954
Yards: 7469, Par: 72, USGA: 74.1, Holes: 18, Pro: Steve Hare
Aurora CC, Prairie St. & Western Ave., Aurora, 60506, 312-892-3785
Yards: 6550, Par: 72, USGA: 70.5, Holes: 18, Pro: Bob Ackerman
Baker Park CC, 1095 Cambridge Rd., Kewanee, 61443, 309-852-2872
Yards: 6501, Par: 71, USGA: 68.4, Holes: 18
Midland CC, RR 2, Kewanee, 61433, 309-852-4508
Yards: 6850, Par: 72, USGA: 71.2, Holes: 18, Pro: Wayne Downing
Balmoral Woods GC, 2500 Balmoral Woods Dr., Crete, 60417, 312-672-7448
Yards: 6683, Par: 72, Holes: 18, Pro: Tony Houglin
Barrington Hills CC, W. County Line Rd., Barrington, 60010, 312-381-4200
Yards: 6637, Par: 71, USGA: 71.5, Holes: 18, Pro: Lee Milligan
Bartlette Hille GC, 800 W. 1, Bartlett, 60103, 312-837-2741
Yards: 6300, Par: 71, USGA: 68.3, Holes: 18
Bel Mar GC, RR 3, Belvidere, 61008, 815-547-8973
Yards: 1650, Par: 71, USGA: 67.4, Holes: 18, Pro: Randy Schairer
Belk Park GC, Belk Park Rd., Wood River, 62095, 618-254-9065
Yards: 6585, Par: 72, USGA: 71.2, Holes: 18
Benton CC, RR 2, Benton, 62812, 618-439-0921
Yards: 6330, Par: 72, USGA: 68.9, Holes: 9, Pro: Gary Squires
Beverly CC, 8700 S. Western Ave., Chicago, 60620, 312-238-4203
Yards: 6700, Par: 71, USGA: 71.5, Holes: 18, Pro: Doug Veling
Billy Caldwell GC, 6200 N. Caldwell Ave, Chicago, 60646, 312-792-1930
Yards: 3029, Par: 35, Holes: 9
Biltmore CC, 160 Biltmore Dr., Barrington, 60010, 312-381-9858
Yards: 6358, Par: 71, USGA: 70.4, Holes: 18, Pro: Jim Michaels

Black Horse GC, 201 63rd St., Westmont, 60559,   312-968-3336
Yards: 1942, Par: 30, Holes: 9, Pro: Mike Tait
Bloomington CC, Towanda Ave., , Bloomington, 61701,   309-829-6166
Yards: 6800, Par: 71, USGA: 70.6, Holes: 18, Pro: Mike Adams
Blue Needles GC, Catlin, 61817,   217-427-5536
Par: 72, Holes: 18
Bob-O-Link GC, 1120 Crofton Ave., Highland Park, 60035,   312-432-0917
Yards: 6713, Par: 72, USGA: 72.5, Holes: 18, Pro: Gary Groh
Bon Vivant CC, Rt. 102 & Career Center Rd., Bourbonnais, 60914,
815-935-0403   Yards: 7498, Par: 72, USGA: 76.2, Holes: 18, Pro: John Krutilla
Bonnie Brook GC, N. Lewis Ave., Waukegan, 60087,   312-336-5538
Yards: 6655, Par: 72, USGA: 70.5, Holes: 18, Pro: Ed Staffan
Bonnie Dundee G & CC, Rts. 1, E. Dundee, 60118,   815-426-5511
Yards: 6195, Par: 70, USGA: 67.9, Holes: 18, Pro: Jim Ervin
Brae Loch CC, Rt. 45, Grayslake, 60030, 312-223-5542
Yards: 6025, Par: 70, USGA: 69.5, Holes: 18
Briarwood CC, 355 Deerfield Rd., Deerfield, 60015,   312-945-2660
Yards: 6545, Par: 71, USGA: 71.3, Holes: 18, Pro: Joe Zelazny
Brook Hill GC, Rantoul, 61866,   217-893-1200
Par: 72, Holes: 18
Brook Park GC, N. Maplewood, Rantoul, 61866,   217-893-1200
Yards: 6370, Par: 72, USGA: 68.0, Holes: 18, Pro: Mike Duran
Brookwood CC, 271 S. Addison, Wood Dale, 60191,   312-595-4330
Yards: 6156, Par: 71, USGA: 69.7, Holes: 18, Pro: Greg Befera
Bryn Mawr CC, 6600 North Crawford, Lincolnwood, 60069,   312-478-2014
Yards: 6382, Par: 72, USGA: 69.9, Holes: 18, Pro: Ken Bartosh
Buena Vista GC, N. 1st St, De Kalb, 60115,   815-758-4812
Yards: 2700, Par: 32, Holes: 9, Pro: Rich Zonca
Buffalo Grove GC, 48 Raupp Blvd., Buffalo Grove, 60089,   312-537-5819
Yards: 6800, Par: 72, USGA: 69.9, Holes: 18, Pro: Carmen Mouinaro
Bunn Park GC, 2500 S. 11th St., Springfield, 62703,   217-522-2633
Yards: 6300, Par: 72, USGA: 69.0, Holes: 18, Pro: Dale Schofield
Bureau Valley CC, SR-26, Princeton, 64356,   815-879-6531
Yards: 3462, Par: 36, USGA: 68.9, Holes: 9, Pro: Kai Vandemore
Burnham Woods GC, 14201 Burnham, Burnham, 62318, 312-862-9043
Yards: 6480, Par: 72, Holes: 18
Burr Hill CC, 5 N. 748 Burr Rd., St. Charles, 60174,   312-584-8236
Yards: 6390, Par: 72, USGA: 70.5, Holes: 18, Pro: Terry Cayland
Butler National Golf, 2616 York Rd., Oak Brook, 60521,   312-990-3333
Yards: 6600, Par: 72, USGA: 74.0, Holes: 18, Pro: Errie Ball
Butterfield CC, Summit & 1st Street, Hinsdale, 60521,   312-323-1000
Yards: 6530, Par: 72, USGA: 71.2, Holes: 18
Calumet CC, W. 175th & Dixie Hwy, Homewood, 60430,   312-799-5050
Yards: 6533, Par: 71, USGA: 71.4, Holes: 18, Pro: Bill Kuikman
Cantigny Golf & Tennis Club, 27 West 270 Mack Road, Wheaton, 60187
Holes: 27
Canton CC, 1920 N. Main St., Canton, 61520,   309-647-5419
Yards: 6319, Par: 71, Holes: 18
Cardinal GC, Effingham, 62401,   217-868-2860
Yards: 5899, Par: 72, USGA: 68.0, Holes: 18
Carlinville CC, Hwy 4 South, Carlinville, 62626,   217-854-6516
Yards: 3094, Par: 36, Holes: 9
Carriage Greens CC, 8700 Carriage Greens Dr., Darien, 60559,   312-985-9280
Yards: 3076, Par: 35, USGA: 69.1, Holes: 18, Pro: Dave Eubanks
Carthage GC, Carthage Park, Carthage, 62321,   217-357-3625
Yards: 2805, Par: 35, Holes: 9, Pro: Bob Rigney

Cary CC, 2400 Grove Lane, Cary, 60013, 312-639-3161
Yards: 6135, Par: 72, USGA: 67.9, Holes: 18, Pro: Bob Keith
Casey CC, 13th Street, Casey, 62420, 217-932-2030
Yards: 3010, Par: 35, USGA: 67.2, Holes: 9
CC of Decatur, 135 N. CC Rd., Decatur, 62521, 217-429-7823
Yards: 6338, Par: 72, USGA: 69.7, Holes: 18, Pro: George Wrede
CC of Peoria, 4700 N. Grand View Dr., Peoria Heights, 61614, 309-685-1212
Yards: 6068, Par: 72, USGA: 69.6, Holes: 18, Pro: Kevin Fitzerald
Cedar Crest CC, RR 3, Quincy, 62301, 217-223-1210
Yards: 2800, Par: 35, USGA: 71.5, Holes: 9
Cedardell GC, S. Hale St., Plano, 60545, 312-552-3242
Yards: 2938, Par: 36, USGA: 67.8, Holes: 9
Chalet GC, 945 W. Rawson Bridge Rd., Cary, 60013, 312-639-9732
Yards: 5400, Par: 70, USGA: 65.2, Holes: 18
Champaign CC, 1211 Prospect St., Champaign, 81820, 217-356-1391
Yards: 6361, Par: 71, USGA: 68.8, Holes: 18, Pro: Larry Brady
Chanute AFB GC, Chanute AFB, 60410, 217-495-3063
Yards: 6800, Par: 72, USGA: 71.1, Holes: 18, Pro: Gene DeGenere
Charleston GC, CC Rd., Charleston, 61920, 217-345-9711
Yards: 6200, Par: 36, USGA: 68.7, Holes: 9
Cherry Hills GC, 191st & Kedzie Ave., Flossmoor, 60422, 312-799-5600
Yards: 2267, Par: 33, USGA: 32.6, Holes: 9, Pro: D. Falaschette
Cherry Hills CC, 175th & Western, Homewood, 708-799-5600
Yards: 6270, Par: 72, Holes: 27
Chester CC, SR-3 N, Chester, 62233, 618-826-3168
Yards: 6270, Par: 36, USGA: 72.6, Holes: 9
Chevy Chase GC, 1000 N. Milwaukee Ave., Whelling, 60090, 312-537-0082
Yards: 6700, Par: 72, USGA: 71.4, Holes: 18, Pro: V. Verstraete
Chicago Heights CC, 1112 Scott Ave., Chicago, 60610, 312-755-9222
Yards: 3672, Par: 36, Holes: 9, Pro: Randy Cochran
Chick Evans GC, 6145 Golf Rd., Morton Grove, 60053, 312-965-5353
Yards: 5681, Par: 71, USGA: 67.5, Holes: 18
Clay Country G & CC, RR 2, Flora, 62839, 618-662-2500
Yards: 3022, Par: 35, Holes: 9
Clinton CC, Clinton, 61727, 217-935-2918
Yards: 2821, Par: 35, USGA: 67.0, Holes: 9
Clinton Hill CC, 3700 Old Collinsville Rd., Belleville, 62221, 618-277-3700
Yards: 6600, Par: 71, USGA: 71.3, Holes: 18, Pro: Brain Maine
Cloverleaf GC, Fosterberg Rd., Alton, 62002, 618-462-3022
Yards: 5872, Par: 70, Holes: 18
Colonial GC, US Hwy 51 S, Sandoval, 62882, 618-247-3307
Columbia GC, RR 1, Columbia, 62236, 618-286-9653
Yards: 6200, Par: 70, USGA: 67.8, Holes: 18, Pro: Bob Furkin
Cool Creek Rec. Area, RR 1, Highland, 62249, 618-675-3500
Yards: 2631, Par: 36, Holes: 9
Country Lakes, 5S-100 Fairway Drive, Naperville, 60540, 312-420-1060
Yards: 7000, Par: 73, Holes: 18
Country Side GC, 2607 W. Lincoln St., De Kalb, 60115, 815-758-5249
Yards: 2355, Par: 34, Holes: 9
Country View GC, Rt. 2, Geneseo, 61254, 309-441-5272
Yards: 2865, Par: 35, Holes: 9
Countryside GC, W. Hawley Rd. and Rt. 83, Mundelein, 60060, 312-566-5544
Yards: 6267, Par: 72, USGA: 69.5, Holes: 18
Cress Creek CC, 1215 Royal St., George Dr., Naperville, 60540, 312-355-7300
Yards: 5615, Par: 72, USGA: 69.7, Holes: 18, Pro: Frank Witt

Crestwicke CC, SR-13, Bloomington, 61701, 309-829-8092
Yards: 6518, Par: 72, USGA: 70.5, Holes: 18, Pro: Rick Sellers
Crystal Lake CC, 721 CC Rd., Crystal Lake, 60014, 815-459-1068
Yards: 6400, Par: 71, USGA: 69.9, Holes: 18, Pro: J. Anderson
Crystal Woods GC, 5915 S. SR-47, Woodstock, 60098, 815-338-3111
Yards: 6300, Par: 72, USGA: 69.1, Holes: 18
Da De Co GC, Rt 1, Ottawa, 61350, 815-434-0145
Yards: 2985, Par: 35, Holes: 9
Danville CC, Denmark Rd., Danville, 61832, 217-442-5213
Yards: 6300, Par: 71, USGA: 69.8, Holes: 18, Pro: Neil T. Moore
Danville Elks CC, 332 E. Liberty Lane, Danville, 61832, 217-442-8876
Yards: 6565, Par: 72, USGA: 71.3, Holes: 18, Pro: Greg Flesher
Deer Creek GC, 26201 S. Western, University Park, 708-672-6667
Yards: 6755, Par: 72, Holes: 36
Deer Park CC Inc., SR-71, LaSalle, 61301, 815-667-4239
Yards: 7115, Par: 72, Holes: 18
Deer Run GC, Rt. 136, Hamilton, 62341, 217-847-3623
Yards: 3000, Par: 36, USGA: 69.9, Holes: 9
Deerfield Park, 1201 Sanders Rd., Deerfield, 60015, 312-945-8333
Yards: 6780, Par: 74, USGA: 72.7, Holes: 18
Deerpath Park GC, 500 W. Deerpath Ave., Lake Forest, 60045, 312-234-1968
Yards: 6097, Par: 70, USGA: 68.1, Holes: 18, Pro: Don Kennedy
Detweiller GC, 8412 N. Galena Rd., Peoria, 61615, 309-692-7518
Yards: 1847, Par: 29, USGA: 55.1, Holes: 9, Pro: Louis Carter Jr
Earl F. Elliot GC, Lyford & Mill Roads, Rockford, 61107, 815-332-5130
Yards: 6393, Par: 72, USGA: 69.4, Holes: 18, Pro: Dave Claeyssens
Earlville CC Inc., Oakstreet, Earlville, 60518, 815-246-9436
Yards: 2500, Par: 32, USGA: 31.4, Holes: 9
East Fork GC, RR 6, Olney, 62450, 618-395-3505
Yards: 800, Par: 27, Holes: 9
Edgebrook GC, 6100 North Central Ave., Chicago, 60646, 312-631-7522
Yards: 4626, Par: 66, Holes: 18
Edgewood GC, RR 3, Auburn, 62615, 217-438-3221
Yards: 6400, Par: 72, USGA: 70.5, Holes: 18, Pro: Elaine Nitz
Edgewood GC, 10684 Edgewood Rd., Polo, 61064, 815-946-3636
Yards: 2798, Par: 35, USGA: 33.1, Holes: 9
Edgewood Park GC, SR-89, McNabb, 60026, 815-882-2317
Yards: 3200, Par: 36, USGA: 35.1, Holes: 9
Edgewood Valley CC, 7500 Willow Spring Rd., LaGrange, 60525, 312-246-2800
Yards: 6562, Par: 72, USGA: 71.8, Holes: 18, Pro: Jim Schreiber
Effingham CC, W. Rt. 40, Effingham, 62401, 217-347-0423
Yards: 6300, Par: 72, USGA: 67.7, Holes: 18, Pro: Dave Martin
Egyptian CC, US Hwy 51, Mounds, 62964, 618-745-6412
Yards: 6009, Par: 72, Holes: 9
El Paso GC, RR 1, El Paso, 61738, 309-527-5225
Yards: 6070, Par: 70, Holes: 18, Pro: Lane Vance
Elgin CC, 37 W. 267 Weld Rd., Elgin, 60123, 312-741-1716
Yards: 6500, Par: 72, Holes: 18, Pro: Chris Jacques
Elliot GC, Mill and Lyford Roads, Rockford, 61112, 815-332-5130
Yards: 6800, Par: 72, USGA: 69.9, Holes: 18, Pro: David Claeyssen
Ellwood Greens GC, Ellwood Gr. Rd., Genoa, 60135, 815-784-5678
Yards: 6875, Par: 72, USGA: 72.6, Holes: 18, Pro: Wally Ansted
Elmwood GC, 1404 Eiler Rd., Belleville, 62223, 618-538-5826
Yards: 3030, Par: 36, Holes: 9, Pro: William Ross
Emerald Hill Inc., E. Lincoln Hwy., Sterling, 61081, 815-625-7200
Yards: 3200, Par: 36, Holes: 18

Evanston GC, 44401 W. Dempster, Skokie, 60076,   312-676-0300
Yards: 6500, Par: 70, USGA: 71.2, Holes: 18, Pro: Hal Miller
Evergreen G & CC, 9140 S. Western Ave., Chicago, 60620,   312-238-6680
Yards: 6355, Par: 71, Holes: 18
Exmor CC, 700 Vine St., Highland Park, 60035,   312-432-3600
Yards: 6592, Par: 72, USGA: 71.6, Holes: 18, Pro: John Cleland
Fairlakes GC, Secor, 61771,   309-744-2222
Par: 66, Holes: 18
Fairmont GC, 4000 Collinsville Rd., Fairmont City, 61841,   618-874-9554
Yards: 2248, Par: 33, Holes: 9, Pro: Howard Popphim
Faries GC, 61 Faries Par, Decatur, 62526, 217-422-2211
Yards: 6561, Par: 72, Holes: 18, Pro: Richard Hamel
Flossmoor CC, West 195th & Western, Flossmoor, 60422,   312-798-4700
Yards: 6455, Par: 72, USGA: 71.3, Holes: 18, Pro: David Ogilvie
Fondulac GC, Springfield Rd., E. Peoria, 61611,   309-699-4222
Yards: 1255, Par: 27, Holes: 9
Ford Hills CC, R.R. 4, Geneseo, 61254,   309-944-5418
Yards: 3025, Par: 35, Holes: 9
Forest Hills CC, 5135 Forest Hills Rd., Rockford, 61111,   815-877-4280
Yards: 6691, Par: 72, USGA: 71.6, Holes: 18, Pro: Robert Pegoraro
Forest Preserve National, 16300 163rd & Central Ave., Oak Forest, 60452,
312-429-6886   Yards: 7170, Par: 72, USGA: 71.9, Holes: 18, Pro: George Kallish
Foss Park GC, 3121 Argonne Dr., North Chicago, 60064,   312-689-1633
Yards: 6454, Par: 72, USGA: 70.5, Holes: 18
Four Winds GC, SR-176, Mundelein, 60060,   312-566-8502
Yards: 6500, Par: 70, USGA: 70.2, Holes: 18, Pro: Frank Hebert
Fox Bend GC, State Rt. 34, Oswego, 60543,   312-554-3939
Yards: 6660, Par: 71, USGA: 69.1, Holes: 18, Pro: Leon McNair
Fox Run Links, 333 Plum Grove Rd., Elk Grove Village, 60007,   312-980-4653
Yards: 6350, Par: 70, USGA: 70.4, Holes: 18
Franklin County CC, Rt. 2, West Frankfort, 62896,   618-932-2723
Yards: 6615, Par: 71, USGA: 71.0, Holes: 18, Pro: Gene Carello
Freeport CC, S. Park Blvd., Freeport, 61032,   815-232-2012
Yards: 6433, Par: 70, USGA: 70.1, Holes: 18, Pro: John Green
Fulton CC, Rt. 1, Cattail Rd., Fulton, 21252,   815-589-2440
Yards: 6335, Par: 36, USGA: 69.7, Holes: 9
Galena GC, Turnpike Rd., Galena, 61036,   815-777-9826
Yards: 2985, Par: 36, USGA: 33.3, Holes: 9
Genesco CC, RR 1, Geneseo, 61254,   309-944-2671
Yards: 2706, Par: 35, USGA: 66.0, Holes: 9
Geneva GC, 831 South St., Geneva, 60134,   312-232-0624
Yards: 2940, Par: 34, USGA: 67.9, Holes: 9, Pro: Albert Staudt
Gibson Wood GC, Monmouth Park, Monmouth, 61462,   309-734-9968
Yards: 6362, Par: 71, USGA: 70.9, Holes: 18, Pro: Tim Sweborg
Gillespie CC, R.R. 1, Gillespie, 62033,   217-839-2703
Yards: 2378, Par: 31, Holes: 9
Glen Eagles GC—#1, 123rd & Bell Ave., Lemont, 60439,   312-257-5466
Yards: 6090, Par: 70, USGA: 68.6, Holes: 18
Glen Flora GC, 2200 N. sheridan Rd., Waukegan, 60087,   312-244-6300
Yards: 6288, Par: 70, USGA: 70.2, Holes: 18, Pro: Ken Henry
Glen View Club, Golf Rd., Golf, 60029,   312-729-6500
Yards: 6500, Par: 72, USGA: 70.8, Holes: 18, Pro: Ed Oldfield
Glendale GC, 5 N. 181 Glen Ellyn Rd., Bloomingdale, 60108,   312-529-6232
Yards: 6385, Par: 72, USGA: 69.8, Holes: 18, Pro: Tom Winter
Glenview N.A.S. GC, Naval Air Station, Glenview, 60025,   312-657-2443
Yards: 6535, Par: 72, USGA: 70.2, Holes: 18, Pro: Sy Wolf

Glenview Park GC, 800 Shermer Rd., Glenview, 60025,   312-724-0250
Yards: 6800, Par: 70, USGA: 68.5, Holes: 18, Pro: David Rowlands
Glenwoodie Club, 193rd & State St., Glenwood, 60425,   312-758-1212
Yards: 6670, Par: 72, USGA: 71.8, Holes: 18, Pro: Dave Mose
Gold Hills, RR 2, Colchester, 62326,   309-837-2930
Yards: 2962, Par: 35, Holes: 9
Golden Acres GC—#1, 162 Roselle Rd., Schaumburg, 62283,   312-885-9000
Yards: 3265, Par: 36, Holes: 9, Pro: Lou Janis
Grand Marias GC, 4500 Pocket Rd., E. St. Louis, 62208,   618-398-9999
Yards: 6506, Par: 72, USGA: 72.0, Holes: 18
Green Acres Club, 916 Dundee Rd., Northbrook, 60065,   312-291-2238
Yards: 6540, Par: 72, USGA: 71.3, Holes: 18, Pro: Dick Lanscioni
Green Garden CC, Frankford, 60423,   815-469-3350
Par: 72, Holes: 18
Green Hills CC, Old Fairfield Rd., Mt. Vernon, 62864,   618-244-3747
Yards: 6012, Par: 71, USGA: 68.2, Holes: 18, Pro: Jerry Tucker
Green River GC, Rt 92, Walnut, 61376,   815-379-2227
Yards: 2750, Par: 34, USGA: 32.7, Holes: 9, Pro: Roger Shule
Greenshire GC, 3809 Lewis Ave., Waukegan, 60085,   312-244-2066
Yards: 1265, Par: 27, Holes: 9, Pro: Ed Steffan
Greenview GC, R.R. 5, Centralia, 62801,   618-532-7395
Yards: 5639, Par: 72, USGA: 70.1, Holes: 18, Pro: Tom Wargo
Greenville CC, Vandalia Rd., Greenville, 62246,   618-664-1341
Yards: 3334, Par: 36, USGA: 33.1, Holes: 9
Harbor Ridge CC, 4150 N. State Rt. 59, Antioch, 60002,   312-395-3004
Yards: 6170, Par: 71, USGA: 69.1, Holes: 18
Hardin County GC, State Rt. 1, Cave in Rock, 62919,   618-289-4587
Yards: 6000, Par: 35, Holes: 9
Hazy Hills GC, US-51, Hudson, 61748,   309-726-9200
Yards: 2900, Par: 35, Holes: 9, Pro: Joe Ellenberger
Heather Ridge GC, 5864 Manchester Dr., Gurnee, 60031,   312-367-6010
Yards: 2861, Par: 35, USGA: 33.3, Holes: 9
Hickory Hills GC—18 hole cou, 8201 95th St., Hickory Hills, 60457,
312-598-6460   Yards: 6081, Par: 71, USGA: 67.9, Holes: 18
Hickory Knoll GC, 24745 Monaville St., Lake Villa, 60046,   312-356-8640
Yards: 1900, Par: 30, Holes: 9
Hickory Point GC, Weaver Rd., RR 1, Decatur, 62526,   217-877-5181
Yards: 6870, Par: 72, USGA: 71.0, Holes: 18, Pro: Boby Scherer
Highland CC, RFD 2, Highland, 62249,   618-654-9092
Yards: 6566, Par: 36, USGA: 35.7, Holes: 9
Highland Park GC, 1613 S. Main St., Bloomington, 61701,   309-829-6636
Yards: 5825, Par: 70, USGA: 66.9, Holes: 18, Pro: Tom Guttschow
Highland Park, 1201 Park Ave. W, Highland Park, 60035,   312-433-4000
Yards: 6522, Par: 70, USGA: 69.0, Holes: 18, Pro: Jim Sobb
Highland Springs GC, 9500 35th St. West, Rock Island, 61201,   309-787-5814
Yards: 6500, Par: 72, USGA: 70.8, Holes: 18
Highland Woods GC, 2775 North Ela Rd., Hoffman Estates, 60195,
312-359-5850 Yards: 6510, Par: 72, USGA: 71.6, Holes: 18, Pro: Dick Knopp
Highview GC, 1921 Colby Lane, Rockford, 61111,   815-282-9795
Yards: 900, Par: 27, Holes: 9, Pro: Chuck Behrens
Hillcrest CC, SR-53, Long Grove, 60047,   312-438-8281
Yards: 6727, Par: 72, USGA: 72.1, Holes: 18, Pro: Steve Benson
Hillcrest G & Rec Area, RR 1, Orion, 61273,   309-526-9787
Yards: 1829, Par: 30, Holes: 9
Hillcrest GC, 1829 Washington Rd., Washington, 61571,   309-444-9033
Yards: 3090, Par: 59, Holes: 18, Pro: Ben Brubaker

Hilldale CC, 1655 Ardwick Dr., Hoffman Estates, 60195, 312-310-1100
Yards: 6302, Par: 71, USGA: 70.2, Holes: 18, Pro: Garry Hopkins
Hillsboro CC, City Lake Rd., Hillsboro, 62049, 217-532-2045
Yards: 3249, Par: 36, USGA: 35.4, Holes: 9, Pro: Earl Williams
Hinsdale GC, Rt. 83 & 47th St., Clarendon Hills, 60514, 312-986-5330
Yards: 6475, Par: 71, USGA: 70.8, Holes: 18, Pro: Dick Hart
Homestead GC, Fairway Dr., SR-5, Mt. Vernon, 62864, 618-242-5015
Yards: 2613, Par: 35, Holes: 9
Hubbard Trail CC, Rt. 2, Hoopeston, 60942, 217-748-6759
Yards: 3086, Par: 35, USGA: 69.2, Holes: 9, Pro: Jim Opp
Idlewild CC, Dixie Hwy. & Flossmoor Rd., Flossmoor, 60422, 312-798-0514
Yards: 6393, Par: 72, USGA: 70.5, Holes: 18, Pro: Larry Anderson
Illini CC, 1601 Illini R.d, Springfield, 62704, 217-546-2830
Yards: 6522, Par: 71, USGA: 70.5, Holes: 18, Pro: Chuck Rowland
Illinois State Univ. GC, Gregory St., Normal, 61761, 309-438-8065
Yards: 6326, Par: 71, USGA: 69.7, Holes: 18, Pro: Harland Kilborn
Indian Bluff GC, 6200 78th Ave., Milan, 61263, 309-799-3868
Yards: 5674, Par: 70, USGA: 66.8, Holes: 18, Pro: Craig Miller
Indian Boundary GC, 8600 W. Forest Preserve Dr., Chicago, 60634,
312-625-9630   Yards: 6003, Par: 70, Holes: 18
Indian Creek G&CC, Fairbury, 61739, 815-692-2655
Par: 35, Holes: 9
Indian Hills GC, SR-2, Mt. Vernon, 62864, 618-244-4905
Yards: 6100, Par: 72, USGA: 69.7, Holes: 18, Pro: Randy Arnett
Indian Hills GC, Indian Trail Dr., Centralla, 62864
Indian Hills GC, 1 Indian Hills Rd., Winnetka, 60093, 312-251-4584
Yards: 6325, Par: 71, USGA: 70.6, Holes: 18, Pro: Richard Wagley
Indian Lakes GC, 250 W. Schick Rd., Bloomingdale, 60108, 312-529-0200
Yards: 6580, Par: 72, USGA: 72.4, Holes: 18, Pro: Randy McPherran
Indian Oaks CC, Preserve Rd., Shabbona, 60550, 815-824-2202
Yards: 3551, Par: 37, USGA: 36.5, Holes: 9, Pro: Curt Biarnesen
Indian Springs CC, RR 2, Saybrook, 61770, 309-475-4111
Yards: 3255, Par: 36, USGA: 70.8, Holes: 9, Pro: Tom Kearfott
Indian Valley CC, Rt. 83 & 45, Mundelein, 60060, 312-566-1313
Yards: 6173, Par: 72, USGA: 68.1, Holes: 18
Ingersoll GC, W. State & Daisyfield Rd., Rockford, 61101, 815-968-9742
Yards: 5938, Par: 70, Holes: 18, Pro: Dave Claeyssen
Inwood GC, US-52, Joliet, 60436, 815-725-1407
Yards: 6296, Par: 71, Holes: 18
Iron Horse GC, 1765 N. Milwaukee Ave., Libertyville, 60048, 312-362-8700
Yards: 690, Par: 27, Holes: 9
Itasca CC, Walnut & Orchard Rd., Itasca, 60143, 312-773-1800
Yards: 6762, Par: 72, USGA: 72.2, Holes: 18, Pro: Phil Benson
Jackson CC, CC Rd., Murphysboro, 62966, 618-684-2387
Yards: 5897, Par: 71, USGA: 66.6, Holes: 18, Pro: Jesse Barge
Jackson Park GC, 64th & Stony Island Ave., Chicago, 60629, 312-853-3636
Yards: 5538, Par: 69, Holes: 18
Jacksonville CC, CC Rd., Jacksonville, 62650, 217-245-7717
Yards: 6500, Par: 72, USGA: 69.0, Holes: 18, Pro: Pete Kuklinski
Jasper County CC, SR-1, Newtn, 62448, 618-783-3790
Yards: 3121, Par: 36, Holes: 9
Joe Louis The Champ GC, 131st & Halstead St, Riverdale, 60627, 312-849-1731
Yards: 6524, Par: 71, USGA: 69.1, Holes: 18
Joliet CC, 1009 Spencer Rd., Joliet, 60433, 815-723-9613
Yards: 6440, Par: 72, USGA: 70.7, Holes: 18, Pro: John Walsh

Kankakee Elks, RR 3, St. Anne, 60964, 815-937-9547
Yards: 6600, Par: 71, USGA: 68.8, Holes: 18, Pro: Ed McCollough
Kankakee, 2900 Cobb Blvd., Kankakee, 60901, 815-933-6615
Yards: 5721, Par: 70, USGA: 66.9, Holes: 18, Pro: Paul Reinking
Kaskaskia CC, R.R. 2, Arcola, 61910, 217-268-3001
Yards: 2999, Par: 35, Holes: 9
Kaufman Park GC, US-24 West, Eureka, 61530, 309-467-2523
Yards: 2767, Par: 34, Holes: 9, Pro: Richard Holdley
Kellogg CC—18 hole course, 7716 Randor St., Peoria, 61615, 309-691-0293
Yards: 6370, Par: 72, USGA: 68.4, Holes: 18, Pro: Louis Carter Jr
Kellogg GC, 7716 Radnor, Peoria, 61615, 309-691-0293
Yards: 6370, Par: 72, Holes: 18
Ken Loch Golf Links, 1 S. 601 Finley Rd., Lombard, 60148, 312-620-9665
Yards: 1840, Par: 30, Holes: 9
Kishwauke CC, 1901 Sycamore Rd., De Kalb, 60115, 815-758-6848
Yards: 6057, Par: 72, USGA: 70.4, Holes: 18, Pro: Dave O'Neal
Knight's of Col Par 3, 700 S 36th St., Quincy, 62301, 217-222-1000
Yards: 1300, Par: 27, Holes: 9
Knollwood GC, 1890 Waukegan Rd., Lake Forest, 60045, 312-234-1600
Yards: 6607, Par: 72, USGA: 72.2, Holes: 18, Pro: Sherman Finger
Lacoma GC—9 hole, 8080 Dunleith Dr., East Dubuque, 61025, 815-747-3874
Yards: 1000, Par: 27, Holes: 9, Pro: Dana Schrack
Lacoma GC—18 hole, 8080 Dunleith Dr., East Dubuque, 61025, 815-747-3874
Yards: 6661, Par: 71, Holes: 18, Pro: Dana Schrack
Lacon CC, SR-17, Lacon, 61540, 309-246-7650
Yards: 2142, Par: 34, USGA: 33.5, Holes: 9, Pro: Gary Ehringer
Lagrange CC, 620 S. Brainard, La Grange, 60525, 312-352-0066
Yards: 6587, Par: 71, USGA: 71.6, Holes: 18, Pro: Wm. Johnstone
Lake Barrington Shores GC, 40 Shore Line Road, Barrington, 60010, 312-382-4240 Yards: 6392, Par: 71, USGA: 70.4, Holes: 18, Pro: Chas. Carpenter
Lake Bluff GC, Blair Park, Lake Bluff, 60044, 312-234-6771
Yards: 6457, Par: 72, USGA: 69.9, Holes: 18, Pro: C. McDernmand
Lake Bracken CC, RR 3, Galesburg, 61401, 309-343-5915
Yards: 6024, Par: 70, USGA: 67.8, Holes: 18, Pro: Joe Butler
Lake Calhoun GC, LaFayette Hwy. 17, LaFayette, 61449, 309-995-3343
Yards: 3015, Par: 36, USGA: 68.4, Holes: 9, Pro: Greg Stalter
Lake Carroll CC, Ironwood Boulevard, Shannon, 61078, 815-493-2808
Yards: 3394, Par: 36, Holes: 9, Pro: Duane Kloepping
Lake Erie, Lake Erie Dr., Erie, 61250, 309-659-2250
Yards: 3055, Par: 36, USGA: 68.0, Holes: 9
Lake Park GC, 1175 Howard St., Des Plaines, 60018, 312-827-7930
Yards: 1515, Par: 54, Holes: 18
Lake Shore CC, 1255 Sheridan Rd., Glencoe, 60022, 312-835-3000
Yards: 6500, Par: 71, USGA: 71.7, Holes: 18, Pro: Bob Koschman
Lakeview CC, US Rt. 45, Loda, 60948, 217-386-2335
Yards: 3220, Par: 36, USGA: 70.3, Holes: 9
Lakewoiod Golf Ass'n., SR-78, Bath, 62617, 309-546-2930
Yards: 3250, Par: 36, USGA: 36.1, Holes: 9
Lakewood GC, Havana, 62644, 309-546-2274
Par: 36, Holes: 9
Lansing CC, 186th & Wentworth Ave., Lansing, 60438, 312-474-7500
Yards: 4600, Par: 71, Holes: 18
Ledges CC, 7111 McCurry Rd., Roscoe, 61073, 815-389-9981
Yards: 6708, Par: 72, USGA: 71.6, Holes: 18, Pro: Phil Beyers
Leisure Village GC, 7313 E. Leisure Village, Fox Lake, 60020, 312-587-6795
Yards: 906, Par: 27, Holes: 9

Lena GC, W. Lena St., Lena, 61048, 815-369-5513
Yards: 2805, Par: 35, USGA: 33.0, Holes: 9
Leroy CC, R.F.D. 1, Leroy, 61752, 309-962-3421
Yards: 2850, Par: 36, USGA: 68.0, Holes: 9, Pro: Todd Zimmerman
Lincoln Elks Club, R.R. 1, Lincoln, 62656, 217-732-4010
Yards: 6000, Par: 71, USGA: 68.9, Holes: 18, Pro: Rick Pettit
Lincoln Greens, 700 E. Lake Dr., Springfield, 62707, 217-786-4000
Yards: 6600, Par: 72, USGA: 71.0, Holes: 18, Pro: Miles Horton
Lincolnshire CC—#1, 390 E. Richton Rd., Crete, 60417, 312-672-5411
Yards: 6120, Par: 72, USGA: 70.3, Holes: 18, Pro: J. Niestodziany
Lincolnshire Fields CC, 2000 Byrnebruck St., Champaign, 61821, 217-352-1911
Yards: 6792, Par: 72, USGA: 70.5, Holes: 18, Pro: John Mulliken
Links GC, Nichols Park, Jacksonville, 62650, 217-243-3212
Yards: 6435, Par: 72, USGA: 69.0, Holes: 18, Pro: Gary Church
Litchfield GC, Hillsboro Rd., Litchfield, 62056, 217-324-4115
Yards: 3040, Par: 35, Holes: 9
Lochaven CC, Lochaven Rd., Alton, 62002, 618-466-2441
Yards: 6421, Par: 72, USGA: 70.1, Holes: 18, Pro: Mike Halcomb
Lockport G & Rec Club, High Rd., Lockport, 60441, 815-838-8692
Yards: 2455, Par: 33, Holes: 9
Lone Oak CC, Rt. 1, Carrollton, 62016, 217-942-6166
Yards: 2100, Par: 32, Holes: 9
Longwood CC, 3200 E. Steger Rd., Steger, 60475, 312-758-1811
Yards: 6500, Par: 70, USGA: 69.2, Holes: 18, Pro: Bob Tintari
Macktown GC, 2221 Freeport Rd., Rockton, 61072, 815-624-9931
Yards: 5800, Par: 71, USGA: 66.2, Holes: 18
Macomb CC, Hickory Grove, Macomb, 61455, 309-837-2132
Yards: 3286, Par: 36, USGA: 34.7, Holes: 9, Pro: Gary Sutton
Madison GC, 2735 Martin Luther King Jr. Dr, Peoria, 61604, 309-673-7161
Yards: 5332, Par: 69, Holes: 18
Manteno Muni GC, Barnard Rd., Manteno, 61342, 815-468-8827
Yards: 6500, Par: 72, USGA: 67.0, Holes: 18, Pro: John Krutilla
Maple Crest GC, 6851 Joliet Rd., LaGrange, 60525, 312-246-2893
Yards: 3463, Par: 45, Holes: 12
Maple Lane CC, RR 1, Elmwood, 61529, 309-742-8212
Yards: 3220, Par: 35, Holes: 9
Marissa Recr. Area GC, Marissa, 62257, 618-295-2889
Yards: 3500, Par: 36, Holes: 9
Marriot Lincolnshire GC, 1 Marriott Dr., Chicago, 60015
Mattoon G & CC, CC Rd., Mattoon, 61938, 217-234-8831
Yards: 6450, Par: 72, Holes: 18, Pro: Ike Bailey
McHenry CC, 820 N. John St., McHenry, 60050, 815-385-3435
Yards: 6300, Par: 71, USGA: 69.6, Holes: 18, Pro: Don Habjan
McLeansboro GC, RR-1, McLeansboro, 62859, 618-643-2400
Yards: 3100, Par: 36, Holes: 9
Meadow Woods CC, SR-161, Centralia, 62801, 618-532-1121
Yards: 3004, Par: 36, Holes: 9
Medinah CC—#1, Medinah Rd., Midinah, 62666, 312-773-1700
Yards: 6660, Par: 70, USGA: 72.8, Holes: 18, Pro: Robert Hickman
Mendota GC, RR 2, Mendota, 61342, 815-538-7241
Yards: 6015, Par: 36, USGA: 68.2, Holes: 9, Pro: Louis Lang
Metropolis CC, US-45, Metropolis, 62960, 618-524-4414
Yards: 5731, Par: 34, Holes: 18
Mid-Iron GC, 1250 Bell Road, Lemont, 708-257-3340
Yards: 1717, Par: 31, Holes: 9

Midlane GC, 14565 Yorkhouse Rd., Wadsworth, 60083, 312-244-1990
Yards: 6449, Par: 72, USGA: 71.1, Holes: 18
Midlothian CC, 147th & Cicero Ave., Midlothian, 60445, 312-233-1946
Yards: 6675, Par: 72, USGA: 70.5, Holes: 18, Pro: Don Pauley
Minnie Monesse GC, Yellowhead Twp., Grant Park, 60940, 815-465-6653
Yards: 6200, Par: 71, USGA: 68.1, Holes: 18, Pro: Mark English
Monmouth CC, CC Lane, Monmouth, 61462, 309-734-7909
Yards: 3025, Par: 34, USGA: 68.0, Holes: 9, Pro: Gary Trotter
Monticello GC, 720 W. Marion St., Monticello, 61856, 217-762-2831
Yards: 3004, Par: 36, Holes: 9
Mount Mariah CC, Rt. 1, Nauvoo, 62354, 217-453-2417
Yards: 2565, Par: 34, Holes: 9
Mt. Hawley CC, 7724 N. Knoxville, Peoria, 61614, 309-691-6731
Yards: 6350, Par: 72, USGA: 70.7, Holes: 18
Mt. Prospect GC, 600 See Gwum, Mt. Prospect, 60056, 312-259-4200
Yards: 6100, Par: 71, Holes: 18, Pro: Tom Norton
Naperville CC, 25 W. 570 Chicago Ave., Naperville, 60540, 312-355-0747
Yards: 6450, Par: 71, USGA: 70.5, Holes: 18, Pro: Ken Sirois
Nelson Park GC, 200 N. Nelson Blvd., Decatur, 62521, 217-422-7241
Yards: 4800, Par: 65, USGA: 61.0, Holes: 18, Pro: Rick Anderson
Newman GC, 2219 W. Nebraska Ave., Peoria, 61604, 309-674-1663
Yards: 6387, Par: 71, Holes: 18
North County CC, 703 West Market, Redbud, 62278, 618-282-7963
Yards: 3000, Par: 35, Holes: 9
North Shore CC, 1340 Glenview Rd., Glenview, 60025, 312-724-9240
Yards: 6688, Par: 72, USGA: 72.2, Holes: 18, Pro: Bill Ogden
Northmoor G & CC—#1, 820 Edgewood Rd., Highland Park, 60035,
312-432-6092   Yards: 3600, Par: 36, USGA: 70.3, Holes: 9, Pro: Harvey Bott Jr.
Northmoor GC, 5805 N. Knoxville St., Peoria, 61614, 309-691-8361
Yards: 6127, Par: 70, USGA: 67.1, Holes: 18, Pro: Louis Carter Jr
Norton Knolls GC, Reel St., Oakland, 61943, 217-346-3102
Yards: 2800, Par: 34, USGA: 31.2, Holes: 9, Pro: Allen Parkes
Oak Brook GC, 2606 York Rd., Oak Brook, 60521, 312-990-3032
Yards: 6145, Par: 72, USGA: 68.9, Holes: 18, Pro: Vince DiTella
Oak Brook GC, RR 3 Box 327B, Edwardsville, 62025, 618-656-5600
Yards: 6300, Par: 71, USGA: 68.2, Holes: 18, Pro: Larry Suhre
Oak Club of Genoa GC, Genoa, 60135, 815-784-5678
Par: 72, Holes: 18
Oak Glen Golf, SR-33, Robinson, 62454, 618-592-3030
Yards: 5797, Par: 35, USGA: 67.0, Holes: 9
Oak Hills GC, 13248 S. 76th Ave., Palos Heights, 60463, 312-448-5544
Yards: 2950, Par: 35, USGA: 34.0, Holes: 9, Pro: Terry Lowe
Oak Leaf CC, R.R. 2, Girard, 62640, 217-627-3015
Yards: 2236, Par: 32, Holes: 9
Oak Meadows GC, 900 N. Wood Dale Rd., Addison, 60101, 312-595-0071
Yards: 6718, Par: 71, USGA: 71.9, Holes: 18, Pro: Mike Buros
Oak Park CC, Armitage Ave. & Thatcher, Elmwood Park, 60635, 312-456-7600
Yards: 6800, Par: 72, USGA: 71.2, Holes: 18, Pro: Steve Dunning
Oak Run GC, RR 1, Dahinda, 61243, 309-879-2582
Yards: 3229, Par: 36, USGA: 35.3, Holes: 9, Pro: R. W. Stinger
Oak Springs GC, R.R. 1, St. Anne, 60964, 815-937-1648
Yards: 6354, Par: 72, USGA: 69.6, Holes: 18
Oak View CC, SR-94, Aledo, 61231, 309-582-7916
Yards: 2257, Par: 33, Holes: 9
Oaks GC, The, R.R. 1, Springfield, 62707, 217-528-5544
Yards: 6150, Par: 70, USGA: 67.0, Holes: 18, Pro: Chris Bivens

Oakwood CC, US-6, Moline, 61265,   309-799-5558
Yards: 6588, Par: 71, USGA: 72.1, Holes: 18, Pro: Kurt Kretchman
Old Elm Club, 800 Old Elm Rd., Highland Park, 60035,   312-432-6272
Yards: 6365, Par: 73, USGA: 69.6, Holes: 18, Pro: Dow Wegrzwn
Old Oak CC, 143rd & Parker Rd., Orland Park, 60462,   312-349-3344
Yards: 6357, Par: 71, USGA: 68.2, Holes: 18, Pro: A. J. Lieponis
Old Orchard CC, RR 2, Pittsfield, 62363,   217-285-9041
Yards: 3005, Par: 36, USGA: 69.0, Holes: 9
Old Wayne GC—18 hole course, Klein Road, West Chicago, 60185,
312-231-1350   Yards: 6590, Par: 72, USGA: 71.4, Holes: 18, Pro: Frank Kruloc
Olympia Fields CC, 2800 CC Dr., Olympia Fields, 60461,   312-748-0495
Yards: 6567, Par: 72, USGA: 71.7, Holes: 18, Pro: John Spiropalua
Orchard Hills CC, 38342 N. Green Bay Rd., Waukegan, 60087,   312-336-5118
Yards: 6529, Par: 72, USGA: 70.9, Holes: 18
Oregon GC, Daysville Rd., Oregon, 61061,   815-732-7405
Yards: 2990, Par: 35, USGA: 33.6, Holes: 9, Pro: Ken Ledene
Palisades GC, 6002 SR-84, Savanna, 61074,   815-273-2141
Yards: 2551, Par: 33, Holes: 9, Pro: Ronald Hagen
Palos CC—18 hole course, 131st SW Hwy., Palos Park, 60464,   312-448-6550
Yards: 6450, Par: 72, USGA: 70.0, Holes: 18
Pana CC, SE of edge of Pana, Pana, 62557,   217-562-2641
Yards: 2711, Par: 35, Holes: 9, Pro: Biaigo Frisina
Par 3 GC—#1, 2205 S. Neil St., Champaign, 61820,   217-359-3722
Yards: 909, Par: 27, Holes: 9, Pro: Robert Nelson
Par 3 GC, Wolf Rd. & 62nd St., LaGrange, 60525,   312-246-9848
Yards: 1737, Par: 27, Holes: 9
Park Forest Mun. CC, 200 Forest Blvd., Park Forest, 60466,   312-747-0303
Yards: 1630, Par: 27, Holes: 9, Pro: Wayne Soloman
Park Ridge CC, 636 N. Prospect Ave., Park Ridge, 60068,   312-823-3101
Yards: 6800, Par: 70, Holes: 18, Pro: Ken Weiler
Parkview GC, 2200 E. Broadway, Pekin, 61554,   309-346-8494
Yards: 5908, Par: 70, USGA: 66.4, Holes: 18
Pasfield Park GC, 1700 W. Lawrence, Springfield, 62704,   217-787-0517
Yards: 2379, Par: 34, USGA: 31.0, Holes: 9, Pro: Nick Hoffman
Pekin CC, 310 CC Dr., Pekin, 61554,   309-346-6888
Yards: 6843, Par: 72, USGA: 70.8, Holes: 18, Pro: Dean Grinon
Perry County CC, RR 2, Tamaroa, 62888,   618-357-8712
Yards: 6000, Par: 70, Holes: 18, Pro: Larry Emery
Pestwick CC, 601 Prestwick Dr., Frankfort, 60423,   815-469-2136
Yards: 6300, Par: 72, USGA: 71.6, Holes: 18, Pro: Jim Arendt
Peter "N" Jans GC, 1031 Central St., Evanston, 60201,   312-475-9173
Yards: 3608, Par: 34, Holes: 18, Pro: Patty McLean
Phillips Park GC, US Hwy 30, Aurora, 60507,   312-898-7352
Yards: 5931, Par: 71, USGA: 67.0, Holes: 18, Pro: Ted Brodeur
Pine Crest GC, SR 10 & 29 N, Mason City, 62443,   217-482-3349
Yards: 2766, Par: 35, USGA: 35.0, Holes: 9, Pro: Bill Brickell
Pine Hills GC, S. Ottawa Twp. Rt. 4, Ottawa, 61350,   815-434-3985
Yards: 3200, Par: 35, USGA: 67.9, Holes: 9, Pro: Tim Spula
Pine Meadow GC, 1 Pine Meadow Lane, Mundelein, 60060,   312-566-4653
Yards: 7129, Par: 72, USGA: 69.5, Holes: 18, Pro: Joe Jemsek
Pinnacle CC, Knoxville Rd, Milan, 61264,   309-787-5446
Yards: 6238, Par: 71, USGA: 69.7, Holes: 18, Pro: Larry GIllam
Pistakee GC, 815 W. Bay Rd., Pistakee, 60959,   815-385-9854
Yards: 3027, Par: 36, Holes: 9
Plum Tree Natl. GC, 19511 Lemboke Rd., Harvard, 60033,   815-943-7474
Yards: 6648, Par: 72, USGA: 71.5, Holes: 18, Pro: George Jackson

Pontiac Elks CC, Pontiac, 61764, 815-842-1249
Par: 72, Holes: 18
Popular Creek GC, 1400 Eric Drive, Hoffman Estates, 60195, 312-884-0219
Yards: 6122, Par: 70, USGA: 68.9, Holes: 18, Pro: Jim Karnas
Pottawatomie GC, N. 2nd Ave., St. Charles, 60174, 312-584-8356
Yards: 3005, Par: 36, USGA: 69.0, Holes: 9, Pro: Jim Wheeler
Prairie Lake GC, Rt. 2 Miller Twp., Marseilles, 61341, 815-795-5107
Yards: 3630, Par: 37, USGA: 67.5, Holes: 9, Pro: "Harpo"
Prestbury CC, Buckingham Dr., Aurora, 60504, 312-466-4177
Yards: 2750, Par: 33, USGA: 64.1, Holes: 9, Pro: Ron Braunsky
Prophet Hills CC, Rt. 2, Prophetstown, 61277, 815-537-5226
Yards: 2772, Par: 35, Holes: 9
Quail Creek, Rt. 1, Robinson, 62454, 618-544-8674
Yards: 6131, Par: 72, USGA: 70.5, Holes: 18, Pro: Rick Bundy
Quail Meadows GC, 2215 Highview Rd., Washington, 61571, 309-694-3139
Yards: 6902, Par: 72, USGA: 71.5, Holes: 18, Pro: Bob Pruitt
Quincy CC, 24th & State St., Quincy, 62301, 217-222-1052
Yards: 6149, Par: 70, USGA: 70.0, Holes: 18, Pro: Lynn Rosely
Rail GC Inc., Peoria Rd., R.R. 5, Rt. 124 N, Springfield, 62702, 217-525-0365
Yards: 6883, Par: 72, USGA: 72.5, Holes: 18, Pro: Vince Alfonso
Ramsey Lake GC, Ramsey Lake Rd., Ramsey, 62080, 618-423-2261
Yards: 2750, Par: 35, Holes: 9, Pro: Tim Reiss
Randall Oaks GC, 37 W. 361 Binnie Rd., W. Dundall, 60185, 312-428-5661
Yards: 6129, Par: 72, USGA: 67.7, Holes: 18, Pro: Marvin Oglesby
Ravinia Green GC, 1200 Sanders Rd., Riverwoods, 62561, 312-945-6200
Yards: 6700, Par: 72, USGA: 70.9, Holes: 18, Pro: Jim Holmes
Ravisloe CC, 179th & Park Ave., Homewood, 60430, 312-799-3500
Yards: 3535, Par: 70, USGA: 70.3, Holes: 18, Pro: Tony Makarek
Red Barn CC, Wagon Wheel Resort, Rockton, 61109, 815-624-8711
Yards: 1600, Par: 28, Holes: 9, Pro: G. Flemming
Richland County CC, RR 6, Olney, 62450, 618-395-1661
Yards: 3005, Par: 35, Holes: 9, Pro: Pat Reed
Ridge CC, 10522 S. California, Chicago, 60608, 312-238-9400
Yards: 6069, Par: 70, USGA: 68.6, Holes: 18, Pro: Vince Milweski
Ridgemoor Country, 6601 W. Gunnison St., Chicago, 60656, 312-867-8400
Yards: 6454, Par: 72, USGA: 70.5, Holes: 18, Pro: Paul Colton
River Forest GC, 15 W. 469 Grand Ave., Elmhurst, 60126, 312-279-5444
Yards: 6497, Par: 71, USGA: 71.1, Holes: 18
River Oaks GC, 1 Park Ave., Calumet City, 60409, 312-868-4090
Yards: 6416, Par: 72, USGA: 70.0, Holes: 18
Riverside GC, 26th & Des Planes, N. Riverside, 60546, 312-447-3700
Yards: 6039, Par: 70, USGA: 69.9, Holes: 18, Pro: Bill Heald
Riverview Gardens, Murphysboro, 62966, 618-687-2244
Par: 27, Holes: 9
Rob Roy CC, 505 E. McDonald Rd., Prospect Heights, 60070, 312-253-4544
Yards: 3126, Par: 36, USGA: 68.5, Holes: 9, Pro: Jim Hahn
Robert Black GC, 2045 W. Pratt, Chicago, 60645, 312-853-3636
Yards: 2600, Par: 33, Holes: 9, Pro: Ignatius Vitale
Rock Island Arsenal GC, Rock Island Arsenal, Rock Island, 61201,
309-793-1604   Yards: 6244, Par: 71, USGA: 68.6, Holes: 18, Pro: Hank Stukart
Rock River CC, 3901 Dixon Rd., Rock Falls, 61071, 815-625-2322
Yards: 5240, Par: 70, USGA: 68.1, Holes: 18, Pro: Paul Attard
Rock Spring GC, Rock Springs Park, Alton, 62002, 618-465-9898
Yards: 3053, Par: 35, Holes: 9
Rockford CC, 2500 Willoughby & Oxford, Rockford, 61107, 815-968-9811
Yards: 6617, Par: 71, USGA: 71.5, Holes: 18, Pro: Jack Halverson

Rogala Public GC, W. Rt. 16, Matoon, 61938, 217-235-5581
Yards: 3069, Par: 36, USGA: 37.3, Holes: 9
Rolling Green CC, 750 North Rand Rd., Arlington Heights, 60004, 312-253-0400
Yards: 6336, Par: 72, USGA: 70.4, Holes: 18, Pro: Bill Ventresca
Rolling Greens CC, RR 1, Mt. Sterling, 62353, 217-773-9085
Yards: 3225, Par: 36, Holes: 9
Rolling Hills GC, Pierce Lane, Godfrey, 62035, 618-466-8363
Yards: 2551, Par: 35, Holes: 9
Royal Links, Fort Jesse & Airport Rds., Bloomington-Normal, 61701,
309-662-9440 Yards: 1219, Par: 27, Holes: 9
Ruth Lake CC, 6200 S. Madison, Hinsdale, 60521, 312-986-2060
Yards: 6250, Par: 71, USGA: 69.9, Holes: 18, Pro: Pat Dorgan
S. Glasgow's Westview GC–18, S. 36th St., Quincy, 62301, 217-223-7499
Yards: 6485, Par: 71, USGA: 70.6, Holes: 18, Pro: Steve Liter
Saint Elmo GC, RR 2, Saint Elmo, 62458, 618-827-3390
Yards: 3250, Par: 36, USGA: 70.4, Holes: 9, Pro: Gary Smith
Salem CC, South Marion, Salem, 62881, 618-548-2975
Yards: 3011, Par: 36, Holes: 9
Saline County G & CC, R.F.D. 3, Eldorado, 62930, 618-273-9002
Yards: 5973, Par: 70, USGA: 68.3, Holes: 18
Salt Creek GC—#1, PO Box 338, Itasca, 60143, 312-773-0184
Yards: 2104, Par: 31, Holes: 9, Pro: Greg W. Genz
Sandy Hollow GC, 2500 Sandy Hollow Rd., Rockford, 61109, 815-398-5980
Yards: 6128, Par: 71, USGA: 69.4, Holes: 18, Pro: Dave Claeyssen
Scott AFD GC, 375th Air Base Group, Scott AFB, 62225, 618-744-1400
Yards: 6524, Par: 72, USGA: 71.0, Holes: 18
Scovill GC, 3909 W. Main St., Decatur, 62522, 217-429-6243
Yards: 5615, Par: 70, USGA: 66.0, Holes: 18, Pro: Gary Schlosser
Scripps Park GC, R.R. 2, Rushville, 62681, 217-322-4444
Yards: 2880, Par: 35, Holes: 9
Shady Lawn—18 hole, 615 Dixie Hwy., Beecher, 60401, 312-946-2801
Yards: 6133, Par: 72, USGA: 67.8, Holes: 18, Pro: Brett Luckas
Shagbark GC, Onarga twp., RR 1, Onarga, 60955, 815-268-7691
Yards: 6106, Par: 36, USGA: 71.0, Holes: 9, Pro: Lewis Razzano
Shambolee GC, R.R. 1, Petersburg, 62675, 217-632-2140
Yards: 3603, Par: 36, USGA: 36.0, Holes: 9, Pro: Mike Monigolld
Shaw Creek GC, 300 ½Miller St., Bushnell, 61422, 309-772-3422
Yards: 2996, Par: 36, Holes: 9
Shawnee Hills CC, RR 4, Harrisburg, 62946, 618-253-7294
Yards: 3012, Par: 36, Holes: 9, Pro: Walt Siensglusz
Shelby CC, Rt. 4, Shelbyville, 64565, 217-774-3030
Yards: 3000, Par: 35, USGA: 67.9, Holes: 9
Shewami CC, 116 E. Walut, Watseka, 60970, 815-429-3769
Yards: 5801, Par: 71, USGA: 67.2, Holes: 18, Pro: Ken Cospa
Shiloh GC, 2400 Dowe Memorial Dr., Zion, 60099, 312-746-9733
Yards: 2900, Par: 36, Holes: 9
Short Hills CC, 2500 11th St., East Moline, 61244, 309-755-0618
Yards: 6366, Par: 71, USGA: 71.3, Holes: 18, Pro: Rbt. Van Fleet
Silver Oaks GC, Braidwood, 60408, 815-478-3371
Holes: 9
Silver Ridge GC, 54 Silver Ridge Sub,3069 North, Oregon, 61061, 815-734-4440
Yards: 3103, Par: 36, USGA: 35.6, Holes: 9, Pro: Liz Weir
Sinnissippi Park GC, 1300 N. Second St., Rockford, 61107, 815-226-0593
Yards: 3230, Par: 36, Holes: 9, Pro: Dave Clayssen
Skokie GC, 500 Washington, Glencoe, 60022, 312-835-0600
Yards: 6600, Par: 72, USGA: 72.3, Holes: 18, Pro: Robert Powers

Soangetaha CC, Lake Rice, Galesburg, 61401, 309-342-5410
Yards: 6224, Par: 72, USGA: 69.9, Holes: 18, Pro: John Jambor
South Shore GC, Rt. 2, River Rd., Momence, 60954, 815-472-4407
Yards: 6226, Par: 72, USGA: 68.1, Holes: 18, Pro: Jim Kasier
South Side, W. Grove Rd., Decatur, 62521, 217-428-4851
Yards: 6115, Par: 71, USGA: 58.9, Holes: 18, Pro: M. Welovich
Southwestern Lakes GC, RR 1, Percy, 62272, 618-497-2749
Yards: 3340, Par: 37, Holes: 9, Pro: Doby Burns
Spartan Meadows GC, Spartan Drive, Elgin, 60123, 312-695-2303
Yards: 6850, Par: 72, USGA: 69.9, Holes: 18, Pro: Wm. Fetty
Springbrook GC, 29 W. 231 83rd St., Naperville, 60565, 312-420-4215
Yards: 6459, Par: 72, USGA: 69.5, Holes: 18, Pro: John Long
Spring Creek GC, RR 1, Spring Valley, 61362, 815-894-2137
Yards: 6406, Par: 72, USGA: 69.9, Holes: 18, Pro: Mary Dagraedt
St. Andrews GC—#1, SR-59, W. Chicago, 60185, 312-231-3100
Yards: 6403, Par: 71, USGA: 70.3, Holes: 18
St. Catherines-Villa GC, Old Carpenter Rd., Edwardsville, 62025, 618-656-4224
Yards: 2856, Par: 35, Holes: 9
St. Charles GC, 4N 666 RT. 25, St. Charles, 60174, 312-377-9000
Yards: 6571, Par: 71, USGA: 71.2, Holes: 18, Pro: Regi Starzyk
St. Clair CC, S. 78th St., Belleville, 62223, 618-398-3402
Yards: 6600, Par: 72, USGA: 68.0, Holes: 18, Pro: Paul Hooser
Stauton CC, RR 1, Stauton, 62088, 618-635-2430
Yards: 3000, Par: 36, Holes: 9
Stockton Atwood GC, 3502 S. Golf Rd., Stockton, 61085, 815-947-3011
Yards: 3255, Par: 36, Holes: 9
Stonehenge GC, W. State Rt. 22 & Harbor Rd., Barrington, 60010, 312-381-8600
Yards: 7155, Par: 72, USGA: 71.5, Holes: 18, Pro: Scott Kulovsck
Streator CC, RR 4, Streator, 61364, 815-673-5551
Yards: 6224, Par: 72, USGA: 69.3, Holes: 9, Pro: Jack Wilson
Sugar Creek GC, 500 E. Van Buren, Villa Park, 62996, 312-834-3325
Yards: 2245, Par: 31, Holes: 9
Sullivan CC, RR 1, Sullivan, 61951, 217-728-4406
Yards: 3222, Par: 36, USGA: 70.3, Holes: 9, Pro: Tom Lowry
Summertime Nine GC, Salem, 62881, 618-822-6242
Par: 34, Holes: 9
Sun, Fun, Golf & Swim, Sun & Fun Drive, Decatur, 62522, 217-877-6622
Yards: 1280, Par: 28, Holes: 9
Sunset GC, Sunset Lane, Top of Sunset Hil, Mt. Morris, 61054, 815-734-4839
Yards: 3143, Par: 36, Holes: 9
Sunset Hills CC—18 hole cour, 1620 Summit Dr., Pekin, 61554, 309-347-7553
Yards: 6516, Par: 71, USGA: 69.9, Holes: 18, Pro: Fran Bourdeau
Sunset Ridge CC, 2100 Sunset Ridge Rd., Northbrook, 60065, 312-446-5222
Yards: 6562, Par: 71, USGA: 71.3, Holes: 18, Pro: Tom Wilcox
Sunset Valley GC, 1390 Sunset Rd., Highland Park, 60035, 312-432-7140
Yards: 6400, Par: 72, USGA: 69.8, Holes: 18, Pro: Tony Moselly
Swan Hills GC, R.R. 2, Avon, 61415, 309-465-3127
Yards: 3250, Par: 36, Holes: 9, Pro: Jim Owens
Sycamore Community GC, Rt. 64, Sycamore, 60178, 815-895-3884
Yards: 5931, Par: 71, USGA: 68.0, Holes: 18, Pro: Don Chavez
Sycamore Hills CC, RR #6 Clinton Rd., P.O.Box 968, Paris, 61944, 217-465-4031
Yards: 6125, Par: 72, USGA: 68.9, Holes: 18, Pro: Kelly Spaulding
Tall Oaks CC, Toluca, 61369, 815-452-9392
Par: 35, Holes: 9
Tam GC, 6700 E. Howard, Niles, 60648, 312-965-9697
Yards: 2414, Par: 33, USGA: 31.4, Holes: 9, Pro: L. Abernethy

Tamarack CC, 800 Tamarack Lane, O'Fallon, 62269, 618-632-6666
Yards: 6300, Par: 72, USGA: 69.5, Holes: 18, Pro: Howard Krener
Taylorville CC, Old State Rt. 29, Lincoln Trai, Taylorville, 62546, 217-824-5161
Yards: 2788, Par: 34, Holes: 9, Pro: Andy Kremphsky
Terrace Hills GC, 8515 Algouquin Rd., Algouquin, 60102, 312-658-4653
Yards: 6600, Par: 72, USGA: 69.1, Holes: 18
Terry Park GC, R.R. 1, Palmyra, 62674, 217-436-2203
Yards: 2456, Par: 33, Holes: 9
Thorngate CC, 600 Sanders Rd., Deerfield, 60015, 312-945-1105
Yards: 6435, Par: 71, USGA: 70.1, Holes: 18, Pro: Mike Harrigan
Thunderbird CC, 1010 E. NW Hwy., Barrington, 60010, 312-381-6500
Yards: 6200, Par: 70, USGA: 67.3, Holes: 18, Pro: Walt Wynarczyk
Timber Lake CC, 5501 W. Farmington Rd., Peoria, 61604, 309-674-2171
Yards: 2428, Par: 33, Holes: 9
Timber Trails CC, 11350 Plainfield Rd., LaGrange, 60525, 312-246-0275
Yards: 6197, Par: 71, USGA: 68.9, Holes: 18, Pro: Tom Byrd
Timberlake GC, R.R. 3, Sullivan, 61951, 217-797-6496
Yards: 2970, Par: 35, USGA: 69.1, Holes: 9, Pro: Larry Endsley
Tri City CC, RFD 1, Villa Grove, 61956, 217-268-3001
Yards: 2759, Par: 34, Holes: 9
Tri-City CC, RR 1, Augusta, 62311, 309-458-3226
Yards: 2637, Par: 34, Holes: 9
Triple Lakes GC, Triple Lakes Rd., Millstadt, 62260, 618-476-9985
Yards: 3127, Par: 35, Holes: 18
Troy Zigfield GC, 1501 75th St., Woodbridge, 60191, 312-985-9860
Yards: 1064, Par: 27, Holes: 9, Pro: Tim Troy
Tuckaway GC, SR-394, Crete, 60417, 312-946-2259
Yards: 5952, Par: 71, USGA: 66.9, Holes: 18, Pro: Marc Adduci
Tuckaway GC, Goodenow & Stony Island, Richton Park, 708-946-2259
Yards: 6185, Par: 71, Holes: 18
Turnberry CC, Turnbery Trail, Crystal Lake, 60014, 815-455-0501
Yards: 6620, Par: 72, USGA: 71.1, Holes: 18, Pro: Ralph Backe
Twin Creeks GC, Streator, 62364, 815-672-4220
Par: 36, Holes: 9
Twin Lakes GC, 400 W. 59th St., Westmont, 60559, 312-852-7167
Yards: 1688, Par: 29, Holes: 9
Twin Oaks GC, SR-9, Blandsville, 61420, 309-652-9519
Yards: 3004, Par: 35, USGA: 35.4, Holes: 9
Twin Oaks GC, SR-127, Greenville, 62246, 618-749-5611
Yards: 3190, Par: 36, USGA: 68.9, Holes: 9
Twin Orchard CC—#1, Old McHenry Rd., Long Grove, 60047, 312-634-3800
Yards: 6697, Par: 72, USGA: 72.1, Holes: 18, Pro: Earl Puckett
Twin Ponds GC, 4411 Northwest Hwy., Crystal Lake, 60014, 815-459-1110
Yards: 1351, Par: 28, Holes: 9, Pro: John Swenson
Union County CC, Anna, 62906, 618-833-7912
Par: 72, Holes: 18
University of Illinois GC—#1, 104 Huff Gym, Savoy, 61874, 217-359-5613
Yards: 6596, Par: 72, USGA: 72.0, Holes: 18
Urban Hills CC, 23520 Crawford Ave, Richton Park, 60471, 312-747-0306
Yards: 6881, Par: 72, USGA: 69.9, Holes: 18, Pro: Bruce Meyer
Urbana G & CC, CC Rd., Urbana, 61801, 217-367-8449
Yards: 6523, Par: 72, USGA: 70.6, Holes: 18, Pro: Jack Anrico
VA Hospital GC, Roosevelt Rd. & 5th Ave., Maywood, 60153, 312-261-6700
Yards: 685, Par: 24, Holes: 8
VA Hospital GC, SR-137, North Chicago, 60064, 708-688-1900
Yards: 3080, Par: 36, Holes: 9, Pro: Joe Sisolak

Valley Lo Sports Club, 2200 Tanglewood Dr., Glenview, 60025, 312-729-5550
Yards: 2208, Par: 55, Holes: 18, Pro: Don Gricus
Valley View Club, Cambridge, 61238, 309-937-2300
Yards: 2820, Par: 36, USGA: 34.8, Holes: 9
Vandalia G & VV, 1110 S. 8th St., Vandalia, 62471, 618-283-1365
Yards: 2604, Par: 35, USGA: 67.4, Holes: 9
Vermillion Hills CC, Terrysville R.d, Danville, 61832, 217-446-9226
Yards: 3100, Par: 35, USGA: 69.3, Holes: 9, Pro: Ed Biehl
Victorian GC, 11369 North Main Street, Rockton, 61072, 815-624-2057
Holes: 20
Villa Olivia CC, US Rt. 20 & Naperville Rd., Bartlett, 60103, 312-289-5200
Yards: 6100, Par: 70, USGA: 68.9, Holes: 18, Pro: Charley Tawse
Village Green CC, 2501 N. Midlothian Rd., Mundelein, 60060, 312-566-7373
Yards: 6235, Par: 70, USGA: 69.2, Holes: 18
Virginia CC, Virginia, 62691, 217-452-3488
Par: 35, Holes: 9
Waterloo CC, SR-3, Waterloo, 62298, 618-939-9810
Yards: 2511, Par: 34, Holes: 9
Wedgewood GC, Caton Farm Rd. & Rt. 59, Plainfield, 60544, 815-436-5677
Yards: 6756, Par: 72, USGA: 70.5, Holes: 18, Pro: Bob Murphy
Wee-Ma-Tuk Hills CC, RR 2, Cuba, 61427, 309-789-6208
Yards: 6269, Par: 72, USGA: 69.9, Holes: 18
Westgate Valley CC—#1, 131 Ridgeland Ave., Palos Heights, 60463,
312-385-1810   Yards: 6400, Par: 72, USGA: 68.2, Holes: 18, Pro: Ken Buss
Westlake CC, Westlake Dr., Jerseyville, 62052, 618-498-3713
Yards: 3000, Par: 35, Holes: 9
Westmoreland CC, 2601 Old Glenview Rd., Wilmette, 60091, 312-251-4600
Yards: 6643, Par: 72, USGA: 71.7, Holes: 18, Pro: Gary Vinder
White Pines GC—#1, 500 W. Jefferson St., Bensenville, 60106, 312-766-3360
Yards: 6394, Par: 72, USGA: 70.5, Holes: 18, Pro: Pete Longo
Wildwood GC, 2702 Wildwood Dr., Decatur, 62521, 217-429-4509
Yards: 1343, Par: 27, USGA: 26.0, Holes: 9
Willow Run GC, Mokena, 60448, 815-485-2119
Yards: 2950, Par: 37, Holes: 9
Wilmette GTC, Lake Ave & Harms Rd., Wilmette, 60091, 312-256-6100
Yards: 6068, Par: 70, USGA: 68.6, Holes: 18, Pro: Dean Lind
Windmills GC, Rio, 61472, 309-872-5321
Par: 32, Holes: 9
Wing Park GC, Wing Street, Elgin, 60123, 312-741-4819
Yards: 3195, Par: 36, Holes: 9, Pro: William Fetty
Winnetka GC, 1300 Oak St., Winnetka, 60093, 312-446-1488
Yards: 6472, Par: 71, Holes: 18
Wolf Creek GC, Pontiac, 61764, 815-842-9008
Par: 72, Holes: 18
Woodland CC, 902 E. Richardsn, Farmer City, 61842, 309-928-3215
Yards: 3072, Par: 36, USGA: 69.4, Holes: 9
Woodruff CC, Geougar Rd., Joliet, 60436, 815-722-1598
Yards: 5563, Par: 68, USGA: 64.8, Holes: 18, Pro: John Plat
Woodstock CC, 103120 CC Rd., Woodstock, 60098, 815-338-5355
Yards: 3000, Par: 35, USGA: 68.5, Holes: 9, Pro: Steve Hulka
Wyaton Hill GC, Rt. 5, Princeton, 64356, 815-872-2641
Yards: 6142, Par: 36, USGA: 33.7, Holes: 9, Pro: Max Halberg
Yorktown GC, Belleville, 62220, 618-233-2000
Par: 54, Holes: 18

Angel Hill GC, Rossville, 46065, 317-379-3533
Par: 36, Holes: 9
Augusta Hills GC, Albion, 46701, 219-636-2778
Par: 35, Holes: 9
Bass Lake CC, Knox, 46534, 219-772-2432
Par: 72, Holes: 18
Beachwood GC, Woodlawn Dr., Gary, 46222
Beacon Hills GC, Laporte, 46350, 219-324-4777
Par: 36, Holes: 9
Beeson Park GC, Winchester, 47394, 317-584-5151
Par: 36, Holes: 9
Benton County CC, Fowler, 47944, 317-884-1864
Par: 35, Holes: 9
Bicknell CC, Bicknell, 47512, 812-735-4518
Par: 70, Holes: 18
Big Boulder GC, Milford, 46542, 219-658-5927
Par: 31, Holes: 9
Birchtree GC, New Carlisle, 46552, 219-654-7311
Par: 67, Holes: 18
Bogey GC, Borden & Sellersburg Rd, Charlestown, 47111
Holes: 9
Briar Leaf GC, Laporte, 46350, 219-326-1992
Par: 72, Holes: 18
Broadmoor G&CC, 4300 W 81st Ave., Merrillville, 46410, 219-769-5444
Yards: 6300, Par: 72, Holes: 18
Brockway GC, Lapal, 46051, 317-534-4194
Par: 36, Holes: 9
Brownsburg GC, Brownsburg, 46112, 317-852-5530
Par: 36, Holes: 9
Calumet GC, 3920 W Ridge, Gary, 219-980-9484
Yards: 2700, Par: 35, Holes: 9
Canterbury Green CC, Fort Wayne, 46835, 219-486-4229
Par: 58, Holes: 18
Carroll County CC, Delphi, 46923, 317-564-2155
Par: 36, Holes: 9
Cedar Lake GC, Howe, 46746, 219-562-3923
Par: 71, Holes: 18
Chippendale GC, Kokomo, 46902, 317-453-7079 Par: 71, Holes: 27
Christian Creek GC, 116 W. Bristol St., South Bend, 46514
Clear Creek GC, Huntington, 46750, 219-344-1665
Par: 36, Holes: 9
Cold Springs GC, Hamilton, 46742, 219-488-2920
Par: 58, Holes: 18
Colonial Oaks Golf Club, 8218 Huguenard Rd., Fort Wayne, 46818,
219-489-5121 Yards: 5743, Par: 71, USGA: 67.1, Holes: 18, Pro: Pat Riley
Community GC, Pittsboro, 46167, 317-892-3335
Par: 35, Holes: 9
Cool Lake GC, Lebanon, 46052, 317-325-9271
Par: 70, Holes: 18
Country Meadows Golf Resort, Fremont, 46737, 219-495-4525
Par: 71, Holes: 18
Cressmoor CC, Hobart, 46342, 219-942-9300
Par: 72, Holes: 18
Crestview GC, Muncie, 47302, 317-289-6952
Par: 72, Holes: 27

Crooked Lake GC, Columbia City, 46725, 219-691-2157
Par: 36, Holes: 9
Decatur GC, Highway 224 W, Decatur, 46733
Holes: 9
Deer Valley GC, Franklin, 46131, 317-738-4441
Par: 36, Holes: 9
Eaton Creek GC, Route 1 Box 122, Fremont, 46737
Holes: 9
Eberhart-Petro Muni GC, Mishawaka, 46544, 219-255-5508
Par: 70, Holes: 18
Edwood Glen GC, West Lafayette, 47906, 317-463-1100
Par: 70, Holes: 18
Elbel Park GC, 26595 Auten Rd., South Bend, 46628
Elk Run GC, Aurora, 47001, 812-926-3595
Par: 34, Holes: 9
Elks CC, Seymour, 47274, 812-522-1662
Par: 70, Holes: 18
Etna Acres GC, Andrews, 46702, 219-468-2906
Par: 36, Holes: 9
Fountain Head GC, Plymouth, 46563, 219-936-4405
Par: 72, Holes: 18
Frazanda GC, Huntington, 46750, 219-468-2579
Par: 36, Holes: 9
The Garrett CC, Garrett, 46738, 219-357-3616
Par: 34, Holes: 9
Geneva Hills CC, Clinton, 47842, 317-832-8384
Par: 72, Holes: 18
GG of Brown County, Nashville, 47448, 812-988-4818
Par: 36, Holes: 9
Grand Oak GC, 29755 Carolina Trace Road, West Harrison, 47060
Holes: 18
Grand Oak GC, 28755 Carolina Trace Road, West Harrison, 47060
Holes: 18
Green Acres CC, Paoli, 47454, 812-723-2110
Par: 35, Holes: 9
Green Acres GC, Kokomo, 46901, 317-883-5771
Par: 72, Holes: 18
Griffith GC, 1901 N. Cline, Griffith, 219-932-3223
Yards: 2653, Par: 54, Holes: 18
Hart GC, Marion, 46952, 317-662-8236
Par: 72, Holes: 18
Hazelden CC, Brook, 47922, 219-275-7771
Par: 70, Holes: 18
Helfrich GC, 1550 Mesker Park Dr., Evansville, 47712, 812-428-0667
Yards: 6008, Par: 71, Holes: 18, Pro: Don Bisesi
Hendricks County GC, Danville, 46122, 317-745-3190
Par: 35, Holes: 9
Hickory Hills GC, Bluffton, 46714, 219-824-4510
Par: 36, Holes: 9
Hidden Valley GC, Angola, 46703, 219-665-6064
Par: 35, Holes: 9
Highland Hills GC, Roann, 46974, 219-982-2679
Par: 60, Holes: 18
Honeywell GC, Wabash, 46992, 219-563-8663
Par: 72, Holes: 18

Hoosier Hills GC, Cory, 47846, 812-864-2304
Par: 34, Holes: 9
Idlewold G&CC, Pendleton, 46064, 317-778-2053
Par: 71, Holes: 18
Indian Lakes GC, Batesville, 47006, 812-623-3660
Par: 36, Holes: 9
Indian Oaks GC, Peru, 46970, 317-473-7312
Par: 36, Holes: 9
Indian Ridge CC, Hobart, 46342, 219-942-6850
Par: 72, Holes: 18
Indian Springs GC, Trafalgar, 46181, 317-878-5926
Par: 32, Holes: 9
Jasper Muni GC, Jasper, 47546, 812-482-4600
Par: 71, Holes: 18
Juday Creek GC, Granger, 46530, 219-277-4653
Par: 72, Holes: 18
Kendallville Elks CC, Kendallville, 46755, 219-347-1500
Par: 36, Holes: 9
La Fontaine GC, Huntington, 46750, 219-356-5820
Par: 72, Holes: 18
La Grange CC, La Grange, 46761, 219-463-2906
Par: 71, Holes: 18
Lake Hills G&CC, 10001 W. 85th Ave., St. John, 46373, 219-365-8601
Yards: 5888, Par: 72, Holes: 27
Lake James GC, Angola, 46703, 219-833-3967
Par: 72, Holes: 18
Lake View GC, Marion, 46953, 317-998-7671
Par: 35, Holes: 9
Lakeside CC, Milan, 47031, 812-654-2440
Par: 34, Holes: 9
Lakeview CC, Eaton, 47338, 317-396-9010
Par: 72, Holes: 18
Lakeview GC, Loogootee, 47553, 812-295-9559
Par: 35, Holes: 9
Larimer Greens GC, 1017 Larimer Drive, Goshen, 46526, 219-533-1828
Par: 72, Holes: 18
Linton Muni GC, Linton, 47441, 812-847-4790
Par: 71, Holes: 18
Logansport CC, Logansport, 46947, 219-722-1110
Par: 71, Holes: 18
Lugene Links CC, Lake Village, 46536, 219-992-3337
Par: 36, Holes: 9
Maplewood GC, Muncie, 47303, 317-284-8007
Par: 72, Holes: 18
Matthews Park Muni GC, Clinton, 47842, 317-832-9016
Par: 36, Holes: 9
Maxwelton GC, Syracuse, 46567, 219-457-3504
Par: 72, Holes: 18
McArthur GC, 140 & Indianapolis, East Chicago, 219-391-8474
Yards: 1370, Par: 27, Holes: 9
Mohawk Hills GC, Carmel, 46032, 317-844-3112
Par: 35, Holes: 9
Moss Creek GC, Winamac, 46996, 219-595-7115
Par: 35, Holes: 9
Muscatatuck CC, North Vernon, 47265, 812-346-4615
Par: 36, Holes: 9

Nappanee Muni GC, Nappanee, 46550,   219-773-2725
Par: 36, Holes: 9
New Salisbury GC, New Salisbury, 47161,   812-347-2076
Par: 35, Holes: 9
North Branch GC, Greensburg, 47240,   812-663-6062
Par: 36, Holes: 9
Norwood GC, Huntington, 46750,   219-356-5929
Par: 71, Holes: 18
Oak Grove GC, Oxford, 47971,   317-385-2713
Par: 71, Holes: 18
Oak Knoll GC, Whitcomb Street, Crown Point, 46307,   219-663-3349
Yards: 5803, Par: 70, Holes: 18
Palmira G&CC, 1211 W. 109, St. John, 46373,   219-365-4331
Yards: 6878, Par: 71, Holes: 18
Pebble Brook GC, State Road 32 West, Noblesville, 46060
Holes: 18
Pheasant Valley CC, 3838 W 141 St., Crown Point,   219-663-5000
Yards: 6800, Par: 72, Holes: 18
Pleasant Run GC, 601 N. Arlington Ave, Indianapolis, 46219
Princeton CC, Princeton, 47670,   812-385-5669
Par: 35, Holes: 9
Riverbend GC, Fort Wayne, 46803,   219-485-2732
Par: 72, Holes: 18
Rochester Elks GC, Rochester, 46975,   219-223-4427
Par: 35, Holes: 9
Rolling Hills GC, Logansport, 46947,   219-722-3646
Par: 55, Holes: 18
Sandy Creek GC, Seymour, 47274,   812-522-8164
Par: 72, Holes: 18
Sandy Pines GC, Demotte, 46310,   219-987-3611
Par: 36, Holes: 18
Scherwood CC, 600 E. Joliet, Schererville,   219-865-2554
Yards: 6800, Par: 72, Holes: 18
South Bend GC, 25800 Country Club Dr., South Bend, 46619
South Gleason Park GC, 3400 Jefferson, Gary, 46401,   219-980-1089
Yards: 6300, Par: 71, Holes: 18
South Shore CC, 14400 Lakeshore Drive, Cedar Lake,   219-374-6070
Yards: 5644, Par: 70, Holes: 18
Spring-O-Mint GC, Bremen, 46506,   219-546-2640
Par: 72, Holes: 18
Stonehenge GC, Warsaw, 46580,   219-269-2902
Par: 32, Holes: 9
Summertree GC, 2323 W 101st Street, Crown Point, 46307,   219-663-0800
Yards: 6696, Par: 71, Holes: 18
Swanlake GC, 5319 Plymouth/La Pointe Trail, Plymouth, 46563,   219-936-9798
Par: 72, Holes: 36
Sycamore GC, North Manchester, 47965,   219-982-2279
Par: 72, Holes: 18
Tameka Woods GC, Trafalgar, 46181,   317-878-5926
Par: 72, Holes: 18
Tippecanoe GC, Monticello, 47960,   219-583-9977
Par: 72, Holes: 18
Tomahawk Hills GC, Jamestown, 46147,   317-676-6002
Par: 36, Holes: 9
Tri-State Univ. Zollner GC, Angola, 46703,   219-665-5812
Par: 72, Holes: 18

Turkey Creek Country Park GC, 6400 Harrison, Merrillville, 46410, 219-980-5170   Yards: 6300, Par: 70, Holes: 18
Turkey Run GC, Waveland, 47989,   317-435-2048
Par: 72, Holes: 18
Union City CC, Union City, 47390,   513-968-6518
Par: 36, Holes: 9
Wawasee G&CC, Syracuse, 46567,   219-457-3961
Par: 72, Holes: 18
Wedgewood GC, Rome City, 46784,   219-854-3788
Par: 70, Holes: 18
Westwood GC, Scottsburg, 47170,   812-752-3233
Par: 35, Holes: 9
Wicker Memorial Park GC, RTE. 41 and 6th, Highland, 46322,   219-838-9809
Par: 72, Holes: 18
Winding Branch GC, Cambridge City, 47327,   317-478-5638
Par: 72, Holes: 18

3730 G&CC, Box 61, Lowden, 52255,   319-944-7695   *Iowa*
Pro: Robert Mannen
5 x 80 G&CC, RR #1, Box 163, Menlo, 50164,   515-524-2345
Pro: Robert M Kane
Ackley CC, S. State Street, Ackley, 50601,   515-847-3475
Pro: Bonnie Poley
Albia CC, RR #3 Box 41, Albia, 52531,   515-932-5002
Pro: Jim Campbell
Alta G&CC, 601 East 6th Street, Alta, 51002,   712-284-2442
Pro: Loren Sherman
American Legion Rec., Marshalltown, 50158
American Legion CC, Box 82, Shenandoah, 51601,   712-246-2967
Pro: Jim Bonwell
Ames G&CC, RR 4, Ames, 50010,   515-232-8334
Pro: Jon Ward
Ankeny G&CC, 9268 NW 16th Street, Ankeny, 50021,   515-964-3647
Pro: Norma Righi
Aplington Rec. Complex, Highway 20 West, Aplington, 50604,   319-347-6059
Appanoose G&CC, RR #3, Box 821, Centerville, 52544,   515-856-2222
Pro: John Riggall
Audubon G&CC, South Division Street West, Audubon, 50025,   712-563-2348
Pro: Allan Jacobson
Aurelia GC, Aurelia, 51005,   712-434-5498
Pro: Steve Volkert
Avoca GC Inc, 1920 Willow, Avoca, 51521,   712-343-6979
Pro: Lorraine Mann
Backbone G&CC, Box 436, Strawberry Point, 52076,   319-933-4545
Pro: Betty Keppler
Ballard G&CC, Box 352, Huxley, 50124,   515-597-2266
Pro: Terry Frantum
Beaver Hills GC, P.O. Box 483, Cedar Falls, 50613,   319-266-9172
Pro: K. Dorrington
Beaver Meadows G&CC, Highway 14 N, Parkersburg, 50665,   319-346-1870
Pro: Maryann Bergman
Paullina GC, Box 327, Paullina, 51046,   712-448-3477
Pro: Steve Harton
Bedford GC, Highway 148, Bedford, 50833,   712-523-3126
Pro: Bob McCoy

Belle Plaine CC, 13th Avenue N, Belle Plaine, 52208,   319-442-3443
Pro: Paul Pippert
Belmond CC, RR, P. O. Box 37, Belmond, 50421,   515-444-4183
Pro: Jerry Wilhite
Bloomfield CC, P.O. Box 74, Bloomfield, 52537,   515-664-2089
Pro: Mary Owens
Brooklyn-Victor CC, P.O. Box 191, Brooklyn, 52211, 515-522-7608
Pro: Roger Nelson
Brooks GC, Hwy 71 North, Box 449, Okoboji, 51355,   712-332-5011
Pro: Larry Jansen
Burlington GC, 2124 Sunnyside, Burlington, 52601,   319-752-3720
Pro: Jack Richards
Byrnes Park GC, 1000 Fletcher Avenue, Waterloo, 50701,   319-234-9271
Par: 72, Holes: 18, Pro: Mark Lemon
Carroll CC, Highway 30 East, P.O. Box 426, Carroll, 51401,   712-792-1255
Pro: Joe Ward
Cedar Crest CC, Box 46, Columbus Junction, 52738,   319-728-2158
Pro: John Carpenter
Cedar Rapids CC, 550 27th Drive SE, Cedar Rapids, 52403,   319-362-4878
Pro: Jock Olson
Charles City CC, P.O. Box 68, Charles City, 50616,   515-228-6465
Pro: Ginny Franke
Cherokee CC, N. 11th Street, Cherokee, 51012,   712-225-3900
Pro: Pete Wildemann
Clinton CC, 1501 Harrison Drive, Clinton, 52732,   319-242-7032
Pro: Max Hines
Colfax GC, RR #2, Box 67, Colfax, 50054,   515-674-3776
Pro: Jim Hay
Conrad Grove Rec Inc, Box 220, Conrad, 50621,   515-366-2211
Pro: Mike Stubbs
Coon Rapids GC, P.O. Box 174, Coon Rapids, 50058,   712-684-2880
Pro: Mike Clouser
Countryside GC, Box 428, Armstrong, 50514,   712-864-3048
Pro: Harold Craig
Cresco CC, P.O. Box 4, Cresco, 52136,   319-547-2374
Pro: Jerry Stevicks
Crestwood Hills GC, Anita, 50020,   712-762-3803
Pro: Laveda Pine
Crow Valley GC, P.O. Box 856, Bettendorf, 52722,   319-359-1676
Pro: Jerry Mortier
Davenport GC, 490 E. Valley Dr., Box 27, Pleasant Valley, 52767,   319-332-4050
Pro: S. Stephenson
Dayton G & CC, Dayton, 50530,   515-547-2712
Pro: George Florea
Deerwood GC Inc, RR #1, Box 44, New London, 52645,   319-367-5216
Pro: John Alden
Denison CC, Donna Reed Drive, P.O. Box 422, Denison, 51442,   712-263-9809
Des Moines G & CC, P.O. Box 65520, West Des Moines, 50625,   515-225-1148
Pro: Scott Howe
Dubuque G & CC, 1800 Randall Place, Dubuque, 52001,   319-583-9158
Pro: Steve Groves
Dyersville G & CC, P.O. Box 237, Dyersville, 52040,   319-875-8497
Pro: June Platz
Dysart Recreation Inc., RR #2, Box 8, Dysart, 52224,   319-476-3207
Pro: Jean Hennings
Eagle Grove CC, P. O. Box 347, Eagle Grove, 50533,   515-448-4166

Echo Valley CC, 760 County Line Rd., Des Moines, 50321, 515-285-0101
Pro: Dave Bianchi
Edmundson GC, South M Extension, Oskaloosa, 52577, 515-673-5120
Pro: Jeff Smith
Ellis Park GC, 2000 Ellis Blvd. N.W., Cedar Rapids, 52404, 319-398-5180
Elmcrest CC, 1000 36th Street NE, Cedar Rapids, 52402, 319-363-7980
Pro: Larry Gladson
Elmhurts CC, 2214 So. 11th Street, Box 54, Oskaloosa, 52534, 515-673-5234
Pro: Max Shields
Elmwood CC, 1734 Country Club Lane, Marshalltown, 50158, 515-753-8111
Pro: Jerry Johnson
Emerald Hills GC, Box 517, 808 US 71, Arnolds Park, 51331, 712-332-5672
Pro: Bette Benit
Fairfield G & CC, 905 E. Harrison, Box 549, Fairfield, 52556, 515-472-3798
Pro: Marilyn Kane
Fairview GC, E. Muscatine Ave, Iowa City, 52240, 319-351-9454
Pro: Bob Mitchell
Fawn Creek CC, RR #3, Anamosa, 52205, 319-462-4155
Pro: Milt Meeks
Fillmore Fairways GC, 1780 Fairway Rd., Cascade, 52033, 319-852-3377
Flint Hills GC, RR #5, Box 269, Burlington, 52601, 319-752-8855
Pro: Gerry Walker
Fonda GC, Fonda, 50540, 712-288-6419
Forest City GC, P.O. Box 286, Forest City, 50436, 515-582-3250
Par: 34, Holes: 9, Pro: Craig Johnson
Fort Dodge, P. O. Box 1416, Fort Dodge, 50501, 515-955-8551
Pro: Craig Graham
Fort Madison CC, Box 353 High Point, Fort Madison, 52627, 319-372-1765
Pro: Rod Rogers
Fremont County GC, RR #1, Sidney, 51652, 712-374-2347
Pro: Jack Gibson
Friendly Fairways GC, Radcliffe, 50230, 515-899-7969
Pro: Lee Amundson
Gates Park GC, Waterloo, 50701, 319-291-4485
Par: 72, Holes: 18
Gateway Rec. Inc., Box 767, Monroe, 50170, 515-259-3246
Pro: Judy Brodersen
Geneva G & CC, 2507 Mulberry Ave, Muscatine, 52761, 319-262-8894
Pro: Steve Meckel
Glenwood Golf Corp, P. O. Box 170, Glenwood, 51534, 712-527-9798
Gowrie G & CC, P. O. Box 205, Gowrie, 50543, 515-352-3320
Pro: Ardell Gudbaur
Green Acres Club, Box 131, Donnellson, 52625, 319-835-5011
Green Valley CC, P. O. Box 2581, Sioux City, 51106, 712-276-4891
Pro: Helen Bobo
Greene County CC, S Elm St., P O Box 186, Jefferson, 50129, 515-386-4178
Greenfield G & CC, P. O. Box 96, Greenfield, 50849, 515-743-2113
Pro: Terry Buckner
Greenview GC I, P. O. Box 577, West Branch, 52358, 319-643-2100
Par: 36, Holes: 9, Pro: Mike McCarty
Grinnell CC, 13th & Park St, Grinnell, 50112, 515-236-5955
Pro: Terry Miller
Guthrie Center G & CC, Hwy 44 East, Guthrie Center, 50115, 515-747-3558
Pro: Gifford Covault
Guttenberg GC, Guttenburg, 52052, 319-252-1211

Hampton CC, RR #2, Hampton, 50441, 515-456-3256
Pro: Cathy Cooper
Happy Hollow, Corning, 50847, 515-322-4333
Pro: K. Wynn
Harlan G & CC, 2503 12th, Harlan, 51537, 712-755-5951
Pro: T. J. Gute
Hawarden GC, Highway 10 & Country Club Rd, Hawarden, 51023,
712-552-9917 Pro: Glenn Olsen
Hickory Grove CC, RR 1, Oelwein, 50662, 319-283-2674
Par: 36, Holes: 9, Pro: Barbara Darland
Hidden Hills GC, Davenport, 52804, 319-332-5616
Par: 70, Holes: 18
Highland GC, P. O. Box 105, Iowa Falls, 50126, 515-648-4021
Pro: Jakki Lyman
Highland Park GC, 944 17th Street NE, Mason City, 50401, 515-423-9693
Pro: John Pritchard
Hillcrest CC, P. O. Box 82, Adel, 50003, 515-993-4320
Pro: Tim Holmes
Hillcrest CC, P. O. Box 261, Mount Vernon, 52314
Pro: Robert Kupfer
Holstein Town & Country, Koemehl Drive, Holstein, 51025, 712-368-2530
Pro: Robert Lister
Hubbard Recreation Club, P. O. Box 339, Hubbard, 50122
Pro: Mike Doering
Humboldt CC, Highway 3 East, Humboldt, 50548, 515-332-1447
Pro: Marvin Buhr
Hyperion Field Club, 7390 NW Beaver Drive, Johnston, 50131, 515-276-1596
Pro: Ross Debuhr
Ida Grove G & CC, East Second St, Box 67, Ida Grove, 51445, 712-364-3684
Pro: Dallas Jensen
Indian Creek CC, 2401 Indian Creek Rd., Marion, 52302, 319-377-4489
Pro: Dick Williams
Indian Hills G & CC, Route 2, Box 110, Wapello, 52653, 319-868-7747
Pro: Ron Gerst
Indian Hills GC, Spirit Lake, 51360, 712-336-4768
Par: 35, Holes: 9
Jesup CC, Old Highway 20, Box 542, Jesup, 50648, 319-827-9152
Pro: Pat Wold
Jewell G & CC, Jewell, 50130, 515-827-5631
Pro: L. R. Walker
Kalona GC, P. O. Box 354, Kalona, 52247, 319-656-2000
Pro: James Hauth
Keokuk CC, 3318 Middle Rd., Keokuk, 52632, 319-524-2002
Pro: Ed Biehl
Knoll Ridge, Box 115, North English, 52316, 319-664-3700
Lacoma Golf, Box 47, East Dubuque, 61025, 815-797-3879
Pro: Dana Schrack
Lagos Acres, 203 N. County Line Rd., Keota, 52248, 515-636-3411
Pro: Ed Adam
Lake City CC, Hiway 175 E., Lake City, 51449, 712-464-3344
Pro: Hazel Holm
Lake Creek CC, RR 1, Storm Lake, 50588, 712-732-1548
Pro: Curt Nelson
Lake Mac Bride GC, RR #4, Solon, 52333, 319-644-2500
Par: 36, Holes: 9, Pro: Thomas Wolfe

Lake Panorama Nat. GC, E. Panorama Drive, Box 517, Panora, 50216, 515-755-2080 Pro: Doug Meredith
Lakeshore GC, P. O. Box 1545, Council Bluffs, 51502,   712-366-1639
Pro: Dave Hilgenberg
Lakeside GC, RR Box 83, Jefferson, 50129,   515-738-2403
Pro: Helen Durbin
Lakeside Muni GC, RR #2, Fort Dodge, 50501,   515-576-7237
Pro: Paul Panek
Laporte City GC, Rt 2, Laporte City, 50657,   319-342-2249
Pro: Bob Wood
Latimer Golf Inc., Box 644, Latimer, 50452,   515-579-6090
Pro: Duane Nielsen
Lemars Muni GC, 935 Park Lane SW, Lemars, 51031,   712-546-6849
Pro: Karen Garvey
Lincoln Valley Golf, RR #1, State Center, 50247,   515-483-2054
Pro: Jill Alles
Little Sioux G & CC, P. O. Box 413, Sioux Rapids, 50585,   712-283-2162
Logan-Mo. Valley CC, RR 2, Box 34, Logan, 51546,   712-644-3050
Pro: Harley Erickson
Lost Island GC, RR, Ruthver, 51358,   712-837-4804
Pro: Ray Freeburg
Manchester G & CC, RR #1, Manchester, 52057,   319-927-4155
Pro: Nick Bernhard
Maquoketa CC, P. O. Box 926, Maquoketa, 52060,   319-652-4515
Pro: Gaylon Gohlman
Marcus Community CC, Hiway 143-3, Marcus, 51035,   712-376-4492
Pro: Maxine Ludwig
Marengo GC, RR Box 331, Marengo, 52301,   319-642-3508
Pro: V. Brunseen
Mason City GC, Box 948, Mason City, 50401,   515-424-2173
Pro: Billy Kammeyer
Meadow Hills GC, E. Rocksylvania Ave., Box 191, Iowa Falls, 50126, 515-648-4421   Pro: Keith Rau
Meadowbrook G & CC, P. O. Box 202, Hartley, 51346,   712-728-2060
Par: 37, Holes: 9, Pro: Bill Loder
Meadowbrook GC, Wellsburg, 50680,   515-869-5224
Pro: Al Blake
Meadows G&CC, Moville, 51039,   712-873-9130
Par: 36, Holes: 9
Meadowview CC, 1500 Maple Street, Central City, 52214,   319-438-1063
Pro: Chris Nelson
Monticello GC, P. O. Box 173, Monicello, 52301,   319-465-3225
Pro: Dennis Ortgies
Mt. Ayr G & CC, Mt. Ayr, 50854,   515-464-2430
Pro: Karen Bender
Mt. Pleasant G & CC, Rt. 3, Mt. Pleasant, 52641,   319-986-6157
Pro: Gene Ripp
Nashua Town & CC, Highway 218 South, Nashua, 50658,   515-435-4466
Pro: Ruby Riley
New Hampton CC, Box 212, New Hampton, 50659,   515-394-4340
Pro: Bob Messersmith
Newell GC, Newell, 50568,   712-272-4424
Pro: Bev Jorgensen
Newton CC, P. O. Box 652, Newton, 50208,   515-792-1589
Pro: Ciamak Hojati

Nishna Hills GC, Box 95,East 14th Street, Atlantic, 50022, 712-243-9931
Par: 69, Holes: 18, Pro: Tim Denham
Northwood CC, Hwy 65 North. RR #3, Northwood, 50459, 515-324-1662
Oakland Acres GC, RR 1, Box 238, Grinnell, 50112, 515-236-7111
Par: 69, Holes: 18, Pro: Michael Johnson
Oakleaf CC, P. O. Box 25, Reinbeck, 50669, 319-345-2079
Par: 36, Holes: 9, Pro: Don Keith
Oaks GC, RR #1, Ames, 50010, 515-232-9862
Pro: Steve Carr
Oakwood GC, Box 220, Conrad, 50621, 515-366-2211
Pro: Mike Stubbs
Onawa CC, Box 358, Onawa, 51040, 712-423-1481
Pro: Linda Johnson
Oneota G & CC, P. O. Box 234, Decorah, 52101, 319-382-4407
Pro: John Jasper
Osceola CC, 400 East Fayette St, Osceola, 50213, 515-342-3717
Otter Valley CC, RR #2, George, 51237, 712-475-3861
Pro: Thomas Rokusek
Ottumwa CC, East Golf Avenue, Ottumwa, 52501, 515-684-5491
Pro: L. M. Deevers
Ottumwa Muni GC, Rt. 5, Ottumwa, 52501, 515-682-7946
Pro: Mike Steffen
Pella G & CC, 600 Elm Street, Box 43, Pella, 50219, 515-628-4564
Pro: Joe Gowdy
Perry G & CC, Box 426, Perry, 50220, 515-465-3852
Pro: Jerry Thornburg
Pheasant Ridge GC, 3205 W. 12th Street, Cedar Falls, 50613, 319-266-9040
Par: 72, Holes: 18, Pro: Norm Luttinen
Pine Knolls CC, Box 6, Knoxville, 50138, 515-842-5586
Pro: Susan Visser
Pine Lake CC, Box 428, Eldora, 50627, 515-858-3167
Pro: Jay Braska
Esterville G & CC, Box 384, Esterville, 51334, 712-362-4755
Par: 36, Holes: 9, Pro: Darrel Schnell
Pioneer Town & CC, Manly, 50456, 515-454-2414
Pro: Phil Hoyne
Pleasant Valley GC, 405 N. 1st, Thornton, 50479, 515-998-2117
Pro: Daryl Buchholtz
Pleasant Valley GC, 1301 S. Gilbert St, Iowa City, 52240, 319-337-2622
Pro: Tom Hein
Pleasantville G & CC, P. O. Box 8, Pleasantville, 50225, 515-947-4031
Pro: Mary Ann Crowl
Plum Creek GC, Highway 18 West, Fredricksburg, 50630, 319-237-6401
Pro: Ross Edwards
Pocahontas GC, Box 147, Pocahontas, 50574, 712-335-4375
Pro: Betty Bollard
Ponderosa GC, 600 S. 60, West Des Moines, 50265, 515-225-1766
Pro: Paul Latta
Porky's Red Carpet, 1409 Newell, Waterloo, 50703, 319-235-1242
Pro: Ed Dolan
Prairie Knolls Inc., 509 E. Walnut, New Sharon, 50207, 515-637-4200
Pro: Marla Whitehead
Red Oak CC, Box 413, RR #1, Red Oak, 51566, 712-623-4281
Par: 72, Holes: 18, Pro: Norma Dean
Rice Lake G & CC, RR #2, Lake Mills, 50405, 515-592-8022
Pro: Kurtis Helgeson

Rickville CC, Riceville, 50466, 515-985-9976
Par: 35, Holes: 9
River Bend Muni GC, 720 Forest Avenue, Story City, 50248, 515-733-2611
Pro: John Morgan
River Road GC, RR #2, Algona, 50511, 515-295-7351
Pro: Kent Hoover
River View GC, Box 37, Keosauqua, 52565, 319-293-3200
Pro: Alan Mahon
Rock River G & CC, RR 1, Rock Rapids, 51246, 712-472-3168
Pro: Tom Vinson
Rockford G & CC, Rockford, 50468, 515-756-3314
Pro: William Weigand
Rolling Hills GC, Hull, 51239
Holes: 9
Round Grove G & CC, Greene, 50636, 515-823-5621
Pro: Diane Marquard
Sac CC, South 9th Street, Sac City, 50583, 712-662-7342
Pro: Jim Hoft
Sac County G & CC, Jcty. 71 & 175, Wall Lake, 51466, 712-668-4410
Pro: Nacy Flynn
Sanborn G & CC, Western Avenue, Sanborn, 51248, 712-729-5600
Pro: R. Vanden Hoek
Sandy Hollow GC, RR #1, Sioux Center, 51250, 712-722-4866
Pro: Brad Vermeer
SDigourney G & CC, Box 284, Sigourney, 52591, 515-622-3400
Pro: Luann Crouse
Sheaffer GC, RR 1 Box 229, Fort Madison, 52627, 319-528-6214
Pro: Emil Roewert
Sibley G & CC, 11th Avenue, Sibley, 51249, 712-754-2729
Pro: Dan Mulder
Silvercrest G & CC, Box 247, Decorah, 52101, 319-382-5296
Pro: Ruth Branhagen
Sioux City CC, 40th & Jackson, Sioux City, 51104, 712-277-4612
Pro: Bob Reith
Sioux City Boat Club, 1201 Council Oak Drive, Sioux City, 51109, 712-233-1342
Pro: C. E. Jenell
Sioux G & CC, Alton, 51003, 712-756-4513
Pro: Al Pottebaum
Slippery Elm GC, Box 286, Klemme, 50449, 515-587-2670
Pro: Milvern Barz
Sloan Comm. Rec. Corp., Sloan, 51055, 712-428-9993
Pro: Wayne Peterson
South Hardin Rec. Area, P. O. Box 294, Union, 50258, 515-486-2335
Pro: M. Munsinger
South Hills GC, Waterloo, 50701, 319-291-4268
Par: 72, Holes: 18
South Winn G & CC, P. O. Box 396, Calmar, 52132
Spencer G & CC, 2200 W. 18th, Spencer, 50301, 712-262-6734
Pro: Dave Brostrom
Spencer Muni GC, 1320 4th Avenue SW, Spencer, 51301, 712-262-7783
Pro: S. Landhuis
Sport Hill CC, 712 Long Street, Williamsburg, 52361, 319-668-2225
Pro: Pat Scott
Spring Hills CC, RR, Box 353, Mallard, 50562, 712-425-9582
Pro: Marilyn Schultz

Spring Valley GC, RR, Box 110 B, Livermore, 50558, 515-379-1259
Pro: Gerald Berte
Springbrook CC, RR #3, Box 186, Dewitt, 52742, 319-659-3187
Pro: Dave Kent
St. Andrews GC, 1866 Blairs Ferry Rd NE, Cedar Raipds, 52402, 319-393-9915
Pro: Mike Hall
Sunny Brae G & CC, RFD Box 177, Osage, 50461, 515-732-3435
Pro: Dick Harkenson
Sunnyside CC, 1600 Olympic Drive, Waterloo, 50701, 319-234-1125
Pro: Andy Devine
Tama—Toledo CC, 806 W 13th, Tama, 52339, 515-484-2027
Pro: Bob Balvin
Tara Hills CC, Van Horne, 52346, 319-228-8771
Par: 36, Holes: 9
Terrace Hills GC, 8700 NE 46th Ave, Altoona, 50009, 515-967-3932
Pro: Joe Riding
Thunder Hills CC, RR #1, Peosta, 52068, 319-556-3363
Pro: Paul Gansen
Tipton G & CC, RR 1, Tipton, 52772, 319-886-2848
Pro: L. Geadelmann
Toad Valley GC, RR #2, Runnells, 50237, 515-967-9575
Par: 71, Holes: 18, Pro: Dan Brady
Town & Country GC, Box 36, Grundy Center, 50638, 319-824-3712
Pro: Gordon Akers
Traer G&CC, Traer, 50675, 319-478-2700
Par: 35, Holes: 9
Treynor Rec. Area, Treynor, 51575
Pro: Darlene Walters
Twin Lakes GC, Winfield, 52659, 319-257-6253
Twin Pines Muni GC, 3800 42nd St NE, Cedar Rapids, 52402, 319-398-5183
Pro: Bob Higgins
Urbandale G & CC, 4000 Clive Rd, Urbandale, 50322, 515-276-5496
Pro: Tamie Osby
Valley Oaks, Hart Mill Road, Clinton, 52732, 319-242-7221
Pro: Ted Lewis
Veenker Memorial, Strange Rd., Ames, 50011, 515-294-6727
Par: 72, Holes: 18, Pro: Julie Manning
Wakonda Club, 3915 Eleur Drive, Des Moines, 50321, 515-285-1934
Pro: Terry Beardsley
Wapsi Oaks CC, Calamus, 52759, 319-246-2216
Par: 35, Holes: 9
Wapsipinicon CC, Route #2, Amamosa, 52205, 319-462-3930
Pro: Gene Lawrence
Wapsipinicon GC, Golf Club Rd., Independence, 50644, 319-334-6576
Pro: John Arend
Washington G & CC, Box 62, Washington, 52353, 319-653-2080
Pro: James Lloyd
Waveland GC, 4908 University, Des Moines, 50311, 515-271-4706
Pro: L. Castagnoli
Waverly G & CC, P. O. Box 356, Waverly, 50677, 319-352-3855
Pro: Bo Blake
Wellman GTC, Wellman, 52356
Pro: Ival Redlinger
Wesley Hillside GC, Wesley, 50483, 515-679-4262
West Bend G & CC, RR 1, Box 145, West Bend, 50597, 515-887-6217
Pro: Ray Anderson

West Liberty G & CC, Box 75, West Liberty, 52776, 319-627-2920
West Union CC, P.O. Box 122, Echo Valley Rd., West Union, 52175, 319-422-3482 Pro: L. Langreck
Westwood GC, 2807 1st Ave. West, Newton, 50208, 515-792-3087
Pro: Larry Stewart
Whittemore GC, RR, Whittemore, 50598, 515-884-2774
Pro: Linda Farrell
Wildwood Muni GC, 3rd & South Iowa St, Charles City, 50616, 515-228-9887
Par: 36, Holes: 9, Pro: Richard Wynn
Willow Creek GC, 6300 Army Post Rd., Des Moines, 50321, 515-285-4558
Par: 71, Holes: 27, Pro: Dan Clark
Willow Run C, Box 690, 940 E. Fayette, Denver, 50622, 319-984-5762
Pro: Roger Claiser
Willow Vale GC, West Main, Mapleton, 51034, 712-882-1002
Pro: Tim Hupke
Woods Edge GC, RR, Edgewood, 52042, 319-928-6428
Pro: Steve Brady

Abilene CC, RR 4, Abilene, 67410, 913-263-3811   *Kansas*
USGA: 69.3
Allen County CC, Box 362, Rt. 3, Iola, 66749, 316-365-3422
USGA: 34.5
American Legon GC, 1801 W. Central, El Dorado, 67042, 316-321-9805
USGA: 66.7
Arkansas City CC, Box 45, East Kansas Avenue, Arkansas City, 67005,
316-442-5560 USGA: 71.1
Arrowhead Hills GC, P.O. Box 8, New Strawn, 66839, 316-364-8051
USGA: 33.7
Ashland CC, Box 252, Ashland, 67831
USGA: 35.2
Atwood CC, P. O. Box 53, Atwood, 67330, 913-626-9973
USGA: 69.9
Augusta CC, Rt. 1 Box 465, Augusta, 67010, 316-775-7281
USGA: 68.9
Baxter Springs CC, Box 88, Baxter Springs, 66713, 316-856-9898
USGA: 33.8
Bellevue CC, PO Box 272, Atchison, 66002, 913-367-3022
USGA: 67.1
Beloit CC, R.R. #2, Box 84, Beloit, 67420, 913-738-3184
Par: 35, USGA: 32.6, Holes: 9
Brookridge CC, 8223 W. 103rd., Overland Park, 66212, 913-648-1600
USGA: 70.5
Caldwell GC, 306 S. Main St., Caldwell, 67022
USGA: 64.8
Carey Park GC, Box 1212, Hutchinson, 67501, 316-662-9816
USGA: 70.3
Highland CC, R.R. 7, P.O. Box 146, Hutchinson, 67502, 316-663-5301
Cedar Hills GC, Rt. 1, Washington, 67206, 913-325-2424
USGA: 67.4
Cedarbrook GC, Cottonwood Street, Iola, 66749
Holes: 9
Chanute CC, Box 351, Chanute, 66720, 316-431-9560
USGA: 68.9
Clafin GC, P.O. Box 462, Clafin, 67525
Clay Center CC, Box 282, Clay Center, 67432

Clearwater Greens Men's Club, RR 2, Box 48A, Clearwater, 67026, 316-584-2799 USGA: 67.3
Coffeyville CC, Box 264 Rt. 4, Coffeyville, 67337, 316-251-5236 USGA: 73.3
Colby CC, Box 792, Colby, 67701, 913-462-6443
Columbus CC, R.R. #2, Columbus, 66725, 316-674-3383 USGA: 68.5
Concordia CC, P.O. Box 342, Concordia, 66901, 913-243-3305 USGA: 59.0
Crestview CC, 1000 N. 127th East, Wichita, 67206, 316-733-1344 USGA: 71.1
Crestwood CC, Box 654, Pittsburg, 66762, 316-231-6530 USGA: 70.5
Custer Hill GC, Fort Riley Golf Club Bldg 5202, Fort Riley, 66442, 913-239-5412 USGA: 71.8
Deer Creek GC, 7000 133rd Street, Overland Park, 66209 Holes: 18
Dodge City CC, Box 879, Dodge City, 67801, 316-225-5231 USGA: 69.8
Dubs Dread GC, 12601 Hollingsworth Road, Kansas City, 66109, 913-721-1333 Yards: 6987, Par: 72, USGA: 70.4, Holes: 18, Pro: Jay Lispi
Echo Hills GC, 800 East 53rd North, Wichita, 67219, 316-838-0143 USGA: 66.0
El Dorado CC, Box 8, El Dorado, 67042, 316-321-4118 USGA: 70.0
Elkhart GC, P.O. Box 811, Elkhart, 67950 USGA: 68.9
Ellis CC, 1301 Spruce, Ellis, 67637, 913-726-4711 USGA: 65.0
Ellsworth Municipal GC, Box 163, Ellsworth, 67439
Emporia CC, 1800 N. Rural, Box 744, Emporia, 66801, 316-342-0349 USGA: 70.6
Emporia Municipal, Emporia, 66801 USGA: 69.7
Eureka CC, P.O. Box 620, Eureka, 67045, 316-583-5642 USGA: 68.7
Forbes GC, 700 Capehart Road, Topeka, 66619, 913-862-0114 USGA: 70.6
Fort Scott CC, R.R. #5, Box 35, Fort Scott, 66701, 316-223-5060 USGA: 67.6
Four Oaks GC, 201 W. 4th, Pittsburg, 66762, 316-231-8070
Fredonia GC, Box 203, R. R. #3, Fredonia, 66736, 316-378-3270
Ft. Leavenworth GC, Bldg. 324, Ft. Leavenworth, 66027
Ft. Hays Municipal GC, R.R. #2, Box 1337, Hays, 67601, 913-625-9949 USGA: 69.4
Garnett CC, North Park, Box 12, Garnett, 66032, 913-448-9545 USGA: 67.6
Girard GC, Route 4, Girard, 66743, 316-724-8855 USGA: 67.3
Graham County Grass Greens, 7 Eastgate, Hill City, 67642, 913-674-5471
Great Bend Petroleum Club, Box 1305, Great Bend, 67530, 316-792-4306 USGA: 66.7
Green Valley Green GC, 909 North Andover Drive, Andover, 67002, 316-733-4100 Holes: 9
Grove Park GC, P.O. Box 86, Ellinwood, 67526, 316-564-3123 USGA: 58.8

Herington CC, R.R. #3, Herington, 67449, 913-258-2052
Hesston GC, P.O. Box 608, Hesston, 67062-0, 316-327-2331
USGA: 69.9
Hiawatha CC, Rt. 5, Hiawatha, 66434, 913-742-3361
Hidden Lakes GC, 6020 S. Greenwich Rd., Derby, 67037, 316-788-2855
Par: 72, USGA: 69.4, Holes: 18
Highlands GC, Abilene, 67410, 913-263-2093
Par: 36, Holes: 9
Hillcrest GC, Rt. 4, Coffeyville, 67337, 316-251-4590
Hillsboro GC, 606 S. Lincoln, Hillsboro, 67063, 316-947-3846
USGA: 65.3
Holton CC, Box 68, Holton, 66436, 913-486-3829
USGA: 68.0
Horton Lakeview CC, R.R. 2, Box 949, Horton, 66439, 913-486-3829
USGA: 67.8
Hoxie CC, Hoxie, 67740
USGA: 68.8
Hugoton CC, P.O. Box L, Hugoton, 67951
USGA: 69.9
Indian Hills CC, 69th & Mission Rd., Prairie Village, 66208, 913-362-6204
USGA: 70.5
Joyce L. Hamm CC, Box 771, Plains, 67869, 316-563-9987
USGA: 70.3
Kansas City CC, 62nd & Indian Lane, Mission Hills, 66208, 913-362-8100
USGA: 71.7
Katy Parsons GC, R.R. 2, P.O. Box 376, Parsons, 67357, 316-421-4532
USGA: 68.8
Kingman CC, Box 401, Kingman, 67068, 316-532-2373
Kinsley GC, 612 Niles, Kinsley, 67547, 316-659-2124
USGA: 68.4
L. W. Clapp Men's Club, 4611 E. Harry, Wichita, 67218, 316-682-9848
USGA: 69.5
LaCrosse CC, P.O. Box 148, LaCrosse, 67548
Lake Barton CC, Box 666, Great Bend, 67530, 316-653-4255
USGA: 65.4
Lake Perry CC, R.r. #1, Ozawkie, 66070, 913-484-2339
USGA: 63.6
Lake Shawnee GC, 4141 SE East Edge, Topeka, 66609, 913-267-2295
USGA: 68.9
Lakeside Hills GC, 2300 Golf Courts Road, Olathe, 66061, 913-782-4192
Par: 70, USGA: 66.0, Holes: 18
Lakin CC, P.O. Box 492, Lakin, 67860, 316-355-6222
USGA: 69.4
Lamont Hills GC, R.R. 1, Hwy. 368, Vassar, 66543
USGA: 66.2
Larned GC, P.O. Box 329, Larned, 67550
USGA: 67.5
Lawrence GC, 400 Country Club Terr., Lawrence, 66044, 913-843-2866
USGA: 70.3
Leavenworth CC, Box 277, Lansing, 66043, 913-727-6600
USGA: 67.7
Leawood South CC, 12700 Overbrook Road, Leawood, 66209, 913-491-1313
USGA: 70.0
Leoti CC, Leoti, 67861
USGA: 71.1

Liberal CC, Box 601, Liberal, 67901, 316-624-3992
USGA: 71.8
Lindsborg GC, Box 455, Lindsborg, 67456, 913-227-8775
Mac Donald Park GC, 840 N. Yale Ave., Wichita, 67208, 316-685-5391
Yards: 6837, Par: 71, USGA: 69.7, Holes: 18, Pro: Mike Consolver
Manhattan CC, Box 1026 1531 N. 10th, Manhattan, 66502, 913-539-7501
USGA: 69.4
Mariah Hills GC, R.R. 2, Dodge City, 67801, 316-227-7634
USGA: 70.5
Marion CC, Box 111, Marion, 66861, 316-382-8647
USGA: 66.6
Marysville CC, R.R. #2, Marysville, 66508
McPherson CC, Box 1041, R. R. #3, McPherson, 67460, 316-241-3541
USGA: 66.7
Meadowbrook CC, 9101 Nall, Prairie Village, 66207, 913-643-3161
USGA: 71.2
Milburn CC, 7501 W 69th Street, Overland Park, 66204, 913-432-1224
USGA: 71.2
Minneapolis CC, Minneapolis, 67467
Mission Hills CC, 5400 Mission Dr., Shawnee Mission, 66208, 913-722-5400
USGA: 71.3
Newton Public GC, 622 E. 6th, Newton, 67114, 316-283-3873
USGA: 66.4
Oakley CC, 608 E. 5th, Oakley, 67748, 913-672-3081
USGA: 68.0
Oberlin CC, 163 Penn, Oberlin, 67749, 913-475-8990
USGA: 67.8
Osage City CC, Box 527, Osage City, 66523
USGA: 69.7
Osawatomie Men's GC, 829 Pacific, c/o Steve Smith, Osawatomie, 66064,
913-755-4769   Par: 71, USGA: 68.1, Holes: 18
Ottawa CC, Box 255, R.R. #1, Ottawa, 66067, 913-242-6527
USGA: 67.3
Overland Park GC, 12600 Quivira Rd., Overland Park, 66213, 913-897-3809
USGA: 68.6
Paola CC, Box 141, North Pearl Street, Paola, 66071, 913-294-2131
Park Hills CC, Lake Rd., Box 1043, Pratt, 67124, 316-672-7541
USGA: 35.4
Parsons CC, Route 3, P.O. Box 301, Parsons, 67357, 316-421-5290
USGA: 66.8
Pawnee Prairie Men's Club, 1931 S. Tyler, Wichita, 67209, 316-722-6310
USGA: 71.9
Phillipsburg GC, Box 314, Phillipsburg, 67661, 913-543-5545
Pine Bay GC, 6615 S. Grove, Wichita, 67233, 316-524-7300
Yards: 6244, Par: 72, USGA: 70.7, Holes: 18
Pineview CC, Box 388, Atchison, 66002, 913-367-9730
Prairie Dog Recreation Assn. G, Route #3, Box 159, Norton, 67654,
913-877-3341   USGA: 68.5
Prairie Dunes GC, 4812 E. 30th, Hutchinson, 67502, 316-662-0581
USGA: 70.2
Quivira Lake CC, Lake Quivira, Kansas City, 66106, 913-631-7707
USGA: 69.4
Rabbit Creek GC, R.R. #1, Box 128, Louisburg, 66053, 913-837-5476
USGA: 68.9
Republic County Recreation Ass, Box 421, 2208 Country Club Dr., Belleville,
66935, 913-527-6990

Riverside Recreation Assoc., 307 W. Jackson, Box 872, St. Franics, 67756, 913-332-3401   USGA: 70.0
Rolling Acres GC, Rt. 3, McPherson, 67460,   316-241-9765
USGA: 66.0
Rolling Hills CC, 223 South Westlink Drive, Wichita, 67277,   316-722-1181
USGA: 70.1
Rolling Meadows GC, P.O. Box 287, Junction City, 66441,   913-238-4303
USGA: 69.9
Rooks County CC, 702 S. Kansas, Plainville, 67663,   913-434-2213
USGA: 66.2
Russell CC, 326 Main, Russell, 67665,   913-483-2852
USGA: 69.2
Safari Public GC, 701 S. Santa Fe, Chanute, 66720
USGA: 67.1
Salina CC, East Country Club Rd., Box 205, Salina, 67402,   913-827-0388
USGA: 67.5
Salina Elks Lodge #718, Box 418, R.R. #3, Salina, 67402,   913-827-8585
USGA: 67.2
Salina Municipal GC, 2500 E. Crawford St., Salina, 67401,   913-827-6050
USGA: 67.4
Scott City CC, R.R. #1, Box 7, Scott City, 67871,   316-872-7109
Yards: 5440, Par: 68, USGA: 65.4, Holes: 9, Pro: Richard Haston
Sedan CC, 308 E. Bowers, P.O. Box 101, Sedan, 67361, 316-725-9990
USGA: 68.9
Shagbark GC, 3124 Shrine Park Rd., Leavenworth, 66048,   913-682-4451
USGA: 32.2
Sharon Springs GC, Box 89, Sharon springs, 67758
Shawnee CC, 913 E. 29th, Topeka, 66605,   913-233-2373
USGA: 70.2
Silver Lake GC, Ottawa, 66067,   913-566-3733
Par: 36, Holes: 9
Sim Park Men's Club, 800 Amidon, Wichita, 67203,   316-267-5383
Smiley's Golf Complex GC, 10195 Monticello Terrace, Shawnee, 66227
Holes: 18
Smith Center CC, 517 Jarvis, Smith Center, 66967,   913-282-6309
USGA: 33.9
Smoky Hill CC, Box 204, North Hall Str., Hays, 67601,   913-625-7377
USGA: 68.4
Somerset G & CC, 8533 S W 21st, Topike, 66614
USGA: 67.4
Southwind CC, South Star Rd., Box 1115, Garden City, 67846,   316-275-2117
USGA: 70.4
Spring Hill Municipal GC, North Summit Road, Arkansas City, 67005,
316-442-9879   USGA: 68.1
St. Andrews GC, 11099 W 135th St., Overland Park, 66221,   913-897-3804
USGA: 70.0
Stanton County Prairie Pines, Hwy 160 Box 617, Johnson, 67855,   316-492-6818
USGA: 35.0
Sugar Hills GC, Box 791, Goodland, 67735,   913-899-2785
USGA: 70.0
Sugar Valley G & CC, R.R. 2, Mound City, 66056,   913-795-2120
USGA: 72.7
Sycamore Valley GC, R.R. 4, Box 277, Independence, 67301,   316-331-2828
Syracuse CC, Box 802, Syracuse, 67878,   316-384-7833 USGA: 68.8
Tomahawk Hills GC, 17501 Midland Dr., Shawnee, 66218,   913-631-8000
USGA: 69.0

Topeka CC, 2700 Buchanan, Topeka, 66619, 913-354-8561
USGA: 70.5
Topeka Public GC, 2533 S. W. Urish Rd., Topeka, 66614, 913-272-0511
Town & Country Club, 100 W. Blair, P.O. Box 53, Lyons, 67554, 316-257-2962
Twin Lakes GC, McConnell AFB, Bldg. 1336, Wichita, 67221, 316-681-6272
USGA: 70.5
Village Greens, Inc., Box 1, Ozawki, 66070, 913-876-2255
Wamego CC, Country Club Drive, Wamego, 66547, 913-456-2649
USGA: 69.5
Wedgewood GC, 303 Main St., Halstead, 67056
USGA: 65.5
Wichita CC, Box 8105, Wichita, 67206, 316-682-5566
USGA: 72.4
Wichita State University GC, 4201 E. 21st, Wichita, 67208, 316-685-7211
USGA: 69.8
Willowbend GC, 4110 N. Tara Circle, Wichita, 67226
USGA: 71.6
Willow Tree GC, 325 N. Washington, Liberal, 67901, 000-624-7042
USGA: 68.2
Winfield CC, R.R. 3, P.O. Box 501, Winfield, 67156, 316-221-1570
USGA: 70.6
Wolf Creek Golf Links, 18695 Lackman Road, Olathe, 66061, 913-782-6052
USGA: 71.5

---

76 Falls CC, Albany, 42602, 606-387-5908   *Kentucky*
Par: 36, Holes: 9
A. J. Jolly GC, Alexandria, 41001, 606-635-2106
Par: 71, Holes: 18
Andover G&CC, 3530 Todds Road, Lexington, 40509
Holes: 18
Barren River Lake State Resort Park, Lucas, 42156, 502-646-2151
Par: 35, Holes: 9
Beattyville CC, Beattyville, 41311, 606-464-9286
Par: 34, Holes: 9
Beechland GC, Burlington, 41005, 606-525-9864
Par: 70, Holes: 18
Ben Hawes State Park GC, Owensboro, 42301, 502-685-2011
Par: 72, Holes: 27
Best Western Park Mammoth GC, Park City, 42160, 502-749-4104
Par: 70, Holes: 18
Bob-O-Link GC, Lawrenceburg, 40342, 502-839-4029
Par: 71, Holes: 18
Boone Links GC, Country Club Drive, Florence, 41042
Holes: 9
Boone Links, Florence, 41042, 606-371-7553
Par: 72, Holes: 18
Bright Leaf Resort GC, Harrodsburg, 40330, 606-734-5481
Par: 35, Holes: 18
Cabin Brook GC, Versailles, 40383, 606-873-8404
Par: 36, Holes: 9
Calvert City G&CC, Calvert City, 42029, 502-395-5831
Par: 72, Holes: 18
Cardinal Hills GC, Bedford, 40006, 502-255-7770
Par: 36, Holes: 9
Carter Caves State Resort Park, Olive Hill, 41164, 606-286-4411
Par: 35, Holes: 9

Caveland Par 3 GC, Cave City, 42127,   502-773-2377
Par: 36, Holes: 9
Cedar-Fil GC, Bardstown, 40004,   502-348-8981
Par: 36, Holes: 9
Clear Creek GC, Route 8 Box 49AB, Shelbyville, 40065
Holes: 9
Crescent Hill GC, Louisville, 40231,   502-896-9193
Par: 36, Holes: 9
Cynthiana CC, Cynthiana, 41031,   606-234-5364
Par: 36, Holes: 9
Devou Park GC, Covington, 41016,   606-431-8030
Par: 34, Holes: 9
Doe Valley CC, Brandenburg, 40108,   502-422-3397
Par: 71, Holes: 18
Eagle Creek CC, Dry Ridge, 41035,   606-428-1772
Par: 71, Holes: 18
Elkhorn CC, Jenkins, 41537,   606-832-2118
Par: 72, Holes: 9
Fairway GC, Wheatley, 40389,   502-463-2338
Par: 70, Holes: 18
General Butler State Resort Park, Carrollton, 41008,   502-732-4384
Par: 36, Holes: 9
Griffin Gate GC, Lexington, 40511,   606-254-4101
Par: 72, Holes: 18
Hazard GC, Hazard, 41701,   606-436-5320
Par: 34, Holes: 9
Henderson Muni GC, Henderson, 42420,   502-826-0517
Par: 32, Holes: 9
Henry County CC, New Castle, 40050,   502-845-2375
Par: 72, Holes: 18
Hickory Hills CC, Liberty, 42539,   606-787-7368
Par: 36, Holes: 9
Hobson Grove GC, Bowling Green, 42101,   502-781-2877
Par: 36, Holes: 9
Hurstbourne GC, 8222 Shelbyville Rd., Louisville, 40222
Indian Springs GC, Barbourville, 40906,   606-546-5607
Par: 36, Holes: 9
Jenny Wiley State Resort Park, Prestonsburg, 41653,   606-886-2711
Par: 34, Holes: 9
John James Audubon State Park, Henderson, 42420,   502-826-2247
Par: 36, Holes: 9
Kearney Hills GC, 3403 Kearney Road, Lexington, 40511
Holes: 18
Kenlake State Resort Park, Hardin, 42048,   502-474-2211
Par: 30, Holes: 9
Kenton County GC, Independence, 41051,   606-371-3200
Par: 70, Holes: 18
Kenton Station GC, Maysville, 41056,   606-759-7154
Par: 35, Holes: 9
Kentucky Dam Village GC, Hwy. 641, Paducah, 42044,   502-362-4271
Yards: 6525, Par: 72, Holes: 18, Pro: Ken Stull
Knob View GC, Lebanon Junction, 40033,   502-833-2253
Par: 36, Holes: 9
L&N GC, Brooks, 40109,   502-955-9987
Par: 71, Holes: 18

Lake Cumberland State Resort Park, Jamestown, 42629, 502-343-3111
Par: 36, Holes: 9
Lakeside GC, Lexington, 40502, 606-263-5315
Par: 72, Holes: 18
LaRue County CC, Hodgenville, 42748, 502-358-9727
Par: 35, Holes: 9
Lexington GC, Paris Pike, Lexington, 40555
Lincoln Trail CC, Vine Grove, 40175, 502-877-2181
Par: 72, Holes: 18
Marion CC, Marion, 42064, 502-965-9241
Par: 72, Holes: 18
Meadows GC, Clay City, 40312, 606-663-4000
Par: 36, Holes: 9
Middlesboro CC, Middlesboro, 40965, 606-248-3831
Par: 36, Holes: 9
Miller Memorial GC, Murray, 42071, 502-762-2238
Par: 71, Holes: 18
Morehead State Univ. GC, Morehead, 40351, 606-783-2866
Par: 36, Holes: 9
My Old Kentucky Home State Park, Bardstown, 40004, 502-348-3528
Par: 35, Holes: 9
Ohio County CC, Hartford, 42347, 502-298-7210
Par: 35, Holes: 9
Paducah GC, Holt Rd., Paducah, 42002
Park Place Resort GC, Park City, 42160, 502-749-9466
Par: 70, Holes: 18
Paul R. Walker GC, Bowling Green, 42101, 502-843-9821
Par: 35, Holes: 9
Paxton Park GC, 841 Berger Rd., Paducah, 42001, 502-444-9514
Par: 71, Holes: 18
Pennyrile Forest State Resort Park, Dawson Springs, 42408, 592-797-3421
Par: 36, Holes: 9
Pine Mountain State Resort Park, Pineville, 40977, 606-337-6195
Par: 34, Holes: 9
Pine Valley GC, Elizabethtown, 42701, 502-737-8300
Par: 72, Holes: 18
Quail Chase GC, 7000 Cooper Chapel Rd., Louisville, 40229
Holes: 18
Rolling Meadows GC, Catlettsburg, 41129, 606-739-4140
Par: 35, Holes: 9
Rough River Dam State Resort Park, Falls of Rough, 40119, 502-257-2311
Par: 27, Holes: 9
Seneca GC, Louisville, 40231, 502-458-9298
Par: 72, Holes: 18
Shelbyville CC, Shelbyville, 40065, 502-633-0542
Par: 72, Holes: 18
Stearns GC, Stearns, 42647, 606-376-2666
Par: 35, Holes: 9
Skyline Golf & Recreation Ctr, Hopkinsville, 42748, 502-885-0943
Par: 36, Holes: 9
Sportland GC, Winchester, 40391, 606-744-9959
Par: 72, Holes: 18
Sundowner GC, Ashland, 41105, 606-329-9093
Par: 33, Holes: 9
Tates Creek GC, 1400 Gainesway Dr., Lexington, 40502, 606-272-3428
Yards: 6240, Par: 72, USGA: 69.5, Holes: 18, Pro: Al Chrouser Jr

Tri-County CC, Corbin, 40701, 606-528-2166
Par: 35, Holes: 9
Twin Oaks GC, Covington, 41016, 606-581-2410
Par: 70, Holes: 18
Western Hills Muni GC, Hopkinsville, 42748, 502-885-6023
Par: 72, Holes: 18
Windridge CC, Owensboro, 42301, 502-684-4324
Par: 70, Holes: 18
Woodson Bend Resort GC, Burnside, 42519, 606-561-5311 Par: 72, Holes: 18
World of Sports GC, Florence, 41042, 606-371-8255
Par: 58, Holes: 18

Alpine Golf, 8311 Shreveport Hwy., Pineville, 71360, 318-640-4030   *Louisiana*
Yards: 6050, Par: 72, Holes: 9
Audubon GC, New Orleans, 70113, 514-865-8260
Par: 68, Holes: 18
Brechtel GC, 3700 Behrman Pl., New Orleans, 70114, 504-362-4761
Yards: 5820, Par: 70, USGA: 65.8, Holes: 18, Pro: F. Frederickson
Bringhurst GC, City Park, 1306 Murray St., Alexandria, 71301, 318-445-9759
Yards: 981, Par: 27, Holes: 9
Chennault Park GC, Milhaven Road, Rt. 6, Monroe, 71203, 318-329-2454
Yards: 7044, Par: 72, Holes: 18
City Park GC, Mudd Ave., Lafayette, 70502, 318-261-8385
Yards: 6000, Par: 71, Holes: 18
City Park GC, 1442 City Park Ave., Baton Rouge, 70895, 504-287-8229
Yards: 2858, Par: 34, Holes: 9
Clark Park GC, Hwy. 19, Baker, 70714, 504-775-9008
Yards: 2863, Par: 35, Holes: 9
Delhi GC, Hwy. 80 East, Delhi, 71232, 318-878-2532
Yards: 2832, Par: 35, Holes: 9
Frasch GC, Picard Road, P.O. Box 207, Sulphur, 70663, 318-527-8693
Yards: 6000, Par: 72, Holes: 18
Greenwood GC, Lavey Lane, Baker, 70714, 504-775-9166
Yards: 6596, Par: 72, Holes: 18
Howell Park CC, 5511 Winbourne Ave., Baton Rouge, 70805, 504-357-9292
Yards: 5700, Par: 70, Holes: 18
Huntington Park GC, 8300 Pines Road, Shreveport, 71129, 318-686-8001
Yards: 7295, Par: 72, USGA: 71.4, Holes: 18, Pro: "Digger" Odell
Lake Texoma Resort GC, PO Box 279, Kingston, 73439, 405-564-3333
Holes: 18, Pro: Johnny Keithley
Lakeside Park GC, 2200 Milam, Shreveport, 71103, 318-226-6378
Yards: 2456, Par: 32, Holes: 9
Leesville Muni GC, Leesville, 71446, 318-239-2526
Par: 35, Holes: 9
Les Vieux Chenes GC, Hwy. 89, Rt. 2, Box 15 G.C., Lafayette, 70505,
318-837-1159   Yards: 6800, Par: 71, Holes: 18
LSU GC, LSU Campus, Athletic Dept., Baton Rouge, 70803, 504-388-3394
Yards: 6407, Par: 70, Holes: 18
Mallard Cove GC, Chennault Base, P.O. Box 119, Lake Charles, 70602,
318-491-1241   Yards: 5869, Par: 72, Holes: 18
NSU Recreation Complex, Hwy. 1-Bypass, P.O. Box 5225-N, Natchitoches,
71458, 318-352-6133   Yards: 2808, Par: 35, Holes: 9
Par Three Golf, 5006 Jefferson Paige Road, Shreveport, 71109, 318-636-3162
Yards: 3485, Par: 59, Holes: 18
Pine Hills Golf & CC, Britton Road, P.O.Box 280, Calhoun, 71225, 318-644-5370
Yards: 7020, Par: 72, USGA: 72.5, Holes: 18, Pro: J.E. Wood

Plaquemines Parish Commissiom, Hwy. 39, Braithwaite, 70040, 504-682-0081
Yards: 6775, Par: 72, Holes: 18
Port Sulphur GC, Hwy. 23 South, P.O. Box 345, Port Sulphur, 70083,
504-564-2761   Yards: 3115, Par: 36, Holes: 9
Querbes Park GC, 3500 Beverly Place, Shreveport, 71104,   318-865-2367
Yards: 6162, Par: 71, Holes: 18
Sharon Meadows GC, Hwy. 19, Rt. 1, box 197-N, Ethel, 70730,   504-654-2104
Yards: 2793, Par: 34, Holes: 9
Spring Bayou GC, Spring Bayou Road, Rt. 3, Box, Marksville, 71351,
318-253-9264   Yards: 2900, Par: 34, Holes: 9
Toro Hills Inn GC, Hwy. 171, Alexandria, 71449
Trails End Golf, Hwy. 9 S., P. O. Box 696, Arcadia, 71001,   318-263-2206
Yards: 2652, Par: 36, Holes: 9
Twin Oaks CC, Crowville Road, P.O. Box 168, Winnsboro, 71295,   318-435-4626
Yards: 6200, Par: 71, Holes: 9
Webb Memorial GC, 1351 Country Club Dr., Baton Rouge, 70806,   504-383-4919
Willowdale CC, Hwy. 90, Rt. 2, Luling, 70070,   504-785-8276
Yards: 6529, Par: 72, Holes: 18

Apple Valley GC, Pinewoods Rd., Lewiston, 04240,   207-784-9773   *Maine*
Holes: 9
Aroostook Valley GC, Russell Rd., Fort Fairfield, 04742
Augusta CC, Rt. 202, Manchester, 04351,   207-623-3021
Holes: 18
Bath CC, Whiskeag Rd., Bath, 04530
Holes: 9
Biddeford-Saco CC, Old Orchard Rd., Saco, 04072,   207-282-5883
Holes: 9
Birch Point GC, Lakeshore Dr., Madawaska, 04756,   207-895-6957
Holes: 9
Boothbay Region CC, Country Club Rd., Boothbay, 04537,   207-633-6085
Holes: 9
Bridgton Highlands CC, Bridgton, 04009,   207-647-3491
Holes: 9
Bucksport GC, Duckscove Rd., Rt. 46, Bucksport, 04416,   207-469-7612
Par: 36, Holes: 9
Cape Arundel GC, Old River Road, Kennebunkport, 04046,   207-967-3494
Yards: 5869, Par: 69, USGA: 68.2, Holes: 18, Pro: Ken Raynor
Caribou CC, New Sweden Rd., Caribou, 04736,   207-493-3933
Holes: 9
Castine GC, Battle Ave., Castine, 04421,   207-326-8844
Holes: 9
Causeway Club, Southwest Harbor, 04679,   207-244-3780
Holes: 9
Cobbosse Colony GC, Monmouth, 04259, 207-258-4182
Holes: 9
Dexter Muni GC, Sunrise Ave., Dexter, 04930,   207-924-6477
Yards: 2586, Par: 35, Holes: 9
Fort Kent GC, St. John Rd., Fort Kent, 04743,   207-834-3149
Holes: 9
Foxcroft GC, Milo Rd., Dover-Foxcroft, 04426,   207-564-8887
Holes: 9
Freeport CC, Old County Rd., Freeport, 04032,   207-865-4922
Yards: 3000, Par: 36, Holes: 9
Gorham CC, McLellan Rd., Gorham, 04038,   207-839-3490
Yards: 6509, Par: 71, Holes: 18

Grandview GC, Palmyra, 04965,   207-938-4947
Yards: 3087, Par: 36, Holes: 9
Great Chebeague GC, Chebeague Island, 04017,   207-846-9478
Holes: 9
Great Cove GC, Jonesboro, 04648
Holes: 9
Green Acres Inn & GC, Hartford, 04943,   207-597-2333
Yards: 1775, Par: 32, Holes: 9
Grindstone Necl GC, Grindstone Ave., Winter Harbor, 04693,   207-963-7760
Holes: 9
Hampden CC, Western Ave., Hampden, 04444,   207-862-9999
Holes: 9
Hermon Meadow GC, Rt 2, Billings Rd., Bangor, 04401,   207-848-3741
Par: 72, Holes: 18
Hillcrest GC, Millinocket, 04462,   207-723-8410
Holes: 9
Houlton Community GC, Nickerson Lake Rd., Houlton, 04730,   207-532-2662
Yards: 3002, Par: 36, Holes: 9
Island CC, Rt. 15A, Sunset, Deer Isle, 04627
Holes: 9
Johnson W. Parks GC, Hartland Ave., Pittsfield, 04967,   207-487-5545
Yards: 3000, Par: 35, Holes: 9
Katahdin CC, Park St., Milo, 04463
Holes: 9
Kebo Valley GC, Eagle Lake Rd., Bar Harbor, 04609,   207-288-3000
Yards: 6102, Par: 70, Holes: 18
Kenduskeag Valley GC, Rt. 15, Kenduskeag, 04450
Holes: 9
Lake Kezar CC, Rt. 5, Lovell, 04051,   207-925-2462
Holes: 9
Lakeview GC, Prairie Rd., Burnham, 04922,   207-948-5414
Holes: 9
Lakewood GC, Rt. 201, Madison, 04950,   207-474-5955
Yards: 3087, Par: 36, Holes: 9
Meadowhill Athletic Club GC, U.S. 201, off Park St., Farmingdale, 04938,
207-623-9831   Yards: 3112, Par: 36, Holes: 9
Mingo Springs GC, off Rt 4 & Mingo Loop Rd., Rangeley, 04970,   207-864-5021
Yards: 6000, Par: 70, Holes: 18
Natanis GC, Webber Pond Rd., Vassalboro, 04989,   207-622-3561
Yards: 5935, Par: 71, Holes: 18
North Haven Club, Iron Point Rd., North Haven, 04853,   207-867-4696
Holes: 9
Northeast Harbor GC, Northeast Harbor, 04662,   207-276-5335
Holes: 15
Northport GC, Northport, 04961,   207-338-2270
Holes: 9
Norway CC, Norway, 04268,   207-743-9840
Holes: 9
Old Orchard Beach CC, Cascade & Ross Rd., Rt. 98, Old Orchard Beach
04064, 207-934-4513   Yards: 3006, Par: 36, Holes: 9
Paris Hill CC, Paris, 04271,   207-743-2371
Holes: 9
Penobscot Valley GC, Ornono, 04473
Pine Ridge GC, West River Rd., Waterville, 04901
Holes: 9

Piscataquis CC, Dover Rd., Guilford, 04443, 207-876-3203
Holes: 9
Pleasant Hill CC, Chamberlain Rd., Scarborough, 04074, 207-883-9340
Holes: 9
Poland Spring CC, Rt. 26, Poland Springs, 04274, 207-998-6002
Yards: 6410, Par: 71, USGA: 70.6, Holes: 18
Portland GC, 11 Foreside Dr., Portland, 04105
Presque Isle CC, Parkhurst Siding Rd., Presque Isle, 04769
Holes: 9
Prospect Hill GC, 694 S Main Street, Auburn, 04210, 207-782-9220
Holes: 18
Province Lake CC, Rt. 153, Parsonsfield, 04271
Holes: 9
Purpoodock Club, Spurwink ave., Cape Elizabeth, 04107, 207-799-0821
Holes: 18
Riverside Muni GC—#1, 1158 Riverside St., Portland, 04103, 207-797-3524
Yards: 6502, Par: 72, Holes: 18
Riverside Muni GC—#2, 1158 Riverside St., Portland, 04103, 207-797-3524
Yards: 3152, Par: 36, Holes: 9
Spring Valley CC, Gorham Rd., Rt. 114, Scarborough, 04074
Holes: 9
Squaw Mountain Resort GC, on Moosehead Lake, Greenville, 04441,
207-695-3049   Yards: 2563, Par: 34, Holes: 9
Summit GC, Poland, 04273, 207-998-4515
Holes: 9
Tarratine GC, Golf Club Rd., Isleboro, 04848, 207-734-2248
Holes: 9
Twin Falls GC, Spring St., Westbrook, 04092, 207-854-5397
Holes: 9
Union CC, Union, 04862
Holes: 9
Waterville CC, Off I-95, Oakland, 04963, 207-465-2838
Holes: 18
Wawenock CC, Rt. 129, Walpole, 04573, 207-563-3938
Holes: 9
Webhannet GC, Old River Road, Kennebunk Beach, 04043
Western View GC, Bolton Hill Rd., Augusta, 04330, 207-622-5309
Par: 35, Holes: 9
White Birches GC, Thorsen Rd., off Rt. 1, Ellsworth, 04605, 207-667-5682
Yards: 2600, Par: 32, Holes: 9
Willowdale GC, off US Rt. 1, Scarborough, 04074, 207-883-9351
Yards: 5980, Par: 70, Holes: 18
Wilson Lake CC, Weld Rd., Wilton, 04294, 207-645-2016
Holes: 9
Woodland Terrace Motel & GC, Brewer, 04412, 207-989-3750
Holes: 9
Woodlands GC, 39 Woods Road, Falmouth, 04105
Holes: 18
Woodsman's CC, Rt. 11N, Portage, 04768
Holes: 9

Annapolis CC, 2638 Carrollton Rd., Annapolis, 21403, 301-263-6771   *Maryland*
Holes: 9
Baltimore GC, 11500 Mays Rd., Baltimore, 21093
Bay Club GC, PO Box 682, Ocean City, 21842
Holes: 18

Black Rock GC, Rt 2 Box 438, Smithsburg, 21783
Holes: 18
Blue Heron GC, Route 8, Stevensville, 21666, 301-643-5721
Holes: 9
Bowie G & CC, P. O. Box 590, Bowie, 20715, 301-262-8141
Holes: 18
Breton Bay G & CC, Leonardtown, 20650, 301-475-2300
Holes: 18
Caroline County CC, Pealiquor Rd., Denton, 21629, 301-479-1425
Holes: 18
Carroll Park GC, 2100 Washington Blvd., Baltimore, 21230, 301-752-9150
Holes: 9
Clifton Park GC, 2701 St. Lo Driver, Baltimore, 21213, 301-243-3500
Holes: 18
Diamond Ridge GC, Dogwood & Ridge Rds., Woodlawn, 21207, 301-944-2446
Holes: 18
Dwight D. Eisenhower GC, P.O. Box 484, Crownsville, 21030, 301-849-8341
Holes: 18
Elks GC, P. O. Box 1602, Salisbury, 21801, 301-749-2695
Holes: 9
Enterprise GC, 3000 Enterprise Rd., Mitchellville, 20716, 301-249-2040
Holes: 18
Falls Road GC, 10800 Falls Rd., Potomac, 20854, 301-299-5156
Holes: 18
Font Hill GC, 10135 Frederick Rd., Ellicott City, 21043, 301-465-1558
Holes: 18
Forest Park GC, 2900 Hillsdale Rd., Baltimore, 21207, 301-448-2293
Holes: 18
Glenn Dale GC, Old Prospect Hill Rd., Glenn Dale, 20769, 301-262-1166
Holes: 18
Golf Gridiron, 301 Mitchell Drive, Reisterstown, 21136, 301-833-7721
Holes: 9
Great Oaks Landing Resort & Co, Box 527, Chestertown, 21620, 301-778-2100
Holes: 9
Hagerstown Muni GC, 2 South Cleveland Ave., Hagerstown, 21740,
301-733-8630
Holes: 9
Henson Creek GC, 7200 Sunnyside Ln., Ft. Washington, 20744, 301-567-4646
Holes: 9
Golden Triangle GC, 2231 Johns Hopkins Rd., Gambrills, 21054, 301-721-1170
Holes: 9
Laytonsville gC, 7130 Dorsey Rd., Laytonsville, 20879, 301-948-5288
Holes: 18
Longview GC, Padonia Rd., Timonium, 21093, 301-628-6362
Holes: 18
Marlboro CC, P.O. Box 29, Upper Marlboro, 20870, 301-952-1350
Par: 72, Holes: 18
Mt. Pleasant GC, 6001 Hillen Rd., Baltimore, 21239, 301-254-5100
Holes: 18
Nassawango CC, P.O. Box 266, Snow Hill, 21863, 301-632-3114
Holes: 18
Naval Ordnance Station GC, Indian Head, 20640, 301-743-4662
Holes: 9
Needwood GC, 6724 Needwood Rd., Derwood, 20855, 301-948-1075
Holes: 27

Oakland CC, P.O. Box 209 Golf Course Rd., Oakland, 21550, 301-334-3883
Holes: 18
Ocean City Golf & Yacht Club, Rt. 2, Box 251, Berlin, 21811, 301-641-1779
Holes: 36
Oxon Run GD, 3000 23rd Pkwy., Oxon Run, 20021, 301-894-2200
Holes: 18
Paint Branch GC, 4690 University Blvd., College Park, 20740, 301-935-0330
Holes: 9
Pine Ridge GC, Dulaney Valley Rd., Lutherville, 21093, 301-252-1408
Holes: 18
Prospect Bay GC, Prospect Bay Rd., Grasonville, 21638, 301-827-6924
Holes: 18
Redgate Muni GC, 14500 Avery Rd., Rockville, 20853, 301-340-2404
Holes: 18
Rocky Point GC & Driving Range, 1935 Back River Neck Rd., Essex, 21221,
301-391-2906 Holes: 18
Sligo Creek Parkway GC, 9701 Sligo Creek Pkwy., Silver Spring, 20901,
301-585-6006 Holes: 9
Swan Point GC, Issue, 20645, 301-259-2074
Holes: 18
University of Maryland GC, College Park, 20740, 301-262-2321
Holes: 18
Village Green, McHenry, 21541, 301-387-5581
Holes: 18
Western Maryland College GC, Pennsylvania Ave., Westminster, 21157,
301-848-7667 Holes: 9
White Plains GC, Box 68, White Plains, 20695, 301-645-1300
Par: 70, Holes: 18
Wicomico Shores Muni GC, Rt. 234 & 236, Chaptico, 20621, 301-884-4601
Holes: 18
Winter Quarters GC, Winters Quarters Dr., Pocomoke City, 21851,
301-957-1171 Holes: 9
Worthington Valley CC, 12425 Greenspring Ave., Owings Mills, 21117,
301-356-9890 Holes: 18

Agawam CC, Agawam, 01001, 413-786-2194 *Massachusetts*
Yards: 6000, Par: 71, Holes: 18
Amesbury G & CC, Amesbury, 01913, 508-388-5153
Yards: 3125, Par: 35, Holes: 9
Amherst GC, Amherst, 01002, 413-256-6894
Yards: 3100, Par: 35, Holes: 9
Ashfield Community GC, Ashfield, 01330, 413-628-4413
Yards: 4088, Par: 33, Holes: 9
Bass River GC, High Bank Road, South Yarmouth, 02664, 508-398-9079
Yards: 6154, Par: 72, Holes: 18
Bay Path GC, East Brookfield, 01515, 508-867-8161
Yards: 3000, Par: 36, Holes: 9
Beaver Brook CC, Haydenville, 01039, 413-268-7229
Yards: 3310, Par: 36, Holes: 9
Blandford CC, Blandford, 01008, 413-848-2414
Yards: 2350, Par: 33, Holes: 9
Blue Rock GC, 48 Todd Road, South Yarmouth, 02664, 508-352-9839
Yards: 2790, Par: 54, Holes: 18
Braintree Golf Assoc., South Braintree, 02184, 617-843-9781
Yards: 3180, Par: 70, Holes: 9

Brewster GC, Brewster, 02631, 617-896-3785
Yards: 6130, Par: 70, Holes: 9
Brookline GC, Chestnut Hill, 02135, 617-566-9300
Yards: 6300, Par: 71, Holes: 18
Candlewood GC, Ipswich, 01938, 617-356-5377
Yards: 2170, Par: 33, Holes: 9
CC of New Seabury, Mashpee, 02649, 617-428-8585
Yards: 7175, Par: 72, Holes: 18
Cedar Glen GC, Saugus, 01906, 617-233-3609
Yards: 3040, Par: 36, Holes: 9
Chemawa CC, North Attleborough, 02760, 617-761-8754
Yards: 2879, Par: 36, Holes: 9
Chequesset Yacht & CC, Wellfleet, 02667, 617-349-3704
Yards: 2950, Par: 35, Holes: 9
Cherry Hill GC, North Amherst, 01059, 413-253-9935
Yards: 6120, Par: 37, Holes: 9
Clauson's Inn & Golf Resort, North Falmouth, 02556, 617-563-2255
Yards: 6548, Par: 72, Holes: 18
Clearview CC, Millbury, 01527, 617-753-9201
Yards: 3038, Par: 35, Holes: 9
Colonial CC, Wakefield, 01880, 617-245-9300
Yards: 6825, Par: 71, Holes: 18
Cotuit-Highground GC, Cotuit, 02635
Yards: 1200, Par: 28, Holes: 9
Country Club of Billerica, Billerica, 01821, 617-667-8061
Yards: 3315, Par: 36, Holes: 9
Cranwell GC, Lenox, 01240, 413-637-1030
Yards: 6170, Par: 70, Holes: 18
Crystal Springs GC, Haverhill, 01830, 617-374-9621
Yards: 6490, Par: 71, Holes: 18
Cummaquid GC, Cummaquid, 02637, 617-362-2022
Yards: 3100, Par: 35, Holes: 9
D. Wm. Field GC, 331 Oak Street, Brockton, 02401, 508-580-7855
Yards: 5972, Par: 70, Holes: 18
Dennis Highlands GC, 825 Old Bass River Road, Dennis, 02638, 508-385-8347
Yards: 6500, Par: 71, Holes: 18
Dennis Pines GC, Golf Course Road, East Dennis, 02641, 617-385-8347
Yards: 7029, Par: 72, Holes: 18
Dunfey's GC, Hyannis, 02601, 617-775-7775
Par: 54, Holes: 18
Dunroamin CC, Gilbertville, 04031, 617-477-8880
Yards: 2950, Par: 35, Holes: 9
East Mountain CC, Westfield, 01085, 413-568-1539
Yards: 6100, Par: 71, Holes: 18
Easton CC, South Easton, 02375, 617-238-9090
Yards: 6000, Par: 72, Holes: 9
Eastward HO! CC, Chatham, 02633, 617-945-0620
Yards: 6350, Par: 71, Holes: 18
Edgewood GC, Southwick, 01077, 413-569-6826
Yards: 6050, Par: 69, Holes: 18
Egremont CC, Great Barrington, 01230, 413-528-4222
Par: 18, Holes: 72
Elmcrest CC, E. Longmeadow, 01028, 413-525-6641
Yards: 6441, Par: 70, Holes: 18
Falmouth CC, 630 Carriage Shop Road, Falmouth, 02540, 508-548-3211
Yards: 6535, Par: 72, Holes: 18

Far Corner Farm GC, Boxford, 01921, 617-352-9838
Yards: 6719, Par: 72, Holes: 18
Fire Fly CC, Seekonk, 02771, 617-336-6622
Yards: 3866, Par: 54, Holes: 18
Forest Park CC, Adams, 01220, 413-743-0775
Yards: 2525, Par: 34, Holes: 9
Foxborough CC, Foxborough, 02035, 617-543-4661
Yards: 6370, Par: 72, Holes: 18
Franconia Muni GC, Springfield, 01101, 413-734-9349
Yards: 6350, Par: 71, Holes: 18
Fresh Pond GC, Cambridge, 02114, 617-354-9130
Yards: 6226, Par: 70, Holes: 9
Gardner Muni GC, Gardner, 01440, 617-632-9703
Yards: 5980, Par: 71, Holes: 9
Geaa GC, Pittsfield, 01201, 413-442-3585
Yards: 3190, Par: 35, Holes: 9
George Wright GC, 429 West Street, Hyde Park Boston, 02136, 617-361-8313
Yards: 6400, Par: 70, Holes: 18
Glen Ellen CC, Millis, 02054, 617-742-3922
Yards: 6600, Par: 71, Holes: 18
Granberry Valley GC, Oak St., Hyannis, 02645
Grasmere CC, Falmouth, 02540, 617-540-1655
Yards: 2740, Par: 54, Holes: 18
Great Neck GC, Wareham, 02571, 617-295-2617
Yards: 3010, Par: 54, Holes: 18
Green Harbor GC, 624 Webster Street, Marshfield, 02050, 617-834-7303
Yards: 6211, Par: 71, Holes: 18
Green Hill Muni GC, Worcester, 01613, 617-852-0915
Yards: 6300, Par: 71, Holes: 18
Greenock CC, Lee, 01238, 413-243-3323
Yards: 3000, Par: 35, Holes: 9
Halifax CC, Halifax, 02338, 617-293-9181
Yards: 6760, Par: 72, Holes: 18
Happy Valley GC, Lynn, 01901, 617-592-8238
Yards: 6000, Par: 70, Holes: 18
Harwich Port GC, Harwich Port, 02646, 617-432-0250
Yards: 5286, Par: 70, Holes: 9
Heather Hill GC, Plainville, 02762, 617-695-9895
Yards: 6450, Par: 71, Holes: 18
Heritage CC, Charlton, 01507, 617-248-5111
Yards: 6370, Par: 71, Holes: 18
Heritage Hill CC, Lakeville, 01930, 508-947-7743
Par: 54, Holes: 18
Herring Run GC, Taunton, 02780, 617-822-1797
Yards: 3000, Par: 34, Holes: 9
Hickory Hill, Methuen, 01844, 617-686-0822
Yards: 6900, Par: 71, Holes: 18
Hidden Hollow CC, Rehoboth, 02769, 617-252-9392
Yards: 2905, Par: 35, Holes: 9
Highland GC, N. Truro, 02666, 617-487-9723
Yards: 2980, Par: 34, Holes: 9
Hillcrest CC, Leicester, 01524, 508-892-9361
Yards: 5850, Par: 71, Holes: 12
Holly Ridge GC, Country Club Road, South Sandwich, 02563, 617-428-5577
Yards: 2934, Par: 54, Holes: 18

Holly Ridge GC, Country Club Road, S. Sandwich, 02563
Holes: 18
Holyoke CC, Holyoke, 01040, 413-539-9133
Yards: 6800, Par: 72, Holes: 9
Island CC, Oak Bluffs, 02557, 617-693-2002
Yards: 6190, Par: 70, Holes: 18
Island Inn GC, Beach Rd., Buzzards Bay, 02557
Iyanough Hills GC, RTE. 132, Hyannis, 02601, 617-362-2606
Yards: 3240, Par: 36, Holes: 9
L. J. Martin GC, 85 Park Road, Weston, 02193, 617-891-1110
Yards: 6800, Par: 72, Holes: 18
Lakeview GC, Hamilton, 01936, 617-468-9584
Yards: 2040, Par: 31, Holes: 9
Lakewood CC, Natick, 01760, 617-655-1118
Yards: 6475, Par: 71, Holes: 18
Larry Gannon Muni Course, Lynn, 01901, 617-592-8238
Yards: 5924, Par: 70, Holes: 18
Little Harbor CC, Little Harbor Road, Wareham, 02571, 508-295-2617
Yards: 3095, Par: 56, Holes: 18
Lost Brook GC, 750 University Ave, POB 772, Norwood, 02062, 617-769-2550
Yards: 3104, Par. 54, Holes: 18, Pro: Alan Greim
Lynnfield Center GC, Lynnfield, 01940, 617-334-9877
Yards: 2500, Par: 34, Holes: 9
Maplewood GC, LKunenburg, 01773, 617-582-6694
Yards: 2690, Par: 35, Holes: 9
Marion GC, Marion, 02738, 617-897-9885
Yards: 3350, Par: 34, Holes: 9
Marlborough CC, Marlborough, 01752, 617-485-1660
Yards: 3210, Par: 36, Holes: 9
Maynard CC, Maynard, 01754, 617-897-9885
Yards: 3350, Par: 34, Holes: 9
Miacomet GC, Nantucket, 02554, 617-228-9764
Yards: 3333, Par: 37, Holes: 9
Middlebrook CC, Rehoboth, 02769, 617-252-9395
Yards: 2984, Par: 35, Holes: 9
Mill Valley Golf Links, Belchertown, 01007, 413-323-4079
Yards: 3609, Par: 36, Holes: 9
Mink Meadows GC, Vineyard, 02568, 617-693-0600
Yards: 3100, Par: 35, Holes: 9
Mohawk Meadows GC, Deerfield, 01342, 413-773-7710
Yards: 2910, Par: 36, Holes: 9
Monoosnock CC, Leominster, 01453, 617-534-9619
Yards. 3050, Par. 35, Holes 9
Mt. Everett GC, Gt Barrington, 01230 413-528-4222
Yards: 5850, Par 72, Holes: 18
Mt. Hood GC, Slayton Road, Melrose, 02176, 617-665-8139
Yards: 5500, Par: 69, Holes: 18
Needham GC, Needham, 02136, 617-444-9692
Yards: 6078, Par· 72, Holes: 9
Newton Commonwealth GC, Newton, 02158, 617-244-4763
Par: 70, Holes: 18
Nichols College GC, Dudley, 01570, 617-943-9837
Yards: 6482, Par 71, Holes 9
North Hill CC, Duxbury, 02332, 617-934-5800
Yards. 3290, Par 36, Holes 9

Northfield CC, East Northfield, 01260,   413-498-5311
Yards: 2930, Par: 36, Holes: 9
Norton CC, Norton, 02766,   617-285-3840
Yards: 6300, Par: 71, Holes: 18
Oak Ridge GC, W. Gill Rd., Gill, 01376,   413-863-9693
Yards: 2952, Par: 36, USGA: 68.7, Holes: 9, Pro: Bill Macklin
Orchard GC, South Hadley, 01075,   413-538-2543
Yards: 6595, Par: 71, Holes: 18
Oxford GC, North Oxford, 01540,   617-892-9188
Yards: 6167, Par: 71, Holes: 18
Pakachoag GC, Auburn, 01501,   617-755-4292
Yards: 3375, Par: 36, Holes: 9
Paul Harney GC, 74 Club Valley Drive, East Falmouth, 02535,   508-563-3454
Yards: 3700, Par: 59, Holes: 18
Pine Knoll GC, East Longmeadow, 01028,   413-525-7647
Yards: 1827, Par: 54, Holes: 18
Pembroke CC, West Elm, Pembroke, 02359,   617-826-5191
Yards: 6429, Par: 71, Holes: 18
Pheasant Run GC, Leominster, 01453,   617-537-9293
Yards: 1315, Par: 27, Holes: 9
Pine Crest GC, Berlin, 01503,   617-838-9404
Yards: 2405, Par: 33, Holes: 9
Pine Meadow GC, Lexington, 02173,   617-862-9632
Yards: 2840, Par: 35, Holes: 9
Pine Oaks GC, Easton, 02334,   617-238-2320
Yards: 3000, Par: 34, Holes: 9
Pine Valley CC, Brockton, 02403,   617-583-9525
Yards: 2915, Par: 33, Holes: 9
Pittsfield Gen. A. A., Pittsfield, 01201,   413-442-3585
Yards: 6195, Par: 69, Holes: 9
Pleasant Valley GC, Armsby Rd., Worcester, 01527
Plymouth CC, Plymouth, 02360,   617-746-0476
Yards: 6200, Par: 69, Holes: 18
Pocasset GC, Club House Dr., Pocasset, 02559,   617-563-9851
Yards: 6300, Par: 72, Holes: 18
Ponkapoag GC, Canton, 02021,   617-828-0645
Yards: 6555, Par: 72, Holes: 18
Pontoosuc Lake CC, Pittsfield, 01201,   413-445-4217
Yards: 6100, Par: 70, Holes: 18
Poquoy Brook CC, Lakeville, 01347,   617-947-9834
Yards: 6900, Par: 72, Holes: 18
Rehoboth CC, Rehoboth, 02769,   617-252-6259
Yards: 6355, Par: 70, Holes: 18
Reservoir Heights GC, Lakeville, 01347,   617-947-6630
Yards: 6385, Par: 72, Holes: 9
Ridder Farm GC, East Bridgewater, 02333,   617-447-9003
Yards: 6135, Par: 71, Holes: 18
Riverside GC, Weston, 02193,   617-894-4903
Yards: 6475, Par: 72, Holes: 18
Rochester GC, Rochester, 02770,   617-763-5155
Yards: 5500, Par: 70, Holes: 9
Rockland GC, Rockland, 02370,   617-878-5836
Yards: 3600, Par: 54, Holes: 18
Rolling Green, Andover, 01810,   617-475-4006
Yards: 1500, Par: 27, Holes· 9

Saddle Hill CC, Hopkinton, 01748, 617-435-4630
Yards: 6245, Par: 72, Holes: 18
Sagamore Spring GC, 1287 Main St, POX 8, Lynnfield, 01940, 617-334-3151
Yards: 6135, Par: 71, Holes: 18
Saint Mark's GC, Southborough, 01772, 617-485-9816
Yards: 5710, Par: 67, Holes: 9
Salem CC, Peabody, 01960, 617-532-2540
Yards: 6750, Par: 72, Holes: 18
Sandy Burr CC, Wayland, 01778, 617-358-7211
Yards: 6800, Par: 71, Holes: 18
South Shore CC, Hingham, 02043, 617-749-1720
Yards: 6375, Par: 71, Holes: 18
Southampton CC, Southampton, 01982, 413-527-9815
Yards: 6000, Par: 70, Holes: 18
St. Anne CC, Agawam, 01001, 413-786-2088
Yards: 6412, Par: 72, Holes: 18
Stockbridge GC, Stockbridge, 01101, 413-298-3423
Yards: 6400, Par: 71, Holes: 18
Stone-E-Lea CC, Attleboro, 02703, 617-222-9735
Yards: 5200, Par: 70, Holes: 18
Strawberry Valley GC, Abington, 02351, 617-878-9797
Yards: 3325, Par: 36, Holes: 9
Sun Valley CC, Rehoboth, 02769, 617-336-9825
Yards: 6300, Par: 71, Holes: 18
Suspiro CC, Somerset, 02725, 617-675-2539
Yards: 3070, Par: 35, Holes: 9
Swansea CC, Swansea, 02777, 617-379-9886
Yards: 6855, Par: 72, Holes: 18
Tekoa CC, Westfield, 01085, 413-562-9859
Yards: 3000, Par: 35, Holes: 9
Tony Conigliaro, Nahant, 01908, 617-581-1300
Par: 27, Holes: 9
Touisset CC, Swansea, 02777, 617-678-7991
Yards: 6380, Par: 71, Holes: 18
Twin Springs GC, Bolton, 01740, 617-779-8273
Yards: 2754, Par: 35, Holes: 9
Tyngsboro CC, Tyngsborough, 01879, 617-649-7334
Yards: 3100, Par: 33, Holes: 12
Veterans GC, Springfield, 01101, 413-783-7264
Yards: 6330, Par: 72, Holes: 18
Wachusett CC, West Boylston, 01583, 617-835-4484
Yards: 6625, Par: 72, Holes: 18
Wading River GC, Norton, 02766, 617-222-9883
Yards: 2289, Par: 54, Holes: 18
Wareham CC, Wareham, 01778, 617-759-5742
Yards: 6700, Par: 72, Holes: 18
Wayland CC, Wayland, 01778, 617-358-4882
Yards: 6285, Par: 70, Holes: 18
Westboro CC, Westborough, 01581, 617-366-7714
Yards: 3150, Par: 35, Holes: 9
Whaling City CC, New Bedford, 02741, 617-996-9393
Yards: 7000, Par: 74, Holes: 18
Whippernon Club, Russell, 01071, 413-862-3606
Yards: 5186, Par: 29, Holes: 9
Willowdale GC, Mansfield, 02048, 617-339-3197
Yards: 1900, Par: 30, Holes: 9

Winchendon CC, Winchendon, 04175, 617-297-9897
Par: 70, Holes: 18
Winchendon School GC, 172 Ash St., Fitchburg, 01475
Worthington GC, Worthington, 01098, 413-238-9731
Yards: 2825, Par: 35, Holes: 9

A-Ga-Ming GC, W. Torch Lake Dr., Elk Rapids, 49648, 616-264-5081 *Michigan*
Yards: 6520, Par: 72, USGA: 71.3, Holes: 18
Alpena GC, 1135 Golf Course Rd., Alpena, 49707, 517-354-5052
Par: 71, USGA: 69.5, Holes: 18
Alpine GC, 6320 Alpine Ave. NW, Comstock Park, 49321, 616-784-1064
Yards: 6467, Par: 71, Holes: 18
Alwyn Downs GC, 1225 S. Kalamazoo, Marshall, 49068, 616-781-3905
Yards: 6350, Par: 72, Holes: 18
Antrim Dells GC, US-31, Atwood, 48412, 616-599-2679
Yards: 6700, Par: 72, USGA: 72.1, Holes: 18
Arrowhead GC—#1, 2797 Lapeer Rd., Pontiac Twp., 48057, 313-373-6860
Yards: 3287, Par: 36, Holes: 9
Arrowhead GC, 1201 E. Gun Rd., Caro, 48723, 517-673-2017
Yards: 2798, Par: 35, Holes: 9
Arrowhead GC, 2170 Alden Nash, NE, Lowell, 49331, 616-897-7264
Yards: 6100, Par: 72, Holes: 18
Au Sable River GC, 4450 E. Bissonette, Oscoda, 49750, 517-739-7760
Yards: 6700, Par: 70, Holes: 18
Bald Mountain GC—#1, 3350 Kern Road, Lake Orion, 48035, 313-373-1110
Yards: 6850, Par: 71, Holes: 18
Bay County GC, 584 W. Hampton, Essexville, 48732, 517-892-2161
Yards: 6700, Par: 72, USGA: 71.3, Holes: 18
Bear Lake Golf Assn., Hwy. 31 S, Bear Lake, 49614, 616-864-3817
Yards: 6085, Par: 72, Holes: 18
Beaver Island GC, St. James, Beaver Island, 49720, 616-448-2301
Yards: 3260, Par: 35, Holes: 9
Bedford Valley GC, 23161 Wabascon Rd., Battle Creek, 49017, 616-965-3384
Yards: 7010, Par: 72, Holes: 18
Beech Hollow GC, 7494 Hospital Rd., Freeland, 48623, 517-695-5427
Yards: 5900, Par: 72, Holes: 18
Beechwood Greens GC, 1161 W. Frances Rd., Mt. Morris, 48458, 313-686-4200
Yards: 1995, Par: 31, Holes: 9
Bel-Aire GC, M-88 Highway, Bellaire, 49615, 616-533-8942
Yards: 3300, Par: 37, Holes: 9
Belle Isle GC, Oakwood & Riverbank Rds., Detroit, 48226, 313-267-7130
Yards: 1881, Par: 29, Holes: 9
Belle River GC, 12564 Belle River Rd., Memphis, 48041, 313-392-2121
Yards: 6700, Par: 72, Holes: 18
Belvedere GC, Ellsworth Rd., Charlevoix, 49720, 616-547-2611
Yards: 6701, Par: 72, USGA: 71.8, Holes: 18
Bent Pine GC, Whitehall, 49461, 616-766-2045
Par: 72, Holes: 18
Big Spruce GC, N US-45, Bruce Crossing, 49912, 906-827-3727
Yards: 2600, Par: 35, Holes: 9
Binder Park Muni GC, 6723 B Srive S, Battle Creek, 49017, 616-966-3459
Yards: 7000, Par: 72, Holes: 18
Blossom Trails GC, 1565 E. Britian Ave., Benton Harbor, 49022, 616-925-4951
Yards: 5808, Par: 69, Holes: 18
Bob-O-Link GC—#1, 47666 Grand River, Novi, 48050, 313-349-2723
Yards: 6895, Par: 72, Holes: 18

Bogie Lake GC, 11231 Bogie Lake Rd., Union Lake, 48085, 313-363-4416
Yards: 6145, Par: 71, Holes: 18
Bonnie Brook GC, 19990 Shiawassee, Detroit, 48219, 313-538-8383
Yards: 4190, Par: 63, Holes: 18
Bonnie View GC, 311 N. Michigan Rd., Eaton, 48827, 517-663-4363
Yards: 3176, Par: 36, Holes: 9
Boyne Mountain GC—Alpine Course, Boyne Falls, 49713, 616-549-2441
Yards: 7017, Par: 72, Holes: 18
Brad Van Pelt's GC, 4377 S. M-52, Owosso, 48867, 517-725-9194
Yards: 2975, Par: 36, Holes: 9
Brae Burn GC, 10860 W. 5 Mile, Plymouth, 48170, 313-453-1900
Yards: 6515, Par: 70, Holes: 18
Bramblewood GC, 2154 Bramblewood Rd., Holly, 48442, 313-634-3481
Yards: 2806, Par: 35, Holes: 9
Briar Hill GC, 950 W. 40th, Fremont, 49412, 616-924-2070
Yards: 5895, Par: 71, USGA: 66.2, Holes: 18
Briarwood GC, 2900 92nd St., Caledonia, 49316, 616-698-8720
Yards: 6050, Par: 71, Holes: 18
Broadmoor GC, 7725 Kraft, Caledonia, 49316, 616-891-8000
Yards: 6506, Par: 72, Holes: 18
Brooklane GC, 44115 W. 6 Mile Rd., Northville, 48167, 313-348-1010
Yards: 3600, Par: 60, Holes: 18
Brookshire GC, 205 W. Church St., Williamston, 48895, 517-655-2028
Yards: 2712, Par: 35, Holes: 9
Brookside GC, 6451 Ann Arbor-Saline Rd., Saline, 48176, 313-429-4276
Yards: 6412, Par: 72, Holes: 18
Brookside Golf GC, 1518 S. Johnson Rd., Gowen, 49326, 616-984-2381
Yards: 2900, Par: 35, Holes: 9
Bruce Hills GC, 6771 Traf Rd., Romeo, 48065, 313-752-7244
Yards: 2984, Par: 35, Holes: 9
Bryn Mawr GC, Dowagiac, 49047, 616-782-5827
Par: 70, Holes: 18
Burning Oak GC, Higgins Lake, 48627, 517-821-9821
Par: 72, USGA: 69.5, Holes: 18
Burr Oak GC, 3491 N. Parma Rd., Parma, 49269, 517-531-4741
Yards: 6289, Par: 72, USGA: 69.7, Holes: 18
Burroughs Farms GC—#1, 5341 Brighton Rd., Brighton, 48116, 313-227-4541
Yards: 6235, Par: 71, USGA: 68.5, Holes: 18
Butternut Brook GC, 2200 Island Hwy., Charlotte, 48813, 517-543-0570
Yards: 6455, Par: 71, Holes: 18
Byron Hills GC, 7330 Burlingame Ave., Byron Center, 49315, 616-878-1522
Yards: 6500, Par: 72, Holes: 18
Cadillac CC, M-55, Cadillac, 49601, 616-775-9442
Yards: 6000, Par: 70, Holes: 18
Calumet GC, Golf Course Rd., Calumet, 49913, 906-337-3911
Yards: 3152, Par: 36, Holes: 9
Candlestone GC, 8100 N. Storey, Belding, 48809, 616-794-1580
Yards: 6800, Par: 72, Holes: 18
Caro GC, 1080 E. Caro Rd., Caro, 48723, 517-673-7797
Yards: 2984, Par: 35, Holes: 9
Caseville Golf, Griggs Rd., Caseville, 48725, 517-856-2613
Yards: 2810, Par: 35, Holes: 9
CC of Reese, 2280 S. Reese Rd., Reese, 48757, 517-868-4991
Yards: 2911, Par: 35, Holes: 9
Cedar Glen GC, 36860 25 Mile Rd., New Baltimore, 48047, 313-725-8156
Yards: 3100, Par: 35, Holes: 9

Cedar Hills GC, 7525 Cedar Run Rd., Traverse City, 49684
Yards: 1292, Par: 27, Holes: 9
Cedarview Golf, 800 Hogsback, Mason, 48854, 517-676-1942
Yards: 1100, Par: 27, Holes: 9
Centennial Acres GC, 12479 Dow Rd., Sunfield, 48890, 517-566-8055
Yards: 3290, Par: 36, Holes: 9
Centerview GC, N. Adrian Hwy., Adrian, 49221, 517-263-8081
Yards: 6647, Par: 71, Holes: 18
Century Oaks GC, 4570 M-142, Elkton, 48731, 517-375-4419
Yards: 2965, Par: 35, Holes: 9
Chandler Park GC, Chandler Park Dr., Detroit, 48213, 313-267-7150
Yards: 5235, Par: 66, Holes: 18
Chardell GC, 4646 Howe Rd., Bath, 48808, 517-641-4123
Yards: 3116, Par: 36, Holes: 9
Charlevoix GC, Central Ave., Charlevoix, 49720, 616-547-2171
Yards: 3000, Par: 36, Holes: 9
Chase H. Hammond GC, 2454 N. Putnam Rd., Muskegon, 49445, 616-766-3035
Yards: 6600, Par: 72, Holes: 18
Cheboygan G & CC, Old Mackinaw Rd., Cheboygan, 49721, 616-627-4264
Yards: 6100, Par: 70, Holes: 18
Cherrywood GC, 7910 Whiteford Center Rd., Ottawa Lake, 49267,
313-856-6669   Yards: 3005, Par: 35, Holes: 9
Cheshire Hills GC, Rt. 6, Allegan, 49010, 616-673-9907
Yards: 5335, Par: 70, Holes: 18
Chippewa Hill GC, 5300 Bancroft Rd., Durand, 48429, 517-743-3277
Yards: 3100, Par: 35, Holes: 9
Chisholm Hills GC, 2397 s. Washington Rd., Lansing, 48910, 517-694-0169
Yards: 5700, Par: 70, USGA: 63.1, Holes: 18
Clare City GC, 7795 S. Clare Ave., Clare, 48617, 517-386-3510
Yards: 3275, Par: 36, Holes: 9
Clark Lake GC—18 hole course, 5535 Wesch Rd., Brooklyn, 49230,
517-592-6259   Yards: 7000, Par: 72, Holes: 18
Clarkston GC, 9241 N. Eston, Clarkston, 48016, 313-394-0020
Yards: 2715, Par: 35, Holes: 9
Clinton County GC, 8013 N. US-27, St. Johns, 48879, 517-224-6287
Yards: 3224, Par: 36, Holes: 9
Concord Hills GC, 7331 Pulaski Rd., Concord, 49237, 517-524-8337
Yards: 6525, Par: 72, USGA: 69.7, Holes: 18
Corunna Hills GC, 1840 Legion Rd., Corunna, 48817, 517-743-4693
Yards: 3200, Par: 36, Holes: 9
Courtland Hills GC, 5460 11 Mile Rd., Rockford, 49341, 616-866-1402
Yards: 6700, Par: 71, Holes: 18
Cracklewood GC, 22 Mile Road, Mt. Clemens, 48045
Holes: 18
Crapo Hills GC, West Branch, 48661, 517-345-5479
Par: 35, Holes: 9
Crest View GC, 6279 96th Avenue, Zeeland, 49464, 616-875-8101
Yards: 6200, Par: 72, Holes: 18
Crestview GC, 900 West D Avenue, Kalamazoo, 49007, 616-349-1111
Yards: 6025, Par: 70, USGA: 67.1, Holes: 18
Crooked Creek GC, 9387 Gratiot Rd., Saginaw, 49603, 517-781-0050
Yards: 6071, Par: 72, Holes: 18
Crystal Falls GC, Crystal Falls, 49920, 906-875-9919
Yards: 3025, Par: 36, Holes: 9
Crystal Golf—#1, 2122 Strait Tow Blvd., Crystal, 48818, 517-235-6616
Yards: 2800, Par: 35, Holes: 9

Crystal Lake GC, US-31 ½ Mile N. of Beulah, Beulah, 49617, 616-882-4061
Yards: 3248, Par: 36, Holes: 9
Currie Muni—#1, 1006 Currie Pkwy., Midland, 48640, 517-839-9600
Yards: 6486, Par: 72, Holes: 18
Dama Farms GC, 410 E. Marr Rd., Howell, 48843, 517-546-4635
Yards: 6400, Par: 72, Holes: 18
Dearborn Hills GC, 1300 S. Telegraph, Dearborn, 48128, 313-277-9625
Yards: 6025, Par: 70, Holes: 18
Deer Run GC, 3200 Hanover Rd., Horton, 49246, 517-688-3350
Yards: 3245, Par: 36, Holes: 9
Deer Run GC, 13955 Cascade, Lowell, 49331, 616-897-8481
Yards: 7151, Par: 74, Holes: 18
Deme Acres GC, 17655 Albain Rd., Petersburg, 49270, 313-279-1151
Yards: 5730, Par: 71, Holes: 18
Demor Hills GC, Rte. 1 Ranger Hwy., Morenci, 49256, 517-458-6679
Yards: 6100, Par: 72, Holes: 18
Devils Lake GC, 14600 US-223, Manitou Beach, 49253, 517-547-7440
Yards: 3100, Par: 36, Holes: 9
Diamond Lake GC, Golf Lane, Cassopolis, 49031, 616-445-3143
Yards: 2724, Par: 35, Holes: 9
Dowagiac Elks GC, Riverside Drive, Dowagiac, 49047, 616-782-5685
Yards: 3011, Par: 37, Holes: 9
Drummond Island GC, Drummond Island, 49726, 906-493-5406
Yards: 3128, Par: 36, Holes: 9
Dundee GC, 13851 S. Custer Rd., Dundee, 48131, 313-529-2321
Yards: 3000, Par: 36, Holes: 9
Dun Rovin GC, 16377 Haggerty Rd., Plymouth, 48170, 313-420-0144
Yards: 6850, Par: 72, USGA: 71.0, Holes: 18
Dunham Hills GC, 13561 Dunham, Milford, 48042, 313-887-9170
Yards: 6908, Par: 72, USGA: 72.8, Holes: 18
Dutch Hollow GC, 8500 E. Lansing Rd., Durand, 48429, 517-288-3960
Yards: 6000, Par: 71, Holes: 18
Eastern Hills GC, 6075 E.G. Ave., Kalamazoo, 49004
Yards: 6700, Par: 72, Holes: 18
Edgewood Forest GC, 2160 Sage Lake Road, Prescott, 48756, 517-873-5427
Yards: 2547, Par: 35, Holes: 9
Edgewood Hills BC, 1270 W. Monroe Rd., St. Louis, 48880, 517-681-3404
Yards: 3253, Par: 36, Holes: 9
Edmore Tennis & CC, Edmore, 48829, 517-427-3241
Yards: 3000, Par: 36, Holes: 9
El Dorado GC, 2869 N. Pontiac Trail, Walled Lake, 48088, 313-624-1736
Yards: 3100, Par: 34, Holes: 9
El Dorado GC, 3750 W. Howell Rd., Mason, 48854, 517-676-2854
Yards: 6307, Par: 72, Holes: 18
Elk Rapids GC, 724 Amos, Elk Rapids, 49629, 616-264-8891
Yards: 3106, Par: 36, Holes: 9
Ella Sharp Muni GC, 2880 Fourth St., Jackson, 49203, 517-788-4066
Yards: 6027, Par: 71, Holes: 18
Elmbrook GC, 420 Hammond Rd., Traverse City, 49684, 616-946-9180
Yards: 6165, Par: 72, Holes: 18
English Hills GC, 1300 4 Mile Rd., Walker, 49504, 616-784-3420
Yards: 4635, Par: 69, Holes: 18
Evergreen GC, 16124 W. Cadmus Rd., Hudson, 49247, 517-448-8017
Yards: 2700, Par: 36, USGA: 66.6, Holes: 9, Pro: Andy Montvai
Fairview Hills GC, 148 N. Caldwell Rd., Mio, 48647, 517-848-5810
Yards: 3180, Par: 36, Holes: 9

Fairway Estates GC, 6150 14th Ave., Hudsonville, 49417,   616-842-4040
Yards: 6247, Par: 72, USGA: 71.9, Holes: 18
Family Golf, 4200 Whitehall Rd., Muskegon, 49445,   616-766-2217
Yards: 1118, Par: 27, Holes: 9
Faulkwood Shores GC, 300 S. Hughes Rd., Howell, 48843,   517-546-4180
Yards: 7045, Par: 72, USGA: 74.3, Holes: 18
Fawn Crest GC, 663 Seaman Rd., Wellston, 49689,   616-848-4174
Yards: 2340, Par: 33, Holes: 9
Fellows Creek GC, 2936 Lotz Rd., Canton, 48188, 313-728-1300
Yards: 6210, Par: 72, Holes: 18
Fern Hill GC, 17600 Clinton River Rd., Mt. Clemens, 48044,   313-286-4700
Yards: 6035, Par: 71, Holes: 18
Forest Akers - MSU GC—#1, Harrison Rd., E. Lansing, 48824,   517-355-1635
Yards: 6812, Par: 71, USGA: 72.5, Holes: 18
Fox Hills, 485 Fox Farm Rd., Manistee, 49660,   616-723-3809
Yards: 2340, Par: 33, Holes: 9
Frankfort GC, 1857 Golf Lane, Frankfort, 49635,   616-352-4101
Yards: 2552, Par: 34, Holes: 9
Fruitport GC, 6330 S. Harvey, Muskegon, 49444
Yards: 5725, Par: 71, Holes: 18
G M Hazard GC, Sandusky, 48471,   313-648-2256
Par: 36, Holes: 9
Garland GC—#1, County Road 489, Lewiston, 49756,   517-786-2274
Yards: 6700, Par: 72, USGA: 72.9, Holes: 18
Gauss's Green Valley GC, 5751 Brooklyn Rd., Jackson, 49201,   517-764-0270
Yards: 5000, Par: 65, Holes: 18
Gaylord CC, M-32 West, Gaylord, 49735,   616-546-3377
Yards: 6582, Par: 72, Holes: 18
Genesee Valley GC, 5499 Miller Rd., Swartz Creek, 48473,   313-732-1401
Yards: 6772, Par: 72, Holes: 18
George Young Rec. GC, Iron River, 49935,   906-265-3401
Holes: 18
Georgetown GC, 1365 King George, Ann Arbor, 48104,   313-971-5500
Yards: 1272, Par: 28, Holes: 9
Giant Oaks GC—#1, 1024 Valetta Dr., Temperence, 48182,   313-847-6733
Yards: 6700, Par: 72, Holes: 18
Giant Oaks GC—#2, 1024 Valetta Dr., Temperence, 48182,   313-847-6733
Yards: 2100, Par: 29, Holes: 9
Gladstone GC, Days River, Gladstone, 49837,   906-428-9646
Yards: 2920, Par: 35, Holes: 9
Gladwin Heights GC, 3551 W. M-61, Gladwin, 48624,   517-426-9941
Yards: 5900, Par: 71, Holes: 18
Glen Oaks GC, 30500 13 Mile Rd., Farmington Hills, 48018,   313-851-8356
Yards: 6390, Par: 70, Holes: 18
Glenbrier GC, 4178 Locke Rd., Perry, 48872,   517-625-3800
Yards: 6000, Par: 71, Holes: 18
Glenhurst GC, 25345 W. 6 Mile Rd., Redford, 48240,   313-592-8758
Yards: 5600, Par: 70, Holes: 18
Glenlore GC, 2000 Sleeth Rd., Milford, 48042,   313-363-7997
Yards: 2100, Par: 54, Holes: 18
Glenn Shores GC, 111 Blue Star Hwy., South Haven, 49090,   616-227-3226
Yards: 2985, Par: 35, Holes: 9
Godwin Glen GC—#1, Johns Road, South Lyon, 48178,   313-437-0178
Yards: 3455, Par: 36, USGA: 72.5, Holes: 9
Gogebic GC, Country Club Rd., Ironwood, 49938,   906-932-2515
Yards: 3000, Par: 35, Holes: 9

Goodrich GC, 10080 Hegel Rd., Goodrich, 48438, 313-636-2493
Yards: 5380, Par: 70, Holes: 18
Gracewil Pines GC, 5400 Trailer Park Rd., Jackson, 49201, 517-764-4200
Holes: 18
Grand Beach GC, Perkins Blvd., Grand Beach, 48439, 616-469-4888
Yards: 2830, Par: 36, USGA: 66.2, Holes: 9
Grand Blanc GC, 5270 Perry, Grand Blanc, 48439, 313-694-5960
Yards: 6404, Par: 72, USGA: 70.9, Holes: 18
Grand Ledge GC, 5811 St. Joe, Hwy, Grand Ledge, 48837, 517-627-2495
Yards: 6676, Par: 72, Holes: 18
Grand Prairie GC, 3620 Grand Prairie Rd., Kalamazoo, 49007, 616-385-9806
Yards: 1720, Par: 30, Holes: 9
Grand Rapids—18 Hole Course, 4300 Leonard NE, Grand Rapids, 49506,
616-949-2820   Yards: 6500, Par: 72, USGA: 69.5, Holes: 18
Gratiot CC, 1508 N. State Rd., Ithaca, 48847, 517-875-4612
Yards: 3576, Par: 35, Holes: 9
Graver Lake GC, 25320 May St., Edwardsburg, 49112, 616-663-6463
Yards: 2700, Par: 35, Holes: 9
Grayling CC, Grayling, 49738, 517-348-9941
Yards: 3005, Par: 36, Holes: 9
Great Lakes Golf, 3113 Carpenter, Ypsilanti, 48197, 313-971-1165
Yards: 2105, Par: 54, Holes: 18
Green Acres GC, 7323 Dixie Hwy., Bridgeport, 48722, 517-777-3510
Yards: 6312, Par: 72, USGA: 69.8, Holes: 18
Green Hills GC, 1699 N. M-13, Pinconning, 48650, 517-697-3011
Yards: 6300, Par: 71, Holes: 18
Green Hills GC, 2411 W. Silver Lake Rd., Traverse City, 49684, 616-946-2975
Yards: 3400, Par: 36, Holes: 9
Green Meadows GC, 1555 Strasburg Rd., Monroe, 48161, 313-242-5566
Yards: 6448, Par: 70, USGA: 70.5, Holes: 18
Green Oaks GC, 1775 Clark Rd., Ypsilanti, 48197, 313-485-0881
Yards: 6235, Par: 71, Holes: 18
Green Tee Par 3 GC, 2233 Oakville-Waltz Rd., New Boston, 48164,
313-654-6427   Yards: 1495, Par: 27, Holes: 9
Green Valley GC, 25379 W. Fawn, Sturgis, 49091, 616-651-6331
Yards: 5500, Par: 68, Holes: 18
Greenbriar GC, 14820 Wellwood Rd., Brooklyn, 49230, 517-592-6952
Yards: 2400, Par: 33, Holes: 9
Greenbrier GC, 9350 N. Lapeer Rd., Mayville, 48744, 517-843-6675
Yards: 5703, Par: 72, Holes: 18
Groesbeck GC, 1600 Ormond St., Lansing, 48906, 517-483-4232
Yards: 6200, Par: 72, USGA: 69.4, Holes: 18, Pro: None
Gull Lake View's—Stonehedge, 15300 East "D" Ave. (M-89), Augusta, 49012,
616-731-2300   Yards: 5775, Par: 72, USGA: 68.8, Holes: 18, Pro: Woody Capron
Gun Ridge GC, 4460 Gun Lake Rd., Hastings, 49053, 616-948-8366
Yards: 2600, Par: 35, Holes: 9
Hadley Acres GC, 3797 S. Hadley, Hadley, 48440, 313-797-4820
Yards: 3200, Par: 36, Holes: 9
Hampton GC, 2600 Club Dr., Rochester, 48063, 313-852-3250
Yards: 2036, Par: 32, Holes: 9
Hankard Hills GC, 10251 Resort Rd., Pleasant Lake, 49272, 517-769-2507
Yards: 2600, Par: 34, Holes: 9
Harley's GC—#1, 2280 Union Lake Rd., Union Lake, 48085, 313-363-0202
Yards: 2905, Par: 35, Holes: 9
Harper Metro GC, 37575 Harper, Mt. Clemens, 48043, 313-465-5800
Yards: 1225, Par: 27, Holes: 9

Hartland Glen GC, 12400 Highland Rd., Hartland, 48029, 313-887-3777
Yards: 7045, Par: 72, Holes: 18
Hastings GC, 1550 N. Broadway, Hastings, 49058, 616-945-2756
Yards: 6277, Par: 72, Holes: 18
Heart of the Lakes GC, Case Rd., Brooklyn, 49230, 517-592-2110
Yards: 2660, Par: 34, Holes: 9
Heather Club, 900 Upper Scottsboro Way, Bloomfield Hills, 4013
Holes: 9
Heather Highlands GC—#2, 600-A Highlands Drive, Harbor Springs, 49740,
313-634-6800   Yards: 2052, Par: 31, Holes: 9
Heather Hills GC, 3100 McKail Rd., Almont, 48003, 313-798-3120
Yards: 6363, Par: 35, Holes: 18
Hi-Lo GC, 47th St., Bloomingdale, 49026, 616-427-5265
Yards: 1100, Par: 27, Holes: 9
Hickory Hills GC, 2307 Orland, Wixom, 48096, 313-624-4733
Yards: 2865, Par: 35, Holes: 9
Hickory Hollow GC, 49001 North Ave., Mt. Clemens, 48043, 313-949-9033
Yards: 6340, Par: 73, USGA: 69.1, Holes: 18
Hickory Knoll GC—#1, 3065 W. Alice St., Whitehall, 49461, 616-893-9245
Yards: 2825, Holes: 9
Hickory Woods GC, 5415 Crane Rd., Ypsilanti, 48197, 313-434-4653
Yards: 2685, Par: 34, Holes: 9
Hidden Valley GC, Shelbyville, 49344, 616-672-7866
Par: 60, Holes: 18
Highland Hills GC, 450 E. Alward Rd., Dewitt, 48820, 517-669-9873
Yards: 6500, Par: 72, Holes: 18
Highland Hills GC, 2075 Oakland Dr., Highland, 48031, 313-887-4481
Yards: 6315, Par: 72, Holes: 18
Hillsdale Public GC, 2171 Bankers Road, Hillsdale, 49242, 517-437-3434
Yards: 2850, Par: 35, Holes: 9
Hilltop GC, 47000 Powell, Plymouth, 48170, 313-453-9800
Yards: 6404, Par: 70, Holes: 18
Hilton Shanty Creek—#1, Shanty Creek Rd., Ballaire, 49615, 616-533-8621
Yards: 6559, Par: 72, USGA: 71.1, Holes: 18
Highland GC, US-2 & 41, Bark River, 49829, 906-466-7457
Yards: 6224, Par: 71, Holes: 18
Holiday Greens GC, Holiday Inn, 5665 E. Pickard S, Mt. Pleasant, 48858,
517-772-2905   Yards: 3722, Par: 63, Holes: 18
Holland Lake GC, 1100 E. Holland Lake Rd., Sheridan, 48884, 517-291-5757
Yards: 3140, Par: 36, Holes: 9
Huron GC, E.M.U. Whitaker Road, Ypsilanti, 48197
Holes: 18
Huron Hills GC, 3465 E. Huron River Dr., Ann Arbor, 48104, 313-971-9841
Yards: 5120, Par: 68, Holes: 18
Huron shores GC, 1441 N. Lakeshore, Port Sanilac, 48469, 313-622-9961
Yards: 2749, Par: 35, Holes: 9
Idyl Wyld GC, 35780 5 Mile Rd., Livonia, 48152, 313-464-6325
Yards: 6072, Par: 71, Holes: 18
Independence Green GC, 24360 Washington Ct., Farmington Hills, 48018,
313-471-6800   Yards: 3425, Par: 56, Holes: 18
Indian Hills GC, 4811 Nakoma Dr., Okemos, 48864, 517-349-1919
Yards: 2700, Par: 33, Holes: 9
Indian Lake GC, Manistique, 49854, 906-341-5600
Yards: 3127, Par: 36, Holes: 9
Indian Lake Hills GC, Rt. 2 Brush Lake Rd., Eau Claire, 49111, 616-782-2540
Yards: 6205, Par: 71, USGA: 69.3, Holes: 18

Indian Run GC, 6359 E. RS Ave., Scotts, 49088, 616-327-1327
Yards: 7000, Par: 72, Holes: 18
Indian Trails GC, 2776 Kalamazoo Ave. SE, Grand Rapids, 49507, 616-245-2021
Yards: 5089, Par: 68, Holes: 18
Indianhead Mtn. GC, Indianhead Mtn. Rd., Wakefield, 49968, 906-229-5181
Yards: 1300, Par: 27, Holes: 9
Interlochen GC, 10586 US 31 S., Interlochen, 49643, 616-275-7311
Yards: 6300, Par: 71, Holes: 18
Ironwood GC, 6900 E. M-59, Howell, 48843, 517-546-3211
Yards: 3189, Par: 36, Holes: 9
Ironwood GC, 3750 64th St., Byron Center, 49315, 616-538-4000
Yards: 5500, Par: 71, Holes: 18
Iyopawa Island GC, Iyopawa Island, Coldwater, 49036, 517-238-2216
Yards: 2818, Par: 36, Holes: 9
Jenkins GC, 1001 Homer Rd., Litchfield, 49252, 517-542-3121
Yards: 3135, Par: 36, Holes: 9
Kaufman GC, 4829 Clyde Park SW, Wyoming, 49509, 616-538-5050
Yards: 6875, Par: 72, Holes: 18
Kearsley Lake Muni GC, 4266 E. Pierson, Flint, 48506, 313-736-0930
Yards: 6520, Par: 72, Holes: 18
Keweenaw Mtn. GC, US-41, Copper Harbor, 49918, 906-289-4403
Yards: 3189, Par: 36, Holes: 9
Kimberley Oaks GC, 1100 W. Walnut, St. Charles, 48655, 517-865-8261
Yards: 6485, Par: 72, USGA: 71.9, Holes: 18
Kinchelow Mem. GC, Bailey Rd., Kinross, 49752, 906-495-5706
Yards: 3472, Par: 36, Holes: 9
King Par GC, G-5140 Flushing Rd., Flushing, 48433, 313-732-2470
Yards: 800, Par: 27, Holes: 9
Kingster GC, 20820 Inkster Rd., Romulus, 48174, 313-782-5136
Yards: 3853, Par: 61, Holes: 18
L'Anse GC, US-41, L'Anse, 49946, 906-524-6600
Yards: 3600, Par: 36, Holes: 9
Lake Cora Hills GC, County Rd., 671, Paw Paw, 49079, 616-657-4074
Yards: 6164, Par: 72, Holes: 18
Lake Isabella GC, 7000 N. Clubhouse Dr., Weidman, 48893, 517-644-2300
Yards: 6725, Par: 72, Holes: 18
Lake Leann GC, 119 Fairway Blvd., Somerset Ctr., 49282, 517-688-3445
Yards: 2850, Par: 35, Holes: 9
Lake Monterey GC, 3765 28th, Dorr, 49314, 616-896-8118
Yards: 4712, Par: 65, Holes: 18
Lake O'The Hills GC, 2101 Lac DuMont, Haslett, 48840, 517-339-9445
Yards: 1500, Par: 27, Holes: 9
Lake of the North GC, Mancelona Rd., Gaylord, 49659, 616-585-6800
Yards: 3550, Par: 36, USGA: 72.8, Holes: 9
Lake Wood Shores GC, 7751 Cedar Lake Rd., Oscoda, 49750, 517-739-2075
Yards: 6528, Par: 72, USGA: 72.9, Holes: 18
Lakeland Hills GC, 5119 Page, Jackson, 49201, 517-764-5292
Yards: 6070, Par: 72, Holes: 18
Lakes of the North-Pineview, Pineview Dr., Mancelona, 49659
Holes: 9
Leaning Tree GC, 7890 Smiths Creek Rd., Smiths Creek, 48074, 313-367-3528
Yards: 3071, Par: 37, Holes: 9
Ledge Meadows GC, 1801 Grand Ledge Hwy, Grand Ledge, 48837,
517-627-7492   Yards: 3400, Par: 36, Holes: 9
Lemontree GC, 48356 Denton Rd., Belleville, 48111, 313-699-2800
Yards: 3400, Par: 36, Holes: 9

Les Cheneaux GC, Snows Channel, Cedarville, 49719,   906-484-2424
Yards: 3010, Par: 35, Holes: 9
Leslie Park GC, 2120 Traver Rd., Ann Arbor, 48105,   313-668-9011
Yards: 6690, Par: 72, Holes: 18
Lilac Brothers GC, 9090 Armstrong Rd., Newport, 48166,   313-586-9902
Yards: 7052, Par: 72, Holes: 18
Lincoln GC, 4907 N. Whitehall Rd., Muskegon, 49445,   616-766-2226
Yards: 6100, Par: 72, Holes: 18
Lincoln GC, 3485 Lake Michigan Dr., Grand Rapids, 49504,   616-453-6348
Yards: 5864, Par: 72, USGA: 67.7, Holes: 18
Lincoln Hills GC, 2666 W. 14 Mile Rd., Birmingham, 48010,   313-647-4468
Yards: 3350, Par: 35, Holes: 9
Lincoln Hills GC, No. Lakeshore Dr., Ludington, 49431, 616-843-4666
Yards: 6032, Par: 70, USGA: 69.0, Holes: 18
Links at Pinewood GC, 8600 PGA Drive, Walled Lake, 48088,   313-669-9800
Yards: 7000, Par: 72, Holes: 18
Loch Lomond GC, 5267 s. Dort Hwy., Flint, 48507,   313-742-1434
Yards: 2700, Par: 34, USGA: 64.8, Holes: 9
Lower Huron Metro GC, 17845 Savage Rd., Belleville, 48111,   313-697-9181
Yards: 1372, Par: 54, Holes: 18
Ludington Hills GC, 5369 W. Chauves Rd., Ludington, 49431,   616-843-3660
Yards: 6035, Par: 70, Holes: 18
Lum International GC, 5191 Lum Rd., Lum, 48452,   313-724-0851
Yards: 2960, Par: 36, Holes: 9
Mac Log Hills GC, 3990 Willis Rd., Milan, 48160,   313-434-4800
Yards: 2470, Par: 33, Holes: 9
Macomb GC, 21111 23 Mile Rd., Mt. Clemens, 48044
Macon GC, 11066 Macon Hwy., Macon, 49236,   517-423-4259
Yards: 2900, Par: 36, Holes: 9
Manistee G & CC, 700 Bryant Ave., Manistee, 49660,   616-723-2509
Yards: 6031, Par: 70, Holes: 18
Maple Grove GC, 6360 Secor Rd., Lambertville, 48144,   313-856-6777
Yards: 3015, Par: 56, Holes: 18
Maple Hills GC, 16344 C Ave., E. Augusta, 49012,   616-731-4430
Yards: 2960, Par: 35, Holes: 9
Maple Hills GC, 555 Ivanrest Ave. Sw, Grandville, 49418,   616-538-0290
Yards: 4500, Par: 68, Holes: 18
Maple Lane GC—#1, 33203 Maple Lane, Sterling Heights, 48077,   313-754-3020
Yards: 5926, Par: 71, Holes: 18
Maple Leaf GC, 158 N. Mackinaw, Linwood, 48634,   517-697-3531
Yards: 6015, Par: 70, Holes: 18
Marks GC, N. Main St., Lawton, 49065
Yards: 2950, Par: 36, Holes: 9
Marquette GC, Grove St., Marquette, 49855,   906-225-0721
Yards: 6000, Par: 71, USGA: 69.9, Holes: 18
Marquette Trails GC, Rt. 1 Big Star Lake Rd., Baldwin, 49304,   616-898-2450
Yards: 3300, Par: 36, Holes: 9
Marysville GC, 2080 River Rd., Marysville, 48040,   313-364-4653
Yards: 6331, Par: 72, USGA: 71.3, Holes: 18
Mason Hills GC, 2692 Tomlinson, Mason, 48854,   517-676-5366
Yards: 6700, Par: 72, Holes: 18
Meadowlane GC, 3356 44th St., SW, Kentwood, 49508,   616-698-8034
Yards: 5500, Par: 72, Holes: 18
Meceola CC, Big Rapids, 49307,   616-796-9004
Par: 36, Holes: 9

Metro Beach GC, 31300 Metro Parkway, Mt. Clemens, 48043, 313-463-4581
Yards: 1271, Par: 54, Holes: 18
Mi-Ro GC, 396 Chase Rd., Douglas, 49406, 616-857-2271
Yards: 3125, Par: 36, Holes: 9
Middle Channel GC, 2306 Golf Course Rd., Harsens Island, 48028,
313-748-9922 Yards: 6100, Par: 72, Holes: 18
Milham Muni GC, 4200 Lovers Lane, Kalamazoo, 49002, 616-344-7639
Yards: 6712, Par: 72, USGA: 71.3, Holes: 18
Mill Creek, 15886 Speaker Rd., Imlay City, 48444, 313-395-7495
Yards: 3046, Par: 36, Holes: 9
Indian River GC, 6460 Chippewa Rd., Indian River, 49749, 616-238-7011
Yards: 3085, Par: 36, Holes: 9
Mill Race GC, 200 Adrian Rd., Jonesville, 49250, 517-849-9439
Yards: 3150, Par: 36, Holes: 9
Missaukee GC, 5300 s. Morey, Lake City, 49651, 616-825-2756
Yards: 5850, Par: 71, Holes: 18
Mission Hills GC, 14830 Sheldon Rd., Plymouth, 48170, 313-453-1047
Yards: 6425, Par: 71, USGA: 68.9, Holes: 18
Mitchell Creek GC, 2846 3 Mile Rd., Traverse City, 48684, 616-941-5200
Yards: 3200, Par: 36, Holes: 9
Morrison Lake GC, Portland Rd., Saranac, 48881, 616-642-9528
Yards: 5555, Par: 70, Holes: 18
Mott Park Muni GC, 2401 Nolan Dr., Flint, 48505, 313-766-7077
Yards: 2942, Par: 36, Holes: 9
Mulberry Fore GC, 955 N. Main, Nashville, 49073, 517-852-0760
Yards: 3203, Par: 36, Holes: 9
Mulberry Fore GC, 955 N. Main Street, Nashville, 49873
Holes: 9
Mulberry Hills GC, 3530 Noble Rd., Oxford, 48051, 313-628-2808
Yards: 6470, Par: 72, Holes: 18
Mullenhurst GC, Mullen Rd., Delton, 49046, 616-623-8383
Yards: 5625, Par: 71, Holes: 18
Mullett Lake GC, Mullette Lake, 49761, 616-627-5971
Yards: 3282, Par: 36, Holes: 9
New Hawthorne Valley GC, 31002 W. Warren, Westland, 48185, 313-422-3440
Yards: 2881, Par: 35, Holes: 9
Newberry CC, M-124, Newberry, 49868, 906-293-8422
Yards: 1575, Par: 35, Holes: 9
Normandy Oaks GC, 4234 Delemere, Royal Oak, 48073, 313-549-7070
Yards: 2802, Par: 34, USGA: 65.4, Holes: 9
North Kent GC, 11029 Stout Ave. NE, Rockford, 49341, 616-866-2659
Yards: 6000, Par: 70, Holes: 18
North Star GC, 4550 s. Bagley Rd., Ithaca, 48847, 517-875-3841
Yards: 5960, Par: 70, Holes: 18
Northbrook GC, 21690 27 Mile Rd., Washington, 48094, 313-749-3415
Yards: 6460, Par: 72, Holes: 18
Northville GC, 19025 Newburgh, Northville, 48167, 313-591-9720
Yards: 5800, Par: 71, Holes: 18
Northwood GC, 9025 W. 32nd St., Fremont, 49412, 616-924-3380
Yards: 6100, Par: 71, Holes: 18
Oak Crest GC, Norway, 49807, 906-563-5891
Yards: 6006, Par: 72, USGA: 68.6, Holes: 18
Oakland Hills GC, 11619 H, Drive N, Battle Creek, 49016, 616-965-0809
Yards: 6265, Par: 72, Holes: 18
Oakland Hills GC, 8716 Oakland Dr., Portage, 49081, 616-327-1493
Yards: 6540, Par: 71, Holes: 18

Oakland Hills GC, 3951 W. Maple Rd., Detroit, 48012
Oasis Golf Center, 39500 5 Mile Rd., Plymouth, 48170, 313-420-4653
Yards: 2295, Par: 54, Holes: 18
Oceana GC, 3333 W. Weaver Rd., Shelby, 49455, 616-861-4211
Yards: 6108, Par: 73, Holes: 18
Old Channel Trail GC, RTE 3 Old Channel Trail, Montague, 49437,
616-894-5076 Yards: 6166, Par: 71, Holes: 18
Olde Mill GC, 6091 W. XY ave., Schoolcraft, 49087, 616-679-4685
Yards: 6540, Par: 71, Holes: 18
Olivet GC, 6819 Old US-27, Olivet, 49076, 616-749-9051
Yards: 3007, Par: 36, Holes: 9
Orchard Hills—18 Hole Course, 714 125th Ave., Shelbyville, 49344,
616-672-7096 Yards: 6200, Par: 71, Holes: 18
Ot-Well-Egan GC, 1058 Lincoln Rd., Allegan, 49010, 616-673-8261
Yards: 3187, Par: 36, Holes: 9
Overbrook GC, 6234 West Grant, Middleton, 48856, 517-236-5357
Yards: 2850, Par: 35, Holes: 9
Oxford Hills, 300 E. Drahner Dr., Oxford, 48051, 313-628-2518
Yards: 6449, Par: 72, Holes: 18
Oyler GC, 2480 Duck Lake Rd., Whitehall, 49461, 616-766-2045
Yards: 6103, Par: 72, Holes: 18
Paint Creek GC, 2375 Stanton Rd., Lake Orion, 48035, 313-693-4695
Yards: 3000, Par: 36, Holes: 9
Palmer Park GC, 19013 Woodward, Detroit, 48203, 313-876-0428
Yards: 5729, Par: 69, Holes: 18
Par-Mor GC, 2591 E. M-78, E. Lansing, 48823, 517-332-3432
Yards: 2400, Par: 33, Holes: 9
Park Shore GC, Park Shore Rd., Cassopolis, 49031, 616-445-2834
Yards: 3106, Par: 35, Holes: 9
Parkview GC, 4600 s. Sheridan Dr., Muskegon, 49444, 616-773-8814
Yards: 2000, Par: 54, Holes: 18
Paw Paw Lake GC, Paw Paw Ave., Watervliet, 49098, 616-463-3831
Yards: 5457, Par: 70, Holes: 18
Pebble Creek GC, 55535 10 Mile Rd., South Lyon, 48178, 313-437-5411
Yards: 3347, Par: 36, Holes: 9
Pictured Rocks GC, H-58, Munising, 49862, 906-387-2146
Yards: 3125, Par: 36, Holes: 9
Pierce Park Muni GC, 2302 Brookside, Flint, 48503, 313-766-7297
Yards: 2354, Par: 54, Holes: 18
Pine Brook GC, 4575 County Line Rd., Richmond, 48062, 313-727-7029
Yards: 3100, Par: 36, Holes: 9
Pine Creek GC, 50521 Huron River Dr., Belleville, 48111, 313-483-5010
Yards: 2653, Par: 56, Holes: 18
Pine Hill GC, US 31 North, Brutus, 49716, 616-529-6574
Yards: 4600, Par: 64, Holes: 18
Pine Hills GC, 6603 N. Woodbury, Laingsburg, 48848, 517-651-7781
Yards: 2319, Par: 34, Holes: 9
Pine Knob GC, 5580 Waldon Rd., Clarkston, 48016, 313-625-0700
Yards: 6403, Par: 71, Holes: 18
Pine Knoll GC, 1200 E. Michigan, Battle Creek, 49017, 616-964-8807
Yards: 2527, Par: 35, Holes: 9
Pine Lake GC, 1018 Haslett Rd., Haslett, 48840, 517-339-8281
Yards: 6000, Par: 68, Holes: 18
Pine Mountain GC, Pine Mountain Rd., Star Rte., Iron Mountain, 49801,
906-774-2747 Yards: 2527, Par: 34, Holes: 9

Pine River CC & Ranch, 2244 Pine River Rd., Standish, 48658, 517-846-6819
Yards: 3300, Par: 36, USGA: 71.8, Holes: 9
Pine Shores GC, 709 Fred W. Moore, St. Clair, 48079, 313-329-4294
Yards: 2825, Par: 35, Holes: 9
Pine Trace GC, 3600 Pine Trace Blvd., Rochester Hills, 48309
Holes: 18
Pine View GC—#1, 52065 Pulver Rd., Three Rivers, 49093, 616-279-5131
Yards: 6317, Par: 72, USGA: 69.9, Holes: 18
Pines GC (The), 5050 Byron Center Ave. SW, Wyoming, 49509, 616-538-8380
Yards: 5900, Par: 70, Holes: 18
Pineview GC, Houghton Lake, 48629, 517-366-9806
Yards: 3120, Par: 36, Holes: 9
Pipestone Creek GC, 6768 Naomi Rd., Eau Claire, 49111, 616-944-1611
Yards: 4402, Par: 67, Holes: 18
Pleasant Hills GC, 4452 E. Millbrook, Mt. Pleasant, 48858, 517-772-0487
Yards: 6100, Par: 71, Holes: 18
Plum Brook GC, 13390 Plumbrook Dr., Sterling Heights, 48077, 313-264-9411
Yards: 6300, Par: 71, USGA: 67.5, Holes: 18
Plym Park Mun. GC, 401 Marmont, Niles, 49120, 616-684-7331
Yards: 3112, Par: 36, Holes: 9
Pontiac GC, 4335 Elizabeth Lake Rd., Pontiac, 48054, 313-835-4477
Yards: 6276, Par: 72, USGA: 70.1, Holes: 18
Portland CC, Divine Hwy., Portland, 48875, 517-647-4521
Yards: 6006, Par: 71, USGA: 68.0, Holes: 18
Prairie Creek GC, 704 W. Webb, Dewitt, 48820, 517-669-3091
Yards: 6105, Par: 71, Holes: 18
Prairie River GC, 1015 Brink Rd., Bronson, 49028, 517-369-6745
Yards: 3260, Par: 36, Holes: 9
Quincy GC, 60 Miller, Quincy, 49082, 517-639-4491
Yards: 2842, Par: 34, Holes: 9
Rackham GC, 10100 10 Mile Rd., Huntington Woods, 48070, 313-564-4939
Yards: 6438, Par: 71, Holes: 18
Raisin Valley GC, 4057 Comfort Rd., Tecumseh, 49286, 517-423-2050
Yards: 5600, Par: 72, Holes: 18
Rammler GC—#1, 38180 Utica Rd., Sterling Heights, 48077, 313-264-4101
Yards: 6131, Par: 71, USGA: 69.3, Holes: 18
Ravenna GC, 11566 Hts. Ravenna Rd., Ravenna, 49451, 616-853-6736
Yards: 2956, Par: 36, Holes: 9
Red Arrow GC, 1041 King, Kalamazoo, 49001, 616-345-8329
Yards: 1500, Par: 29, Holes: 9
Red Cedar Muni GC, 203 S. Clippert, Lansing, 48912, 517-332-9161
Yards: 2585, Par: 34, Holes: 9
Red Oaks GC, 29600 John R., Madison Heights, 48071, 313-541-5030
Yards: 2490, Par: 31, Holes: 9
Ridge View GC, 10360 W. Main, Kalamazoo, 49009, 616-375-8821
Yards: 6500, Par: 71, Holes: 18
Ridgeview GC, 5200 Flat River Trail, Belding, 48809, 616-794-1860
Yards: 2000, Par: 31, Holes: 9
River Bend—18 Hole Course, 1370 W. State Rd., Hastings, 49058, 616-945-3238
Yards: 6000, Par: 72, Holes: 18
River Forest GC, 3571 Rue Foret, Flint, 48504, 313-732-9240
Yards: 1165, Par: 27, Holes: 9
Riverside CC, 14th Ave., P. O. Box 164, Menominee, 49858, 906-863-9937
Yards: 5978, Par: 71, USGA: 69.2, Holes: 18, Pro: Mike Wietor
Riverview CC, 1201 S. Oneida St., P.O. Box 4, Appleton, 54915, 414-733-2354
Yards: 6078, Par: 70, USGA: 69.0, Holes: 9, Pro: Larry Helminen

Riverwood GC—#1, 1313 Broomfield Rd., Mt. Pleasant, 48858,   517-772-5726
Yards: 2400, Par: 25, Holes: 9
Rochester GC, 655 Michelson, Rochester, 48063,   313-852-4800
Yards: 6400, Par: 72, Holes: 18
Rogell GC, 18601 Berg Rd., Detroit, 48219,   313-935-5331
Yards: 6018, Par: 70, Holes: 18
Rogers City CC, 4325 Golf Course Rd., Rogers City, 49779,   517-734-4909
Yards: 3110, Par: 36, Holes: 9
Rogue River GC, 12994 Paine Ave., Sparta, 49345,   616-887-7182
Yards: 5670, Par: 70, Holes: 18
Rolling Green GC, 5170 Weiss, Saginaw, 48603,   517-799-1450
Yards: 2267, Par: 33, Holes: 9
Rolling Hills GC, 3274 Davison Rd., Lapeer, 48446,   313-664-2281
Yards: 6320, Par: 72, Holes: 18
Rolling Hills GC, 3100 Baldwin St., Hudsonville, 49426,   616-669-9768
Yards: 6018, Par: 71, Holes: 18
Rolling Hills GC, Cass City, 48726,   517-872-3569
Par: 35, Holes: 9
Rolling Meadows GC, 6484 Sutton Road, Whitmore Lake, 48189,   313-662-5144
Yards: 6415, Par: 70, Holes: 18
Romeo GC, 14600 E. 32 Mile Rd., Romeo, 48065,   313-752-9673
Yards: 6348, Par: 72, Holes: 18
Rouge Park GC, 11701 Burt Rd., Detroit, 48228,   313-935-3761
Yards: 6327, Par: 72, Holes: 18
Royal Oak GC, 3417 Don Soper Dr., Royal Oak, 48073,   313-549-3600
Yards: 3043, Par: 35, USGA: 67.2, Holes: 9
Royal Scott GC, 4722 W. Grand River, Lansing, 48906,   517-321-3071
Yards: 6750, Par: 71, USGA: 70.9, Holes: 18
Rush Lake GC, 3199 Rush Lake Rd., Pinckney, 48169,   313-878-9790
Yards: 6545, Par: 72, Holes: 18
Rustic Glen GC, 12090 W. Michigan, Saline, 48176,   313-429-7679
Yards: 3120, Par: 36, Holes: 9
Salem Hills GC, 8810 W. 6 Mile Rd., Northville, 48167,   313-437-2152
Yards: 7108, Par: 72, USGA: 72.2, Holes: 18
Salt River GC, 33633 23 Mile Rd., New Baltimore, 48047,   313-725-0311
Yards: 6220, Par: 71, Holes: 18
San Marino GC, 26634 Halstead Rd., Farmington Hills, 48018,   313-476-5910
Yards: 3299, Par: 36, Holes: 9
Sandy Lanes Par 3 GC, 2204 Yankee St., Niles, 49120,   616-684-7331
Yards: 2800, Par: 27, Holes: 9
Sandy Ridge GC, 2750 W. Lauria Rd., Midland, 48640,   517-631-6010
Yards: 6110, Par: 71, Holes: 18
Saskatoon GC—#1, 9038 92nd St., Alto, 49302,   616-891-8652
Yards: 3011, Par: 35, Holes: 9
Sauganash GC, Three Rivers, 49093,   616-278-7825
Yards: 5780, Par: 72, Holes: 18
Scenic Golf, 8364 W. Fillon Rd., Pigeon, 48755,   517-453-3350
Yards: 6000, Par: 72, USGA: 68.5, Holes: 18
Schuss Mountain GC, Schuss Mountain Drive, Mancelona, 49659,
616-587-9162   Yards: 6394, Par: 72, USGA: 71.5, Holes: 18, Pro: Rodger Jabara
Scott Lake GC, 911 Hayes NE, Comstock Park, 49321,   616-784-1355
Yards: 6300, Par: 72, Holes: 18
Seifert's Golf, 2193 W. Grand Blanc Rd., Grand Blanc, 48439,   313-655-4722
Yards: 1005, Par: 27, Holes: 9
Shady Hollow GC, 34777 Smith, Romulus, 48174,   313-721-0403
Yards: 6200, Par: 72, Holes: 18

Shenandoah GC, 5600 Walnut Lake Rd., W. Bloomfield, 48033, 313-682-4300
Yards: 7000, Par: 72, Holes: 18
Sherwood on Hill GC, 6625 Third St., Gagetown, 48735, 517-665-9971
Yards: 2439, Par: 34, Holes: 9
Shoreview GC, 5741 Lake Shore Rd., Port Huron, 48060, 313-385-3542
Yards: 3000, Par: 31, Holes: 9
Shuss Mountain GC, Shuss Mountain Rd., Traverse City, 49659
Silver Lake GC, 2602 W. Walton Blvd., Pontiac, 48055, 313-673-1611
Yards: 3150, Par: 36, Holes: 9
Silver Lake GC, 15649 US-12 Devils Lake Hwy, Brooklyn, 49230, 517-592-8036
Yards: 1320, Par: 27, Holes: 9
South Haven GC, Blue Star Mem. Hwy., South Haven, 49090, 616-637-3896
Yards: 6700, Par: 72, Holes: 18
Southgate GC, 14600 Reaume Pky., Southgate, 48195, 313-285-9770
Yards: 3424, Par: 58, Holes: 18
Southmoor GC, 4312 S. Dort Hwy., Burton, 48529, 313-743-4080
Yards: 5300, Par: 70, Holes: 18
Sparrow Hawk GC, 2618 Seymour Rd., Jackson, 49201, 517-787-1366
Yards: 3155, Par: 36, USGA: 69.8, Holes: 9
Spring Lake GC, 6060 Maybee Rd., Clarkston, 48016, 313-625-3731
Yards: 6570, Par: 72, Holes: 18
Spring Port Hills GC, Harrisville, 48740, 517-724-5611
Par: 36, Holes: 9
Spring Valley GC, 2635 E. Beaver Rd., Kawkawin, 48631, 517-686-0330
Yards: 5954, Par: 36, Holes: 9
Spring Valley GC, E. US-10, Hersey, 49639, 616-832-5041
Yards: 3442, Par: 36, Holes: 9
Springbrook GC, 1600 Avenue A, Springfield, 49015, 616-964-9313
Yards: 3300, Par: 36, Holes: 9
Springbrook GC, 42545 Ryan Rd., Sterling Heights, 48077, 313-739-6230
Yards: 3175, Par: 36, Holes: 9
Springbrook Hills GC, Springvale Rd., Walloon Lake, 49796, 616-535-2413
Yards: 6260, Par: 72, Holes: 18
Springdale GC, 300 Strathmore, Birmingham, 48009, 313-644-2254
Yards: 3190, Par: 33, Holes: 9
Springfield Oaks GC, 12450 Andersonville Rd., Davisburg, 48019, 313-625-2540
Yards: 6085, Par: 72, Holes: 18
Springport Hills GC, 5184 East Springport Rd., Harrisville, 48740, 517-724-5611
Yards: 2911, Par: 36, Holes: 9
St. Clair Shores GC, 22185 Masonic Blvd., St. Clair Shores, 48082,
313-294-2000   Yards: 6035, Par: 71, Holes: 18
St. Ignace GC, West US-2, St. Ignace, 49781, 906-643-8071
Yards: 3070, Par: 36, Holes: 9
St. Joe Valley GC, 24953 M-86, Sturgis, 49091, 616-467-6275
Yards: 5215, Par: 68, Holes: 18
States GC, 20 W. Ave., Vicksburg, 49097, 616-649-1931
Yards: 6272, Par: 72, Holes: 18
Sugar Springs GC, 1930 W. Sugar River Rd., Gladwin, 48624, 517-426-4391
Yards: 6462, Par: 72, USGA: 72.6, Holes: 18
Sultana Par 3—#1, 22201 Pennsylvania, Wyandotte, 48192, 313-285-7480
Yards: 1236, Par: 27, Holes: 9
Sunny Acres GC, 30750 Little Mack, Roseville, 48066, 313-293-1410
Yards: 2406, Par: 32, Holes: 9
Sunnybrook GC—#1, 7191 17 Mile Rd., Sterling Heights, 48077, 313-977-9759
Yards: 6310, Par: 70, Holes: 18

Swan Valley GC, 9499 Geddes Rd., Saginaw, 48603, 517-781-4411
Yards: 6189, Par: 70, Holes: 18
Swanee's Twin Knolls GC, 10400 Mack Island Rd., Grass Lake, 49240,
517-522-8944 Yards: 2850, Par: 36, Holes: 9
Swartz Creek Muni GC—#1, 1902 Hammersburg, Flint, 48503, 313-766-7043
Yards: 6748, Par: 72, Holes: 18
Sycamore GC, 1526 E. Mt. Hope, Lansing, 48910, 517-374-0151
Yards: 2343, Par: 33, Holes: 9
Sylvan Glen GC, 5725 Rochester Rd., Troy, 48098, 313-879-0040
Yards: 6199, Par: 70, USGA: 71.9, Holes: 18
Tabor Farms Resort GC, 6020 River Road, Sodus, 49126, 616-925-6404
Yards: 3060, Par: 36, Holes: 9
Tall Oaks GC, 14310 Wahrman Rd., Romulus, 48174, 313-941-3372
Yards: 2564, Par: 56, Holes: 18
Tamaracks GC, Harrison, 48625, 517-539-3864
Par: 35, Holes: 9
Tawas G & CC, 1002 Monument Rd., Tawas, 48763, 517-362-6262
Yards: 6558, Par: 72, Holes: 18
Taylor Meadows GC, 25360 Ecourse, Taylor, 48180
Holes: 18
Tecumseh CC, P.O. Box 219, Tecumseh, 49286
USGA: 69.5, Pro: Bruce Fridd
Terrace Bluff GC, Lake Bluff Rd., Gladstone, 48837, 906-428-2343
Yards: 6198, Par: 72, Holes: 18
Thornapple Creek GC, 6415 West F Ave., Kalamazoo, 49009, 616-342-2600
Yards: 6800, Par: 72, Holes: 18
Thorne Hills GC, 12915 Sumpter Rd., Carleton, 48117, 313-587-2332
Yards: 3159, Par: 36, Holes: 9
Thunder Bay GC, M-32 East, Hillman, 49746, 517-742-4875
Yards: 3085, Par: 36, Holes: 9
Timber Ridge, 16339 Park Lake Road, East Lansing, 48823
Holes: 9
Tomac Woods GC, 14827 26½ Mile Rd., Albion, 49224, 517-629-8241
Yards: 7200, Par: 72, Holes: 18
Torrey Pines GC, 12312 Torrey Rd., Fenton, 48430, 313-629-1212
Yards: 6545, Par: 72, Holes: 18
Travis Pointe CC, 2829 Travis Point Rd., Ann Arbor, 48104
USGA: 72.2, Pro: Jon Gates
Twin Birch GC, County Rd. 612, Kalkaska, 49646, 616-258-9691
Yards: 3055, Par: 36, Holes: 9
Twin Brooks GC, 1005 McKeighan Rd., Chesaning, 48616, 517-845-6403
Yards: 3352, Par: 36, Holes: 9
Twin Knolls, Grass Lake, 49240, 517-522-8944
Par: 36, Holes: 9
Twin Oaks GC, 6371 N. US-27, St. Johns, 48879, 517-224-7342
Yards: 3265, Par: 36, Holes: 9
Twin Oaks GC—#1, 6710 Freeland Rd., Freeland, 48623, 517-695-9746
Yards: 2755, Par: 35, Holes: 9
Tyrone Hills GC, 8449 Hwy. US-23, Fenton, 48430, 313-629-5011
Yards: 6300, Par: 72, USGA: 68.1, Holes: 18, Pro: Denis Husse
University Park GC, 2100 Marquette, Muskegon, 49443, 616-773-0023
Yards: 3136, Par: 36, Holes: 9
Valley View Inn GC, 8240 Genuine Rd., Shepherd, 48883, 517-828-6618
Yards: 6400, Par: 72, Holes: 18
Valley View Farms GC, 1435 S. Thomas Rd., Saginaw, 48603, 517-781-1248
Yards: 6318, Par: 71, Holes: 18

Vassar G & CC, 3509 Kirk Rd., Vassar, 48768, 517-823-7221
Yards: 6616, Par: 72, Holes: 18
Verona Hills GC, 3175 Sand Beach Rd., Bad Axe, 48413, 517-269-8132
Yards: 6500, Par: 71, Holes: 18
Vienna Greens GC, 1184 E. Tobias Rd., Clio, 48420, 313-686-1443
Yards: 6200, Par: 72, Holes: 18
Village Green GC, 8104 Bingham, Newaygo, 49337, 616-652-6513
Yards: 2848, Par: 34, USGA: 65.4, Holes: 9
Walnut Woods GC, 7446 4th Ave., Gobles, 49055, 616-628-2070
Yards: 4980, Par: 66, Holes: 18
Warfield Greens GC, 34255 Utica Rd., Fraser, 48026, 313-293-9887
Yards: 1650, Par: 29, Holes: 9
Warren Valley GC—#1, 26116 W. Warren, Dearborn Heights, 48127,
313-561-1040   Yards: 6246, Par: 72, Holes: 18
Warwick Hills GC, 95 S. Saginaw, Flint, 48439
Waterloo GC, 11347 Trist Rd., Grass Lake, 49240, 517-522-8527
Yards: 2794, Par: 35, Holes: 9
Waverly Muni GC, 3619 W. Saginaw, Lansing, 48917, 517-321-9094
Yards: 3377, Par: 36, Holes: 9
Wawonowin GC, County Rd. 478, Ishpemming, 49849, 906-485-1435
Yards: 6347, Par: 72, Holes: 18
Wesburn GC, 5617 S. Huron River Dr., Rockwood, 48179, 313-379-3555
Yards: 6200, Par: 72, Holes: 18
West Branch CC, 198 s. Fairview, W. Branch, 48661, 517-345-2501
Yards: 6457, Par: 72, USGA: 71.2, Holes: 18
West Brook GC, 47666 Back Rd., Detroit, 48050
West Ottawa GC, 6045 136th St., Holland, 49423, 616-399-1678
Yards: 6247, Par: 70, Holes: 18
West Shore GC, 14 Ferry St., Douglas, 49406, 616-857-2500
Yards: 5320, Par: 66, USGA: 63.6, Holes: 18
Westland Muni GC, 500 s. Merriman Rd., Westland, 48185, 313-721-6660
Yards: 2860, Par: 34, Holes: 9
Whiffletree Hill GC, 15700 Homer Rd., Concord, 49237, 517-524-6655
Yards: 6315, Par: 70, Holes: 18
Whispering Willows GC, 20500 Newburgh Rd., Livonia, 48152, 313-476-4493
Yards: 6256, Par: 71, Holes: 18
White Birch Hills GC, 360 Ott Rd., Bay City, 48706, 517-662-6523
Yards: 5300, Par: 70, Holes: 18
White Deer GC, 1309 Bright Angle Dr., Prudenville, 48651, 517-366-5812
Yards: 6400, Par: 72, Holes: 18
Whiteford Valley GC—#1, 8440 Old US-223, Ottawa Lake, 49267, 313-856-4545
Yards: 6525, Par: 71, Holes: 18
Wilderness GC, Cecil Bay Road, Carp Lake, 49718, 616-537-4973
Yards: 2625, Par: 35, USGA: 68.4, Holes: 9
Willow Brook GC, 232 Galbraith Line, Melvin, 48454, 313-387-9898
Yards: 3070, Par: 36, Holes: 9
Willow Brook GC, 311 W. Maple, Byron, 48418, 313-266-4660
Yards: 6100, Par: 72, Holes: 18
Willow Creek GC, 3252 Heeney Rd., Stockbridge, 49285, 517-851-7856
Yards: 2850, Par: 35, Holes: 9
Willow Ridge GC, 3311 N. River Rd., Port Huron, 48060, 313-982-7010
Yards: 2894, Par: 36, Holes: 9
Willow Springs Golf & CC, 7335 Oak Rd., Millington, 48768, 517-871-9703
Yards: 4975, Par: 68, Holes: 18, Pro: Jerry Sauer
Willow Tree G&CC, Melvin, 48454, 313-387-9898
Par: 36, Holes: 9

Winding Creek GC, 8600 Ottogan St., Holland, 49423, 616-396-4516
Yards: 6800, Par: 72, USGA: 71.9, Holes: 18
Windmill Farms GC, State St., Mancelona, 49659, 616-587-5570
Yards: 795, Par: 27, Holes: 9
Windy Hill GC, 2236 S. Isles Rd., Sandusky, 48471, 313-648-2712
Yards: 2850, Par: 36, Holes: 9
Winters Creek GC, 13200 Northland Dr., Big Rapids, 49307, 616-796-2613
Yards: 6048, Par: 72, USGA: 70.3, Holes: 18
Wolverine GC, 17201 25 Mile Rd., Mt. Clemens, 48043, 313-781-5544
Yards: 6495, Par: 72, Holes: 18
Woodland GC, 100 Kristen Dr., Sandusky, 48471, 313-648-2400
Yards: 3002, Par: 35, Holes: 9
Woodland GC, 7635 W. Grand River, Brighton, 48116, 313-229-9663
Yards: 4855, Par: 67, Holes: 18
Wyandotte Hills GC, Twin Lakes Toivola, Houghton, 49965, 906-288-3720
Yards: 2650, Par: 34, Holes: 9
Wyndiwicke GC, 3711 Niles Rd., St. Joseph, 49085, 616-429-8411
Yards: 6886, Par: 72, Holes: 18
Yankee Springs GC, Bowens Mill Rd., Wayland, 49348, 616-795-9047
Yards: 6207, Par: 72, Holes: 18
Ye Nyne Olde Holles GC, East Jordan, 49651, 616-582-7609
Yards: 2970, Par: 35, Holes: 9

Afton Alps GC, 6600 Teller Avenue South, Hastings, 55033, *Minnesota*
612-436-5245 Holes: 9
Albany Golf Club PC, 500 Church Avenue, Box 338, Albany, 56307,
612-845-2505 Yards: 6092, Par: 73, USGA: 68.0, Holes: 18, Pro: P. Wallenstein
Angushire Golf Course PC, 117 4th Street South, Waite Park, 56387,
612-251-9619
Yards: 5512, Par: 35, USGA: 64.8, Holes: 18
Anoka-Greenhaven GC PC, P.O. Box 244, Anoka, 55303, 612-427-3180
Yards: 5927, Par: 71, USGA: 68.5, Holes: 18
Arrowhead CC, Emmons, 56029, 507-297-5767
Par: 36, Holes: 9
Arrowhead Country Club PC, P.O.Box 639, Alexandria, 56308, 612-762-1124
Yards: 6350, Par: 36, USGA: 68.9, Holes: 18
Arrowwood GC, 2100 Arrowwood Ln., St. Cloud, 56308, 612-762-1124
Yards: 5067, Par: 63, USGA: 63.0, Holes: 18
Babbit Golf Club PC, Box 280, Babbit, 55706, 218-827-2603
Yards: 6048, Par: 35, USGA: 67.9, Holes: 9
Baker II Park GC, 3425 Park View Drive, Minneapolis, 55431
Holes: 9
Baker Park GC PC, 3025 Parkview Dr., Hamel, 55340, 612-473-7418
Yards: 6224, Par: 66, USGA: 69.4, Holes: 18
Balmoral GC, Rt 3 Box 119, Battle Lake, 56515, 218-864-5414
Yards: 6132, Par: 72, Holes: 18
Bellwood Oaks Golf Club PC, P.O. Box 306, Hastings, 55033, 612-437-9944
Yards: 6591, Par: 73, USGA: 70.8, Holes: 18
Bemidji Town & CC, Birchmont NE, Bemidgi, 56601, 218-751-9215
Yards: 6179, Par: 72, USGA: 69.0, Holes: 18
Benson Muni GC, 2222 Atlantic Ave., Benson, 56215, 612-842-7901
Yards: 6007, Par: 72, USGA: 67.9, Holes: 18
Birchwood Golf Course PC, Golf Course Rd. P.O. Box 328, Pelican Rapids,
56572, 218-863-6486 Yards: 2448, Par: 34, USGA: 31.1, Holes: 9
Blackduck GC PC, Blackduck, 56630, 218-835-7757
Yards: 6122, Par: 36, USGA: 67.5, Holes: 9

Blooming Prairie CC, Blooming Prairie, 55917,   507-583-2887
Holes: 9
Blueberry Hills CC PC, Box 245, Deer River, 56636,   218-246-8411
Yards: 6090, Par: 36, USGA: 67.0, Holes: 9
Bluff Creek GC PC, 1025 Creekwood, Chaska, 55331,   612-445-5685
Yards: 6196, Par: 70, USGA: 69.0, Holes: 18
Bracketts Crossing GC, Lakeville, 55044,   612-435-7600
Holes: 18
Braemar GC PC, 6364 Dewey Hill Rd., Edina, 55435,   612-941-2072
Yards: 6368, Par: 71, USGA: 70.2, Holes: 18, Pro: John Valliere
Brainerd CC, Brainerd, 56401,   218-829-5733
Yards: 6034, Par: 71, Holes: 18
Breezy Point Resort GC, Route 371, Breezy Point, 56472
Holes: 9
Brightwood Hills, 1975 Silver Lake Rd., New Brighton, 55112,   612-633-7776
Yards: 1556, Par: 30, USGA: 27.2, Holes: 9
Brooklyn Park GC, Osseo, 55369
Holes: 9
Brookside GC, Park Rapids, 56470,   218-732-4093
Holes: 9
Brooktree Municipal GC PC, 1369 Cherry St., Owatonna, 55060,   507-451-0730
Yards: 6383, Par: 71, USGA: 70.5, Holes: 18
Buffalo Heights GC PC, Hwy. 25 So., Buffalo, 55313,   612-682-2854
Yards: 6241, Par: 36, USGA: 68.7, Holes: 9
Burl CC, Mound, 55364,   612-472-4909
Holes: 18
Cannon CC, Cannon Falls, 55509,   507-263-3126
Holes: 9
Carriage Hills Country Club PC, 3535 Wescott Hills Dr., Eagan, 55123,
612-452-7211   Yards: 5914, Par: 71, USGA: 67.6, Holes: 18
Castle Green CC, St. Paul, 55101, 612-464-6233
Par: 27, Holes: 9
Castle Highlands GC, Bemidji, 56601,   218-586-2681
Holes: 18
Castlewood Golf Course PC, 21350 Forest Blvd N, Forest Lake, 55025,
612-464-6233   Yards: 3166, Par: 36, USGA: 34.6, Holes: 9, Pro: Jake Jacobson
Cedar Hills Golf & Ski Club, Eden Prairie, 55344,   612-934-1977
Par: 27, Holes: 9
Cedar River CC, Adams, 55909,   507-582-3595
Holes: 18
Centerbrook GC PC, 5500 North Lilac Dr., Brooklyn Center, 55430,
612-561-3468   Yards: 2778, Par: 27, USGA: 53.0, Holes: 9
Chomonix GC PC, 6580 W. Shadow lake Dr., Lino Lakes, 55014,   612-482-8484
Yards: 6337, Par: 36, USGA: 69.9, Holes: 9
Cimarron Public GC, Lake Elmo, 55042,   612-436-6188
Par: 27, Holes: 9
Clarks Grove GC PC, Route 1 Box 22a, Clarks Grove, 56016,   507-256-7737
Yards: 3036, Par: 30, USGA: 53.6, Holes: 9
Cleary lake Park GC PC, 18106 Texas Ave., Prior Lake, 55437,   218-447-2171
Yards: 1656, Par: 30, USGA: 56.0, Holes: 9
Climax GC, Box 244, Climax, 56523
Yards: 2847, Par: 36, Holes: 9
Coffee Mill G & CC, Wabasha, 55981,   612-565-4332
Holes: 9
Cokato Town & CC, Cokato, 55321,   612-286-2007
Par: 36, Holes: 9

Columbia GC PC, 3300 Central Ave. NE, Minneapolis, 55418,   612-789-2627
Yards: 6131, Par: 71, USGA: 68.8, Holes: 18
Como GC PC, 1431 N. Lexington Pkwy, St. Paul, 55108,   612-489-3171
Yards: 6700, Par: 70, Holes: 18
Cottonwood CC, Cottonwood, 56229,   507-423-6335
Holes: 9
Country Hills GC, Shakopee, 55379
Holes: 18
Country View GC, St. Paul, 55101,   612-484-9809
Par: 54, Holes: 18
Crestwood Golf & Ski, Alexandria, 56308
Holes: 27
Crow Greens CC PC, P.O. Box 689 1445 Country Rd., Watertown, 55388,
612-955-2223   Yards: 5586, Par: 36, USGA: 65.0, Holes: 9
Cuyuna CC, Deerwood, 56444,   218-523-3489
Holes: 9
Dahlgreen GC, 6940 Dahlgreen Road, Chaska, 55318,   612-448-7463
Yards: 6641, Par: 72, Holes: 18
Dawson Golf Association PC, Dawson, 56232
Yards: 5674, Par: 35, USGA: 64.6, Holes: 9
Daytona Club PC, 14740 Lawndale Lane, Dayton, 55327,   612-427-6110
Yards: 6232, Par: 72, USGA: 69.3, Holes: 18, Pro: Bruce McCann
Deer Run GC, 8610 Victoria Dr., Victoria, 55386,   612-443-2351
Yards: 6256, Par: 71, Holes: 18
Dodge CC, Dodge Center, 55927,   507-374-2374
Holes: 9
Driftwood Family Resort & Golf, Pine River, 56474,   218-568-4221
Holes: 9
Dwan GC PC, 3301 West 110th St., Bloomington, 55431,   612-887-9602
Yards: 5275, Par: 68, USGA: 64.8, Holes: 18
Eagle View GC PC, Itasca Star Route, Park Rapids, 56470,   218-732-7102
Yards: 3617, Par: 64, USGA: 56.1, Holes: 18
Eastwood GC PC, Eastwood Road S.E., Rochester, 55904,   507-281-6173
Yards: 6177, Par: 70, USGA: 68.7, Holes: 18
Edenvale GC PC, 14500 Valley View Rd., Eden Prairie, 55344,   612-937-9347
Yards: 5952, Par: 70, USGA: 68.7, Holes: 18
Edinburgh USA, 8700 Edinburgh Crossing, Minneapolis, 55443,   612-424-7060
Yards: 6335, Par: 72, USGA: 71.3, Holes: 18
Eko Backen GC, Scandia, 55073,   612-433-2422
Holes: 9
Elk River CC, Elk River, 55330,   612-441-4111
Holes: 18
Elm Creek GC PC, 18940 Hwy. 55, Plymouth, 55446,   612-478-6716
Yards: 4117, Par: 63, USGA: 59.7, Holes: 18
Enger Park GC PC, 1801 West Skyline Blvd., Duluth, 55811,   218-722-5044
Yards: 6047, Par: 72, USGA: 67.8, Holes: 18
Eveleth Municipal GC PC, P.O. Box 649, Eveleth, 55734,   218-741-1577
Yards: 6152, Par: 36, USGA: 69.1, Holes: 9
Faribault G & CC, Faribault, 55332,   507-334-3810
Par: 72, Holes: 18
Farmer's Golf And Health Club, Box 33, Sanborn, 56083,   507-648-3629
Yards: 2996, Par: 36, USGA: 34.5, Holes: 9, Pro: Richard Meyers
Fertile Duffers GC, Fertile, 56540
Par: 27, Holes: 9
Fiddlestix Golf Course PC, South Highway 47 Box 23, Isle, 56342,
612-676-3636   Yards: 2800, Par: 36, USGA: 66.1, Holes: 9, Pro: Jeff Searles

Fifty Lakes CC, Fifty Lakes, 56448
Holes: 9
Fort Snelling GC PC, Box 20515, Bloomington, 55420,   612-726-9331
Yards: 5362, Par: 35, USGA: 64.4, Holes: 9
Fosston, Fosston, 56542,   218-435-6535
Holes: 9
Fountain Valley GC, Farmington, 55024,   612-463-2121
Holes: 18
Fox Hollow GC, 4780 Palmgren Avenue, Rogers, 55374
Holes: 18
Francis A. Gross GC PC, 2201 St. Anthony Blvd., Minneapolis, 55418,
612-789-2542   Yards: 6362, Par: 71, USGA: 69.9, Holes: 18
Frazee GC PC, Box 236, Frazee, 56544,   218-334-3831
Yards: 5338, Par: 71, USGA: 65.6, Holes: 18
French Lake Open GC PC, 10370 9th Place North, Maple Grove, 55369
Yards: 2864, Par: 30, USGA: 52.3, Holes: 9
Fritzs Resort G & CC, Nisswa, 56468,   218-568-8988
Par: 27, Holes: 9
Garrison GC, Garrison, 56450
Par: 27, Holes: 9
Gem Lake Hills GC PC, 4039 Scheunemann Rd., White Bear Lake, 55110,
612-429-8715   Yards: 3362, Par: 57, USGA: 55.3, Holes: 18
Glencoe CC, Glencoe, 55336,   612-864-3023
Par: 36, Holes: 9
Graceville GC, Graceville, 56240,   612-748-7557
Holes: 9
Grand View Lodge, S. 134 Nokomis, Nisswa, 56468,   800-345-9625
Yards: 3100, Par: 35, Holes: 9, Pro: Andrew Smith
Grandy Nine GC PC, Route 2, Stanchfield, 55080,   612-689-1417
Yards: 5174, Par: 35, USGA: 63.1, Holes: 9
Green Valley Recreation GC, Lake Park, 56554,   218-532-7447
Par: 34, Holes: 9
Greenhaven CC, Anoka, 55303
Holes: 18
Greenwood GC, Wyoming, 56601,   612-462-4653
Yards: 2827, Par: 36, Holes: 9
Gunflint Hills GC PC, Box 62, Grand Marais, 55604,   218-387-9988
Yards: 2126, Par: 31, USGA: 59.1, Holes: 9
Hampton Hills GC PC, 5313 North Juneau Lane, Minneapolis, 55442,
612-559-9800   Yards: 6085, Par: 72, USGA: 67.7, Holes: 18
Harmony GC, Harmony, 55939
Holes: 9
Havana Hills Par-3 GC, Owatonna, 55060,   507-451-2577
Par: 27, Holes: 9
Hawley Golf and CC PC, Hwy. 10 Box 734, Hawley, 56549,   218-483-4808
Yards: 5877, Par: 70, USGA: 66.3, Holes: 18
Hayden Hills GC PC, 618 West Hyden Lake Rd., Champlin, 55316,
612-421-0060   Yards: 2842, Par: 30, USGA: 52.2, Holes: 9
Hazeltine National GC, 1900 Hazeltine Blvd., Minneapolis, 55318
Headwaters GC, Park Rapids, 56470,   218-732-4832
Par: 72, Holes: 18
Heart of the Valley GC PC, Ada, 56510,   218-784-4746
Yards: 2955, Par: 37, USGA: 33.5, Holes: 9, Pro: Sheldon Johnson
Hendricks GC, Hendricks, 56136,   507-275-3852
Holes: 9

Hiawatha GC PC, 4553 Longfellow Ave. South, Minneapolis, 55407,
612-724-7715   Yards: 6630, Par: 73, USGA: 71.0, Holes: 18
Hibbing Municipal GC PC, 7th Ave & 16th St, Hibbing, 55746,   218-263-4230
Yards: 2657, Par: 34, USGA: 62.8, Holes: 9
Hidden Greens GC PC, 14176 210th St. East, Hastings, 55033,   612-437-3085
Yards: 5954, Par: 72, USGA: 68.3, Holes: 18
Hidden Haven CC, 20520 NE Polk Street, Cedar, 55011,   612-434-4626
Holes: 9
Highland Nine GC, St. Paul, 55101,   612-699-6082
Par: 35, Holes: 9
Highland Park GC PC, 1403 Montreal Ave., St. Paul, 55116,   612-699-6082
Yards: 6116, Par: 72, USGA: 68.4, Holes: 27
Holiday Park GC, Hayward, 56043,   507-373-3886
Par: 27, Holes: 9
Hollydale GC, 4710 Holly Lane No., Plymouth, 55446,   612-559-9847
Yards: 5922, Par: 71, USGA: 68.1, Holes: 18
Howards Barn & GC, Fifty Lakes, 56448,   218-763-2038
Holes: 9
Hoyt Lakes CC PC, Hoyt Lakes, 55750,   218-225-2841
Yards: 6716, Par: 36, USGA: 71.2, Holes: 9
Ironman GC, Detroit Lakes, 56501,   218-847-5592
Par: 54, Holes: 18
Ironwood GC, Mankato, 56001
Holes: 9
Island View CC, Waconia, 55387,   612-448-5335
Holes: 18
Jackson GC, Jackson, 56143,   507-847-2660
Holes: 9
Jonathan Pri-30 GC, Chaska, 55318
Par: 30, Holes: 9
Karlstad GC, Karlstad, 56732
Holes: 9
Kenyon CC, Kenyon, 55946,   507-789-6307
Holes: 9
Kerkhoven Community GC, Kerkhoven, 56252
Holes: 9
Kimball GC PC, Co Rd 150, Kimball, 55353,   612-398-2285
Yards: 3196, Par: 36, USGA: 34.8, Holes: 9
Lake Miltona GC, Miltona, 56354
Holes: 9
Lake View Executive GC, Detroit Lakes, 56501,   218-847-8942
Holes: 18
Lakefield Golfers, INC. PC, Box 807, Lakefield, 56150,   507-662-5755
Yards: 5258, Par: 34, USGA: 64.5, Holes: 9
Lakeside GC, Waseca, 56093,   507-835-2574
Holes: 18
Lakeview Golf of Orono PC, 710 N. Shore Drive West, Mound, 55364,
612-472-3459   Yards: 5376, Par: 69, USGA: 62.3, Holes: 18
Lakeview-Two Harbors GC PC, Two-Harbors, 55616,   218-834-2255
Yards: 5848, Par: 36, USGA: 66.8, Holes: 9
Lakeway GC PC, Route 1 Box 129, Dalton, 56342,   218-589-8591
Yards: 4754, Par: 35, USGA: 61.2, Holes: 9
Lancaster Muni GC, Lancaster, 56735
Holes: 9
Lewiston CC PC, Route 2, Lewiston, 55952,   507-523-9000
Yards: 6128, Par: 35, USGA: 67.6, Holes: 9

Lindstrom Par-3 GC, Lindstrom, 55045
Par: 27, Holes: 9
Litchfield GC PC, P.O. Box 706, Litchfield, 55355,   612-693-6059
Yards: 6007, Par: 70, USGA: 67.6, Holes: 18
Little Crow CC, Spicer, 56288,   612-354-2296
Holes: 18
Lone Pine CC PC, 15451 Howard Lake Rd., Shakopee, 55379,   612-445-3575
Yards: 4824, Par: 68, USGA: 62.5, Holes: 18
Long Prairie CC, Long Prairie, 56347,   612-732-3312
Par: 36, Holes: 9
Loon Lake GC PC, R.R. 3 Box 192, Jackson, 56143,   507-847-4036
Yards: 5982, Par: 36, USGA: 66.2, Holes: 9
Lutsen Lodge GC, Lutsen, 55612,   218-663-7296
Holes: 18
Luverne CC, Luverne, 56156,   507-283-4383
Par: 35, Holes: 9
Ma-Cal-Grove CC, Caledonia, 55912,   507-724-2733
Holes: 9
Mahnomen CC PC, Rt. 2 Box 58, Mahnomen, 56557,   218-935-5188
Yards: 2979, Par: 36, USGA: 33.6, Holes: 9
Majestic Oaks GC, 701 Bunker Lake Blvd., Ham Lake, 55304,   612-755-2140
Yards: 6337, Par: 72, USGA: 70.4, Holes: 18, Pro: Bill Folkes
Manitou Ridge GC PC, 3200 N. McKight Rd., White Bear Lake, 55110,
612-777-2987   Yards: 5820, Par: 70, USGA: 67.1, Holes: 18
Maple Hills GC PC, Rt. 4, Frazee, 56544,   218-847-9532
Yards: 5884, Par: 36, USGA: 66.0, Holes: 9
Marshall High School GC, Marshall, 56258,   507-532-2278
Par: 27, Holes: 9
Mayflower CC PC, Fairfax, 55332,   507-426-9964
Yards: 6172, Par: 35, USGA: 68.0, Holes: 9
Meadowbrook GC PC, 201 Meadowbrook Rd., Hopkins, 55343,   612-929-2077
Yards: 6376, Par: 72, USGA: 70.0, Holes: 18
Mendota Heights Par-3 GC, St. Paul, 55101,   612-454-9822
Par: 27, Holes: 9
Milaca GC, Milaca, 56353,   612-983-2110
Holes: 9
Millers Crestwood GC PC, Rt. 6 Box 211, Alexandria, 56308,   612-762-8223
Yards: 5042, Par: 36, USGA: 62.8, Holes: 9
Minneopa GC PC, Rt. #9 Box 133, Mankato, 56001,   507-625-5777
Par: 33, USGA: 32.6, Holes: 9, Pro: Ken Bohks
Minnesota State Prison, Stillwater, 55082, 612-779-2700
Holes: 9
Minniowa GC PC, Hwy. 169 N., Elmore, 56027,   507-943-3149
Yards: 6006, Par: 35, USGA: 66.3, Holes: 9
Mississippi National Golf Link, 409 Golf Links Dr., Red Wing, 55066,
612-388-1874   Yards: 6182, Par: 71, USGA: 69.5, Holes: 18, Pro: Sam Drodofsky
Montgomery GC PC, Montgomery, 56069,   612-364-5602
Yards: 6520, Par: 36, USGA: 70.3, Holes: 9
Monticello CC PC, Co. Rd. 39 West P.O. Box 651, Monticello, 55362,
612-295-4653   Yards: 6104, Par: 72, USGA: 70.0, Holes: 18
Moorhead Village Green GC PC, 3420 Village Green Blvd., Moorhead, 56560,
218-299-5366   Yards: 6596, Par: 36, USGA: 70.6, Holes: 9
Moose Lake gC, Moose Lake, 55767,   218-485-4886
Yards: 2500, Par: 34, Holes: 9
Mora CC, RR 1, Mora, 55051,   612-679-2317
Yards: 3300, Par: 36, Holes: 9

Mount Frontenac GC, Box 119, Frontenac, 55026, 612-388-5826
Yards: 2823, Par: 36, USGA: 66.5, Holes: 9
New Hope Village GC PC, 4401 Xylon Ave. North, New Hope, 55428,
612-537-1149 Yards: 2674, Par: 27, USGA: 52.8, Holes: 9
New Prague CC, New Prague, 56071, 612-758-3126
Holes: 18
Normandale GC PC, 4800 West 7th St., Edina, 55435, 612-835-4653
Yards: 1575, Par: 27, USGA: 74.0, Holes: 9, Pro: Bob Goodrich
North Branch Gc PC, Box 387, North Branch, 55056, 612-674-9989
Yards: 2122, Par: 33, USGA: 62.4, Holes: 9
Northern Hills GC PC, 4805 41 Ave. N.W., Rochester, 55901, 507-281-6170
Yards: 5936, Par: 72, USGA: 67.4, Holes: 18
Oak Glen CC, 1599 McKusick Rd., Stillwater, 55082, 612-439-6981
Yards: 6310, Par: 72, Holes: 27
Oak Knolls GC, Red Lake Falls, 56750, 218-253-4423
Holes: 9
Oak Ridge GC PC, Box 475, Hallock, 56728, 218-843-2155
Yards: 5668, Par: 36, USGA: 65.2, Holes: 9
Oak Ridge CC, Detroit Lakes, 56501, 218-439-6192
Par: 36, Holes: 9
Oak View GC PC, Box 123, Freeborn, 56032, 507-863-2288
Yards: 6004, Par: 36, USGA: 68.2, Holes: 9
Oakcrest GC PC, Box 69, Roseau, 56751, 218-463-3016
Yards: 6254, Par: 36, USGA: 68.9, Holes: 9
Oakdale CC, Buffalo Lake, 55314, 612-833-5518
Holes: 9
Oaks CC PC, Box 86, Hayfield, 55940, 507-477-3115
Yards: 6045, Par: 72, USGA: 68.0, Holes: 18
Orchard Gardens GC PC, Cty. Rd. #5 & 155th St., Burnsville, 55337,
612-435-5771 Yards: 3054, Par: 27, USGA: 54.3, Holes: 9
Orono GC PC, 265 Orono Orchard Rd. Box 66, Crystal Bay, 55323,
612-473-9904 Yards: 2139, Par: 33, USGA: 60.3, Holes: 9
Ortonville GC PC, 315 Madison Ave., Ortonville, 56278, 612-839-3428
Yards: 6182, Par: 72, USGA: 67.1, Holes: 18
Owatonna CC, Box 446, Owatonna, 55060, 507-451-1363
Yards: 6312, Par: 72, Holes: 18
Pebble Creek CC PC, 14000 Club House Drive, Becker, 55308, 612-261-4653
Yards: 6355, Par: 72, USGA: 69.9, Holes: 18, Pro: Geo. Shortridge
Perham Lakeside GC, Perham, 56573, 218-346-6070
Par: 36, Holes: 9
Phalen GC PC, 1772 Landfond Ave., St. Paul, 55104, 612-778-0424
Yards: 5872, Par: 70, USGA: 67.3, Holes: 18
Pheasant Run GC PC, 10705 Cty. Rd. 116, Rogers, 55374, 612-428-8244
Yards: 6019, Par: 71, USGA: 68.2, Holes: 18, Pro: Lyle Johansen
Pierz Municipal GC, Rt. 3 Box 93, Pierz, 56364, 612-468-6270
Yards: 5948, Par: 35, USGA: 68.0, Holes: 9
Pine Creek GC, La Crescent, 55947, 507-895-2410
Holes: 9
Pine Hill GC, Carlton, 55718
Par: 27, Holes: 9
Pine River CC, Box 196, Pine River, 56474, 218-587-4774
Yards: 3127, Par: 36, USGA: 34.5, Holes: 9
Pinewood Estates GC, Elk River, 55330, 612-441-3451
Holes: 9
Piper Hills Golf Club PC, 140 1st St. S.E., Box 535, Plainview, 55964,
507-534-2613 Yards: 3086, Par: 36, USGA: 68.3, Holes: 9

Pipestone CC, Pipestone, 56164, 507-825-2592
Holes: 9
Pokegama CC PC, 3910 Golf Course Rd., Grand Rapids, 55744, 218-326-0785
Yards: 6526, Par: 72, USGA: 71.2, Holes: 18
Pomme De Terre CC, Morris, 56267, 612-589-1009
Holes: 9
Prairie View Municipal GC PC, P.O. Box 279, Worthington, 56187,
507-372-7896   Yards: 5994, Par: 71, USGA: 67.4, Holes: 18
Preston GC PC, Hwy. 16 West, Preston, 55965, 507-765-4485
Yards: 5448, Par: 35, USGA: 67.5, Holes: 9
Purple Hawk CC, Cambridge, 55508, 612-689-3800
Par: 72, Holes: 18
Quadna Mountain Lodge & CC, 100 Quadna Rd., Hill City, 55748,
218-697-8444   Yards: 3115, Par: 36, Holes: 9
Red Oak GC PC, 710 N. Share Drive W., Mound, 55364, 612-472-3999
Yards: 2376, Par: 27, USGA: 50.5, Holes: 9
Red Rock GC, Hoffman, 56339, 612-986-2342
Holes: 9
Rich Springs GC PC, RR 1, Cold Springs, 56320, 612-685-8810
Yards: 6278, Par: 71, USGA: 69.4, Holes: 18
Rivers Edge CC, Watertown, 55388, 612-955-2223
Par: 36, Holes: 9
Riverside GC PC, Box 387, Stephen, 56757, 218-478-2735
Yards: 2700, Par: 35, USGA: 32.3, Holes: 9
Riverside Town & CC, Winnebago, 56098, 507-893-3677
Holes: 9
Riverview GC, Box 32, New Richland, 56072, 507-465-3516
Yards: 3200, Par: 36, Holes: 9
Rolling Green Fairways PC, 1422 Oak Beach Dr., Fairmont, 56031,
507-235-5998   Yards: 2352, Par: 27, USGA: 50.1, Holes: 9
Rolling Hills GC PC, Rt. 2, Pelican Rapids, 56572, 218-532-2214
Yards: 5426, Par: 35, USGA: 65.2, Holes: 9
Rolling Hills GC PC, R.R. #2 Box 86, Westbrook, 56183, 507-274-5166
Yards: 5630, Par: 36, USGA: 63.4, Holes: 9
Rum River GC, Princeton, 55371, 612-389-5109
Par: 35, Holes: 9
Rushford GC, Rushford, 55971
Holes: 9
Sandstone Muni GC, Sandstone, 55072
Holes: 9
Sauk Center CC PC, Lakeshore Dr. Box 173, Sauk Centre, 56378, 612-352-3860
Yards: 3195, Par: 37, USGA: 68.7, Holes: 9
Savanna Golf & Supper Club, Rt 4, Mc Gregor, 55760, 218-426-3117
Yards: 3254, Par: 36, Holes: 99
Sawmill GC, 11177 N Mc Kusick Rd, Stillwater, 55082, 612-439-7862
Yards: 6365, Par: 70, Holes: 18
Scottdale GC PC, 19400 Natchez Ave., Prior Lake, 55372, 612-435-7182
Yards: 6290, Par: 36, USGA: 68.9, Holes: 9
Shor-Tee GC, RT 1 Box 85, Waterville, 56096, 507-362-4471
Yards: 767, Par: 27, Holes: 9, Pro: Bill Sautbine
Shoreland CC, Box 516, St. Peter, 56082, 507-931-4400
Yards: 5575, Par: 69, Holes: 18
Silver Cedar GC, Annandale, 55302
Par: 27, Holes: 9
Silver Springs GC PC, P.O. Box 246, Monticello, 55362, 612-338-2207
Yards: 6651, Par: 72, USGA: 71.1, Holes: 18

Sneaky Pines GC, Cass Lake, 56633
Holes: 9
Soldiers Memorial Field GC, Box 1102, Rochester, 55903,   507-281-6176
Yards: 5706, Par: 70, USGA: 67.0, Holes: 18, Pro: Tim Higgins
Springfield CC, Springfield, 56087,   507-723-5888
Holes: 9
Sugar Hills GC, Grand Rapids, 55744,   218-326-9461
Par: 34, Holes: 9
Sundance GC PC, 15240 113th Ave. North, Osseo, 55369,   612-420-4700
Yards: 6400, Par: 72, USGA: 70.1, Holes: 18, Pro: Aaron McClay
Swan Lake CC, Pengilly, 55775,   218-885-1198
Holes: 9
Theodore Wirth GC PC, Glenwood Pkwy. & Plymouth Nort, Minneapolis,.
55422, 612-522-4584   Yards: 6129, Par: 72, USGA: 68.7, Holes: 18
Tianna CC, Walker, 56484,   218-547-1712
Yards: 6323, Par: 72, Holes: 18
Tracy CC, Tracy, 56175,   507-629-4666
Holes: 9
Twenty-Nine Pines CC, Mahtowa, 55762,   218-389-3136
Holes: 9
Twin Pines GC PC, RR #1 Box 89, Bagley, 56621,   218-694-2454
Yards: 6342, Par: 36, USGA: 68.9, Holes: 9
University GC PC, Larpenteur and Fulham, St. Paul, 55113,   612-627-4000
Yards: 6123, Par: 71, USGA: 69.3, Holes: 18
University of Minnesota Golf, St. Paul, 55101,   612-627-4001
Holes: 18
V A Hospital Pitch & Putt Golf, St. Cloud, 56301,   612-252-1670
Par: 27, Holes: 9
Vallebrook GC, 101 Oallebrook Rd., P.O.Box 11, Lakefield, 56150,   507-662-5755
Yards: 2718, Par: 34, USGA: 32.4, Holes: 9
Valley GC PC, Route 4 Box 318, Willmar, 56201,   612-235-6790
Yards: 4970, Par: 35, USGA: 62.1, Holes: 9
Valley High CC, Houston, 55943,   507-896-3239
Holes: 9
Valleywood GC PC, 4851 W. 125th St., Apple Valley, 55124,   612-423-2171
Yards: 6083, Par: 71, USGA: 68.0, Holes: 18
Vermilion Fairways GC PC, Vermilion Fairways, Cook, 55723,   218-666-2679
Yards: 6490, Par: 36, USGA: 69.9, Holes: 9
Veterans GC, Dawson, 56232
Holes: 9
Viking Meadows GC, 1788 Viking Blvd. NE, Wyoming, 55092,   612-434-4205
Yards: 6310, Par: 72, Holes: 18
Wadena CC PC, P.O. Box 446, Wadena, 56482,   218-631-4010
Yards: 6030, Par: 36, USGA: 67.8, Holes: 9
Wapicada GC, St. Cloud, 56379,   612-251-7804
Par: 72, Holes: 18
Warren Riverside CC PC, Warren, 56762,   218-745-4028
Yards: 5780, Par: 36, USGA: 67.2, Holes: 9
Waseca Lakeside CC, Waseca, 56093,   507-835-2574
Par: 71, Holes: 18
Watona Park GC PC, 116 West Main St., Madelia, 56062,   507-642-3608
Yards: 6138, Par: 36, USGA: 68.5, Holes: 9
Wells GC PC, P.O. Box 96, Wells, 56097,   507-553-3313
Yards: 4108, Par: 32, USGA: 58.6, Holes: 9
Westfield GC PC, 1460 W. Fifth St., Winona, 55987,   507-452-6901
Yards: 3300, Par: 36, USGA: 36.0, Holes: 9, Pro: Rodney Sines

Wheaton CC PC, Wheaton, 56296, 612-563-4079
Yards: 5828, Par: 34, USGA: 66.0, Holes: 9
Willmar GC, Willmar, 56201, 612-235-1166
Par: 72, Holes: 18
Willow Creek GC, Box 68, Rochester, 55903, 507-285-0305
Par: 72, Holes: 18
Willow Creek GC PC, Rt. 1, Barnesville, 56514, 218-493-4486
Yards: 5476, Par: 36, USGA: 64.9, Holes: 9
Willow Greens GC, Stewartville, 55976
Holes: 9
Winthrop GC, Winthrop, 55396, 507-674-5828
Holes: 9
Woodbury Golf & Fitness Club, Woodbury, 55125, 612-735-4401
Par: 27, Holes: 9
Woodland Creek GC, 830 West Main Street, Anoka, 55303, 612-417-7500
Holes: 9
Zumbrota GC, Zumbrota, 55992, 507-635-2821

Amory GC, Hwy 25 N, Amory, 38821, 601-256-9003   *Mississippi*
Yards: 6200, Par: 36, Holes: 9
Annandale GC, 837 Mannsdale Rd., Jackson, 39110
Bel Air Park, Country Club Road, Tupelo, 38801, 601-841-6440
Biloxi Par 3 GC, Pope Ferry Rd., Biloxi, 39532, 601-388-3631
Par: 54, Holes: 18
Bovina R&C Complex GC, Vicksburg, 39180, 601-636-2260
Yards: 6283, Par: 72, Holes: 18
Clear Creek GC, Rt. 5 Box 322 C, Vicksburg, 39180, 601-638-9395
Yards: 6680, Par: 72, Holes: 18, Pro: Jack Slocum
Delta St Univ GC, P.O. Box 3271, Cleveland, 38733, 601-846-4585
Yards: 3020, Par: 36, Holes: 9
Green Hills CC, Beaver Lake Rd., P. O. Box 61, Purvis, 39475, 601-794-6427
Yards: 6126, Par: 71, Holes: 18
Grove Park GC, Ave D, Jackson, 39213, 601-982-9728
Par: 36, Holes: 9, Pro: Walter Welch
Gulfport Par 3, 700 34th St., Gulfport, 29503, 601-868-3809
Par: 54, Holes: 18
Hattiesburg GC, 1 Country Club Dr., Laurel, 39401
Hickory Hills GC, Hickory Hills Dr., Gautier, 38755, 601-497-5150
Yards: 7049, Par: 72, Holes: 18
Hinds Jr College GC, Hwy 18, P. O. Box 1145, Raymond, 39154, 601-857-5993
Yards: 6100, Par: 72, Holes: 18
Holiday GC, East Goodman Road, Olive Branch, 38654, 601-895-3500
Iuka CC, Oldham Rd., P. O. Box 596, Iuka, 38852, 601-423-9981
Yards: 2666, Par: 36, Holes: 9
Jackson CGC, P. O. Box 358, Hurley, 39555, 601-588-6111
Yards: 3100, Par: 36, Holes: 9, Pro: Ralph Cumbest
Lake Hillsdale GC, Rt. 3 Box 220, Lumberton, 39455, 601-796-9012
Yards: 2584, Par: 34, Holes: 9
Lakeview GC, Causeyville Rd., Meridan, 39309, 601-693-3301
Par: 72, Holes: 18
Lakeview GC, Rt 2 Box 7, Summit, 39666, 601-276-9311
Yards: 3400, Par: 36, Holes: 9
Laurel GC, Hwy. 84, Laurel, 39440
LeFleurs Bluff Park GC, Riverside Drive, Jackson, 39202, 601-987-3998
Millbrook CC, Highway 11 North, Picayune, 39466, 601-798-8711

Nik Nar CC, P. O. Box 5703, Pearl, 39208,   601-939-9964
Yards: 3025, Par: 36, Holes: 9
Oxford CC, 315 CC Rd., P.O. Box 50, Oxford, 38655,   601-234-5811
Yards: 3100, Par: 36, Holes: 9
Pass Christian Isles GC, 159 Country Club Dr., Pass Christian, 39650,
601-452-3830   Yards: 6195, Par: 72, Holes: 18, Pro: Mike Burke
Pearl River Valley CC, Hwy 26 W, Rt. 3 Box 186, Poplarville, 39470,
601-795-8887 Yards: 6470, Par: 72, Holes: 18, Pro: Bryan Amacker
Pine Hill CC, P.O. Box 397, Gloster, 39638,   601-225-7741
Yards: 2600, Par: 35, Holes: 9
Rainbow Bay GC, 4500 Pass Rd., Bilouxi, 39531,   601-388-9670
Yards: 5957, Par: 71, Holes: 18, Pro: Dewey Stewart
Sonny Guy Muni GC, 3200 Woodrow Wilson Dr., Jackson, 39209,   601-960-1905
Yards: 6531, Par: 72, Holes: 18
St. Andrews GC, #2 Golfing Green Dr., Ocean Springs, 39564,   601-875-7730
Yards: 6037, Par: 72, USGA: 68.6, Holes: 18, Pro: Bobby Burch
Starkville CC, S. Montgomery, P. O. Box 226, Starkville, 39759,   601-323-1818
Yards: 3150, Par: 36, Holes: 9, Pro: Richard Kelley
Sunkist GC, Biloxi, 39532,   601-388-3961
Yards: 6121, Par: 72, Holes: 18
Tramark GC, Washington Ave., Box 6631, Gulfport, 39506,   601-863-7808
Par: 72, Holes: 18
Twin Pines, Highway 42 East, Hattiesburg, 39402,   601-544-8318
University of Mississippi GC, College Hill Rd., Oxford, 38655,   601-234-4816
Yards: 6420, Par: 72, Holes: 18, Pro: Ernest Ross
University of S. Mississippi, 406 Westhills Dr., Hattiesburg, 39406,
601-264-1872   Yards: 6200, Par: 72, Holes: 18, Pro: James Carpenter

---

A.L. Gustin Jr. GC, Stadium Blvd., Columbia, 65201, 314-882-6016   *Missouri*
Yards: 6400, Par: 70, Holes: 18
Albany CC, 224 W. Wood, Albany, 64402,   816-726-3961
Yards: 3069, Par: 36, Holes: 9
American Legion GC, 3681 route MM, Hannibal, 63401
Yards: 2705, Par: 35, Holes: 9
Arcadia Valley CC, P.O. Box 43, Hwy 72, Ironton, 63650,   314-546-9508
Yards: 3142, Par: 36, Holes: 9
Arthur Hills GC, Route 2, Mexico, 65265,   314-581-1330
Yards: 3022, Par: 36, Holes: 9
Aurora GC, RR 1, K Hwy., Aurora, 65605,   417-678-3353
Yards: 3250, Par: 35, Holes: 9
Ballwin GC, 333 Holloway Rd., Ballwin, 63011,   314-227-1750
Yards: 3171, Par: 36, Holes: 9
Belton Muni GC, 4200 Bong Ave., Belton, 64012,   816-331-6777
Yards: 6800, Par: 72, Holes: 18
Bent Oak GC, P.O. Box 537, White Rd., Oak Grove, 64075,   816-625-3028
Yards: 6804, Par: 72, Holes: 18
Blue River GC, 6901 Elmwood, Kansas City, 64132,   816-523-5830
Yards: 4580, Par: 66, Holes: 18
Bolivar GC, P.O. Box 163, West Hwy 32, Bolivar, 65613,   417-326-6600
Yards: 3285, Par: 36, Holes: 9
Bridgeton-Berry Hill GC, 11919 Berry Hill Dr., Bridgeton, 63044,   314-731-7979
Yards: 3117, Par: 36, Holes: 9
Brookfield CC, P.O. Box 95, Hwy 11 East, Brookfield, 64628,   816-258-3400
Yards: 3060, Par: 36, Holes: 9

Butler Country Club, S. Main St. Rd., Butler, 64730, 816-679-3637
Yards: 3100, Par: 36, Holes: 9
California CC, P.O. Box 46, California, 65018, 314-796-2089
Yards: 3353, Par: 36, Holes: 9
Cameron Memorial GC, 816 N. Chestnut St., Cameron, 64429, 816-632-2626
Yards: 2900, Par: 36, Holes: 9
Cape Jaycees Muni GC, A.C. Brase Arena Building, Cape Girardeau, 63701,
314-334-2031   Yards: 5715, Par: 70, Holes: 18
Carthage GC, West of City, Carthage, 64836, 417-358-8724
Yards: 6342, Par: 71, Holes: 18
Caruthersville CC, P.O. Box 875, Hwy 84, Caruthersville, 63830, 314-333-1443
Yards: 5987, Par: 71, Holes: 9
Cassville GC, RR 2, Box 112 South, Cassville, 65625, 417-847-2399
Yards: 6604, Par: 72, Holes: 18
Cedar Creek CC, Turkey Mountain Estates #1, Shell Knob, 65747, 417-858-6461
Yards: 1346, Par: 29, Holes: 9
Cedar Oak Public GC, Route 4, Box 160B, Stockton, 65785, 417-276-3193
Yards: 2720, Par: 35, Holes: 9
Chapel Woods GC, Route 5, Box 89, Lee's Summit, 64063, 816-795-8870
Yards: 6366, Par: 72, Holes: 18
Chesterfield GC, 815 River Valley Rd., Chesterfield, 63017, 314-469-1432
Yards: 5500, Par: 68, Holes: 18
Claycrest GC, P.O. Box 90, Liberty, 64068, 816-781-6522
Yards: 6200, Par: 72, Holes: 18
Clinton CC, P.O. Box 212, Clinton, 64735, 816-885-2521
Yards: 2914, Par: 36, Holes: 9
Cottonwood GC, Desoto, 63020, 314-586-8803
Yards: 3335, Par: 36, Holes: 9
Country Club of Blue Springs, 1600 N. Circle Dr., Blue Springs, 64015,
816-229-8103   Yards: 6536, Par: 72, Holes: 18
Crackerneck GC, 18800 E. 40 Hwy, Independence, 64050, 816-795-8800
Yards: 6160, Par: 71, Holes: 18
Creve Coeur GC, 11400 Olde Cabin Rd., Creve Coeur, 63141, 314-432-1806
Yards: 2986, Par: 35, Holes: 9
Cuba Lakes G&CC, Route 2, Box 9A, Cuba, 65453, 314-885-2234
Yards: 2825, Par: 34, Holes: 9
Deer Run G&CC, P.O. Box 869, Van Buren, 63965
Yards: 3025, Par: 36, Holes: 9
Duncan Hills GC, 400 E. Duncan Dr., Savannah, 64485, 816-324-3796
Yards: 5734, Par: 35, Holes: 9
Eagle Springs GC, 2575 Redman Road, St. Louis, 63136
Holes: 9
El Dorado Springs Muni GC, 301 S. High, El Dorado Springs, 64744,
417-876-9968   Yards: 3269, Par: 36, Holes: 9
Eldon GC, Route 1, Box 75, Eldon, 65026, 314-392-4172
Yards: 6170, Par: 72, Holes: 9
Elk River CC, Route TT & Hwy 90, Neol, 64854, 417-475-3208
Yards: 3334, Par: 36, Holes: 9
Elm Hills GC, Route 7, Sedalia, 65301, 816-826-6171
Yards: 2795, Par: 34, Holes: 9
Elmwood GC, #9 Elmwood, Washington, 63090, 314-239-6841
Yards: 3100, Par: 36, Holes: 9
Fairview GC, P.O. Box 7162, St. Joseph, 64507, 816-364-9055
Yards: 6740, Par: 72, Holes: 18
Forest Park Muni GC, 5600 Clayton Rd., St. Louis, 63110, 314-367-1337
Yards: 5868, Par: 70, Holes: 27

Frank E. Peters Muni GC, Twin Lakes Park, Nevada, 64772, 417-667-8233
Yards: 3201, Par: 35, Holes: 9
Fredericktown CC, P.O. Box 69, Fredericktown, 63645, 314-783-6236
Yards: 5954, Par: 36, Holes: 9
Grandview GC, 1825 E. Norton, Springfield, 65803, 417-833-9962
Yards: 6102, Par: 70, Holes: 18
Greene Hills GC, Willard, 65781, 417-742-3086
Par: 70, Holes: 18
Hidden Valley Golf Links, Route 1, Clever, 65631, 417-743-2860
Yards: 6900, Par: 73, Holes: 18
Hodge Park GC, 6800 N.E. Barry Rd., Kansas City, 64156, 816-781-4152
Yards: 6194, Par: 71, Holes: 18
House Springs Public GC, 5791 Dulin Creek Rd., House Springs, 63051,
314-671-0560   Yards: 2797, Par: 36, Holes: 9
Hub Golf & Swim Club, 2222 Hub Club Dr., Bethany, 64424, 816-425-8121
Yards: 2360, Par: 34, Holes: 9
Incline Village GC, 1240 Fairway Dr., Foristell, 63348, 314-673-2941
Par: 36, Holes: 9
Indian Foothills, P.O. Box 202, Marshall, 65340, 816-886-7128
Yards: 3007, Par: 36, Holes: 9
Indian Rock GC, P.O. Box 1129, Laurie, 65038, 314-372-3023
Yards: 3395, Par: 36, Holes: 9
Innsbrook Estates CC, One Innsbrook Estates Dr., Wright City, 63390,
314-928-3366   Yards: 6465, Par: 70, Holes: 18
Kemper Golf Course, Hwy 40 West, Boonville, 65233, 816-882-9998
Yards: 2720, Par: 35, Holes: 9
Kennett CC, P.O. Box 606, Kennett, 63857, 314-888-9945
Yards: 6324, Par: 72, Holes: 18
Keth Memorial GC, Central Missouri State Univ., Warrensburg, 64093,
816-429-4182   Yards: 6068, Par: 71, Holes: 18
Kirksville CC, Box 1050, Kirksville, 63501, 816-665-5335
Yards: 6500, Par: 71, Holes: 18
L A Nickell GC, Columbia, 65201, 314-445-4213
Par: 70, Holes: 18
La Plata Muni GC, RR 2, La Plata, 63549, 816-332-4584
Yards: 2825, Par: 35, Holes: 9
Lake Country Resort, Route 3, Box 91, Galena, 65656, 417-538-2273
Par: 32, Holes: 9
Lake of the Woods GC, Columbia, 65201, 314-474-7011
Par: 71, Holes: 18
Lake Valley G&CC, Lake Road 54-79, P.O. Box 317, Camdenton, 65020,
314-346-7218   Yards: 6114, Par: 72, USGA: 69.3, Holes: 18
Lakeview GC, General Delivery, Hamilton, 65041, 816-583-9940
Par: 33, Holes: 9
Lakewood GC, P.O. Box 1149, Fenton, St. Louis County, 63026, 314-343-5567
Yards: 2530, Par: 34, Holes: 9
Lamar CC, P.O. Box 87, Lamar, 64759, 417-682-3977
Yards: 2971, Par: 35, Holes: 9
Lebanon CC, P.O. Box 1070, Lebanon, 65536, 417-532-2901
Yards: 3171, Par: 36, Holes: 9
Lockwood Muni GC, Lockwood City Hall, Lockwood, 65682, 417-232-4221
Yards: 3165, Par: 35, Holes: 9
Loutre Shore CC, P.O. Box 148, Hermann, 65041, 314-486-2781
Yards: 3310, Par: 36, Holes: 9
Mark Twain CC, Star Route, Paris, 65275
Par: 36, Holes: 9

Marshfield CC, P.O. Box 334, Marshfield, 64706, 417-468-9961
Yards: 3058, Par: 35, Holes: 9
Meadow Lake CC, Route 4, Clinton, 64735, 816-885-5124
Yards: 6200, Par: 71, Holes: 18
Minor Park GC, 11105 Holmes Rd., Kansas City, 64134, 816-942-4033
Yards: 5560, Par: 72, Holes: 18
Montgomery County GC, 429 Hensley St., Montgomery City, 63361,
314-564-3010 Yards: 2769, Par: 35, Holes: 9
Mosswood Meadows, P.O. Box 283, Monroe City, 63456, 314-735-2088
Yards: 3310, Par: 36, Holes: 9
Mound City CC, North end of Nebraska St., Mound City, 64470, 816-442-5780
Yards: 3200, Par: 36, Holes: 9
Mt. Vernon Muni GC, Hwy CC, Mt. Vernon, 65712, 314-466-9999
Yards: 2900, Par: 35, Holes: 9
Neosho Muni GC, Route 6, Box 318, Neosho, 64850, 417-451-1543
Yards: 6168, Par: 71, Holes: 18
Normandie Park GC, 7605 St. Charles Rock Rd., St. Louis, 63133, 314-862-4884
Yards: 6258, Par: 71, USGA: 69.6, Holes: 18, Pro: M. Ferzacca
Oak Hills CC, Box 441, Dixon, 65459, 314-759-9808
Yards: 2600, Par: 34, Holes: 9
Oak Hills Golf Center, 932 Ellis Blvd., Jefferson City, 65101, 314-636-4232
Yards: 5746, Par: 70, Holes: 18
Oak Meadow CC, P.O. Box 1256, Rolla, 65401, 314-364-6767
Yards: 6488, Par: 70, Holes: 18
Oakmont Community GC, HCR 2, Box 650, Ridgedale, 65739, 417-334-1572
Yards: 3000, Par: 36, Holes: 9
Osage CC, P.O. Box 521, Linn, 65051, 314-897-3631
Yards: 3003, Par: 35, Holes: 9
Oscar Bloom GC, 3000 N. Glenstone, Springfield, 65803, 417-833-9962
Yards: 1175, Par: 27, Holes: 9
Owensville CC, Route 2, Peaceful Valley Lake, Owensville, 65006
Yards: 2076, Par: 32, Holes: 9
Paddock GC, 50 Country Club Lane, Florissant, 63033, 314-741-4334
Yards: 6311, Par: 72, USGA: 70.1, Holes: 18
Paradise Valley G&CC, P.O. Box 459, Valley Park, 63088, 314-225-5157
Yards: 6000, Par: 70, Holes: 18
Piedmont Canyon GC, P.O. Box 265, Piedmont, 63957, 314-223-7908
Yards: 3201, Par: 35, Holes: 9
Pointe Royale GC, Box 23, Branson, 65616, 417-334-4477
Yards: 6175, Par: 70, Holes: 18
Pomme de Terre G&CC, Route 1, Box 273, Wheatland, 65779, 417-282-6544
Yards: 3100, Par: 35, Holes: 9
Poplar Bluff Muni GC, Box 481AA, Poplar Bluff, 63901, 314-686-6286
Yards: 3250, Par: 36, Holes: 9
Prairie Ridge GC, Route 4, Box 315, Sedalia, 65301, 816-827-5424
Yards: 2679, Par: 36, Holes: 9
Quail Creek GC, 6022 Wells Rd., St. Louis, 63128, 314-487-1988
Yards: 6800, Par: 72, Holes: 18
Randel Muni GC, W. First St., Mountain Grove, 65711, 417-926-5700
Par: 36, Holes: 9
Richland G&CC, Route 1, Box 675, Richland, 65556, 314-765-4825
Yards: 3035, Par: 36, Holes: 9
River Oaks GC, 14204 St. Andrews Dr., Kansas City, 64063
Riverside GC, 1210 Larkin-Williams Rd., Fenton, 63026, 314-343-6333
Yards: 5169, Par: 69, Holes: 18

Rock Port G&CC, Box 235, Rock Port, 64482, 816-744-2590
Yards: 2539, Par: 34, Holes: 9
Rockwood GC, 2400 Maywood, Independence, 64052, 816-252-2002
Yards: 6000, Par: 70, Holes: 18
Rockwood GC, 2400 Maywood, Kansas City, 64052
Royal Meadows GC, 10501 E. 47th St., Kansas City, 64133, 816-353-1323
Yards: 8959, Par: 72, Holes: 27
Ruth Park GC, 8211 Groby, University City, 63130, 314-727-4800
Yards: 2808, Par: 34, Holes: 9
Salisbury Muni GC, Hwy 129 South, P.O. Box 77, Salisbury, 65281, 816-388-5721
Yards: 2795, Par: 35, Holes: 9
Schifferdecker GC, 6th & Schifferdecker, Joplin, 64801, 417-624-3533
Yards: 6123, Par: 71, Holes: 18
Shamrock Hills GC, 3160 S. 291 Hwy, Lee's Summit, 64063, 816-537-6556
Yards: 6500, Par: 17, Holes: 18
Shawnee Bend Muni GC, Box 68, Warsaw, 65355, 816-438-6115
Yards: 3300, Par: 36, Holes: 9
Shelbina Lakeside GC, RR 3, Box 93, Shelbina, 65747, 314-588-4755
Yards: 5699, Par: 36, Holes: 9
Shirkey GC, Hwy 13 South, Richmond, 64085, 816-776-9965
Yards: 6969, Par: 71, Holes: 18
Siler's Shady Acres GC, 6000 S. National, Springfield, 65807, 417-881-9060
Yards: 6000, Par: 69, Holes: 18
Southview GC, 162nd & 71 Hwy, Belton, 64012, 816-331-4042
Yards: 6300, Par: 72, Holes: 27
St. Andrews GC, 2121 St. Andrews Lane, St. Charles, 63301, 314-946-7777
Yards: 5868, Par: 68, Holes: 18
St. Charles GC, 500 Friedens Rd., St. Charles, 63301, 314-946-6190
Yards: 3020, Par: 36, Holes: 9
St. James GC, Hwy 68 South, St. James, 65559, 314-265-8688
Yards: 3373, Par: 36, Holes: 9
St. Peters Muni GC, P.O. Box 9, St. Peters, 63376, 314-278-2227
Yards: 3295, Par: 37, Holes: 9
Stanberry GC, 303 N. Park, Stanberry, 64489, 816-783-2700
Yards: 2949, Par: 36, Holes: 9
Stockton CC, P.O. Box H, Stockton, 65785, 417-276-5417
Yards: 6710, Par: 36, Holes: 9
Sun Valley GC, Elsberry, 63343, 314-898-2613
Yards: 3158, Par: 35, Holes: 9
Swope Memorial GC, 6900 Zoo Dr., Swope Park, Kansas City, 64132,
816-523-9081 Yards: 6000, Par: 71, Holes: 18
Taneycomo GC, Route 1, Box 196-1, Forsyth, 65653, 417-546-5454
Yards: 2626, Par: 35, Holes: 9
Tarkio GC, 1107 Poplar, Box 235, Tarkio, 64491, 816-736-4776
Yards: 3200, Par: 36, Holes: 9
Teetering Rocks Executive Link, 8307 Westridge, Kansas City, 64138,
816-356-1111 Yards: 1800, Par: 31, Holes: 9
Thayer CC, P.O. Box 82, Thayer, 65791, 417-264-7854
Yards: 6718, Par: 36, Holes: 9
Tower Tee GC, 6727 Heege Rd., Affton, 63123, 314-351-1353
Yards: 2000, Par: 54, Holes: 18
Univ. of Missouri–Rolla GC, Rolla, 65401, 314-341-4217
Yards: 3002, Par: 36, Holes: 9
Valley Hills CC, Grain Valley, 64029, 816-229-3032
Par: 72, Holes: 18

Warrenton GC, P.O. Box 339, Warrenton, 63383,   314-456-8726
Yards: 5800, Par: 70, Holes: 18
Wedgewood CC, P.O. Box 505, Cabool, 65689,   417-926-5374
Yards: 6373, Par: 72, Holes: 9
West Plains CC, 1402 Country Club Dr., West Plains, 65775,   417-256-7197
Yards: 6146, Par: 70, Holes: 18
Whitmoor CC, Weldon Springs, 63384,   314-926-2266
Yards: 6900, Par: 72, Holes: 27
Willow Springs CC, P.O. Box 316, Willow Springs, 65793,   417-469-1214
Yards: 3165, Par: 35, Holes: 9
Windbrook GC, 10306 N.W. Hwy 45, Parkville, 64152,   816-741-9520
Yards: 6300, Par: 71, Holes: 18

Airport GC, S off Hwy 13 W, Wolf Point, 59201,   406-653-2161 *Montana*
Holes: 9
Anaconda CC, Opportunity, 59250,   406-797-3220
Holes: 9
Anaconda GC, Black Eagle, N of Missouri Riv, Great Falls, 59401,   406-761-1078
Holes: 9
Beaver Creek GC, US 2 S, Havre, 59501,   406-265-7861
Holes: 9
Beaverhead CC, NE on MT 41, Dillon, 59725,   406-683-9933
Holes: 9
Big Muddy GC, N of town along Big Muddy Cree, Redstone, 59257
Holes: 9
Bill Roberts Muni GC, N of Carroll College on Benton, Helena, 59601,
406-442-2191   Holes: 18
Briarwood CC, 3429 Briarwood Blvde., Billings, 59101,   406-248-2702
Holes: 18
Butte CC, E of Harrison ave on E. Warren, Butte, 59701,   406-494-3383
Holes: 18
Cabinet View CC, S off US 2, Libby, 59923,   406-293-7332
Holes: 9
Chinook GC, off US 2 W, Chinook, 59523,   406-357-2244
Holes: 9
Choteau CC, N of Choteau, Choteau, 59422,   406-466-2020
Par: 35, Holes: 9
Crystal Lakes, E of Crystal Lakes turnoff fm, Fortine, 59918,   406-882-4455
Holes: 18
Cut Bank G & CC, 501 E. Main, Cut Bank, 59427,   406-873-2574
Holes: 9
Deer Lodge GC, W on Millwaukee Ave., Deer Lodge, 59722,   406-846-1625
Holes: 9
Exchange City GC, Jct. Central Ave & 19th St. W, Billings, 59101,   406-652-2553
Holes: 18
Fairmont Hot Springs GC, 101 High Country, Anaconda, 59711,   406-797-3241
Holes: 18
Fallon County GC, S on MT 7 thru Baker, E at Fal, Baker, 59313
Holes: 9
Fort Custer GC, N on MT 47, then W, Hardin, 59034,   406-665-2597
Holes: 9
Glacier GC, N of Jct. US 2 & MT 49, East Glacier, 59434,   406-226-4411
Holes: 9
Hamilton GC, SE Hamilton off Golf Course Rd, Hamilton, 59840,   406-363-4251
Holes: 18

Heaven on Earth, 50 mi S of Ulm along Smith Riv, Millegan, 59301, 406-452-7365 Holes: 6
Highland View GC, 2903 Oregon ave., Butte, 59701, 406-494-7900
Holes: 9
Highlands GC, 102 Ben Hogan Dr., Missoula, 59803, 406-728-7360
Holes: 9
Jawbone Creek GC, W of Jct US 12 & US 191 on Cen, Harlowton, 59036, 406-632-9960 Par: 36, Holes: 9
Lake Hills GC, 1930 Clubhouse Way, Billings, 59105, 406-252-9244
Yards: 6489, Par: 72, USGA: 69.7, Holes: 18, Pro: Jon Wright
Laurel GC, P.O. Box 247, Laurel, 59044
Lewistown Elks CC, SE of Lewiston off Spring Cree, Lewistown, 59457, 406-538-7075 Holes: 9
Livingston CC, S end of Livingston, Livingston, 59047, 406-222-1031
Holes: 9
Madison Meadows GC, W on Mt 287, Ennis, 59729, 406-682-7468
Holes: 9
Marias Valley G & CC, I-15 Exit 358 S of Shelby, Shelby, 59474, 406-434-5940
Holes: 9
Meadowlark GC, 300 Country Club Dr., Great Falls, 59403
Missoula GC, 3850 Old Hwy. 93, Misoula, 59806
Par 3 on 93, Highway 93 South, Whitefish, 59337
Par: 27, Holes: 9
Pine Ridge CC, N/NW ½mi from Jct US 12 & 8, Roundup, 59072, 406-323-2880
Holes: 9
Plains GC, NW of Plains, Plains, 59859
Plentywood GC, Sheridan St., N of town, Plentywood, 59254, 406-765-2532
Holes: 9
Polson CC, Eastside of Polson, Polson, 59860, 406-883-2440
Holes: 9
Pondera G & CC, N on 4th Ave, Conrad, 59425, 406-278-3402
Par: 34, Holes: 9
Red Lodge Elks G & CC, SW edge of Red Lodge, Red Lodge, 59068, 406-446-3344 Par: 72, Holes: 18
Riverside GC, 2500 Springhill Rd., Butte, 59715
Robert O. Speck Muni GC, NE Great Falls off 25th St. S, Great Falls, 59401, 406-761-1078 Holes: 18
Rolling Hills GC, Jct. US 212 & MT 59, Broadus, 39317, 406-436-9984
Holes: 9
Scobey GC, SW of Scobey, Scobey, 59263, 406-487-9995
Holes: 9
Signal Point GC, Hwy 387 NE of Ft. Benton, Fort Benton, 59442, 406-622-9950
Holes: 9
Sleeping Buffalo GC, 17 mi E of Malta, Malta, 59538, 406-527-3370
Holes: 9
Miles City Town & CC, SW of Miles City, Miles City, 59301, 406-232-1600
Holes: 9
Stevensville GC, N of Stevensville, Stevensville, 59870, 406-777-3636
Holes: 9
Stillwater GC, S off MT 78, Columbus, 59019, 406-322-4298
Holes: 9
Sunnyside GC, W edge of Glasgow, Glasgow, 59230, 406-228-9937
Holes: 9
Thompson Falls GC, NW of Thompson Falls, Thompson Falls, 59873, 406-827-3438 Holes: 9

University of Montana GC, E side of Missoula at UM, Missoula, 59801,
406-728-8629   Holes: 9
Valley View GC, 302 Kagy Blvd., Bozeman, 59338,   406-586-2145
Par: 72, Holes: 18
Yellowstone GC, RT #6 Bobby Jones Blvd., Billings, 59106
Yards: 6643, Par: 72, USGA: 69.6, Holes: 18, Pro: Don Tolson

Ainsworth CC (Munic. Golf), Ainsworth, 69210,   402-387-1658   *Nebraska*
Holes: 9
Airport GC, Arthur, 69121
Par: 27, Holes: 9
Albion CC, Albion, 68620,   402-395-2900
Holes: 9
Alliance Muni GC, Alliance, 69301,   308-762-1446
Holes: 18
Alma Muni GC, Alma, 68920,   308-928-2341
Holes: 9
Antelope CC, Neligh, 68756,   402-887-5211
Holes: 9
Applewood GC, Omaha, 68108,   402-444-4656
Holes: 18
Arnold CC, Arnold, 69120,   308-848-2715
Holes: 9
Ash Hollow GC, Blue Hill, 68930, 402-753-3031
Holes: 9
Ashland CC, Ashland, 68003,   402-944-3388
Holes: 18
Atkinson-Stuart CC, Atkinson, 68713,   402-925-5330
Holes: 9
Aurora CC, Aurora, 68818,   402-694-3662
Holes: 9
Base GC, Bellevue, 68005,   402-294-3663
Holes: 9
Bassett CC, Bassett, 68714,   402-684-3449
Holes: 9
Bay Hills GC, Plattsmouth, 68048,   402-298-8191
Par: 36, Holes: 9
Beatrice CC, Beatrice, 68310,   402-223-2710
Holes: 18
Benkelman GC, Benkelman, 69021,   308-423-5210
Holes: 9
Benson Park GC, Omaha, 68108,   402-444-4626
Holes: 18
Blair GC, Blair, 68008,   402-426-2941
Holes: 9
Bloomfield-Wausa GC, Bloomfield, 68718,   402-586-2507
Holes: 9
Broken Bow CC, Broken Bow, 68822,   308-872-6444
Holes: 9
Buffalo Ridge GC, Kearney, 68847,   308-237-9833
Holes: 9
Callaway GC, Callaway, 68825,   308-836-2610
Holes: 9
Cambridge GC, Cambridge, 69022,   308-697-4768
Holes: 9

Capehart GC, Bellevue, 68005,   402-292-1680
Holes: 18
Cedar Hills GC, Omaha, 68108,   402-391-1956
Holes: 9
Cedar View CC, Laurel, 68745,   402-256-3184
Holes: 9
College Heights GC, Crete, 68333,   402-826-9944
Holes: 18
Cottonwood Green GC, Spalding, 68065
Holes: 9
Country Club Tenth Hole, Plainview, 68769,   402-582-3445
Holes: 9
Court House & Jail Rock GC, Bridgeport, 69336,   308-262-9925
Par: 36, Holes: 9
Covington Links, So. Sioux City, 68776,   402-494-9841
Par: 71, Holes: 18
Cozad CC, Cozad, 69130,   308-784-2585
Holes: 9
Crawford CC, Crawford, 69339,   308-665-1462
Holes: 9
Crofton Lakeview GC, Crofton, 68730
Holes: 9
Curtis CC, Curtis, 69025,   308-367-4122
Holes: 9
Dannebrog GC, Dannebrog, 68831,   308-226-2422
Holes: 9
David City CC, David City, 68632,   402-367-4292
Holes: 9
Deer Park GC, Valentine, 69201,   402-376-1271
Holes: 18
Elk Creek CC, Nelson, 68961,   402-222-3611
Holes: 9
Elk's Country Club, Columbus, 68601,   402-564-4930
Holes: 18
Elkhorn Acres GC, Stanton, 68779,   402-439-2191
Holes: 9
Elkhorn Valley GC, Hooper, 68031,   402-654-3512
Holes: 9
Elks Lodge & CC, Hastings, 68901,   402-462-6113
Holes: 9
Elmwood Park GC, Omaha, 68108,   402-444-4683
Holes: 18
Enders Lake GC, Enders, 69027,   308-394-5491
Holes: 9
Fairbury CC, Fairbury, 68352,   402-729-5314
Holes: 9
Fairplay GC, Norfolk, 68701,   402-371-9877
Holes: 9
Fairview GC, Pawnee City, 68420
Holes: 9
Falls City CC, Falls City, 68355,   402-245-3624
Holes: 18
Field Club GC, Omaha, 68108,   402-345-6343
Holes: 9
Firethorn GC, Lincoln, 68501,   402-488-6467
Holes: 18

Fonner View GC, Grand Island, 68802, 308-382-0202
Par: 27, Holes: 9
Fontenelle Hills CC, Bellevue, 68005, 402-296-2500
Holes: 9
Fontenelle Park GC, Omaha, 68108, 402-444-5019
Holes: 9
Franklin GC, Franklin, 68939, 308-425-3614
Holes: 9
Friend CC, Friend, 68359, 402-947-6501
Par: 27, Holes: 9
Fullerton CC, Fullerton, 68638, 308-536-2428
Holes: 9
Gordon CC, Gordon, 69343, 308-282-1146
Holes: 9
Gothenburg GC, Gothenburg, 69138, 308-537-8782
Holes: 9
Grand Island Muni GC, Grand Island, 68802, 308-381-5340
Holes: 18
Greeley CC, Greeley, 68842
Holes: 9
Happy Hollow GC, 1701 S. 105th St., Omaha, 68124, 402-391-2341
Holes: 18
Hartington Town & CC, Hartington, 68739, 402-254-7312
Par: 27, Holes: 9
Hay Springs GC, Hay Springs, 69347
Par: 27, Holes: 9
Hayes Center GC, Hayes Center, 69032
Holes: 9
Hebron CC, Hebron, 68370, 402-768-6350
Holes: 9
Hemingford Muni GC, Hemingford, 68348
Holes: 9
Henderson Golf Assn., Henderson, 68371, 402-723-4828
Holes: 9
Hidden Acres Recreation Area, Beatrice, 68310, 402-228-2146
Holes: 9
Hidden Hills CC, Geneva, 68361, 402-759-9930
Holes: 9
Highland GC, 12627 Pacific, Omaha, 68154, 402-333-7500
Holes: 18
Hillcrest CC, Lincoln, 68501, 402-489-8181
Holes: 18
Holmes Park GC, 3701 S. 70th, Lincoln, 68506, 402-488-8012
Holes: 18
Hillcrest GC, Fremont, 68025, 402-727-4403
Holes: 9
Hillside GC, Sidney, 69162, 308-254-2311
Par: 36, Holes: 9
Hilltop CC, Wahoo, 68066, 402-443-3338
Holes: 9
Holdrege CC, Holdrege, 68949, 308-995-5744
Holes: 18
Imperial GC, Imperial, 69033
Holes: 9
Indian Trails CC, Beemer, 68716, 402-528-3404
Holes: 18

Kearney CC, Kearney, 68847, 308-234-3151
Holes: 18
Kimball City-County GC, Kimball, 69145, 308-235-2222
Holes: 9
Knolls GC, 11630 Sahler St., Omaha, 68164, 402-493-1740
Yards: 5813, Par: 71, USGA: 68.0, Holes: 18, Pro: Mike Jansen
Knolls GC, Lincoln, 68506, 402-423-1776
Par: 27, Holes: 9
Lake Maloney GC, North Platte, 69101
Holes: 18
Lakeside CC (Elwood), Lexington, 68850, 308-785-2818
Holes: 9
Lakeview GC, Ralston, 68127, 402-339-2522
Holes: 9
Lawrence GC, Lawrence, 68957, 402-756-7591
Holes: 9
Lochland CC, Hastings, 68901, 402-462-4151
Holes: 18
Logan Valley GC, Wakefield, 68784, 402-287-2343
Par: 27, Holes: 9
Loup City GC, Loup City, 68853, 308-745-9982
Holes: 9
Maple Village GC, Omaha, 68108, 402-444-3623
Holes: 9
Meadow Brook GC, Omaha, 68108, 402-391-1958
Holes: 9
Mid-County GC, Arapahoe, 68922, 308-962-5555
Holes: 9
Minden GC, Minden, 68959, 308-832-1965
Holes: 9
Miracle Hills GC, Omaha, 68108, 402-498-0220
Holes: 18
Mullen GC, Mullen, 69152, 308-546-2445
Holes: 9
Norfolk CC, Norfolk, 68701, 402-379-1188
Holes: 18
North Platte CC, North Platte, 69101, 308-532-7550
Holes: 18
O'Neill County Club, O'Neill, 68763, 402-336-1676
Holes: 9
Oakland GC, Oakland, 68045, 402-685-6258
Holes: 9
Ogallala CC, Ogallala, 69153, 308-284-4358
Holes: 9
Omaha CC, Omaha, 68108, 402-571-7777
Holes: 18
Ord GC, Ord, 68862, 308-728-9970
Holes: 9
Oshkosh CC, Oshkosh, 69154, 308-772-3560
Par: 36, Holes: 9
Overton GC, Overton, 68863
Holes: 9
Pinelake GC, Lincoln, 68501, 402-489-9948
Par: 27, Holes: 9
Pines CC, The, 7516 N. 286th, Valley, 68064, 402-359-4311
Yards: 6655, Par: 72, USGA: 68.8, Holes: 18, Pro: Don Dravland

Platteview CC, Springfield, 68059, 402-291-7255
Holes: 18
Plattsmouth CC, Plattsmouth, 68048, 402-298-8033
Holes: 9
Potter GC, Potter, 69156
Holes: 9
Prairie Hills Golf, Pleasanton, 68866, 308-388-5115
Holes: 9
Ravenna CC, Ravenna, 68869, 308-452-3664
Holes: 9
Ridgeview CC, Chadron, 69337, 308-432-4468
Holes: 9
Riverside GC, Grand Island, 68802, 308-382-2648
Holes: 9
Riverview GC, Inc., Scottsbluff, 69361, 308-635-1555
Holes: 18
Rolling Green GC, Morrill, 69358, 308-247-2817
Holes: 9
Rushville GC, Rushville, 69360
Holes: 9
Ryan Hill CC, Osceola, 68651, 402-747-6661
Holes: 9
Sargent-Comstock GC, Sargent, 68874
Holes: 9
Schuyler CC, Schuyler, 68861, 402-352-2900
Holes: 9
Scotia GC, Scotia, 68875
Holes: 9
Scottsbluff CC, Scottsbluff, 69361, 308-632-8297
Holes: 18
Seward CC, Seward, 68434, 402-643-6650
Holes: 9
Skyline GC, Elkhorn, 68022, 402-289-3545
Holes: 18
South Ridge GC, So. Sioux City, 68776, 402-494-9758
Par: 35, Holes: 9
Southern Hills CC, Hastings, 68901, 402-463-8006
Holes: 18
Spring Lake GC, Omaha, 68108, 402-444-4630
Holes: 9
Springview CC, Springview, 68778
Holes: 9
St. Paul CC, St. Paul, 68873, 308-754-4203
Holes: 9
Superior CC, Superior, 68978, 402-879-9983
Holes: 9
Sutherland GC, Sutherland, 69165
Holes: 9
Syracuse CC & GC, Syracuse, 68446, 402-269-2924
Holes: 9
Tara Hills GC, Papillion, 68128, 402-592-7550
Holes: 9
Taylor Creek GC, Madison, 68748, 402-454-3925
Holes: 9
Tecumseh GC, Tecumseh, 68450, 402-335-2337
Holes: 9

Tiburon CC, 10302 S 169th Street, Omaha, 68136
Holes: 18
Town & Country GC, Humphrey, 68642
Holes: 9
Trenton Muni GC, Trenton, 69044
Holes: 9
Valley View GC, Central City, 68826,   308-946-9872
Holes: 9
Valley View GC, Gibbon, 68840,   308-468-5884
Holes: 9
Van Berg Park & GC, Columbus, 68601,   402-564-0761
Holes: 9
Wauneta CC, Wauneta, 69045
Holes: 9
Wayne CC & GC, Wayne, 68787,   402-375-1152
Par: 71, Holes: 18
Willow Green GC, North Platte, 69101,   308-532-6955
Holes: 9
Wood River CC, Wood River, 68883,   308-583-2225
Holes: 9
Wymore CC, Wymore, 68466,   402-645-8084
Holes: 9
York CC, York, 68467,   402-362-3

Angel Park GC, 222 South Rainbow #17, Las Vegas, 89128,   *Nevada*
702-254-0560   Holes: 18
Arcadian Greens, Logandale, 89021,   702-397-2431
Par: 37, Holes: 9
Black Mountain CC, Henderson, 89015,   702-565-7933
Yards: 6775, Par: 72, Holes: 18, Pro: Randy Tickner
Boulder City Muni GC, Boulder City, 89005,   702-293-9236
Yards: 6561, Par: 72, Holes: 18, Pro: Gale Parcell
Brookside GC, Reno, 89510,   702-322-6009
Yards: 5860, Par: 70, Holes: 9, Pro: Jerry Brown
Carson Valley CC, Gardnerville, 89410, 702-265-3181
Yards: 5739, Par: 72, Holes: 18
Chimney Rock GC, Wells, 89835,   702-752-3928
Yards: 3050, Par: 35, Holes: 9, Pro: Lenny W. Stroup
Craig Ranch GC, 628 W. Craig Rd., North Las Vegas, 89030,   702-642-9700
Yards: 6001, Par: 70, USGA: 67.0, Holes: 18, Pro: Sam Camerano
Desert Rose GC, 5483 Clubhouse Drive, Las Vegas, 89122,   702-438-4653
Yards: 6511, Par: 71, USGA: 68.7, Holes: 18, Pro: Ron Fogler
Dunes Hotel GC, 3650 Las Vegas Blvd., Las Vegas, 89109,   702-737-4746
Yards: 6571, Par: 72, USGA: 71.8, Holes: 18
Eagle Valley West GC, Carson City, 89701,   702-887-2380
Yards: 6245, Par: 72, Holes: 18, Pro: Tom Duncan
Fallon GC, Fallon, 89406,   702-423-4616
Yards: 3213, Par: 36, Holes: 9, Pro: Preston Kyle
Glenbrook GC, Glenbrook, 89413,   702-749-5201
Yards: 6133, Par: 32, Holes: 9, Pro: Warren MacCarty
Hyatt At Lake Tahoe GC, 955 Fairway Dr., Reno, 89450
Jackpot GC, Jackpot, 89825,   702-755-2264
Yards: 6700, Par: 72, Holes: 18, Pro: Billy Downs
Lakeridge GC, 1200 Razorbank Rd., Reno, 89505,   702-825-2200
Yards: 6717, Par: 71, Holes: 18, Pro: Cork Corl

Las Vegas GC, Las Vegas, 89114, 702-646-3003
Yards: 6700, Par: 72, Holes: 18, Pro: Ron Fogler
Legacy GC @ Green Valley, 8501 Green Valley Parkway, Henderson, 89015
Holes: 18
Los Prados CC, Las Vegas, 89114, 702-645-5696
Yards: 4752, Par: 66, Holes: 18, Pro: Keith Flatt
Mason Valley CC, Yerington, 89447, 702-463-3300
Yards: 6638, Par: 69, Holes: 9
North Las Vegas Community, North Las Vegas, 89030, 702-649-7171
Yards: 1128, Par: 27, Holes: 9
Painted Desert, 5555 Painted Mirage Dr., Las Vegas, 89129, 702-645-2568
Yards: 6323, Par: 72, USGA: 70.9, Holes: 18, Pro: Scott Greet
Ruby View GC, Elko, 89801, 702-738-6212
Yards: 6743, Par: 72, Holes: 18, Pro: Rick Longhurts
Sahara GC, 1911 E. Desert Inn Rd., Las Vegas, 89109, 702-796-0013
Yards: 6418, Par: 71, USGA: 71.1, Holes: 18, Pro: Monty Kaser
Sierra Sage GC, Reno, 89510, 702-972-1564
Yards: 6500, Par: 71, Holes: 18, Pro: Mike Mitchell
Spring Creek GC, Elko, 89801, 702-753-6331
Yards: 6258, Par: 71, Holes: 18, Pro: John Heller
Toana Vista GC, 2319 Pueblo Blvd., West Wendover, 89883, 702-664-4300
Yards: 6911, Par: 72, USGA: 67.3, Holes: 18, Pro: Milan Swillor
Tropicana GC, 3801 Las Vegas Blvd. So., Las Vegas, 89109, 702-739-2457
Yards: 6109, Par: 70, USGA: 69.8, Holes: 18, Pro: Tim Webster
Walker Lake CC, Hawthorne, 89415, 702-945-7705
Yards: 5200, Par: 68, Holes: 9, Pro: Pete Summerell
Washoe County GC, Reno, 89510, 702-785-4286
Yards: 6468, Par: 72, Holes: 18, Pro: Barney Bell
Winnemucca Muni GC, Winnemucca, 89445, 702-623-9920
Yards: 3250, Par: 36, Holes: 9, Pro: Bill Phillips

Abenaqui CC, Central Rd., Rye Beach, 03871, 603-964-5335   *New Hampshire*
Yards: 6216, Holes: 18, Pro: James Sheerin
Amherst CC, 70 Ponemah Rd., Rte 122, Amherst, 03031, 603-673-6352
Yards: 6665, Par: 72, Holes: 18, Pro: Ted Bishop
Androscoggin Valley CC, Rte #2, Gorham, 03581, 603-466-9468
Yards: 6025, Par: 72, USGA: 68.0, Holes: 18, Pro: Peter M. Dennis
Angus Lea GC, West Main St. Box 18, Hillsboro, 03244-0, 603-464-5404
Yards: 4270, Par: 66, USGA: 60.8, Holes: 18, Pro: Russ Niven
Bald Peak Colony Club, Box 201, Melvin Village, 03850
Beaver Meadow CC, 1 Beaver Meadow St., Concord, 03301, 603-228-8954
Yards: 6300, Par: 72, USGA: 69.0, Holes: 18, Pro: Ed Deshaies
Bethlehem CC, Main St., Bethlehem, 03574, 603-869-5745
Yards: 5756, Par: 70, USGA: 66.7, Holes: 18, Pro: "Fred" Ghioto
Bethlehem GC, Bethlehem, Littleton, 03576
Bretwood GC, S. Surry Road, Keene, 03431
Holes: 9
Buckmeadow GC, Route 101A Box 42, Amherst, 03031
Charmingfar GC, S. Rd., Manchester, 03034
Charmingfare Golf Links, 313 South Road, Candia, 03034, 603-483-2307
Yards: 6500, Par: 72, USGA: 70.0, Holes: 18, Pro: Rich Thibeault
Claremont CC, Box 563, Claremont, 03743, 603-542-9550
Cochecho CC, Box 267 Gulf Road, Dover, 03820, 603-742-8580
Colebrook CC, R 1 Box 2, Colebrook, 03576, 603-237-5566
Yards: 2891, Par: 36, Holes: 9
Concord CC, Country Club Lane, Concord, 03301

Den Brae GC, Rte 127, Sanborton, 03253, 603-934-9818
Yards: 2921, Par: 36, Holes: 9
Derryfield CC, 625 Mammoth Rd., Manchester, 03104, 603-669-0235
Yards: 6020, Par: 70, Holes: 18, Pro: Jeff Taylor
Dublin Lake Club, Box 90, Dublin, 03444
Eagle Mountain House, Carter Notch Road, Jackson, 03846, 603-383-4347
Yards: 2126, Par: 32, Holes: 9, Pro: Brian Duchesne
East Kingston GC, Rte 107 P.O. Box 2, East Kingston, 03827, 603-642-4414
Yards: 3169, Par: 35, USGA: 67.2, Holes: 9
Exeter CC, Box 1088, Exeter, 03833, 603-778-8080
Farmington CC, Henry Wilson Hwwy., Farmington, 03835, 603-755-2412
Yards: 2400, Par: 64, Holes: 9, Pro: Warren Tickle
Farnum Hill Golf & CC, West Lebanon Rd., Rte. 4 Ex. 1, Lebanon, 03766,
603-448-3323 Yards: 2908, Par: 36, Holes: 9, Pro: Lyman Doane Sr.
Goffstown CC, Rte 13, Goffstown, 03045, 603-774-5031
Yards: 3288, Par: 36, Holes: 9, Pro: Mark Larrabee
Green Meadow GC—Course #1, Rte 3A, Hudson, 03051, 603-889-1555
Yards: 6350, Par: 71, Holes: 18, Pro: Phil Friel
Highland Links Colony, Mt. Prospect Rd., Plymouth, 03264, 603-536-3452
Yards: 1700, Par: 30, Holes: 9, Pro: Joe Clark
Hominy Hill GC, 92 Mercer Rd., Red Bank, 07722
Hoodkroft CC, Route 102, East Broadway, Derry, 03038, 603-434-0651
Yards: 6436, Par: 71, USGA: 70.7, Holes: 9, Pro: R. Berberian
Hooper GC of Walpole, Box 311 Prospect Hill, Walpole, 03608, 603-756-4020
Indian Mound GC, Old Rte 16B, Center Ossipee, 03814, 603-539-7733
Yards: 3215, Par: 36, USGA: 68.2, Holes: 9, Pro: Paul Downey
Intervale CC, 1491 Front Street, Manchester, 03102, 603-623-9180
Yards: 2981, Par: 36, Holes: 18, Pro: Robert Drew
John H. Cain GC, P.O. Box 676, Newport, 03773, 603-863-9818
Yards: 5586, Par: 68, USGA: 66.8, Holes: 18, Pro: Chuck LaRoche
Keene CC, Box 264, Jeebe, 03431, 603-352-0135
Kingswood CC, Main St., Wolfeboro, 03894, 603-569-3569
Yards: 5800, Par: 71, USGA: 67.5, Holes: 18, Pro: Dave Pollini
Laconia CC, 607 Elm St., Lakeport, 03246, 603-524-1274
Yards: 6253, Par: 72, Holes: 18, Pro: Mike Marquis
Lake Sunapee CC, Country Club Lane, New London, 03257, 603-526-6040
Yards: 6371, Par: 70, USGA: 70.9, Holes: 18, Pro: Chris Doyle
Londonderry CC, Kimball Rd., Londonderry, 03053, 603-432-9789
Yards: 1245, Par: 27, Holes: 9
Manchester CC, 180 South River Rd., Bedford, 03102
Maplewood CC, Rt. 302 Box 238, Bethlehem, 03574
Mojalaki CC, 4656 Prospect St., P.O. Box 10, Franklin, 03235, 603-934-3033
Yards: 6222, Par: 70, USGA: 69.0, Holes: 9, Pro: Ed LaPierre
Monadnock CC, Box 97, Peterborough, 03458, 603-924-7769
Yards: 3152, Par: 54, USGA: 51.2, Holes: 18
Mount Washington GC, RTE 302, Bretton Woods, 03575, 603-278-1000
Yards: 6154, Par: 71, Holes: 18, Pro: Dean Webb
Mountain View House Golf Club, Mountian View Rd., Whitefield, 03598,
603-837-2511 Yards: 2873, Par: 35, Holes: 9, Pro: Jim Frazer
New Hampshire GC, Kearsarge Valley Rd., Concord, 03260
Nippo Lake GC, Province Road, Barrington, 03825, 603-664-2030
Yards: 2529, Par: 34, Holes: 9, Pro: Alan Orluk
Niticook Landing GC, 150 Lowell Road, Litchfield, 03051
Holes: 18
North Conway CC, Norcross Circle, Box 555, North Conway, 03860,
603-356-9391 Yards: 6659, Par: 71, USGA: 69.9, Holes: 18, Pro: John MacDonald

Pine Valley Golf Links, Old Gage Hill Rd., Pelham, 03076,   603-635-8305
Yards: 2900, Par: 35, Holes: 9, Pro: Todd Madden
Oak Hill GC, Pease Rd. RD 2, Meredith, 03253,   603-279-4438
Yards: 2234, Par: 34, USGA: 30.0, Holes: 9
Panorama GC, Panorama, Littleton, 03576,   603-255-3400
Pheasant Ridge CC, Country Club Rd., Gilford, 03246,   603-524-7808
Yards: 6116, Par: 70, USGA: 68.7, Holes: 18, Pro: Jim Buckley
Pine Grove Springs CC, P.O. Box 56, Rte 9A, Spoffard, 03878,   603-363-4433
Yards: 3000, Par: 36, Holes: 9
Plausawa Valley CC, 42 Whittemore Road, Pembroke, 03275
Holes: 9
Portsmouth CC, Country Club Lane, P.O.Box 87, Greenland, 03840,
603-436-9791   Yards: 6202, Par: 72, Holes: 18, Pro: Tony Loch
Profile Club, Inc., Franconia, Greenland, 03580,   603-823-9568
Rochester CC, Church St., Gonic, 03867,   603-332-0985
Yards: 6585, Par: 72, Holes: 18, Pro: Tony Kaloustizn
Rockingham CC, Route 108, Newmarket, 03857,   603-659-6379
Yards: 5900, Par: 35, USGA: 69.0, Holes: 9, Pro: Bruce Hauschel
Sky Meadow CC, Sky Meadow Drive, Nashua, 03062,   603-888-9000
Yards: 6316, Par: 70, USGA: 69.9, Holes: 18
Sunningdale CC, 301 Green St., Somersworth, 03878,   603-742-8056
Par: 36, Holes: 9, Pro: Dich Meade
Sunset Hill House GC, Sunset Rd., Sugar Hill, 03585,   603-823-5522
Yards: 1977, Par: 33, Holes: 9, Pro: B. Carmichael
Upper Mountclair GC, 177 Hepburn, Newark, 07012
Valley View CC, RFD #1, Rt. 13, Dunbarton, 03045,   603-774-5031
Yards: 6336, Par: 72, USGA: 70.2, Holes: 9, Pro: Mark Larrabee
Waumbeck GC, The, RTE 2, Littleton, 03586
Waumbek Inn & CC, Jefferson, 03583,   603-586-7777
Wentworth-by-the-Sea, Wentworth Road, Portsmouth, 03801,   603-433-5010
Yards: 5752, Par: 70, USGA: 66.1, Holes: 18, Pro: Dan Franzoso
Whip-Poor-Will GC, Marsh Rd., Hudson, 03051,   603-889-9706
Yards: 3050, Par: 36, Holes: 9, Pro: Bill Meier
Woodbound Inn, Woodbound Rd., Jaffrey, 03452-1, 603-532-8341
Yards: 1158, Par: 27, Holes: 9

Apple Mountain GC, RD 2, Box 24, Belvedere, 07823,   201-453-3023 *New Jersey*
Yards: 6500, Par: 71, USGA: 69.0, Holes: 18, Pro: Robert Dacey
Ashbrook GC, 1210 Raritan Rd., Scothc Plains, 07207,   201-756-0414
Holes: 18
Avalon GC, 1510 Route 9 North—Swainton, Cape May Court House, 08210,
609-465-4389   Holes: 18
Basking Ridge GC, 185 Madisonville Road, Basking Ridge, 07920
Beckett GC, Kings Highway, Swedesboro, 08085,   609-467-4700
Par: 72, Holes: 27
Bel Aire GC—18 Hole, State Hwy. 34 & Allaire Rd., Allenwood, 08720,
201-449-6024 Par: 60, Holes: 18
Bey Lea GC, RD #1 Bay Ave., Toms River, 08753,   201-349-0566
Yards: 6251, Par: 72, USGA: 69.3, Holes: 18
Blackwood CC, Little Gloucester & Cole Roads, Blackwood, 08012,
609-227-3171 Holes: 27
Blair Academy GC, Blair Academy, Blairstown, 07825,   201-362-6218
Holes: 9
Bowling Green GC, 53 Schoolhouse Rd., Milton, 07438,   201-697-8688
Yards: 6689, Par: 72, USGA: 70.8, Holes: 18, Pro: Tom Staples

Brigantine CC, Roosevelt Blvd. & East Shore D, Brigantine, 08203, 609-266-1388   Holes: 18
Buena Vista CC, Hwy. 40 & Country Club Lane, Buena, 08310,   609-697-1200
Holes: 18
Bunker Hill GC, Bunker Hill Rd., Griggstown, 08540,   201-359-6335
Holes: 18
Cedar Greek GC, Tilton Blvd & Forest Hills Par, Bayville, 08721,   201-269-4460
Holes: 18
City of East Orange GC, Parsonage Hill Road, Short Hills, 07078, 201-379-6775   Holes: 18
Cohanzick CC, Fairton Road, Bridgeton, 08302,   609-455-2127
Par: 17, Holes: 18
Colonial Terrace GC, 105 Wickapecko Dr., Wanamassa, 07712,   201-775-3636
Holes: 9
Covered Bridge GC, 23 Kilmer Dr., Morganville, 07726,   201-536-9864
Pro: Don Ross
Cranbury GC, 9 Southfield Rd., Cranbury, 08512,   609-799-0341
Yards: 5939, Par: 70, USGA: 69.0, Holes: 18
Cream Ridge GC, David Station Rd., Cream Ridge, 08514,   609-259-2849
Pro: Bill Marine
Cruz Farm CC, Farmingdale, 07727,   201-938-3378
Par: 70, Holes: 18
Culver Lake GC, East Shore Road, Culver Lake, 08515,   201-948-5610
Holes: 9
Darlington GC, 327 Campgaw Road, Mahwah, 07430,   201-327-8770
Yards: 5909, Par: 72, USGA: 67.3, Holes: 18, Pro: Brian Stambaugh
Eastlyn GC, Italia Avenue, Vineland, 08360,   609-691-5558
Par: 62, Holes: 18
Fairway Mews CC, Allaire Rd., Spring Lake, 07762,   201-499-9716
Pro: Todd Tooley
Farmstead G & CC, Germany Flats Road, Andover, 07848,   201-383-1666
Holes: 27, Pro: Scott Pruden
Francis Byrne GC, Pleasant Valley Way, West Orange, 07083,   201-736-2306
Holes: 18, Pro: Bob Schubert
Galloping Hill GC, Union & Kenilworth Blvd., Union, 07083,   201-686-1556
Holes: 27, Pro: Terry McCormack
Gambler Ridge GC, Box 109, Burlington Path Rd., Cream Ridge, 08514, 609-758-3588   Par: 71, Holes: 18, Pro: Brian Jodoin
Golden Pheasant GC, Eayerstown Rd & Country Club D, Lumberton, 08048, 609-267-4276   Holes: 18
Golf Farm Course, Haddonfield–Berlin Road, Gibbsboro, 08026,   609-428-1766
Holes: 9
Green Knoll GC, 587 Garreston Rd., Somerville, 08876,   201-722-1300
Holes: 27, Pro: Anthony DeMaio
Green Pond GC, Green Pond Rd., Rockaway, 07866,   201-983-9494
Holes: 9
Green Tree CC, Somers Point Road, Mays Landing, 08330,   609-625-9131
Par: 70, Holes: 18
Hamilton Trails CC, Egg Harbor Ave & Mill Road, McKee City, 07428, 609-641-6824   Holes: 9
Hanover CC, Larrison Rd., Jacobstown, 08562,   609-758-8301 Holes: 18, Pro: Lin Cesario
Haworth GC, 5 Lakeshore Drive, Haworth, 07641,   201-384-7300
Holes: 18
Hendricks Field GC, Franklin Ave., Belleville, 07109,   201-751-0178
Holes: 18, Pro: Bob Schubert

Hidden Hills GC, State Highway 24, Washington Township, 07840, 201-852-5694   Holes: 18, Pro: Arnold D'Andrea
High Mountain GC, Ewing Avenue, Franklin Lakes, 07417,   201-891-4653
Holes: 18
High Point CC, Clove Road, Montague, 07827,   201-293-3282
Par: 73, Holes: 18
Hillman Golf Land, 700 River Drive, Elmwood Park, 07407,   201-796-1265
Holes: 9
Holland Orchards CC, Mariboro, 07746,   201-462-9304
Holly Hills GC, Alloway—Friesburg Road, Alloway Township, 08001,
609-935-2412   Holes: 18
Indian Spring GC, Elmwood Road & Old Marlton Pik, Marlton, 08053,
609-983-0222   Holes: 18
Jumping Brook G & CC, Jumping Brook Rd., Neptune, 07753,   201-922-8200
Holes: 18, Pro: Harold Cahoon
Knob Hill CC, 360 Rt. 33, Englishtown, 07726,   201-446-4800
Holes: 18, Pro: John Piotrowski
Knoll CC, Knoll and Green Bank Road, Parsippany, 07054,   201-263-7111
Holes: 18, Pro: Steele King
Kresson GC, Gibbsboro Road, Kresson, 07405,   609-424-1212
Holes: 18
Lakewood GC, Country Club DR., Lakewood, 08701,   201-363-8124
Yards: 6248, Par: 71, Holes: 18, Pro: Rob Lawson
Latona CC, Cumberland & Oak Road, Buena, 08310,   609-692-8149
Holes: 9
Laurel Oak GC, Haddonfield—Berlin Road, Rt, Gibbsboro, 08026,   609-435-0990
Holes: 9
Lincoln Park Golf Range, Route 1 & Duncan Avenue, Jersey City, 07303,
201-435-5660   Par: 27, Holes: 9
Mays Landing CC, McKee Ave & Cates Road, McKee City, 07428,   609-641-4411
Holes: 18
Meadows CC, 79 Two Bridges Rd., Lincoln Park, 07035,   201-696-7212
Pro: Peter Cherone
Millburn Township GC, White Oak Ridge Road Park, Short Hills, 07078,
201-379-4156
Mountain View GC, Bear Tavern Road, Trenton, 08650,   609-882-4093
Holes: 18, Pro: Steve Bowers
Oak Ridge GC, 136 Oak Ridge Rd., Clark, 07066,   201-574-0139
Yards: 6001, Par: 70, USGA: 68.2, Holes: 18, Pro: Joe Cruise
Hominy Hill GC, Mercer Rd., Colts Neck, 07722,   201-462-9222
Yards: 7059, Par: 72, USGA: 71.7, Holes: 18
Ocean Acres GC, 93 Bucaneer Lane, Manahawkin, 08050,   201-597-9393
Holes: 18, Pro: Jack Fox
Ocean City GC, Bay Ave between 22nd & 28th Av, Ocean City, 08226,
609-399-1315   Par: 36, Holes: 9
Ocean County GC, Tuckerton, 08087,   609-296-2444
Par: 72, Holes: 18
Old Orchard CC, Monmouth Road, Eatontown, 07724,   201-542-9139
Holes: 18
Old Tappan GC, 83 DeWolf Rd., Old Tappan, 07675
Orchard Hills GC, 404 Paramus Rd., Paramus, 07652,   201-447-3778
Holes: 9
Overpeck GC, East Cedar Lane, Teaneck, 07666,   201-837-3020
Holes: 18
Paramus G & CC, 314 Paramus Rd., Paramus, 07652,   201-447-6067
Holes: 18, Pro: Jake Zastko

Pascack Brook GC, 15 River Vale Rd., River Vale, 07675, 201-664-5886
Holes: 18
Passaic Country GC, 209 Totowa Rd., Wayne, 07470, 201-694-0887
Pro: Alex Cupo
Peace Pimpe GC, Cook Lane, Denville, 07834, 201-627-2867
Pro: Sidney Lee
Pennsauken CC, 380 Haddonfield Road, Pennsauken, 08110, 609-662-4961
Holes: 18
Pinch Brook GC, 234 Ridgedale Avenue, Florham Park, 07932, 201-334-1320
Holes: 18
Pine Brook GC, 1 Covered Bridge Blvd., Englishtown, 07726, 201-536-7272
Par: 61, Holes: 18
Pinecrest G & CC, Hammonton, 08095, 609-561-6110
Par: 72, Holes: 18
Pitman GC, Jefferson Road, Pitman, 08071, 609-589-8081
Holes: 18
Plainfield CC (West), 9 Woodland & Maple Ave., Edison, 08817, 201-769-3672
Pro: Ed Famula
Pomona GC, Mossmill & Odessa Avenue, Pomona Township, 08240,
609-965-3232 Holes: 9
Preakness GC, 209 Totowa Road, Wayne, 07470, 201-694-0887
Holes: 36
Princeton CC, Route 1–Wheeler Way, Princeton, 08540, 609-452-9382
Holes: 18, Pro: Steve Bowers
Princeton Meadows CC, 70 Hunters Glen Road, Plainsboro, 08536,
609-799-4000 Holes: 18
Quail Brook GC, New Brunswick Road, Franklin Township, 08322,
201-560-9190 Holes: 18
Rock View Club, River Road, Montague, 07827, 201-293-9991
Holes: 9
Rockleigh GC, 15 Paris Ave., Rockleigh, 07647, 201-768-6353
Yards: 6243, Par: 72, Holes: 27
Ron Jaworski's Eagles Nest, Woodbury - Glassboro Road, Sewell, 08080,
609-468-3542 Par: 71, Holes: 18
Scotch Hills GC, Jerusalem Rd., Scotch Plains, 07076, 201-245-9671 Holes: 9,
Pro: John Turnbull
Seasons GC at Great Gorge, PO Box 637, McAfee, 07428, 201-827-6000
Yards: 6325, Par: 70, USGA: 70.7, Holes: 27, Pro: Thomas Manziano
Shark River GC, 320 Old Corlies Avenue, Neptune, 07727, 201-922-4141
Holes: 18
Spooky Brook GC, Elizabeth Ave., East Millestone, 08873, 201-873-2241
Holes: 18
Spring Meadow G & CC, Allarie Road, Wall Township, 07727, 201-449-0806
Yards: 5448, Par: 70, USGA: 65.1, Holes: 18
Stone Harbor GC, Route 9, Cape May Court House, 08210, 609-465-9270
Holes: 18
Stony Brook GC, Stony Brook Road, Hopewell Township, 08525, 609-466-2220
Holes: 18
Summit Municipal GC, River Rd., Summit, 07901, 201-277-6828
Sunset Valley GC, W. Sunset Rd., Pompton Plains, 07444, 201-835-1515
Holes: 18, Pro: Dave Nelson
Tamarack GC, 97 Hardenburg Lane, E. Brunswick, 08816, 201-821-8881
Holes: 36, Pro: Ed Heuser
Tara Green GC, 1111 Somerset St., Franklin Township, 08873, 201-247-8284
Holes: 9, Pro: Mike Bonetate

Warrenbrook GC, 500 Warrenville Road, Warren, 07060, 201-754-8400
Holes: 18
Wedgewood CC, Hurffville Road, Turnersville, 08012, 609-227-5522
Par: 72, Holes: 18
Weequahic Park GC, Elizabeth Avenue, Newark, 07306, 201-923-1838
Holes: 18, Pro: Jim Feastor
Wildwood G & CC, RD 2—Golf Club Rd, Cape May Court House, 08210,
609-465-7823   Holes: 18
Willowbrook CC, Bridgeboro Road, Moorestown, 08057, 609-461-0131
Holes: 18
Woodbury CC, 467 Cooper Street, Woodbury, 08096, 609-845-9882
Holes: 9

Alamogordo Muni GC, 2351 Hamilton Rd., Alamogordo, 88310   *New Mexico*
505-437-0290   Yards: 6424, USGA: 69.0, Holes: 9, Pro: Dave Halleman
Angel Fire GC, Drawer B, Angel Fire, 88710,   800-633-PINE
Yards: 6275, USGA: 69.0, Holes: 18
Arroyo Del Oso GC, 7001 Osuna Rd., Albuquerque, 87109,   505-884-7505
Yards: 6545, USGA: 69.9, Holes: 27, Pro: Guy Wimberly
Artesia CC, 510 West Texas, POB 707, Artesia, 88210,   505-746-6732
Yards: 6245, USGA: 68.4, Holes: 18, Pro: S. Cranford
Carrizozo Muni GC, Hwy 380, Carrizozo, 88301,   505-648-2451
Yards: 6552, Par: 36, USGA: 68.4, Holes: 9
Civitan GC, 2200 N. Dustin, Farmington, 87401,   505-327-7701
Par: 27, Holes: 9, Pro: Anthony Montano
Clayton GC, PO Box 4, Clayton, 88415,   505-374-9957
Yards: 6324, USGA: 68.0, Holes: 18, Pro: Arch Tiembly
Clovis Muni GC, 1200 Norris, Clovis, 88101,   505-762-0249
Yards: 6061, USGA: 67.2, Holes: 9, Pro: Troy Gann
Conchas Dam State Park GC, PO Box 905, Conchas Dam, 88416,   505-868-9970
Yards: 6727, USGA: 68.8, Holes: 9
Cree Meadows CC, 310 Country Club Dr., POB 2274, Ruidoso, 88345,
505-257-5815   Yards: 5766, USGA: 66.2, Holes: 18, Pro: Jack Warlick
Dos Lagos GC, North 4th St., PO Box O, Anthony, 88021,   505-882-2830
Yards: 6226, Par: 72, USGA: 68.5, Holes: 18, Pro: Mike Olson
Double Eagle Country Club & Re, 10035 Country Club Lane NW,
Albuquerque, 87114,   505-898-0960
Yards: 6629, Par: 72, USGA: 70.0, Holes: 18, Pro: Tom Nielsen
Eunice Muni GC, PO Box 1235 Carlsbad Hwy., Eunice, 88231,   505-394-2881
Yards: 6350, USGA: 68.5, Holes: 9
Gallup Muni GC, PO Box 1477, 1111 Susan Dr., Gallup, 87301,   505-863-9224
Yards: 6416, USGA: 69.0, Holes: 18, Pro: Alex Alvarez
Hidden Valley CC, #29 Road 3025, POB 1450, Aztec, 87410,   505-334-3248
Yards: 6104, USGA: 68.5, Holes: 9, Pro: M. Armstrong
Hobbs CC, Carlsbad Hwy West Box 760, Hobbs, 88240,   505-393-5212
Yards: 6164, USGA: 68.4, Holes: 18, Pro: Fred Bond
Ladera GC, 3401 Ladera Dr. NW, Albuquerque, 87120,   505-836-4449
Yards: 6618, USGA: 69.9, Holes: 27, Pro: Don Zamora
Lake Carlsbad GC, 901 N. Muscatel, Carlsbad, 88220,   505-885-5444
Yards: 5891, USGA: 66.5, Holes: 27, Pro: John A. Heaton
Las Cruces CC, PO Box 876 Hwy 70 East, Las Cruces, 88005,   505-526-8731
Yards: 6153, USGA: 68.6, Holes: 18, Pro: Richard Garcia
New Mexico Tech GC, #1 Canyon Rd., Socorro, 87801,   505-835-5335
Yards: 6550, USGA: 71.0, Holes: 18, Pro: Russ Moore
New Mexico Military Inst. GC, 201 West 19th St., Roswell, 88201,   505-622-6033
Yards: 6365, USGA: 69.3, Holes: 18, Pro: Pete Chavez

New Mexico State Univ. GC, Box 3595 Univ Park Station, Las Cruces, 88003, 505-646-4131   Yards: 6659, USGA: 71.2, Holes: 18, Pro: Herb Wimberly
New Mexico Highlands Univ. GC, Mills Avenue, Las Vegas, 87701, 505-425-7711   Yards: 6109, USGA: 67.3, Holes: 9, Pro: Gene Torres
Oasis G&CC, Box AC Stagecoach Rd., Elephant Bute, 87935,   505-744-5224 Yards: 6850, Par: 37, USGA: 70.3, Holes: 9, Pro: Bill Hurley
Ocotillo Park GC, Lovington Hwy North POB 146, Hobbs, 88240,   505-393-5561 Yards: 6372, USGA: 69.3, Holes: 18, Pro: Douglas Lyle
Paradise Hills GC, 10035 Country Club NW., Albuquerque, 87114
Pendaries Lodge GC, POB 820, Rociada, 87742, 505-425-6076 Yards: 6080, USGA: 67.7, Holes: 18
Pinon Hills, 800 Municipal Drive, Farmington, 87401 Holes: 18
Ponderosa Pines GC, Rt. 4 Box 4680, Cloudcroft, 88317,   505-682-2995 Par: 34, Holes: 9
Puerto Del Sol GC, 1800 Girard SE, Albuquerque, 87106,   505-265-5636 Yards: 5496, USGA: 65.0, Holes: 9, Pro: Jack Hardwick
Raton CC, Gardner Rd., Raton, 87740,   505-445-8113 Yards: 5946, Par: 35, USGA: 66.6, Holes: 9
Santa Fe CC, PO Box 211 Airport Rd., Santa Fe, 87501,   505-471-0601 Yards: 6707, USGA: 70.2, Holes: 18, Pro: Joe Tiano
Santa Rosa G&CC, 121 North 4th St., Santa Rosa, 88435,   505-472-3949 Yards: 6517, USGA: 68.8, Holes: 9
Scott Park Muni GC, Silver City, 88061,   505-538-5041 Yards: 5816, Par: 72, USGA: 66.4, Holes: 18, Pro: Jim Smith
Spring River GC, 1612 West 8th St., Roswell, 88201,   505-622-9506 Yards: 6300, USGA: 67.6, Holes: 18, Pro: Ron Doan
Tierra Del Sol CC, POB 496, Belen, 87002,   505-865-5056 Yards: 6368, USGA: 69.5, Holes: 27, Pro: Keith Crist
Truth or Consequences Muni GC, 700 Marie St., Truth or Consequences, 87901 505-894-2603   Yds: 6412, Par: 36, USGA: 73.4, Holes: 9, Pro: G. Whitehead
Tucumcari Muni GC, PO Box 1188, Tucumcari, 88401,   505-461-1849 Yards: 6643, Par: 36, USGA: 70.4, Holes: 9, Pro: Mike Loudder
Zuni Mountain GC, PO Box 2128, Grants-Milan, 87021,   505-287-9239 Yards: 6570, USGA: 69.8, Holes: 9, Pro: Ray Cragun

---

1000 Acres GC, Stony Creek, 12878,   518-696-5246   *New York* Yards: 2900, Par: 35, Holes: 9
Adirondack GC, PO Box 96, Rock Rd., Peru, 12972,   518-643-8403 Holes: 18
Afton GC, Afton, 13730,   607-639-2454 Yards: 6200, Par: 72, Holes: 18
Alder Creek GC, Adler Creek, 13301,   315-831-5388 Par: 36, Holes: 9
Alexandria Bay GC, Alexandria Bay, 13607,   315-482-9846 Yards: 3045, Par: 35, Holes: 9
Amherst Audubon Par 3 GC, Williamsville, 14221,   716-631-7139 Yards: 990, Par: 27, Holes: 9
Amherst Audubon GC, Williamsville, 14221,   716-631-7139 Yards: 6600, Par: 71, Holes: 18
Amsterdam GC, Amsterdam, 14706,   518-842-4265 Yards: 6370, Par: 71, Holes: 18
Antlers CC, Ft. Johnson, 12072,   518-829-7423 Par: 70, Holes: 18
Apalachin GC, Apalachin, 13732,   607-625-2682 Yards: 2750, Par: 36, Holes: 9

Arrowhead GC, Syracuse, 13220, 315-656-9563
Yards: 6790, Par: 72, Holes: 18
Au Sable Valley GC, Au Sable Forks, 12912, 518-647-8666
Yards: 2599, Par: 34, Holes: 9
Barberlea GC, Nunda, 14517, 716-468-2116
Yards: 5800, Par: 69, Holes: 18
Batavia CC, Batavia, 14020, 716-343-7600
Par: 72, Holes: 18
Battenkill GC, Greenwich, 12834, 518-692-9179
Yards: 2944, Par: 35, Holes: 9
Battle Island GC, Fulton, 13069, 315-593-3408
Yards: 5973, Par: 72, Holes: 18
Bay Meadows GC, Glens Falls, 12801, 518-792-1650
Yards: 4835, Par: 64, Holes: 18
Bay Park GC, East Rockaway, Long Island, 11518, 516-593-8840
Pro: G. MacGilvary
Be Ge GC, Old Route 17, Chemung, 14825, 607-565-2618
Holes: 18
Beaver Island GC, 2136 W. Oakfield Rd., Grand Island, 14072, 716-773-4668
Yards: 6595, Par: 72, Holes: 18, Pro: Hal Carlson
Bedford Creek GC, Sackets Harbor, 13685, 315-646-3400
Par: 36, Holes: 9
Beekman CC, Beekman Rd., Hopewell Junction, 12533, 914-226-7700
Yards: 6420, Par: 71, Holes: 27, Pro: Jim Bergholtz
Bege's GC, Waverly, 14892, 607-565-2618
Yards: 2199, Par: 54, Holes: 18
Bellport CC, Main St., Bellport, 11713, 516-286-7045
Yards: 6220, Par: 71, Holes: 18
Belwood Park GC, New Windsor, 12550, 914-564-9913
Pro: Jim Petro
Belwood Park GC, New Windsor, 12550, 914-564-9913
Yards: 640, Par: 27, Holes: 9
Bemus Point GC, Bemus Point, 14712, 716-386-2893
Yards: 3109, Par: 36, Holes: 9
Bend of the River GC, Hadley, 12835, 518-696-3415
Par: 35, Holes: 9
Bergen Point GC, P.O. Box 1384, Bergen Ave., Long Island, 11704, 516-661-8282 Pro: Kevin J. Smith
Big Oak GC, Geneva, 14456, 315-789-9419
Yards: 3100, Par: 35, Holes: 9
Birch Run CC, Alleghany, 14706, 716-373-3113
Par: 35, Holes: 9
Blue Hill GC, Blue Hill Rd., Pearl River, 10965, 914-735-2094
Yards: 6375, Par: 71, Holes: 18, Pro: Jim Stewart
Blue Huron Hills GC, Macedon, 14502, 315-986-2007
Yards: 6779, Par: 71, Holes: 18
Bluff Point GC, Plattsburgh, 12901, 518-563-3420
Yards: 6540, Par: 72, Holes: 18
Brae Bum GC, Dansville, 14437, 716-335-3101
Yards: 2759, Par: 34, Holes: 9
Braemar GC, Spencerport, 14559, 716-352-5360
Yards: 6409, Par: 72, Holes: 18
Brantingham GC, Brantingham, 13312, 315-348-8861
Yards: 5300, Par: 71, Holes: 18
Brentwood CC, 100 Pennsylvania Ave., Brentwo, Long Island, 11717, 516-273-6633 Pro: R. Loughlin

Brentwood GC, Dix Hills, 11746, 516-273-6633
Yards: 6173, Par: 72, Holes: 18
Brighton Park GC, 70 Brompton Rd., Buffalo, 14150
Brighton Park GC, Tonawanda, 14150, 716-875-8721
Yards: 6485, Par: 72, Holes: 18
Bristol Harbour GC, Canandaigua, 14424, 716-396-2460
Yards: 6700, Par: 71, Holes: 18
Brockport GC, Brockport, 14420, 716-638-5334
Yards: 6619, Par: 72, Holes: 18
Brookfield GC, Greenfield Center, 12833, 518-893-7458
Yards: 6527, Par: 71, Holes: 18
Brooklawn GC, Syracuse, 13220, 315-463-1831
Yards: 4965, Par: 64, Holes: 18
Bryncliff CC, Varysburg, 14167, 716-535-7300
Par: 73, Holes: 18
Burden Lake GC, Nassau, 12123, 518-674-8917
Yards: 2958, Par: 36, Holes: 9
Burden Lake CC, Averill Park, 12018, 518-674-2142
Par: 36, Holes: 9
Caledonia CC, Caledonia, 14423, 716-538-9956
Par: 72, Holes: 18
Camillus GC, Camillus, 14423, 315-672-3770
Yards: 6200, Par: 73, Holes: 18
Camroden GC, Rome, 13440, 315-865-5771
Yards: 3044, Par: 36, Holes: 9
Canajoharie GC, Canajoharie, 13317, 518-673-3929
Yards: 3007, Par: 35, Holes: 9
Canasawacta GC, Norwich, 13815, 607-336-2685
Yards: 6271, Par: 70, Holes: 18
Cantiague Park, W. John St., Hicksville, Long Island, 11801, 516-681-7611
Pro: Gene Miller
Casolwood GC, Canastota, 13032, 315-697-9164
Par: 71, Holes: 18
Cassadaga GC, Cassadaga, 14718, 716-595-3003
Yards: 3000, Par: 35, Holes: 9
Castle Inn GC, Olean, 14760, 716-372-1050
Yards: 1580, Par: 27, Holes: 9
Catatonk GC, Candor, 13743, 607-659-4600
Yards: 6222, Par: 72, Holes: 18
Cato GC, Cato, 13033, 315-626-2291
Yards: 2953, Par: 35, Holes: 9
Cazenovia Park GC, Buffalo, 14150, 716-825-9811
Yards: 3057, Par: 36, Holes: 9
Cedar River GC, Indian Lake, 12842, 518-648-5906
Yards: 2800, Par: 36, Holes: 9
Cedar View GC, Rooseveltown, 13683, 315-764-9104
Yards: 6800, Par: 72, Holes: 18
Cedars GC, Cutchogue, 11935, 516-734-6363
Yards: 1120, Par: 27, Holes: 9
Cedars GC, Cutchogue, Long Island, 11935, 000-734-6363
Yards: 1120, Par: 27, Holes: 9
Central Valley GC, Smith Clove Road, Central Valley, 10917, 914-928-6924
Yards: 5639, Par: 71, USGA: 67.5, Holes: 18, Pro: Wendy Wolf
Chautauqua GC, Chautauqua, 14722, 716-357-6211
Yards: 3400, Par: 36, Holes: 27

Chautauqua Point GC, Mayville, 14757, 716-753-7271
Yards: 2652, Par: 70, Holes: 9
Cheektowaga Muni GC, Town Hall, Cheektowaga, 14227, 716-686-3445
Holes: 18
Chemung GC, Waverly, 14982, 607-565-2323
Par: 69, Holes: 18
Chenango Valley GC, Chenango Forks, 13746, 607-648-5251
Yards: 6005, Par: 72, Holes: 36
Chestnut Hill GC, Darien Center, 14040, 716-547-3613
Yards: 6358, Par: 72, Holes: 18
Chili CC, Scottsville, 14546, 716-889-9325
Par: 72, Holes: 18
Christopher Morley Park GC, Searingtown Rd., North Hills, Long Island,
11040, 516-621-9107 Pro: Pascal Lordi
Churchville GC, Churchville, 14428, 716-274-7770
Yards: 6186, Par: 72, Holes: 18
Clayton CC, Clayton, 13624, 315-686-4242
Par: 35, Holes: 9
Clearview GC, 202-12 Willets Pt. Blvd., Bays, New York, 11360, 718-229-2570
Pro: T. Chateauvert
Clinton Fine GC, Star Lake, 13690, 315-848-3570
Yards: 2854, Par: 36, Holes: 9
Cobble Hill GC, Elizabethtown, 12932, 518-873-9974
Yards: 3033, Par: 35, Holes: 9
Cobleskills GC, Cobleskill, 14724, 518-234-4045
Yards: 5968, Par: 36, Holes: 9
College GC, Delhi, 13753, 607-746-4281
Yards: 3085, Par: 36, Holes: 9
College Hill GC, P.O. Box 587, N. Clinton St., Poughkeepsie, 12601,
914-486-9112 Pro: Bruck Flesland
Colonial GC, Tannersville, 12485, 518-589-9807
Yards: 5436, Par: 35, Holes: 9
Colonie Hill GC, 63 Blydenburgh Rd., Hauppauge, Long Island, 11787
Commack Hills Golf & CC, P.O. Box 173, Hauppauge Rd., Long Island, 11725
Conewango GC, Randolph, 14772, 716-358-5409
Par: 72, Holes: 18
Countryside GC, Boonville, 13309, 315-942-5442
Yards: 3056, Par: 36, Holes: 9
Crab Meadow GC, Waterside Ave, Northport, Long Island, 11768,
516-757-8830 Pro: Tony Sidor
Crab Meadow GC, Northport, 11768, 516-757-8800
Yards: 6557, Par: 72, Holes: 18
Craig Wood GC, Lake Placid, 12946, 518-523-2591
Yards: 6554, Par: 72, Holes: 18
Cranebrook GC, Auburn, 13021, 315-252-7887
Yards: 1837, Par: 29, Holes: 9
Cronin's Vacationland GC, Warrensburg, 12885, 518-623-9336
Yards: 6121, Par: 70, Holes: 18
Crystall Springs GC, Vernon, 13476, 315-829-3210
Par: 35, Holes: 9
Dande Farms GC, Akron, 14001, 716-542-9229
Yards: 6475, Par: 71, Holes: 18
Deerfield CC, 2879 Clarkson-Parma TL Rd., Brockport, 14420, 716-392-4131
Yards: 6704, Par: 72, USGA: 71.9, Holes: 27, Pro: John Gruber
Deerwood GC, North Tonawanda, 14120, 716-695-8525
Yards: 6827, Par: 72, Holes: 18

Delaware Park GC, Buffalo, 14150,   716-835-2533
Yards: 5359, Par: 68, Holes: 18
Delphi Falls GC, Delphi Falls, 13051,   315-662-3611
Yards: 4317, Par: 68, Holes: 18
Delta Knolls GC, Rome, 13440,   315-339-1280
Yards: 1259, Par: 27, Holes: 9
Dimmock Hill GC, Binghamton, 13905,   607-729-5511
Par: 33, Holes: 9
Dinsmore Memorial GC, Box 182,, Staatsburg, 12580,   914-889-4100
Yards: 5750, Par: 70, Holes: 18, Pro: Ralph Montoya
Dix Hills GC, 527 Half Hollow Rd., Dix Hills, 11746,   516-271-4788
Yards: 2574, Par: 35, Holes: 9, Pro: Clifton George
Dix Hills Park GC, Vanderbilt Pkwy., Dix Hills, Long Island, 11743,
515-499-8005   Pro: Tony Sidor
Dix Hills Muni GC, Dix Hills, 11746,   516-499-8005
Yards: 1882, Par: 29, Holes: 9
Dogwood Knolls GC, Rt. 376, Hopewell Junction, 12533,   914-226-7317
Pro: Bob Finnegan
Douglaston GC, 6320 Marathon Pkwy., Douglaston Queens, 11363,
718-224-6566   Yards: 5482, Par: 67, Holes: 18, Pro: Helen G. Finn
Drumlins West GC, Syracuse, 13220,   315-446-4555
Yards: 6005, Par: 70, Holes: 18
Dryden Lake GC, Dryden, 13053,   607-844-9173
Par: 33, Holes: 9
Dunwoodie GC, Wasylenko Lane, Yonkers, 10701,   914-969-9217
Pro: Andrew Macko
Dyker Beach GC, 86th St., 7th Ave., Brooklyn, 11228,   718-836-9722
Yards: 6548, Par: 71, USGA: 68.8, Holes: 18, Pro: Ray Wood
Eastporte GC, 7 Lake Bridge Drive, Kings Park, Long Isl., 11754,   516-269-1031
Holes: 9
Easy Part GC, Oswego, 13126,   315-343-7906
Yards: 2133, Par: 32, Holes: 9
Edgewood GC, Laurens, 13796,   607-432-2713
Yards: 5674, Par: 72, Holes: 9
Eisenhower GC, Hempstead Tpke., East Meadow, Long Island, 11554,
516-794-0390   Pro: Pat Lordi
Elkdale GC, Salamanca, 14779,   716-945-5553
Yards: 6132, Par: 70, Holes: 18
Elm Tree Golf Course, Rt. 13, Cortland, 13045,   607-753-1341
Yards: 6130, Par: 70, USGA: 67.5, Holes: 18, Pro: Bruce Martins
Elms GC, The, Sandy Creek, 13145,   315-387-5297
Par: 70, Holes: 18
Ely Park GC, Binghamton, 13865,   607-772-7231
Yards: 6001, Par: 71, Holes: 18
Emerald Crest GC, Fulton, 13069,   315-593-1016
Yards: 3000, Par: 35, Holes: 9
En-Joie GC, Endicott, 13760,   607-785-1661
Yards: 6521, Par: 72, Holes: 18
Endwell Greens GC, Endwell, 13760,   607-785-4653
Yards: 6800, Par: 72, Holes: 18
Evergreen CC, East Greenbush, 12061,   518-477-6224
Par: 72, Holes: 18
Evergreen GC, Bolivar, 14715,   716-928-1270
Yards: 2976, Par: 36, Holes: 9
Evergreen, Schodack, 12156,   518-477-6224
Yards: 5800, Par: 70, Holes: 18

Ford Hill CC, Whitney Point, 13862, 607-692-8938
Par: 71, Holes: 36
Fore by Four GC, Gouverneur, 13642, 315-287-3711
Par: 35, Holes: 9
Forest Park GC, Park Lane S., Forest Park, New York, 11421, 718-296-0999
Pro: Tom Strafaci, Jr
Fox Hollow Run GC, 15856 Lynch Road, Holley, 14470, 716-638-6125
Holes: 9
Fox Hollow Run GC, 15816 Lynch Road, Holley, 14470, 716-637-2649
Holes: 18
Foxfire GC, Baldwinsville, 13027, 315-638-2930
Yards: 6900, Par: 72, Holes: 18
Frear Park GC, Troy, 12180, 518-270-4600
Yards: 5903, Par: 71, Holes: 18
Galway GC, Galway, 12074, 518-882-6395
Yards: 1340, Par: 28, Holes: 9
Garrison GC, Garrison, 10524, 914-424-3604
Yards: 6500, Par: 72, Holes: 18
Genegantslet GC, Greene, 13778, 607-656-8191
Yards: 6300, Par: 70, Holes: 18
Genesee Valley GC, 1000 E. River Rd., Rochester, 14623, 716-274-7750
Yards: 6195, Par: 71, Holes: 36
Gleneagles GC, Lake Placid, 12946, 518-523-3443
Holes: 18
Golden Oak GC, RTE 79 Rd. 2, Binghamton, 13865
Golden Oaks Inn & GC, Windsor, 13865, 607-655-9961
Par: 69, Holes: 18
Gouverneur GC, Gouverneur, 13642, 315-287-2130
Yards: 6476, Par: 71, Holes: 9
Grandview GC, Angola, 14006, 716-549-4930
Yards: 2060, Par: 33, Holes: 9
Grandview GC, Box 237, Pfafftown, 27040, 919-924-8229
Yards: 6329, Par: 71, Holes: 18
Granit GC, Lower Granit Rd., Kerhonkson, 12446, 914-626-3141
Yards: 5828, Par: 71, Holes: 18, Pro: John Magaletta
Green Acres GC, Harwich St., Kingston, 12401, 914-331-7807
Yards: 2854, Par: 36, Holes: 9
Green Lakes GC, Fayetteville, 13066, 315-637-5515
Yards: 6212, Par: 71, Holes: 18
Green Mansions GC, Chestertown, 12817, 518-494-9975
Yards: 2722, Par: 36, Holes: 9
Green Mansions GC, Warrensburg, 12885, 518-494-7222
Par: 36, Holes: 9
Greenview GC, West Monroe, 13167, 315-668-2244
Yards: 6299, Par: 35, Holes: 27
Greenwood GC, Clarence Center, 14032, 716-741-3395
Yards: 3351, Par: 36, Holes: 9
Griffins' Greens GC, Oswego, 13126, 315-343-2996
Yards: 5445, Par: 70, Holes: 18
Dutch Hollow GC, Owasco, 13130, 315-784-5052
Par: 71, Holes: 18
Grossinger GC, Grossinger, 12734, 914-292-5000
Yards: 6406, Par: 71, USGA: 71.0, Holes: 27
Grygiel's Pine Hills GC, Frankfort, 13340, 315-733-5030
Yards: 5900, Par: 69, Holes: 18

Halmet G&CC (The), P.O.Box 173m Gayooayge & Comma, Commack, 11725, 516-499-0345   Yards: 6309, Par: 71, Holes: 18, Pro: Ed DiMattia
Hancock GC, Hancock, 13783,   607-736-2480
Par: 36, Holes: 9
Harbour Pointe GC, Waterport, 14571,   716-682-3922
Yards: 5610, Par: 70, Holes: 18
Heatherwood GC, Nesconset Hwy., Route 347., Long Island, 11720,
516-473-9000   Pro: Chris McGuckin
Hidden Hills GC, P.O. Box 337, Pomono, 10512
Hidden Valley GC, Whitesboro, 13492,   315-736-9953
Yards: 6500, Par: 71, Holes: 18
Hidden Walins GC, RTE 30, Kingston, 12455
Hidden Waters GC at Kass Inn, Margaretville, 12455,   914-586-4849
Par: 71, Holes: 18
Highlands GC, Garrison, 10524,   914-424-3727
Yards: 4400, Par: 68, Holes: 9
Hiland GC, Haviland Road, Glens Falls, 12801,   518-761-4053
Yards: 6956, Par: 72, Holes: 18
Hill & Dale GC, Hill & Dale Rd., Carmel, 10512,   914-225-9886
Pro: B. S. Palmer
Hillendale GC, Ithaca, 14850,   607-273-2363
Par: 35, Holes: 9
Hillview GC, Fredonia, 14063,   716-679-4574
Yards: 6149, Par: 70, Holes: 18
Holiday GC, Gloversville, 12078,   518-725-3704
Yards: 3070, Par: 37, Holes: 9
Holiday Valley Golf & Ski, Ellicottville, 14731,   716-699-2346
Par: 72, Holes: 18
Holland Meadows GC, Gloversville, 12078,   518-883-3318
Yards: 3333, Par: 59, Holes: 18
Hollow Hills GC, 49 Ryder Ave., Dix Hills, Long Island, 11746,   516-242-0010
Pro: Joe Bifulco
Hollow Hills GC, Dix Hills, 11746,   516-242-0010
Yards: 2640, Par: 35, Holes: 9
Homewack Lodge GC, Spring Glen, 12483,   914-647-6800
Yards: 2500, Par: 36, Holes: 9
Hoosick Falls GC, Hoosick Falls, 12090,   518-686-4210
Yards: 3000, Par: 34, Holes: 9
Hornell GC, Hornell, 14843,   607-324-1735
Yards: 3100, Par: 36, Holes: 9
Huff House GC, Anawanda Lake Rd., Roscoe, 12776
Yards: 1800, Par: 27, Holes: 9
Hulett's GC, Hulett's Landing, 12841,   518-499-1234
Yards: 1780, Par: 34, Holes: 9
Huntington G & T, 1506 W. Herico Tpke., Huntingt, Long Island, 11743
Hyde Park GC, Niagara Falls, 14302,   716-297-2067
Yards: 6500, Par: 70, Holes: 36
Imperial Resort & CC, The, Swan Lake, 12783,   914-292-8000
Par: 71, Holes: 18
Indian Hills GC, Painted Post, 14870,   607-523-7315
Par: 72, Holes: 18
Indian Island GC, Rierhead, Long Island, 11901,   516-727-7776
Pro: Box Fox
Indian Valley Par 3 GC, Shrub Oak, 10588,   914-245-9816
Par: 27, Holes: 9

Inlet GC, Inlet, 13360, 315-357-3503
Yards: 5900, Par: 70, Holes: 18
Ironwood GC, Baldwinsville, 13027, 315-635-9826
Par: 35, Holes: 9
Island Valley GC, Fairport, 14450, 716-586-1300
Yards: 2903, Par: 35, Holes: 9
Ives Hill GC, Watertown, 13601, 315-782-1771
Yards: 6700, Par: 72, Holes: 18
J. Victor Skiff GC, Saratoga Springs, 12866, 518-584-2006
Yards: 1627, Par: 29, Holes: 9
James Baird State Park GC, Rd. #1 Box 239C, Pleasant Valley, 12569,
914-889-4100   Yards: 6667, Par: 71, USGA: 71.2, Holes: 18, Pro: Brad David
Jones Beach GC, Wantagh, 11793
Yards: 1010, Par: 54, Holes: 18
Kass Inn GC, Margaretville, 12455, 914-586-9844
Katsbaan GC, Old Kings Highway, Saguerties, 12477
Holes: 9
Kissena Park GC, 164-15 Booth Mem. Dr., Flushin, New York, 11365,
718-939-4594
Pro: Dale Shankland
Knickerbocker GC, Cincinnatus, 13040, 607-863-3800
Yards: 5580, Par: 35, Holes: 9
Kutsher's CC, Kutsher Rd., Monticello, 12701, 914-794-6000
Yards: 6638, Par: 72, Holes: 18, Pro: Steve Downey
La Tourette GC, 1001 Richmond Hill Rd., Staten Island, 10306, 718-351-1889
Pro: Chas. Kilkenny
Lake Anne CC, Clove Rd., Monroe, 10950, 914-783-9025
Pro: Marvin Green
Lake Breeze GC, Watkins Glen, 14891, 607-535-4413
Yards: 2929, Par: 36, Holes: 9
Lake Placid Club GC, Lake Placid Club Dr., Plattsburgh, 12901
Lake Pleasant GC, Lake Pleasant, 12108, 518-548-7071
Yards: 2888, Holes: 9
Lake Shore GC, Rochester, 14623, 716-663-5578
Yards: 6300, Par: 70, Holes: 18
Latourette GC, 100 London Rd., New York, 10306
Latta Lea GC, Rochester, 14623, 716-663-9440
Yards: 1001, Par: 27, Holes: 9
Le Roy CC, Le Roy, 14482, 716-768-9764
Par: 71, Holes: 18
Leatherstocking GC, Nelson Ave., Utica, 13326
Lido GC, Lido Dr., Lido Beach, Long Island, 11561, 516-431-8778
Pro: Leo Tabick
Little Falls GC, Little Falls, 13365, 315-823-4442
Yards: 3150, Par: 36, Holes: 9
Liverpool GC, Liverpool, 13088, 315-457-7170
Yards: 6412, Par: 71, Holes: 18
Livingston GC, Geneseo, 14454, 716-243-9939
Yards: 6500, Par: 71, Holes: 18
Loch Ledge GC, Rt. 118, Box 187, Yorktown Heights, 10598, 914-962-2922
Pro: Orlando Fiore
Lochmor GC, Loch Sheldrake, 12759, 914-434-9079
Yards: 6286, Par: 72, Holes: 18, Pro: Rick Knox
Lyndon GC, Fayetteville, 13066, 315-446-1885
Yards: 4795, Par: 65, Holes: 18

Malone GC, Malone, 12953, 518-483-2926
Yards: 6688, Par: 72, Holes: 36
Maple Hill GC, Marathon, 13803, 607-849-3285
Par: 70, Holes: 18
Maple Moor GC, North St., White Plains, 10605, 914-946-1830
Pro: Rick Paonessa
Marine Park GC, 2800 Flatbush Ave., Brooklyn, New York, 11234, 718-338-7114
Pro: Neil Barbella
Mark Twain GC, Elmira, 14901, 607-737-5770
Yards: 6820, Par: 72, Holes: 18
Marvin's GC, Macedon, 14502, 315-986-4455
Yards: 6000, Par: 70, Holes: 18
Massena GC, Massena, 13662, 315-769-2293
Yards: 6566, Par: 71, Holes: 18
McCann GC, 155 Wilbur Blvd., Poughkeepsie, 12603, 914-454-1968
Yards: 6524, Par: 72, Holes: 18, Pro: Ron Jensen
Meadow Brook GC, Weedsport, 13166, 315-834-9358
Par: 35, Holes: 9
Meadow Brook GC, Winthrop, 13697, 315-389-4562
Yards: 3150, Par: 36, Holes: 9
Meadowgreens GC, Ghent, 12075, 518-828-0663
Yards: 3011, Par: 36, Holes: 9
Mechanicville CC, Mechanicville, 12118, 518-664-3866
Par: 36, Holes: 9
Merrick Road Park GC, 2550 Clubhouse Rd., Merrick, Long Island, 11566,
516-378-5401   Pro: Bob Hyde
Middle Island CC, Box 205, Yaphank Rd., Middle I, Long Island, 11953,
516-924-5100
Yards: 9915, Par: 72, USGA: 71.9, Holes: 27, Pro: Michael Wands
Middle Island GC, Middle Island, 11953, 516-924-5100
Yards: 6610, Par: 72, Holes: 27
Mill Road Acres GC, Latham, 12110, 518-783-7244
Yards: 1720, Par: 29, Holes: 9
Mohansic GC, Taconic State Pkwy., Yorktown Heights, 10598, 914-962-4065
Yards: 6329, Par: 70, Holes: 18, Pro: John Paonessa
Mohawk Valley GC, Utica, 13326,   315-866-0204
Yards: 3153, Par: 36, Holes: 9
Moriah GC, Port Henry, 12974, 518-546-7472
Yards: 2100, Par: 32, Holes: 9
Mosholu GC, Jerome & Bainbridge Aves. Bron, New York, 10467, 212-822-4845
Pro: Dale Shankland
Nevele CC, Ellenville, 12428, 914-647-6000
Par: 71, Holes: 18
Newark Valley GC, Newark Valley, 13811, 607-642-3376
Par: 69, Holes: 18
Newman GC, Ithaca, 14850, 607-273-6262
Yards: 3400, Par: 36, Holes: 9
Niagara County GC, Lockport, 14094, 716-439-6051
Yards: 6464, Par: 72, Holes: 18
Nick Stoner GC, Caroga Lake, 12032, 518-835-4211
Yards: 5500, Par: 70, Holes: 18
North Country GC, Champlain, 12919, 518-297-5814
Yards: 6523, Par: 72, Holes: 18
North GC, Rouses Point, 12979, 518-297-5814
Yards: 6523, Par: 72, Holes: 18

North Shore GC, Cleveland, 13042, 315-675-8101
Par: 35, Holes: 9
North Woodmere GC, Hungry Harbor Rd., N. Woodmere, Long Island, 11598,
516-791-2919 Pro: Gene Miller
Northern Pines GC, Cicero, 13039, 315-699-2939
Yards: 6161, Par: 70, Holes: 9
Northern Pines GC, Clay, 13041, 315-699-2939
Par: 35, Holes: 9
Northport Veterans Hospital GC, Northport, Long Island, 11768,
516-261-4400 Pro: Sam Baruchov
Northway Heights GC, Ballston Lake, 12019, 518-877-7082
Par: 72, Holes: 18
Oak Ridge CC, Route 1, Box W 391-A, Alexandria Bay, 13607, 315-482-2918
Holes: 9
Oneida CC, Oneida, 13421, 315-363-8879
Par: 63, Holes: 18
Orchard Valley GC, Newrow, 13811, 315-677-5180
Par: 71, Holes: 18
Orchard Valley GC, Lafayette, 13084, 315-677-5180
Yards: 3121, Par: 36, Holes: 9
Oriskany Hills GC, Oriskany, 13424, 315-736-4540
Yards: 3000, Par: 35, Holes: 9
Otsego GC, Springfield Center, 13468, 607-547-9290
Yards: 2900, Par: 35, Holes: 9
Oyster Bay GC, Woodbury, Long Island, 11101, 516-364-3977
Pro: Steve Matuza
Pap-Pap's Par 3, Albion, 14411, 716-589-4004
Yards: 1500, Par: 27, Holes: 9
Pelham & Split Rock GCs, 870 Shore Road Bronx, New York, 10464,
212-885-1258 Pro: John Connelly
Peninsula GC, 50 Nassau Road, Massapequa, 11758, 516-798-9776
Yards: 3277, Par: 37, USGA: 71.6, Holes: 9, Pro: George Tavalaro
Philip J. Rotella Municipal GC, Thiellis Mt. Ivy Rd., Thiellis, 10984,
914-354-1616 Pro: Howard Pierson
Pine Grove GC, Camillus, 13031, 315-672-9272
Par: 72, Holes: 18
Pine Hills CC, 162 Wading River Rd., Manorvil, Long Island, 11949,
516-878-4343 Pro: Roger Tooker
Pine Meadows GC, Clarence, 14031, 716-741-3970
Par: 31, Holes: 9
Pine Plains GC, Pine Plains, 12567, 518-398-7101
Yards: 7300, Par: 73, Holes: 18
Pinehurst GC, Westfield, 14787, 716-326-4424
Yards: 3200, Par: 36, Holes: 9
Pines GC, South Fallsburg, 12779, 914-434-6000
Yards: 2330, Par: 32, Holes: 9
Pines GC, The, Pulaski, 13142, 315-298-9970
Par: 36, Holes: 9
Pinnacle GC, Addison, 14801, 607-359-2767
Yards: 3235, Par: 36, Holes: 9
Pitch and Putt GC, Flushing Meadow Park, Corona, New York, 10001,
718-271-8182
Pleasant Knolls GC, Oneida, 13421, 315-363-2939
Par: 35, Holes: 9
Pleasant View Lodge & GC, Freehold, 12431, 914-738-3399
Holes: 9

Pleasant View GC, Freehold, 12431, 518-634-2523
Par: 36, Holes: 9
Pope's Grove GC, Syracuse, 13220, 315-487-9075
Yards: 1339, Par: 29, Holes: 9
Potsdam Town & CC, Potsdam, 13676, 315-265-2141
Par: 36, Holes: 9
Putnam Golf, Swim & Tennis Club, Hill St., Mahopac, 10541, 914-628-3451
Pro: Jim Cassia
Quaker Ridge GC, Griffen Ave., White Plains, 10583
Queensbury GC, Lake George, 12845, 518-793-3711
Yards: 6100, Par: 70, Holes: 18
Queensbury GC, R123, Glens Falls, 12845
Rainbow GC, Greenville, 12083, 518-966-5343
Yards: 3000, Par: 36, Holes: 9
Raymondville GC, Raymondville, 13678, 315-769-2759
Yards: 3500, Par: 35, Holes: 9
Red Hook GC, Red Hook, 12571, 914-758-8652
Par: 35, Holes: 9
Ricci Meadows GC, Albion, 14411, 716-682-3280
Yards: 6015, Par: 71, Holes: 18
Rip Van Winkle GC, Palenville, 12463, 518-678-9779
Yards: 3120, Par: 36, Holes: 9
River Oaks GC, 201 Whitehaven Rd., Grand Island, 14072, 716-773-3336
Yards: 6588, Par: 72, USGA: 71.0, Holes: 18
Riverbend GC, New Berlin, 13411, 607-847-8481
Yards: 2964, Par: 35, Holes: 9
Riverside CC, Central Square, 13036, 315-676-7714
Par: 58, Holes: 18
Riverton GC, West Henrietta, 14586, 716-334-6196
Par: 36, Holes: 9
Robert Moses GC, Fire Island, 11782
Yards: 1300, Par: 54, Holes: 18
Robert Van Patten GC, Clifton Park, 12065, 518-877-5400
Yards: 7100, Par: 73, Holes: 27
Rock Hill GC CC, Clancy Rd., Manorville, 11949, 516-878-2250
Yards: 6465, Par: 72, USGA: 71.3, Holes: 18, Pro: George Cosgrove
Rockland Lake State Park GC, P.O. Box 190, Rte. 9W, Congers, 10920,
914-268-7275 Yards: 6864, Par: 72, Holes: 36, Pro: Bill Osetek
Rockview GC, Old Mine Rd., Port Jervis, 12771
Rogues Roost GC, Bridgeport, 13030, 315-633-9406
Par: 71, Holes: 18
Rolling Hills of Medford, 3325 Rte. No. 112, Medford, Long Island, 11963,
516-732-8694
Roundup Ranch GC, Downsville, 13755, 607-363-7300
Par: 36, Holes: 9
Rustic G&CC, Dexter, 13634, 315-639-6800
Par: 36, Holes: 9
Sacandaga GC, Northville, 12134, 518-863-4887
Yards: 3012, Par: 36, Holes: 9
Sag Harbor GC, Sag Harbor, Long Island, 11963, 516-725-9739
Pro: Dennis Rozzi
Sagamore GC, Bolton Landing, 12814, 518-644-9400
Yards: 6900, Par: 70, Holes: 18
Salmon Creek GC, Spencerport, 14559, 716-352-4300
Yards: 6300, Par: 72, Holes: 18

Sandy Pond GC, Riverhead, Long Island, 11901, 516-727-3462
Pro: Ed Bucholz
Saranac Inn GC, Saranac Lake, 12982, 518-891-1402
Yards: 6550, Par: 72, Holes: 18
Saranac Lake GC, Ray Brook, 12977, 518-891-2675
Yards: 3163, Par: 36, Holes: 9
Saratoga Spa GC—Championship, Saratoga State Park, Glens Falls, 12866,
518-584-2008   Yards: 6319, Par: 72, Holes: 18
Saratoga Spa GC—Par 29, Saratoga State Park, Glens Falls, 12866,
518-584-2007   Yards: 1627, Par: 29, Holes: 9
Sauquoit Knolls GC, Sauquoit, 13456, 315-737-8959
Yards: 3100, Par: 35, Holes: 9
Saxon Woods GC, Mamaroneck Rd., Scarsdale, 10583, 914-725-3814
Pro: Tony Masciola
Schenectady GC, Schenectady, 12301, 518-382-5155
Yards: 6700, Par: 72, Holes: 18
Schroon Lake Muni GC, Schroon Lake, 12870, 518-532-9539
Par: 36, Holes: 9
Scotts Corners GC, Montgomery, 12549, 914-457-9141
Par: 36, Holes: 9
Scotts Oquaga Lake House GC, Deposit, 13754, 607-467-3094
Par: 67, Holes: 18
Seneca GC, Baldwinsville, 13027, 315-635-5695
Yards: 5901, Par: 71, Holes: 9
Serenity Hills GC, Friendship, 14739, 716-973-7907
Yards: 2756, Par: 36, Holes: 9
Shamrock GC, Oriskany, 13424, 315-336-9585
Yards: 3400, Par: 35, Holes: 9
Shawangunk CC, Ellenville, 12428, 914-647-6090
Par: 34, Holes: 9
Shawnee GC, Sanborn, 14132, 716-694-5144
Yards: 3280, Par: 36, Holes: 9
Shelther Island CC, Shelter Island, Long Island, 11964, 516-749-8863
Pro: Bill Congden
Shephard Hills GC, Roxbury, 12474, 607-326-7121
Yards: 3066, Par: 36, Holes: 9
Sheridan Park GC, Tonawanda, 14150, 716-875-8721
Yards: 6534, Par: 71, Holes: 18
Shorewood GC, Dunkirk, 14048, 716-366-1880
Yards: 6625, Par: 72, Holes: 18
Silver Lake GC, 915 Victory Blvd., Staten Is., New York, 10301, 718-448-4693
Pro: Ed Sorge
South Shore GC, 200 Huguenot Ave., Staten Is., New York, 10312, 718-984-0101
Pro: Greg Deangelo
Six-S GC, Belfast, 14711, 716-373-3113
Yards: 6210, Par: 72, Holes: 18
Skene Valley CC, Route 2 Norton Road, Whitehall, 12887, 518-499-1685
Yards: 3350, Par: 36, Holes: 9
Skyline GC, Brewerton, 13029, 315-699-5338
Par: 71, Holes: 18
Skyridge GC, Chittennango, 13037, 315-687-6900
Par: 35, Holes: 9
Sleepy Hollow GC, Rome, 13440, 315-336-4110
Yards: 4852, Par: 68, Holes: 18
Smallwood GC, Smallwood, 12778, 914-583-4211

Smithtown Landing CC, 496 Landing Ave., Smithtown, Long Island, 11787, 516-360-7618 Pro: Mike Hebron
Smithtown Landing GC, Smithtown, 11787, 516-360-7618
Yards: 6200, Par: 71, Holes: 18
Soaring Eagles GC, Horseheads, 14845, 607-739-0551
Par: 72, Holes: 18
Sodus Bay Heights GC, Sodus Point, 14555, 315-483-6777
Yards: 6286, Par: 72, Holes: 18
South Hills CC, Jamestown, 14701, 716-487-1471
Par: 72, Holes: 18
South Park GC, Buffalo, 14150, 716-825-9504
Yards: 2713, Par: 35, Holes: 9
Spa Championship GC, Saratoga Springs, 12866, 518-584-2535
Yards: 6950, Par: 72, Holes: 18
Sprain Lake GC, 290 E. Grassy Sprain Rd., Yonkers, 10710, 914-779-9827
Pro: Tom Avezzano
Spring Lake GC, Plainview Dr., Wading River, Long Island, 11792
St. Bonaventure GC, St. Bonaventure, 14778, 716-372-7692
Yards: 2970, Par: 36, Holes: 9
St. Lawrence G&CC, Canton, 13617, 315-386-4600
Par: 72, Holes: 18
St. Lawrence State Park GC, Ogdensburg, 13669, 315-393-2286
Yards: 2811, Par: 35, Holes: 9
Stadium GC, Schenectady, 12301, 518-374-9104
Yards: 6419, Par: 71, Holes: 18
Stamford GC, Stamford, 12167, 607-652-7398
Yards: 6490, Par: 70, Holes: 18
Stevensville CC, Swan Lake, 12783, 914-292-8000
Yards: 6800, Par: 71, Holes: 18, Pro: Jim Calderone
Stone Creek CC, Watertown, 13601, 315-785-8091
Par: 37, Holes: 9
Stone Dock G&CC, High Falls, 12440, 914-687-9944
Par: 36, Holes: 9
Stonehedges GC, Groton, 13073, 607-898-3754
Yards: 6100, Par: 72, Holes: 18
Sullivan County G&CC, Liberty, 12754, 914-292-3900
Par: 36, Holes: 9
Sullivan GC, RTE 52, Monticello, 12754
Sunny Hill GC, Greenville, 12083, 518-634-7698
Par: 66, Holes: 18
Sunnyside Par 3 GC, Glens Falls, 12866, 518-792-0148
Yards: 800, Par: 27, Holes: 9
Sunset Valley GC, Lakewood, 14750, 716-664-7508
Yards: 2771, Par: 57, Holes: 18
Swan Lake GC, Manorville, 11949, 516-369-1818
Yards: 6800, Par: 72, Holes: 18
Swan Lake GC, 388 River Dr., Manorville, Long Island, 11949, 516-369-1818
Pro: Jon Schippers
Sweetland Pines GC, 5795 Sweetland Road, Stafford, 14143, 716-343-7659
Holes: 9
Sycamore Greens GC, Duanesburg, 12056, 518-355-6145
Yards: 5777, Par: 70, Holes: 18
Syosset GC INC., 585 Jericho Tpke., Syosset, Long Island, 11101, 516-921-9803
Pro: Frank Weber
Tall Tree GC, Rt. 25A, Rocky Point, 11778, 516-744-3200
Yards: 4715, Par: 65, Holes: 18, Pro: E. Acquavella

Tamacy's GC, Adams, 13605, 315-232-4842
Yards: 3014, Par: 35, Holes: 9
Tanner Valley GC, Syracuse, 13220, 315-492-9856
Yards: 6005, Par: 71, Holes: 18
Tee-Bird GC, Fort Edward, 12828, 518-792-7727
Yards: 6140, Par: 70, Holes: 18
Tennanah Lake GC, Roscoe, 12776, 914-794-2900
Terry Hills GC, 5122 Clinton St. Rd., Batavia, 14020, 716-343-0860
Yards: 6038, Par: 72, USGA: 68.7, Holes: 18, Pro: Nick Rotondo
Thendara GC, Thendara, 13472, 315-369-3136
Yards: 6435, Par: 72, Holes: 18
Thompson Park GC, Watertown, 13601, 315-782-6929
Yards: 6200, Par: 72, Holes: 18
Thousand Islands GC, At Wellesley Island, Alexandria Bay, 13607,
325-482-9454   Yards: 6000, Par: 72, Holes: 18
Ticonderoga CC, Ticonderoga, 12883, 518-585-9776
Par: 71, Holes: 18
Tioga GC, Nichols, 13812, 607-699-3881
Par: 71, Holes: 18
Top of the World GC, Lake George, 12845, 518-668-2062
Yards: 2868, Par: 36, Holes: 9
Town Isle GC, Kirkville, 13082, 315-656-9049
Yards: 3175, Par: 70, Holes: 18
Tri-County GC, Forestville, 14062, 716-965-2053
Yards: 6434, Par: 71, Holes: 18
Trumansburg GC, Trumansburg, 14886, 607-387-8844
Par: 35, Holes: 9
Tupper Lake GC, Tupper Lake, 12986, 518-359-3701
Yards: 6200, Par: 71, Holes: 18
Turin Highlands GC, Turin, 13473, 315-348-9912
Par: 72, Holes: 18
Twin Brooks GC, Waddington, 13694, 315-388-4480
Yards: 6600, Par: 71, Holes: 18
Poxabogue GC, Moutauk Highway Box 890, Wainscott, 11975, 516-537-0025
Yards: 1706, Par: 30, Holes: 9, Pro: Wm. Manelski
Twin Hickory GC, Hornell, 14843, 607-324-1441
Yards: 6560, Par: 72, Holes: 18
Twin Ponds GC, New York Mills, 13417, 315-736-9303
Yards: 6125, Par: 70, Holes: 18
Twin Village GC, Roscoe, 12776, 607-498-9983
Par: 32, Holes: 9
Valley View GC, Utica, 13326, 315-732-8755
Yards: 6651, Par: 71, Holes: 18
Van Cortlandt Park GC, Van Cortlandt Park West & Bail, Bronx, 10471,
212-543-4585   Yards: 5953, Par: 70, USGA: 67.7, Holes: 18, Pro: William Castner
Vassar GC, Poughkeepsie, 12601, 914-473-1550
Pro: Harry Vinall
Victor Hills GC, Victor, 14564, 716-924-3480
Yards: 3209, Par: 36, Holes: 9
Wakely Lodge GC, Indian Lake, 12842, 518-648-5011
Yards: 2700, Par: 34, Holes: 9
Walden CC, Box 32, Walden, 12586, 914-457-5100
Pro: Walt Merrill
Wateridge at East Port GC, Eastport, LI, 11941, 516-862-7676
Holes: 18

Watertown GC, Thompson Pk., Watertown, 13601, 315-782-4040
Yards: 5984, Par: 72, USGA: 68.1, Holes: 18, Pro: Stuart Jamieson
Watkins Glen GC, Watkins Glen, 14891, 607-535-2340
Yards: 2950, Par: 36, Holes: 9
Wayne Hills GC, Lyons, 14489, 315-946-6944
Yards: 6600, Par: 72, Holes: 18
Webster GC, Webster, 14580, 716-265-1201
Yards: 6000, Par: 70, Holes: 18
Wellesley Island GC, Alexandria Bay, 13607, 315-482-9622
Yards: 2730, Par: 35, Holes: 9
Wellsville GC, Wellsville, 14895, 716-268-7623
Yards: 6200, Par: 70, Holes: 18
West Hill GC, Camillus, 13031, 315-672-8677
Yards: 2788, Par: 54, Holes: 18
West Sayville GC, Montauk Hwy., W. Sayville, Long Island, 11796,
516-567-1704   Pro: Fred Gipp
Wester East GC, Webster, 14580
Yards: 6600, Par: 72, Holes: 18
Western Turnpike GC, Gulderland, 12084, 518-456-0786
Par: 72, Holes: 27
Westport GC, Westport, 12993, 518-962-4470
Par: 72, Holes: 18
Whispering Hills GC, Conesus, 14435, 716-346-2100
Yards: 6500, Par: 72, Holes: 18
Whispering Pines GC, Schenectady, 12301, 518-355-2724
Yards: 2350, Par: 55, Holes: 18
White Birch GC, Lyndonville, 14098, 716-765-2630
Yards: 1265, Par: 27, Holes: 9
Wildwood GC, Cicero, 13039, 315-699-7222
Yards: 4800, Par: 62, Holes: 18
Wildwood GC, Clay, 13041, 315-699-5255
Par: 72, Holes: 18
Willowbrook GC, Cortland, 13045, 607-756-7382
Par: 36, Holes: 9
Willowbrook GC, Lockport, 14094, 716-434-0111
Yards: 6003, Par: 71, Holes: 18
Willowbrook GC, Watertown, 13601, 315-782-8192
Yards: 9389, Par: 72, Holes: 27
Willowcreek GC, Big Flats, 14814, 607-562-8898
Par: 72, Holes: 27
Willows GC, Rexford, 12148, 518-399-1920
Yards: 7000, Par: 73, Holes: 18
Willsboro GC, Willsboro, 12996, 518-963-8989
Par: 35, Holes: 9
Windham Ridge Club, Windham Ridge Road, PO Box, Windham, 12496,
518-734-3005   Yards: 6053, Par: 71, Holes: 18
Winding Brook CC, Valatie, 12184, 518-758-9117
Par: 72, Holes: 18
Windy Wes GC, Archerville Park, Wallkill, 12589
Holes: 18
Winged Foot GC, Fenimore Rd., White Plains, 10543
Wolcott GC, Wolcott, 14509, 315-594-8295
Yards: 2881, Par: 35, Holes: 9

Apple Valley CC, Rt. 1, Lake Lure, 28746, 704-625-9111   *North Carolina*
Holes: 18

Arrowhead GC, Mebane-Oaks Rd., Mebane, 27302, 919-563-5255
Yards: 6555, Par: 72, Holes: 18
Asheboro Muni GC, 421 Country Club Rd., Asheboro, 27203, 919-625-4158
Yards: 3175, Par: 35, Holes: 9
Asheville Buncombe GC, 226 Fairway Dr., Asheville, 28805, 704-298-1867
Yards: 6412, Par: 72, USGA: 70.6, Holes: 18, Pro: Ted Tipton
Ayden G&CC, Ayden, 28513, 919-746-3389
Yards: 6784, Par: 72, Holes: 18
Bald Head Island Club, Bald Head Island, 28706, 919-457-5000
Yards: 7040, Par: 72, Holes: 18
Bald Mountain CC, Rt 1, Lake Lure, 28746, 704-625-9111
Yards: 6689, Par: 72, Holes: 18
Beacon Ridge CC, Beacon Ridge, 28516, 919-673-2950
Yards: 6143, Par: 72, Holes: 18
Bean Rivage Plantation, Wilmington, 28402, 919-395-1300
Yards: 6885, Par: 72, Holes: 18
Beaver Creek GC, Rt. 2, Dobson, 27017, 919-374-5670
Yards: 3032, Par: 36, Holes: 9
Beaver Ridge GC, Rt 7, Rocky Rd., Lenoir, 28645, 704-754-4653
Yards: 6000, Par: 70, Holes: 18
Beech Mountain GC, Club House Rd. RT 2, Hickory, 28604, 704-387-2372
Yards: 5675, Par: 72, USGA: 68.0, Holes: 18
Bel-Aire GC, Pleasant Ridge Rd., Greensboro, 27406, 919-668-2413
Yards: 6500, Par: 72, Holes: 18
Bent Creek Golf Resort, Bent Creek, 27504, 615-436-3947
Yards: 5895, Par: 72, Holes: 18
Bethania GC, 5801 Tobaccoville Rd., P.O. Bo, Bethania, 27010, 919-924-5226
Yards: 6365, Par: 72, Holes: 18
Black Mountain, 225 W. State St., Black Mountain, 28711, 704-669-2710
Yards: 6087, Par: 71, Holes: 18
Blue Mountain Lodge & CC, Mars Hill, 28754, 704-689-9990
Par: 72, Holes: 18
Bogue Banks GC, Pineknoll Shores, 28662, 919-726-1034 Par: 73, Holes: 18
Boone GC, Highway 321, Boone, 28607, 704-264-8760
Yards: 6400, Par: 71, USGA: 67.0, Holes: 18, Pro: Joe Maples
Booneville GC, Box 339, Booneville, 27011, 919-367-7561
Yards: 3381, Par: 36, Holes: 9
Briarcreek GC, High Shoals, 27077, 704-922-4208
Par: 72, Holes: 18
Brierwood Estates GC, Shallotte, 28459, 919-754-6614
Yards: 6607, Par: 72, Holes: 18, Pro: Benjamin Ward
Brookwood GC, Mills Gap Rd., Arden, 28704, 704-684-6278
Yards: 2834, Par: 35, Holes: 9
Brushy Mtn. GC., Lenoir Rd., Taylorsville, 28681, 704-632-4804
Yards: 6637, Par: 72, Holes: 18
Cape Golf & Racquet Club, Wilmington, 28402, 919-799-3110
Yards: 6700, Par: 72, Holes: 18
Cardinal CC, Rt. 3, Box 350-1, Selma, 27576, 919-284-3647
Yards: 6218, Par: 72, Holes: 18
Carolina Lakes, Hwy. 87, Sanford, 27330, 919-499-5421
Yards: 6337, Par: 70, Holes: 18
Carolina Pines CC, Carolina Pines Blvd., New Bern, 28560, 919-444-1000
Yards: 6955, Par: 71, Holes: 18
Carolina Shores, P.O. Box 205, Calabash, 28459, 919-579-2181
Yards: 6757, Par: 72, Holes: 18

Cashie G&CC, Windsor, 27983, 919-794-4942
Yards: 6193, Par: 72, Holes: 9
Catawba Valley GC, New Highway 70 East, Hickory, 28601, 704-324-6304
Yards: 2100, Par: 31, Holes: 9
Cedar Grove GC, Hillsborough, 27278, 919-732-8397
Par: 71, Holes: 18
Cedarbrook CC, Elkin, 28621, 919-835-2320
Yards: 6841, Par: 72, Holes: 18
Cedarwood GC, Hwy. 51, Charlotte, 28134, 704-542-0206
Yards: 6900, Par: 71, Holes: 18
Chanticleer GC, Hwy. 17, Hampstead, 28443, 919-270-2883
Yards: 6630, Par: 71, Holes: 18
Charlotee GC, 2465 Mecklenburg Ave., Charlotee, 28205
Chatuge Shores, Rt. 2, Myers Chapel Rd., Hayesville, 28904, 704-387-5853
Yards: 6324, Par: 72, Holes: 18
Cherokee Hills, Box 647, Murphy, 28906, 704-837-5853
Yards: 6300, Par: 72, Holes: 18
Cheviot Hills GC, 7301 North Blvd., Raleigh, 27604, 919-876-9920
Yards: 6500, Par: 71, Holes: 18
Confederate Acres GC, Woods Road, Graham, 27253, 919-227-4815
Yards: 6070, Par: 70, Holes: 18
Connestee Falls, Brevard, 28712, 704-885-2005
Yards: 6605, Par: 72, Holes: 18
Corbin Hills GC, Box 964, Salisbury, 28144, 704-636-0672
Yards: 6639, Par: 72, Holes: 18
Crestview GC, Hwy. 18, Ennice, 28623, 919-657-3471
Yards: 5885, Par: 72, Holes: 9
Crooked Creek, Crooked Creek Rd., Hendersonville, 28739, 704-692-2011
Yards: 6586, Par: 71, Holes: 18
Crowders Mountain G&CC, Gastonia, 28052, 704-739-7681
Par: 72, Holes: 18
Crystal Springs GC, Miller Road, Charlotte, 28134, 704-588-2640
Yards: 6356, Par: 71, Holes: 18
Cullasaja Club, Highlands, 28741, 704-526-4104
Yards: 7100, Par: 72, Holes: 18
Cummings Cove, 3000 Cummings Rd., Hendersonville, 28739, 704-891-9412
Yards: 6008, Par: 70, Holes: 18
Cypress Lake GC, Rt. 1, Hope Mills, 28348, 919-483-0359
Yards: 6615, Par: 72, Holes: 18
Dan Valley GC, Route 2, Stoneville, 27048, 919-548-6808
Yards: 3001, Par: 35, Holes: 9
Dawn Acres GC, Hwy. 68, Stokesdale, 27357, 919-643-5397
Yards: 6365, Par: 71, Holes: 18
Denton GC, Rt. 3, Box 235, Denton, 27239, 704-869-3456
Yards: 3100, Par: 36, Holes: 9
Dogwood Valley GC, Box 176, Caroleen, 28019, 704-657-6214
Yards: 2943, Par: 36, Holes: 9
Duck Haven GC, 1202 Eastwood Road, Wilmington, 28403, 919-791-7983
Yards: 6431, Par: 72, Holes: 18
Duck Woods CC, Kitty Hawk, 27949, 919-261-2609
Yards: 6106, Par: 72, Holes: 18
Eagle Crest GC, Rt. 2, Box 145, Garner, 27529, 919-772-0580
Yards: 6253, Par: 71, Holes: 18
Eastwood GC, 4400 The Plaza, Charlotte, 28215, 704-537-7904
Yards: 6083, Par: 71, Holes: 18

Echo Farms CC, 4114 Echo Farms Blvd., Wilmington, 28403, 919-791-9318
Yards: 7023, Par: 72, Holes: 18
Elk River Club, Banner Elk, 28604, 704-898-9773
Yards: 6900, Par: 72, Holes: 18
Fairfield GC, Hwy. 62 East, High Point, 27260, 919-431-2913
Yards: 2845, Par: 27, Holes: 9
Fairfield Harbour GC—Country Club, 750 Broad Creek, New Bern, 28560,
919-638-8011   Yards: 6310, Par: 72, USGA: 71.3, Holes: 18, Pro: Tom Johnson
Fairfield Mountains GC—Apple, Route 1, Lake Lure, 28746, 704-625-9111
Yards: 6297, Par: 72, USGA: 70.5, Holes: 18
Fairfield Mountains GC—Bald Mountain, RTE 1, Lake Lure, 28746,
704-625-9111   Yards: 6125, Par: 72, Holes: 18
Fairwoods-On-Seven, Pinehurst, 28374, 919-295-6144
Yards: 7114, Par: 72, Holes: 18
Forest City Muni GC, Clay Street, Forest City, 28043, 704-245-2474
Yards: 6400, Par: 72, Holes: 18
Forest Hills CC, Box 1599, Cullowhee, 28723, 704-293-5442
Yards: 3035, Par: 35, Holes: 9
Fox Squirrel CC, Boiling Springs Lakes, Southport, 45861, 919-845-2625
Yards: 6762, Par: 72, Holes: 18
Foxwood GC, Rt. 1, Box 382-A, Salisbury, 28144, 704-637-2528
Yards: 6175, Par: 72, Holes: 18
Franklin GC & Lodge, P.O.Box 320, Franklin, 28734, 704-524-2288
Par: 36, Holes: 9
Gallagher Trails GC, Box 10, High Shoals, 28077, 704-922-4208
Yards: 6424, Par: 72, Holes: 18
Gastonia Muni GC, Niblick Drive, Gastonia, 28052, 704-865-1996
Yards: 6474, Par: 71, Holes: 18
Gastonia National GC, 2801 Linwood Road, Gastonia, 28052, 704-866-6945
Yards: 6474, Par: 71, Holes: 18
Gillespie Park GC, 306 E. Florida St., Greensboro, 27406, 919-373-2439
Yards: 3465, Par: 37, Holes: 9
Glen Cannon CC, P.O.Box 1155, Brevard, 28712, 704-884-9160
Yards: 6294, Par: 72, Holes: 18
Glen Oaks G&CC, Spruce Pine, 28777, 704-765-7436
Yards: 6277, Par: 72, Holes: 18
Goldsboro GC, S. Slocumb Street Ext., Goldsboro, 27530, 919-735-0411
Yards: 6728, Par: 72, Holes: 18
Governors Club, Chapel Hill, 27514, 919-968-8500
Yards: 7080, Par: 72, Holes: 18
Grassy Creek, 101 Grassy Creek Rd., Spruce Pine, 28777, 704-765-7436
Yards: 6267, Par: 72, Holes: 18
Green Acres GC—#1, 311 Exit at US 220, Randleman, 27317, 919-498-2247
Yards: 5290, Par: 68, Holes: 18
Green Hills GC, Rt. 5, Box 282, Rocky Mount, 27801, 919-443-7103
Yards: 3070, Par: 36, Holes: 9
Green Meadows GC, Kelly Rd., Mt. Holly, 28120, 704-827-9264
Yards: 5591, Par: 70, Holes: 18
Green Oaks GC, Hamby Branch Rd., Concord, 28025, 704-786-4412
Yards: 6250, Par: 72, Holes: 18
Green Valley GC, Linwood Road, Box 1091, Gastonia, 28052, 704-739-7681
Yards: 6545, Par: 72, Holes: 18
Greenbriar Hills GC, 5002 Old Dowd Road, Charlotte, 28208, 704-392-0538
Yards: 2600, Par: 34, Holes: 9
Greenbrier GC, New Bern, 28560, 919-636-3700
Yards: 6924, Par: 72, Holes: 18

Hampton Heights GC, 1700 Fifth Street, N.E., Hickory, 28601, 704-328-5010
Yards: 6448, Par: 71, Holes: 18
Hemlock GC, Power Dam Rd., Walnut Cove, 27052, 919-591-7934
Yards: 5400, Par: 70, Holes: 18
Henry River GC, Hickory, 28603, 704-294-0380
Par: 70, Holes: 18
High Hills GC, Route 6, Lenoir, 28645, 704-758-1403
Yards: 6000, Par: 71, Holes: 18
High Vista CC, High Vista, 27259, 704-891-8047
Yards: 6715, Par: 72, Holes: 18
Highlands Falls CC, Highlands, 28741, 704-526-4101
Yards: 6111, Par: 70, Holes: 18
Hillcrest CC, 3018 N. Sharon Amity Rd., Charlotte, 28205, 704-536-6472
Yards: 2775, Par: 35, Holes: 9
Hillcrest GC, 2450 Stratford Rd., Winston-Salem, 27103, 919-765-9961
Yards: 6840, Par: 72, Holes: 27
Holly Forest GC, 4000 Hwy. 64 W., West Sapphire, 28774, 704-743-3441
Yards: 6155, Par: 70, Holes: 18
Hound Ears Club, P.O. Box 188, Blowing Rock, 28605, 704-963-4321
Yards: 6150, Par: 72, USGA: 68.3, Holes: 18, Pro: Tom Adams
Hyland Hills GC, 1420 US 1 N, Southern Pines, 28387, 919-692-7581
Yards: 6726, Par: 72, Holes: 18
Indian Trails G & CC, Country Club Hills, Grifton, 28530, 919-524-5485
Yards: 6335, Par: 72, Holes: 18
Indian Valley Muni GC, Indian Valley Drive, Burlington, 27215, 919-584-7871
Yards: 6610, Par: 70, Holes: 18
Jamestown Park GC, 200 East Fork Rd., Jamestown, 27282, 919-454-4912
Yards: 6637, Par: 72, Holes: 18
Jonesville GC, Swan Creek Road, Jonesville, 28642, 919-835-5041
Yards: 2992, Par: 36, Holes: 9
Keer Lake CC, Neathery's Bridge Rd., Henderson, 27536, 919-492-1895
Yards: 6432, Par: 72, Holes: 18
Kenmure, P.O.Box F, Flat Rock, 28731, 704-697-1200
Yards: 6509, Par: 72, Holes: 18
Knollwood Fairways, Midland R.d, Southern Pines, 28387, 919-692-3572
Yards: 2609, Par: 35, Holes: 9
Lake Gaston Estates GC, Box 673, Warrenton, 27589, 919-257-1500
Yards: 3165, Par: 36, Holes: 9
Lake Lure Muni GC, Rt. 1, Box 100, Lake Lure, 28746, 704-725-4472
Yards: 3011, Par: 35, Holes: 9
Lake Royale GC, PO Box 278, Bunn, 27508
Holes: 9
Lake Toxaway GC, Lake Toxaway, 28747, 704-966-4661
Yards: 6100, Par: 72, Holes: 18
Lake-Winds GC, Hwy. 501 North, Rougemont, 27572, 919-471-4653
Yards: 6365, Par: 72, Holes: 18
Lakewood GC, 147 Old Thomasville Rd., High Point, 27260, 919-882-2690
Yards: 683, Par: 27, Holes: 9
Lakewood GC, Rt. 16, Box 200, Statesville, 28677, 704-873-6441
Yards: 6375, Par: 72, Holes: 18
Land 'O Lakes GC, Rt 1 Box 120A, Whiteville, 28472, 919-642-5757
Yards: 6093, Par: 70, USGA: 67.4, Holes: 18, Pro: Tony Mackey
Landfall, Wilmington, 28402, 919-256-6111
Yards: 6997, Par: 72, Holes: 18
Larkhaven GC, Inc., Camp Stewart Road, Charlotte, 28215, 704-545-4693
Yards: 6622, Par: 72, Holes: 18

Laurel Ridge CC, Laurel Ridge, 28644,   704-452-0545
Yards: 6814, Par: 72, Holes: 18
Lenoir GC, Lenoir, 28645,   704-754-5093
Yards: 6223, Par: 71, Holes: 18
Lexington GC, 200 Country Club Blvd., Lexington, 27292,   704-246-2770
Yards: 5803, Par: 70, Holes: 18
Lincolnton CC, Box 541, Lincolnton, 28092,   704-735-1382
Yards: 6211, Par: 72, Holes: 9
Links O Tryon, P.O.Drawer O, Tryon, 28782,   803-468-4995
Yards: 6708, Par: 72, Holes: 18
Linville GC, c/o Eseeola Lodge, P.O. Box 98, Linville, 28646,   704-733-4363
Yards: 6286, Par: 72, USGA: 69.6, Holes: 18, Pro: Burl Dale
Linville Land Harbor GC, Linville, 28646,   704-733-2868
Yards: 5153, Par: 69, Holes: 18
Linville Ridge G&CC, Linville, 28646, 704-898-9741
Yards: 6736, Par: 72, Holes: 18
Linwood Springs GC, Gastonia, 28052,   704-867-1642
Yards: 6332, Par: 72, Holes: 18
Loch Haven GC, Sandhill Rd., Rockingham, 28379,   919-895-3295
Yards: 5800, Par: 71, Holes: 18
Lockwood Golf Links, Holden Beach, 28462,   919-842-5666
Yards: 6801, Par: 72, Holes: 18
Lodge GC (The), Laurinburg, 28352,   919-277-0311
Par: 72, Holes: 18
Long Creek GC, Bethania, 27010,   919-924-5226
Par: 72, Holes: 18
Longleaf CC, Pinehurst, 28374,   919-692-6100
Yards: 5605, Par: 71, Holes: 18
Longview GC, 6321 Ballinger Rd., Greensboro, 27410,   919-294-4018
Yards: 6306, Par: 70, Holes: 18
Lost Diamond Valley GC, 111 High Land Lake Rd., Flat Rock, 28731,
704-692-0143   Yards: 2522, Par: 32, Holes: 9
Lyn-Rock GC, 636 Valley Dr., Eden, 27288,   919-623-6110
Yards: 5860, Par: 70, Holes: 18
Mallard Head GC, Rt. 6, Box 217, Mooresville, 28155,   704-663-0431
Yards: 7200, Par: 72, Holes: 18
Maple Leaf GC, Kernersville, 27284,   919-769-9122
Yards: 6028, Par: 71, Holes: 18
Marion Lake, Hwy. 126, Marion, 28761,   704-652-6232
Yards: 6400, Par: 70, Holes: 18
McCanless GC, Rt. 10, Box 27, Salisbury, 28144,   704-637-1235
Yards: 5519, Par: 70, Holes: 18
Meadow Greens CC, Eden, 27288,   919-623-6381
Yards: 6274, Par: 71, Holes: 18
Midland CC, Pinehurst, 28374,   919-295-3241
Yards: 3093, Par: 36, Holes: 9
Mike Rubish Golf City, Durham-Chapel Hill Blvd., Durham, 27707,
919-489-9655   Yards: 984, Par: 27, Holes: 9
Mill Creek GC, Rt 1, Old Highway 64 West, Franklin, 28734,   704-524-4653
Yards: 6300, Par: 72, Holes: 18
Minnesott CC, Arapaho, 28510,   919-249-0813
Par: 72, Holes: 18
Monroe GC, Hwy. 601 S., Monroe, 28110,   704-289-3041
Yards: 3200, Par: 36, Holes: 9
Monticello GC, Box 457, Brown Summit, 27214,   919-656-3211
Yards: 2845, Par: 35, Holes: 9

Mooresville Muni GC, West Wilson Ave., Mooresville, 28115, 704-663-2539
Yards: 6348, Par: 71, Holes: 18
Morehead City CC, Morehead, 27557, 919-726-4917
Yards: 6383, Par: 72, Holes: 18
Mountain Brook GC, Albemarle, 28001, 704-983-4653
Par: 72, Holes: 18
Mountain Glenn GC, P.O. Box 326, Newland, 28657, 704-733-5809
Yards: 6790, Par: 72, Holes: 18
Mountain View GC, Hwy. 127 South, Hickory, 28601, 704-294-0380
Yards: 6500, Par: 72, Holes: 18
Mountain View GC, Waynesville, 28786, 704-648-1311
Par: 36, Holes: 9
North Shore CC, North Topsail Island, 27864, 919-327-2410
Yards: 6900, Par: 72, Holes: 18
Oak Grove GC, Rt. 2, Box 193, Bladenboro, 28320, 919-648-4239
Yards: 3060, Par: 36, Holes: 9
Oak Hills GC, 4008 Oakdale Rd., Charlotte, 28216, 704-394-2834
Yards: 6274, Par: 72, USGA: 69.6, Holes: 18, Pro: G.W.Picklesimer
Ocean Harbour Golf Links, 10301 Sommerset Drive, Calabash, 28459
Holes: 18
Ocean Isle Beach GC, Rte 6, Box 16, Ocean Isle Beach, 28459, 919-579-2610
Yards: 6130, Par: 72, USGA: 68.9, Holes: 18
Old Fort GC, Golf Course Road, Old Fort, 28762, 704-668-4256
Yards: 3202, Par: 36, Holes: 9
Old Mill G & CC, Rt. 1, Box 18-A, Winton, 27986, 919-358-4671
Yards: 3255, Par: 36, Holes: 9
Olde Point G&CC, Hampstead, 28443, 919-270-2403
Yards: 7002, Par: 72, Holes: 18
Oyster Bay GC, Lakeshore Dr., Sunset Beach, 28459, 803-272-6399
Yards: 6435, Par: 70, USGA: 70.2, Holes: 18
Paradise Valley GC, 10025 N. Tryon St., Charlotte, 28206, 704-596-2874
Yards: 2774, Par: 35, Holes: 9
Paschal GC, Box 571, Wake Forest, 27587, 919-556-5861
Yards: 2575, Par: 35, Holes: 9
Peachtree Hills CC, P.O. Box 267, Spring Hope, 27882, 919-478-5745
Yards: 2718, Par: 35, Holes: 9
Pebble Creek Executive GC, Rt. 8, Hwy. 74E, Indian Trail, 28079, 704-821-7276
Yards: 2251, Par: 54, Holes: 18
Pilot Knob Park, Pilot Mountain, 27041, 919-368-2828
Yards: 6300, Par: 70, Holes: 18
Pine Burr GC, Hwy. 401 South, Lillington, 27546, 919-893-5788
Yards: 6537, Par: 72, Holes: 18
Pine Hollow GC, Hwy. 70-A, Clayton, 27520, 919-553-4554
Yards: 6266, Par: 71, Holes: 18
Pine Knolls GC, 1100 Quail Hollow Rd., Kernersville, 27284, 919-993-5478
Yards: 6310, Par: 72, Holes: 18
Pine Mountain GC, Rt. 1, Box 205, Connelly Springs, 28612, 704-433-4950
Yards: 5100, Par: 68, Holes: 18
Pine Tree GC, 1680 Pine Tree Lane, Kernersville, 27284, 919-993-5598
Yards: 6800, Par: 71, Holes: 18
Pine Wild CC, Pinehurst, 28374, 919-295-5625
Yards: 7350, Par: 71, Holes: 18
Piney Point GC, Norwood, 28128, 704-474-3985
Yards: 6300, Par: 72, Holes: 18
Plantation GC, Reidsville, 27320, 919-342-6191
Yards: 6260, Par: 71, Holes: 18

Plantation GC, 1323 Hwy. 70 West, Clayton, 27520, 919-553-5247
Yards: 3015, Par: 36, Holes: 9
Ponderosa GC, Rt. 3, P.O. Box 573, Stoneville, 27048, 919-573-9025
Yards: 2680, Par: 35, Holes: 9
Ponderosa GC, P.O. Box 208, Olivia, 28368, 919-499-4013
Yards: 6642, Par: 73, Holes: 18
Quail Ridge GC, Sanford, 27330, 919-776-6623
Yards: 6875, Par: 72, Holes: 18
Quaker Meadow GC, Inc., Rt. 10, Box 3, Morganton, 28655, 704-437-2677
Yards: 6702, Par: 71, Holes: 18
Quaker Neck GC, Trenton, 28585, 919-224-5736
Par: 71, Holes: 18
Raleigh Golf Assoc. GC, 1527 Tryon Rd., Raleigh, 27603, 919-772-9987
Yards: 6097, Par: 70, Holes: 18
Reedy Creek GC, Four Oaks, 27524, 919-934-7502
Yards: 6401, Par: 72, Holes: 18
Reems Creek GC, Pink Fox Cove Road, Weaverville, 28787
Holes: 18
Renaissance GC, Charlotte, 28228, 704-357-3375
Yards: 7465, Par: 72, Holes: 18
Reynolds Park GC, Reynolds Park Rd., Winston-Salem, 27101, 919-784-4900
Yards: 6328, Par: 72, Holes: 18
Richmond Pines CC, US 1 N, Rockingham, 28379, 919-895-3279
Yards: 6200, Par: 72, Holes: 18
River Bend GC, Shelby, 28150, 704-482-4286
Yards: 6555, Par: 72, Holes: 18
River Bend Plantation CC, Shoreline Drive, New Bern, 28560, 919-638-2819
Yards: 3436, Par: 36, Holes: 9
River Mont GC, Rt. 1, Box 136, Siloam, 27047, 919-374-2384
Yards: 6013, Par: 72, Holes: 18
Riverside CC, P.O. Box 906, Jacobs Road, Pembroke, 28372, 919-521-2100
Yards: 6200, Par: 72, Holes: 18
Riverside CC, Box 428, Robbins, 27325, 919-464-3686
Yards: 6804, Par: 72, Holes: 18
Riverview GC, Box 8, Pine Hall, 27042, 919-548-6908
Yards: 3309, Par: 35, Holes: 9
Roaring Gap GC, Roaring Gap, 28668, 919-363-2861
Yards: 6400, Par: 72, Holes: 18
Rock Creek CC, Rt. 2, Box 440, N. Wilkesboro, 28659, 919-696-2146
Yards: 2931, Par: 36, Holes: 9
Rolling Hills GC, Sunset Drive, Salisbury, 28144, 704-633-8125
Yards: 6056, Par: 72, Holes: 18
Royster Memorial GC, 901 West Sumter St., Shelby, 28150, 704-482-4996
Yards: 2815, Par: 35, Holes: 9
Ru-Bob Par Three, Old Wilson Road, Rocky Mount, 27801, 919-446-9444
Yards: 1000, Par: 27, Holes: 9
Rutherford Muni GC, Hospital Drive, Rutherfordton, 28139, 704-287-3406
Yards: 3000, Par: 36, Holes: 9
Sandy Ridge GC, 2025 Sandy Ridge Rd., Colfax, 27235, 919-668-0408
Yards: 6000, Par: 72, Holes: 18
Sanford GC, Route 5, Box 678, Sanford, 27330, 919-776-0415
Yards: 6069, Par: 71, Holes: 18
Sapphire Lakes, Sapphire, 28774, 704-966-9200
Yards: 6805, Par: 72, Holes: 18
Scothurst CC, P.O. Box 88, Lumber Bridge, 28357, 919-843-5357
Yards: 6900, Par: 72, Holes: 18

Sea Scape GC, Rt. 158, Box 110, Kitty Hawk, 27949,   919-261-2158
Yards: 6122, Par: 71, Holes: 18
Sea Trails Golf Links, 651 Clubhouse Road, Sunset Beach, 28459
Holes: 18
Seven Devils GC, P.O. Box 2690, Hwy. 105, Boone, 28607,   704-963-6565
Yards: 6240, Par: 71, Holes: 18
Seven Lakes CC, NC Hwy. 211, West End, 27376,   919-673-3442
Yards: 7000, Par: 72, Holes: 18
Shamrock GC, Burlington, 27215,   919-226-7045
Yards: 6416, Par: 72, Holes: 18
Shillelagh GC, Rt. 1, Box 202, Burlington, 27215,   919-449-4882
Yards: 6231, Par: 70, Holes: 18
Silver Creek GC, Swansboro, 28584,   919-393-8058
Yards: 7030, Par: 72, Holes: 18
Sippihaw GC, Inc., Rt. 4, Box 1, Fuquay-Varina, 27526,   919-552-9693
Yards: 6080, Par: 72, Holes: 18
South Brunswick Islands GC, P.O. Box 100, Shallotte, 28459,   919-754-4660
Yards: 6800, Par: 72, Holes: 18
Southern Wayne CC, Box 127, Mt. Olive, 28365,   919-658-4269
Yards: 6100, Par: 71, Holes: 18
Southwick GC, Graham, 27253,   919-227-2582
Yards: 6100, Par: 70, Holes: 18
Stanly County CC, Badin, 28009,   704-422-3683
Yards: 5908, Par: 72, Holes: 18
Star Hill G&CC, Swansboro, 28584,   919-393-8111
Yards: 3003, Par: 36, Holes: 27, Pro: R. T. Burney
Sugar Hollow GC, Banner Elk, 28604,   704-898-9383
Holes: 18
Sugar Mountain GC, Box 69, Banner Elk, 28604,   704-898-4521
Yards: 4000, Par: 64, Holes: 18
Sumner Hills GC, Rt. 3, High Point, 27260,   919-431-1953
Yards: 6013, Par: 72, Holes: 18
Sunset Hills GC, 800 Radio Road, Charlotte, 28216,   704-399-0980
Yards: 6200, Par: 72, Holes: 18
Topsail Greens, Hampstead, 28443,   919-270-4444
Yards: 6492, Par: 72, Holes: 18
Twin Cedars GC, Twin Cedars Rd., Mocksville, 27028,   704-634-5824
Yards: 6623, Par: 71, Holes: 18
Twin Lakes GC, 1706 Curtis Road, Chapel Hill, 27514, 919-933-1024
Yards: 3026, Par: 35, Holes: 9
Twin Oaks GC, Rt. 2, Hilltop Road, Jamestown, 27282,   919-855-5278
Yards: 2300, Par: 54, Holes: 18
Twin Oaks GC, 3250 Twin Oaks Drive, Statesville, 28677,   704-872-3979
Yards: 6368, Par: 72, Holes: 18
Univ. of NC-Finley GC, Finley Golf Club Rd., Chapel Hill, 27515,   919-962-2349
Yards: 6580, Par: 72, Holes: 18
Uwharrie G&CC, Rt. 5, Asheboro, 27203,   919-857-2651
Yards: 6480, Par: 72, Holes: 18
Wake Forest CC, Wake Forest, 27587,   919-556-3416
Yards: 7079, Par: 72, Holes: 18
Warrenton Golf & CC, Box 14B, Rt. 3, Warrenton, 27589,   919-257-9803
Yards: 5774, Par: 72, Holes: 18
Washington Yacht & CC, Rt. 2, Box 177, Washington, 27889,   919-946-3245
Yards: 6711, Par: 72, Holes: 18
Wedgewood gC, Old Stantonsburg Rd., Wilson, 27893,   919-237-4761
Yards: 6358, Par: 72, Holes: 18

Wendell CC, Wendell, 27591, 919-365-7337
Yards: 6142, Par: 71, Holes: 18
Westport GC, 251 Golf Course Dr., Denver, 28037, 704-483-5604
Yards: 6833, Par: 71, Holes: 18
Westwood GC, Andrews Road, Durham, 27705, 919-383-3896
Yards: 890, Par: 27, Holes: 9
Whispering Pines CC—South Co, Whispering Pines, 28327, 919-949-2311
Yards: 6010, Par: 71, Holes: 18
White Lake GC, Elizabethtown, 28337, 919-862-8796
Par: 72, Holes: 18
White Pines CC, Rt. 5, Mt. Airy, 27030, 919-786-6616
Yards: 3500, Par: 36, Holes: 9
Whiteville CC, Whiteville, 28472, 919-642-3623
Yards: 3190, Par: 36, Holes: 9
Wil-Mar GC, Rt. 5, Box 257-F, Raleigh, 27604, 919-266-6305
Yards: 6000, Par: 71, Holes: 18
Wildwood Green GC, Raleigh, 27612, 919-846-8376
Yards: 5512, Par: 70, Holes: 18
Willow Creek GC, Box 1579, Boone, 28607, 704-963-4025
Yards: 3600, Par: 27, Holes: 9
Willow Valley GC, Boone, 28607, 704-963-6551
Yards: 3122, Par: 27, Holes: 9
Wilmington GC, 311 S. Wallace Ave., Wilmington, 28403, 919-791-0558
Yards: 6414, Par: 71, Holes: 18, Pro: Lawrence Cook
Wilshire GC, 1570 Bridgeton Road, Winston-Salem, 27107, 919-788-7016
Yards: 6404, Par: 71, USGA: 67.0, Holes: 18, Pro: George Veach
Winston Lake Park GC, New Walkertown Road, Winston-Salem, 27105,
919-727-9659 Yards: 6374, Par: 71, Holes: 18
Wolf Creek GC, 1222 Fillman Dr., Reidsville, 27320, 919-349-7660
Yards: 3100, Par: 35, Holes: 9
Wolf Laurel Resort, Rt. 3, Mars Hill, 28754, 704-689-4111
Yards: 6252, Par: 72, Holes: 18
Woodbridge Golf Links, Kings Mountain, 28086, 704-482-0353
Yards: 6708, Par: 72, Holes: 18
Woodlake GC, P.O.Box 648, Vass, 28394, 919-245-4031
Yards: 7003, Par: 72, USGA: 73.4, Holes: 18
Zebulon CC, Route 3, Box 118, Zebulon, 27597, 919-269-8311
Yards: 5646, Par: 72, Holes: 18

Aasen GC, Minot, 58701   *North Dakota*
Holes: 9
Apple Creek CC, Bismarck, 58501, 701-223-5955
Holes: 18
Apple Grove GC, RR 5, Box 412, Minot, 58701, 701-852-5460
USGA: 55.3, Holes: 9, Pro: Ardis Aasen
Ashley CC, P. O. Box 127, Ashley, 58413, 701-288-9566
Yards: 4398, USGA: 63.9, Holes: 9, Pro: Ralph Grams
Beaver Valley GC, ℅ Reuben Kautz, P.O. Box 85, Wishek, 58495, 701-452-9249
Holes: 9, Pro: Lorren Henke
Beulah Muni GC, Box 844, Beulah, 58523, 701-873-2929
Yards: 5864, Par: 70, USGA: 66.7, Holes: 9, Pro: Ray Simms
Birchwood, Route 1, Box 74, Bottineau, 58318, 701-263-4283
Yards: 2354, Par: 33, USGA: 61.5, Holes: 9, Pro: D. Bergstrom
Bois De Sioux GC, N. 4th and 13th Ave., Fargo, 58075, 701-642-3673
Yards: 6551, Par: 72, USGA: 70.3, Holes: 18, Pro: Mark Holm

Bottineau CC, Bottineau, 58318,   701-228-3857
Holes: 9
Cando GC, Cando, 58324,   701-968-3813
Yards: 5474, Par: 70, Holes: 9, Pro: Emerson Neuman
Carrington GC, Southeast of City, Carrington, 58421,   701-652-2601
Yards: 5700, Par: 72, USGA: 65.8, Holes: 9, Pro: Leonard Opp
Cavalier CC, Cavalier, 58220,   701-265-4506
Yards: 5380, Par: 72, USGA: 64.7, Holes: 9, Pro: Roger Erickson
Columbus, Box 25, Columbus, 58727,   701-939-4005
Holes: 9, Pro: Wiley Post
Cooperstown Swimming Pool, Cooperstown, 58425,   701-797-2137
Holes: 9
Crosby CC, Crosby, 58730,   701-965-6157
Holes: 9
Crossroads Golf Assoc., c/o Mike L. Halpern, 107 South M, Glen Ullin, 58631,
701-348-3678   Yards: 2998, Par: 72, USGA: 68.0, Holes: 9, Pro: Mike L. Halpern
Drake GC, Drake, 58736
Holes: 9
Drayton GC, North Main St., P.O. Box 280, Drayton, 58225,   701-454-6547
Yards: 4768, Par: 68, USGA: 61.3, Holes: 9, Pro: Kelly Dakken
Edgewater CC, Hwy. 23 West, P. O. Box 131, New Town, 58763,   701-627-9407
Yards: 6320, Par: 72, USGA: 69.4, Holes: 9, Pro: Jack Smith
Edgewood Men's Golf Assoc., North Elm St., Box 1845, Fargo, 58107,
701-232-2824   Yards: 6045, Par: 71, USGA: 66.6, Holes: 18, Pro: Dave Kingsrud
El Zagel Par 3 GC, Fargo, 58102,   701-232-8156
Holes: 9
Elgin GC, Elgin, 58533
Yards: 5565, Par: 68, USGA: 64.9, Holes: 9
Ellendale CC, Ellendale, 58432,   701-349-4292
Yards: 5578, Par: 72, USGA: 64.9, Holes: 9, Pro: Dan Diemert
Enderlin GC, Enderlin, 58027,   701-437-2369
Holes: 9
Fair Oaks GC, Grafton, 58237,   701-352-3956
Par: 72, USGA: 65.8, Holes: 9, Pro: Ray Morgan
Fargo CC, Fargo, 58102,   701-237-9122
Holes: 18
Fessenden GC, P. O. Box 602, Fessenden, 58438,   701-547-9598
Yards: 2732, Par: 70, USGA: 64.3, Holes: 9, Pro: Charles Kunz
Forman GC, Box 307, Forman, 58032,   701-724-9347
Yards: 6178, Par: 72, USGA: 67.5, Holes: 9, Pro: Larry Bartz
Gackle CC, Box 354, Gackle, 58442,   701-485-3540
Yards: 3096, Par: 72, USGA: 68.1, Holes: 9, Pro: Mark Lehr
Garden Gate GC, Dunseith, 58329
Holes: 9
Garrison CC, Box 729, Garrison, 58540,   701-337-5420
Par: 72, USGA: 67.2, Pro: Wes Cumings
Gerald Schroeder Memorial Park, Harvey, 58341
Holes: 9
Grand Forks GC, Country Rd. 6, Grand Forks, 58201,   701-772-4831
Yards: 6524, Par: 72, USGA: 70.7, Holes: 18, Pro: J.D. Duval
Green Goose GC, Northwood, 58267,   701-587-5373
Holes: 9
Heart River GC, Southwest of City, Box 1245, Dickinson, 58601,   701-225-9412
Yards: 6444, Par: 72, USGA: 70.7, Holes: 18, Pro: Rod Stecher
Hillsboro GC, Hillsboro, 58045,   701-436-5556
Holes: 9

Jamestown CC, Jamestown, 58401, 701-252-5521
Holes: 9
Jamestown Hillcrest, Jamestown, 58401, 701-252-4320 Holes: 9
Kenmare CC, Box 397, Kenmare, 58746, 701-385-4093
Yards: 5096, Par: 66, USGA: 63.3, Holes: 9, Pro: Gary Hagen
Kulm City Park, Kulm, 58456
Holes: 9
Lakewood Town & CC, Devils Lake, 58301, 701-662-2408
Holes: 9
Lamoure Memorial GC, LaMoure, 58271, 701-825-6845
Holes: 9, Pro: Dallas Johnson
Langdon CC, Langdon, 58249, 701-256-5938
Yards: 6014, Par: 72, USGA: 68.0, Holes: 9, Pro: Scott Stewart
Leeds GC, Leeds, 58346, 701-446-2858
Holes: 9
Leonard GC, Box 398, Leonard, 58251, 701-645-2491
Yards: 6016, Par: 72, USGA: 67.9, Holes: 9, Pro: C. N. Richards
Lincoln Park GC, Elks Drive, P.O. Box 248, Grand Forks, 58201, 701-775-4871
Yards: 5950, Par: 71, USGA: 66.3, Holes: 18, Pro: Paul O'Leary
Linton CC, P.O. Box 698, Linton, 58522, 701-254-4603
Yards: 6093, Par: 36, USGA: 68.2, Holes: 9, Pro: S.J.Schumacher
Lisbon Bissell GC, Rt. #1, P.O. Box 30, Lisbon, 58054, 701-683-4510
Yards: 6028, Par: 72, USGA: 68.0, Holes: 9, Pro: Ken Kaspari
Mandan GC, 1002 7th St. SW, P.O. Box 721, Mandan, 58554, 701-667-3272
Yards: 5648, Par: 70, USGA: 65.7, Holes: 9, Pro: Larry Souther
Maple River GC, P. O. Box 662, West Fargo, 58078, 701-282-5415
Yards: 6356, Par: 72, USGA: 69.8, Holes: 9, Pro: Duane Siverson
Westhope CC, Box 248, Westhope, 58793, 701-245-6553
Yards: 5566, Par: 70, USGA: 65.0, Holes: 9, Pro: Lois Rosendahl
Mayville GC, West Midway, Mayville, 58257, 701-786-3659
USGA: 67.7, Holes: 9, Pro: Mike Bakken
McVille GC, McVille, 58254
Minot Air Force Base, Minot, 58701, 701-723-1110
Holes: 9
Minot GC, 1 Minot Country Club, Minot, 58722
Mohall CC, Mohall, 58761, 701-756-6948
Holes: 9
Mott GC, P.O. Box 216, Mott, 58646, 701-824-2277
Yards: 6022, Par: 72, USGA: 67.8, Holes: 9, Pro: Ron Benson
New Town CC, New Town, 58763, 701-627-9407
Holes: 9
Oakes GC, Oakes, 58474, 701-742-2405
Holes: 9
Oxbow CC, Hickson, 58044
Painted Woods GC, Highway 83, Box 609, Washburn, 58577, 701-462-8480
Yards: 5526, Par: 72, USGA: 65.3, Holes: 9, Pro: Brad Larson
Park River City Park, Park River, 58270
Holes: 9
Pembina GC, Pembina, 58271
Holes: 9
Prairiewood GC, Fargo, 58102, 701-232-1445
Holes: 9
Rolette CC, Rolette, 58366, 701-246-3644
Holes: 9

Rolla CC, Box 26, Rolla, 58367,   701-477-6202
Yards: 6000, Par: 72, USGA: 66.8, Holes: 9, Pro: Doug Mongeon
Rugby GC, Rugby, 58368,   701-776-6917
Holes: 9
Sandager Park, Lisbon, 58054
Holes: 9
Seeman Park, Linton, 58552
Holes: 9
Souris Valley Golf Shop, Minot, 58701,   701-839-1819
Holes: 18
Stanley GC, Box 1002, Stanley, 58784,   701-628-2135
Par: 72, USGA: 67.2, Holes: 9, Pro: Al Aune
Steele GC, Steele, 58482
USGA: 60.3, Holes: 9
Tioga G & CC, NW of City, P.O. Box 651, Tioga, 58852,   701-664-9442
Yards: 6220, Par: 72, USGA: 66.5, Holes: 9, Pro: Ted Blikre
Tom O'Leary GC, Box 2063, Bismarck, 58502,   701-223-9919
Par: 70, USGA: 66.5, Holes: 9, Pro: Floyd Keimele
Underwood GC, Underwood, 58576
Par: 72, Holes: 9, Pro: Rick Wilke
Velva GC—18 Hole Course, Velva, 58790
Holes: 18
Walhalla CC, P.O. Box 122, Walhalla, 58282,   701-549-2357
USGA: 66.3, Holes: 9, Pro: George Kopf
Watford City GC, East of City, Bos 53, Watford City, 58854,   701-842-2074
Yards: 5588, Par: 72, USGA: 67.1, Holes: 9, Pro: Tim Taylor
Williston CC, Williston, 58801,   701-572-6500
Holes: 9
Williston Municipal GC, P.O. Box 1153, Williston, 58801,   701-774-1321
Yards: 5922, Par: 72, USGA: 67.2, Holes: 9, Pro: Al Bervig

Acacia CC, 26899 Cedar Road, Cleveland, 44122,   216-442-2686   *Ohio*
Holes: 18, Pro: Randy Padavick
Adams County CC, West Union, 45693,   513-544-8021
Par: 33, Holes: 9
Alliance CC, 25 E. Milton St., Alliance, 44601
Andover GC, Andover, 44003,   216-203-9930
Par: 35, Holes: 9
Apple Hills GC, 8233 Seasons Road, Streetsboro, 44248, 216-673-0512
Holes: 9, Pro: Carson Heiner
Aqua Marine CC, 216 Miller Road, Avon Lake, 44012,   216-933-2000
Holes: 18, Pro: Joe Kristoski
Arrowhead CC, 3435 Orchard Hill Dr. NW, N. Canton, 44720
Arrowhead Lakes GC, 5314 Mulhauser Road, Hamilton, 45011
Holes: 9
Ash Hills GC, 2544 Niles-Cortland Rod, Cortland, 44410,   216-637-3841
Par: 35, Holes: 9
Ashtabula CC, 4338-48 Lake Road W., Ashtabula, 44004,   216-964-7952
Holes: 18, Pro: Deae Nicholson
Astrohurst CC, 7000 Dunham Road, Halton Hills, 44146,   216-439-3636
Holes: 18, Pro: Paul Tirpak
Auburn Springs CC, 10001 Stafford Road, Chagrin Falls, 44022,   216-543-4449
Holes: 18
Auglaize CC, State Route 111 S, Defiance, 43512,   419-393-2211
Yards: 6189, Par: 72, USGA: 69.1, Holes: 18, Pro: John Grimes

Aurora CC, Hudson Road, Aurora, 44202, 216-562-5300
Holes: 18, Pro: Donald Haftman
Avon Dale GC, 38490 Detroit Road, Avon, 44011, 216-934-4398
Holes: 18
Avon Oaks CC, 32300 Detroit Road, Avon, 44011, 216-871-4638
Holes: 18, Pro: Don Antenucci
Baird's Wayside GC, Findlay, 45840, 419-423-5089
Par: 35, Holes: 9
Baker's Acres GC, 594 Northwest Avenue, Tallmedge, 44278, 216-928-8728
Holes: 18
Barberton Brookside CC, 3727 Golf Course Drive, Barberton, 44203,
216-825-4539 Holes: 18
Bath GC, 531 N Madina Line Road, Bath, 44256, 216-666-9981
Holes: 18
Beaver Creek Par-3 GC, 12360 St. Rt. 7, Lisbon, 44432, 216-385-5315
Holes: 9
Beaver Creek Meadows GC, 12774 St. Rt. 7, Lisbon, 44432, 216-385-3020
Holes: 18
Bedford Trails GC, 713 Bedford Road, Cotsville, 44436, 216-536-2234
Holes: 9
Beechmont CC, 29600 Chagrin Blvd, Cleveland, 44122, 216-292-6687
Holes: 18, Pro: Robert Bourne
Beechwood GC, Arcanum, 45304, 513-678-4422
Par: 72, Holes: 18
Belmont CC, 29601 Bates Rd., Perrysburg, 43551
USGA: 69.1, Pro: John Perrotti
Berkshire Hills CC, PO Box 611, Chesterland, 44026, 216-729-9511
Holes: 18, Pro: Ray Petty
Big Bend GC, Uhrichsville, 44683, 614-922-1766
Par: 66, Holes: 18
Big Springs GC, 1101 Barlow Road, Hudson, 44236, 216-655-2267
Holes: 18, Pro: Ralph Obert
Big Walnut GC, Sunbury, 43074, 614-548-5189
Par: 32, Holes: 9
Blackbrook CC, 8900 Lake Shore Blvd., Mentor, 44060, 216-951-0010
Holes: 18, Pro: John J. Austin
Blackhawk GC, 8830 Dustin Rd., Columbus, 43021, 614-965-1042
Yards: 6013, Par: 71, USGA: 68.3, Holes: 18
Bluffton GC, 8575 N. Dixie Hwy., Bluffton, 45817, 419-358-6230
Yards: 6285, Par: 72, USGA: 67.7, Holes: 18, Pro: Larry Shute
Bob-O-Link GC, 2399 Applegrove Rd. NW, N. Canton, 44720
Bob-O-Link GC, 4141 Center Road, Avon, 44011, 216-835-0676
Holes: 27
Boston Hills GC, 105 E. Hines Hill Road, Hudson, 44236, 216-650-0934
Par: 71, Holes: 18
Bowling Green State Univ GC, Mercer & Poe Roads, Bowling Green, 43402
USGA: 69.0, Pro:
Bowling Green CC, 851 Country Club Dr., Bowling Green, 43402, 419-352-5546
Par: 35, USGA: 32.8, Holes: 9, Pro: Jim Edgeworth
Brandywine CC, 6904 Salisbury Rd., Maumee, 43537, 419-866-3444
Yards: 6636, Par: 71, USGA: 70.3, Holes: 27, Pro: Gene Boni
Brentwood GC, 3056 Grafton Road, Grafton, 44044, 216-322-9254
Holes: 18
Briar Hill GC, Millersburg, 44654, 216-674-3921
Par: 36, Holes: 9

Briardale Greens GC, 585 East 222, Euclid, 44123, 216-289-8574
Holes: 18
Briarwood GC, 2737 Edgerton Road, Broadview Heights, 44147, 216-237-5271
Holes: 27
Bridgeview GC, 2738 Agler Rd., Columbus, 43224, 614-471-1565
Yards: 5252, Par: 72, USGA: 66.7, Holes: 18
Bristolwood GC, PO Box 149, Bristolville, 44402, 216-889-3771
Par: 36, Holes: 9
Bronzewood GC, Rt. 2, Kinsman-Pymatuning Rd., Kinsman, 44428,
216-876-5300   Holes: 18
Brook Ledge GC, 1621 Bailey Road, Cuhahoga Falls, 44221, 216-923-1627
Holes: 18
Brookside CC, 1800 Canton Ave., NW, Canton, 44706
Brookside GC, 1299 Olivesburg Rd., Ashland, 44906
Brunswick Hills GC, PO Box 187, Brunswick, 44212, 216-225-7370
Par: 72, Holes: 18
Buckeye Hills CC, Greenfield, 45123, 513-981-4136
Par: 70, Holes: 18
Buckrun GC, 29742 Buck Road, Salem, 44460, 216-549-3359
Holes: 9
Bunker Hill GC, 3068 Pearl Road, Medina, 44256, 216-722-4174
Holes: 18
Burning Tree GC, Newark, 43055, 614-522-3464
Par: 36, Holes: 9
Buttermilk Falls GC, Georgetown, 45121, 513-378-9970
Par: 35, Holes: 9
Candywood GC, 765 Scoville Road, Vienna, 44473, 216-399-4217
Holes: 18
Canfield CC, 9399 Leffingwell Road, Canfield, 44406, 216-533-3053
Holes: 18
Canterbury GC, 22000 S. Woodland Rd., Cleveland, 44122
Holes: 18
Carlisle GC, 39708 Slife Road, Grafton, 44044, 216-458-8011
Par: 71, Holes: 18
Casement Club, The, 349 Casement Avenue, Box 150, Painesville, 44077,
216-354-4443   Holes: 9
Catawba Island Club, 4235 E. Beach Club Rd., Port Clinton, 43452
USGA: 67.6, Pro: Chuck Redmond
Chagrin Valley CC, 4700 S O N Center Road, Chagrin Falls, 44022,
216-248-4314
Holes: 18, Pro: James Chapman
Champion Links GC, 4891 Clover Crest Drive, Warren, 44483, 216-847-0383
Par: 72, Holes: 18
Chapel Hills GC, 3381 Austinsburg Road, Ashtabula, 44004
Holes: 18
Chardon Lakes GC, 470 South Street, Chardon, 44024, 216-286-9938
Holes: 18, Pro: Don Tincher
Cherokee Hills GC, 5740 Center Road, Valley City, 44280, 216-225-6122
Par: 70, Holes: 18
Cherry Ridge GC, Box 27, Elyria, 44035, 216-324-3713
Holes: 9
Chestnut Hill GC, 6548 Rte. 44, Ravena, 44266, 216-296-4384
Holes: 9, Pro: Roger Stevens
Chippewa GC, 23550 W. State Rte. 579, Curtice, 43402
USGA: 69.6, Pro: Bill Brown

Chippewa GC, 12147 Shank Road, Doylestown, 44230,   216-658-6126
Par: 72, Holes: 18
Clearview GC, PO Box 20196, E. Canton, 44730
Cliffside GC, Gallipolis, 45631,   614-446-4653
Par: 72, Holes: 18
Clover Crest GC, 4891 Clover Crest Drive, Warren, 44483
Colonial Hills GC, 10985 Harding Hwy., Harrod, 45850,   419-649-3350
Yards: 6200, Par: 72, USGA: 68.8, Holes: 18, Pro: John Yerick
Columbia Hills CC, 16200 E. River Road, Columbia Station, 44028,
216-236-8277 Holes: 18, Pro: John H. Grimm
Congress Lake Club, Hartville, Warren, 43632
Conneaut Shores GC, 726 Whitney Road, Conneaut, 44030,   216-593-5403
Par: 36, Holes: 9
Coolridge GC, 591 Benhol Blvd., Mansfield, 44905,   419-522-1452
Holes: 9
Copeland Hills GC, 41703 Metz Road, Columbiana, 44408,   216-482-3221
Holes: 18
Copley Green GC, 2266 Jacoby Road, Copley, 44321
Country Acres GC, Route 4, Ottawa, 45875,   419-532-3434
Par: 71, USGA: 69.6, Holes: 18, Pro: James Miller
Country Club of Ashland, 1333 S. Center St., Ashland, 44805
Country Club of Hudson, 2155 Middleton Road, Hudson, 44236,   216-650-1192
Holes: 18, Pro: James Camp
Country Club, The, 2825 Lander Road, Pepper Pike Village, 44124,
216-831-9252   Holes: 18, Pro: Bob Keller
Countryside GC, 1421 Struthers Coitsville Road, Lowellville, 44436,
216-755-0016   Holes: 18
Cranberry Hills GC, 8005 S. R. 100, New Washington, 44854,   419-492-2192
Par: 35, Holes: 9
Creekwood GC, 6372 Mills Creek Lane, North Ridgeville, 44039,   216-748-3188
Par: 72, Holes: 18
Crooked Tree GC, 3595 Mason-Montgomery Rd., Mason, 45040
Holes: 18
Deer Creek GC, 7691 E. Liberty St. SE, Hubbard, 44425,   216-534-1395
Holes: 9
Deer Creek GC, 20635 Waterloo Rd., Mt. Sterling, 43143,   614-869-3088
Deer Lake GC, 6300 Lake Road West, Geneva, 44041,   216-466-8450
Par: 72, Holes: 18
Deer Track GC, 9488 Leavitt Road, Elyria, 44035,   216-986-5881
Holes: 18, Pro: Tony Dulio
Delphos CC, P.O. Box 227, Delphos, 45833
USGA: 69.8, Pro: Don Cook
Detwiler GC, 4001 North Summit St., Toledo, 43611
USGA: 69.0, Pro: Rob Ross
Dick Williams Memorial GC, Sodom Hutching Road, Vienna, 44473,
216-394-2900   Holes: 9
Dogwood GC, S. Newton Falls Road, Diamond, 44412,   216-538-2305
Holes: 18
Donnybrook GC, 3265 Schotten Road, Hubbard, 44425,   216-534-1872
Holes: 9
Doplon Park GC, 1800 Station, Columbia Station, 44028
Doughton GC, 2600 Seifert-Lewis Rd, Hubbard, 44425,   216-568-7005
Holes: 18
Eagles Nest GC, Goshen, 45122,   513-722-1241
Par: 71, Holes: 18

East Liverpool CC, PO Box 16, East Liverpool, 43920,   216-385-0624
Holes: 9, Pro: Dick Schwartz
East Palestine CC, Rt. 170, East Palestine, 44413,   216-426-9761
Holes: 9
Echo Valley GC, RFD #1, Box 325, Wellington, 44090,   216-647-2065
Holes: 9
Edgewater GC, 6900 Market Ave N, North Canton, 44721
Elks GC, 451 Danville Pk., Hillsboro, 45133,   513-393-2940
Yards: 3240, Par: 72, USGA: 70.0, Holes: 9, Pro: Karl Roller
Elks GC, Wilmington, 45177,   513-382-9049
Par: 36, Holes: 9
Elm GC, The, Athens, 45701,   614-592-2877
Par: 35, Holes: 9
Elms CC, Rte. 92, Massillon, 44646,   216-833-2668
Par: 71, Holes: 27
Elyria CC, 41625 Oberlin Road, Elyria, 44035,   216-322-6391
Holes: 18
Emerald Valley CC, 4397 Leevitt Road, Lorain, 44053,   216-282-5663
Par: 35, Holes: 9
Emerald Woods GC, Boone & Snell Roads, Columbia Station, 44028,
216-236-8940   Holes: 36
Erie Shores GC, 7298 Lake Road East, North Madison, 44057,   216-428-3164
Holes: 18, Pro: Tom Weiss
Estate Club, The, Lancaster, 43130,   614-654-4444
Par: 71, Holes: 18
Fairlawn CC, 200 North Wheaton Road, Akron, 44313,   216-864-2121
Holes: 18
Fairview GC, Findlay, 45840,   419-422-5035
Par: 35, Holes: 9
Fairway Pines, 731 Bacon Road, Painesville, 44077
Holes: 18
Findlay CC, P.O. Box 1126, Findlay, 45839
USGA: 70.4, Pro: Tom Herzan
Firestone CC, 452 Warner Road, Akron, 44319,   216-644-8441
Holes: 36
Five Waters GC, Midvale, 44653,   614-922-9019
Par: 64, Holes: 18
Flying B GC, 13223 W Middletown Road, Salem, 44460,   216-337-8138
Holes: 18
Fonderlac CC, 1140 Paulin Road, Poland, 44514, 216-549-3995
Holes: 18, Pro: John Scotford
Forest Hills GC, Glouster, 45732,   614-767-4623
Par: 35, Holes: 9
Forest Hills CC, 12882 Diagonal Road, La Grange, 44050,   216-323-2829
Holes: 18
Forest Hills GC, Heath, 43056,   614-323-GOLF
Par: 36, Holes: 9
Forest Hills GC, PO Box 7016, Mansfield, 44905,   419-589-3331
Par: 57, Holes: 18
Forest Hills GC, Chesapeak, 45619,   614-867-4445
Par: 35, Holes: 9
Forest Oaks GC, RR 1, Southington, 44470,   216-898-2852
Par: 70, Holes: 27
Fostoryia CC, P.O. Box 68, Fostoria, 44830
USGA: 69.4, Pro: David Sanford

Fowler's Mill GC, 13095 Rockhaven Road, Chesterland, 44026, 216-286-9545
Holes: 27, Pro: Lamott Smith
Fox Den Fairways GC, 2770 Call Road, Stow, 44224, 216-673-3443
Holes: 18, Pro: Thomas McKinney
Franklin GC, Franklin, 45005, 513-746-0310
Par: 35, Holes: 9
Fremont CC, 2340 E. State St., Fremont, 43420, 419-332-2646
Yards: 6374, Par: 71, USGA: 70.2, Holes: 18, Pro: Chris Aseltine
Friendly Meadows GC, Hamersville, 45130, 513-379-1050
Par: 72, Holes: 18
Front 9 GC, 1667 East Bailey Road, Cuyehaga Falls, 44221, 216-923-1627
Holes: 9, Pro: Betty Ashton
Gahanna Muni GC, Gahanna, 43230, 614-471-0579
Par: 35, Holes: 9
Geauga Hidden Valley CC, 17261 Thompson Road, Thompson, 44086,
216-298-3912 Holes: 9
Geneva on the Lake GC, Golf Avenue, Geneva On The Lake, 44041,
216-466-8797 Holes: 18, Pro: Charles Webb
Gleneagles GC, 1667 E. Bailey Rd, Cuyahoga Falls, 44221
Glengarry CC, 8665 Hill Ave., Holland, 43528
USGA: 70.0, Pro: Steven Chandler
Glenwood GC, W Main St., Ashland, 44805
Grandview G&CC, PO Box 361, Middlefield, 44062, 216-834-1824
Par: 70, Holes: 18
Grantwood Recreation Center GC, 38855 Aurora Road, Solon, 44139,
216-248-4646 Holes: 18, Pro: Robert Garrett
Granville GC, 527 Newark Rd., Columbus, 43023
Great Trails GC, Minera, 44657
Green Hills GC, 1105 Tallmadge Rd, Kent, 44240, 216-678-2601
Holes: 9
Green Ridge GC, 29150 Ridge Road, Wickliffe, 44092, 216-943-0007
Holes: 9, Pro: James Bond
Green Valley GC, 88088 Cleveland, New Philadelphia, 44663, 216-364-2812
Par: 72, Holes: 18
Green Valley GC, Zanesville, 43701, 614-452-7105
Par: 59, Holes: 18
Grove City GC, Grove City, 43123, 614-875-2497
Par: 70, Holes: 18
Harbor Hills CC, Hebron, 43025, 614-928-3596
Par: 36, Holes: 9
Hawthorne Valley CC, 27840 Aurora Road, Solon, 44139, 216-232-9129
Holes: 18, Pro: Leo Zampedro
Heather Downs CC, 3910 Heather Downs Blvd., Toledo, 43614
USGA: 69.5, Pro: David Horne
Hedgewood GC, 29800 Center Ridge Road, Westlake, 44145, 216-835-4440
Holes: 18
Hemlock Springs GC, 4654 Cold Springs Road, Geneva, 44041, 216-466-4044
Holes: 18
Henry Stambaugh GC, 202 Gypsy Lane, Youngstown, 44505, 216-743-5370
Holes: 9, Pro: Tom Ciminelli
Hiawatha GC, Mt. Vernon, 43050, 614-393-2886
Par: 72, Holes: 18
Hickory Flat Greens GC, West Lafayette, 43845, 614-545-7796
Par: 72, Holes: 18
Hickory Grove GC, Rt. 294 Box 26, Harpster, 43323, 614-496-2631
Yards: 6351, Par: 72, USGA: 68.9, Holes: 18, Pro: Milt Boucher

Hickory Grove GC, PO Box 8, Jefferson, 44047, 216-576-3776
Par: 72, Holes: 18
Hickory Hills GC, State Rte. 18 W., Hicksville, 43526, 419-542-6400
Yards: 3047, Par: 71, USGA: 66.2, Holes: 9, Pro: Dick Leazier
Hickory Nut GC, 23601 Royalton Road, Columbia Station, 44028, 216-236-8008
Holes: 18
Hidden Lake GC, Tipp City, 45371, 513-667-8880
Par: 72, Holes: 18
Hidden Valley GC, Delaware, 43015, 614-363-1739
Par: 28, Holes: 9
Highland Meadows GC, P.O. Box 197, Sylvania, 43560
USGA: 70.8, Pro: Dave Samaritoni
Highland Park GC, 3550 Greek Rd., Cleveland, 44114, 216-751-4361
Holes: 36, Pro: Ed Dalton
Hillcrest GC, 800 Bigelow Ave., Findlay, 45840
Hillcrest CC, Montpelier, 43543, 419-485-3368
Par: 71, Holes: 18
Hilliard Lakes CC, 31666 Hilliard Blvd, Westlake, 44145, 216-871-9578
Holes: 18
Hillsboro Elks GC, 451 Danville Pike, Cincinnati, 45133
Hilltop GC, Manchester, 45144, 513-549-2904
Par: 36, Holes: 9
Hol-Hi GC, 81 Vaughn Road, Akron, 44319, 216-644-9815
Holes: 18
Hubbard GC, 6322 W. Liberty Street S.E., Hubbard, 44425, 216-534-9026
Holes: 18, Pro: David Coller
Hueston Woods Lodge GC, Brown Rd., Cincinnati, 45056
Hyde-A-Way GC, Route 1, Beloit, 44609, 216-584-2200
Holes: 9
Indian Hollow GC, 16525 Indian Hollow Road, Grafton, 44044, 216-355-5344
Holes: 18
Inverness GC, 4601 Dorr St., Toledo, 43615
USGA: 71.5, Pro: Don Perne
Ironton CC, Ironton, 453638, 614-532-2511
Par: 70, Holes: 18
Ironwood GC, 1015 W. Leggett St., Wauseon, 43567
USGA: 70.0, Pro: Dale Holmes
Ironwood GC, 445 State Road, Hinckley, 44233, 216-278-7171
Holes: 18, Pro: Frank Disanto
J. E. Good Park GC, 530 Nome Avenue, Akron, 44320, 216-864-0020
Holes: 18
Jamaica Run GC, 8781 Jamaica Road, Germantown, 45327
Holes: 18
Jaycee Public GC, Zanesville, 43701, 614-452-1860
Par: 71, Holes: 18
Jaymar GC, Pomeroy, 45769, 614-992-2342
Par: 34, Holes: 9
Juli-Fe View CC, PO Box 308, Orrville, 44667, 216-684-1010
Holes: 18, Pro: Carl D. Rehm
Kalu GC, Canfield, 44406
Kent State University GC, 2346 State Route 59, Kent, 44240, 216-672-2500
Par: 69, Holes: 18
Maplecrest GC, 219 Tallmadge Road, Kent, 44240, 216-673-2722
Holes: 18, Pro: Jim Franklin
Ketenring CC, 211 Carpenter Rd., Defiance, 43512
USGA: 67.6, Pro: Donald Ott

Keys GC, Bogart and Bass, Sandusky, 44610, 419-433-5585
Par: 36, Holes: 9
Kirtland CC, 39438 Kirtland Road, Willoughby, 44094, 216-951-8422
Holes: 18, Pro: Joe Talley
Knollbrook GC, 8421 Richman Road, Lodi, 44254, 216-948-1482
Par: 35, Holes: 9
L C Boles Memorial GC, College of Wooster, Wooster, 44691, 216-264-9851
Par: 36, Holes: 9
Lake Forest CC, Atterbury Blvd., Hudson, 44236, 216-656-3804
Holes: 18, Pro: David Morgan
Lake Front GC, 14500 South Avenue Ext., Columbiana, 44408, 216-482-3466
Par: 35, Holes: 9
Lake View GC, E. Maple, Hartville, 44632
Lakeland GC, St. Paris, 43072, 513-663-4707
Par: 36, Holes: 9
Lakeside GC, PO Box 127, Lake Milton, 44429, 216-547-2797
Holes: 18, Pro: Al Blazek
Lakewood CC, 2613 Bradley Road, Westlake, 44145, 216-871-5338
Holes: 18, Pro: Jerry Boykin
Lakewood GC, Georgetown, 45121, 513-378-4200
Par: 68, Holes: 18
Larch Tree GC, Trottwood, 45426, 513-854-1951
Par: 72, Holes: 18
Leaning Tree GC, PO Box 106, 3770 Broadview Rd, Richfield, 44286,
216-659-4900   Holes: 18
Lee Win GC, 12688 Salem-Warren Road, Salem, 44460, 216-337-8033
Holes: 18
Legend Lake GC, 11135 Auburn Road, Chardon, 44024, 216-285-3110
Holes: 18
Leisure Time Rec. Center GC, 4561 Darrow Road, Stow, 44224, 216-688-4162
Holes: 9, Pro: Philip Baker
Licking Springs Trout & GC, Newark, 43055, 614-366-2770
Par: 72, Holes: 18
Links at Renissence, 26376 John Road, Olmstead Township, 44138,
216-235-0501   Holes: 18, Pro: Bryan Lagton
Links GC, 26111 John Road, Olmstead Township, 44138, 216-235-0501
Holes: 18, Pro: Bryan Lagton
Little Apple GC, 366 South Main Street, Bellville, 44813, 419-886-4400
Holes: 18
Little Scioto CC, Wheelersburg, 45694, 614-776-9976
Par: 36, Holes: 9
Locust Hills GC, Springfield, 45504, 513-265-5152
Par: 72, Holes: 27
Lorain CC, 5445 Beaver Crest Drive, Lorain, 44053, 216-282-9106
Holes: 18
Lost Creek CC, P.O. Box 297, Lima, 45802
USGA: 68.3, Pro: Kim Boehlke
Lost Nation GC, 38890 Hodgeon Road, Willoughby, 44094, 216-953-4280
Holes: 18
Loudon Meadows GC, 11072 Columbus Ave. West, Fostoria, 44830,
419-435-8500
Yards: 5980, Par: 71, USGA: 66.7, Holes: 18, Pro: Donald Karns
Loyal Oak GC, 2989 S Cleve-mass Road, Barberton, 44283, 216-825-9815
Holes: 27, Pro: Arthur Gruber
Lyon's Den GC, Rtes 93 & 21, Canal Fulton, 44614

Madison CC, 6131 Chapel Road, North Madison, 44057, 216-428-2641
Holes: 18, Pro: Thomas Fussaro
Mahoning CC, 700 E. Liberty Street, Girard, 44420, 216-545-2519
Par: 70, Holes: 18
Manakiki GC, 35501 Eddy Road, Willoughby, 44094, 216-942-2500
Holes: 18
Maple Ridge GC, 8921 Center Road, Austinburg, 44010, 216-969-1369
Holes: 18
Marion CC, P.O. Box 374, Marion, 43302
USGA: 70.1, Pro: Ross Carley
Mastick Woods GC, 4101 Fulton Parkway, Cleveland, 44144, 216-267-5626
Holes: 9
Mayfair CC, 2229 Raber Road, Uniontown, 44685, 216-699-2209
Holes: 36, Pro: Dan Simmons
Mayfield CC, 1545 Sheridan Road, South Euclid, 44121, 216-382-3958
Holes: 18, Pro: Charles E. Wood
Meadowbrook GC, 1 Pheasant Run Drive, La Grange, 44050, 216-458-5035
Holes: 9
Meadowlake GC, 1211 38th St. NE, Canton, 44714
Meadowood GC, 29694 Center Ridge Rd., Westlake, 44145
Meander GC, 6985 Mill Creek Blvd, Youngstown, 44512, 216-538-3933
Holes: 9
Medina CC, 5588 Wedgewood Road, Medina, 44256, 216-725-6621
Holes: 27
Mid Pines GC, 39300 Aurora, Solon, 44139, 216-248-0282
Holes: 9
Midway GC, 9488 Levitt Rd., Elyria, 44036
Mills Creek GC, Sandusky, 44870, 419-625-3993
Par: 36, Holes: 9
Millstone Hills GC, Euclid Road, New London, 44851, 419-929-6477
Par: 72, Holes: 18
Mogadore CC, Mogadore, 44260, 216-628-2611
Par: 71, Holes: 18
Mohawk GC, P.O. Box 506, Tiffin, 44883
USGA: 71.1, Pro: Ken Corliss
Mohican Hills GC, Jeromesville, 44840, 419-368-3303
Par: 72, Holes: 18
Mount Gilead GC, P.O. Box 64, Mount Gilead, 43338
USGA: 66.8, Pro: Roger Hensel
NCR GC, 4435 Dogwood Tr., Kettering, 45429
Neumann GC, 7215 Bridgetown Rd., Cincinnati, 45248
New Garden GC, 30975 ST 172, East Rochester, 44625, 216-223-1773
Par: 35, Holes: 9
North Olmstead GC, 5840 Canterbury Road, North Olmstead, 44070,
216-777-0220   Holes: 9
Northmoor CC, Celina, 45822, 419-394-4896
Par: 70, Holes: 18
Northwood GC, 635 Champion St E, Warren, 44483, 216-847-7608
Par: 36, Holes: 9
Norwalk Elks GC, Norwalk, 44857, 419-668-8535
Par: 35, Holes: 9
Oak Grove GC, 14901 German Church Road, Atwater, 44201, 216-823-0290
Par: 71, Holes: 18
Oak Harbor Club, Oak Harbor, 43449, 419-898-1493
Par: 72, Holes: 18

Oak Knolls GC, 6700 State Route 43, Kent, 44240, 216-673-6713
Holes: 36, Pro: Jon Megenek
Oakwood CC, 1516 Warreneville Ctr. Road, Cleveland, 44121, 216-291-8679
Holes: 18, Pro: George Bigham
Oaks GC, The, Lima, 45802, 419-999-2586
Par: 72, Holes: 18
Oberlin GC, 200 Pyle Road, Oberlin, 44074, 216-774-9221
Holes: 18, Pro: Jack Durban
Ohio Prestwick CC, 2220 Raber Rd., Uniontown, 44685
Old Avalon GC, 9794 E. Market St., Warren, 44484
Orchard Hills CC, P.O. Box 608, Bryan, 43506
USGA: 69.1, Pro: John Lindert
Ottawa Park GC, 1 Walden Pond, Toledo, 43606, 419-472-2059
Yards: 5478, Par: 71, USGA: 65.4, Holes: 18, Pro: Rob Ross
Oxbow GC, Belpre, 45714, 614-423-6771
Par: 71, Holes: 18
P & J Par 3 GC, 6349 Mahonig Avenue, Warren, 44481, 216-847-0104
Par: 27, Holes: 9
Painesville CC, 84 Golf Drive, Painesville, 44077, 216-354-3469
Holes: 18
Paradise Lake CC, 1900 Randolph Road, Suffield, 44260, 216-628-1313
Holes: 18, Pro: John Rainieri
Parkview GC, 320 Som Center Road, Cleveland, 44143, 216-442-8560
Holes: 18
Pebble Creek GC, 4300 Algire Road, Lexington, 44904, 419-884-3434
Holes: 18
Penn Terra GC, Lewisburg, 45338, 513-962-4515
Par: 35, Holes: 9
Pepper Pike Club GC, 2800 S O M Center Road, Cleveland, 44124,
216-831-9466   Holes: 18, Pro: Carol Alaqua
Pepperidge GC, 6825 North Ridge Road, North Madison, 44057, 216-428-1398
Holes: 9
Pheasant Run GC, 1 Pheasant Run Dr., Elyria, 44964
Pike Run GC, Ottawa, 45875, 419-523-4669
Par: 36, Holes: 9
Pine Brook GC, 1316 N. Durkee Road, Grafton, 44044, 216-748-2939
Par: 70, Holes: 18
Pine Meadows GC, 15518 S.R. 62, Salem, 44460, 216-537-2626
Holes: 9
Pine Ridge CC, 30601 Ridge Road, Wickliffe, 44092, 216-944-6596
Holes: 18, Pro: Tom Haas
Pine Valley GC, 469 Reimer Rd Rd 2, Wadsworth, 44281, 216-335-3375
Holes: 18, Pro: Steve Stajcer
Pleasant Hill GC, Middletown, 45042, 513-539-7220
Par: 71, Holes: 18
Pleasant Hill GC, 12626 Butternut Road, Chardon, 44024, 216-286-9961
Holes: 27
Pleasant Valley CC, 3830 Hamilton Road, Medina, 44256, 216-725-5770
Holes: 18
Pleasant Valley GC, Payne, 45880, 419-263-2037
Par: 36, Holes: 9
Pleasant View GC, 14605 Louisville St., NE, Paris, 44669
Plum Brook CC, 3712 Galloway rd., Sandusky, 44870
USGA: 69.2, Pro: Robert Carver
Portage CC, 140 North Portage Path, Akron, 44303, 216-836-4994
Holes: 18, Pro: Rod Johnston

Possum Run Golf & Swim Club, 1313 S. Main Street, Mansfield, 44907, 419-756-1026   Par: 70, Holes: 18
Powderhorn GC, PO Box 487, Madison, 44057,   216-428-5951
Par: 70, Holes: 18
Prestwick G&CC, 4096 Cadwallader, Cortland, 44410,   216-637-7901
Par: 36, Holes: 9
Punderson GC, 11755 Kinsman, Newbury, 44065,   216-564-5465
Yards: 6600, Par: 72, USGA: 72.0, Holes: 18, Pro: John King
Raccoon Valley GC, Granville, 43023,   614-587-0921
Par: 72, Holes: 18
Rawiga CC, 10353 Rawiga Road, Seville, 44273,   216-336-2220
Holes: 18, Pro: Don Olney
Red Oaks CC, Bloomingdale, 43910,   614-944-1400
Par: 36, Holes: 9
Riceland GC, RFD 2, Orrville, 44667,   216-683-1876
Par: 71, Holes: 18
Ridge Top GC, 7441 Tower Road, Medina, 44256,   216-725-5500
Holes: 18, Pro: Bob Emery
Ridgewood GC, 6505 Ridge Road, Parma, 44129,   216-888-1057
Holes: 18
Riverbend GC, Miamiburg, 45342,   513-859-8121
Par: 72, Holes: 18
Riverby Hills GC, 16571 W. River Rd., Bowling Green, 43402
USGA: 70.3, Pro: Dan Connelly
Riverside GC, Sprague and Columbia Rd., Olmsted Falls, 44138,   216-235-8006
Holes: 18
Riverside GC, Sardis, 43946,   614-483-1536
Par: 72, Holes: 27
Riverview GC, 3903 St. Rt. #82 SW, Newton Falls, 44444,   216-898-5674
Holes: 18
Robins' Ridge GC, Senecaville, 43780,   614-685-6029
Par: 68, Holes: 18
Rocky Fork Golf & Tennis, Hillsboro, 45133,   513-393-9004
Par: 71, Holes: 18
Rocky River GC, Metroparks, 4101 Fulton Pkwy., Cleveland, 44144,
216-331-1070   Holes: 27
Rolling Acres GC, Nova, 44859,   419-652-3160
Par: 72, Holes: 18
Rolling Acres Golf & Swim, 7814 Infirmary Road, Ravenna, 44266,
216-296-4103
Holes: 9
Rolling Greens GC, 15900 Mayfield Road, Huntsburg, 44046,   216-636-5171
Par: 71, Holes: 18
Rolling Greens GC, 7656 Lutz NW, Canal Fulton, 44614
Root 62 GC, RD No. 1, Salem, 44460
Rossmont GC, 3730 Medina Road, Akron, 44313,   216-666-8109
Holes: 18, Pro: Michael Bishop
Round Lake GC, Rte 179, Lakeville, 44638
Royal Crest GC, 23310 Royalton Road, Columbia Station, 44028,   216-236-5644
Holes: 18
Running Fox GC, Chillocothe, 45601,   614-775-9955
Par: 72, Holes: 18
Rustic Hills CC, 5399 River Styx Road, Medina, 44256,   216-725-4281
Holes: 9
Rustic Woods GC, 18000 Station Road, Columbia Station, 44028,   216-236-8234
Holes: 18

Saint Bernard GC, 5364 W. Streetsboro Road, West Richfield, 44286, 216-659-3451   Holes: 18, Pro: Dan Kaczor
Saint Denis GC, 18660 Chardon Road, Chardon, 44024,   216-285-2183
Holes: 18
Saint Mikes GC, Defiance, 43512,   419-497-4675
Par: 36, Holes: 9
Salem GC, 1957 S. Lincoln, Salem, 44460,   216-332-0111
Holes: 18, Pro: Jerome Szwedko
Salem Hills GC, Salem, 44460,   216-337-8033
Par: 70, Holes: 18
Salt Fork GC, Salt Fork State Park P.O. Box, Cambridge, 43725,   614-432-7185
Yards: 6200, Par: 71, USGA: 69.0, Holes: 18, Pro: Peter Asman
Sawmill Creek GC, 2401 Cleveland Rd.,P.O.Box 358, Huron, 44839,
419-433-3800 Holes: 18
Sebring CC, Box 2 North Benton, Sebring, 44449,   216-584-9231
Holes: 9, Pro: Frank Loftus
Seneca GC, 1901 Edgerton Road, Broadview Heights, 44147,   216-526-2111
Holes: 36, Pro: Rene Powell
Seneca Hills GC, Tiffin, 44883,   419-447-9446
Par: 70, Holes: 18
Sequoia GC, Mentor Aveneu, Willoughby, 44094,   216-946-3154
Holes: 9, Pro: Tom Daniels
Sevakeen GC, 29742 Buck Rd., Salem, 44460
Seven Hills CC, 11700 William Penn Ave, Hartville, 44832
Shaker Heights CC, 3300 Courtland Blvd., Cleveland, 44122,   216-991-3660
Holes: 18
Shamrock GC, 4436 Powell Road, Powell, 43065
Holes: 18
Sharon GC, Route 94, Box 6, Sharon Center, 44274,   216-253-4533
Holes: 18, Pro: Henry Friede
Shawnee GC, Star Route 125, P.O.Box 98, Portsmouth, 45662,   614-858-6681
Par: 71, Holes: 18
Shawnee GC, PO Box 516, Kent, 44278,   216-673-2111
Par: 71, Holes: 18
Shawnee Hills GC, Metroparks, 4101 Fulton Ave, Cleveland, 44144,
216-232-7184   Holes: 18, Pro: Joseph Wehmer
Spring Hills GC, 6571 Cleve-mass Road, Clinton, 44216,   216-825-2439
Holes: 18
Shawnee Country Club, The, 1700 Shawnee Rd., Lima, 45805
USGA: 68.3, Pro: Bill Hughes
Shelby CC, 3885 Laser Road, Shelby, 44875,   419-347-1824
Holes: 18, Pro: D. Weisenberger
Silver Lake CC, 1325 Graham Rd., Cuyahoga Falls, 44224,   216-688-6816
Holes: 18, Pro: Donald Spears
Skyland GC, 2085 Center Rd., Hinckley, 44233,   216-225-5698
Holes: 18
Skyland Pines GC, 3550 Columbus Rd NE, Canton, 44719
Sleepy Hollow GC, Clyde, 43410,   419-547-0770
Par: 71, Holes: 18
Sleepy Hollow GC, 9445 Brecksville Rd., Brecksville, 44141,   216-526-4285
Holes: 18, Pro: Charlie Sifford
Sleepy Hollow CC, PO Box 2848, Alliance, 44601,   216-821-8865
Holes: 18, Pro: Deon L. Good
South Toledo GC, 3915 Heatherdowns Blvd., Toledo, 43614,   419-385-4678
Yards: 6191, Par: 71, USGA: 67.0, Holes: 18, Pro: Greg A. Fish

Spring Lakes GC, 2745 Grandview Road, Lake Milton, 44429, 216-654-4100
Holes: 18
Spring Valley GC, 5851 Breezehill Rd SW, Canton, 44626
Spring Valley CC, PO Box 1168, Elyria, 44035, 216-777-6451
Holes: 18, Pro: M. Caronchi
Springvale CC, 5871 Canterbury Road, North Olmsted, 44070, 216-777-4415
Holes: 18
Spruce Tree Village GC, 5852 Cleveland Road, Wooster, 44691, 216-345-8010
Holes: 9
Spuyten Duyval GC, 9501 W. Central Ave., Sylvania, 43560
USGA: 66.3, Pro: Bruce Denno
Squaw Creek CC, 761 Youngstown-Kingsville Rd S, Vienna, 44473,
216-539-5008 Holes: 18
Stillwater Ridge GC, West Milton, 45383, 513-698-5806
Par: 36, Holes: 9
Stillwater Valley GC, Versailles, 45380, 513-526-3041
Par: 36, Holes: 9
Sugar Bush GC, 11186 North Street SR 88, Garrettsville, 44231, 216-527-4202
Par: 72, Holes: 18
Sugar Creek GC, P.O. Box 24, Elmore, 43416, 419-862-2551
Par: 71, USGA: 64.9, Holes: 18, Pro: George Rodewalt
Sugar Isle GC, New Carlisle, 45344, 513-845-8699
Par: 72, Holes: 18
Sugarcreek GC, Sugar Creek, 44681, 216-852-9989
Par: 72, Holes: 18
Sun Valley CC, 2678 Sand Rd, Port Clinton, 43452
Sunnyhill GC, 3734 Sunnybrook Road, Kent, 44240, 216-673-1785
Par: 71, Holes: 27
Sweetbriar GC, 750 Jaycox Road, Avon Lake, 44012, 216-933-9001
Holes: 27, Pro: Mark Wise
Switzerland of Ohio GC, Beallsville, 43716, 614-926-9985
Par: 35, Holes: 9
Sycamore Hills GC, 14 Sycamore Drive, Norwalk, 44857, 419-668-8460
Par: 36, Holes: 9
Sycamore Hills GC, 3728 W. Hayes Ave., Fremont, 43420, 419-332-5716
Yards: 6220, Par: 70, USGA: 66.4, Holes: 18, Pro: Douglas Michael
Sycamore Spring GC, 11492 County Rd. 25, Arlington, 45814, 419-365-5109
Yards: 3257, Par: 36, USGA: 67.6, Holes: 9, Pro: Mike Hicks
Sycamore Valley GC, 1651 Akron-Peninsula Rd., Akron, 44313, 216-928-3329
Holes: 9, Pro: David Springer
Sylviania CC, 5201 Corey Rd., Sylvania, 43560
USGA: 70.3, Pro: Douglas Nelson
Table Rock GC, Centerburg, 43011, 614-625-6859
Par: 72, Holes: 18
Tamarac GC, 599 Stevic Rd., Lima, 45805, 419-331-2951
Par: 72, USGA: 68.5, Holes: 27, Pro: John Pielemeier
Tamaron CC, 2162 Alexis Rd., Toledo, 43613
USGA: 66.1, Pro: Brad Pietras
Tamer Win G&CC, 2940 Niles Cortland Road, Cortland, 44410, 216-637-2881
Par: 71, Holes: 18
Tanglewood CC, 8745 Tanglewood Trail, Chagrin Falls, 44022, 216-543-7010
Holes: 18, Pro: Jim Dale
Tannenhauf GC, 11411 McCallum Ave., Alliance, 44601, 216-823-4402
Yards: 6364, Par: 72, USGA: 70.2, Holes: 18, Pro: J. Williamson
Thornwood GC, Fremont, 43420, 419-334-2451
Par: 34, Holes: 9

Thunder Hill CC, Griswold Road, Madison, 44957, 216-298-3474
Holes: 18
Thunderbird Hills GC, Rte 13, Huron, 44839
Tippacanoe CC, PO Box 86, Canfield, 44406, 216-758-2380
Holes: 18, Pro: George BElline
Toledo CC, The, P.O. Box 14409, Toledo, 43614
USGA: 68.8, Pro: Don Kotnik
Trumbull CC, 600 Golf Drive N.E., Warren, 44483, 216-372-5127
Holes: 18, Pro: Bob Woodfin
Turkeyfoot Lake GC, 294 W. Turkeyfoot Lake Rd., Akron, 44319, 216-644-5971
Yards: 6070, Par: 72, USGA: 68.8, Holes: 27
Twin Lakes GC, 2700 Austinburg Road, Mansfield, 44004, 419-529-3777
Par: 71, Holes: 18
Twin Lakes CC, 1519 Overlook, Kent, 44240, 216-673-3515
Holes: 9, Pro: Tim Starett
Twin Lakes GC, Bellevue, 44811, 419-483-2842
Par: 36, Holes: 9
Twin Oaks Par 3, 2700 Austinburg Road, Ashtabula, 44004, 216-998-2423
Par: 27, Holes: 9
Twin Springs GC, 32985 St. Rt. 172, Lisbon, 44432, 216-222-2335
Holes: 9
Upper Lansdowne Golf Links, Ashville, 43103, 614-093-2989
Par: 36, Holes: 9
Valleaire CC, 6969 Boston Road, Hinckley, 44233, 216-237-9191
Holes: 18
Valley GC, 41784 Cherry Fork Rd., Columbiana, 44408, 216-482-9464
Holes: 9
Valley View GC, Lancaster, 43130, 614-687-1112
Par: 71, Holes: 18
Valley View GC, 1212 Cuyahoga Street, Akron, 44313, 216-928-9419
Holes: 27
Valley View GC, State Rte 598, Crestline, 44827
Valley Vista GC, Bainbridge, 45612, 614-634-2221
Par: 36, Holes: 9
Valleywood GC, Airport Hwy., Swanton, 43558, 000-826-3991
Yards: 6058, Par: 71, USGA: 67.4, Holes: 18, Pro: Tracy Grant
Vermillion CC, Vermillion, 44089, 216-967-3492
Par: 36, Holes: 9
Veterans Memorial Park GC, Kenton, 43326, 419-674-4573
Par: 35, Holes: 9
Vienna Short Holes GC, 900 Youngstown-Kingsville Rd, Vienna, 44473,
216-856-2245   Par: 27, Holes: 9, Pro: Jack Hutchinson
Village Green Muni GC, PO Box 253, North Kingsville, 44068, 216-224-0931
Par: 71, Holes: 18
Vink's GC, Mentor, 44060
Vista View Village & GC, Nashport, 43830, 614-453-4758
Par: 71, Holes: 18
Walden Golf & Tennis Club, 700 Bissell Road, Aurora, 44202, 216-562-6966
Holes: 18, Pro: D. Antenucci
Wapakoneta CC, P.O. Box 2004, Wapakoneta, 45895
USGA: 64.2, Pro:
Waverly GC, Waverly, 45690, 614-947-7422
Par: 36, Holes: 9
West Gate GC, 3781 State Route 5, Newton Falls, 44444, 216-872-7984
Par: 29, Holes: 9

West's Mogadore CC, 197 N. Cleveland Avenue, Mogadore, 44260, 216-628-2611   Holes: 18, Pro: Dennis Pifer
Westbrook CC, 1098 Springmill Street, Mansfield, 44906,   419-747-2556   Holes: 18, Pro: Don Priest
Western Reserve G&CC, PO Box 128, Sharon Center, 44274,   216-239-9906   Holes: 18, Pro: Bernard Steward
Westfield CC, County Road 97, Westfield Center, 44251,   216-887-0391   Holes: 36
Westlake City Meadowood GC, 29694 Center Ridge Road, Westlake, 44145, 216-835-6440   Holes: 9
Westville Lake CC, 858 Case Rd 2, Beloit, 44609,   216-537-4042   Holes: 9
Westwood CC, 22625 Detroit Road, Rocky River, 44116,   216-331-2120   Holes: 18
Weymouth Valley GC, 3946 Weymouth Road, Medina, 44256,   216-725-6297   Holes: 18
Whisky Run G&CC, Quaker City, 43773,   614-679-2082   Par: 36, Holes: 9
Whispering Pines GC, 947 East Park Avenue, Columbiana, 44408, 216-482-3733   Holes: 9
White Oak CC, Sardinia, 45171,   513-444-2888   Par: 35, Holes: 9
Wildfire GC, New Concord, 43762,   614-826-7606   Par: 66, Holes: 18
Wilkshire GC, St Rte 212, Bolivar, 44612
Willard CC, RD 3 Rt 162, Willard, 44890,   419-935-0252   Holes: 9, Pro: Bill Pfefferle
Willoughby GC, 38886 Mentor Avenue, Willoughby, 44094,   216-942-4051   Holes: 9
Willow Bend GC, 115 Hospital Dr., Van Wert, 45891   USGA: 65.0, Pro:
Willow Creek GC, 15905 Darrow Road, Vermilion, 44089
Willow Run GC, Reynoldsburg, 43068,   614-927-1932   Par: 71, Holes: 18
Windmill Lakes GC, 6544 State Route 14, Ravena, 44266,   216-297-0440   Holes: 18, Pro: Herb Page
Windwood Hollow GC, Edon, 43518,   419-272-3310   Par: 36, Holes: 9
Windy Hill GC, PO Box 418, Conneaut, 44030,   216-594-5251 Holes: 18
Windy Hills GC, Rockbridge, 43149,   614-385-7886   Par: 36, Holes: 9
Woody Ridge GC, 6362 State Route 598, Shelby, 44675,   419-347-1588   Par: 72, Holes: 18
Wooster CC, 1251 Oak Hill Rd., Wooster, 44691,   216-263-1988   Holes: 18, Pro: Gary Helshhans
Wyandot GC, Centerburg, 43011,   614-625-5370   Par: 72, Holes: 18
Yankee Run GC, 7610 Warren Sharon Road, Brookfield, 44403,   216-448-8096   Holes: 18
Youngstown CC, 1402 Country Club Lane, Youngstown, 44505,   216-759-1040   Holes: 18, Pro: William S. Cox
Zoar Village GC, RD 2, Dover, 44622

Adams GC, 6001 Tuxedo Blvd., Bartlesville, 74003,   918-333-2045   *Oklahoma*   Holes: 18

Al & Em GC, 607 W. Osage, Marlow, 73055,   405-658-3021
Par: 71, Holes: 18
Altus AFB GC, Bldg 35, Altus, 73523
Alva Golf & CC, P.O. Box 42, Alva, 73717
Yards: 6668, Par: 72, USGA: 68.0, Holes: 18
Arrowhead State Park & Resort, 18 mi. S of I-40 on US-69, Canadian, 74425,
918-339-2769   Par: 72, Holes: 18
Atoka GC, 1 mi. N on US-75, Atoka, 74525,   405-889-7171
Holes: 9
Beaver Pioneer Park CC, P.O. Box 1214, Beaver, 73932
Bermuda Hills GC, Rt 1-Box 116A, Warner, 74469,   918-463-5118
Yards: 6800, Par: 72, Holes: 18, Pro: Ken Pruitt
Blackwell CC, Rt 2-Box 95, Blackwell, 74613,   405-363-1228
Holes: 9
Boiling Springs GC, Rt 2-Box 204-1A, Woodward, 73801,   405-256-1206
Holes: 18
Brent Bruehl GC, 1400 Airport Road, Purcell, 73080,   405-527-5114
Holes: 9
Bristow Golf & CC, 6th and Main, Bristow, 74010, 918-367-3343
Yards: 6052, Par: 72, Holes: 18
Broadmoore GC, 500 Willow Pine Dr., Moore, 73160, 405-794-1529
Holes: 18
Brookside GC, 9016 Shields, Oklahoma City, 73160,   405-632-9666
Holes: 9
Cedar Creek GC, P.O. Box 218, Broken Bow, 74728,   405-494-6456
Yards: 3270, Par: 36, USGA: 70.0, Holes: 9
Cedar Lake GC, Bldg # 4746, Fort Sill, 73503
Cedar Ridge GC, 10302 S. Garnett Rd., Broken Arrow, 74011
Chandler Municipal GC, 1 mi N., then 1 mi W, Chandler, 73834,   405-258-2947
Holes: 9
Cherokee Grove GC, Rt 1-Box 136, Grove, 74344,   918-786-9852
Yards: 6480, Par: 72, USGA: 69.1, Holes: 9, Pro: Vince Bizik
Cherry Springs GC, PO Box 1718, Tahlequah, 74464
Holes: 18
Chickasha CC, P.O. Box 1264, Chickasha, 73018
Choctaw CC, Rt 1—Box 144, Poteau, 74953,   918-647-3488
Yards: 6174, Par: 71, USGA: 68.4, Holes: 9, Pro: Aaron Ridenour
Pryor Municipal GC, Star Rt 4-Box 115, Pryor, 74361,   918-825-3056
Holes: 18
Clinton Municipal GC, Rt 4-Box 336, Clinton, 73601,   405-323-5958
Holes: 9
Comanche GC, 1800 Country Club Rd., Comanche, 73529,   405-439-8879
Yards: 2986, Par: 36, Holes: 9
Cordell Golf and CC, 1½ mi W, Cordell, 73632,   405-832-2975
Holes: 9
Coves, Rt 2-Box 142, Afton, 74331
Cushing CC, 4 Mi E on 9th St., Cushing, 74023,   918-225-9068
Yards: 6292, Par: 70, USGA: 69.5, Holes: 18, Pro: Johnny Johnson
Dietrich Memorial GC, E on Country Club Rd., Anadarko, 73005,
405-247-5075 Holes: 9
Doby Springs GC, 8 mi W. 1½ mi N on US-64, Buffalo, 73834,   405-735-2654
Holes: 9
Dornick Hills CC, P.O. Box 1787, Ardmore, 73401
Drumright CC, 1 mi W on Sh-33, Drumright, 74030,   918-352-9424
Yards: 3035, Par: 36, Holes: 9, Pro: Howard Morphew

Durant CC, P.O. Box 811, Durant, 74701, 405-924-0622
Yards: 5302, Par: 71, USGA: 67.8, Holes: 18
El Reno CC, P.O. Box 98, El Reno, 73036, 405-262-5240
Par: 35, Holes: 9
Elk City Golf & CC, 2 Mi So. on Hwy 6, Elk City, 73648, 000-225-3556
Yards: 5639, Par: 71, Holes: 18
Elks Golf & CC, P.O. Box 1178, Shawnee, 74801
Elks Golf & CC, P.O. Box 520, Duncan, 73533
Yards: 6116, Par: 72, USGA: 69.1, Holes: 18, Pro: Don Atchison
Elks Golf & CC, P.O. Box 775, Altus, 73521
Yards: 6041, Par: 72, Holes: 18
Fairview Lakeside CC, 108 Woodcreek, Fairview, 73737, 405-227-3225
Par: 35, Holes: 9
Falconhead Resort & CC, 605 Falconhead Dr., Burneyville, 73430,
405-276-9284 Yards: 6448, Par: 72, USGA: 71.0, Holes: 18, Pro: Rick Harrington
Firelake GC, Rt 5-Box 151, Shawnee, 74801, 405-275-4471
Holes: 18
Fort Cobb GC, 4 mi N on SH-9, Fort Cobb, 73038, 405-643-2398
Yards: 6344, Par: 70, Holes: 18, Pro: Jim Pasby
Fort Still GC, P.O. Box 3128, Fort Still, 73503
Fountainhead GC, HC 60-452, Checotah, 74426, 918-689-3209
Yards: 6489, Par: 72, USGA: 69.2, Holes: 18
Frederick CC, Drawer "E", Frederick, 73542
Yards: 3146, Par: 36, Holes: 9
Gil Morgan GC, End of 7th St., Wewoka, 74884, 405-257-3292
Holes: 9
Golf Club of OKLA, The, 20400 E. 141 St-So, Broken Arrow, 74013
Greens GC, S. Williams Circle, Burns Flat, 73624, 405-562-3961
Holes: 9
Greens Golf & CC, 13100 Green Valley Dr., Oklahoma City, 73120
Guthrie Golf & CC, P.O. Box 1315, Guthrie, 73044
Haskell County Recreation Club, Country Club East, Stigler, 74462,
918-867-8884 Holes: 9
Hennessey Golf & CC, P.O. Box 66, Hennessey, 73742
Yards: 6093, Par: 72, Holes: 18
Henryetta CC, P.O. Box 597, Henryetta, 74437, 918-652-8664
Holes: 9
Heritage Hills GC, 1 mi W of SH-88 from Will Roge, Claremore, 74017,
918-341-0055 Holes: 18
Hillcrest CC, P.O. Box 637, Bartlesville, 74003
Hobart CC, P.O. Box 891, Hobart, 73651
Hugo CC, Rt 2, Hugo, 74342, 405-326-6549
Par: 35, Holes: 9
Idabel CC, Rt. 3, Box 36, Idabel, 74745, 405-326-6130
Yards: 3035, Par: 35, Holes: 9, Pro: T. J. Eidson
Indian Springs CC, 16006 E. 131st, Broken Arrow, 74011
Jimmie Austin GC, Seminole Municipal Park, Seminole, 74868, 405-382-3365
Par: 71, Holes: 18
Kah-Wah-Z CC, 2 Mi E on SH-18, Fairfax, 74637, 918-642-3221
Yards: 2987, Par: 37, Holes: 9
Keystone GC, Cleveland, 74020
Kicking Bird GC, 1600 E. Danforth, Edmond, 73034, 405-341-5350
Yards: 5852, Par: 70, USGA: 68.1, Holes: 18, Pro: Steve Ball
Kingfisher Muni GC, 723 S. 8th St., Kingfisher, 73750, 405-375-3941
Holes: 9

La Fortune Park GC, 5501 S. Yale, Tulsa, 74135, 918-496-2822
Yards: 6484, Par: 72, USGA: 70.9, Holes: 18, Pro: Jerry Jones
Lake Murray GC, 7 mi S on US-77, Ardmore, 73402, 405-223-6613
Yards: 2780, Par: 35, Holes: 9
Lakeside CC, 1 mi N, 3 mi W, Longdale, 73755, 405-227-3225
Holes: 9
Lakeside GC, 9500 S. Eastern, Moore, 73160, 405-799-5051
Holes: 9
Lakeside GC, 3 mi N on US-177, Stillwater, 74075, 405-372-9610
Holes: 18
Lakeside Park GC, 211 East Texas, Walters, 73752, 405-875-2703
Par: 36, Holes: 9
Lakewood GC, Ada, 74820, 405-332-5151
Par: 35, Holes: 9
Latimer Country GC, Rt 2-Box 136, Wilburton, 74578, 918-465-9954
Yards: 2980, Par: 35, Holes: 9, Pro: Mel Richardson
Laverne Golf & CC, 1 mi S and 1 mi W off US-283, Laverne, 73848,
405-921-5528 Holes: 9
Lawton CC, 4601 W. Gore, Lawton, 73505
Lawton GC, S. 11th St. and King Blvd., Lawton, 73502, 405-353-4493
Par: 72, Holes: 18
Lew Wentz GC, E. on Lake Road, Ponca City, 74601, 405-762-5167
Yards: 6354, Par: 71, Holes: 18, Pro: Ron Locke
Lincoln Park GC—East Course, 4001 NE Grand Blvd., Oklahoma City, 73111,
405-424-1421 Yards: 6508, Par: 70, Holes: 18
Lindsay Muni GC, 611 SE 2nd, Lindsay, 73052, 405-756-3611
Yards: 6554, Par: 72, Holes: 18
McAlester CC, P.O. Box 1122, McAlester, 74502
Meadowlake GC, 1 mi. S. on Rupe St., Enid, 73703, 405-234-3080
Yards: 6412, Par: 71, USGA: 68.8, Holes: 18, Pro: S.C.Kealiher
Miami CC, 1915 Cleveland, Miami, 74354
Mohawk Park GC—Pecan Valley, 41st North & Park Road, Tulsa, 74115,
918-425-6871 Yards: 6300, Par: 70, USGA: 66.0, Holes: 18, Pro: Arthur Bennett
Muskogee CC, 2400 N. Country Club Dr., Muskogee, 74403
Weatern Hills GC, RTE 1, Muskogee, 74441
Nowata CC, 517 W. Delaware, Nowata, 74048, 918-273-1353
Yards: 2679, Par: 33, Holes: 9
Oak Tree GC, P.O. Box 660, Edmond, 73083
Yards: 5986, Par: 71, Holes: 18, Pro: Brent Goodger
Oak Tree GC, 1515 Oak Tree Dr., Oklahoma City, 73034
Oaklahoma City Golf & CC, 7000 N.W. Grand Blvd., Oklahoma City, 73116
Oaks CC, P.O. Box 9339, Tulsa, 74157
Oaks Hills Golf & CC, P.O. Box 1393, Ada, 74920
Oakwood CC, 1601 N. Oakwood Rd., Enid, 73701
Oilfield Rec Assn GC, SH-76 S, Healdton, 73438, 405-229-9930
Yards: 6696, Par: 73, Holes: 18
Okeene GC, 315 S. Phillips St., Okeene, 73763, 405-822-3435
Yards: 5902, Par: 70, USGA: 66.7, Holes: 9, Pro: Scott Brady
Oklahoma GC, 20400 S. 100 41th, Tulsa, 74013
Okmulgee CC, P.O. Box 788, Okmulgee, 74447
Page Belcher GC, 6666 S. Union, Tulsa, 74132, 918-446-1529
Holes: 18
Pawhuska Golf & CC, P.O. Box 1048, Pawhuska, 74058
Pawnee GC, Rt 1-Box 202, Pawnee, 74058, 918-762-3785
Yards: 2819, Par: 35, Holes: 9, Pro: Bud Boss

Perry Golf & CC, P.O. Box 230, Perry, 73077,   405-336-2326
Yards: 3059, Par: 35, Holes: 9
Ponca City CC, P.O. Box 1150, Ponca City, 74602
Quail Creek Golf & CC, 3501 Quail Greek Rd., Oklahoma City, 73120
Quartz Mountain Resort, Rt 1-Box 35, Lone Wolf, 73655,   405-563-2520
Yards: 5660, Par: 35, Holes: 9, Pro: Elmer Shelton
Rock Creek GC, HC 69-Box 230, Hugo, 74743,   405-326-6130
Yards: 6179, Par: 71, USGA: 68.0, Holes: 9, Pro: Hassen Dow
Rolling Hills CC, P.O. Box 449, Catoosa, 74015,   000-266-2208
Yards: 6425, Par: 72, USGA: 72.0, Holes: 18, Pro: Frank Gobbell
Roman Nose Park GC, Rt. 1, Box 2-9, Watonga, 73772,   405-623-7989
Yards: 2965, Par: 35, Holes: 9, Pro: John P. Kelly
Sapulpa Muni GC, 1 mi W on US-66, Sapulpa, 74066,   918-224-0237
Holes: 18
Sayre Municipal GC, ¼ mi. S, Sayre, 73662,   405-928-9046
Holes: 9
Sequoyah GC, P.O. Box 948, Tahlequah, 74464
Shattuck Municipal GC, P.O. Box 228, Shattuck, 73828,   405-938-9879
Holes: 9
Shawnee Golf & CC, P.O. Box 1574, Shawnee, 74801
South Lakes GC, 9253 South Elwood Street, Jenks, 74037
Holes: 18
Southern Hills CC, P.O. Box 702298, Tulsa, 74170
Stillwater CC, 5215 Country Club Dr., Stillwater, 74074
Stone Creek GC, 6666 S. Union, Tulsa, 74132
Stroud Municipal GC, 1 mi N on US-66, Stroud, 74079,   918-968-2105
Holes: 9
Sulphur Hills GC, P.O. Box 512, Sulphur, 73086,   405-622-5057
Par: 36, Holes: 9
Sunset CC, Rt 1-Box 193, 547 Sunset Blvd., Bartlesville, 74003
Sunset Hills CC, N. 5th St. and Sunset Lane, Guymon, 73942,   405-338-7404
Holes: 18
Surry Hills CC, 11340 Surrey Hills Blvd, Yukon, 73099
Tahlequah City GC, 101 S. Cherokee, Tahlequah, 74464,   918-456-3761
Holes: 9
Tinker A.F.B. GC, 2854 ABG/FSRG-Bldg 6601, Tinker AFB, 73145,   000-734-2909
Yards: 6141, Par: 72, USGA: 69.0, Holes: 18
Tishomingo GC, P.O. Box 751, Tishomingo, 73460,   405-371-2604
Holes: 9
Trails GC, The, 3200 S. Berry Rd., Norman, 73069
Tropser Park GC, 2301 S.E. 29 Street, Oklahoma City, 73129,   405-677-8874
Holes: 18, Pro: Steve Carsib
Tulsa CC, 701 N. Union, Tulsa, 74101
Twenty Greens GC, 5 mi E. off US-66, Catoosa, 74015,   918-266-3893
Holes: 18
Twin Hills GC, 3401 NE 36th, Oklahoma City, 73121
Twin Oaks GC, Rt 2-Box 149, Duncan, 73533,   405-255-8927
Holes: 9
University Lake GC, 302 S. 21st St., Enid, 73701,   405-234-5131
Holes: 9
Vinta CC, P.O. Box 881, Vinita, 74301
Walnut Creek CC, 6501 S. Country Club Dr., Oklahoma City, 73159
Watonga GC, P.O. Box 94, Watonga, 73772
Yards: 2901, Par: 36, Holes: 9
Waurika GC, 1220 W. Anderson, Waurika, 73573,   405-228-3581
Holes: 9

Waynoka GC, ½ mi E, Waynoka, 73860, 405-824-2261
Holes: 9
Weatherford GC, Route 3, Rader Park, Weatherford, 73096, 405-772-3832
Yards: 5778, Par: 70, USGA: 66.4, Holes: 18, Pro: Lee Cargile
Westbury CC, 10000 Thompson Ave., Yukon, 73099, 405-324-0707
Holes: 18
Western Hills Guest Ranch, 6 mi E on SH-51, Wagoner, 74467, 918-772-7281
Par: 70, Holes: 18
Wildhorse GC, P.O. Box 364, Velma, 73091
Willow Lake GC, Rt 1-Hwy 99 North, Stroud, 74079
Woodward Muni GC, P.O. Box 1165, Woodward, 73802, 405-256-9028
Yards: 3073, Par: 35, Holes: 9

Alderbrook GC, 7300 Alderbrook Rd., Bay City, 97141, 503-842-6413   *Oregon*
Yards: 5474, Par: 69, Holes: 18
Alpine Meadows GC, Enterprise, 97828, 503-426-3246
Yards: 3178, Par: 35, Holes: 9
Baker GC, Baker, 97814, 503-523-2358
Yards: 3018, Par: 35, Holes: 9
Bandon Face Rock GC, Bandon, 97411, 503-347-9441
Yards: 2168, Par: 32, Holes: 9
Battle Creek GC, 6161 Commercial St. SE, Salem, 97306, 503-585-1402
Yards: 5830, Par: 71, USGA: 67.4, Holes: 18, Pro: C. Lynn Baxter
Black Butte Ranch GC, P.O.Box 8000, Black Butte Ranch, 97759, 503-595-6689
Yards: 6800, Par: 72, Holes: 18
Broadmoor GC, Portland, 97208, 503-281-1337
Yards: 6269, Par: 72, Holes: 18
Cedar Bend GC, Gold Beach, 97444, 503-247-6911
Yards: 3000, Par: 36, Holes: 9
Christmas Valley GC, Christmas Valley, 97641, 503-576-2333
Yards: 3393, Par: 36, Holes: 9
Circle Bar GC, Westfir, 97492, 503-782-3541
Yards: 3365, Par: 36, Holes: 9
Colonial Valley GC, Grants Pass, 97526, 503-479-5568
Yards: 1587, Par: 29, Holes: 9
Colwood National GC, Portland, 97208, 503-254-5515
Yards: 6422, Par: 72, Holes: 18
Condon GC, Condon, 97823, 503-384-2711
Yards: 3131, Par: 36, Holes: 9
Crooked River GC, Crooked River, 97701, 503-923-6343
Yards: 2601, Par: 36, Holes: 9
Devils Lake GC, Lincoln City, 97367, 503-994-8442
Yards: 2673, Par: 36, Holes: 9
Echo Hills, Echo, 97826, 503-376-8244
Yards: 2884, Par: 36, Holes: 9
Elkhorn Valley GC, Mehama, 97384, 503-897-3368
Yards: 3235, Par: 36, Holes: 9
Estacada Springwater GC, Estacada, 97023, 503-630-4586
Yards: 2938, Par: 36, Holes: 9
Eugene GC, 255 Country Club Rd., Eugene, 97401, 503-344-5121
Yards: 6406, Par: 72, USGA: 71.0, Holes: 18
Evergreen GC, Mt. Angel, 97362, 503-845-6522
Yards: 3034, Par: 35, Holes: 9
Forest Hills CC, Reedsport, 97467, 503-271-2626
Par: 36, Holes: 9

Forest Hills GC, Cornelius, 97113,   503-648-8559
Yards: 6244, Par: 72, Holes: 18
Frontier Golf, Canby, 97013,   503-266-4435
Yards: 1030, Par: 27, Holes: 9
Gil Morgan Municipal GC, End of East 7th St., Wewoka, 74884
Yards: 3225, Par: 36, Holes: 9
Glaze Meadow GC, Sisters, 97759,   503-595-6400
Yards: 6266, Par: 72, Holes: 18
Glendoveer GC, Portland, 97208,   503-253-7505
Yards: 5803, Par: 71, Holes: 18
Golf City GC, Corvallis, 97333,   503-753-6213
Yards: 881, Par: 28, Holes: 9
Grants Pass GC, Grants Pass, 97526,   503-476-0849
Yards: 6353, Par: 72, Holes: 18
Greenlea GC, Boring, 97009,   503-663-3934
Yards: 1525, Par: 30, Holes: 9
Greshma G&CC, Greshma, 97030,   503-665-3352
Par: 72, Holes: 18
Hawk Creek GC, Neskowin, 97149,   503-392-4120
Yards: 2306, Par: 33, Holes: 9
Illinois Valley GC, Cave Junction, 97523,   503-592-3151
Yards: 3075, Par: 36, Holes: 9
Kentuck GC, North Bend, 97459,   503-756-4464
Yards: 5404, Par: 70, Holes: 18
King City GC, King City, 97224,   503-639-7986
Yards: 2444, Par: 33, Holes: 9
Kinzua Hills GC—#1, Fossil, 97830
Yards: 4233, Par: 65, Holes: 18
Lakeridge G & CC, Lakeview, 97630,   503-947-3855
Yards: 3382, Par: 36, Holes: 9
McNary GC, 6255 River Rd. N., Salem, 97303,   503-393-4653
Yards: 6258, Par: 71, USGA: 68.1, Holes: 18, Pro: Richard Brown
McNary GC, Umatilla, 97882,   503-922-3006
Yards: 6000, Par: 70, Holes: 18
Meriwether Natl GC, RTE 6, Hillsboro, 97123,   503-648-4143
Yards: 6408, Par: 72, Holes: 18
Milton-Freewater GC, Milton-Freewater, 97862,   503-938-7284
Yards: 1800, Par: 30, Holes: 9
Mountain View CC, John Day, 97845,   503-575-0170
Yards: 3005, Par: 36, Holes: 9
Mountain View GC, 27195 SE Kelso Rd., Boring, 97009,   503-663-4869
Yards: 6135, Par: 71, USGA: 67.5, Holes: 18, Pro: Jack Beaudoin
Nine Peaks G & CC, Madras, 97741,   503-475-3511
Yards: 3023, Par: 36, Holes: 9
Oak Knoll GC, Ashland, 97520,   503-482-4311
Yards: 3130, Par: 36, Holes: 9
Olalla Valley GC, Toledo, 97391,   503-335-2121
Yards: 3052, Par: 36, Holes: 9
Ontario GC, Ontario, 97914,   503-889-9022
Yards: 6895, Par: 72, Holes: 18
Oregon City GC, Oregon City, 97045, 503-656-2846
Yards: 5940, Par: 71, Holes: 18
Orenco Woods GC, Orenco, 97045,   503-648-1836
Yards: 2625, Par: 35, Holes: 9
Orion Greens GC, Bend, 97701,   503-388-3999
Yards: 2200, Par: 31, Holes: 9

Pineway GC, Lebanon, 97355, 503-258-8919
Yards: 3070, Par: 36, Holes: 9
Portland Meadows GC, Portland, 97208, 503-289-3405
Yards: 2095, Par: 31, Holes: 9
Progress Downs GC, Progress, 97536, 503-646-5166
Yards: 6149, Par: 71, Holes: 18
Ranch Hills GC, Mulino, 97042, 503-632-6848
Yards: 3010, Par: 36, Holes: 9
Rivergreens Golf, Gladstone, 97027, 503-656-1033
Yards: 2307, Par: 54, Holes: 18
Riverside GC, 8105 NE 33rd, Portland, 97211, 503-282-7265
Riverwood GC, Dundee, 97115, 503-864-9901
Yards: 2853, Par: 36, Holes: 9
Rose City GC, 2200 NE 71st, Portland, 97213, 503-253-4744
Yards: 6166, Par: 72, Holes: 18
Santiam GC, Stayton, 97383, 503-769-3485
Yards: 6131, Par: 72, Holes: 18
Seaside GC, Seaside, 97138, 503-738-5261
Yards: 2610, Par: 35, Holes: 9
Shadow Butte Muni GC, Ontario, 97914, 503-889-9022
Par: 72, Holes: 18
Springfield CC, Springfield, 97477, 503-747-2517
Yards: 3062, Par: 71, Holes: 18
St. Helens GC, Warren, 97053, 503-397-0358
Yards: 2967, Par: 36, Holes: 9
Sandelie GC, West Linn, 97068, 503-655-1461
Yards: 5947, Par: 71, Holes: 18
Stewart Park GC, Roseburg, 97470, 503-672-4592
Yards: 2909, Par: 35, Holes: 9
Summerfield G & CC, Tigard, 97223, 503-620-1200
Yards: 2475, Par: 33, Holes: 9
Sunset Bay GC, Charleston, 97420, 503-888-9301
Yards: 3035, Par: 36, Holes: 9
Sunset Grove GC, Forest Grove, 97116, 503-357-6044
Yards: 2830, Par: 36, Holes: 9
Sutherlin Knolls GC, Sutherlin, 97479, 503-459-4422
Yards: 6506, Par: 71, Holes: 18
Valley GC, Hines, 97738, 503-573-6251
Yards: 3190, Par: 36, Holes: 9
Vernonia GC, Vernonia, 97064, 503-429-6811
Yards: 3000, Par: 36, Holes: 9
Waverly GC, 110 SE Waverly Dr., Portland, 97222, 503-654-6521
West Delta Park GC, 3500 N. Victory Blvd., Portland, 97217, 503-289-1818
Yards: 6397, Par: 72, Holes: 18
Willow Creek CC, Heppner, 97836, 503-676-5437
Yards: 1650, Par: 30, Holes: 9
Wilson's Willow Run, Boardman, 97818, 503-481-4381
Yards: 1753, Par: 31, Holes: 9

American Legion GC, Mt. Union, 17066, 814-542-9087 *Pennsylvania*
Par: 74, Holes: 18
Armitage GC, Orrs Bridge Rd., Mechanicsburg, 18934, 717-737-5344
Holes: 18, Pro: Gerry Dougherty
Arnold's Course, Mifflinville, 18631, 717-752-7022
Par: 70, Holes: 18
Aronimink GC, ST. Davids Rd., Philadelphia, 19073

Arrowhead GC, RD 2, Douglassville, 19518, 215-582-4258
Arrowhead GC, Weavertown Rd., Amityville, 15311, 215-582-4258
Yards: 6035, Par: 71, USGA: 69.7, Holes: 27
Beaver Bend Chip & Putt, Pleasant View Rd, Hummelstown, 17036,
717-566-5858   Holes: 18
Bon Air GC, McCormick Rd., Coraopolis, 15108, 412-262-2992
Briarwood GC, 4775 W. Market, York, 17404, 717-792-9776
Par: 72, Holes: 18
Broken Tee GC, Green Valley Rd., Carmichaels, 15320, 412-966-5138
Buffalo GC, Rt 356, Freeport, 16229, 412-353-2440
Burn Brae GC, Twining & Susquehanna Rd.s, Dresher, 19025, 215-659-9917
Yards: 6815, Par: 71, USGA: 68.8, Holes: 18
Cambrian Hills GC, Barnesboro, 15714, 814-247-8521
Par: 36, Holes: 9
Carradam GC, North Huntingdon, 15642, 412-863-6860
Par: 72, Holes: 18
Castle Hills GC, 110 W. Oakwood Way, New Castle, 16105, 412-652-8122
Holes: 18
Cedarbrook GC, Cedarbrook Dr., Pittsburgh, 15012, 412-929-8300
Cedarbrook GC, RT 5 & I-70, Belle Vernon, 15012, 412-929-8300
Holes: 36
Center Square GC, Skippack Rk. & Whitehall Rd., Center Point, 19422,
215-584-4288   Yards: 6460, Par: 71, USGA: 68.5, Holes: 18
Cherrington CC, 1700 Beaver Grade Rd., Coraopolis, 15108, 412-269-4666
Holes: 18
Cherry Hills Inn GC, RD 3, McDonald, 15057, 412-926-9121
Cherry Valley GC, Stroudsburg, 18360, 717-421-1350
Par: 71, Holes: 18
Chippewa GC, Bentleyville, 15314, 412-239-4841
Holes: y
Chukker Valley GC, Rts. 73 & 663, Gilbertsville, 19525, 215-754-7597
Par: 72, USGA: 71.4, Holes: 27
Clingan's Tanglewood GC, Pulaski, 16143, 412-964-8702
Par: 72, Holes: 18
Cobbs Creek GC, 72nd St & Lansdowne Ave., Philadelphia, 19131,
215-473-5440   Yards: 6130, Par: 70, Holes: 27
Colonial GC, Uniontown, 15401, 412-439-3150
Par: 71, Holes: 18
Conley's CC Inn, 740 Pittsburgh Rd., Butler, 16001, 412-586-7711
Cool Springs GC, 1530 Hamilton Rd., Pittsburgh, 15234, 412-881-9877
Crafton Public GC, Thornburg Rd., Pittsburgh, 15205, 412-921-6203
Cricket Hill GC, Hawley, 18428, 717-226-4366
Par: 70, Holes: 18
Cross Creek GC, RD. 3 RTE 85, Oil City, 16354, 814-827-9611
Yards: 6480, Par: 70, USGA: 70.9, Holes: 18
Cross Creek Resort, Rt 8 4 Mi So of Titusville, Titusville, 16354, 814-827-9611
Cumberland GC, Carlisle, 17013, 717-249-5538
Par: 72, Holes: 18
Down River G&CC, Everett, 15537, 814-652-5193
Par: 72, Holes: 18
Eagles Mere GC, 1 Country Club Rd., Williamsport, 17731
Ebensburg GC, Ebensburg, 15931, 814-472-9936
Par: 36, Holes: 9
Edgewood Pines GC, Hazleton, 18201, 717-788-1101
Par: 72, Holes: 18

Evergreen Park GC, Analomink, 18320,   717-421-7721
Par: 35, Holes: 9
Exeter GC, Reading, 19606,   215-779-1211
Par: 70, Holes: 18
Fairway GC, Country Club Lane, Warrington, 18976,   215-343-9979
Yards: 5300, Par: 65, Holes: 18
Falcon Ridge CC, 1550 Mayview Rd., Pittsburgh,   412-257-8900
Flatbush GC, 355 Clouser Road, Littlestown, 17731
Holes: 18
Fort Cherry GC, RD 4, McDonald, 15057,   412-926-4181
Fox Hollow GC, Quakertown, 18951,   215-538-1920
Par: 71, Holes: 18
Foxburg CC, Foxburg, 16036,   412-659-3196
Par: 34, Holes: 9
Franklin Park GC, Rochester Rd., Pittsburgh,   412-364-7688
Franklin Park Boro GC, 2168-B Reiss Run Rd., Swkly,   412-364-2447
Frosty Valley Golf Links, 1300 Boyce Rd., Bridgeville, 15017,   412-941-5003
General Washington GC, 2750 Egypt Rd., Audobon, 19407,   215-666-7602
Yards: 6300, Par: 72, USGA: 69.4, Holes: 18
Gilbertsville GC, Gilbertsville, 19525,   215-323-3222
Par: 71, Holes: 18
Glenbrook GC, Stroudsburg, 18360,   717-421-3680
Par: 72, Holes: 18
Golf Course at Shepherd Hills, 1160 S. Krocks Rd., Wescosville, 18106,
215-391-0644   Par: 70, Holes: 18
Gospel Hill GC, Reese Road, Erie, 16510,   814-899-5700
Grandview Club, York, 17403, 717-764-2674
Par: 72, Holes: 18
Grandview GC, Grampion, 16838,   814-236-3669
Par: 72, Holes: 18
Great Cove GC, Mc Connellsburg, 17233,   717-485-5876
Par: 36, Holes: 9
Green Acres GC, R.D. 4, Rt. 408, Titusville, 16354,   814-827-3589
Green Hills GC, Birdsboro, 19508,   215-856-7672
Par: 36, Holes: 9
Green Pond CC, 3604 Farmersville Rd., Bethlehem, 18017,   215-691-9453
Yards: 6070, Par: 71, Holes: 18
Greenwood GC, Route 220, Altoona, 16601,   814-942-0898
Hailwood GC, 562 Park Ave. Ext., Meadville, 16335,   814-333-2505
Hartstown Level GC, Hartstown, 16131,   412-932-3017
Heritage Hills Golf Resort, 2700 Mt. Rose, York, 17402
Holes: 18
Hi-Level GC, Cranberry, 16319,   814-797-1813
Par: 71, Holes: 18
Hi-Point GC, Jacksonville & Bristol Rds., Ivyland,   215-672-6110
Yards: 6560, Par: 72, USGA: 71.1, Holes: 18
Hickory Heights GC, Spring Grove, 17362,   717-225-4247
Par: 70, Holes: 18
Hidden Springs GC, Horsham Rd., Horsham, 19044,   215-672-4141
Yards: 6800, Par: 70, USGA: 72.3, Holes: 36
Hidden Valley GC, Hidden Valley Premier Resort, Craighead Dr., 15501,
814-443-6454
Hiland GC, 106 St. Wendlin Rd., Butler, 16001,   412-287-9180
Honey Run G&CC, 3131 S. Salem Church Rd., York, 17404,   717-792-9771
Horsham Valley GC, Babylon Rd., Horsham,   215-646-4707
Yards: 5210, Par: 66, Holes: 18

Incredible GC, 3300 Hartzdale Dr., Camp Hill, 17011, 717-731-5454
Ivan Wood GC, E. Side Road, Conneaut Lake, 16316, 814-382-8438
Jeffersonville GC, Ridge Pike, Jeffersonville, 15344, 215-539-0422
Yards: 6488, Par: 71, USGA: 68.7, Holes: 18
John Byrne GC, Eden & Leon Sts., Philadelphia, 19145, 215-632-8666
Yards: 4858, Par: 66, Holes: 18
Juniata GC, M & Cayuga Sts., Philadelphia, 19124, 215-743-4060
Yards: 4530, Par: 63, Holes: 18
Karakung GC, Philadelphia, 19104, 215-877-8707
Par: 72, Holes: 18
Kimberton GC, Rte. 23, Phoenixville, 19460, 215-933-8836
Yards: 6500, Par: 72, USGA: 69.0, Holes: 18
King's Mountain Resort GC, Rockwood, 15557, 814-926-2021
Par: 36, Holes: 9
Krendale GC, 131 N. Eberhart Rd., Butler, 16001, 412-482-4065
Lake Arthur CC, Butler, 16001, 412-865-2765
Par: 72, Holes: 18
Lake Vue North GC, Butler, 16001, 412-586-7097
Par: 72, Holes: 18
Lakewood GC, Central City, 15926, 814-754-4142
Par: 34, Holes: 9
Lancaster GC, 1466 New Holland Dike, Lancaster, 17601
Langhorne CC, N. Bellvue Ave., Langhorne, 19047, 215-757-6951
Yards: 6000, Par: 69, Holes: 18
Lehman GC, Route 118, Wilkes-Barre, 18701, 717-675-1686
Lenape Heights GC, Route 66, Ford City, 16226, 412-763-2201
Limekiln GC, Rtes. 152 & 463, Prospectville, 19076, 215-643-0643
Yards: 6233, Par: 70, USGA: 68.2, Holes: 18
Limerick GC, Royersford, 19468, 215-495-6945
Par: 71, Holes: 18
Linden Hall Golf Resort, Perryopolis, 15473, 412-461-2424
Lindenwood GC, Linden Rd., Canonsburg, 15317, 412-745-9889
Holes: 18
Lykens Valley GC, Millersburg, 17061, 717-692-3664
Par: 70, Holes: 18
Mahoning Valley GC, Tamaqua, 18252, 717-386-4515
Par: 70, Holes: 18
Mandana GC, RTE 1, Grantville, 17028, 717-469-2400
Par: 72, Holes: 18
Manor Valley GC, Export, 15632, 412-744-4242
Par: 72, Holes: 18
Maplecrest GC, Portage, 15946, 814-736-9398
Par: 36, Holes: 9
Marada GC, Rt 30, Clinton, 15026, 412-899-2600
Holes: 9
Meadow Lane GC, Hamil Rd., Indiana, 15701, 412-465-5604
Meadowbrook GC, State Rd., Phoenixville, 19640, 215-933-2929
Yards: 6800, Par: 74, USGA: 70.0, Holes: 9
Meadowink GC, 4076 Bulltown Rd., Murrysville, 15668, 412-327-8243
Holes: 18
Middlecreek GC, Rockwood, 15557, 814-926-3524
Par: 35, Holes: 9
Middletown CC, N Bellevue Ave., Langhorne, 19047, 215-757-6953
Mill Race GC, Benton, 17814, 717-925-2040
Par: 70, Holes: 18

Moccasin Run GC, Atglen, 19310,   215-593-2600
Par: 72, Holes: 18
Monroe Valley GC, Jonestown, 17038,   717-865-2375
Par: 72, Holes: 18
Montgomeryville GC, Rtes. 202 & 309, Montgomeryville, 17752,   215-855-6112
Yards: 6300, Par: 70, USGA: 69.5, Holes: 18
Mount Odin Park GC, Greensburg, 15601,   412-834-2640
Par: 70, Holes: 18
Mount Pocono GC, Mt. Pocono, 18344,   717-839-9070
Par: 34, Holes: 9
Mountain Manor GC, Marshall Creek, E. Stroudsburg, 18335
Mountain Valley GC, Mahanoy City, 17948,   717-467-2242
Par: 71, Holes: 18
Mountain View Golf Resort, 7 Mi. West of Gettysburg, Fairfield, 17320,
717-642-5848   Yards: 6035, Par: 71, USGA: 69.0, Holes: 18
Mullberry Hill GC, Mullberry Hill Rd., Mt. Pleasant, 15666,   412-547-1909
Par: 72, Holes: 18
Murrysville GC, Sardis Road, Murrysville, 15668,   412-327-0726
Neshaminy Valley GC, Almshouse Rd., Jamison, 18929,   215-343-6930
Yards: 6090, Par: 71, USGA: 69.0, Holes: 18
Northampton Valley CC, Rt. 332, Richboro, 18954,   215-355-2234
Yards: 6560, Par: 71, USGA: 70.5, Holes: 18
Norvelt GC, Route 981, Mt. Pleasant, 15666,   412-423-5400
Oakbrook GC, Route 30, Jennerstown, 15547,   814-629-5892
Oakland Beach GC, Route 18 N, Oakland, 15225,   814-382-5665
Oakland Beach GC, Rt. 18 North, Conneaut Lake, 16316,   814-382-5665
Oakmont East GC, Hutton Rd., Pittsburgh, 15139
Overlook GC, 2040 Lititz Pike, Lancaster, 17601,   717-569-9551
Yards: 6187, Par: 70, Holes: 18
Park GC, Rt. 618, Conneaut Lake, 16316,   814-382-4971
Perry GC, Shoemakersville, 19555,   215-562-3510
Par: 70, Holes: 18
Pine Grove GC, Route 208, Pine Grove, 17963,   412-458-9942
Piney Run GC, Garrett, 15542,   814-634-8660
Par: 35, Holes: 9
Pittsburgh-North GC, 3800 Bakerstown Rd., Gbsna,   412-443-3800
Plasant Valley GC, Rd. 1, York, 17363
Pleasant Valley GC, Stewartstown, 17363, 717-993-2184
Par: 72, Holes: 18
Pleasant Valley GC, Vintondale, 15961,   814-446-6244
Par: 72, Holes: 18
Pocono Farms GC, Tobyhanna, 18466,   717-894-8441
Par: 72, Holes: 18
Ponderosa GC, Hookstown, 15050,   412-947-4745
Par: 71, Holes: 18
Rich Maiden, RD2, Fleetwood, 19522,   215-391-0644
Riverside GC, Cambridge Springs, 16403,   814-398-4692
Riverside GC, RD. 2, Erie, 16403
Riverview GC, Bunola Road, Elizabeth, 15037,   412-384-7596
Rolling Acres GC, Beaver Falls, 15010,   412-843-6736
Par: 72, Holes: 27
Rolling Green GC, Route 136, Monongahela, 15063,   412-222-9671
Rolling Hills GC, Pulaski, 16143,   412-964-8201
Par: 71, Holes: 18
Rolling Turf GC, Smith Rd., Schwenksville, 19473,   215-287-7297
Yards: 1985, Par: 38, Holes: 12

Roosevelt GC, 20th St. & Pattison Ave., Philadelphia, 19138,   215-462-8997
Yards: 6333, Par: 71, Holes: 18
Sandy Hill GC, Gibsonia, 15044,   412-443-1908
Par: 35, Holes: 9
Saucon Valley GC, Saucon Valley Rd., Bethlehem, 18015
Saxon GC, Millerstown, 17062,   412-353-2130
Schenley Park GC, Schenley Park, Oakland,   814-682-9848
Shamrock Public GC, Grove City-Slippery Rock Rd., Slippery Rock, 16057,
412-794-3030
Sheraton Inn-Greensburg GC, Greensburg, 15601,   412-836-6060
Par: 29, Holes: 9
Silver Spring GC, 136 Sample Bridge Rd, Mechanicsburg, 18934,   717-766-0462
Par: 70, Holes: 18
Skippack GC, Stump Hall & Cedar Rds., Cedars, 19423,   215-584-GOLF
Yards: 6010, Par: 71, USGA: 69.2, Holes: 18
Skippack GC, Skippack, 19474,   215-584-GOLF
Par: 70, Holes: 18
Sleepy Hollow GC, 4 Mi on Rt.427, Wyattsville Rd, Franklin, 16323,
814-374-4111
Sleepy Hollow GC, Route 427, Wyattsville,   814-374-4111
Somerton Springs GC, 49 Bustleton Ave., Feasterville, 19047,   215-355-1776
Yards: 2200, Par: 56, Holes: 18
Speer's Public GC, Route 417, Dempsytown,   814-676-3890
Speer's Public GC, Rt. 417, Dempsyetown Road, Oil City, 16301,   814-676-3890
Sportsman's GC, 3800 Langlstown Rd, Harrisburg, 17112,   717-545-0023
Par: 71, Holes: 18
Springfield GC, 400 W. Sproul Rd., Springfield, 19064,   215-543-9860
Yards: 5348, Par: 69, USGA: 64.9, Holes: 18
Standing Stone GC, Huntingdon, 16652,   814-643-4800
Par: 70, Holes: 18
Stonecrest GC, Wampum, 16157,   412-535-8971
Par: 71, Holes: 18
Sugarloaf GC, Sugarloaf, 18249,   717-384-4097
Par: 72, Holes: 18
Suncrest GC, Rt 8, Butler, 16001,   412-586-5508
Sunset GC, Sunset Dr., Middletown, 17057,   717-944-5415
Holes: 18
Sweet Valley GC, Sweet Valley, 18656,   717-477-5426
Par: 31, Holes: 9
Sylvan Hills GC, Hollidaysburg, 16648,   814-695-4769
Par: 35, Holes: 9
Tam O'Shanter of Pennsylvania, I-80 Route 18 North, West Middlesex, 16159,
412-981-3552   Holes: 18
Tamiment GC, Tamiment, 18371,   717-588-6652
Par: 72, Holes: 18
Thunderbird GC, Quakertown, 18951,   215-536-9974
Yards: 6193, Par: 71, USGA: 69.6, Holes: 18
Turbot Hills GC, Milton, 17847,   717-742-7455
Par: 71, Holes: 18
Twin Lakes GC, Rittenhouse & Forty Foot Rds., Mainland, 19451,   215-256-9548
Yards: 6250, Par: 70, USGA: 69.6, Holes: 18
Twin Lakes CC, RD 1, Allentown, 18104,   215-395-3369
Holes: 18
Twin Woods GC, 2924 E. Orvilla Rd., Hatfield, 19440, 215-822-9263
Yards: 3200, Par: 36, Holes: 9

Valley Forge GC, 401 N. Gulph Rd., King of Prussia, 19406, 215-337-1776
Yards: 6001, Par: 71, USGA: 68.9, Holes: 18
Valley Green G&CC, RD 2, Greenburg, 15601, 412-837-6366
Valley Green GC, 1227 Valley Green Rd., Etters, 17319, 717-938-4200
Holes: 18
Walnut Creek GC, East Lake Road, Jamestown, 16134, 412-932-5219
Walnut Lane GC, Walnut Lane & Henry Ave., Philadelphia, 19128,
215-482-3370 Yards: 5100, Par: 62, Holes: 18
Waynesboro GC, Waynesboro, 17268, 717-762-3734
Par: 36, Holes: 9
Westover GC, S. Schuylkill Ave., Norristown, 19403, 215-539-4502
Yards: 6477, Par: 70, USGA: 69.4, Holes: 18
Whispering Pines GC, R.D. 4, Meadville, 16335, 814-337-9702
White Birch GC, Barnesville, 15714, 717-467-2525
Par: 69, Holes: 27
Whitemarsh Valley GC, Thomas Rd and Germantown, Philadelphia, 19444
Wilkes-Barre GC, Wilkes-Barre, 18701, 717-472-3590
Par: 72, Holes: 18
Willow Brook, 1364 Howertown Rd., Catasauqua, 18032, 215-264-9904
Willow Run Inn & GC, Berwick, 18603, 717-752-2794
Par: 72, Holes: 18
Windyhill GC, 603 Windy Hill, Plum Boro, 15239, 412-793-7771
Wiscasset GC, Mt. Pocono, 18344, 717-839-7155
Par: 36, Holes: 9
Wood's GC, 559 W. Germantown Pike, Norristown, 19403, 215-279-0678
Yards: 3076, Par: 54, Holes: 18
Woodlawn GC, Pittsburgh, 412-224-4720
Yorktowne GC, 1605 Loucks Rd., York, 17404, 717-764-2224

Bristol GC, 95 Tupelo Street, Bristol, 02809, 401-253-9844 *Rhode Island*
Yards: 6060, Par: 71, Holes: 9
Country View GC, Colwell Street, Burrillville, 02917, 401-568-7157
Yards: 6235, Par: 70, Holes: 18
Coventry Pine CC, Harkney Hill Road, Coventry, 02816, 401-397-5592
Yards: 3160, Par: 35, Holes: 9
Exeter CC, Victory Highway, Exeter, 02822, 401-295-1178
Yards: 6390, Par: 72, Holes: 18
Fairlawn GC, Sherman Avenue, Lincoln, 02865, 401-334-3937
Yards: 1400, Par: 27, Holes: 9
Foster CC, Harrison & Johnson Roads, Foster, 02825, 401-397-5990
Yards: 6187, Par: 72, Holes: 18
Goddard State Park, Ives Road, Warwick, 02818, 401-884-9834
Yards: 3021, Par: 36, Holes: 9
Green Valley CC, 371 Union Street, Portsmouth, 02871, 401-847-9543
Yards: 6500, Par: 71, Holes: 18
Jamestown CC, East Shore Road, Jamestown, 02835, 401-423-9930
Yards: 3344, Par: 72, Holes: 9
Laurel Lane GC, 309 Laurel Lane, West Kingston, 02892, 401-783-3844
Yards: 5806, Par: 71, Holes: 18, Pro: Rick Holley Jr
Lindhbrook CC, Alton-Woodville Road, Hope Valley, 02832, 401-539-8641
Yards: 2814, Par: 54, Holes: 9
Metacomet GC, 500 Veterans Mamorial Pkwy., Providence, 02914
Midville CC, Lombardi Lane, West Warwick, 02893, 401-828-9215
Yards: 3200, Par: 70, Holes: 9
Montaup CC, Anthony Road, Portsmouth, 02871, 401-683-9882
Yards: 6300, Par: 71, Holes: 18

Pocasset CC, 807 Bristol Ferry Road, Bristol, 02809, 401-683-2266
Yards: 2770, Par: 34, Holes: 9
Pond View CC, Shore Road, Westerly, 02891, 401-322-7870
Yards: 3257, Par: 36, Holes: 18
Rolling Greens, Ten Rod Road, North Kingstown, 02852, 401-294-9859
Yards: 3059, Par: 35, Holes: 9
Seaview CC, 150 Gray Street, Warwick, 02886, 401-739-6311
Yards: 3000, Par: 36, Holes: 9
Silver Spring GC, Pawtucket Avenue, East Providence, 02914, 401-434-9697
Yards: 1668, Par: 32, Holes: 9
Triggs Memorial GC, 1533 Chalkstone Ave., Providence, 02908, 401-272-4653
Yards: 6619, Par: 72, Holes: 18, Pro: John Tusher
Washington GC, 174 Station Street, Coventry, 02816, 401-828-9891
Yards: 3015, Par: 71, Holes: 9
Winnapaug GC, Shore Rd., Westerly, 02891, 401-596-9164
Yards: 5919, Par: 72, Holes: 18
Woodland Golf & CC, 655 Old Baptist Road, North Kingstown, 02852,
401-294-2872   Yards: 3189, Par: 70, Holes: 9

Arthur Hills GC, Hwy. 278, Hilton Head Island, 29938   *South Carolina*
Azalea Sands GC, Hwy. 17 S, North Myrtle Beach, 29582, 803-272-6191
Yards: 6287, Par: 72, USGA: 69.0, Holes: 18
Bay Tree Golf Plantation, Rt 2, Hwy 9, North Myrtle Beach, 29582,
803-249-1487   Yards: 6363, Par: 72, USGA: 70.0, Holes: 18
Beachwood GC, 1520 Highway 17 South, North Myrtle Beach, 29582,
803-272-6168   Yards: 6202, Par: 72, USGA: 69.7, Holes: 18, Pro: Dave Hill, Jr
Berkeley GC, Moncks Corner, 29461, 803-899-9312
Yards: 6696, Par: 72, Holes: 18
Bishopville CC, Bishopville, 29010, 803-428-3675
Yards: 3400, Par: 36, Holes: 9
Bonnie Brae, Greenville, 29602, 803-277-9838
Yards: 6575, Par: 72, Holes: 18
Boscobel G & CC, Pendleton, 29670, 803-646-3991
Yards: 6796, Par: 71, Holes: 18
Burning Ridge GC—East Course, Box 1147, Myrtle Beach, 29578, 803-448-3141
Yards: 6216, Par: 72, USGA: 68.9, Holes: 18
Calhoun CC, St. Matthews, 29135, 803-823-2465
Yards: 6482, Par: 71, Holes: 18
Carolina CC, Loris, 29569, 803-756-3975
Yards: 6040, Par: 36, Holes: 9
Carolina Downs CC, York, 29745, 803-684-5878
Yards: 6900, Par: 72, Holes: 18
Carolina Shores GC, Hwy 17 N., N. Myrtle Beach, 29597, 919-579-2181
Yards: 6231, Par: 72, USGA: 71.0, Holes: 18
Cat Island GC, Beaufort, 29902, 803-524-0300
Yards: 6610, Par: 71, Holes: 18
Cedar Knoll GC, Allendale, 29621, 803-584-4785
Yards: 1530, Par: 27, Holes: 9
Cedar Springs GC, Greenwood, 29646, 803-374-3396
Yards: 6225, Par: 70, Holes: 9
Cherry Hill CC, Andrews, 29510, 803-264-5422
Yards: 6242, Par: 71, Holes: 18
Chester GC, Chester, 29706, 803-377-1677
Yards: 6811, Par: 72, Holes: 18

Chickasaw Point GC, Westminster, 29693, 803-972-3700
Yards: 6516, Par: 72, Holes: 18
Clarendon G & CC, Manning, 29102, 803-435-8752
Yards: 6624, Par: 72, Holes: 18
Cokesbury Hills GC, Hodges, 29653, 803-374-7820
Yards: 1857, Par: 30, Holes: 9
Conway GC, P.O. Box 94, Conway, 29526, 803-365-3621
Yards: 6076, Par: 71, Holes: 9
Cooper's Creek GC, Pelion, 29123, 803-894-3666
Yards: 6550, Par: 72, Holes: 18
County Club of Callawassie, Ridgeland, 29936, 803-785-7888
Yards: 6960, Par: 72, Holes: 18
Crestwood GC, Denmark, 29042, 803-793-3651
Par: 35, Holes: 9
Darlington CC, Darlington, 29532, 803-393-2196
Yards: 6200, Par: 72, Holes: 18
Deertrack GC—North Course, P.O. Box 14430 Hwy 17 South, Surfside Beach,
29587, 803-650-2146   Yards: 6428, Par: 72, USGA: 70.7, Holes: 18
Dogwood Hills CC, Walterboro, 29488, 803-538-2731
Yards: 3111, Par: 35, Holes: 9
Dunes Golf and Beach Club, 9000 N. Ocean Blvd., Myrtle Beach, 29577,
803-449-5914
Dusty Hills CC, Marion, 29571, 803-423-2721
Yards: 6120, Par: 72, Holes: 18
Eagle Landing GC, Hanahan, 29406, 803-797-1667
Yards: 4300, Par: 72, Holes: 18
Eagle Nest GC, P.O. Box 746, North Myrtle Beach, 29597, 803-249-1449
Yards: 6393, Par: 72, USGA: 70.5, Holes: 18
Fairwood GC, Union, 29379, 803-427-3055
Yards: 6880, Par: 72, Holes: 18
Fort Mill GC, Fort Mill, 29715, 803-547-2044
Yards: 6865, Par: 72, Holes: 18
Gator Hole, P. O. Box 154, North Myrtle Beach, 29582, 803-249-3543
Yards: 5600, Par: 70, USGA: 67.9, Holes: 18
Gauley Falls, Pickens, 69671, 803-878-2030
Yards: 6514, Par: 72, Holes: 18
George Miller CC, Summerville, 29483, 803-873-2219
Yards: 6200, Par: 71, Holes: 18
Green Hills GC, Lugoff, 29078, 803-438-1917
Yards: 3100, Par: 36, Holes: 9
Hampton County CC, Hampton, 29924, 803-943-2735
Yards: 6100, Par: 72, Holes: 18
Heather Glen Golf Links, P. O. Box 297, North Myrtle Beach, 29582,
803-249-9000 Yards: 6500, Par: 72, Holes: 18
Heather Glen Golf Links, US Highway 17, PO Box 297, Myrtle Beach, 29597,
803-249-9000   Holes: 9
Heritage Club, P.O. Box 1885, Pawleys Island, 29585, 803-237-3424
Yards: 6599, Par: 71, USGA: 72.0, Holes: 18
Hidden Valley CC, West Columbia, 29169, 803-794-8087
Yards: 6700, Par: 72, Holes: 18
High Meadows CC, Abbeville, 29620, 803-446-2043
Yards: 6527, Par: 72, Holes: 9
Highland Park CC, Aiken, 29801, 803-649-6029
Yards: 6300, Par: 70, Holes: 18
Hillandale GC, Greenville, 29602, 803-232-0011
Yards: 5700, Par: 71, Holes: 18

Hillcrest Golf Facility, Orangeburg, 29115, 803-534-3566
Yards: 6722, Par: 72, Holes: 18
Hilton Head National GC, PO Box 5597, Hilton Head Island, 29938
Holes: 18
Indian Wells GC, P. O. Box 15418, Surfside Beach, 2958, 803-651-1505
Yards: 6231, Par: 72, USGA: 69.7, Holes: 27
Jim and Lilie GC, Jackson, 29831, 803-471-9950
Yards: 5481, Par: 70, Holes: 9
Keowee Key GC, RTE. 2 Hwy. 183, Salem, 29676, 803-944-2222
Yards: 6540, Par: 72, Holes: 18
Kershaw CC, Kershaw, 29067, 803-475-2104
Yards: 3011, Par: 36, Holes: 9
Kings Grant CC, Summerville, 29483, 803-873-7110
Yards: 6712, Par: 72, Holes: 18
Lake Marion GC, Santee Cooper Resort, Santee, 29142, 803-854-2554
Yards: 6223, Par: 72, Holes: 18, Pro: Carroll Pifer
Lakeview GC, Greenville, 29602, 803-277-2680
Yards: 6400, Par: 72, Holes: 18
Legends Golf Complex, PO Box 65, North Myrtle Beach, 29597, 803-236-1112
Holes: 54
Lin Rick GC, RTE. 1 Box 189, Columbia, 29203, 803-754-6331
Yards: 6919, Par: 73, USGA: 70.2, Holes: 18, Pro: Charles Dymock
Long Cove GC, 44 Long Cove Dr., Hilton Head Island, 29928
Midland Valley CC, Aiken, 29801, 803-663-7332
Yards: 6721, Par: 71, Holes: 18
Midway Par 3, Myrtle Beach, 29577, 803-448-4713
Yards: 2127, Par: 81, Holes: 27
Mt. Hope GC, Georgetown, 29440, 803-546-5582
Yards: 6100, Par: 72, Holes: 18
Myrtle Beach Natl. GC—North, Hwy. 501, P.O. Box 1936, Myrtle Beach, 29578, 803-448-2308   Yards: 6769, Par: 72, Holes: 18
Myrtle West GC, PO Box 3371, N. Myrtle Beach, 29582
Holes: 18
Myrtlewood GC—Pines Course, P. O. Box 2095, Myrtle Beach, 29578, 803-449-3121   Yards: 6068, Par: 72, USGA: 68.2, Holes: 18
New Ellenton, New Ellenton, 29809, 803-652-7867
Yards: 5911, Par: 72, Holes: 9
Oaks GC, The, Donalds, 29638, 803-379-2400
Yards: 2080, Par: 33, Holes: 9
Oaks Plantation CC, Goose Creek, 29445, 803-553-2422
Yards: 5400, Par: 35, Holes: 9
Ocean Point GC, Fripp Island, 29644, 803-838-2309
Yards: 6060, Par: 72, USGA: 69.4, Holes: 18, Pro: Bill Totten
Ocean Ridge GC, Edisto Beach, 29438, 803-869-2561
Par: 71, Holes: 18
Oyster Reef GC, High Bluff Rd., P.O. Box 2419, Hilton Head Island, 29925, 803-681-7717   Yards: 6961, Par: 72, USGA: 70.0, Holes: 18, Pro: Pam Phipps
Palmetto GC, 275 Berrie Rd., Aiken, 29801, 803-649-2951
Yards: 6037, Par: 71, Holes: 18
Parkland GC, Greenwood, 29646, 803-229-5086
Yards: 6400, Par: 72, Holes: 18
Pawley's Plantation, Pawleys Island, 29577, 803-237-8497
Yards: 7143, Par: 72, Holes: 18, Pro: Jack Nicklaus
Pawpaw CC, Bamberg, 29003, 803-245-4171
Yards: 6723, Par: 72, Holes: 18

Peach Valley GC, Spartanburg, 29316, 803-583-2244
Yards: 6225, Par: 70, Holes: 18
Pickens County CC, Pickens, 69671, 803-878-6083
Yards: 6400, Par: 72, Holes: 18
Pine Lake GC, Anderson, 29621, 803-296-9960
Yards: 6400, Par: 70, Holes: 18
Pine Lakes Intl GC, Woodside Dr. Box 7099, Myrtle Beach, 29577,
803-449-6459 Yards: 6176, Par: 71, USGA: 69.3, Holes: 18, Pro: "Augie" Swarat
Pine Ridge Club, Inc. GC, Edgefield, 29824, 803-637-3570
Yards: 6928, Par: 72, Holes: 18
Pineland CC, Nichols, 29581, 803-526-2175
Yards: 6800, Par: 72, Holes: 18
Pineland Plantation GC, Mayesville, 29104, 803-495-3550
Yards: 7080, Par: 72, Holes: 18
Pinetuck GC, Rock Hill, 29730, 803-327-1141
Yards: 6600, Par: 71, Holes: 18
Pleasant Point Plantation Resort, Beaufort, 29902, 803-524-5015
Yards: 6700, Par: 72, Holes: 18
Pocalla Springs GC, 1700 Hwy. 15 S., Sumter, 29150, 803-481-8322
Yards: 5442, Par: 72, USGA: 65.4, Holes: 18
Port Royal Plantation—Robber, Hilton Head, 29928, 803-681-3671
Yards: 6711, Par: 72, Holes: 18
Possum Trot GC, Possum Trot Rd., P. O. Box 297, N. Myrtle Beach, 29597,
803-272-5341 Yards: 6966, Par: 72, USGA: 70.3, Holes: 18, Pro: Michael Friend
Quail Creek GC, P. O. Box 2940, Myrtle Beach, 29578, 803-448-7906
Yards: 6800, Par: 72, USGA: 70.3, Holes: 18, Pro: Howard McMeekin
Raccoon Run GC, RFD #6, Box 104, Myrtle Beach, 29577, 803-650-2644
Yards: 6799, Par: 73, USGA: 72.6, Holes: 18
River Club, P.O. Box 1885, Pawleys Island, 29585, 803-237-8755
Yards: 6283, Par: 72, USGA: 69.0, Holes: 18
Robbers Roost GC, P. O. Box 68, North Myrtle Beach, 29597, 803-249-1471
Yards: 6356, Par: 72, USGA: 72.1, Holes: 18
Rolling "S" GC, Waterloo, 29384, 803-677-3457
Yards: 5594, Par: 72, Holes: 18
Rose Hill GC, Hilton Head, 29928, 803-757-2160
Yards: 6506, Par: 72, Holes: 18
Saluda Valley GC, Williamston, 29697, 803-847-7102
Yards: 6400, Par: 72, Holes: 18
Santee National GC, PO Drawer 190, Santee, 29142
Holes: 18
Seagull GC, Box 196, Pawleys Island, 29589, 803-237-4285
Yards: 6300, Par: 72, USGA: 70.0, Holes: 18
Sedgewood CC, 9560 Garners Ferny Rd., Hopkins, 29061, 803-776-2177
Yards: 6031, Par: 72, Holes: 18, Pro: Ronnie Smoak
Seniors Country Club, Myrtle Beach, 29577, 803-249-8000
Yards: 7065, Par: 72, Holes: 18
Shadowmoss GC, Charleston, 29401, 803-556-8251
Yards: 6701, Par: 72, Holes: 18
Sigfield Golf Resort, Summerton, 29148, 803-478-7000
Yards: 6868, Par: 72, Holes: 18
Spring Lake CC, York, 29745, 803-684-4898
Yards: 700, Par: 72, Holes: 18
Star Fort National GC, Ninety Six, 29666, 803-543-2757
Yards: 6900, Par: 72, Holes: 18
Surf Golf and Beach Club, P. O. Box 47, North Myrtle Beach, 29597,
803-249-1524 Yards: 6859, Par: 72, USGA: 70.0, Holes: 18, Pro: George Hendrix

Sweetwater CC, Barnwell, 29812, 803-259-5004
Yards: 6400, Par: 71, Holes: 18
Tidewater GC, Highway 17, North Myrtle Beach, 29582, 314-965-8787
Holes: 18
Tifton GC, Darlington, 29532, 803-393-5441
Yards: 6140, Par: 72, Holes: 18
Timberlake Plantation, Chapin, 29036, 803-345-9909
Yards: 6703, Par: 72, Holes: 18
Twin Lakes CC, Dillon, 29536, 803-774-9101
Yards: 5669, Par: 71, Holes: 18
Ware Shoals GC, Ware Shoals, 29692, 803-456-2623
Yards: 3120, Par: 35, Holes: 9
Waterway Hills GC, P. O. Box 1936, Myrtle Beach, 29578, 803-449-6488
Yards: 6081, Par: 72, USGA: 68.8, Holes: 27
Whispering Pines GC, P.O.Box 1146, Hardeeville, 29927, 803-784-2426
Yards: 6100, Par: 71, Holes: 18, Pro: Vic Allmon
White Pines CC, Camden, 29020, 803-432-7442
Yards: 3095, Par: 36, Holes: 9
White Pines CC, Camden, 29020, 803-432-7442
Yards: 3095, Par: 36, Holes: 9
White Plains, Pageland, 29728, 803-672-7200
Yards: 6596, Par: 72, Holes: 18
Willbrook CC, Pawleys Island, 29585, 803-237-4627
Yards: 6895, Par: 72, Holes: 18
Witch Golf Links, Highway 544, Myrtle Beach, 29578
Holes: 18

Aberdeen CC, Aberdeen, 57401, 605-225-8135   *South Dakota*
Yards: 5765, USGA: 65.8, Holes: 18
Alcester GC, Alcester, 57701, 605-934-1839
Yards: 2358, USGA: 30.4, Holes: 18
Arrowhead GC, 3675 Sheridan Lake Rd., Rapid City, 57702
Yards: 5933, Par: 71, USGA: 67.2, Holes: 18, Pro: Dave Walters
Belle Fourche CC, Belle Fourche, 57717, 605-892-3472
Yards: 3025, USGA: 33.7, Holes: 9
Boulder Canyon CC, Sturgis, 57785, 605-347-5108
Yards: 3063, USGA: 33.2, Holes: 9
Britton GC, Britton, 57430, 605-448-2512
Yards: 2636, USGA: 32.0, Holes: 9
Brookings CC, Brookings, 57006, 605-693-3215
Yards: 6327, USGA: 69.1, Holes: 18
Burke GC, Burke, 57523, 605-775-9190
Yards: 3267, USGA: 33.9, Holes: 9
Cactus Heights GC, Sioux Falls, 57101, 605-332-9675
Yards: 3091, USGA: 34.6, Holes: 9
Central Valley GC, Hartford, 57033, 605-528-3971
Yards: 2976, Par: 36, USGA: 33.3, Holes: 9
Chamberlain CC, Chamberland, 57325, 605-734-9951
Yards: 2942, USGA: 32.7, Holes: 9
Clark GC, Clark, 57225, 605-532-5871
Yards: 2652, USGA: 31.6, Holes: 9
Clear Lake GC, Clear Lake, 57226, 605-874-2641
Yards: 2804, USGA: 34.0, Holes: 9
Colman GC, Colman, 57017
Yards: 2723, USGA: 32.2, Holes: 9

Dell Rapids GC, Dell Rapids, 57022,   605-428-3498
Yards: 3081, Par: 36, USGA: 33.5, Holes: 9
Edgebrook GC, Brookings, 57006,   605-692-6995
Yards: 5980, USGA: 68.1, Holes: 18
Elks Lodge, Rapid City, 57701,   605-393-0522
Yards: 2849, USGA: 33.0, Holes: 9
Elmwood GC, 2604 W. Russel Ave., Sioux Falls, 57104
Yards: 6567, USGA: 70.9, Holes: 27
Eureka GC, Eureka, 57437
Yards: 2661, USGA: 32.1, Holes: 9
Firesteel G&CC, Mitchell, 57301,   605-996-2084
Yards: 3187, USGA: 34.3, Holes: 9
Fisher's Grove CC, Frankfort, 57440,   605-472-9914
Yards: 2668, USGA: 31.8, Holes: 9
Flandreau Park GC, Flandreau, 57028,   605-997-3031
Yards: 2884, USGA: 32.9, Holes: 9
Gettysburg CC, Gettysburg, 57442,   605-765-2656
Yards: 2988, USGA: 32.6, Holes: 9
Glenridge GC, Irene, 57037,   605-263-3546
Yards: 2535, USGA: 31.5, Holes: 9
Gregory GC, Gregory, 57533,   605-835-8134
Yards: 3129, USGA: 33.6, Holes: 9
Hart Ranch Resort, Rapid City, 57701,   605-341-5700
Yards: 3074, USGA: 34.9, Holes: 9
Hiawatha GC, Canton, 57013,   605-987-2474
Yards: 2971, USGA: 32.9, Holes: 9
Highmore GC, Highmore, 57345
Yards: 2878, USGA: 32.6, Holes: 9
Hillsview GC, Pierre, 57501
Yards: 6372, USGA: 69.4, Holes: 18
Huron CC, Huron, 57350,   605-352-2113
Yards: 3158, USGA: 34.4, Holes: 9
Kingsbury County CC, De Smet, 57231,   605-854-3134
Yards: 3053, USGA: 33.3, Holes: 9
Lake 16 GC, Kimball, 57355
Yards: 2313, USGA: 30.2, Holes: 9
Lake Platte GC, Platte, 57369,   605-337-3300
Yards: 2666, USGA: 31.6, Holes: 9
Lake Region GC, Arlington, 57212,   605-983-5437
Yards: 2924, USGA: 33.1, Holes: 9
Lakeview Muni GC, Mitchell, 57301,   605-996-1424
Yards: 6315, USGA: 68.7, Holes: 18
Lead CC, Lead, 57754,   605-584-1852
Yards: 3190, USGA: 34.2, Holes: 9
Lee Park GC, Aberdeen, 57401,   605-622-7092
Yards: 6401, USGA: 69.6, Holes: 18
Lemmon GC, Lemmon, 57638,   605-374-3176
Yards: 2918, USGA: 33.3, Holes: 9
Madison G&CC, Madison, 57042,   605-256-3991
Yards: 3139, USGA: 34.3, Holes: 9
McCook CC, Salem, 57058,   605-425-2073
Yards: 3073, USGA: 34.8, Holes: 9
Meadowbrook GC, Huron, 57350,   605-352-1535
Yards: 3172, USGA: 34.3, Holes: 9
Milbank CC, Milbank, 57252, 605-432-4124
Yards: 3001, Par: 36, USGA: 33.7, Holes: 9

Miller CC, Miller, 57362,   605-853-2652
Yards: 2905, USGA: 32.8, Holes: 9
Minnehaha CC, Sioux Falls, 57101,   605-336-1085
Yards: 6000, USGA: 68.4, Holes: 18
Mission GC, Mission, 57555
Yards: 2827, USGA: 32.8, Holes: 9
Mobridge CC, Mobridge, 57601,   605-845-2848
Yards: 2992, USGA: 33.2, Holes: 9
Moccasin Creek CC, Aberdeen, 57402,   605-226-0900
Yards: 6469, USGA: 69.5, Holes: 18
Newell GC, Newell, 57760,   605-456-2195
Yards: 3010, USGA: 32.9, Holes: 9
North Shore, Faith, 57626
Yards: 2987, USGA: 34.6, Holes: 9
Par-Mar Valley CC, Parker, 57053,   605-297-4819
Yards: 2833, USGA: 33.3, Holes: 9
Parkston CC, Parkston, 57366,   605-928-3092
Yards: 2802, USGA: 33.2, Holes: 9
Rocky Knolls GC, Custer, 57730,   602-673-4481
Yards: 2974, USGA: 33.7, Holes: 9
Scotland GC, Scotland, 57059,   605-583-4244
Yards: 2820, USGA: 32.4, Holes: 9
Southern Hills CC, Hot Springs, 57747,   605-745-6400
Yards: 2779, USGA: 33.7, Holes: 9
Spearfish Canyon CC, Spearfish, 57783,   605-642-7156
Yards: 3025, USGA: 34.9, Holes: 9
Springfield GC, Springfield, 57062,   605-369-5525
Yards: 2995, USGA: 33.9, Holes: 9
Tomahawk Lake CC, Deadwood, 57732,   605-578-9979
Yards: 3136, USGA: 34.3, Holes: 9
Valley View CC, Sisseton, 57262,   605-698-3742
Yards: 2808, USGA: 32.3, Holes: 9
Vermillion GC, Vermillion, 57069,   605-624-4550
Yards: 2996, USGA: 33.5, Holes: 9
Watertown CC, 552 S. Lake Dr., Watertown, 57201,   605-886-3554
Yards: 6213, Par: 72, USGA: 68.5, Holes: 18, Pro: Larry Hayn
Watertown Muni GC, Watertown, 57201,   605-886-3618
Yards: 6250, USGA: 67.4, Holes: 18
Webster CC, Webster, 57274,   605-345-3971
Yards: 2898, USGA: 32.4, Holes: 9
Wessington Springs CC, Wessington Springs, 57382
Yards: 2156, USGA: 29.5, Holes: 9
Westward Ho CC, Sioux Falls, 57101,   605-336-3737
Yards: 6466, USGA: 70.6, Holes: 18
Winner CC, Winner, 57580,   605-842-9981
Yards: 3078, Par: 35, USGA: 33.8, Holes: 9

Adamsville GC, Old Shiloh Rd., Adamsville, 38310,   901-632-0678   *Tennessee*
Par: 36, Holes: 9
Bays Mountain GC, Chris-Haven Dr., Knoxville, 37865,   615-577-8172
Par: 70, Holes: 18
Bent Creek GC, Rt 3 Hwy 321, Gatlinburg, 37738,   615-436-3947
Yards: 6084, Par: 72, USGA: 68.0, Holes: 18, Pro: Mark Wallace
Brainerd GC, 5203 Old Mission Rd., Chattanooga, 37411,   615-894-7131
Par: 72, Holes: 18

Briarwood GC, PO Box 95, Crab Orchard, 37723, 615-484-5285
Yards: 5950, Par: 72, USGA: 70.3, Holes: 18, Pro: Norm Renaud
Brown Acres, 406 Brown Rd., Chattanooga, 37421, 615-894-9001
Par: 72, Holes: 18
Carroll Lake GC, Hwy. 22, McKenzie, 38201, 901-352-2998
Par: 71, Holes: 18
Cedar Hills GC, Martel Rd., Lenoir City, 37771, 615-986-6521
Par: 71, Holes: 18
Chattanooga G&CC, Riverview Rd., Chattanooga, 37405, 615-266-6178
Par: 70, Holes: 18
Clinchview G&CC, Hwy. 11W, Bean Station, 37708, 615-586-9958
Par: 72, Holes: 18
Concord Golf, E. Brainerd Rd., Chattanooga, 37421, 615-894-4536
Par: 67, Holes: 18
Copper Basin G&CC, Hwy. 64, Copperhill, 37317, 615-496-3579
Par: 71, Holes: 9
Creek's Bend GC, 5900 Hixson Pk., Chattanooga, 37415, 615-842-5911
Par: 70, Holes: 18
Crockett G&CC, Country Club Rd., Alamo, 38001, 901-696-8645
Par: 36, Holes: 9
Crooked Creek GC, Oneida, 37841, 615-569-9880
Par: 36, Holes: 9
Cumberland Bend, Hwy. 56, Gainesboro, 38562, 615-268-0259
Par: 36, Holes: 9
Dandridge C&CC, Valley Home Rd., Dandridge, 37725, 615-397-2655
Par: 72, Holes: 18
Davy Crockett Park GC, 4380 Rangeline Road, Memphis, 38127, 901-358-3375
Yards: 6120, Par: 72, USGA: 70.0, Holes: 18, Pro: "Buddy" McEwen
Dead Horse Lake, Sherrill Lane, Knoxville, 37932, 615-693-5270
Par: 71, Holes: 18
Edmund Orgill Park, 9080 Bethuel Rd., Millington, 38053, 901-872-3610
Par: 71, Holes: 18
Emory G&CC, West Hills Subdivision, Harriman, 37748, 615-882-9977
Par: 35, Holes: 9
Fairfield Glade (4 Courses), Peavine Rd., Crossville, 38555, 800-251-6778
Forrest Crossing, Riverview Dr., Franklin, 37064, 615-794-9400
Par: 72, Holes: 18
Fox Meadows, 3064 Clark, Memphis, 38104, 901-362-0232
Par: 71, Holes: 18
Galloway, 3815 Walnut Grove, Memphis, 38117, 901-685-7805
Par: 71, Holes: 18
Hardeman County CC, Hwy. 64 West, Bolivar, 38008, 901-658-2731
Par: 36, Holes: 9
Harpeth Hills, 2424 Old Hickory, Nashville, 37221, 615-259-6399
Par: 72, Holes: 18
Heatherhurst GC, PO Box 1500, Fairfield Glades, 38555
Holes: 9
Henry County CC, Country Club Road, Puryear, 38251, 901-247-3264
Par: 36, Holes: 9
Henry Horton GC, Hwy. 31A RTE. 1, Chapel Hill, 37034, 615-364-2319
Par: 72, Holes: 18
Hickory Valley, 2453 Hickory Valley, Chattanooga, 37421, 615-894-1576
Par: 35, Holes: 9
Hillcrest CC, Off Hwy. 64, Pulaski, 38478, 615-363-5630
Par: 36, Holes: 9

Hohenwald GC, Hwy. 99, Hohenwald, 38462, 615-796-5421
Par: 36, Holes: 9
Holston Hills GC, 5200 Holston Hills Rd., Knoxville, 37914
Holston Valley GC, Bristol, 37620, 615-878-2021
Par: 70, Holes: 18
Hunters Point GC, Lebanon, 37087, 615-444-7521
Par: 72, Holes: 18
King College, 1000 E. State St., Bristol, 37620, 615-968-2331
Par: 70, Holes: 9
Knoxville GC, 3925 Schaad Rd., Knox, 37921, 615-691-7143
Yards: 6800, Par: 72, USGA: 68.2, Holes: 18, Pro: Tim Bridgman
Lakeside GC, Paint Ferry Rock Rd., Kingston, 37763, 615-376-5397
Par: 35, Holes: 9
Lambert Acres, Old Walland Hwy., Maryville, 37801, 615-982-9838
Par: 72, Holes: 18
Madisonville GC, Hwy. 411 N., Madisonville, 37354, 615-442-9240
Par: 36, Holes: 9
Magic Valley, Eva Road, Camden, 38320, 901-584-9964
Par: 36, Holes: 9
Mason Rudolph, 1514 Golf Club Ln., Clarksville, 37043, 615-647-0354
Par: 35, Holes: 9
McCabe Park, Murphy Rd. & 46th, Nashville, 37202, 615-297-9138
Par: 35, Holes: 27
McDonald GC, Gundown Rd., Rogersville, 37857, 615-272-8143
Par: 36, Holes: 9
Milan G&CC, Hwy. 70-79, Milan, 38358, 901-686-0616
Par: 72, Holes: 18
Moccasin Bend GC, Moccasin Bend Rd., Chattanooga, 37405, 615-267-3585
Par: 72, Holes: 18
Montgomery Bell State Park GC, P.O. Box 39, Burns, 37029, 615-797-2578
Yards: 6915, Par: 71, USGA: 71.1, Holes: 18, Pro: D. Hartsfield
Morristown G&CC, Valley Home Rd., Morristown, 37813, 615-586-9953
Par: 35, Holes: 9
Mountainbrook GC, 1001 Reads Lake, Chattanooga, 37415, 615-870-4040
Par: 34, Holes: 9
Municipal GC, Golf Course Rd., Dyersburg, 38024, 901-286-0354
Par: 71, Holes: 18
Nolichuckey GC, Rt. 7, Greenville, 37743, 615-639-1622
Holes: 9
Paris CC, Hwy. 79 E, Paris, 38242, 901-642-0591
Par: 36, Holes: 9
Paris Landing GC, RTE. 1, Buchanan, 38222, 901-644-1332
Yards: 6479, Par: 72, USGA: 71.6, Holes: 18, Pro: Keith Hickman
Percy Warner Park, Forrest Park Dr., Nashville, 37205, 615-352-9958
Par: 34, Holes: 9
Pickwick Landing St. Pk., Hwy 57, Pickwick Dam, 38365, 901-689-3149
Par: 72, Holes: 18
Pine Hill, 1005 Alice, Memphis, 38106, 901-775-9434
Par: 71, Holes: 18
Pine Lakes GC, Singleton Station, Rockford, 37853, 615-970-9018
Par: 71, Holes: 18
Pine Oaks GC, 1709 Buffalo, Johnson City, 37604, 615-926-5451
Par: 71, Holes: 18
Poplar Meadows, Everett Stewart, Union City, 38261, 901-885-3650
Par: 36, Holes: 9

Rhodes Golf Center, 2400 Metrocenter, Nashville, 37228, 615-242-2336
Par: 36, Holes: 9
Rivermont G&CC, off Hixson Pk., Chattanooga, 37415, 615-877-7506
Par: 70, Holes: 18
Riverview, Huff Ferry Rd., Loudon, 37774, 615-986-6972
Par: 36, Holes: 9
Riverview, S. 17th & Sevier, Nashville, 37202, 615-259-6399
Par: 29, Holes: 9
Roan Valley, Hwy. 421, Mountain City, 37683, 615-727-7931
Par: 72, Holes: 18
Rolling Hills GC, P.O.Box 1034 Candies Lane, Cleveland, 37364, 615-472-7129
Yards: 6200, Par: 72, USGA: 70.0, Holes: 18, Pro: Jeff Curtis
Sculley GC, McKellar Airport, Jackson, 38301, 901-424-4500
Par: 36, Holes: 9
Sequatchie Valley G&CC, Swedens Cove Rd., South Pittsburg, 37380,
615-837-6532   Par: 36, Holes: 9
Sewanee Golf & Tennis, Hwy. 64, Sewanee, 37375, 615-598-1104
Par: 36, Holes: 9
Silver Lake GC, Silver Lake Rd., Church Hill, 37642, 615-357-3441
Par: 70, Holes: 9
Smithville GC, Smithville, 37166, 615-597-6648
Par: 36, Holes: 9
South Hills GC, 795 Tuskegee Dr., Oak Ridge, 37830, 615-483-5747
Par: 36, Holes: 9
Southwest Point, Hwy. 58 S., Kingston, 37763, 615-376-9075
Par: 72, Holes: 18
Sparta G&CC, Gaines St., Sparta, 38583, 615-738-5836
Par: 36, Holes: 9
Steel Creek Park, P.O.Box 754, Bristol, 37620, 615-764-6411
Par: 36, Holes: 9
Swan Lake, Dunbar Cave Rd., Clarksville, 37043, 615-648-0479
Par: 71, Holes: 18
Tri-City, Rt. 2, P.O.Box 18, Blountville, 37617, 615-323-4178
Par: 71, Holes: 18
Twin Creeks GC, Rt. 2, Box 2660, Chuckey, 37641, 615-257-5192
Holes: 9
Two Rivers, Two Rivers Pkwy., Nashville, 37214, 615-889-9748
Par: 72, Holes: 18
Valleybrook G&CC, Valleybrook Rd., Chattanooga, 37415, 615-842-4646
Par: 72, Holes: 18
Wallace Hills GC, Rt.4, Box 14, Maryville, 37801, 615-984-4260
Par: 72, Holes: 27
Waterville GC, Dalton Pike, Cleveland, 37311, 615-472-8515
Par: 72, Holes: 18
Weakley Country CC, Rock Hill Rd., Sharon, 38255, 901-456-2323
Par: 36, Holes: 9
White Plains GC, Route 13 Box 104, Cookeville, 38501
Holes: 18
Whittle Springs, 3113 Valley View, Knoxville, 37917, 615-525-1022
Par: 72, Holes: 18

Abernathy CC, PO Box 55, Abernathy, 79311, 806-328-5261   *Texas*
Holes: 9
Academy of Golf, 25 Club Estates Parkway, Austin, 78738, 512-261-7100
Pro: Clayton Cole

Albany GC, PO Box 157, Albany, 76430, 915-762-3746
Holes: 9, Pro: Mike Snead
Alice Muni GC, PO Box 646, Alice, 78332, 512-668-6940
Holes: 18, Pro: Rick Monsevais
Alpine CC, Bos 985 Loop Rd., Alpine, 79831, 915-837-2752
Yards: 5938, USGA: 66.4, Holes: 9
Alpine GC, Rt. 9, Box 610, Longview, 75601, 214-753-4515
Holes: 18, Pro: Mike Williams
Alvin G&CC, PO Box 981, Alvin, 77511, 713-331-4541
Holes: 9, Pro: Rex Casey
Amarillo Public GC, 3805 Moberly Dr., Amarillo, 79111, 806-335-1142
Holes: 18, Pro: Todd Posey
Andrews County GC, Golf Course Rd., Andrews, 79714, 915-523-2461
Holes: 18, Pro: Alan Pursley
Anson Muni GC, Rt. 1, box 1, Anson, 79501, 915-823-9822
Holes: 9
Aquarena Springs GC, PO Box 1107, San Marcos, 78666, 512-392-2710
Holes: 9, Pro: Bobby Schauer
Archer City CC, Box 851, Archer City, 76351, 817-574-4322
Holes: 9
Ascarte GC, 6900 Delta, El Paso, 79985, 915-772-7381
Yards: 6185, USGA: 69.2, Holes: 27, Pro: Manny Martinez
Aspermount City GC, PO Box 622, Aspermount, 79502, 817-989-3381
Holes: 9
Babe Zaharias GC, PO Box 1151, Port Arthur, 77640, 409-722-8286
Holes: 18, Pro: Johnny Barlow
Battle Lake GC, Route 1, Box 82, Mart, Malakoff, 76664, 817-876-2837
Holes: 18, Pro: Gary Hammer
Bay Forest GC, 201 Bay Forest Dr., La Porte, 77571, 713-471-4653
Holes: 18, Pro: Alex Osmond
Bay G&CC, 400 Half Moon Way, Runaway Bay, 76026, 817-575-2225
Holes: 18, Pro: Mac McCall
Bayou Din GC, Route 2, Box 2722, Beaumont, 77705, 409-796-1327
Holes: 18, Pro: Ed Campbell
Bayou GC, P.O. Box 3611, Texas City, 77590, 409-948-8362
Holes: 18, Pro: Claude Harmon
Birmingham GC, Box 728, Rusk, 75785, 214-683-2041
Par: 36, Holes: 9, Pro: Milt Harris
Blue Lake GC, Rt. 3, Box 246, Marble Falls, 78654, 512-598-5524
Holes: 9
BlueBonnet Country, Route #2 Box 3471, Navasota, 77868, 409-894-2207
Yards: 6707, Par: 72, Holes: 18, Pro: Ron Byrd
Booker CC, Box 221, Booker, 79005, 806-658-9663
Holes: 9
Bosque Valley GC, Box 759, Meridian, 76665, 817-435-2692
Par: 36, Holes: 9, Pro: Matt Child
Brady Muni CC, Highway 87 West, Brady, 76825, 915-597-6010
Holes: 9
Brazoria Bend GC, Rt. 3 Box 102, Rosharon, 77583, 713-431-2954
Yards: 3700, Par: 36, USGA: 69.0, Holes: 9, Pro: Larry Bushee
Breckenridge CC, Box 72, Breckenridge, 76024, 817-559-3466
Holes: 9
Bridgeport G&CC, PO Box 305, Bridgeport, 76026, 817-683-9438
Holes: 9, Pro: Lonny Benham
Brock Park GC, 8201 John Ralston Rd., Houston, 77004, 713-458-1350
Holes: 18, Pro: Jody Hawkins

Brookhaven GC, 3333 Golfing Green Dr., Dallas, 75234
Brownsville CC, 1800 W. San Marcelo, Brownsville, 78520, 512-541-2582
Par: 70, Holes: 18, Pro: Johnny Aguillon
Bryan GC, 206 West Villa Maria, Bryan, 77801, 409-823-0126
Holes: 18, Pro: Jerry Honza
Butler Park Pitch & Putt GC, 201 Lee-Barton Drive, Austin, 78704,
412-477-9025   Holes: 9
Canadian GC, PO Box 1, Canadian, 79014, 806-323-5512
Holes: 9
Canyon CC, Rt. 1, Box 213, Canyon, 79015, 806-499-3397
Holes: 9, Pro: Alan Coe
Cape Royale GC, P.O. Box 321, Cold Springs, 77331, 713-353-4176
Holes: 18, Pro: Ron Phillips
Caprock GC, Box 220, Post, 79356, 806-495-3029
Holes: 9, Pro: D. H. Bartlett
Carmack Lake GC, Rte. 1, Box 228, Converse, 78109, 512-658-3806
Holes: 18, Pro: Don Carmack
Carpenter's Par 3 GC, 5223 Hamilton Wolfe, San Antonio, 78229, 512-696-3143
Holes: 9
Carrizo Springs Muni GC, Rt. 2, Box 44, Carrizo Springs, 78834, 512-876-2596
Holes: 9, Pro: C.V. Speer Jr.
Casa Blanca GC, PO Box 141, Laredo, 78040, 512-727-9218
Holes: 18, Pro: Carlos Guerra
Cedar Creek GC, 8250 Dogleg Left Dr., San Antonio, 78255, 512-695-5050
Holes: 18, Pro: Jim Traina
Cedar Crest GC, 1800 Southerland, Dallas, 75203
Chambers Country GC, #1 Pinchback Dr., Anahuac, 77514, 409-267-3236
Yards: 6664, Par: 72, USGA: 69.5, Holes: 18, Pro: Hal Underwood
Chambers County GC, Box 1208, Anahuac, 77514, 409-267-3236
Holes: 18, Pro: Hal Underwood
Champions GC, 13722 Champions Dr., Houston, 77069
Channelview GC, 8306 Sheldon Rd., P.O. Box 660, Channelview, 77503,
713-452-2183   Holes: 18, Pro: Paul Luna
Chase Oaks GC, 7201 Chase Oaks Blvd., Plano, 75023, 214-517-7777
Holes: 27, Pro: Rick DeLoach
Cherokee CC, Box 1069, Henderson Hwy., Jacksonville, 75766, 214-586-2141
Holes: 18, Pro: Wanda Hendrix
Chester W. Ditto Muni GC, 801 Brown Blvd, Arlington, 76011, 817-275-5941
Holes: 18, Pro: Clint Baak
Cielo Vista GC, 1510 Hawkins, El Paso, 79925, 915-591-4927
Yards: 6600, Par: 72, USGA: 69.0, Holes: 18, Pro: Mark Pelletier
Clarendon CC, Star Rt. 2, Box 48A, Clarendon, 79226, 806-874-2166
Holes: 18, Pro: Eddie Baker
Clay County CC, Henrietta, 76365, 817-538-4339
Holes: 9, Pro: Don Parker
Clear Creek GC, 3902 Fellows Rd., Houston, 77047, 713-738-8000
Holes: 18, Pro: Greg Dillon
Clear Lake GC, 1202 Reseda Dr., Houston, 77062, 713-488-0252
Holes: 18, Pro: Jeff Sheehan
Cleveland Golf & Health Club, P.O. Box 519, Cleveland, 77328, 713-593-0323
Holes: 9, Pro: Paul Hendrix
Coleman CC, PO Box 128, Coleman, 76834, 915-625-2922
Holes: 9, Pro: Jack Birdwell
Colonial GC, 3735 Country Club Circle, Fort Worth, 76109
Columbus GC, 1617 Walnut, Columbus, 78934, 409-732-5575
Holes: 9, Pro: Dan Meyers

Comanche Creek GC, Mason, 76856, 915-347-5798
Holes: 9
Comanche Trail GC, PO Box 391, Big Spring, 79720, 915-263-7271
Holes: 18, Pro: Al Patterson
Conroe Golf Center, 12000 Highway I-45, P.O. Box 3, Conroe, 77305,
409-273-4002 Holes: 27, Pro: Rick Lewis
Copperas Cove GC, Box 188, Coperas Cover, 76522, 817-547-2606
Holes: 9
Copperas Hollow GC, Rt. 5, Box 316A, Caldwell, 77836, 409-567-4422
Holes: 9
Cottonwood Creek GC, 5200 Bagby, Waco, 76711, 817-752-2474
Holes: 18, Pro: Dale Morgan
Cottonwood Creek GC, 1001 South Ed Carey Drive, Harlingen, 78552,
512-425-4887 Holes: 9, Pro: Sid Latimer
Country Campus Public GC, Route 3 Box 558, Huntsville, 77340, 409-291-0008
Yards: 5940, Par: 72, Holes: 18, Pro: John Medley
Country Club of Merkel, 200 Country Club Rd., Merkel, 79536, 915-928-5514
Holes: 9
Crane CC, Box 532, Crane, 79731, 915-558-2651
Holes: 9, Pro: Stan Allen
Cuero Muni GC, Rt. 4, Box 122, Cuero, 77954, 512-275-3233
Holes: 9, Pro: Stanley Koenig
Cummins Creek CC, Giddings, 78942, 409-542-3777
Par: 36, Holes: 9
Cypress Creek CC, Route 1, Box 95, Scroggins, 75480, 214-860-2155
Holes: 9
D.J.'s Golf Center, Inc., 2043 S. Richey, Pasadena, 77502, 713-473-9060
Dallas Athletic GC, 4111 La Prada, Dallas, 75228
Decatur GC, Box 16, Decatur, 76234, 817-627-3789
Holes: 9
Deer Trail GC, Route 1, Box 58, Woodville, 75979, 409-283-7985
Par: 36, Holes: 9, Pro: Eric Carrington
Devine GC, 116 Malone Dr., Devine, 78016, 512-663-9943
Par: 36, Holes: 9, Pro: Kevin Yanity
Diboll Muni GC, Box 145, Diboll, 75941, 409-829-5086
Holes: 9, Pro: Dewey Wolf
Eagle Lake Recreation Center, P.O. Box 845, Eagle Lake, 77434, 409-234-5981
Holes: 9, Pro: Larry Broeshe
Eagle Pass GC, PO Box 483, Eagle Pass, 78852, 512-773-9761
Holes: 9
Ebony GC, 300 W. Palms, Edinburg, 78539, 512-381-1244
Holes: 0, Pro: Walter Shirah
Echo Creek CC, Rt. 1, Box 10, Murchison, 75778, 214-852-7094
Holes: 9, Pro: John Brewer
Edna CC, PO Box 563, Edna, 77957, 512-782-3010
Holes: 9
Eldorado GC, Box 1115, Eldorado, 76936, 915-853-2036
Holes: 9
Electra CC, Rt. 2, Electra, 76360, 817-495-3832
Holes: 9
Elk Hollow GC, Rt. 10, Paris, 75460, 214-785-6586
Par: 36, Holes: 9, Pro: Pete Witter
Elm Grove GC, 3203 Milwaukee, Lubbokc, 79407, 806-799-7801
Holes: 18, Pro: Terry Harvick
Fairway Farm Golf & Hunt Club, Drawer T, San Augustine, 75972,
409-275-2334 Holes: 18

Fairway Farm GC, Hwy. 21 E., Lufkin, 75972
Fairways GC, 2524 West Spur 54, Harlingen, 78550,   512-423-9098
Par: 27, Holes: 9
Falfurrias GC, Box 556, Falfurrias, 78355,   512-325-5348
Holes: 9, Pro: Bond Cosby
Farwell CC, Rt. 2, Farwell, 79325,   806-481-9910
Yards: 6520, USGA: 69.0, Holes: 9, Pro: C. Fontanilla
Feather Bay G&CC, Rte. 1, Box 800, Brownwood, 76801,   915-784-6741
Holes: 9, Pro: Jack Blundell
Firewheel Golf Park GC, PO Box 462074, Garland, 75046,   214-205-2795
Holes: 36, Pro: Jerry Andrews
First Colony GC, 1650 Hwy. 6 South, Sugar Land, 77478,   713-265-4653
Holes: 18, Pro: Paul Levy
Floydada CC, Box 8, Floydada, 79235,   806-983-2769
Holes: 9, Pro: Danny Riddle
Flying C. GC, HCR, San Antonio, 78003
Flying L Resort GC, PO Box HCR1, Box 32, Bandera, 78003,   512-796-3001
Par: 72, Holes: 18
Fort Brown Muni GC, PO Box 3027, Brownsville, 78520,   512-541-0394
Holes: 18, Pro: Robert Lucio
Fort Clark Springs CC, PO Box 1328, Brackettville, 78832,   512-563-9204
Par: 70, Holes: 18, Pro: Karl Chism
Fort Ringgold GC, 111 Pete Diaz Ave., Rio Grande City, 78582,   512-487-5666
Holes: 9
Fox Creek GC, Route 3, Box 128F, Hempstead, 77445,   409-826-2131
Holes: 18
Freeport Municipal GC, 830 Slaughter Rd., Freeport, 77541,   409-233-8311
Par: 72, Holes: 18, Pro: A. R. Nichols
Freestone County CC, Box 517, Teague, 75860,   817-739-3272
Holes: 9, Pro: Billy Newlin
Friendswood CC, #3 Country Club Drive, Friendswood, 77546,   713-331-4396
Holes: 18, Pro: Chas. Henley Jr
Frisch Auf Valley CC, P.O. Box 101, La Grange, 78945,   409-968-6113
Par: 36, Holes: 9, Pro: Margaret Burton
Gabe Lozano Senior Golf Center, 4401 Old Brownsville Rd., Corpus Christi, 78405, 512-883-3696 Holes: 18, Pro: Bruce Haddad
Gaines County GC, PO Box 308, Seminole, 79360,   915-758-3808
Holes: 9, Pro: Dale Newman
Gainesville Muni GC, 200 S. Rusk, Gainesville, 76240,   817-665-2161
Holes: 18
Garden Valley Resort, Rt. 2, Box 501, Lindale, 75771,   214-882-6107
Yards: 5995, Par: 71, USGA: 68.0, Holes: 18
Gatesville CC, PO Box 638, Gatesville, 76528,   817-865-6917
Holes: 18
Giddings CC, PO Box 838, Giddings, 78942,   409-542-3777
Holes: 9, Pro: Allen Jones
Gladewater CC, Rt. 1, Box 66, Gladewater, 75647,   214-845-4566
Holes: 9
Glenbrook Park GC, 8205 North Bayou Dr., Houston, 77207-2,   713-644-4081
Holes: 18, Pro: Gene Hill
Graham CC, PO Box 576, Graham, 76046,   817-549-7721
Holes: 9, Pro: Lloyd R. Moody
Granbury CC, Box 398, Granbury, 76048,   817-573-9912
Holes: 9
Grand Prairie Muni GC, 3203 S.E. 14th St., Grand Prairie, 75051,   214-263-0661
Holes: 27, Pro: Jan Smith

Grapevine Municipal GC, 3800 Fairway Dr., Grapevine, 76051, 817-481-0422
Yards: 6369, Par: 72, USGA: 69.5, Holes: 18, Pro: James M. Smith
Grayson County College GC, 610 Grayson Drive, Denison, 75020,
214-786-9719 Par: 72, Holes: 18, Pro: Mike Hurley
Green Meadows GC, 6138 Franz Rd., Katy, 77449, 713-391-3670
Yards: 5440, Par: 70, USGA: 65.4, Holes: 18, Pro: Mike McRoberts
Greenbriar G&CC, Box 246, Moody, 76557, 817-853-2927
Par: 70, Holes: 18, Pro: Frank Normand
Grover C Keeton GC, 2323 Jim Miller, Dallas, 75217
Gus Wortham Park GC, 7000 Capitol Ave., Houston, 77207-7, 713-921-3227
Holes: 18, Pro: Paul Reed
Hallettsville Golf Association, P.O. Box 433, Hallettsville, 77964, 512-798-7190
Par: 35, Holes: 9, Pro: Rick Barrow
Hancock Park GC, PO Box 666, Lampasas, 76550, 512-556-3202
Holes: 9
Hancock Park GC, 811 East 41st, Austin, 78751, 512-453-0276
Holes: 9
Haskell CC, Rt. 1, Box 190, Haskell, 79521, 817-864-3400
Holes: 9, Pro: Jack Medford
Hatch Bend CC, PO Box 141 Porft Lavaca, Port Isabel, 77979, 512-552-3037
Holes: 9
Hearne Muni GC, 405 Norwood, Hearne, 77889, 409-279-3112
Holes: 9
Hempstead GC, P.O. Box 186, Hempstead, 77445, 409-826-3212
Yards: 6575, Par: 72, USGA: 72.3, Holes: 9
Henry Homberg GC, PO Box 20436, Beaumont, 77720, 409-842-3220
Holes: 18, Pro: Ronald Pfleider
Hermann Park GC, P.O. Box 8071, Houston, 77004
Yards: 6332, Par: 71, Holes: 18, Pro: Elroy Marti, Jr
Highland Lakes GC, Box 194, Buchanan Dam, 78609, 512-793-2859
Holes: 9, Pro: Johnny Tyson
Highland Lakes GC, Buchanan Dam, 78609, 512-793-2859
Par: 36, Holes: 9
Highland Lakes CC, PO Box 4826, Lago Vista, 78641, 512-267-1685
Par: 72, Holes: 18, Pro: Denis Ching
Hillcrest GC, 3401 Fairway, Alvin, 77511, 713-331-3505
Yards: 2356, Par: 33, Holes: 9, Pro: Charles Wilson
Hillside Acres CC, Rt. 1, Hale Center, 79041, 806-839-2188
Holes: 9
Hogan Park GC, PO Box 10136, Midland, 79702, 915-685-7360
Holes: 27, Pro: Shaun McDonald
Holiday Hills CC, Rt. 3, Box 92C, Mineral Wells, 76067, 817-325-8403
Holes: 18, Pro: Mac Spikes
Holly Lake Ranch GC, PO Box 711, Hawkins, 75765, 214-769-2397
Holes: 18, Pro: Jeff Davis
Hondo GC, PO Box 2, Hondo, 78861, 512-426-8825
Holes: 9, Pro: Bernie Yanity
Horizon Golf & Tennis Club, 16000 Ashford Street, El Paso, 79927,
915-852-3150 Yards: 6514, Par: 71, USGA: 70.8, Holes: 18
Horseshoe Bend CC, 305 Lipan Trail, Weatherford, 76086, 817-594-6454
Holes: 9
Houston Golf Practise, 10115 Southwest Freeway, Houston, 77031,
713-541-3119
Houston Golf Academy, 4035 South Hwy. 6, Houston, 77082, 713-493-3276
Par: 27, Holes: 9, Pro: Rodney Boling

Houston Golf Range, 1030 Witte Road, Houston, 77055, 713-973-6233
Par: 27, Holes: 9, Pro: Ernie Cho
Houston Hills GC, 9720 Ruffino Rd., Houston, 77031, 713-933-2300
Holes: 9, Pro: Chuck Berson
Huber GC, Box 2831, Borger, 79008, 806-273-2231
Holes: 18, Pro: "Andy" Anderson
Hyatt Bear Creek GC, W. Airfield Dr. & Bear Creek, Dallas-Ft Worth Airpor,
75261, 214-453-0140 Holes: 36, Pro: Larry Box
Independence GC, Box 198, Gonzales, 78629, 512-672-9926
Holes: 9
Indian Shores Golf Club, 2141 Whitefeather Trail, Crosby, 77532,
713-324-2592 Par: 36, Holes: 9, Pro: L. Jacobson
Iraan CC, Box 356, Iraan, 79744, 915-639-8892
Holes: 9
Jacksboro G&CC, 309 N. 8th St., Jacksboro, 76056, 817-567-9416
Holes: 9, Pro: James Gammon
James Connally GC, Box 4638, Waco, 76705, 817-799-6561
Holes: 18, Pro: Jack Barger
Jersey Meadow GC, 8502 Rio Grande, Houston, 77040, 713-896-0900
Holes: 18, Pro: Brad Schaffner
Jimmy Clay GC, PO Box 5553, Austin, 78763, 512-444-0999
Holes: 18, Pro: Joe Balander
John C. Beasley Muni GC, City of Beesville,Atn: GC Mgr, Beeville, 78102,
512-358-4295 Par: 36, Holes: 9
Junction GC, Box 656, Junction, 76849, 915-446-2968
Holes: 9
Karnes County CC, PO Box 123, Kenedy, 78119, 512-583-3200
Holes: 9
Killeen Muni GC, Roy Reynolds Dr., 400 N 2nd, Killen, 76541, 817-699-6034
Holes: 18
Kingwood Cove GC, 805 Hamblen, Kingwood, 77339, 713-358-1155
Holes: 18, Pro: Scott Curiel
Kingwood GC, 1700 Lake Kingwood Trail, Houston, 77347
Kurt Cox GC, 11890 O'Connor, San Antonio, 78233, 512-655-3131
Holes: 9, Pro: Kurt Cox
Kurth-Landrum GC, Southwestern Univ., Box 335, Georgetown, 78626,
512-863-1333 Holes: 9
L.B. Houston GC, 11223 Luna Rd., Dallas, 75229, 214-670-6322
Yards: 6280, Par: 72, Holes: 18, Pro: Leonard Jones
L. E. Ramey GC, PO Box 1359, Kingsville, 78363, 512-592-1101
Holes: 18, Pro: Jerry Honza
Lady Bird Johnson Muni GC, 101 Glenmore, Fredericksburg, 78624,
512-997-4010 Par: 36, Holes: 9, Pro: Denis Allen
Lajitas Resort GC, Star Route 70, Box 400, Terlingua, 79852, 915-424-3211
Holes: 9
Lake Arlington GC, 1616 Green Oaks W., Fort Worth, 76016
Lake Arlington Muni GC, PO Box 13215, Arlington, 76013, 817-451-6101
Holes: 18, Pro: Clint Baack
Lake Cisco CC, PO Box 389, Cisco, 76437, 817-442-2725
Holes: 9
Lake Creek GC, PO Box 453, Munday, 76371, 817-422-4458
Holes: 9
Lake Houston GC, 27350 Afton Way, Huffman, 77336, 713-324-1841
Holes: 18, Pro: Jack Forester
Lake Park GC, Box 464, Lewisville, 75067, 214-436-5332
Holes: 18, Pro: Frank Jennings

Lake Whitney GC, Rt. 1, Box 2075, Whitney, 76692, 817-694-2313
Par: 70, Holes: 18
Lakeside GC, Eastland, 76448, 817-629-2117
Par: 36, Holes: 9
Lakeside GC, PO Box 2654, San Angelo, 76902, 915-949-2069
Holes: 9, Pro: John Manage
Lakewood GC, 6430 Gaston Ave, Dallas, 75214
Lakewood Recreation Center GC, Rt. 1,, Rising Star, 76471, 817-643-7792
Holes: 9
Lancaster's Country View GC, 240 West Beltline Rd., Lancaster, 75146,
214-227-0995   Holes: 18, Pro: David Hersman
Landa Park Muni GC, 1445 Agarita Trail, New Braunfels, 78132, 512-625-3225
Holes: 18, Pro: B. G. Halbert
LaVista G&CC, 2000 Northwest Loop 11, Wichita Falls, 76307, 817-855-0771
Holes: 18, Pro: Larry Hickman
Lazy Oaks GC, PO Box 1509, Bandera, 78003, 512-796-3117
Holes: 18
Leaning Pine GC, 494 Laughlin AFB, Del Rio, 78843, 512-298-5451
Holes: 9
Lee's Par 3, PO Box 310059, New Braunfels, 78131, 512-620-4653
Par: 27, Holes: 9
Legends GC, Box 596, Stevenville, 76401, 817-968-2200
Holes: 18
Leon Valley GC, Box 267, Belton, 76513, 817-939-5271
Holes: 18, Pro: Carlie Tice
Lion's Muni GC, 2901 Enfield Rd., Austin, 78703, 512-477-6963
Holes: 18, Pro: Lloyd Morrison
Littlefield CC, Box 767, Littlefield, 79339, 806-385-3309
Holes: 9, Pro: Mike Nix
Live Oak CC, Box 63, Weatherford, 76086, 817-594-7596
Holes: 9
Live Oak GC, 602 Lakeway Drive, Austin, 78734, 512-261-7573
Holes: 18, Pro: Larry Bishop
Livingston Municipal GC, P.O. Box 488, Livingston, 77351, 409-327-4901
Holes: 9, Pro: "Sonny" Nash
Llano Grande GC, Box 1002, Mercedes, 78570, 512-565-3351
Holes: 9, Pro: Al Jones
LLano GC, Route 10, Box 34, Llano, 78643, 915-247-5100
Par: 36, Holes: 9, Pro: David McNeely
Lockhart State Park GC, Rt. 3, Box 69, Lockhard, 78644, 512-398-3479
Holes: 9
Longview CC, 2300 Highway 42, Longview, 75604, 214-759-9251
Par: 70, Holes: 18, Pro: Buster Cupit
Los Ebanos GC, PO Box 14969, Zapata, 78076, 512-765-8103
Holes: 9
Lost Creek GC, Box 26417, Fort Worth, 76116, 817-244-3312
Holes: 18, Pro: Tom Gilbert
Lost Pines GC, PO Box 900, Bastrop, 78602, 512-321-2327
Holes: 9, Pro: Rudy Belmares
Luling GC, PO Box 1255, Luling, 78648, 512-875-5114
Holes: 9
Marfa Muni GC, PO Box 308 Golf Course Rd., Marfa, 79843, 915-729-4043
Yards: 6570, USGA: 69.2, Holes: 9, Pro: E. Villarreal
Marriott's GC at Fossil Creek, 3401 Clubgate Drive, Fort Worth, 76137,
817-847-1900   Holes: 18, Pro: Rocky Papachek

Martin's Valley Ranches & CC, PO Box 1469, Mission, 78572, 512-585-6330
Holes: 18
Max Starcke Park GC, PO Box 591, Seguin, 78155, 512-379-4853 Holes: 18,
Pro: Biff Alexander
Maxwell Muni GC, 1002 S. 32nd, Abilene, 79602, 915-692-2737
Holes: 18, Pro: Dave Hand
McKinney Muni GC, Hwy. 5, McKinney, 75069, 214-542-4523
Holes: 9
Meadow Lakes G&CC, 220 Meadow Lakes Dr., Marble Falls, 78654,
512-693-3300 Par: 72, Holes: 18, Pro: Bill Tombs
Meadow Park GC, PO Box 231, Arlington, 76010, 817-275-0221
Holes: 9, Pro: James Marsh
Meadowbrook CC, Box 224, Palestine, 75801, 214-723-7530
Holes: 9, Pro: Terry Brown
Meadowbrook Muni GC, 1815 Jensen Rd., Fort Worth, 76112, 817-457-4616
Holes: 18, Pro: Gary Dennis
Meadowbrook Municipal GC, 1-18, MacKenzie State Park, Lubbock, 79401,
806-765-6679 Par: 71, USGA: 71.6, Holes: 18, Pro: Steve Shields
Memorial Park GC, PO Box 1749, Uvalde, 78801, 512-278-6155
Holes: 9
Memorial Park GC, 6001 Memorial Dr. Loop, Houston, 77007, 713-862-4033
Holes: 18, Pro: J.B. Hutchens
North Gate CC, 17110 Northgate Forest Dr., Houston, 77068, 713-440-1223
Holes: 18, Pro: Vic Carder
Mesquite Muni GC, 825 N. Hwy. 67, Mesquite, 75149, 214-270-7457
Holes: 18
Mesqutte GC, 825 N. Hwy. 67, Desquite, 75150, 214-270-7457
Yards: 6005, Par: 71, Holes: 18, Pro: David Lipscomb
Mill Creek GC, Salado, 76571, 817-947-5698
Yards: 6052, Par: 71, USGA: 69.3, Holes: 18
Mills County Golf Assoc. GC, Hwy. 16, Goldthwaite, 76844, 915-938-5652
Holes: 9
Mineola CC, PO Box 306, Mineola, 75773, 214-569-2472
Holes: 9, Pro: Vernon Carey
Mission Del Lago Muni GC, 1250 Mission Grande, San Antonio, 78214,
512-627-2522 Holes: 18
Monte Cristo GC, Route 5, Box 958B, Edinburg, 78539, 512-381-0965
Holes: 18, Pro: Jim Brewster
Montgomery County GC, PO Box 8264, Conroe, 77387, 409-273-4002
Par: 27, Holes: 9
Morton CC, 109A Washington, Morton, 79346, 806-266-5941
Holes: 9
Mount Pleasant CC, Box 309, Mount Pleasant, 75455, 214-572-1804
Holes: 9
Mountain Creek GC, Box 700, Robert Lee, 76945, 915-453-2317
Holes: 9
Muleshoe CC, Box 733, Muleshoe, 97347, 806-272-4250
Holes: 9, Pro: Gearold Phipps
Mustang Creek GC, PO Box 209, Taylor, 76574, 512-352-8960
Holes: 9
Mustang Creek CC, HCR-61 Box 4, Ganado, 77962, 512-771-9390
Par: 36, Holes: 9, Pro: Debbie Nitsche
Navasota Municipal GC, P.O. Box 910, Navasota, 77868, 409-825-7284
Holes: 9, Pro: Paul Hubble
Nocona Hills CC, 179 Country Club Dr., Nacona, 75961, 817-825-3444
Par: 71, Holes: 18

North Texas Golf Links, I-35 North, Denton, 76205, 817-387-5180
Par: 70, Holes: 18, Pro: Jerry Griener
Oaklawn CC, Marshall, 75670, 214-938-8522
Par: 36, Holes: 9
Oaks GC, Rt. 2, Box 168, Corsicana, 75110, 214-874-9042
Holes: 9
Old Ocean GC, Box 390, Old Ocean, 77463, 409-647-9902
Holes: 9
Olde Oaks G&CC, Box787, Mexia, 76667, 817-562-2391
Holes: 9, Pro: Kenny Rucker
Oldham CC, PO Box 465, Vega, 79092, 806-267-2595
Holes: 9, Pro: Jim Basford
Olmos Basin GC, 7022 N. McCullough, San Antonio, 78216, 512-826-4041
Holes: 18, Pro: Jerry Hill
Olney CC, Box 111, Olney, Odessa, 76374, 817-564-2424
Holes: 9, Pro: J. C. York
Olton CC, Box 424, Olton, 79064, 806-285-2595
Holes: 9, Pro: Harold W. Payne
Oso Beach Muni GC, PO Box 8335, Corpus Christi, 78412, 512-991-5351
Holes: 18, Pro: Jimmie Taylor
Outdoor Resort Executive Par 3, PO Box 695, Port Isabel, 78578,
512-943-9691 Par: 54, Holes: 18
Outlaw Gap GC, Route 4, Box 1365, Huntsville, 77340, 409-295-5525
Yards: 1365, Par: 27, Holes: 9, Pro: Ray Outlaw
Overton Muni GC, Box 246 Overton, Olton, 75684, 214-834-6414
Holes: 9
Packsaddle GC, PO Box 1898, Kingsland, 78639, 915-388-3863
Holes: 18, Pro: Mark Cornelison
Palacios GC, Drawer G, Palacios, 77465, 512-972-2666
Holes: 9, Pro: Darrell Tedder
Palm View Muni GC, Route 3, Box 1035, McAllen, 78503, 512-687-9591
Holes: 27, Pro: Mimo Hernandez
Palo Duro Creek GC, Box 805, Canyon, 79015, 806-655-1106
Holes: 18, Pro: Wes Malnack
PanhandleCC, Box 770, Panhandle, 79068, 806-537-3300
Holes: 9, Pro: David Mooring
Pasadena Golf Academy, 7506 Spencer, Pasadena, 77505
Pasadena Municipal GC, 73 Greenbriar Dr., Conroe, 77304
Pat Cleburne Muni GC, PO Box 1544, Cleburne, 76031, 817-645-9078
Holes: 18, Pro: Ronnie Humphrey
Peach Tree GC, Rt. 1, Bullard, 75757, 214-894-7079
Holes: 18
Pecan Valley Muni GC, Beenbrook Lake, POB 26632, Fort Worth, 76126,
817-249-1845   Holes: 36, Pro: Charlie Roberts
Pecos County Muni GC, Box 94 Pecos County Airport Rd, Ft. Stockton,
79735, 915-336-7110   Yards: 6543, USGA: 69.3, Holes: 18, Pro: Billy Pounds
Perryton Muni GC, Box 707, Perryton, 79070, 806-435-5381
Holes: 18, Pro: T. Schiffelbein
Phillips CC, Box 444, Borger, 79007, 806-274-6812
Holes: 18, Pro: Larry Joe Reed
Pine Forest GC, PO Box M, Bastrop, 78602, 512-321-1181
Holes: 18, Pro: Joe Priddy
Pine Hill Lake & GC, Frankston, 75763, 214-876-2650
Par: 36, Holes: 9
Pine Ridge GC, 2 W. Plaza, Paris, 75460, 214-785-8076
Holes: 18, Pro: Tim Parker

Pinnacle CC, PO Box 2026, Malakoff, 75148, 214-451-4653
Holes: 9, Pro: Jack Smith
Pirates Galveston Municipal GC, 1700 Sydnor Lane P.O. Box 778, Galveston,
77551, 409-744-2366 Holes: 18, Pro: James Wright
Pitman Muni GC, Box 1982, Herford, 79045, 806-364-2782
Holes: 18, Pro: Brent Warner
Plains Fairway Public GC, Box 1455, Lameda, 79331, 806-872-8100
Holes: 9, Pro: Ron Scott
Plainview CC, Box 1733, Plainview, 79072, 806-293-2445
Holes: 18, Pro: Pete Petersen
Plantation Resort GC, PO Box 1696, Frisco, 75034, 214-733-4653
Holes: 18, Pro: Junior Salinas
Pleasanton CC, 1801 McGuffin Dr., Pleasanton, 78064, 512-569-3486
Par: 36, Holes: 9, Pro: Mike Yanity
Point Venture CC, 422 Venture Blvd., Leander, 78645, 512-267-1151
Holes: 9, Pro: Bob Nesmith
Point Venture CC, Lake Travis, 512-267-1804
Par: 36, Holes: 9
Port Arthur CC, PO Box 486, Port Arthur, 77640, 409-796-1311
Holes: 18, Pro: Gary Freedman
Port Groves GC, 5721 Monroe, Groves, 77619, 409-962-0406
Holes: 9, Pro: Jim Hurley
Quail Creek CC, PO Drawer 2329, San Marcos, 78666, 512-353-1665
Holes: 18, Pro: John Ferguson
Ranch CC, 5901 Glen Oaks Dr., McKinney, 75069, 214-540-2200
Holes: 18, Pro: Burt Buehler
Rankin CC, Rankin, 79778, 915-693-2834
Holes: 9
Ratliff Ranch Golf Links, PO Box 12580, Odessa, 79768, 915-368-4653
Holes: 18, Pro: David Teichmann
Rayburn GC—Blue & Gold, P.O. Box 64, Sam Rayburn, 75951, 409-698-2444
Yards: 6266, Par: 72, Holes: 18
Raymondville Muni GC, 142 S. 7th, Raymondville, 78580, 512-689-9904
Holes: 9, Pro: Charlie Avelar
Red Oak Valley GC, Rt. 1, Box 801, Red Oak, 75154, 214-576-3249
Holes: 18, Pro: Stuart Thiemann
Reeves County GC, 88 Starley Dr., Pecos, 79772, 915-447-2858
Yards: 6132, USGA: 67.4, Holes: 11
River Creek Park GC, Box 246, Burkburnett, 76354, 817-855-3361
Par: 71, Holes: 18, Pro: Tommy Darland
River Place CC, 4207 River Place, Austin, 78730, 512-346-6784
Holes: 18, Pro: Mark Wyatt
Riverbend CC, Route 8, Box 649, Brownsville, 78520, 512-548-0191
Par: 35, Holes: 9
Riverchase GC, 700 Riverchase Drive, Coppell, 75019, 214-462-8281
Holes: 18, Pro: Jeff Johnson
Riverhill GC, P.O.Box 1569, Kerrville, 78029, 512-896-1400
Yards: 6870, Par: 72, USGA: 70.0, Holes: 18, Pro: Bryan Hargrove
Riverside GC, 2600 N. Randolph, San Angelo, 76903, 915-653-6130
Holes: 18
Riverside GC, 5712 E. Riverside Drive, Austin, 78741, 512-389-1070
Holes: 18, Pro: John Ott
Riverside Muni GC, 203 McDonald, San Antonio, 78210, 512-533-8371
Holes: 27, Pro: Roy Truesdell
Riverside Municipal GC, P.O. Box 2234, Victoria, 77901, 512-573-4521
Holes: 18, Pro: Bill Shelton

Riverwood GC, PO Box 657, Vidor, 77662, 409-768-1710
Holes: 18, Pro: James Marshall
Rockwood GC, 1851 Jacksboro Hwy, Fort Worth, 76114, 817-624-1771
Holes: 27, Pro: Kirk Lewis
Rockwood Par 3 GC, 1524 Rockwood Park, Fort Worth, 76114, 817-624-8311
Par: 27, Holes: 9
Sycamore Creek GC, 2423 E. Vickery, Fort Worth, 75105, 817-535-7241
Holes: 18, Pro: Troy Reiser
Ross Rogers GC, 722 N.W. 24th St., Amarillo, 79107, 806-378-3086
Holes: 36, Pro: Sherwin Cox
Rotan GC, 201 W. Snyder, Rotan, 79546, 915-735-2551
Holes: 9
Royal Oaks GC, 7915 Greenville Ave., Dallas, 75231
Salem Road Fairway Range, 2007 College Dr., Victoria, 77901, 512-573-4680
Pro: Wade Pitts
Sammons Park GC, 2220 W. Ave "D", Temple, 76504, 817-778-8282
Holes: 18, Pro: Mitchell Harrel
San Felipe CC, PO Box 1228, Del Rio, 78840, 512-775-3953
Holes: 9, Pro: Phil Branch
San Jacinto College GC, 8060 Spencer Highway, Pasadena, 77505,
713-479-9033   Holes: 9, Pro: Rudy Swedran
San Pedro Par 3 GC, 6102 San Pedro, San Antonio, 78216, 512-349-5113
Par: 27, Holes: 9
San Saba Muni GC, PO Box 475, San Saba, 76877, 915-372-3212
Par: 72, Holes: 18, Pro: Larry McNeely
Sand Hills CC, PO Box 255, Commerce, 75428, 214-886-4455
Holes: 9
Santa Fe Park GC, Box 2565, San Angelo, 76902, 915-657-4485
Holes: 9, Pro: Mike Terrazas
Scott Schreiner Muni GC, One Country Club Dr., Kerrville, 78028,
512-257-4982   Holes: 18, Pro: Guy Cullins
Seagos Par 3 GC, Rt. 1, Box 715, Waco, 76710, 817-848-4831
Par: 27, Holes: 9
Seven Oaks Hotel GC, 1400 Austin Hwy., San Antonio, 782-9, 512-824-5371
Par: 27, Holes: 9
Shadow Hills GC, Box 98300, Lubbock, 79499, 806-793-9700
Holes: 18, Pro: Vergil Smith
Shady Oaks GC, Rt. 1, Baird, 79504, 915-854-1757
Holes: 9, Pro: Gerry McDowell
Shallow Creek CC, Route 3 Box 212B, Gladewater, 75647
Holes: 9
Shamrock CC, PO Box 525, Shamrock, 79079, 806-256-5151
Holes: 9, Pro: Mark Wendt
Sharpstown Park GC, 8200 Bellaire Blvd. P.O. Box 3, Houston, 77036,
713-988-2099   Holes: 18, Pro: Nat Johnson
Shary Muni GC, 2201 Marberry St., Mission, 78572, 512-580-8770
Holes: 18, Pro: Chencho Ramirez
Sherrill Park Muni GC, 2001 Lookout Dr., Richardson, 75080, 214-234-1416
Holes: 36, Pro: Ronny Glanton
Sherrill Park GC, 2001 E. Lookout, Dallas, 75081
Shotgun Red's Bellwood GC, PO Box 50, Rt. 11, Tyler, 75709, 214-597-4871
Holes: 18, Pro: Mick Roberts
Singing Winds GC, PO Box 398, Bronte, 76933, 915-473-7831
Holes: 9
Sinton Muni GC, Box 216, Sinton, 78387, 512-364-9013
Holes: 18

Slaton GC, Rt. 2, Box 158B, Slaton, 79364, 806-828-3269
Holes: 9, Pro: Mike Lewis
Sonora GC, Box 403, Sonora, 76950, 915-387-3680
Holes: 9
South Main GC, 10920 South Main St., Houston, 77025, 713-665-9626
Holes: 9, Pro: Marcos Lopez
Southwest GC, Rt 1, Box 559, Amarillo, 79106, 806-355-7161
Holes: 18, Pro: Guy Bailey
Southwest Golf Center, 10400 Bissonnet, Houston, 77099, 713-933-4447
Southwyck GC, 2901 Clubhouse Dr., Pearland, 77584, 713-436-9999
Holes: 18, Pro: Danny Silianoff
Spur GC, Box 1083, Spur, 79370, 806-271-4355
Holes: 9
Squaw Creek GC, 1605 Ranch House Rd., Willow Park, 76086, 817-441-8185
Holes: 18, Pro: Lynn Vaughn
Star Harbor Muni GC, PO Drawer 949, Malakoff, 75148, 214-489-0091
Holes: 9
Stephen F. Austin GC, Park Road 38, San Felipe, 77473, 409-885-2811
Yards: 5800, Par: 70, USGA: 64.4, Holes: 18, Pro: Bobby Browne
Stevens Park GC, 1005 N. Montclair, Dallas, 75208
Stratford CC, Box 662, Strafford, 79084, 806-396-2259
Holes: 9
Sundown GC, Box 957, Sundown, 79372, 806-229-6186
Par: 35, Holes: 9, Pro: Don Mitchell
Sunset Coiuntry Club, Box 3086, Andrews Hwy., Odessa, 79760, 915-366-1061
Holes: 18
Sunset GC, 4906 E. Main, Grand Prairie, 75050, 214-331-8057
Holes: 9, Pro: Kenny/Bob Mims
Sunset Golf Center, 6615 Hwy. 6 North, Houston, 77052, 713-463-7888
Sweetwater GC, 4400 Palm Royale, Houston, 77479
Sweetwater Muni GC, Rt. 3, Sweetwater, 79556, 915-235-8816
Holes: 18
Tee Time Driving Range, 602 Pruitt Rd., The Woodlands, 77387, 713-298-1186
Tejas GC, Box 326, Stevenville, 76401, 817-965-3904
Holes: 9
Temple Junior College GC, Box 3267, Temple, 76501, 817-778-9549
Holes: 9, Pro: Paul Guillen
Tenison GC, 3501 Samuel Blvd., Dallas, 75223
Texas A&M University GC, Bizzell ST., College Station, 77843, 409-845-1723
Yards: 6020, Par: 70, USGA: 68.8, Holes: 18, Pro: Matthew Schewe
Texas National CC, I-45 North—Willis Exit, POB, Willis, 77378, 713-353-2972
Holes: 18, Pro: Bob Payne
Texas Par Golf Academy, 4035 South Highway 6, Houston, 77082,
713-493-3276   Par: 27, Hole: 9, Pro: Kent Harger
Texas Women's University GC, Box 3926 Univ. Hill Station, Denton, 76201,
817-898-3163   Holes: 18, Pro: John Hamlett
Throckmorton CC, Box 335, Throckmorton, 76083, 817-849-3131
Holes: 9
Tony Butler Muni GC, 2640 South M St., Harlingen, 78550, 512-423-9913
Holes: 27, Pro: Nancy Bunton
Tournament Players Course, 1730 South Millbend Dr., The Woodlands,
77380, 713-367-1100   Yds: 6387, Par: 72, USGA: 70.5, Holes: 18, Pro: M. Callender
Treasure Island GC, 501 Frankford Rd., Lubbock, 79416, 806-795-9311
Holes: 18
Tule Lake GC, Box 843, Tulia, 79088, 806-995-3400
Holes: 9, Pro: Mark Hamersley

Twin Wells Muni GC, 2000 E. Shady Grove, Irving, 75060, 214-438-4340
Holes: 18, Pro: Chuck Barnett
USA Club Repair & Range, 12151 Northwest Freeway, Houston, 77092
USA Club Repair & Range, 2810 Inez Rd., Houston, 77023
Valley Golf Centers GC, Route 1, Box 297F, Pharr, 78577, 512-787-9272
Par: 27, Holes: 9
Valley Inn GC, P.O. Box 3850, Brownsville, 78520, 512-546-5331
Yards: 6109, Par: 71, Holes: 18
Van Horn GC, PO Box 233, Van Horn, 79855, 915-283-2801
Yards: 6073, USGA: 66.8, Holes: 9, Pro: Scott Harris
Village Executive GC, PO Box 1309, Weslaco, 78570, 512-968-6516
Holes: 9
Walden On Lake Conroe GC, 14001 Walden Rd., Houston, 77356
Waller CC, 15347 Penick Road, Waller, 77484, 409-372-3672
Holes: 9, Pro: Fred Wiesner
Ward County GC, North Hwy 18,m PO Box 1693, Monahans, 79756,
915-943-5044
Yards: 6103, USGA: 67.0, Holes: 9, Pro: Douglas J. Ward
Waterwood Natl. GC, Waterwood Box One, Huntsville, 77340, 509-891-5211
Yards: 6258, Par: 71, USGA: 69.7, Holes: 18, Pro: Eddie Dey
Wedgewood CC, Wedgewood Ave., Conroe, 77304, 409-539-4653
Holes: 18, Pro: Mike Welch
Weeks Park Muni GC, 4400 Lake Park Dr., Wichita Falls, 76302, 817-767-6107
Holes: 18, Pro: Chuck Pickering
Weimer GC, P.O. Box 695, Weimer, 78962, 409-725-8624
Par: 36, Holes: 9
Wellington CC, Box 964, Wellington, 79005, 806-447-5050
Holes: 0, Pro: Danny West
Western Oaks CC, Box 7715, Waco, 76710, 817-772-8100
Holes: 18, Pro: Gregg Juster
Western Texas College GC, South College Ave., Snyder, 79549, 915-573-9291
Holes: 9, Pro: Dave Foster
Wildwood GC, PO Box 903, Village Mills, 77663, 409-834-2940
Holes: 18, Pro: Danny Vigreux
Willow Creek GC, 1166 Executive Dr., Abilene, 79062, 915-691-0909
Par: 27, Holes: 9
Willow Springs GC, 202 Coliseum Rd., San Antonio, 78219, 512-226-6721
Holes: 18, Pro: Ken Sealey
Willow Springs GC, Box 116, Haslet, 76052, 817-439-3169
Par: 72, Holes: 18, Pro: David Thatcher
Winkler County GC, PO Box 876, Kermit, 79745, 915-586-9243
Holes: 9, Pro: Lonnie Crosby
Wolf Creek GC, Rt. 3, Box 445, Colorado City, 79512, 915-728-5514
Holes: 9
Woodland Hills GC, 319 Woodland Hills Dr., Nacogdoches, 75961,
409-564-2762 Par: 72, Holes: 18, Pro: C. D. Thomas Jr
Woodlands GC, RT 9, Box 185K, Canyon Lake, 78133, 512-899-3301
Yards: 5797, Par: 70, Holes: 18
World Houston GC, 4000 Greens Rd., Houston, 77032, 713-449-8384
Holes: 18, Pro: Aubrey Culley
Wright Park Muni GC, 2821 Washington, Greenville, 75401, 214-457-2996
Holes: 9, Pro: Bo Hartline
Yaupon GC, 100 Clubhouse Drive, Austin, 78734, 512-261-7572
Holes: 18, Pro: Larry Bishop
Yoakum County GC, Box 1259, Denver City, 79323, 806-592-2947
Holes: 9, Pro: Wiley Osborne

Yoakum Muni GC, PO Box 282, Yoakum, 77995, 512-293-5682
Par: 36, Holes: 9, Pro: Tom Chilek
Yorktown CC, Country Club Rd., Yorktown, 78164, 512-564-9191
Holes: 9, Pro: Warner Borth
Z-Boaz GC, 3240 Lackland, Fort Worth, 76116, 817-738-6287
Holes: 18, Pro: Sam Knight

#1 Country Club, Stansbury Park, 84070, 801-328-1483 *Utah*
Par: 72, Holes: 18
Alpine CC, P.O. Box 220, Highland, 84003, 801-322-3971
Yards: 6492, Par: 72, USGA: 70.0, Holes: 18, Pro: Joey Bonsignore
Bear Lake GC, Sweetwater Resort, Garden City, 84028, 801-946-8742
USGA: 68.8, Pro:
Belmont Springs GC, 5600 W 19200 N, Belmont Springs, 84330, 801-458-3200
Yards: 2766, Par: 36, USGA: 66.7, Holes: 9, Pro: Scott Holmgren
Ben Lomond Golf Course, 1600 North 500 West, Ogden, 84404, 801-782-7754
Yards: 5778, Par: 72, USGA: 65.6, Holes: 18, Pro: Randy Essley
Birch Creek GC, 600 East Center St., Smithfield, 84335, 801-563-6825
Yards: 6770, Par: 72, USGA: 70.0, Holes: 18, Pro: Dan Roskelley
Blanding GC, Blanding, 84511
Par: 32, Holes: 9
Bloomington Hills GC, 1 Mile E. Bloomington, St. George, 84770, 801-673-2029
Bonneville Golf Course, 954 Connor Street, Salt Lake City, 84108,
801-596-5044 Yards: 6553, Par: 72, USGA: 69.0, Holes: 18, Pro: Dick Kramer
Bountiful Springs GC, 1201 N. 1100 W, Woods Cross, 84087, 801-259-1019
Brigham City GC, Jct Hwys 89 & 30, Brigham City, 84302, 801-723-3212
Yards: 6600, Par: 37, USGA: 70.1, Holes: 9, Pro: Reid Goodliffe
Canyon Breeze GC, East Canyon Road, Beaver, 84713, 801-438-9601
Yards: 2847, Par: 34, USGA: 65.2, Holes: 9, Pro: Danny Lindsay
Canyon Hills Park GC, 1200 E. 100 N, Nephi, 84648, 801-623-9930
Yards: 3100, Par: 36, USGA: 68.8, Holes: 9, Pro: John Fillmore
Carbon CC, Hwy 6 Price-Helper, Helper, 84526, 801-637-9949
Yards: 3167, Par: 35, USGA: 69.3, Holes: 9, Pro: Kris Abegglen
Cascade Fairways GC, 1313 East 800 North, Orem, 84057, 801-226-6677
Yards: 4522, Par: 35, USGA: 65.0, Holes: 9, Pro: Herb Stratton
Cedar Ridge GC, 1000 East 900 North, Cedar City, 84720, 801-586-2970
Yards: 3225, Par: 36, USGA: 68.2, Holes: 9, Pro: John Evans
Copper GC, 8975 W. 2500 S., Magna, 84044, 801-250-6396
Yards: 3220, Par: 36, Holes: 9
Cottonwood Club, The, 1780 E. Lakewood Dr., Salt Lake City, 84117,
801-272-5271 Yards: 2040, Par: 27, Holes: 9
Country Club GC, 2400 Country Club Dr., Salt Lake City, 84109
Yards: 6498, Par: 72, USGA: 70.5, Holes: 18
Cove View GC, South Airport Road, Richfield, 84701, 801-896-9987
Yards: 5976, Par: 36, USGA: 68.2, Holes: 9, Pro: John Roberts
Davis Park GC, 1074 E. Nichols Road, Kaysville, 84037, 801-546-4154
Par: 72, USGA: 67.4, Holes: 18, Pro: Pierre Hualde
Dinaland GC, 675 South 2000 East, Vernal, 84078, 801-781-1428
Yards: 3200, Par: 36, USGA: 68.7, Holes: 9, Pro: Kent McCurdy
Dixie Red Hills GC, 1000 North 700 West, P.O. Box, St. George, 84770,
801-634-5852 Yards: 2564, Par: 34, USGA: 65.5, Holes: 9, Pro: Brent Orchard
Dugway GC, 334 B Coyote Cove, Dugway, 84022, 801-831-2305
Yards: 3314, Par: 36, USGA: 69.4, Holes: 9, Pro: John Bugbee
Eagle Mountain GC, 700 S. 780 East, Brigham City, 84302, 801-723-3212
Par: 71, Holes: 18

East Bay GC, 1860 S. East Bay Blvd., Provo, 84601, 801-373-0111
Yards: 6262, Par: 71, USGA: 66.0, Holes: 27, Pro: Kean Ridd
El Monte GC, 1300 Valley Drive, Ogden, 84401, 801-399-8333
Yards: 2950, Par: 35, USGA: 66.2, Holes: 9, Pro: Kent Abegglen
Fore Lakes GC, 1285 West 4700 South, Murray, 84123, 801-266-8621
Yards: 3635, Par: 52, USGA: 59.1, Holes: 18, Pro: Brad Asplund
Forest Dale GC, 2375 South 900 East, Salt Lake City, 84106, 801-483-5420
Yards: 2970, Par: 36, USGA: 67.7, Holes: 9, Pro: Don Dorton
Gladstan GC, #1 Gladstan Drive, Payson, 84651, 800-634-3009
Yards: 5548, Par: 70, USGA: 60.5, Holes: 18, Pro: Jack Lomento
Glendale GC, 1630 W. 2100 South, Salt Lake City, 84119, 801-974-2403
Yards: 6470, Par: 72, USGA: 69.3, Holes: 18, Pro: Tom Reese
Glenmoor GC, 9800 South 4800 West, South Jordan, 84065, 801-255-1742
Yards: 6428, Par: 72, USGA: 69.3, Holes: 18, Pro: Ken Clark
Golf City GC, 1400 E. 5600 South, Ogden, 84403, 801-479-3410
Par: 28, Holes: 9
Granite View Golf Course, 306 South Main St., Milford, 84751, 801-387-2711
Green Valley GC, 1200 S. Dixie Downs Road, St. George, 84770, 801-628-3778
Yards: 1050, Par: 27, USGA: 50.3, Holes: 9, Pro: Mike Smith
Hidden Valley CC, 12000 So. 1700 E., Draper, 84020, 801-571-2951
Hill Air Force Base GC, Bldg. #720, Hill Air Force Bas, Ogden, 84406,
801-777-3272 Yards: 6560, Par: 72, Holes: 18
Hobble Creek GC, Canyon Dr./Hobble Creek Canyon, Springville, 84663,
801-489-6297 Yards: 5950, Par: 71, USGA: 67.1, Holes: 18, Pro: Sonny Braun
Jeremy Ranch, 8770 N. Jeremy Road, Park City, 84060, 801-531-9000
Yards: 7025, Par: 72, USGA: 69.3, Holes: 18, Pro: Pete Scroggle
Jordan River GC, 1200 N. Redwood Rd., Salt Lake City, 801-533-4496
Yards: 1170, Par: 27, Holes: 9
Kanab Muni GC, East Hwy. 89, Kanab, 84741, 801-644-5005
Holes: 9
Logan CC, 710 N. 15th E., Logan, 84321, 801-752-8722
Yards: 6082, Par: 71, Holes: 18
Meadowbrook GC, 4197 S. 1300 W., Salt Lake City, 84123, 801-266-0971
Yards: 6125, Par: 72, USGA: 67.0, Holes: 18, Pro: Jim Healy
Mick Riley GC, 421 East Vine Street, Murray, 84107, 801-266-8185
Yards: 3100, Par: 27, USGA: 67.4, Holes: 9, Pro: Nolan Wathen
Millard County GC, Hinckley, 84635, 801-864-2701
Millsite GC, Ferron, 84523, 801-384-2350
Par: 36, Holes: 9
Moab GC, 2705 S.E. Bench Rd., Moab, 84532, 801-259-6488
Yards: 5502, Par: 72, USGA: 67.0, Holes: 18, Pro: Glen Richeson
Mountain Dell GC, 3387 Cummings Road, Salt Lake, 84109, 801-582-3812
Yards: 6000, Par: 70, USGA: 67.4, Holes: 18, Pro: Tom Sorenson
Mountain View GC, 8660 S. 2400 West, West Jordan, 84088, 801-255-9211
Par: 72, USGA: 67.4, Holes: 18, Pro: Norm Rackley
Mt. Ogden Golf Course, 3000 Taylor Avenue, Ogden, 84403, 801-399-8700
Yards: 5850, Par: 71, USGA: 67.5, Holes: 18, Pro: Steve Wathen
Mulligans GC, 1690 W 400 N, Ogden, 84404
Holes: 9
Nibley Park GC, 2780 S. 700 East, Salt Lake City, 84106, 801-483-5418
Yards: 2900, Par: 34, USGA: 65.0, Holes: 9, Pro: Jeff Waters
Nordic Valley GC, Nordic Valley Way, Eden, 84310, 801-745-3511
USGA: 65.1, Pro: John Hertzke
Oakridge CC, 1492 Shepards Lane, Farmington, 84025, 801-867-2281
Yards: 6462, Par: 72, Holes: 18

Ferron Millsite GC, PO Box 236, Ferron, 84523
Holes: 9
Ogden G&CC, 4197 Washington Blvd., Ogden, 84402, 801-745-0135
Yards: 6439, Par: 73, Holes: 18
Oquirrh Hills GC, 7th & Edgemont, Tooele, 84074, 801-882-4220
Yards: 3005, Par: 35, USGA: 67.7, Holes: 9, Pro: Jerry Braun
Painted Hills GC, 800N. 100 E, Cedar City, 84720, 801-586-9793
Palisade State Park GC, Palisade Park Road, Mantl, 84642, 801-835-4653
Yards: 6068, Par: 36, USGA: 66.9, Holes: 9, Pro: Kirk Abegglen
Paradise Hills GC, 3663 E. Nordic Valley, Liberty, 84310, 801-745-3558
Park Meadows CC, 2000 Meadows Drive, Park City, 84060, 801-649-2460
Yards: 7338, Par: 72, USGA: 70.6, Holes: 18, Pro: Don Branca
Patio Springs CC, Eden, 84310, 801-745-3737
Price Carbon CC, Highway 89 & 30, Helper, 84526, 801-373-9424
Riverside GC, 2701 N. University Ave., Provo, 84601, 801-373-8262
Yards: 6298, Par: 72, Holes: 18
Roosevelt GC, 1155 Clubhouse Drive, Roosevelt, 84066, 801-722-9644
Yards: 3531, Par: 36, USGA: 70.7, Holes: 9, Pro: Brian Ainsworth
Rose Park GC, 1385 N. Redwood Rd., Salt Lake Clty, 84116, 801-596-5030
Yards: 6397, Par: 72, USGA: 67.7, Holes: 18, Pro: Ron Branca
Round Valley GC, 1875 E. Round Valley Dr., Morgan, 84050, 801-829-3796
Yards: 3173, Par: 36, USGA: 68.5, Holes: 9, Pro: Dennis Peterson
Royal Greens GC, 5200 S. 2885 W, Roy, 84067, 801-825-3467
Yards: 3162, Par: 36, USGA: 68.5, Holes: 9, Pro: Bob Betley
Salt Lake CC, 2400 Country Club Dr., Salt Lake City, 84109, 801-466-8751
Yards: 6498, Par: 72, Holes: 18
Sanpete County Palisade GC, Palisade Park, Manti, 84642, 801-835-9151
Schneiter's Pebble Brook, 8968 South 1300 East, Sandy, 84070, 801-566-2181
Yards: 4800, Par: 68, USGA: 58.7, Holes: 18, Pro: Geo. Schneiter
Sherwood Hills GC, Sardine Canyon, US Hwy 80 & 91, Logan, 84404,
801-245-6055 Par: 36, USGA: 68.5, Holes: 9, Pro: Mark Ballif
Skyway GC, 450 N. Country Club Dr., Tremonton, 84337, 801-257-5706
Yards: 2704, Par: 34, USGA: 64.7, Holes: 9, Pro: Ron Fenn
Smithfield GC, 600 E. Center, Smithfield, 84335, 801-563-6825
South Gate GC, 1875 S. Tonaquint Dr., St. George, 84770, 801-628-0000 Par:
69, Holes: 18
Southgate GC, 1975 S. Tonaquint Dr., St. George, 84770, 801-628-0000
Yards: 6141, Par: 69, USGA: 66.0, Holes: 18, Pro: Velma Petersen
Spanish Fork, 5057 S. Zero St., Spanish Fork, 84660, 801-798-8067
Spanish Oaks GC, 2400 E. Powerhouse Rd., Spanish Fork, 84660, 801-798-9816
Yards: 5850, Par: 72, USGA: 67.2, Holes: 18, Pro: Roy Christensen
Spring Meadows GC, 1201 N. 110 West, Bountiful, 84010, 801-295-1019
Par: 36, Holes: 9
St. George GC, 2190 South 1400 East, P.O. Box, St. George, 84770, 801-634-5854
Yards: 6728, Par: 73, USGA: 67.0, Holes: 18, Pro: Reed McArthur
Stansbury Park GC, #1 Country Club, Stansbury Park, 84074, 801-882-4162
Yards: 6432, Par: 72, USGA: 69.8, Holes: 18, Pro: Jeff Green
Summit Park GC, 600 E. Center, Smithfield, 84335, 801-563-6728
Par: 72, Holes: 18
Sunset View GC, North Highway #6, Delta, 84624, 801-864-2508
Yards: 3362, Par: 36, USGA: 68.2, Holes: 9
Sweetwater Park GC, Sweetwater, 84028, 800-662-9166
Par: 36, Holes: 9
Thunderbird GC, Mt. Carmel, 84755, 801-648-2203
Par: 33, Holes: 9
Timpanogos GC, 900 S. University Ave., Provo, 84601, 801-373-9424

Tri City GC, 1400 North 200 East, American Fork, 84003, 801-756-3594
Yards: 6710, Par: 72, USGA: 71.4, Holes: 18, Pro: Gary Naylor
Twin Lakes, 660 N. Twin Lakes Dr., St. George, 84770, 801-673-4441
Yards: 1001, Par: 27, USGA: 46.9, Holes: 9, Pro: John Lagant
University of Utah GC, 100 S. 1900 East, Salt Lake City, 84109, 801-581-6511
Yards: 2621, Par: 34, USGA: 63.6, Holes: 9, Pro: Vinny McGuire
West Bountiful City GC, 1201 North 1100 West, Woods Cross, 84087,
801-295-1019 USGA: 65.1, Pro: Mike Bicky
White Barn GC, 305 W. Pleasant View, Ogden, 84404, 801-782-6202
Yards: 5947, Par: 71, USGA: 68.0, Holes: 18, Pro: Kelly Woodland
Willow Creek CC, 8300 So. 2700 East, Sandy, 84092, 801-942-1621
Yards: 6556, Par: 72, USGA: 71.0, Holes: 18, Pro: Mike Kahler
Wolf Creek Country Club, 3900 N. Wolf Creek Dr., Eden, 84310, 801-745-3365
Yards: 6459, Par: 72, USGA: 70.5, Holes: 18, Pro: Randy Laub

Alburg CC, RR #1, Alburg, 05440, 802-796-3586   *Vermont*
Yards: 6287, Par: 72, USGA: 69.7, Holes: 18
Barre CC, Plainfield, 05667, 802-476-7658
Yards: 6000, Par: 71, Holes: 18
Bellows Falls CC, Route 103, Bellows Falls, 05101, 802-463-9809
Yards: 5807, Par: 70, Holes: 9
Bradford GC, RR #1, Bradford, 05033
Brattleboro CC, P.O. Box 478, Brattleboro, 05301, 802-257-7380
Yards: 6200, Par: 71, Holes: 9
Burlington CC, Inc., P.O. Box 423, Burlington, 05401, 802-864-9532
Yards: 6845, Par: 71, Holes: 18
Bush Hill CC, Box 396, Waterbury, 05676
Copley CC, P.O. Box 51 (off Maple St.), Morrisville, 05661, 802-888-3013
Yards: 5550, Par: 70, USGA: 65.4, Holes: 9, Pro: Tad Lamell
Country Club of Barre, P.O. Box 298, Barre, 05641
Crown Point CC, P.O. Box 413, Springfield, 05156, 802-885-2703
Yards: 6572, Par: 72, Holes: 18
Champlain CC, Route 7, St. Albans, 05478, 802-527-1187
Yards: 6200, Par: 70, USGA: 69.9, Holes: 18, Pro: Duke January
Dorset Field Club, P.O. Box 368, Dorset, 05251
Ekwanok CC, Box 467, Manchester, 05254
Enosburg Falls CC, Inc., P.O. Box 612, Enosburg Falls, 05450, 802-933-8951
Yards: 5568, Par: 36, Holes: 9
Equinox CC, Box 618, Manchester, 05254, 802-362-3223
Yards: 6022, Par: 71, Holes: 18
Farm Resort, Morrisville, 05661, 802-888-3525
Yards: 3019, Par: 36, Holes: 9
Golf Club, Bradford, 05033, 802-222-5207
Yards: 2012, Par: 32, Holes: 9
Golf Club, West Bolton, 05477, 802-434-4321
Yards: 5432, Par: 69, Holes: 18
Haystack GC, RR #1, box 173, Wilmington, 05363, 802-464-5321
Yards: 6164, Par: 72, USGA: 69.8, Holes: 18, Pro: Chuck Deedman
Lake Morey CC, Lake Morey Rd., Fairlee, 05045, 802-333-9575
Yards: 5605, Par: 70, Holes: 18
Lake St. Catherine CC, Lake Rd., Rte. 30, Poultney, 05764, 802-287-9341
Yards: 2973, Par: 36, USGA: 68.8, Holes: 9, Pro: Larry Nichoc
Manchester CC, P.O. Box 947, Manchester Center, 05255, 802-362-2233
Yards: 6724, Par: 72, Holes: 18
Marble Island GC, Malletts Bay, 05446, 802-864-4546
Yards: 2570, Par: 33, Holes: 9

Montague CC, P.O. Box 178, Randolph, 05060,   802-728-3806
Yards: 5780, Par: 34, Holes: 9
Montpelier CC, Drawer E, Montpelier, 05602,   802-223-7457
Yards: 5319, Par: 70, Holes: 9
Mountain View CC, Box 207, Greensboro, 05841,   802-533-7477
Yards: 2502, Par: 35, Holes: 9
Mt. Anthony Golf & Tennis Club, Bank St. - Box 943, Bennington, 05201,
802-447-7079   Yards: 5941, Par: 71, USGA: 69.2, Holes: 18, Pro: Leo Reynolds
Neshobe GC, Inc., P.O. Box 205, Brandon, 05733,   802-247-3611
Yards: 2877, Par: 35, Holes: 9
Newport CC, Newport, 05855,   802-334-2391
Yards: 6102, Par: 72, Holes: 18
Northfield CC, Northfield, 05663,   802-485-4515
Yards: 2950, Par: 35, Holes: 9
Orleans CC, Rte 58, Orleans, 05860,   802-754-2333
Yards: 6123, Par: 72, USGA: 68.5, Holes: 18, Pro: Arthur Mandros
Proctor-Pittsford CC, Corn Hill Road, Pittsford, 05763,   802-483-9379
Yards: 5721, Par: 72, Holes: 9
Quechee Lakes GC, River Rd., White River Junction, 05059
Ralph Myhre, Middlebury, 05753,   802-388-3711
Yards: 6014, Par: 71, Holes: 18
Richford CC, P.O. Box 21, Richford, 05476,   802-848-3527
Yards: 3001, Par: 36, Holes: 9
Rocky Ridges GC, 68 Ledge Road, Hinsburg, 05461,   802-482-2191
Yards: 6000, Par: 72, Holes: 18, Pro: E. Farrington
Rutland CC, P.O. Box 195, Rutland, 05701,   802-773-3254
Yards: 5761, Par: 70, Holes: 18
Sitzmark, Wilmington, 05363,   802-464-3384
Yards: 2000, Par: 54, Holes: 18
St. Johnsbury CC, Route #5 North, St. Johnsbury, 05819,   802-748-9894
Yards: 6004, Par: 37, USGA: 69.2, Holes: 9, Pro: James F. Love
Stamford Valley, Stamford, 05352,   802-694-9144
Yards: 2715, Par: 36, Holes: 9
Tater Hill CC, RFD #1, Chester, 05143,   802-875-2517
Yards: 3227, Par: 36, USGA: 71.4, Holes: 9
White River GC, Route 100, Rochester, 05767,   802-767-3709
Yards: 2700, Par: 34, Holes: 9, Pro: Ray Braune
Wilcox Cove, Grand Isle, 05458,   802-372-8343
Yards: 1705, Par: 32, Holes: 9
Williston GC, P.O. Box 36, Williston, 05495,   802-878-3747
Yards: 5600, Par: 69, USGA: 68.0, Holes: 18, Pro: Wesley Olson
Windsor CC, North Main St., Windsor, 05089,   802-674-6491
Yards: 6500, Par: 72, Holes: 9
Wolf Run, Boston Post Rd., Bakersfield, 05441,   802-933-4007
Yards: 3040, Par: 35, Holes: 9, Pro: Gary Murano

Algonkian Park, on Potomac R., Sterling, 22170,   703-450-4655   *Virginia*
Yards: 6720, Par: 72, Holes: 18
Blacksburg Muni GC, Blacksburg, 24060,   703-961-1137
Yards: 2614, Par: 35, Holes: 9, Pro: Paul Hypes
Blue Hills GC, Mason Mill Rd., Roanoke, 24012,   703-344-7848
Yards: 6547, Par: 71, Holes: 18
Botetourt CC, 15 mi N US 220 & SR 665, Roanoke, 24022,   703-992-1451
Yards: 6176, Par: 71, Holes: 18
Bow Creek GC, 3425 Clubhouse Rd., Norfolk, 23452

Bowling Green CC, 8 mi n US 522/340, SR 658 to S, Front Royal, 22630,
703-635-2024   Yards: 6157, Par: 71, Holes: 18
Brookside Par 3 GC, US 220 Rt. 11, Roanoke, 24022,   703-366-6059
Yards: 900, Par: 27, Holes: 9
Brookwood GC, Quinton, 23141,   804-737-0519
Yards: 6563, Holes: 18
Bryce Resort GC, Vasye, 22810,   703-856-2040
Yards: 6175, Par: 71, USGA: 68.7, Holes: 18, Pro: Vernon Hull
Carpers Valley GC, Winchester, 22601,   703-662-4319
Yards: 6050, Par: 70, Holes: 18
Castle Rock Recreation GC, Rte. 460, Pearisburg, 24134,   703-626-7276
Yards: 5583, Par: 71, Holes: 18, Pro: Buddy Profitt
Caverns CC Resort, PO Box 749, Luray Caverns, 22835,   703-743-6551
Yards: 6452, Par: 72, Holes: 18
Cedar Hill CC, Jonesville, 24263,   703-346-1535
Yards: 6084, Par: 72, Pro: Shannon Evans
Cedar Hill GC, US 29S, Lynchburg, 24506,   804-239-1512
Yards: 7300, Par: 68, Holes: 18
Cedars CC, Chatham, 24531,   804-565-9909
Yards: 6300, Par: 72, Pro:
City of Salem GC, 601 Academy St., Salem, 24153,   703-387-9802
Yards: 2426, Par: 34, Holes: 9
Colonial Hills GC, 7 mi W via US 221, Lynchburg, 24506,   804-525-3954
Yards: 6219, Par: 71, Holes: 18, Pro: J. C. Thomas
Confederate Hills GC, Highland Springs, 23075,   804-737-4716
Par: 72, Holes: 18
Glenrichie CC, Abingdon, 24210,   703-628-3059
Yards: 6500, Par: 72, Holes: 18, Pro: Ed Marlow
Gloucester CC, Gloucester, 23061,   804-693-2662
Yards: 6165, Par: 72, Holes: 9
Golden Eagle GC, The , Tides Inn, Irvington, 22480,   804-438-5000
Yards: 6943, Par: 72, Holes: 18
Goose Creek GC, Leesburg, 22075,   703-729-2500
Yards: 6100, Par: 72, Holes: 18, Pro: Harold Yawberg
Gordon Trent Golf, Stuart, 24171,   703-694-3805
Yards: 4550, Par: 69, Holes: 18, Pro: Leon Martin
Gypsy Hill GC, US 250 W. Churchville Ave., Staunton, 24401,   703-886-9737
Yards: 6115, Par: 71, Holes: 18
Hat Creek GC, Brookneal, 24528,   804-376-2292
Par: 68, Holes: 18
Hollyfield GC, Roanoke, 24022,   703-929-4583
Yards: 3385, Par: 36, Pro:
Holston Hills CC, North R. 11, Marion, 24354,   703-783-7484
Yards: 6229, Par: 72, Holes: 18, Pro: W.H.Atwood
Ingleswide Red Carpet Inn GC, 2 mi N on US 11, Staunton, 24401,
703-885-1201   Yards: 6387, Par: 72, Holes: 18, Pro: Joe Sprouse
Jordon Point CC, Hopewell, 23860,   804-458-0141
Yards: 6092, Par: 72, Holes: 18
Kinderton G & CC, Clarksville, 23927,   804-374-8822
Yards: 6108, Par: 71, Holes: 18, Pro: Bernie Spear
Lakeview GC, Rt 11 Box 212, Harrisonburg, 22801
Holes: 9
Lee Park GC, 3108 Homestead Dr., Petersburg, 23805,   804-733-5667
Yards: 5621, Par: 72, Holes: 18
Leesburg Westpark GC, Leesburg, 22075,   703-777-7023
Par: 71, Holes: 18

Massanutten Village GC, Massanutte Dr., Harrisonburg, 22801, 703-289-9441
Yards: 5956, Par: 72, USGA: 68.2, Holes: 18, Pro: Eddie Jones
McGruder Point GC, 9 Woodlands Road, Hampton, 23663
Holes: 27
Mill Quarter Plantation GC, Powhatan, 23139, 804-598-4221
Par: 72, Holes: 18
Moccasin Hill GC, Gate City, 24251, 703-452-4168
Yards: 5760, Par: 72, Holes: 18, Pro: P. Gardner
Montevista GC, Gibson Station, 22514, 703-861-4014
Yards: 5650, Par: 72, Holes: 18, Pro: Scott Engle
Oak Hill CC, 12638 Patterson Avenue, Richmond, 23233, 804-784-5718
Yards: 6409, Par: 72, Holes: 18
Old Monterey GC, 1112 Tinker Creek Lane, Roanoke, 24019, 703-563-0400
Yards: 6700, Par: 71, Holes: 18
Olde Mill Golf Club, Route 1, Box 84, Laurel Fork, 24352, 703-398-2638
Yards: 6266, Par: 72, Holes: 18
Owls Creek, 411 S. Birdneck Road, Virginia Beach, 23451
Holes: 18
Pen Park GC, Off Rio Road, Charlottesville, 22901, 804-977-0615
Yards: 3002, Par: 70, Holes: 9
Pohick Bay GC, 10301 Gunston Road, Lorton, 22079, 703-339-8585
Yards: 5927, Par: 72, Holes: 18
Poplar Forest GC, P.O. Box H69, Forest, 24551, 804-525-0473
Yards: 3300, Par: 36, Holes: 9, Pro: Peter Dodd
Prince George GC, Petersburg, 23804, 804-991-2251
Yards: 6250, Par: 72, Holes: 18
Rarmington GC, 1 Country Club Cir., Charlottesville, 22901
Red Wing Lake GC, 1080 Prosperity Rd., Virginia Beach, 23451, 804-425-6300
Yards: 7250, Par: 72, USGA: 70.0, Holes: 18, Pro: Jennings House
Ringgold GC, Ringgold, 24586, 804-822-8728
Par: 72, Holes: 18
Saltville GC, Saltville, 24370, 703-496-7779
Yards: 5601, Par: 70, Holes: 9, Pro: John North
Scenic View GC, Chilhowie, 24319, 703-646-3535
Yards: 6170, Par: 72, Holes: 18, Pro: J.M.Wilkinson
Shenandoah Valley GC, 7½ mi N. US 340/522 & SR 65, Front Royal, 22630,
703-636-2641   Yards: 9455, Par: 71, Holes: 27
Skyland Lakes GC, 14 Mi fm Hillsville US 58E Rt., Fancy Gap, 24328,
703-728-4923   Yards: 6319, Par: 71, Holes: 18, Pro: Welch DeBoard
Smithfield Downs, Ltd. GC, at Va 32 & US 258, Smithfield, 23430, 804-357-3101
Yards: 5767, Par: 70, Holes: 18
Spottswood GC, Williamsburg Inn, Williamsburg, 23185, 804-220-7696
Yards: 1880, Par: 31, Holes: 9, Pro: Del Synder
Stone Manor CC, Rt 757 & 653, Goodview, 24095
Holes: 18
Summit GC, Inc., Winchester, 22601, 703-888-4188
Yards: 6397, Par: 71, Holes: 9
Swannanoa GC, Afton, 22920, 703-942-9877
Yards: 5555, Par: 72, Holes: 18
Thorn Spring GC, Pulaski, 24301, 703-980-5851
Yards: 6416, Par: 72, Holes: 18
Tides Tartan GC, The , 1st. Andrews LN., Fredericksburg, 22480
Virginia Tech GC, Blacksburg, 24060, 703-961-6435
Yards: 6131, Par: 74, Holes: 18, Pro: Jay Hardwick
Winton CC, P.O. Box 100, Clifford, 24533, 804-946-7336
Yards: 6400, Par: 71, Holes: 18

Alderbrook Inn GC, E. 300 Country Club Dr., Olympia, 98592, *Washington*
206-898-2560 Yards: 6150, Par: 73, USGA: 69.8, Holes: 18, Pro: Michael Fields
Alta Lake GC, Alta Lake Road, Pateros, 98846, 509-923-2359
Yards: 3000, Par: 36, Holes: 9
American Legion Memorial GC, 144 Wewst Marine View Drive, Everett,
98201, 206-259-4653 Yards: 6265, Par: 72, Holes: 18
Auburn GC, 29630 Green River Road, Auburn, 98002, 206-833-2350
Yards: 6050, Par: 71, Holes: 18
Bellevue Muni GC, 5450—140th N.W., Bellevue, 98005, 206-885-6009
Yards: 5694, Par: 70, Holes: 18
Brookdale GC, 1802 Brookdale Road East, Tacoma, 98445, 206-537-4400
Yards: 6350, Par: 71, USGA: 68.3, Holes: 18, Pro: Tom Parkhurst
Camaloch GC, 223 East Camaloch Drive, Camano Island, 98292, 206-387-3084
Yards: 5741, Par: 72, Holes: 9
Capitol City GC, 5225 Yelm Hwy. SE., Lacey, 98503, 206-491-5111
Yards: 6220, Par: 72, Holes: 18
Carnation GC, 1810 West Snoqualmie River Roa, Carnation, 98014,
206-333-4151 Yards: 5833, Par: 72, Holes: 18
Cedarcrest GC, 6810 84th Place NE, Marysville, 98270, 206-659-3566
Yards: 5390, Par: 71, Holes: 18, Pro: Don Shaw
Cedard G & CC (The), P.O. Box 517, Battle Ground, 98604, 206-687-4233
Yards: 6280, Par: 72, Holes: 18
Centralia-Chehalis Elks GC, 1012 Duffy Street, Centralia, 98531, 206-736-5312
Yards: 5475, Par: 36, Holes: 9
Chevy Chase GC, 7041 Cape George Rd., Port Townsend, 98368, 206-385-0704
Yards: 5400, Par: 68, Holes: 9
Chewelah G & CC, Box 318, Chewelah, 99109, 509-935-6807
Yards: 6200, Par: 36, Holes: 9
Clover Valley CC, 5180 Country Club Way S.E., Port Orchard, 98366,
206-871-2236 Yards: 5289, Par: 69, Holes: 18
Columbia Park GC, 3555 Greenbrook Place, Richland, 99352, 509-586-4069
Yards: 2645, Par: 56, Holes: 18
Colville Elks GC & CC, Box 367, Colville, 99114, 509-684-5508
Yards: 6330, Par: 72, Holes: 18
Crescent Bar GC, Route 2, Box 864, Quincy, 98848, 509-787-1511
Yards: 5978, Par: 70, Holes: 18
Downriver Muni GC, North 3225 Columbia Circle, Spokane, 99205,
509-327-5269 Yards: 6021, Par: 71, Holes: 18
Elks Allenmore GC, 2125 South Cedar, Tacoma, 98405, 206-627-7211
Yards: 6100, Par: 71, Holes: 18
Enumclaw GC, 45220—288th S.E., Enumclaw, 98002, 206-825-2827
Yards: 5629, Par: 70, Holes: 18
Evergreen GC, Box 156, Everson, 98247, 206-966-5417
Yards: 2100, Par: 31, Holes: 9
Fisher Park GC, c/o City of Yakima, 204 East B, Yakima, 98901, 509-575-6075
Yards: 1403, Par: 27, Holes: 9
Foster Golf Links, 13500 Interurban South, Tukwila, 98188, 206-242-4221
Yards: 5280, Par: 68, Holes: 18
Gateway GC, 839 Fruitdale Road, Sedro Woolley, 98284, 206-856-0315
Yards: 5820, Holes: 9
Gig Harbor G & CC, 6909 Artondale Drive N.W., Gig Harbor, 98335,
206-858-2376 Yards: 5452, Par: 35, Holes: 9
Gold Mountain GC, P. O. Box 197, Gorst, 98337, 206-674-2363
Yards: 6146, Par: 72, Holes: 18
Golfgreen GC, 561—7th Avenue, Longview, 98626, 206-425-0450
Yards: 1175, Par: 27, Holes: 9

Grandview GC, 7738 Portal Way, Custer, 98240, 206-366-3947
Yards: 6088, Par: 71, Holes: 18
Green Meadow GC, 7703 N.E. 72nd Avenue, Vancouver, 98661, 206-256-1510
Yards: 6328, Par: 72, Holes: 18
Hangman Valley GC, RT. 3, Box 548, Spokane, 99203, 509-448-1212
Yards: 6119, Par: 71, USGA: 68.8, Holes: 18, Pro: Ken Spence
Harrington G & CC, Box 191, Harrington, 99134, 509-253-4308
Par: 70, Holes: 9
Heritage G & CC, P.O. Box 281A, Ocean Park, 98640, 206-665-4148
Yards: 6200, Par: 69, Holes: 9
Highland GC, 1400 Highlands Parkway North, Tacoma, 98406, 206-759-3622
Yards: 1300, Par: 28, Holes: 9
Highland GC, 300 Yard Drive, Cosmopolis, 98537, 206-533-2455
Yards: 6295, Par: 70, USGA: 67.0, Holes: 18, Pro: Joe Golia
Jackson Park Muni GC, 1000 N.E. 135th, Seattle, 98125, 206-363-4747
Yards: 7011, Par: 72, Holes: 27
Jefferson Park GC, 4101 Beacon S., Seattle, 98104, 206-762-4513
Yards: 5820, Par: 70, USGA: 67.9, Holes: 18, Pro: Joe Thiel
Kent Muni GC, 2020 West Meeker, Kent, 98032
Holes: 18
Kenwanda GC, 14030 Kenwanda Drive, Snohomish, 98290, 206-668-9971
Yards: 5604, Par: 69, Holes: 18
Lake Chelan GC, P. O. Box 1669, Chelan, 98816, 509-682-5421
Yards: 6300, Par: 72, Holes: 18
Lake Cushman GC, Star Route 2, Box 99-7, Hoodsport, 98548, 206-877-5505
Yards: 2909, Par: 69, Holes: 9
Kelso Elks GC, 2222 South River Road, Kelso, 98626, 206-425-1482
Yards: 6777, Par: 72, Holes: 18
Lake Limerick CC, East 790 Street Andrews Drive, Shelton, 98584,
206-426-3581   Yards: 2967, Par: 37, Holes: 9
Leavenworth GC, P. O. Box 247, Leavenworth, 98826, 509-548-7267
Yards: 5648, Par: 71, Holes: 18
Lewis River GC, 3209 Lewis River Road, Woodland, 98674, 206-225-8254
Yards: 6600, Par: 72, Holes: 18
Liberty Lake GC, Liberty Lake, 99019, 509-255-6233
Yards: 5480, Par: 70, Holes: 18
Lipoma Firs GC, PO Box 65, Puyallup, 98371, 206-841-4396
Holes: 9
Lower Valley GC, Route 1, Box 1632, Sunnyside, 98944, 509-837-5340
Yards: 6024, Par: 72, Holes: 9
Madrona Links GC, 3604–22nd Avenue N.W., Gig Harbor, 98335, 206-851-5193
Yards: 6100, Par: 71, Holes: 18
Maplewood G & CC, 13020 S.E. Maple Valley Highwa, Renton, 98056,
206-255-3194   Yards: 5625, Par: 71, Holes: 18
Meadow Park GC—18 Hole Course, 7108 Lakewodd Dr. W., Lakewood, 98467,
206-591-5343   Yards: 5522, Par: 72, Holes: 18
Meadowmeer G & CC, 8530 N.E. Renny Lane, Bainbridge Island, 98110,
206-842-2218   Yards: 2952, Par: 36, Holes: 9
Mount Adams GC, Route 1, Box 1280, Toppenish, 98949, 509-865-4440
Yards: 6400, Par: 72, Holes: 18
Mount Si GC, P. O. Box BB, Snoqualmie, 98065, 206-888-1541
Yards: 5400, Par: 70, Holes: 18
Newaukum Valley GC, 3024 Jackson Highway, Centralia, 98532, 206-748-0461
Yards: 6512, Par: 72, Holes: 18
Nisqually Valley GC, P. O. Box Q, Yelm, 98597, 206-458-3332
Yards: 5832, Par: 71, Holes: 18

North Shore, 4101 N. Shore Blvd. NE., Tacoma, 98422, 206-927-1375
Yards: 6067, Par: 71, USGA: 69.3, Holes: 18, Pro: Scot Solomonson
Oakridge GC, 207 Elma-Monte Road, Elma, 98541, 206-482-3511
Yards: 5700, Par: 70, Holes: 18
Orcas Island GC, Route 1, Box 85, Eastsound, 98245, 206-376-4400
Yards: 5845, Par: 72, Holes: 9
Othello G & CC, Othello, 99344, 509-488-2376
Yards: 6300, Par: 70, Holes: 9
Painted Hills GC, 4403 South Dishman-Minc Roa, Spokane, 99206
Holes: 9
Parkland Putters, 10636 Sales Road, Parkland, 98444, 206-588-2977
Holes: 72
Pasco Muni GC, 2535, North 20th, 99301, 509-545-3440
Yards: 6900, Par: 72, Holes: 18
Peninsula GC, Box 536, Long Beach, 98631, 206-642-2828
Yards: 2084, Par: 33, Holes: 9
Pine Crest GC, 2509 N.W. Bliss Road, Vancouver, 98665, 206-573-2051
Yards: 1261, Par: 27, Holes: 9
Pomeroy GC, Box 400, Pomeroy, 99347, 509-843-1197
Yards: 4084, Par: 31, Holes: 9
Quincy Valley GC, 1705 Road 5 NW, Quincy, 98848
Holes: 9
Ritzville Muni GC, 104 West 19th, Ritzville, 99169, 509-659-9868
Yards: 2812, Par: 35, Holes: 9
Riverside GC, 5799 Riverside Drive, Ferndale, 98248, 206-384-4116
Yards: 3100, Par: 36, Holes: 9
Rock Island GC, 314 Saunders Road, Rock Island, 98850, 509-884-2806
Yards: 5354, Par: 36, Holes: 9
Rolling Hills GC, 2485 N.E. McWilliams Road, Bremerton, 98310, 206-479-1212
Yards: 5487, Par: 68, Holes: 18
Royal Oaks GC, 8917 NE. Fourth Plain Rd., Portland, 98662
San Juan G & CC, P. O. Box 246, Friday Harbor, 98250, 206-378-2254
Yards: 3286, Par: 36, Holes: 9
Semiahmoo Golf & CC, 8720 Semiahmoo Pky., Blaine, 98230, 206-371-7005
Yards: 7005, Par: 72, USGA: 71.6, Holes: 18, Pro: Craig Griswold
Sham Na Pum GC, P. O. Box 14, Richland, 99352, 509-946-1914
Yards: 6244, Par: 70, Holes: 18
Shelton Bayshore GC, East 3800 Highway 3, Shelton, 98584, 206-426-1271
Yards: 6100, Par: 36, Holes: 9
Sheridan Green GC, P. O. Box 454, Republic, 99166, 509-775-3899
Yards: 1000, Par: 5, Holes: 18
Si View GC, P. O. Box "F", North Bend, 98045, 206-888-1817
Yards: 5565, Par: 62, Holes: 18
Similk Beach GC, 1369 Christiansen Road, Anacortes, 98221, 206-293-3444
Yards: 6274, Par: 72, Holes: 18
Snohomish Public GC, 7806—147th Avenue S.E., Snohomish, 98290,
206-568-2676   Yards: 6237, Par: 72, Holes: 18
Spring Valley GC, 1948 Blaine Street, Port Townsend, 98368, 206-385-0752
Yards: 5604, Par: 70, Holes: 9
Sun Country GC, East Nelson Siding Road, Cle Elum, 98926, 509-674-2226
Yards: 2800, Par: 36, Holes: 9
Sun Dance GC, Nine Mile Falls, 99026, 509-466-4040
Par: 70, Holes: 18
Sun Lakes Park Resort GC, Route 1, Box 141, Coulee City, 99115, 509-632-5291
Yards: 2950, Par: 36, Holes: 9

Sun Tides GC, 2215 Pence Road, Yakima, 98901, 509-966-9065
Yards: 5855, Par: 70, Holes: 18
Swallows Nest GC, 1725 Swallows Nest Loop, Clarkston, 99403, 509-758-8501
Yards: 2787, Par: 35, Holes: 9
Tall Chief GC, 1313 West Snoqualmie River Dr., Fall City, 98024, 206-222-5911
Yards: 5600, Par: 70, Holes: 18
Tapteal GC, West Richland, 509-967-2165
Par: 70, Holes: 18
Three Lakes GC, 2695 Golf Drive, Wenatchee, 98801, 509-663-5448
Yards: 5454, Par: 69, Holes: 18
Touchet Valley Muni GC, Route 1, Box 1, Dayton, 99328, 509-382-4851
Yards: 2516, Par: 36, Holes: 9
Tyee Valley GC, 2401 South 192nd Street, Seattle, 98188, 206-878-3540
Yards: 5900, Par: 71, Holes: 18
Valley View GC, Liberty Lake, 99019, 509-928-3484
Yards: 2072, Par: 32, Holes: 9
Veterans Memorial GC, 401 West Reese, Walla Walla, 99362, 509-527-4507
Yards: 6530, Par: 72, Holes: 18
Village Greens GC, 2298 Fircrest Drive S.E., Port Orchard, 98366,
206-871-1222   Yards: 3255, Par: 58, Holes: 18
Walter E. Hall Memorial GC, 1226 West Casino Road, Everett, 98204,
206-353-4653   Yards: 6130, Par: 72, Holes: 18
Wandermere GC, Spokane, 99202, 509-466-8023
Par: 70, Holes: 18
Washington State University, Compton Union Building, 3rd Fl, Pullman,
99163, 509-335-4342   Yards: 5778, Par: 72, Holes: 18
Wayne GC, 16721—96th N.W., Bothell, 98011, 206-486-4714
Yards: 4812, Par: 65, Holes: 18
Wellington Hills G & CC, 7026 Wellington Heights Drive, Woodinville, 98072,
206-483-1981   Yards: 2734, Par: 34, Holes: 9
West Richland Muni GC, 4000 Fallon Drive, West Richland, 99352,
509-967-2165 Yards: 6000, Par: 70, Holes: 18
West Seattle GC, 4470—35th Avenue S.W., Seattle, 98126, 206-932-9792
Yards: 6054, Par: 72, Holes: 18
Westwood GC, 6408 Tieton Drive, Yakima, 98908, 509-966-0890
Yards: 2700, Par: 35, Holes: 9
Willapa Harbor GC, Route 3, Box 441, Raymond, 98577, 206-942-2392
Yards: 3021, Par: 36, Holes: 9

Barbour County CC, Route 1, Philippi, 26416, 304-457-2156   *West Virginia*
Holes: 9
Beaver Creek G&CC, Beaver Creek, 25813, 304-763-9116
Par: 70, Holes: 18
Big Bend GC, Tornado, 25202, 304-727-8006
Yards: 6044, Par: 71, Holes: 18
Brooke Hills Park GC, 140 Gist Drive, Wheeling, 26003, 304-737-1236
Holes: 18
Cato Park Muni GC, Cato Park, Charleston, 25302, 304-348-6359
Holes: 9
Cherry Hill CC, Richwood, 26261, 304-846-9876
Holes: 9
Roane County Field GC, Box 197, Spence, 25276, 304-927-2899
Holes: 9
Clearfork Valley GC, Clear Fork, 24822, 304-682-6209
Par: 72, Holes: 18

Coonskin Park GC, Coonskin Drive, Charleston, 24311,   304-345-8000
Holes: 18
Elks CC, Elkins, 26241,   304-636-2436
Holes: 9
Golf Club of West Virginia, Waverly, 26184,   304-464-4420
Par: 70, Holes: 18
Glenville GC, Box 121, Glenville, 26351,   304-462-9907
Holes: 9
Grand Vue Park GC, P.O. Box 523, Moundsville, 26041,   304-845-9810
Holes: 18
Grandview CC, Beckley, 25801,   304-763-2520
Par: 72, Holes: 18
Greenbrier Valley GC, RTE 60 W. Main St., Lewisburg, 24901,   304-645-3660
Holes: 18
Hawks Nest CC, P.O. Box 299, Gauley Bridge, 25085,   304-632-1361
Par: 36, Holes: 9
Hidden Valley CC, Point Pleasant, 25550,   304-675-9739
Par: 36, Holes: 9
Holly Meadows CC, Parsons, 26287
Holes: 18
Knob Hill GC, Peyton Street, Barboursville, 25504,   304-736-9027
Holes: 9
Lakeview CC, Box 85, Cool Ridge, 25845,   304-785-9917
Holes: 9
Meadow Ponds Golf and West Rid, P.O. Box 365, Cassville, 26527,
304-328-5520 Holes: 9
Mill Creek CC, Box M, Keyser, 26276,   304-289-3160
Holes: 9
Mountain View GC, Morgantown, 26505,   304-594-1111
Par: 72, Holes: 18
Mountaineer G & CC, P.O. Box 100, Jere, 26536,   304-328-5520
Holes: 9
Nicholas Memorial GC, Box 483, Summersville, 26651,   304-872-9850
Holes: 9
North Bend State Park GC, Cairo, 26362,   304-643-2931
Holes: 9
Oglebay Park, Route 88, North, Wheeling, 26003,   304-242-3000
Holes: 18
Orchard Hills GC, Barboursville, 25504,   304-736-1105
Par: 35, Holes: 9
Pocahontas CC, 817 4th Ave., Marlinton, 24954,   304-799-4147
Holes: 9
Poplar Grove CC, Gassaway, 26624,   304-364-8379
Holes: 9
Potomac CC, Polish Pines GC, Keyser, 26276,   304-788-1671
Holes: 9
Riverview CC, Madison, 25130,   304-369-9835
Holes: 9
Riviera CC, Lesage, 25537,   304-736-7778
Par: 72, Holes: 18
Sandy Brae GC, 19 Osborne Mills Rd., Clendenin, 25045,   304-965-7700
USGA: 69.0, Holes: 18
Shawnee GC, Institute, 25112,   304-768-7600
Holes: 9
Sleepy Hollow CC, Charles Town, 25414,   304-725-5210
Par: 72, Holes: 18

St. Marys GC, St. Marys, 26170, 304-684-3557
Par: 32, Holes: 9
Sugarwood GC, Sugarwood Road, Lavalette, 25535, 304-523-6500
Holes: 18
Traidelphia CC, Man, 25635, 304-583-9030
Holes: 18
Twin Falls GC, P. O. Box 1023, Mullens, 25881, 304-294-4000
Par: 71, Holes: 18
Twin Oaks CC, Box 458, Crab Orchard, 25827, 304-253-9258
Holes: 9
Tygart Lake State Park GC, P.O. Box 624, Grafton, 26354, 304-265-3100
Holes: 18
Valley View CC, Box 548. Big Draft Road, White Sulphur Springs, 24986,
304-466-1600   Holes: 18
Waterford Park, Chester, 26034, 304-387-2400
Holes: 9
Western Greenbrier Hills, Rainelle, 25962, 304-438-9050
Holes: 9
Wheeling Park, Wheeling, 26003, 304-242-3770
Holes: 9
Williams GC, Williams Dr., Whelling, 26062
Willow Wood CC, P.O. Box 847, Hinton, 25951, 304-466-3220
Holes: 9
Woodbrier GC, Martinsburg, 25401, 304-274-9818
Holes: 9

Alaskan Motor Inn GC, Rt 3, Kewaunee, 54216, 414-388-3940   *Wisconsin*
Yards: 2839, Par: 36, Holes: 9
Alpine Valley Resort, Hwy. D.P.O. Box 615, East Troy, 53120, 414-642-7374
Yards: 5583, Par: 72, USGA: 66.3, Holes: 27, Pro: Connie Schulte
American Legion Golf Course, Golf Clug Rd., P.O. Box 967, Wausau, 54401,
715-675-3663 Yards: 5344, Par: 68, USGA: 63.7, Holes: 9, Pro: Bill Edwards
Antigo Bass Lake CC, Box 268, Antigo, 54409, 715-623-6196
Yards: 5912, Par: 71, USGA: 68.5, Holes: 18, Pro: Mike Kilas
Arcadia GC, Hwy. 93, Arcadia, 54612, 608-323-3626
Yards: 2738, Par: 35, Holes: 9
Arrowhead Springs GC, 3468 Hwy. 167, Richfield, 53076, 414-628-2298
Yards: 2680, Par: 34, Holes: 9
Auburn Bluffs GC, Campbells Port, 53010, 414-533-4311
Par: 35, Holes: 9
Baraboo CC, 1010 Lake St., Box 383, Baraboo, 53913, 608-356-8195
Yards: 6402, Par: 72, USGA: 70.7, Holes: 9, Pro: Rob Robbins
Bass Lake CC, Box 268, Antigo, 54409, 715-623-6196
Yards: 6203, Par: 71, Holes: 18, Pro: Mike Kulas
Beloit Krueger Men's Club, 1611 Hackett St., Beloit, 53511, 608-362-6503
Yards: 6101, Par: 70, USGA: 69.0, Holes: 18, Pro: Don Tamulis
Big Foot CC, Shabbona Dr., P. O. Box 130, Fontana, 53125, 414-275-2149
Yards: 6436, Par: 73, USGA: 71.8, Holes: 18, Pro: Ronald Romack
Big Oaks GC, 6117 123rd Place, Pleasant Prairie, 53140, 414-694-4200
Yards: 6435, Par: 71, Holes: 18
BlackHawk GC, Palmer Drive, Janesville, 53545, 608-755-0173
Yards: 3097, Par: 36, Holes: 9
BlackhawK CC, 3606 Blackhawk Dr., P.O. Box 5, Madison, 53705, 608-231-2454
Yards: 6034, Par: 72, USGA: 69.3, Holes: 18, Pro: Michael Schnarr
Bloomer Memorial GC, 500 13th Ave, Box 33, Bloomer, 54724, 715-568-1741
Yards: 5348, Par: 66, USGA: 65.6, Holes: 9, Pro: Jon Hassemer

Bluemound G & CC, 10122 W. North Ave., P.O.Box 2, Wauwatosa, 53226, 414-258-4656   Yards: 6347, Par: 70, USGA: 70.6, Holes: 18, Pro: Russ Tuveson
Branch River CC, 3212 N. Union Rd., Cato, 54206,   414-684-3319
Yards: 6448, Par: 71, USGA: 70.5, Holes: 18, Pro: Patrick Furca
Bridgewood GC, US 41 Cecil Street, Neenah, 54956,   414-722-9819
Yards: 6015, Par: 71, Holes: 18, Pro: Lee Miller
Brighton Dale GC, 830-248th Avenue, Kansasville, 53139,   414-878-1440
Yards: 6755, Par: 72, USGA: 71.5, Holes: 27, Pro: K. Schlavensky
Brookfield Hills GC, 16075 Pinehurst Drive, Brookfield, 53005,   414-782-0885
Yards: 4415, Par: 62, Holes: 18, Pro: John Accola
Brown Deer Park GC, 7835 N. Green Bay Rd., Milwaukee, 53209,   414-352-8080
Yards: 6470, Par: 71, USGA: 71.0, Holes: 18
Brynwood GC, 6200 W. Good Hope Rd., Milwaukee, 53223,   414-353-8800
Yards: 6508, Par: 72, USGA: 71.8, Holes: 18, Pro: Carl Unis
Browns Lake GC, 3110 S. Browns Lake Dr., Burlington, 53105,   414-763-6065
Yards: 6415, Par: 72, USGA: 70.2, Holes: 18, Pro: Bill Hagensick
Bull's Eye CC, 1 Airport Ave., P.O. Box 8050, Wisconsin Rapids, 54494,
715-423-2230   Yards: 6387, Par: 72, USGA: 71.3, Holes: 18, Pro: David Andrews
Butte Des Morts GC, Inc., 3600 W. Prospect Ave., Appleton, 54915,
414-738-5555   Yards: 6132, Par: 70, USGA: 69.5, Holes: 18, Pro: William Brodell
Butternut Hills GC, Cty. Rt. B, Sarona, 54870,   715-635-8563
Yards: 2860, Par: 36, Holes: 9
Camelot CC, Hwy 67, P. O. Box 435, Lomira, 53048,   414-269-4949
Yards: 5786, Par: 70, USGA: 67.6, Holes: 18, Pro: Mark Roskopf
Castle Mound GC, W7665 Sylvester Rd., Holmen, 54636,   608-526-3225
Yards: 5747, Par: 72, USGA: 66.9, Holes: 18, Pro: Gary Johnson
CC Estages GC, Fontana, 53125,   414-275-3705
Par: 35, Holes: 9
Cecelia's GC, Rt. 1, Janesville, 53545,   608-754-8550
Yards: 3071, Par: 36, Holes: 9
Cedar Creek CC, N5476 County Ln., Onalaska, 54650,   608-783-8100
Yards: 6751, Par: 71, Holes: 18, Pro: John Schneider
Cedar Springs GC, Rt. 1 Box 64, Manawa, 54949,   414-596-2905
Yards: 5807, Par: 70, USGA: 67.6, Holes: 9, Pro: Dave Schuelke
Chaska GC, Hwy. 10 & 45, P. O. Box 415, Appleton, 54912,   414-757-5757
Yards: 6472, Par: 72, USGA: 70.8, Holes: 18, Pro: Stephanie Jack
Chenequa CC, 6250 N. Hwy. 83, Hartland, 53029,   414-367-3246
Yards: 6371, Par: 71, USGA: 71.3, Holes: 18, Pro: Randy Robel
Cherokee CC, 5000 N. Sherman Ave., Madison, 53704,   608-249-1000
Yards: 6397, Par: 72, USGA: 70.3, Holes: 18, Pro: Larry Tiziani
Chippewa Falls Elks CC, RR 5, P.O. Box 764, Chippewa Falls, 54729,
715-723-7363 Yards: 5769, Par: 70, USGA: 67.1, Holes: 9, Pro: Chuck Harvey
Clear Lake GC, 100 Gulf Drive., P.O. Box 283, Clear Lake, 54005,   715-263-2500
Yards: 5602, Par: 68, USGA: 66.7, Holes: 9, Pro: Douglas Klatt
Clifton Highlands GC, Rt. 1, Prescott, 54021,   715-262-5141
Yards: 6169, Par: 72, USGA: 68.8, Holes: 18, Pro: Bruck Johnson
Clintonville Riverside GC, Golf Club Rd., P. O. Box 188, Clintonville, 54929,
715-823-2991   Yards: 6304, Par: 71, USGA: 69.9, Holes: 9, Pro: William Hurley
Cole Acres GC, RR #1, Cuba City, 53807,   608-744-2476
Yards: 6253, Par: 72, USGA: 68.2, Holes: 9, Pro: James Lacke
Columbus CC, 301 Ingalsbe St., 235 Chapin S, Columbus, 53925,   414-623-5880
Yards: 6250, Par: 74, USGA: 68.5, Holes: 9, Pro: Timothy Hoffman
Coulee Golf Bowl, N4500 Green Coulee Rd., Onalaska, 54650,   608-781-1111
Yards: 6134, Par: 72, USGA: 67.1, Holes: 9, Pro: Wally Hayes
Country Club of Beloit, Inc., 2327 Riverside Dr., P.O.Box 53, Beloit, 53511,
608-364-9000   Yards: 6429, Par: 71, USGA: 70.8, Holes: 18, Pro: Paul Messner

Countryside GC, 3231 Weiler Rd., Kaukauna, 54130, 414-766-2219
Yards: 6140, Par: 71, USGA: 68.9, Holes: 18, Pro: Thomas Schmidt
Crystal Lake GC, County Route C, Plymouth, 53073, 414-892-4834
Yards: 2300, Par: 33, Holes: 9
Cumberland GC, Inc., 499 24th Ave., P. O. Box 595, Cumberland, 54829,
715-822-2791 Yards: 5446, Par: 70, USGA: 65.6, Holes: 9, Pro: Maxine Johnson
Currie Park Men's GC, 3535 N. Mayfair Rd., Wauwatosa, 53222, 414-453-7030
Yards: 6095, Par: 71, USGA: 68.6, Holes: 18, Pro: A. Kowalewski
Darlington CC, 17098 Country Club Rd., Darlington, 53530, 608-776-3377
Yards: 5332, Par: 70, USGA: 63.4, Holes: 9, Pro: A. Hirsbrunner
Decatur Lake GC, P.O.Box 331, Brodhead, 53520, 608-897-2777
Yards: 2940, Par: 35, Holes: 9
Deepwood Ski & Golf, Rt. 1, Wheeler, 54772, 715-658-1500
Yards: 2711, Par: 36, Holes: 9
Deer Run CC, 912 Fairway Dr., Brillon, 54110
Yards: 3160, Par: 36, Holes: 9, Pro: E. Huenerburg
Deertrak GC, W930 Hwy. 0, Aderly, 53066, 414-474-4444
Yards: 5921, Par: 72, USGA: 67.4, Holes: 18, Pro: Don Chapman
Delbrook GC, South 2nd St., Delavan, 53115, 414-728-3966
Yards: 5568, Par: 72, USGA: 69.4, Holes: 18, Pro: Eugene Shreves
Dell View, Hwy 12, Lake Delton, 53940, 608-253-1261
Yards: 5800, Par: 69, USGA: 66.5, Holes: 18, Pro: Bob Kivlin
Dodge Point CC Ltd., R.R. 3, Mineral Point, 53565, 608-987-2814
Yards: 5922, Par: 68, USGA: 67.2, Holes: 9, Pro: Tony Pittz
Dretzka Park Men's GC, 12020 W. Bradley Rd., Milwaukee, 53224,
414-354-7300 Yards: 6617, Par: 72, USGA: 70.8, Holes: 18, Pro: Bill Knight
Eagle Bluff GC, Rt. 1 County Trunk D, P.O.Box, Hurley, 54534, 715-561-3552
Yards: 5842, Par: 69, USGA: 67.7, Holes: 18, Pro: Caeser Tiziani
Eagle Springs GC, Rt. 2 Hwy 99, Eagle, 53119, 414-594-2462
Yards: 3100, Par: 36, Holes: 9
Eau Claire G & CC, 2106 Main St., Eau Claire, 54701, 715-832-3448
Yards: 6119, Par: 71, USGA: 69.4, Holes: 18, Pro: Jim Julsrud
Edelweiss Chalet CC, W4765 Edelweiss Road, P.O. Box, New Glarus, 53574,
608-527-2315 Yards: 6489, Par: 72, USGA: 69.5, Holes: 9, Pro: Roland Buchholz
Edgewater GC, Inc, 1762 West Cedar Creek Rd., Grafton, 53024, 414-377-1230
Yards: 6178, Par: 70, USGA: 68.8, Holes: 9, Pro: A. Brackenbury
Edgewood GC, Oconto, 54153, 414-834-2681
Par: 36, Holes: 9
Elks Lodge GC, Hwy. 137, P. O. Box 364, Ashland, 54806, 715-682-5215
Yards: 6300, Par: 72, USGA: 68.8, Holes: 9, Pro: Gary Jaeger
Ettrick GC, 310 N. Fairway Avenue, Ettrick, 54627, 608-525-6262
Yards: 5852, Par: 70, USGA: 67.3, Holes: 9, Pro: Eugene Hogden
Evergreen CC, Rt. 5, Box 616, Elkhorn, 53121, 414-723-5722
Yards: 6119, Par: 71, USGA: 69.8, Holes: 18, Pro: Lorrie Koppein
Fairview CC, 3659 Riverview Dr., Two Rivers, 54241, 414-794-8726
Yards: 3159, Par: 36, Holes: 9, Pro: Wm. & J. Lane
Far-Vu GC, 414-231-2631
Yards: 6206, Par: 71, Holes: 18
Five Flags CC Estates, Rt. 2, Box 312, Balsam Lake, 54810, 715-825-2141
Par: 36, Holes: 9
Four Seasons GC, Pembine, 54156, 715-324-5244
Yards: 2670, Par: 34, Holes: 9
Fox Hills Resort & Convention, P.O. Box 129, Mishicot, 54228, 414-755-2376
Yards: 6267, Par: 72, USGA: 70.7, Holes: 45, Pro: Bill Boockmeier
Fox Lake GC, Indian Point Rd., P.O. Box 12, Fox Lake, 53933, 414-928-2508
Yards: 6246, Par: 73, USGA: 68.5, Holes: 9, Pro: R. Christianson

Fox Valley GC, CTH UU, P. O. Box 28, Kaukauna, 54130, 414-766-1340
Yards: 6410, Par: 73, USGA: 69.9, Holes: 18, Pro: Donald Erdmann
Foxboro GC, 1020 Cty MM, Oregon, 53575, 608-835-7789
Yards: 3622, Par: 36, Holes: 9
Frederic CC, Inc., Hwy. 35 South, Frederic, 54837, 715-327-8450
Yards: 5598, Par: 70, USGA: 64.6, Holes: 9, Pro: Mary Young
Gateway GC, 4126 Hwy. B, P. O. Box 718, Land O'Lakes, 54540, 715-547-3929
Yards: 6356, Par: 72, USGA: 70.5, Holes: 9, Pro: Mark Hirn
George Williams College GC, Route 67, Box 210, Williams Bay, 53191,
414-245-9507 Yards: 5066, Par: 67, USGA: 63.4, Holes: 18, Pro: Cy Stark
Glen Hills GC, Inc., RR 1, Glenwood City, 54013, 715-265-4718
Yards: 6282, Par: 72, USGA: 69.8, Holes: 18, Pro: Mike Kuhlman
Glenway GC, 3747 Speedway Rd., Madison, 53206, 608-266-4737
Yards: 2298, Par: 32, Holes: 9
Golden Sands Golf Community, 300 Naber Street, Cecil, 54111, 715-745-2189
Yards: 5955, Par: 70, USGA: 67.4, Holes: 18, Pro: Pat Wallrich
Golf Course, The, Three Lakes, 54562, 715-546-2880
Par: 33, Holes: 9
Grand View GC, Inc., 333 N. Olk St., P.O. Box 217, Hortonville, 54944,
414-779-6421 Yards: 5574, Par: 70, USGA: 65.2, Holes: 9, Pro: S. Martzahl
Grant Park Men's GC, 100 Hawthorne Ave., South Milwaukee, 53172,
414-762-4646 Yards: 5174, Par: 67, USGA: 64.1, Holes: 18, Pro: Ted Kaza
Grantsburg GC, 333 W. St. George, Grantsburg, 54840, 715-463-2300
Yards: 4630, Par: 68, USGA: 62.1, Holes: 9, Pro: D. Dahlberg
Green Acres GC, Rt. 1, Pembine, 54156, 715-387-6114
Yards: 5300, Par: 35, Holes: 9
Green Acres GC, Rt. 1, Lake Nebegamon, 54848, 715-374-2567
Yards: 2830, Par: 35, Holes: 9
Greenfield Park Men's GC, 2028 S. 124th St., West Allis, 53227, 414-453-1750
Yards: 5770, Par: 69, USGA: 66.7, Holes: 18, Pro: John Brosman
Hallie GC, 3798 Golf View, Chippewa Falls, 54729, 715-723-8524
Yards: 5283, Par: 70, USGA: 65.6, Holes: 18, Pro: Ed Severson
Hammond GC, Inc., 450 Davis Street, Hammond, 54015, 715-796-2266
Yards: 6173, Par: 72, USGA: 68.1, Holes: 9, Pro: John Girolamo
Hartford CC, 7072 Lee Rd., Hartford, 53027, 414-673-6700
Yards: 6411, Par: 72, USGA: 69.7, Holes: 18, Pro: Earl Dupont, Jr
Hiawatha GC, P.O. Box 287, Tomah, 54660, 608-372-5589
Yards: 6378, Par: 72, USGA: 69.7, Holes: 9, Pro: Kyle Fox
Hickory Grove GC, R.R. 1, Fennimore, 53809, 608-822-3314
Yards: 6332, Par: 72, USGA: 68.5, Holes: 9, Pro: Tino Novinska
Hickory Hills CC, W3095 Hickory Hills Rd., Chilton, 53014, 414-849-2912
Yards: 6066, Par: 70, USGA: 69.0, Holes: 18, Pro: Joseph Nelesen
High Cliff GC, W5055 Golf Course Rd., Menasha, 54952, 414-734-1162
Yards: 5931, Par: 71, USGA: 67.3, Holes: 18, Pro: Lisa Booth
Hillcrest C & CC, 3909 US Hwy. 12, Eau Claire, 54701, 715-832-8623
Yards: 6051, Par: 72, USGA: 69.1, Holes: 18, Pro: Terry Govern
Hillmoor CC, Highway 50 East, P. O. Box 186, Lake Geneva, 53147,
414-248-4570 Yards: 6079, Par: 71, USGA: 69.1, Holes: 18, Pro: Scott Miller
Hilly Haven GC, Rt. 2, DePere, 54115, 414-336-6204
Yards: 2876, Par: 36, Holes: 9
Holiday Lodge CC, Wyeville, 54671, 608-372-9314
Yards: 2900, Par: 35, Holes: 9
Homestead Supper & CC, 3372 Hwy. 13 North, Wisconsin Rapids, 54494,
715-423-7577 Yards: 5424, Par: 68, USGA: 65.3, Holes: 9, Pro: Duane Hafermann
Hudson CC, North Frontage Rd., P.O. Box 6, Hudson, 54016, 715-386-6515
Yards: 6199, Par: 71, USGA: 69.5, Holes: 18, Pro: Dan Loken

Indianhead Golf & Recreation, 966 East Ring Road, Mosinee, 54455, 715-693-6066 Yards: 6120, Par: 70, USGA: 68.7, Holes: 9, Pro: Dewey Doering
Inshalla CC, N11060 Clear Lake Rd., Tomahawk, 54487, 715-453-3130
Yards: 5599, Par: 70, Holes: 18
IOLA Community GC, Inc., RR 2, Iola, 54945, 715-445-3831
Yards: 6412, Par: 72, USGA: 69.4, Holes: 9
Janesville CC, 2615 W. Memorial Dr., P.O. Box, Janesville, 53547, 608-754-5531
Yards: 6307, Par: 72, USGA: 70.6, Holes: 18, Pro: Ken Hulen
Janesville Muni Men's Golf Ass, Cty. Hwy. 14 West, Janesville, 53545,
608-754-9085 Yards: 6322, Par: 70, USGA: 69.9, Holes: 18, Pro: Ken Johnson
Johnson Park Men's GC, 6200 Northwestern Ave., Racine, 53406,
414-637-2840 Yards: 6380, Par: 71, USGA: 69.5, Holes: 18, Pro: M.Bencriscutto
Kenosha CC, 500 13th Avenue, P.O. Box 249, Kenosha, 53140, 414-552-8488
Yards: 6257, Par: 70, USGA: 71.0, Holes: 18, Pro: Tom Befera
Kettle Hills GC, 3375 State Highway 167, Richfield, 53076, 414-255-2200
Yards: 6357, Par: 72, USGA: 70.1, Holes: 18, Pro: David Boda
Kettle Moraine GC, 4299 Highway 67, Dousman, 53118, 414-965-2423
Yards: 6231, Par: 71, USGA: 69.6, Holes: 18, Pro: Jeff Venes
Krueger Muni GC, 1611 Hackett St., Beloit, 53511, 608-362-6503
Yards: 6103, Par: 70, Holes: 18, Pro: Don Tamulis
La Crosse CC, 600 N. Losey Blvd., La Crosse, 54601, 608-784-3257
Yards: 5745, Par: 71, USGA: 67.0, Holes: 18, Pro: Dick Cotter
Lac Belle CC, 6996 Pennsylvania Ave., Oconomowoc, 53066, 414-567-3725
Yards: 6143, Par: 70, USGA: 69.8, Holes: 18, Pro: Rick Rasmussen
Lake Beulah CC, 594 East Shore Drive, Mukwonago, 53149, 414-363-8147
Yards: 5682, Par: 67, USGA: 66.5, Holes: 18, Pro: James Jacobs
Lake Forest Recreation Club, 1531 Golf View Dr., Eagle River, 54521,
715-479-4211 Yards: 5396, Par: 72, USGA: 65.0, Holes: 9, Pro: Tom Beyer
Lake Park GC, N112 W17300 Mequon Rd., P.O.Bo, Germantown, 53022,
414-255-4200 Yards: 6282, Par: 72, USGA: 70.0, Holes: 18, Pro: Lloyd Robinson
Lake Ripley CC, W9574 Hwy. 12, P.O. Box 31, Cambridge, 53523, 608-423-3411
Yards: 6211, Par: 70, USGA: 69.4, Holes: 18, Pro: Richard Lewis
Lake Windsor CC, 4628 Golf Road, P.O. Box 317, Windsor, 53598, 608-846-4440
Yards: 6151, Par: 72, USGA: 69.2, Holes: 27, Pro: Steve Martell
Lakeland Hills CC, RR 1, Lodi, 53555, 608-592-3757
Yards: 5649, Par: 70, USGA: 66.0, Holes: 9, Pro: James Haberli
Lakeshore Men's GC, 2175 Punhoqua St., Oshkosh, 54901, 414-236-5090
Yards: 5526, Par: 68, USGA: 66.9, Holes: 18, Pro: Lou Zwicky
Lakeside CC, W287 N3192, P.O. Box 194, Pewaukee, 53072, 414-691-4630
Yards: 5466, Par: 68, USGA: 65.5, Holes: 9, Pro: Tom Peterman
Lancaster CC, East Lincoln Avenue, Lancaster, 53813, 608-723-4266
Yards: 6006, Par: 72, USGA: 68.0, Holes: 9, Pro: Donald E. Funk
Lincoln GC, 1000 W. Hampton Ave., Glendale, 53209, 414-962-2400
Yards: 2538, Par: 33, Holes: 9
Little River CC, Marinette, 53143, 715-732-2221
Yards: 5893, Par: 71, Holes: 18, Pro: Jean Marineau
Lost Creek GC, 4146 Golf Valley Dr., Sturgeon Bay, 54235, 414-743-6880
Yards: 6552, Par: 72, USGA: 71.1, Holes: 18, Pro: John Muskatevc
Luck CC, 1520 South Shore Dr., Luck, 54853, 715-472-2939
Yards: 5363, Par: 68, USGA: 66.0, Holes: 9, Pro: Janice Nelson
Macdonald's River Bend GC, Rt. 2 Box 136, Melrose, 54642, 608-488-7291
Yards: 2950, Par: 35, Holes: 9
Madeline Island GC, 256 Madeline Island, La Pointe, 54850, 715-747-3212
Yards: 6495, Par: 71, USGA: 70.5, Holes: 18, Pro: Mike Wallrich
Madison Area Retiree Golf Assn, 3747 Speedway Road, Madison, 53705,
608-266-4737 Yards: 4616, Par: 64, USGA: 60.9, Holes: 9, Pro: Robert Muranyi

Maple Birch GC, Tomahawk, 54487, 715-453-3320
Par: 33, Holes: 9
Maple Bluff CC, 500 Kensington Drive, Madison, 53704, 608-249-2144
Yards: 6068, Par: 71, USGA: 70.1, Holes: 18, Pro: John Hall
Maple Grove CC, Route 1, County B, West Salem, 54669, 608-786-1500
Yards: 6307, Par: 71, USGA: 69.0, Holes: 18, Pro: Gary Isakson
Maple Hills GC, Rt. 2, Wittenberg, 54499, 715-253-2448
Yards: 2850, Par: 36, Holes: 9
Maplecrest CC, 9401 18th Street, P.O. Box 141, Somers, 53171, 414-859-2887
Yards: 6414, Par: 70, USGA: 70.9, Holes: 18, Pro: Mickey Gullo
Marshfield CC, 11426 Hwy. B., P.O.Box 531, Marshfield, 54449, 715-384-4409
Yards: 5820, Par: 70, USGA: 66.6, Holes: 18, Pro: Chip Acker
Mayville GC, 325 S. German St., Mayville, 53050, 414-387-9965
Yards: 6086, Par: 72, USGA: 67.6, Holes: 9, Pro: V.Schellpfeffer
Meadow Links GC, 1540 Johnston Dr., Manitowoc, 54220, 414-682-6842
Yards: 5849, Par: 69, USGA: 67.4, Holes: 18, Pro: Wally Hanson
Meadow Springs GC, 424 S. Sanborn Ave., P.O. Box, Jefferson, 53549,
414-674-9986   Yards: 5906, Par: 70, USGA: 67.3, Holes: 9, Pro: Jerry Schuld
Meadowbrook CC, 2149 N. Green Bay Rd., Racine, 53405, 414-637-7461
Yards: 6112, Par: 71, USGA: 70.5, Holes: 18, Pro: Bruck Woodward
Meadowview GC, 800 W. 3 St., Owen, 54460, 715-229-2355
Yards: 3172, Par: 36, Holes: 9
Mellen CC, Mellen, 54546, 715-274-7311
Yards: 2979, Par: 34, Holes: 9
Menomonie CC, 1000 W. Elm Ave., Menomonie, 54751, 715-235-3595
Yards: 5770, Par: 72, USGA: 66.9, Holes: 9, Pro: Marjorie Veum
Merrill Hills CC, W270 S3425, Merrill Hills Road, Waukesha, 53188,
414-548-1100   Yards: 6498, Par: 72, USGA: 72.0, Holes: 18, Pro: Jim Kloiber
Merrill Public GC, O'Day Street, P. O. Box 534, Merrill, 54452, 715-536-2529
Yards: 6375, Par: 72, USGA: 70.2, Holes: 9, Pro: Roger Gifford
Mid-Vallee GC, Inc., Rt. 3 Hwy. 41, De Pere, 54115, 414-532-6674
Yards: 6402, Par: 72, USGA: 69.5, Holes: 18, Pro: Jim Ostrowski
Mill Run Golf, Inc., 3905 Kane Rd., Eau Claire, 54703, 715-834-1766
Yards: 6027, Par: 71, USGA: 65.1, Holes: 18, Pro: Mark Hagen
Milwaukee CC, 8000 N. Range Line Rd., Milwaukee, 53209, 414-354-9224
Yards: 6356, Par: 72, USGA: 71.3, Holes: 18, Pro: M. de la Torre
Milwaukee Golf Connection, 5706 W. Melvina, Milwaukee, 53216,
414-444-2457   Yards: 6617, Par: 72, USGA: 70.8, Holes: 18, Pro: Hanc Spivey
Minocqua CC, 9299 Country Club Rd., P.O. Bo, Minocqua, 54548, 715-356-5216
Yards: 5608, Par: 68, USGA: 66.3, Holes: 9, Pro: Judith Johnson
Missing Links GC, 12950 N. Port Washington Rd., Mequon, 53092,
414-243-5711   Yards: 1270, Par: 27, Holes: 9, Pro: Greg Nikolai
Monona GC, 111 E. Dean Ave., Madison, 53716, 608-266-4736
Yards: 3157, Par: 36, Holes: 9, Pro: Robert Muranyi
Monroe CC, East End 21st St., Monroe, 53566, 608-325-3157
Yards: 5952, Par: 70, USGA: 68.2, Holes: 18, Pro: Michael Muranyi
Moor Downs GC, 438 Prospect Ave., Waukesha, 53186, 414-548-7821
Yards: 2934, Par: 35, Holes: 9, Pro: Tom Adrian
Moundview GC, Highway J. P.O. Box 86, Friendship, 53934, 608-339-3814
Yards: 6360, Par: 72, USGA: 69.7, Holes: 9, Pro: Charles Subera
Moundview GC, Hwy J, Friendship, 53934, 608-339-3814
Yards: 3168, Par: 36, Holes: 9
Muskego Lakes CC, S100 W14020 Loomis Rd., Muskego, 53150, 414-425-6500
Yards: 6003, Par: 61, USGA: 69.3, Holes: 18, Pro: Scott Krause
Mystery Hills GC, Rt. #1 Box 68, Depere, 54115, 414-336-6077
Yards: 6184, Par: 72, USGA: 67.5, Holes: 27, Pro: Skip Holm

Nagawaukee GC, 1897 Maple Ave., Pewaukee, 53072,   414-367-2153
Yards: 6453, Par: 72, USGA: 70.4, Holes: 18, Pro: Peter Schlicht
Nakoma GC, 4145 Country Club Rd., Madison, 53711,   608-238-3141
Yards: 6116, Par: 70, USGA: 69.6, Holes: 18, Pro: Allan Mitchell
Neillsville CC, 603 E. Division, P.O. Box 86, Neillsville, 54456,   715-743-3780
Yards: 6238, Par: 70, USGA: 69.1, Holes: 9, Pro: Tim McQuade
New Berlin Hills GC, 13175 W. Graham St., New Berlin, 53151,   414-782-5005
Yards: 6229, Par: 71, USGA: 70.0, Holes: 18, Pro: Mitch Joannes
New London CC, Route 3, Highway 45 N., P.O.Bo, New London, 54961,
414-982-9993   Yards: 6089, Par: 71, USGA: 68.5, Holes: 9, Pro: Tom Ajack
New Richmond GG, Inc., Rt. 5 Box 36, P.O. Box 7, New Richmond, 54017,
715-246-6724   Yards: 6371, Par: 72, USGA: 70.7, Holes: 18, Pro: Gary Johnson
Nicolet CC, Route 1, Laona, 54541,   715-674-4780
Yards: 4553, Par: 67, Holes: 18, Pro: Steve Amerson
Nippersink Manor GC, RTE. 1 Hwy. P, Genoa City, 53128,   414-279-5281
Yards: 6299, Par: 71, USGA: 69.4, Holes: 18
Norsk Golf Bowl, 207 Golf View Drive, Mount Horeb, 53572,   608-437-3399
Yards: 5704, Par: 70, USGA: 66.4, Holes: 9, Pro: Jack McGinley
North Shore GC, N8421 North Shore Rd., P.O. Bo, Menasha, 54952,
414-739-2386   Yards: 6260, Par: 70, USGA: 70.2, Holes: 18, Pro: George Nackel
North Shore CC, 3100 W. Country Club Dr., Mequon, 53092,   414-242-0820
Yards: 6506, Par: 72, USGA: 71.0, Holes: 27, Pro: Bill Halvorson
Northwoods GC, Rhinelander, 54501,   715-369-2004
Holes: 18
Norwood GC, Rt. 1 Box 813, Lake Nebagamon, 54849,   715-374-3210
Yards: 2015, Par: 31, Holes: 9
Oak Hills GC, 10360 S. Howell, Oak Creek, 53154,   414-762-9994
Yards: 2130, Par: 31, Holes: 9
Oakwood Men's GC, 3720 W. Oakwood Rd., Franklin, 53132,   414-281-6700
Yards: 6658, Par: 72, USGA: 71.1, Holes: 18, Pro: Pat Haberski
Oconomowoc GC, 5261 Brown St., Oconomowoc, 53066,   414-567-9972
Yards: 6314, Par: 70, USGA: 71.8, Holes: 18, Pro: Ed Teresa
Odana Hills GC, 4635 Odana Rd., Madison, 53711,   608-266-4078
Yards: 6360, Par: 72, USGA: 68.7, Holes: 18, Pro: Tom Benson
Ojibwa CC, Rt. 5, P.O. Box 33, Chippewa Falls, 54729, 715-723-8823
Yards: 5580, Par: 68, USGA: 65.0, Holes: 9, Pro: Lynn McDonough
Old Hickory GC, W7596 Hwy. 33 East, P.O. Box 3, Deaver Dam, 53916,
414-887-7179   Yards: 6323, Par: 71, USGA: 70.8, Holes: 18, Pro: Steve Kaiser
Oneida Golf & Riding Club, 207 Country Club Rd., P.O.Box, Green Bay,
54307,   414-494-2366   Yds: 6356, Par: 71, USGA: 71.0, Holes: 18, Pro: J. Thompson
Oshkosh Country Club, 11 W. Ripple Rd., Oshkosh, 54902,   414-231-1076
Yards: 6086, Par: 71, USGA: 69.1, Holes: 18, Pro: John Fulwider
Osseo Golf & Recreation Center, 127 E. Park Ave., P.O. Box 411, Osseo,
54758,   715-597-3215 Yards: 5854, Par: 70, USGA: 67.1, Holes: 9, Pro: Ron Johnson
Ozaukee CC, 10823 North River Rd., P.O. Bo, Mequon, 53092,   414-242-2450
Yards: 6201, Par: 70, USGA: 70.7, Holes: 18, Pro: Robert Brue
Paganica GC, 3850 Silver Lake St., Oconomowoc, 53066,   414-567-0171
Yards: 6678, Par: 72, USGA: 70.2, Holes: 18, Pro: Robert Pancratz
Park Falls CC, Saunders Ave. Box 198, Park Falls, 54552,   715-762-4396
Yards: 6236, Par: 70, USGA: 69.1, Holes: 9, Pro: R. Frankewicz
Pine Acres GC, 3235 Sot Road, Abrams, 54101,   414-826-7765
Yards: 4800, Par: 64, USGA: 61.8, Holes: 9, Pro: Karen Duffy
Pine Crest GC, Box 44, Dellas, 54733,   715-837-1268
Yards: 2741, Par: 35, Holes: 9, Pro: Dale Severson
Pine Hills CC, Route 1, Gresham, 54128,   715-787-3778
Par: 36, Holes: 9

Pine Valley GC, Hwy. 29 & 136th Ave N, 203 136, Marathon, 54448, 715-443-2848 Yards: 5674, Par: 70, USGA: 65.9, Holes: 9, Pro: Rick Lohr
Platteville G & CC, Hwy 80 N, P.O. Box 434, Platteville, 53818, 608-348-3551 Yards: 5794, Par: 71, USGA: 67.2, Holes: 18, Pro: Tim Stoffregen
Pleasant View GC, 4279 Pleasant View Rd., Middleton, 53562, 608-831-6666 Yards: 6193, Par: 72, USGA: 68.9, Holes: 18, Pro: Jeff Bishop
Plum Lake GC, 3160 Club House Rd., Sayner, 54560, 715-542-3375 Yards: 6164, Par: 72, USGA: 68.7, Holes: 9, Pro: Todd Renk
Poplar GC, Rt. #1, Box 796, Poplar, 54864, 715-364-2689 Yards: 3100, Par: 31, Holes: 9, Pro: G. Longville
Portage CC, Country Club Rd., P.O. Box 342, Portage, 53901, 608-742-5121 Yards: 6044, Par: 71, USGA: 68.8, Holes: 18, Pro: Ray Shane
Prairie De Chien CC, RFD 2, P.O. Box 11, Prairie de Chien, 53821, 608-326-6707 Yards: 6036, Par: 70, USGA: 68.8, Holes: 9, Pro: Dick Hoelzer
Prentice Village GC, 403 Center St., Prentice, 54556, 715-428-2127 Yards: 2353, Par: 34, Holes: 9
Princeton Valley GC, 2300 W. Princeton Ave., Eau Claire, 54701, 715-834-3334 Yards: 5964, Par: 72, USGA: 68.2, Holes: 9, Pro: Tom Eisenhuth
Quit-Oui-Oc GC, Inc., 500 Quit-Qui-Oc Lane, P.O. Box, Elkhart Lake, 53020, 414-876-2833 Yards: 5972, Par: 70, USGA: 68.4, Holes: 18, Pro: Tom E. Wiese
Racine CC, 2801 Northwestern Ave., Racine, 53404, 414-637-8537 Yards: 6342, Par: 72, USGA: 71.5, Holes: 18, Pro: Douglas Cameron
Rainbow Springs CC, S103 W33599 Hwy. 99, Mukwonago, 53149, 414-363-4550 Yards: 6702, Par: 72, USGA: 72.4, Holes: 36, Pro: Mark Lychwick
Reedsburg CC, Hwy. 23-33, P.O. Box 125, Reedsburg, 53959, 608-524-3134 Yards: 5906, Par: 72, USGA: 69.6, Holes: 18, Pro: Dan Hillcoat
Reid GC, 1100 East Fremont Street, Appleton, 54915, 414-735-5926 Yards: 5958, Par: 71, USGA: 67.6, Holes: 18, Pro: Cindy Swift
Rhinelander CC, North Eagle St. Hwy. W, P.O.Bo, Rhinelander, 54501, 715-362-2123 Yards: 6096, Par: 70, USGA: 69.8, Holes: 9, Pro: Ron Bosi
Rib Mountain GC, 3605 N. Mountain Rd., Wausau, 54401, 715-845-5570 Yards: 3848, Par: 62, USGA: 57.2, Holes: 9, Pro: Mike Oliva
Richland CC, Hwy. Y, P. O. Box 70, Richland Center, 53581, 608-647-3117 Yards: 5126, Par: 67, USGA: 64.4, Holes: 9
Ridgeway G & CC, 2913 Highway 150, Neenah, 54956, 414-722-2979 Yards: 6390, Par: 72, USGA: 70.3, Holes: 18, Pro: Steve Howe
River Falls GC, County Road M East, P.O. Box 7, River Falls, 54022, 715-425-7253 Yards: 5873, Par: 70, USGA: 67.8, Holes: 18, Pro: Pat Stafford
River Island GC, River Island Dr., Oconto Falls, 54154, 414-846-3303 Yards: 6058, Par: 70, USGA: 68.8, Holes: 9, Pro: Victor Peterson
Riveredge CC, Mill Creek Road, P.O. Box 547, Marshfield, 54449, 715-676-3900 Yards: 6600, Par: 72, USGA: 71.9, Holes: 9, Pro: Mark DeVolder
Rivermoor CC, 30802 Waterford Dr., Waterford, 53185, 414-534-2500 Yards: 6079, Par: 70, USGA: 68.7, Holes: 18, Pro: Rick Swift
Riversbend GC, N96 W18034 County Line Rd., Germantown, 53022, 414-255-6557 Yards: 4548, Par: 66, USGA: 62.1, Holes: 9, Pro: Ronald Manchek
Rock River CC, Route 1, 1 W. Main, Waupun, 53963, 414-324-4340 Yards: 6454, Par: 72, USGA: 71.3, Holes: 9, Pro: Fred McIver
Rolling Meadows Golf Assn., 560 W. Rolling Meadows, P.O.B., Fond du Lac, 54936, 414-921-9369 Yds: 6371, Par: 72, USGA: 69.6, Holes: 18, Pro: G Guenther
Rolling Oaks GC, 440 West Division, Barron, 54812, 715-537-3409 Yards: 5924, Par: 70, USGA: 69.0, Holes: 9, Pro: Lee Johnson
Sandalwood CC, Sandalwood Road, Abrams, 54101, 414-826-7770 Yards: 5943, Par: 72, Holes: 18, Pro: Joe Reinhard
Scenic Valley Golf Assn., Hwys. 80-82-33, P.O. Box 38, Union Center, 53962, 608-462-8691 Yards: 5838, Par: 70, USGA: 67.6, Holes: 9, Pro: Scott Heding

Scenic View CC, 4415 Club Dr., Slinger, 53086, 414-644-5661
Yards: 6120, Par: 71, USGA: 68.7, Holes: 18, Pro: Frank Romano
Sheboygan CC, 4914 Superior Ave., P.O. Box 1, Sheboygan, 53082,
414-458-3533 Yards: 6001, Par: 69, USGA: 70.0, Holes: 18, Pro: Richard Suesens
Sheboygan Town and CC, 6521 County Trunk J, Sheboygan, 53083,
414-467-2509 Yards: 5849, Par: 70, USGA: 66.6, Holes: 27, Pro: Guy Miller
Shoop Park GC, 4510 Lighthouse Dr., Racin, 53401, 414-639-9994
Yards: 2063, Par: 34, Holes: 9
Silver Spring CC, N56 W21318 Silver Spring, Menomonee Falls, 53051,
414-252-4666 Yards: 6323, Par: 72, USGA: 70.1, Holes: 18, Pro: Carrie Van Roo
Skyline GC, 10th & Drectrah, P.O. Box 8, Black River Falls, 54615, 715-284-2613
Yards: 6351, Par: 72, USGA: 69.7, Holes: 9, Pro: Tom Tomter
South Hills CC, 3047 Hwy. 41, Franksville, 53126, 414-835-4441
Yards: 6334, Par: 69, USGA: 69.4, Holes: 18, Pro: Xavier Sandoval
South Hills G & CC, 1175 S. Fond du Lac Ave., POB, Fond du Lac, 54936,
414-921-3636 Yards: 6150, Par: 70, USGA: 69.5, Holes: 18, Pro: Rich Tock
Sparta Municipal GC, 1210 E. Montgomery St., Sparta, 54656, 608-269-3022
Yards: 6055, Par: 71, USGA: 68.5, Holes: 18, Pro: Roger Johnson
Spring Creek GC, W4787 Yandry Rd., Whitewater, 53190, 414-563-4499
Yards: 1644, Par: 27, Holes: 99, Pro: M. Majewski
Spring Green GC, South Lake St., Spring Green, 53588, 608-588-7707
Yards: 2426, Par: 33, Holes: 9
Spring Valley GC, Van Buren Rd., P.O. Box 8, Spring Valley, 54767,
715-778-5513 Yards: 5458, Par: 69, USGA: 65.9, Holes: 18, Pro: Terry Mellum
Spring Valley CC, 23913 Wilmot Rd., Salem, 53168, 414-862-2626
Yards: 6272, Par: 70, USGA: 69.7, Holes: 18, Pro: John Wagner
Spring Valley GC, POB 78, Union Center, 53962, 608-462-8691
Yards: 2921, Par: 36, Holes: 9
Springs GC—White Course, RTE. 3 Golf Course Rd. Box 460, Madison, 53588,
608-588-7707 Yards: 6052, Par: 72, USGA: 68.9, Holes: 18, Pro: Peter Reif
Squires CC, 4970 Country Club Dr., Port Washington, 53074, 414-285-3425
Yards: 5792, Par: 70, USGA: 67.3, Holes: 18, Pro: Shelly Joannes
St. Croix Valley CC, Route 2, P.O. Box 279, St. Croix Falls, 54024, 715-483-3377
Yards: 5628, Par: 70, USGA: 66.6, Holes: 9, Pro: Oralee Schock
St. John's Academy GC, 1101 N. Genesee St., Delafield, 53018, 414-646-3311
Yards: 3152, Par: 36, Holes: 9
Stevens Point CC, 1628 Country Club Dr., P.O. Bo, Stevens Point, 54481,
715-345-8900 Yards: 6379, Par: 72, USGA: 70.6, Holes: 18, Pro: Paul Otto
Stoughton CC, 3165 Shadyside Dr., P.O. Box 2, Stoughton, 53589, 608-873-7861
Yards: 6199, Par: 70, USGA: 70.1, Holes: 9, Pro: Steve Hlavacek
Sundown GC, Crivitz, 54114, 715-854-7833
Yards: 5100, Par: 69, Holes: 18, Pro: M. Jungblut
Sunset Hills Golf & Supper Club, W8884 Hwy. 33 North, P.O. Box, Beaver Dam,
53916, 414-885-4106 Yds: 5950, Par: 71, USGA: 67.6, Holes: 18, Pro: G. Burchardt
Sunset View CC, 1013 Sunset View Rd., Chetek, 54728, 715-859-6211
Yards: 4480, Par: 68, USGA: 60.5, Holes: 9, Pro: Mike Witkowski
Swan Lake Village GC, Hwy 33 East, Portage, 53801, 608-742-2181
Yards: 2988, Par: 35, Holes: 9
Tagalong GC, Birchwood, 54817, 715-354-3458
Yards: 3130, Par: 36, Holes: 9
Tahkodah Hills GC, Lake Owen Dr., Cable, 54821, 715-798-3760
Yards: 2300, Par: 35, Holes: 9
Tee Hi Club House, 580 Tee-Hi Place, Medford, 54451, 715-748-3990
Yards: 2010, Par: 31, Holes: 9, Pro: Gene Wirz
Telemark CC, P.O. Box 277, Hwy. M, Cable, 54821, 715-798-3811
Yards: 6425, Par: 72, Holes: 18, Pro: Geo. Hovlaund

Thal Acres CC, Route 2, P.O. Box 4, Westfield, 53964, 608-296-2850
Yards: 5588, Par: 69, USGA: 66.2, Holes: 18, Pro: R. Hilgendorf
Timber Ridge CC, Hwy. 51, South, P.O. Box 1107, Minocqua, 54548,
715-356-5273 Yards: 6150, Par: 72, USGA: 70.6, Holes: 18, Pro: Brian Baldwin
Timber Terrace GC, 1117 Pumphouse Road, P.O. Box, Chippewa Falls, 54729,
715-726-1500   Yards: 5466, Par: 70, USGA: 66.3, Holes: 9, Pro: M. A. Durch
Towne CC, Inc., 115 Jenson St., P.O. Box 128, Edgerton, 53534,   608-884-4231
Yards: 5392, Par: 68, USGA: 66.0, Holes: 9, Pro: Arnold Wilberg
Traceway GC, 2201 Traceway Dr., Madison, 53704,   608-271-5877
Yards: 1650, Par: 30, Holes: 9
Trapp River GC, Hwy. WW, P.O. Box 1346, Wausau, 54401, 715-675-3044
Yards: 5929, Par: 70, USGA: 66.5, Holes: 18, Pro: Greg Hoenisch
Trenton View GC, 1241 Hwy 33 East, West Bend, 53095,   414-675-6669
Yards: 3276, Par: 36, Holes: 9
Tri-City GC, 3000 Golf Course Rd., P.O. Box, Wisconsin Rapids, 54494,
715-423-1380   Yards: 5692, Par: 68, USGA: 66.7, Holes: 9, Pro: P. McCarville
Tripoli CC, 7401 N. 43rd St., Milwaukee, 53209,   414-351-7200
Yards: 6260, Par: 71, USGA: 70.6, Holes: 18, Pro: Steve Bull
Tuckaway CC, 6901 W. Drexel Ave., Franklin, 53132,   414-425-4280
Yards: 6523, Par: 72, USGA: 71.6, Holes: 18, Pro: Robert Lee
Tumblebrook CC, W287 N1963 Oakton Rd., Pewaukee, 53072
Yards: 6240, Par: 72, Holes: 18, Pro: J. Van Blarcum
Turtle Greens GC, Rt 1 Schroeder Rd., Beloit, 53511, 608-676-4334
Yards: 2404, Par: 34, Holes: 9
Turtleback G & CC, West Allen Rd., Rt. 6, P.O. Bo, Rice Lake, 54868,
715-234-7641   Yards: 5845, Par: 70, USGA: 66.8, Holes: 18, Pro: Arlen Erickson
Tuscumbia GC, Illinois Ave., Green Lake, 54941, 414-294-3240
Yards: 6301, Par: 71, USGA: 70.1, Holes: 18, Pro: Dan Buckley
Twin Lakes CC, 1230 Legion Drive, Twin Lakes, 53181,   414-877-2500
Yards: 5837, Par: 70, USGA: 67.2, Holes: 18, Pro: Aleta Rickert
Tyranena GC, 800 S. Main St., P.O. Box 75, Lake Mills, 53551,   414-648-5013
Yards: 6020, Par: 70, USGA: 68.1, Holes: 9, Pro: John T. Lees
Utica GC, 3350 Knott Rd., P.O. Box 2312, Oshkosh, 54903,   414-233-4446
Yards: 5969, Par: 71, USGA: 67.6, Holes: 18, Pro: James Leher
Valley Golf & Bowl, RR #1, Mondovi, 54755,   715-926-4913
Yards: 5539, Par: 70, USGA: 65.1, Holes: 9, Pro: Gary Norrish
Viking Skyline GC, Hwy. 10, P.O. Box 386, Strum, 54770,   715-695-3306
Yards: 6124, Par: 72, USGA: 68.1, Holes: 9, Pro: Allen Hardy
Village Green GC, 2506 Shawano Ave., Green Bay, 54313,   414-434-0959
Yards: 3259, Par: 36, Holes: 9, Pro: Val Reinhard
Ville du Parc CC, Inc., 12400 N. Ville de Parc, 34W PO, Mequon, 53092,
414-242-1400   Yards: 6388, Par: 72, USGA: 70.8, Holes: 27, Pro: Harry Parker,Jr
Virocqua CC, Hwy 14 South, Virocqua, 54667,   608-637-7615
Yards: 2844, Par: 35, Holes: 9
Viroqua CC, Hwy. 14 S., P.O. Box 347, Viroqua, 54665,   608-637-7615
Yards: 5688, Par: 70, USGA: 67.3, Holes: 9, Pro: Greg Gorman
Voyager Village CC, Star Route No. 4, Danbury, 54830,   715-259-3911
Yards: 6359, Par: 72, USGA: 70.4, Holes: 18, Pro: Tim Smith
Walnut Grove GC, Rt. 2, P.O. Box 4, Cochrane, 54622,   608-248-2800
Yards: 5614, Par: 70, USGA: 65.8, Holes: 9, Pro: Gene Pelowski
Walsh Golf Center Club, 4203 Cty. Hwy. B, La Crosse, 54601,   608-782-0838
Yards: 4346, Par: 64, USGA: 60.0, Holes: 9, Pro: Robert M. Swift
Wanaki GC, N50 W20830 Lisbon Rd., Menomonee Falls, 53051,   414-252-3480
Yards: 6528, Par: 70, USGA: 71.3, Holes: 9, Pro: Brad Nickoli
Wander Springs GC, Route 2, Greenleaf, 54126,   414-864-4653
Yards: 6052, Par: 70, USGA: 68.8, Holes: 9, Pro: Julie Casper

Washington Park GC, 2801 12th St., Racine, 53405, 414-634-9846
Yards: 2690, Par: 35, Holes: 9
Watertown CC, North Water St., P. O. Box 523, Watertown, 53094,
414-261-5009   Yards: 6308, Par: 70, USGA: 69.1, Holes: 18, Pro: Bob Duncan
Waupaca CC, 1330 Ware Street, P.O. Box 274, Waupaca, 54981,   715-258-2339
Yards: 6098, Par: 70, USGA: 70.0, Holes: 9, Pro: Jeffrey Proper
Wausau GC, 208 Country Club Rd., P.O. Box, Schofield, 54476,   715-359-6161
Yards: 6001, Par: 70, USGA: 68.5, Holes: 18, Pro: Al Yates
Waushara GC, Hillside Drive, Wautoma, 54982,   414-787-7012
Yards: 5700, Par: 72, Holes: 18, Pro: Lavern Rick
West Bend CC, 5858 Highway Z, West Bend, 53095,   414-334-9541
Yards: 6450, Par: 73, USGA: 71.0, Holes: 18, Pro: Don Hill
Westbrook Hills GC, American Legion Dr., Plain, 53577,   608-546-4432
Yards: 2411, Par: 33, Holes: 9
Western Lakes GC, W287 N1963 Oakton Rd., P.O. Bo, Pewaukee, 53072,
414-691-0900   Yards: 6236, Par: 72, USGA: 69.3, Holes: 18, Pro: Sean O'Brien
Westhaven GC, 821 Witzel Avenue, Oshkosh, 54901,   414-233-4640
Yards: 5982, Par: 71, Holes: 18
Westmoor CC, 400 S. Moorland Rd., Brookfield, 53005,   414-782-5880
Yards: 6479, Par: 71, USGA: 71.6, Holes: 18, Pro: Thomas Kabler
Westwood CC, HCR3, Box 156, Phillips, 54555,   715-339-3600
Yards: 5888, Par: 70, USGA: 67.7, Holes: 9, Pro: Allan Kress
Weymont Run CC, Rural Route 2, Box 80, Weyauwega, 54983,   414-867-3412
Yards: 6458, Par: 72, USGA: 70.3, Holes: 18, Pro: Richard Seitz
Whistling Wings GC, Hwy. 80, Necedah, 54646,   608-565-7360
Yards: 2400, Par: 27, Holes: 9
Whitetail GC, Box 86, R.R. #3, Colfax, 54730,   715-962-3888
Yards: 6590, Par: 72, USGA: 70.8, Holes: 9, Pro: Walt Boelkhe
Whitewater CC, Highway 89 Rt. #3, P. O. Box 3, Whitewater, 53190,
414-473-3305   Yards: 5874, Par: 70, USGA: 68.2, Holes: 9, Pro: Mary Haggerty
Whitnall Park Men's GC, 5879 So. 92nd St., Hales Corners, 53130,
414-425-2183   Yards: 6169, Par: 71, USGA: 68.6, Holes: 18, Pro: Gerry Clark
Wildwood GC, 10094 Hwy. 70W, P. O. Box 88, Minocqua, 54548,   715-352-3477
Yards: 5372, Par: 68, USGA: 65.6, Holes: 9, Pro: Jim Peck
Willow Run GC, N12 W26506 Golf Rd., Pewaukee, 53072,   414-547-3453
Yards: 6350, Par: 70, USGA: 68.8, Holes: 18, Pro: Jeff Venes
Winagamie GC, 3501 Winagamie Drive, Neenah, 54956,   414-757-5453
Yards: 6355, Par: 73, USGA: 69.5, Holes: 18, Pro: Mary Neinhaus
Windy Acres GC, N1005 Cty. K, Monroe, 53566,   608-325-3240
Yards: 2866, Par: 36, Holes: p, Pro: James Krieger
Winro GC, Box 413, 1200 E. Huron St., Omro, 54963, 414-685-6161
Yards: 2842, Par: 35, Holes: 9
Wisconsin River CC, 705 West River Drive, Stevens Point, 54481,   715-344-9152
Yards: 6213, Par: 71, USGA: 69.5, Holes: 18, Pro: Jim Giddings
Woodside GC, 530 Erie Road, Green Bay, 54301,   414-468-5729
Yards: 6002, Par: 71, Holes: 18, Pro: Buzz Basinski
Yahara Hills GC, 6701 E. Broadway, Madison, 53704,   608-838-3126
Yards: 6564, Par: 72, USGA: 69.3, Holes: 36, Pro: Mark Rechlicz
Yellow Lake GC, 7768 Co. Rd. U, Danbury, 54830
Yards: 2627, Par: 34, Holes: 9

Casper Muni GC, 2120 Allendale Blvd., Casper, 82601,   *Wyoming*
307-234-1037
Cheyenne Airport GC, 4801 Central Ave., Cheyenne, 82009
Cheyenne Muni GC, 4801 Central Avenue, Cheyenne, 82001,   307-637-6418
Douglas GC, Douglas, 82633,   307-358-5099

Kemmerer Field Club, Kemmerer, 83101, 307-877-6954
Par: 36, Holes: 9
Kendrick GC, Big Goose Rd., Sheridan, 82801
Lusk Muni GC, 34 Hwy 273, Lusk, 82225, 307-334-9916
Olive Glenn G&CC, 802 Meadow LN., Cody, 82414, 307-587-5551
Par: 72, Holes: 18
Prairie View GC, 3601 Windmill Rd., Cheyenne, 82009, 307-637-6420
Purple Sage G&CC, Evanston, 82930, 307-789-2383
Par: 36, Holes: 9
Rendezvous Meadows GC, Pinedale, 82941, 307-367-4252
Par: 36, Holes: 9
Riverton CC, Riverton, 82501, 307-856-4779
Par: 72, Holes: 18
Saratoga Inn GC, Saratoga, 82331, 307-326-526J
Par: 36, Holes: 9

Index

458 Index

FREE Newsletter Subscription

Great **Golf** Gazette™

From time to time we will send you a copy of the **Great Golf Gazette** newsletter, which will keep you posted on special golf travel values, air and golf packages, and more! This *free* subscription is available for a limited time only. Subscribe now!

Name _____

Address _____

City _____

State/Zip _____

Send to:
Great Golf Gazette
Lanier Publishing
International, Ltd.
P.O. Box 20429
Oakland, CA 94620

Please answer the following questions and return with this free newsletter subscription order form:

Are you planning a golf vacation within the next year? ___
    If so, how many adults? _____ Children? _____

Are you interested in receiving information on golf course homes and condos for sale?   _____

If so, where? _____

When taking a vacation, do you usually travel by car?_____ air _____ or rail? _____

Lanier Travel Guides
In Book Stores Everywhere!

Lanier Travel Guides have set the standard for the industry:

"All the necessary information about facilities, prices, pets, children, amenities, credit cards and the like. Like France's Michelin..." —New York Times.

"Provides a wealth of information needed to make a wise choice."
—American Council of Consumer Interest.

Golf Resorts International

A wish book and travel guide for the wandering golfer. This guide reviews the creme de la creme of golf resorts all over the world. Beautifully illustrated, it includes all pertinent details regarding hotel facilities and amenities. Wonderful narrative on each hotel's special charm, superb cuisine and most importantly, those fabulous golf courses. Written from a golfer's viewpoint, it looks at the challenges and pitfalls of each course.

Bed & Breakfasts, Inns & Guesthouses
in the United States and Canada

A best selling classic now in its ninth fully-revised edition. Over 6,000 inns listed and access to over 15,000 guesthouses. Includes specialty lists for interests ranging from bird-watching to antiquing. "All the necessary information about facilities, prices, pets, children, amenities, credit cards and the like. Like France's Michelin ..."
— *New York Times*

Condo Vacations
— The Complete Guide

The popularity of Condo Vacations has grown exponentially. In this national guide, details are provided on over 2,000 Condo resorts in an easy to read format with valuable descriptive write-ups. The perfect vacation option for families and a great money saver!

Golf Resorts
— The Complete Guide

This first ever comprehensive guide to over 1,000 golf resorts coast to coast. Includes complete details of each resort facility and golf course particulars. Introductions by A.J. Snyder and Fuzzy Zoeller.

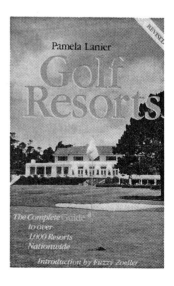

Elegant Small Hotels
— A Connoisseur's Guide

This selective guide for discriminating travelers describes over 200 of America's finest characterized by exquisite rooms, fine dining, and perfect service par excellence. Introduction by Peter Duchin. "Elegant Small Hotels makes a seductive volume for window shopping."
— *Chicago Sun Times*

All-Suite Hotel Guide
The Definitive Directory

The only guide to the all suite hotel industry features over 800 hotels nationwide and abroad. There is a special bonus list of temporary office facilities. A perfect choice for business travelers and much appreciated by families who enjoy the additional privacy provided by two rooms.

AVAILABLE IN BOOK STORES EVERYWHERE

Travel Books from
LANIER GUIDES

ORDER FORM

QTY.	TITLE	EACH	TOTAL
	Golf Courses—The Complete Guide	$14.95	
	Golf Resorts—The Complete Guide	$14.95	
	Golf Resorts International	$19.95	
	Condo Vacations—The Complete Guide	$14.95	
	Elegant Small Hotels	$19.95	
	All-Suite Hotel Guide	$14.95	
	The Complete Guide to Bed & Breakfasts, Inns & Guesthouses	$16.95	
		Sub-Total	$
		Shipping	$3.00 each
		TOTAL ENCLOSED	$

Send your order to:
TEN SPEED PRESS
P.O. Box 7123
Berkeley, California 94707

Allow 3 to 4 weeks for delivery

Please send my order to:

NAME _____

ADDRESS _____

CITY _____ STATE _____ ZIP _____

VOTE

For Your Choice of
GOLF RESORT OF THE YEAR

To the editors of **Golf Resorts, The Complete Guide:**™

I cast my vote for "Golf Resort of the Year" for:

Name of Resort _____

Address _____

Phone _____

Reasons _____

_____

_____

I would also like to (please check one): _____

_____ Recommend a new Course   _____ Comment
_____ Critique   _____ Suggest

Name of Course _____

Address _____

Phone _____

Comment _____

_____

_____

Please send your entries to: **Lanier Publishing
                                International, Ltd.
                                P.O. Box 20429
                                Oakland, CA 94620**